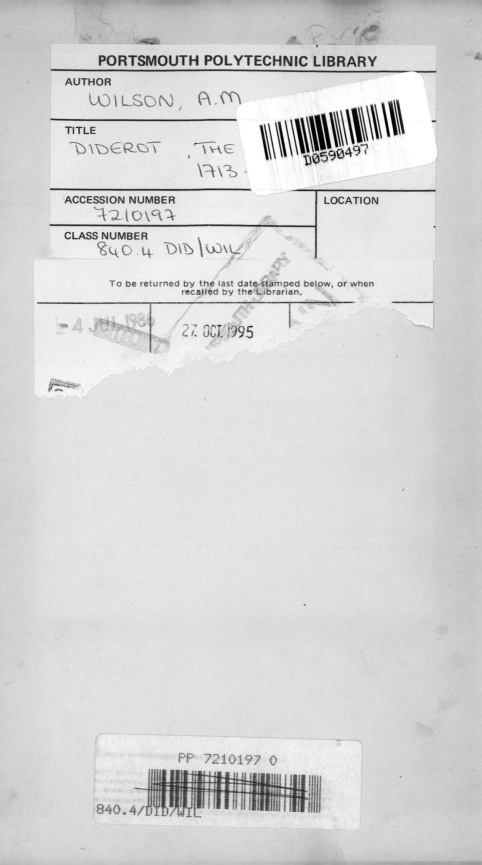

DIDEROT:

THE TESTING YEARS, 1713–1759

WINNER OF THE MODERN LANGUAGE ASSOCIATION OXFORD UNIVERSITY PRESS AWARD TO ENCOURAGE WORK PROVIDING A GREATER UNDERSTANDING OF SIGNIFICANT LITERATURE IN A FOREIGN LANGUAGE.

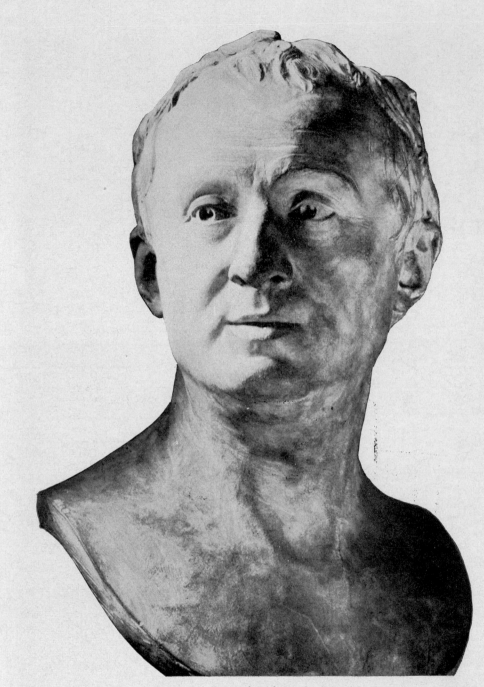

Bust of Diderot, by Houdon (1771)

DIDEROT

THE TESTING YEARS, 1713–1759

By ARTHUR M. WILSON

NEW YORK · OXFORD UNIVERSITY PRESS · 1957

PRINTED IN THE UNITED STATES OF AMERICA

To
C.Z.W. *and* A.M.W., Sr.,
And to
M.Z.G. *and* R.W.G.,
In Gratitude and Appreciation

Preface

A RECENT REVIEWER in *The Times Literary Supplement* remarked, regarding Diderot, that 'among the great minds of the eighteenth century Diderot has received less attention in this country than he deserves.'

Yet interest in Diderot has been increasing markedly of late. Partly this is because of an ever-widening persuasion that he has been too much neglected and too little understood. Partly it is because of the publicity attendant upon the celebration in 1951 of the bicentenary of the *Encyclopédie*. Most of all, it is because of the growing conviction of biographers, historians, and critics that Diderot was not only one of the most representative men of his age but also one of the most glowingly 'modern' figures of the eighteenth century. Certainly for Americans, who are children of the Enlightenment to a degree that is unique among twentieth-century peoples, the life and times of Diderot can have unusual interest and relevancy.

This book has therefore been written in the hope of meeting the needs of two audiences — the general reader and the specialist. The general reader, if he has no previous knowledge about Diderot, has a right to be shown why Diderot and Diderot's times and Diderot's vicissitudes should interest him. As for the specialist, it is hoped that the bibliographical information contained in this book will be useful; and that even for him a conspectus of the early career of Diderot will be of interest.

The reader will discover in the following chapters a good deal more information regarding the contents of the *Encyclopédie* than is usual in biographies of Diderot. By this analysis and description of the contents of such a great work of reference and instruction, it is hoped that the reader will gain a more vivid insight into the intellectual conditions of the Age of Enlightenment.

For every researcher it is a pleasure to record his obligations to the various

libraries that have aided him in his work. In this instance, the author is
under the greatest debt to the Dartmouth College Library and to the Bibliothèque Nationale. Also of very great assistance were the Library of Con-
gress, the Mazarine and the Bibliothèque de l'Arsenal at Paris, the British
Museum, the Bodleian Library, the New York Public Library, the Boston
Public Library, and the university libraries of Harvard, Princeton, Yale,
Iowa, Pennsylvania, Michigan, and Wisconsin. I also hold in grateful recollection all the numerous libraries, from Quebec to San Marino — I fear to list
them lest the enumeration grow tedious — where, during vacation or sabbatical leave, we have sought out the manuscript source or the rare edition
or the comparatively inaccessible book. To the administrations and staffs of
all these institutions I here record my heartfelt thanks.

Research on Diderot has of course entailed the pleasant necessity of wander-
ing about in Paris and Langres, seeking the sites and buildings associated
with events in his life. In this connection I particularly desire to record my
thanks to the Mayor and Deputy Mayor of Langres, M. Beligné and M. l'Abbé
Rabin, for their courtesy and hospitality, as well as to express my appreciation of these qualities in the Librarian of the Municipal Library of Langres,
the late M. Populus.

During the time when this book was in preparation, Dartmouth College
granted me two years of sabbatical leave, as well as a reduction of teaching
duties during one semester. I gratefully acknowledge this assistance, as also
the fellowship granted by the John Simon Guggenheim Memorial Foundation.

Grateful acknowledgment is also made to the Éditions de Minuit, Paris,
for permission to quote from M. Georges Roth's edition of Diderot's *Correspondance;* and to the Librairie Armand Colin, Paris, for permission to quote
from the Dufour-Plan edition of Rousseau's *Correspondance générale.*

Several persons have had the kindness to read this book in manuscript.
It has materially benefited from the judgment of Professor Thomas G. Bergin
of Yale University, Professor W. M. Frohock of Harvard University, Professor Hayward Keniston of Duke University, Professor H. W. Victor Lange
of Cornell University, and Professor Norman L. Torrey of Columbia University. To all of these scholars I desire to acknowledge gratefully my in-
debtedness. I have also been the beneficiary of the counsel of Professors
Charles R. Bagley and François Denoeu, both of Dartmouth College, and
Mr. Bradford Martin, of Thetford Hill, Vermont. Each has offered valuable
suggestions from which I have greatly profited.

Two persons in particular have been of indispensable assistance in bringing this book into being. The first is Professor Ira O. Wade of Princeton University, whose helpful and encouraging suggestions are most gratefully acknowledged. The other is my wife. My debt to her, as research assistant and critic, simply defies description. So does my appreciation.

A.M.W.

Hanover, New Hampshire
March 1957

Contents

Prologue, 3

1. Diderot's Family and Early Childhood, 9

2. Diderot Becomes an Abbé and Goes to Paris, 20

3. Clandestine Marriage, 37

4. First Fruits, 47

5. The Emerging Philosophe, 59

6. The Early History of the *Encyclopédie*, 73

7. Two Very Different Books, 83

8. *Letter on the Blind*, 92

9. Diderot in Prison, 103

10. The Prospectus of the *Encyclopédie,* and *Letter on the Deaf and Dumb,* 117

11. What Readers Found in Volume I of the *Encyclopédie,* 130

12. 'Up till Now, Hell Has Vomited Its Venom Drop by Drop,' 150

13. The *Encyclopédie* Recontinued, 161

14. Italian Opera and French Taste, 173

15. Diderot's Thoughts on the Interpretation of Nature, 187

16. 'Man Is Born To Think for Himself,' 199

17. Business and Pleasure: A New Contract, Mme Geoffrin's Salon, Sophie Volland, 218

18. 'Changing the General Way of Thinking,' 232

19. Growing Tension with Rousseau: 'Only the Bad Man Lives Alone,' 247

20. How To Write a Play: Example and Precept, 260

21. Rising Opposition; D'Alembert's Blunder in Volume VII, 275

22. 'I Used To Have an Aristarchus . . . I Wish To Have Him No Longer,' 291

23. Signs and Portents of Approaching Eclipse, 307

24. *Le Père de Famille* and the 'Discourse on Dramatic Poetry,' 322

25. The Death of the Phoenix, 332

Epilogue, 343

List of Abbreviations, 347

Notes, 349

Bibliography, 399

Index, 405

DIDEROT:

The Testing Years, 1713-1759

The Announcement of an Important Event

IN NOVEMBER of 1750 there took place in Paris what might seem to be nothing more than an inconsiderable occurrence in the realm of letters. An editor of a forthcoming encyclopedia published a prospectus explaining to a hoped-for public what would be the content of his work and the principles of his editorial policy. Yet the work thus announced secured so many readers, the ideas it contained modified current thinking to such a degree, that now the publication of its prospectus is recognized as one of the most important events in the political as well as the intellectual history of the eighteenth century. To symbolize this importance, the French government published in 1950 a reprint in national commemoration of the bicentenary of the event.

The prospectus sought favor in a world familiar to us through the paintings of Nattier, Boucher, and Lancret — a world in which the charming gracefulness and frivolity of the rococo was succeeding to the stately majesty of the baroque. It was the world of wigs, smallclothes, and three-cornered hats; of panniers and beauty patches and pancakes of rouge laid on delicate cheeks. It was the world of the minuet, danced in rooms gleaming with gilt and shimmering with mirrors; of Meissen figurines and of ladies as fragile as the porcelain that portrayed them; the world of the harpsichord, the recorder, and the viola da gamba; of the musket, the frigate, and the balance of power. This was the time when Russia was becoming more important in European diplomacy, when Frederick II of Prussia was astonishing Europe by his temerity and dumbfounding it by his success. It was the time when immense French and British colonial empires were in the making and were providing stakes for great colonial wars. In the American context, it was the time that lay between King George's War and the French and Indian War, between the proud conquest of Louisbourg by the men of Massachusetts and the defeat of Braddock in the western forests. It was a

3

time when the Church patently expected to continue confining men's
thoughts within a narrow orthodoxy, and privileged classes patently expected
to continue enjoying their privileges. Yet it was also a time when the merchant, banking, and professional elements of society were everywhere rising
in esteem and wealth. In 1750 Johann Sebastian Bach had just breathed his
last, Henry Fielding had published *Tom Jones,* Dr. Samuel Johnson was
laboring upon his famous *Dictionary,* and George Washington was eighteen
years old.

The prospectus was published in a country which was far from being be-
nighted. Yet it was one which, in its acceptance of inequalities and in its
denial of civil liberties, fell some distance short of Utopia. It was a society
in which prisons and galleys existed for those confessing the Protestant faith,
where one of the duties of the public executioner was the burning of books,
where valor in the service of one's country could never quite make up for the
lack of noble birth, where a peasantry dressed in rags, where a villager might
find his taxes enormously and arbitrarily increased if the tax collector espied
any chicken feathers on the doorstep, where decent burial could be refused
to those who did not make their peace with the Church, where nothing could
be legally published without undergoing censorship, and where a man could
lawfully be arrested and indefinitely detained without cause being shown.

The prospectus announced a work so new in idea that even its name was
unfamiliar and had to be explained, with learned reference to the Greek
roots: 'The word "Encyclopedia" signifies the interrelationship of the sciences.'
And in order to give a visual presentation of the interrelationships of the
branches of learning, the author appended to his prospectus a much-admired
chart of human knowledge. The visualized relationships in this 'genealogical
tree of all the sciences and all the arts,' avowedly modeled upon a similar
project by Lord Bacon, were to be emphasized constantly in the body of the
work by means of cross reference.

Clearly the author of the prospectus coveted for people, as do present-day
proponents of general education, the pleasure and excitement that comes
from realization of how knowledge is interrelated and interlocked. This
effort at integration was to be one of the proposed work's greatest entice-
ments. It was to be accomplished, wrote the author, by 'indicating the connections, both remote and near, of the beings that compose Nature and which
have occupied the attention of mankind; of showing, by the interlacing of
the roots and branches, the impossibility of knowing well any parts of this
whole without ascending or descending to many others; of forming a general
picture of the efforts of the human mind in all fields and every century; of

presenting these objects with clarity; of giving to each one of them its appropriate length, and, if possible, of substantiating by our success our epigraph [a quotation from Horace]:

> So great is the power of order and arrangement;
> So much grace may be imparted to a common theme.'

The French public had never before been offered just such an opportunity. England had had a successful *Cyclopaedia,* edited by Ephraim Chambers and published in two volumes in 1728. Indeed, it was this *Cyclopaedia* that provided the stimulus for the great work of reference now to be published in France. But the French work promised to outstrip its predecessor in size and coverage. Moreover, it would possess the advantage of being published in a language that, unlike the comparatively little-known English of that day, was the circulating medium of ideas, the common coin, of all educated men.

The work thus announced was to be the result of the combined labor of a considerable number of well-known men of letters, experts, and specialists. It was to consist of ten volumes in folio, of which two were to contain engravings. This size would allow a range of subject matter vastly greater than that of any existing work of reference. It was thus hoped to provide a book 'which one might consult on every subject.' 'The aim of the French Encyclopedia, as set forth in its prospectus,' wrote Frank Moore Colby, the American encyclopedist and essayist, 'was to serve as a reference library for every intelligent man on all subjects save his own. That has remained the aim of general encyclopedias ever since.'

The lack of a comprehensive and extensive encyclopedia is hard for us, who have such an abundance of excellent ones, to understand. But the author of the prospectus was announcing his work at a time when the first edition of the *Encyclopaedia Britannica* was twenty-one years in the future, and he could say quite rightly that no existing work of reference did justice to the great names and the great intellectual accomplishments of the seventeenth century. 'What progress has not since been made in the sciences and the arts?' asked the author of the prospectus, speaking of his puny and outworn predecessors. 'How many truths known today, but only glimpsed then? True philosophy was in its cradle [the author of the prospectus did not care for scholastic philosophy]; the geometry of the infinite was not yet in being; experimental physics was just beginning to show itself; the laws of sound criticism were entirely ignored. Descartes, Boyle, Huyghens, Newton, Leibniz, the Bernoullis, Locke, Bayle, Pascal, Corneille, Racine, Bourdaloue, Bossuet, etc., either did not exist or had not written.'

The *Encyclopédie* was, in fact, very fortunate in its time of publication, for it fitted exactly into the intellectual and social needs of the time. We know now that the eighteenth century was moving more rapidly toward radical change, was more in need of it, than the age itself realized. It was not merely that new conceptions of truth, stemming from current hypotheses about physics and psychology, were having a profoundly unsettling effect upon conventional ideas of morality, religion, and even politics; it was also that the middle classes were daily becoming more qualified to exercise power while being denied their share of it; that a new technology was beginning, whether as cause or effect of the incipient Industrial Revolution; that new theories as to what constitutes the wealth of nations were in gestation; that new doctrines of agricultural husbandry were beginning to be canvassed; and that changing economic conditions were beginning to call attention to such matters as the legal status of peasants and town workers, the supply of labor, the incidence of taxation, and the conditions of occupancy of land.

No doubt the significance of these changes or of these emerging problems was hidden — save in glimpses to a few whom Carlyle would term 'Seers,' and of whom the author of the prospectus was one. But even though the ordinary citizen of the eighteenth century might not recognize the massiveness of the changes that were overtaking his world, he would probably have been aware, however obscurely, that a certain this-worldliness was beginning to overlie the emphasis of preceding generations on other-worldliness. Somehow he now seemed to need to know, or want to know, the names of more objects, the application of more theories, the purpose of more tools, and the geographical location of more places than ever before. The places and objects and relationships of a secular existence were increasingly obtruding themselves upon the attention of the most nonchalant, the most frivolous, the most devout.

The *Encyclopédie* was precisely the means for giving information about these myriads of external objects and relationships, especially as its principal editor, the author of its prospectus, was himself the son of a craftsman and had an extremely lively interest in the technology and craftsmanship of the day. Certainly no one preached the dignity of labor more adroitly than he, and to this purpose he went to great lengths to make his *Encyclopédie* a repository of knowledge concerning the mechanical arts:

. . . Everything accordingly impelled us to have recourse to the workers themselves. We went to the cleverest ones in Paris and in the kingdom. We took the pains of going into their workshops, of questioning them, of writing under their dictation, of developing their thoughts, of educing from them the terms peculiar to their profession, of drawing up tables of such terms, of defining them, of conversing with those persons from whom we had obtained memoranda and (an almost indispensable precaution) of rectifying, in long and frequent conversations with some, what others had imperfectly, obscurely, or unfaithfully explained.

Some crafts were so complicated, the prospectus remarked, that it was necessary to learn to operate the machines and even to construct them before the craft could be accurately described. And the author explained that draftsmen had been sent into the workshops to prepare drawings from which engravings for the *Encyclopédie* would be made.

The promises made by the prospectus were widely welcomed. The *Mercure de France,* remarking that the prospectus was much appreciated by the public, printed lengthy quotations from it. The magisterial and somewhat ponderous *Journal des Sçavans* spoke of the project as 'one of the most interesting and costly since the invention of printing . . .' and spoke with no less approbation of the drawings, 'of which we have seen a very considerable part, [and which] are of great beauty.' And the youthful Adam Smith, writing for the *Edinburgh Review* in 1755, declared that: 'The French work which I just now mentioned, promises to be the most compleat of the kind which has ever been published or attempted in any language.'

The need for the promised work was proved in the most convincing way of all: subscribers' names on the dotted line, subscribers' money in down payments. By the end of April 1751, a little less than six months after the prospectus had been published, there were 1,002 subscribers, each of them paying a deposit of 60 livres for a work scheduled to cost 280 livres in all. By the end of the year the number of subscribers had risen to 2,619, and the number finally rose to about 4000, to say nothing of the subscribers to several editions pirated in Italy and Switzerland. The demand, moreover, was general throughout the Western world. The publishers later asserted that nearly three-fourths of the 4000 subscriptions were taken up in the provinces or by foreigners.

The subscribers got the information they paid for — but conjoined with a special point of view. So distinctive was the particular outlook of the *Encyclopédie* (and of its editor, the author of the prospectus) that it infuriated many persons, while preparing many others for the reforms brought about by the Revolution of 1789. The contents of the *Encyclopédie* will be described in more detail later. Here it suffices to say that the *Encyclopédie* trusted much to the operation of common sense, and was not afraid of change. Essentially, what it advocated can be quite accurately described to American readers as Hamiltonianism plus the Bill of Rights. And because it gave currency to these ideas, it has often been called the Trojan Horse of the *ancien régime*.

There were many people and many vested interests in eighteenth-century France who did not want Hamiltonianism and the Bill of Rights. Their perfervid opposition made the expression of such ideas hazardous, especially since the *Encyclopédie* depended for publication upon an official license, a license which was twice taken away and only very grudgingly and qualifiedly restored. Therefore, to have the tact and energy and courage sufficient to keep the enterprise going, and to combine these with the intellectual breadth requisite in an editor of so vast a work, called for unusual qualities in unusual conjunction. These the author of the prospectus has always been acknowledged to have. 'At the distance of some centuries,' wrote Jean-Jacques Rousseau, '. . . [he] will seem a prodigious man. People will look from afar at that universal head with commingled admiration and astonishment as we look today at the heads of Plato and Aristotle.'

It is this 'prodigious man' who is the subject of this book.

Yet with all his prodigiousness, he still had much to learn — and much to endure — when he wrote his prospectus. Dedicated to the task he had accepted, he fortunately could not foresee the rigors of the years ahead, the enemies he was destined to arouse, the anxieties and frustrations he would have to experience before the mammoth work could be brought to a successful conclusion. In the decade between the publication of the prospectus and the suppression of the *Encyclopédie* in 1759, the Enlightenment in France was taking its characteristic 'set.' Ideas were being tested together with the men holding them. Of no one could this be said with greater aptness than of the young author of the prospectus, destined to become one of the great leaders of the Enlightenment — in some respects the greatest of them all. And because of this very process of testing, much of it painful, some of it unfelt and unseen, the author of the prospectus found himself equipped, ten years after it was written, to cope successfully with the greatest and longest crisis of his life.

This book is the story of that preparation.

CHAPTER I

Diderot's Family and Early Childhood

LANGRES, the pleasant but somewhat austere old Roman town in which Denis Diderot was born, is situated imposingly and rather self-consciously on the northern extremity of the plateau of Langres, so that the land falls sharply away from it on three sides, and one of the principal modes of communication with the outside world is a cog railway connecting it with the nearby Paris-Basel railway line. The city is well remembered by many members of the AEF of 1917–18 as the site of numerous staff and training schools. No doubt many veterans (of both wars) will recall, as in their mind's eye they make the deliberate but exhilarating ascent, the bulk of the massive Charity Hospital, the old towers on the city walls, the second-century Gallo-Roman gate, and the delightful walk on the ramparts around the town, from which one overlooks the nearby plain where the River Marne has its source and can extend one's gaze in the direction of the Vosges and the Alps.

Perhaps they will remember, too, the rather severe-looking old houses, which frequently conceal a Louis XIV interior or screen a Renaissance garden front; the grimy children playing in the streets (Langres, because of its location, is short of playgrounds and water); the rather unusual number of priests and nuns, for Langres is still a conspicuously pious town; and a general air of quietude of which the inhabitants are very proud, speaking as they do of 'the calm of our provincial cities,' in transparent allusion to the bustle of iniquitous Paris.

It is easy for the visitor to Langres to feel a wistfulness for the long ago and far away. Even Diderot himself, never inclined to be unduly sentimental about the native town from which he had emancipated himself — although he was often a touch sentimental about other things — experienced on a visit to Langres in his middle age something of the spell exerted by tranquil and beautiful surroundings in a place where life has been flowing in the same channels for many generations. 'We have here,' he wrote to Sophie Volland, 'a charming promenade, consisting of a broad aisle of thickly verdured trees leading to a small grove . . . . 'tis there that I come afternoons at five. My eyes wander over the most beautiful landscape in the world. . . . I pass hours in this spot, reading, meditating, contemplating nature, and thinking of my love.' [1] The Park of the White Fountain, to the south and through the Gate of the Windmills, is now, as it was when Diderot described it in 1759, a place of beauty and of hushed delight.

Diderot later commemorated the history and antiquities of Langres in an article inserted in the *Encyclopédie*. This exercise in civic piety, couched in sentences uncharacteristically dry and antiquarian, recalled that Langres had been the ancient Andematunum, the capital city of the Lingones; that it was situated in Champagne, fourteen leagues from Dijon, forty from Reims, and sixty-three from Paris; and that it was the seat of a bishop.[2] Diderot might also have remarked that it lies in good wine country, that it had when he wrote a population of about ten thousand, and that it had long been celebrated for the quality of the cutlery that its craftsmen produced.

One of the characteristics for which Diderot became famous was a zest — not to say a weakness — for the divagatious. This intellectual volatility he ascribed, half-whimsically, half-seriously, to the climate of Langres. 'The inhabitants of this district have great wit, too much vivacity, and the inconstancy of weather-vanes,' he wrote. 'This comes, I believe, from the changes in their atmosphere, which passes in twenty-four hours from cold to hot, from calm to stormy, from clear to rainy. . . . Thus they accustom themselves from the most tender infancy to turn to every wind. The head of a man from Langres is set upon his shoulders the way a cock is set upon the top of a belfry. . . . Yet with such a surprising rapidity in their movements, desires, projects, fantasies, and ideas, they have a drawling speech . . . . As for me, I am of my district, except that residence in the capital and assiduous application have somewhat corrected me.' [3]

The appearance of the town reflected then, as it does today, the piety of a community traditionally devoted to Roman Catholicism. There were (and still are) standing in little niches in the housefronts charming madonnas carved in the hard and unweathering stone of the neighborhood. There was (and still is) the cathedral, dedicated to Saint-Mammès, a more than shadowy Cappadocian whose martyred head is said to have been brought to Langres soon after his death, which occurred about 274. There were the churches of Saint-Martin and Saint-Pierre, in the latter of which Diderot was baptized.[4] There was the church of Saint-Didier (now one of the local museums), dedicated to a sainted but somewhat misty bishop of Langres who was martyred about 264 and whose tomb may be seen in the apse of the museum. It is believed to have been the image of this local saint, cradling his mitred and martyred head in his arm, that occupied the Louis XIII niche in the façade of the house in which Diderot grew up.[5] Finally, there was the great crucifix standing in the Place Chambeau, the Place upon which the Diderot home faced. The square is still there, now appropriately named the Place Diderot. The crucifix is not. A statue of Diderot, done in 1884 by Frédéric-Auguste Bartholdi, the sculptor of the Statue of Liberty, has re-placed it. There is little doubt that Diderot would have been vastly amused if he could have foreseen such a triumphant usurpation.

For Diderot came to be an earnest and devoted anticlerical. It is, therefore, all the more piquant to observe that his closest relatives were people who were either extremely pious laymen or else professional religious whose lives were spent in the service of the Church. For example, his mother's brother, Didier Vigneron, was a canon at the local cathedral until his death when Diderot was fifteen years old. Another uncle, Jean Vigneron, was curate at Chassigny, ten miles south of Langres, and died there the year of Diderot's birth. Two uncles of Diderot's mother and two of her cousins had also been country priests, and on the Diderot side of the family, an uncle, Antoine by name, was a Dominican friar.[6] Diderot sprang from a milieu that was not only intimately familiar with the tradition of the Church but also not in the least rebellious against it.

Such had been the way of his ancestors since the names of Diderot and Vigneron first began to appear in the records of the locality. The name Diderot crops up in Langres documents from the middle of the fifteenth century, that of Vigneron from 1558. Both families were of artisan stock, and predominantly devoted themselves through the generations to being either cutlers or tanners. Both families, moreover, displayed a talent for progenitiveness. The Encyclopedist's great-grandfather Vigneron had had nine children; grandfather Vigneron, eleven. Great-grandfather Diderot, for his part, had had fourteen children; grandfather Diderot, nine. Denis Diderot himself was one of a family to which seven children were born.[7]

Into this world, swarming with relatives, Diderot was born on 5 October 1713, the year haughty old Louis XIV had to accept the Treaties of Utrecht which put an end to the exhausting War of the Spanish Succession. But the abundance of Diderot's family connections seems to have left little impression upon him, if one may judge from the rarity of his subsequent allusions to them. He never mentioned his paternal grandfather, although

that Denis Diderot was also the boy's godfather and survived until young
Denis was in his thirteenth year. He never referred in his letters or writings
to his uncle, the Dominican friar, or by name to his aunt and godmother,
Claire Vigneron, though on one occasion, it is true, he included them in
family greetings sent through a friend.[8] And the retiring and no doubt well-
deserving lives of the Diderot collaterals, the cousins and the cousins-german
and the cousins twice removed, have remained, for aught of him, obscure.

Even Diderot's mother figures only infrequently in anything he ever
committed to paper. Angélique Vigneron, the daughter of a merchant
tanner, was born on 12 October 1677, and married Didier Diderot, a master
cutler, in 1711 or the beginning of 1712.[9] It was remarkable for the period
that she was not married before the age of thirty-four. Moreover, she was
eight years older than her husband. Her first child, a son, was born on
5 November 1712, and died soon thereafter.[10] Eleven months later the birth
of a second son, the subject of this biography, partially repaired the loss.
Diderot mentions his mother only four times, but perhaps the depth of
feeling revealed in the last two of these passages atones for the strange lack
of more references. The first two allusions come in letters to his friend,
Friedrich Melchior Grimm, in which Diderot simply remarks that he was
absent when his mother died.[11] The third allusion is in a letter to Sophie
Volland, written when he was forty-seven: 'There are two or three honest
men and two or three honest women in this world, and Providence has
sent them to me. . . . If Providence should speak and say to me, ". . . I have
given thee Didier for father and Angélique for mother; thou knowest what
they were and what they have done for thee. What is remaining for thee
to ask of me?," I don't know what I should say in reply.'[12]

The fourth allusion to his mother dates from 1770, when Diderot was at
Bourbonne-les-Bains and writing an account of the town and the medicinal
properties of its waters. 'When one is in a country, one should inform oneself
somewhat of what goes on there,' he began. Presently, in a characteristic
digression with characteristic dots: 'Now it is midnight. I am alone, and I
bring to mind these good folk, these good parents. . . . O thou, who used
to warm my cold feet in thy hands, O my mother! . . .'[13] Diderot's deep-
seated regard for his mother was displayed by the fact that both his daughters
— the first dying before the second was born — were christened Angélique.

Diderot was extremely fond of his father and often refers to him. Didier
Diderot (born 14 September 1685) was so good an artisan that his surgical
knives, scalpels, and lancets, stamped with his hallmark of a pearl, were

much in demand. A French doctor writing in 1913 spoke with respect of the elder Diderot and of his lancets, 'which he very greatly perfected: better in the hand, they cut more cleanly, and the lancets with the mark of the pearl were sought out by all the doctors teaching medicine. I possess one myself, bequeathed to me by an old physician of Langres, and I understand without difficulty the enthusiasm of contemporaries.' [14] The eminence of Diderot's father in his craft is attested also by the fact that in the Langres Museum at the Hôtel du Breuil there is a pair of small scissors of a design perfected, tradition says, by the elder Diderot.

Diderot's father was, moreover, a man of property who enjoyed a reputation for piety and integrity. During that same night in Bourbonne-les-Bains, his son wrote: '. . . one of the things that has occasioned me the greatest pleasure was the crabbed remark addressed to me by a local man some years after my father's death. I was crossing a street in my city when this man laid his hand on my arm and said, "Monsieur Diderot, you are a good man; but if you think you will ever be the equal of your father, you are mistaken."' [15]

How Diderot felt about his father is well illustrated by a statement that he made six years after the old man had died. Provoked by a dispute with a priest about the character of the Heavenly Father, Diderot made clear his sentiments concerning his earthly one: 'The first years I spent at Paris were considerably disordered; my conduct was more than sufficient to irritate my father, without there being any need to exaggerate it. Nevertheless, calumny had not been wanting. He had been told. . . . What *hadn't* he been told? The opportunity for going to see him presented itself. I did not hesitate. I set out full of confidence in his goodness. I thought that he would see me, that I should throw myself into his arms, that both of us would shed tears, and that all would be forgotten. I thought right.' [16]

Fifteen months after the birth of the future Encyclopedist, the eldest daughter, Denise, was born (27 January 1715). This sister, whom Denis Diderot greatly admired, sometimes referring to her, when they were both in middle age, as 'little sister' and sometimes as 'a female Socrates,' remained a spinster throughout her long life. Sometime in middle age she developed 'a pimple on her nose that became a cancer and entirely destroyed that part of her face.' [17] This affliction, necessitating the use of false noses (she even tried one made of glass), was evidently endured in a spirit of Christian cheerfulness. [18] Diderot's daughter spoke of her aunt as a woman who 'possessed the rare secret of finding heaven on earth,' and Diderot himself wrote in 1770, 'I love my sister to distraction, not so much because she is my sister as because of my taste for things excellent of their kind. How many fine characteristics I could mention of her if I chose!'[19]

Denise was followed in the Diderot family by three other sisters about whom very little is known. The first, Catherine, was born sometime in 1716 and buried 30 August 1718. The second, also named Catherine, was born and baptized on 18 April 1719. Then on 3 April 1720, Angélique Diderot was born. It was an eighteenth-century custom peculiar to Langres and its neighborhood, I have been told — though now quite general in France — to allow persons of extremely tender age to stand as godparents. Thus it was that Angélique's brother stood as godfather for this new sister and boldly signed the baptismal register with his own hand.[20]

It is evident, therefore, that Diderot grew up with considerable experience in being the elder brother of girls. When he left Langres for Paris in 1728 or 1729, his three living sisters were, respectively, about thirteen, nine, and eight years old, although the second Catherine may already have died. In the fullness of time — and, oddly, against the wishes of her family — Angélique became a nun, an Ursuline.[21] His daughter, in her memoirs of Diderot, declares that this sister became insane as a result of overwork in the convent and died at the age of twenty-eight.[22] This incident no doubt was one of the causes of Diderot's dislike of convents, which helped to provide the impetus many years later for his very effective novel, *The Nun*.

The Benjamin of the family was a boy born on 21 March 1722.[23] Didier-Pierre Diderot, as he was named in the baptismal ceremony in which his elder brother served as a proxy godfather, grew up to be a pious and evidently quite thorny Catholic priest, a canon in the cathedral at Langres who accounted his greatest shame to be his brother's impiety. The personal relations of the two brothers, although not hateful, were none too cordial. Each deplored the views of the other while entertaining a stubborn sort of reluctant affection entirely unmixed with respect. The Canon carried his disapprobation to the point of refusing to see his brother's daughter and her children, and when in 1780 he was invited by the mayor and aldermen of Langres to be present at a dinner where the Encyclopedist's bust, done by Houdon, was to be unveiled, he refused. Later, under pretext of some errand or other at the city hall, he went to see the bust by himself.[24]

There is no record of where or from whom Diderot received his elementary schooling. Indeed, there is almost no testimony extant concerning his earliest years, save that his daughter wrote after his death that 'from his tenderest years he gave evidence of extreme sensibility: when he was three years old he was taken to a public execution and came back from it so upset that he was attacked by a violent jaundice.' [25] There are in his works occasional allusions to his early days, as when, criticizing the figures in a landscape by Hubert Robert, he remarked that a Swiss guard in the picture was stiff and 'precisely like those given me one New Year's, when I was small'; [26] or when he observed, perhaps in recollection of his childhood and of the ramparts of Langres, that it is characteristic of children to love to climb; [27] or when, writing in the *Encyclopédie* of the vagaries of orthography, he declared that we get accustomed to pronouncing one language and writing another, 'a bizarre state of affairs which has made so many tears flow in childhood.' [28] Perhaps much of his elementary education he received in his own home, for he wrote late in life that 'arithmetic was one of the first things my parents taught me.' [29] Regardless of how the young Diderot achieved his knowledge of the three R's, by the time he was ten he was qualified to begin his secondary education and in November 1723 (most probably) was enrolled in the lowest form of the Jesuit *collège* at Langres.[30]

The Jesuits exercised in Langres a monopoly of secondary education, just as they frequently did elsewhere in Catholic Christendom.[31] They achieved this pre-eminence as a result of the excellence of their teachers and their emphasis upon the more humane letters, the Latin and Greek which had stood so high in the estimation of cultivated men ever since the Humanists had revived the love of ancient letters. By this emphasis the Jesuits, who were the prime instruments of the Catholic Church in the Counter Reformation, once again showed their cleverness. For in their rigidly standardized curriculum — the *Ratio studiorum* that elaborately regulated Jesuit education everywhere had been promulgated in 1599 — excellent instruction in the ancient literatures was combined with considerable attention to Catholic devotions and thus, from the point of view of the Church, humanistic learning was prevented from becoming too secular.

From his home at Number 6, an edifice still standing and now adorned with a commemorative plaque, the schoolboy Diderot would walk the few steps across the Place Chambeau to the Jesuit *collège,* which stood just off the square at the head of a street since named for him.[32] The *collège* was destroyed by fire in 1746, but was quickly replaced by the present building which also bears his name. In 1770 Diderot referred to it as 'renowned.' It had quite a numerous clientele, perhaps 180 or 200 in the six forms, all of them day students, most of them (but by no means all) from Langres, and coming from diverse social backgrounds, astonishing if one considers what was usual in the tightly knit society of the *ancien régime*. There were noble-

men as well as scions of the upper and lower middle classes, and there was
also, in Diderot's own form, the son of a tinker.[33] Throughout his life
Diderot showed an ability to esteem men for what they were by nature rather
than what they were by rank, and it is not impossible that the relatively
democratic conditions of his schooling habituated him to such a point of
view.

Although Diderot was a sensitive child, he was also a robust one, and
in later years he liked to recall the Spartan aspects of his early education,
much as nineteenth-century Americans were prone to expatiate on the part
played by the little red schoolhouse and the McGuffey readers in making
a nation great and keeping its manners pure. Remembering the scars of ten
slingshot hits on his forehead, he wrote: 'Such was provincial education in
my time. Two hundred boys would divide themselves into two armies. It was
not rare for children, seriously injured, to have to be carried off to their
parents. . . . I remember that . . . my comrades and I got the idea of de-
molishing one of the bastions of my town and passing Holy Week in prison.'
And then, carried away as he so often was by a sort of chain reaction of
associations, and evidently remembering some childhood rival who had
aroused his distaste, he apostrophized an imaginary 'Athenian' who did not
approve of an education that was so Spartan and untrammeled: 'You recoil
at the sight of their disheveled hair and torn clothes. Yet I was that way
when I was young, and I was pleasing — pleasing to even the women and
girls of my home town in the provinces. They preferred me, without a hat
and with chest uncovered, sometimes without shoes, in a jacket and with
feet bare, me, son of a worker at a forge, to that little well-dressed monsieur,
all curled and powdered and dressed to the nines, the son of the presiding
judge of the bailiwick court. . . . They could see in my buttonhole the
token of my attainments in study, and a boy who revealed his soul by frank
and open words and who knew better how to give a blow with his fist than
how to make a bow, pleased them more than a foolish, cowardly, false, and
effeminate little toady.'[34]

Diderot was never above showing off for the girls, and one of his
reminiscences, inspired by this theme and referring to his youthful days in
Paris, has the incidental merit of giving us some notion of his congenital
endowments, at least so far as muscular co-ordination is concerned. 'I was
young,' he wrote. 'I was in love, and very much in love. I was living with
some fellows from Provence who danced from dusk to dawn, and from dusk
to dawn took the hand of the girl I loved and embraced her right under my
eyes. Add to this that I was jealous. I decide to learn to dance. From the

Rue de la Harpe to the far end of the Rue Montmartre I surreptitiously go
for lessons. I keep going to the same dancing master for a long time. Then
I leave him, out of vexation over having learned nothing. I take him up a
second, a third time, and leave off with as much vexation and with just as
little success. What was lacking in me to be a proficient dancer? An ear
for it? I had an excellent one. Lightness? I wasn't heavy on my feet, far
from it. Motive? One could scarcely be animated by one more violent.
What didn't I have? Malleability, flexibility, gracefulness — qualities that
cannot be had for the asking.

'But after having done everything to no purpose in order to learn how
to dance, I learned without difficulty to fence very passably, and without
any other motive than that of pleasing myself.' [35]

At his books Diderot was evidently an apt and quick pupil. Although
in later years he became extremely critical of the value of this education, his
youthful proficiency in it is attested by documents still extant.[36] In the
museum at the Hôtel du Breuil in Langres is a parchment certificate, or
bene merenti, signed by the prefect of studies and probably dating from
August 1728, in which Diderot is called an *'ingeniosum adolescentem'* who
in public exercises had explained and elucidated passages from Quintus
Curtius and Horace, with the praise and applause of all (*'cum laude
plausuque omnium'*). There are also in the same museum two quarto
volumes of some six hundred pages each, a history of the Catholic Church
in Japan by the Reverend Father Grasset, S. J., which Diderot won as
prizes. These edifying volumes, suspiciously fresh and new, with the virginal
appearance, even after two centuries, that books won as prizes are apt to
have, bear inscriptions on their flyleaves indicating that Denis Diderot,
'a young man to be commended on many counts' (*'adolescens multiplici
nomine commendandus'*), had received them on 3 August 1728 as a reward
for securing the second prize in Latin verses and the second prize in translation. It is perhaps of this occasion that Diderot was thinking when he wrote
to Sophie Volland: 'One of the sweetest moments of my life — it happened
more than thirty years ago, though I remember it as though it were yesterday — was when my father saw me coming home from school with my arms
laden with the prizes I had won and around my neck the academic crowns
that I had been given and which, too large for my brow, had let my head
pass through. From the farthest distance that he saw me, he left his work,
came to the door, and began to weep.' [37]

It is always interesting to seek in a mature person the abiding traces of
his early education. In the mature Diderot one can perceive, though in an

extremely contorted and inverted shape, the influence of the religious instruction imparted by his family and by the Jesuits. But much more easily
seen, quite pellucid in the continuity of its effect upon him, is his classical
education, reflected in the frequency of his allusions to ancient authors, in
his enjoyment of the fine points of Latinity and in his fondness for in-
dulging in exegetics, in the trust he reposes in the ancient languages as a
semantic guide, and, most important of all, in his conviction that in the
ancient authors is to be found the acme in genius, in good manners, and in
taste.

References to classic authors are abundant in Diderot's writings and frequently go beyond the casual quotation and passing allusion to be expected in an author whose range was encyclopedic. About 1775 Diderot
wrote for Catherine II a 'Plan for a University for the Government of Russia,' in the course of which he devoted several pages to comments about instruction in Greek and Latin, and incidentally showed how familiar he was
with the idiom and manner of various classic authors.[38] He wrote of his own
experience with the classics: 'Several years in succession I was as religious
about reading a book of Homer before going to bed as a conscientious priest
is about reciting his breviary. At an early age I sucked up the milk of
Homer, Virgil, Horace, Terence, Anacreon, Plato, and Euripides, diluted
with that of Moses and the prophets.'[39] And of Homer in particular he
wrote: 'Let me be pardoned for the little grain of incense I burn before the
statue of a master to whom I owe what I am worth, if I am worth anything.'[40] As a result of his love of the classics, Diderot wrote a long commentary on the works of Seneca; inspired and corrected a critical edition
of Lucretius;[41] elucidated difficult passages in Horace and Virgil;[42] ac-
claimed himself as the 'sacristan' in the 'church' of Pliny's Latinity;[43] wrote
an appreciative estimation (indeed, it is one of Diderot's best pieces) of
Terence;[44] annotated and commented upon the satires of the very difficult
Persius;[45] and composed in Latin numerous inscriptions for statues and
public buildings.

The abiding influence of an education founded on the classics and frequently demanding the use of spoken Latin in the classroom, with a corresponding outlawing of the vernacular, is also revealed in Diderot's interesting advice upon how to learn to read a foreign language. In his own
article 'Encyclopedia,' which he wrote for the fifth volume of the Encyclopédie, he declared, in speaking of linguistic and grammatical matters, that
'Nothing can be more poorly conceived for a Frenchman who knows Latin
than to learn English from an English-French dictionary instead of having

recourse to an English-Latin dictionary. . . . Furthermore, I speak according to my own experience. This method turned out very well for me.' [46]

Diderot's allusions to his childhood are few but full of flavor. In 1773 he was trying to puzzle out a difficult passage in Horace and using the evidence of some very unusual words and constructions. This recalled to him the days of his boyhood and the circumstances of his early education. 'When I used to study Latin under the iron rule of the public schools, a trap that I used to set for my teacher, and one that always worked, was to employ these strange turns of expression. He would cry out against them, he would storm at me, and when he had completely committed himself, what with storming and crying out, I would show by a little quotation that all his abusive remarks applied to Virgil, Cicero, or Tacitus.' [47]

The perversity of the gifted young has ever been the despair — and the secret pride — of the teacher.

CHAPTER 2

Diderot Becomes an Abbé and Goes to Paris

As THE years went by and young Diderot flourished in learning, the question naturally arose as to what should be his career. There was a moment, but only a moment, in which it seemed possible that he might follow his father's trade. For Diderot, impatient of the remonstrances and corrections of his teachers, told his father one day that he didn't want to go to school any more.

'Well, then, do you want to be a cutler?'

'With all my heart.'

So he put on the workshop apron and started in by his father's side. As his daughter tells the story, he spoiled everything he touched, knives, pen-knives — everything. This ended in four or five days when he got up one morning, climbed upstairs to his room, took his books, and went back to school. 'I can stand impatience better than boredom,' he said.[1]

For persons who know only the Diderot of later life — a spirited and emphatic freethinker — it will come as a surprise to learn that at the age of thirteen he signified in a solemn ceremony his intention of becoming a priest. On 22 August 1726, the Bishop of Langres conferred the tonsure on Denis Diderot, a rite consisting of cutting off some locks of the candidate's hair in the form of a cross, the while the future ecclesiastic reads some verses from the Fifteenth Psalm.[2] As a result of this ceremony, Diderot was entitled to be addressed as 'Abbé,' and was expected to wear an abbé's characteristic attire, which consisted not of a soutane worn by priests, but black smallclothes, a short mantle, and an ecclesiastical collar with its white tabs. Thus he became for a time a member of a very numerous class of persons in eighteenth-century French life, for abbés, many of whom never proceeded to holy orders but all of whom were eligible for ecclesiastical benefices, were conspicuous features of the social landscape.

There is nothing to show that young Diderot went through this ceremony against his will. The timing of the ceremony, in all probability, was determined by the hope entertained by Diderot's relatives that he would be allowed to succeed to the lucrative prebend that his uncle, Canon Didier Vigneron, occupied at the local Cathedral of Saint-Mammès. Perhaps because of this consideration Diderot took the tonsure at so early an age, for it was extremely unusual and somewhat irregular, although not precisely uncanonical, to undergo this ceremony before the age of fourteen.

These hopes, however, presently foundered. Canon Vigneron found that his chapter objected to his being succeeded by his young nephew. To circumvent them the Canon went through the proper legal forms for handing over his prebend to the Pope in favor of 'Denis Diderot, tonsured cleric of the diocese of Langres, fourteen years and six months old, and no other.' But five hours after he had sent his representative off to Rome, the Canon died. Apparently his demission was not binding unless the Pope had accepted it while the Canon was still alive. The chapter immediately elected someone else, and the hopes of that career went glimmering.[3]

Soon afterwards, Diderot, influenced of course by his teachers in the Jesuit *collège* where he was becoming markedly successful, began to think of becoming a Jesuit himself. It may have been about this time, too, that he underwent the stress of a devout religious experience. His daughter states that for four or five months during the time that Diderot was desirous of becoming a Jesuit, he fasted, wore a hair shirt, and slept on straw.[4] The following passage from his novel *James the Fatalist,* written in 1773, may therefore be autobiographical in nature: 'There comes a moment during which almost every girl or boy falls into melancholy; they are tormented by a vague inquietude which rests on everything and finds nothing to calm it. They seek solitude; they weep; the silence to be found in cloisters attracts them; the image of peace that seems to reign in religious houses seduces them. They mistake the first manifestations of a developing sexual nature for the voice of God calling them to Himself; and it is precisely when nature is inciting them that they embrace a fashion of life contrary to nature's wish.'[5] It is piquant to learn that Diderot went through such a religious crisis, because in later life he is always assuming the pose, like Lucretius in the beginning pages of *De Rerum Natura,* of freeing men from fear of the gods. Yet even in these later years he now and again felt the tug of a previous persuasion. For instance, he wrote in 1765 of the necessity, in perpetuating a doctrine and an institution, for having concrete symbols that appeal to the imagination through the senses, and he gives as an example the exaltation of the multitude at a Corpus Christi processional, 'an exaltation that sometimes lays hold of even me. I have never seen that long file of priests in their sacerdotal robes, those young acolytes garbed in their white albs, girt up with their wide blue sashes, and casting flowers before the Holy Sacrament; the crowd that precedes and follows them in a religious silence; so many men with their heads bowed down to earth; I have never heard that solemn and affecting plain song of the priests, affectionately replied to by an infinity of voices of men, women, girls, and children, without my feelings being deeply moved and without tears coming to my eyes.' [6]

Apparently it was young Diderot's desire to join the Jesuits that led to his departure from Langres for the rest of his schooling. His daughter, Mme de Vandeul, declares that Diderot intended to leave surreptitiously in company with a Jesuit, but that his father, warned by one of Diderot's cousins, waited up on the appointed night and made an unexpected appearance just as Diderot was creeping down the stairs. To the question as to where he was going at this midnight hour, Diderot replied, 'To Paris, where I am bound to enter the Jesuits.'

'It won't be tonight, though your desires will be accomplished. But first let us get some sleep.' [7]

It is a little hard to believe that an order of the dignity of the Jesuits would recruit its members quite so melodramatically. Mme de Vandeul's extremely valuable account of her father, written in the year of his death, can frequently be proved aberrant in details, although it is so accurate in the main that she has become the ghost writer of many a later biography of Diderot. Her source of information was of course her father, who was not the sort of man to mar a tale in the telling. There may be some exaggeration in this anecdote, just as there is in the statement that he gravely made in an article written for the *Encyclopédie* claiming that his grandmother had had twenty-two children, and by the time she was thirty-three years of age! [8] A personal acquaintance named Taillefer published an account of Diderot only one year after his death, and though this document, too, must be taken with caution, the Taillefer and Vandeul accounts provide some opportunity for reciprocal control. With reference to Diderot's joining the Jesuits, Taillefer says nothing of any attempted flight from Langres.[9]

There is something of a mystery here. Indeed, it may even be that Diderot had fallen out with the Jesuits and that this caused him to go to Paris for the balance of his education. Evidence for such a view is found in something written by Jacques-André Naigeon, the familiar of Diderot during the last twenty years of his life and his would-be Boswell. In the

year of Diderot's death, Naigeon asked Diderot's daughter and her husband
for information about 'the quarrel with the Jesuits,' the context perhaps
implying that this occurred before he went to Paris. 'M. Naigeon desires
to write the life of M. Diderot,' wrote the son-in-law, '[and] persecutes me
to give him an exact and very detailed memorandum of the precise date
of his birth and the principal events of the philosopher's youth, of his early
studies, of his leaving the *collège,* of the quarrel with the Jesuits, of his
age when he was sent to Paris, how many years he stayed at the Collège
d'Harcourt, how many at the Collège de Bourgogne, and with the lawyer
M. Clément de Ris, his adventures with Mme Fréjacques, Mlle La Salette,
etc. . . .'[10] We should like to know more about that quarrel with the
Jesuits and when it occurred. As it stands, it is just another one of the little-
known incidents in a career which was often and surprisingly inscrutable.

At all events and for whatever reason, Diderot left Langres for Paris,
probably in the autumn of 1728, but possibly in 1729, his business being to
finish his last year of study, his 'rhetoric,' in what would now be called a
lycée.[11] Thus began the great adventure, the first going-away-from-home.
There is no indication of his being reluctant to leave Langres, save perhaps
for some sentimental thoughts about Mlle La Salette (a Langres girl born
the same year as he and who, in the course of years, became the mother of
the man who was to marry Diderot's daughter), or about another, but
unidentified, girl of Langres who made a sufficiently lasting impression to
cause him to mention her in a letter to Sophie Volland thirty years later.[12]
His father accompanied him. Down the valley of the Marne they rode —
'my melancholy and tortuous compatriot, the Marne,' he later called it — [13]
traveling, if they went by the slow coach, seven days to reach Paris.[14]

At Paris, Diderot's father made the necessary arrangements for his son's
settling into school, took his leave as though he were going to depart
from the city, and then stayed on in Paris a fortnight just to make certain
that all was going well. Having then been reassured by young Diderot that
he was happy and wanted to stay, and by his son's principal that the boy
was an excellent student even though they had had to discipline him, the
father went back to his knives and lancets at Langres. These incidents are
completely in character, both for father and son. For young Diderot had
thoughtlessly and big-heartedly undertaken to do someone else's work. He
obliged a disconsolate fellow-student who was reluctant to address himself
to the assignment of putting the serpent's seductive speech to Eve into Latin
verse. Diderot's verses were good — too good to have been done by the lad
who was supposed to do them. Both students were 'very roughly handled,'

wrote Mme de Vandeul, 'and my father gave up others' business to occupy himself henceforth exclusively with his own.' [15]

A new phase of his career had begun — and a lasting one, for he was to be a Parisian to the end of his days.

* * * * * *

From the time when he was about sixteen and went to Paris until the time when, at twenty-nine, he was already embarked on a career of letters and was desirous of getting married, little is precisely known of Diderot and of where and how he spent his time. This period of his life is a documentary desert, filled with shimmering mirages of assertion and whimsy, with widely spaced waterholes of verifiable fact upon which the panting searcher stumbles when just about to expire. By the year 1742 it becomes possible to follow his career with some certainty, but meanwhile some thirteen of the most important formative years of his life are shrouded and obscure. Diderot himself seldom spoke of them and, indeed, seems almost intentionally inscrutable about this period. It is amazing that no memoir writer contemporary with Diderot was able to recollect a youthful acquaintance with a man who was constantly resident in the nation's capital and who subsequently became so famous. Yet neither friend nor enemy has spoken from certain, personal knowledge of these years. The earliest notice of him recorded by a contemporary refers to the year 1742.

This account occurs in the memoirs of Johann Georg Wille, a German who lived most of his life in Paris and became one of the most celebrated engravers of the century. His likeness is preserved for us in a magnificent portrait by Greuze, which Diderot himself pronounced to be 'very beautiful' and very like.[16] In the year in which they met, Wille rented lodgings in the Rue de l'Observance, now called the Rue Antoine-Dubois, a very short street which at one end ascends by a stairway to the Rue Monsieur-le-Prince and on the other looked out on the Collège de Bourgogne, the site of which is now occupied by the Ecole de Médecine. 'I was curious to know who might be my neighbors in the house,' wrote Wille, 'and, in order to find out, I went downstairs to my landlord's rooms where by chance I found a very affable young man who in the ensuing conversation informed me that he was seeking to become a proficient man of letters and a still better philosopher, if that was possible; he added that he would be very happy to make my acquaintance, the more because he esteemed artists and loved the arts, because he thought we were of the same age, and because, moreover, he already knew that we were neighbors. I gave him a handclasp and from that moment we were friends. This young man was M. Diderot, since become famous. He occupied the entresol the floor beneath me, had a beautiful library there, and with pleasure lent me the books that might give pleasure to me.' [17]

This makes an engaging and attractive picture. A present-day reader, knowing that this is the picture of a young man about to enter a prodigious career of intellectual virtuosity, and realizing how little is known of the previous formative period, when this mind was broadening its range and deepening its mastery, is tantalized by this fleeting view into those misty years. What experiences had Diderot had to engender and confirm these tastes in philosophy and the arts? How much formal schooling had he had, and in what institutions of learning? How had he supported himself or been supported during all this time?

Even the school he entered on coming to Paris is a matter of conjecture. The evidence is conflicting and confused. A much younger contemporary says that Diderot entered the famous Collège Louis-le-Grand, the school where Voltaire was educated and whose imposing buildings still stand, just across the Rue Saint-Jacques from the Sorbonne.[18] Diderot's daughter and Naigeon declare that he entered the Collège d'Harcourt on the Boulevard Saint-Michel, just across from the Place de la Sorbonne, where the Lycée Saint-Louis now stands.[19] But his daughter also says that he was a school chum of the future Cardinal de Bernis, who indubitably was a student at Louis-le-Grand.[20] This conflicting testimony has touched off a controversy among scholars, nurtured by the fact that the Collèges' records for those years are no longer extant. One authority even argues for the Collège de Beauvais.[21] The recently published inquiry made by Naigeon of Diderot's daughter and son-in-law in 1784, previously alluded to, would seem to settle the matter in favor of the Collège d'Harcourt, but opens up an entirely new vista in suggesting that Diderot was also a student at the Collège de Bourgogne. The matter may be summarized by saying that it is extremely improbable that Diderot attended Louis-le-Grand *exclusively,* if he attended it at all. He probably went to the Collège d'Harcourt instead, but he could very possibly have attended both.

The point is more important than it may seem at first. If it were possible to know with certainty to what college in Paris Diderot belonged, then one could know whether in the important years when he was being introduced to formal philosophy, studied according to the scholastic method with its emphasis on metaphysics and categories and universals and with its strong tincture (at that time) of Cartesianism, he was being taught to see things from the Jesuit or the Jansenist point of view. For Louis-le-Grand was a

Jesuit college, whereas the Collège d'Harcourt was an active center of
Jansenism.[22] Those who dip into the study of seventeenth- and eighteenth-
century France quickly become aware that a chronic struggle went on within
the Catholic Church between these two factions. Moreover, in a society
where Church was as closely knit with State as it was during the *ancien
régime,* these theological disagreements had grave political repercussions.
In the early and middle eighteenth century it was scarcely possible for any
thinking Frenchman to avoid taking a position, even though publicly un-
avowed, in these disputes. Jansenist and Jesuit cordially hated each other,
and freethinkers scoffed at both.

The Jansenists took their name from Cornelis Jansen (1585–1638), Bishop
of Ypres. They constituted a puritanical and fundamentalist sect within
the Catholic Church, which by the time of the latter years of Louis XIV
seemed to be losing out to the Jesuits. The King, seeking uniformity and
orthodoxy, asked the Pope to settle the dispute once for all. The answer was
the papal bull *Unigenitus,* promulgated in 1713, which declared heretical
101 propositions set forth in a popular Jansenist book of devotions. But instead of settling the dispute, the bull only served to inflame it. The Pope's
action was resented by many as too great an interference in French domestic
affairs. Nevertheless, the energetic measures of the government to secure
acceptance of the bull forced the Jansenists undercover. They even published
an underground newspaper, *Les Nouvelles Ecclésiastiques,* which, in spite
of the determined efforts of the police, appeared with mocking and impish
regularity right up to its discontinuation in 1803. Ascetic and dour, stubborn
in adversity and embittered by it, the Jansenists were not the most broad-
minded people of their time. Both sides shocked the liberals of the century,
who feared the authoritarian proclivities of the one as much as those of
the other.

Which group, then, shaped Diderot's thinking during his college years?
Inasmuch as it is known that he was awarded the degree of master of arts in
the University of Paris on 2 September 1732, indicating a formal schooling
of some years' duration at Paris, it is possible to argue that Diderot transferred from the one college to the other following his 'rhetoric' and before
his 'philosophy.'[23] This conjecture has the advantage of reconciling conflicting accounts. It makes it possible for Diderot to have known the future
Cardinal Bernis at the Jesuit Louis-le-Grand, as Mme de Vandeul says he
did, and to have sat there under the famous teacher, Father Porée, as Diderot
claims in his *Letter on the Deaf and Dumb,* and still to have been a student
at the Jansenist Collège d'Harcourt, as his daughter and Naigeon declare

he was.[24] Yet another purpose can be served by this convenient conjecture. Diderot's general editorial policy, as well as the articles he himself wrote for the *Encyclopédie,* reveal a very considerable familiarity with exegetics, but without any special fondness or predilection for them. Therefore, could not the hypothesis that he attended both Jesuit and Jansenist colleges lead to the further one that, having become familiar with the point of view of each, he found himself repelled by both, so that instead of inclining him to the one or the other, each canceled the other out?

What he did immediately after receiving the master of arts degree is no less uncertain. Although it has generally been presumed that he thereupon discontinued his formal schooling, there is nothing in the evidence that demands that this be so. The account his daughter gives of his adventures implies that by this time Diderot, if he ever had the intention of studying for the priesthood, had given it up. This, too, tallies with Naigeon's testimony that while Diderot was a student at the Collège d'Harcourt he stopped wearing his ecclesiastical attire.[25] Documents show that twice during this crepuscular period of Diderot's life he considered entering the law, one document referring to the year 1736 and the other to about 1741.[26] Mme de Vandeul's account is probably accurate as far as it goes, although the biographer might well wish, with a sigh, for greater precision in dates: 'His studies completed, his father wrote to M. Clément de Ris, a solicitor at Paris and a fellow townsman, to take him into the household and have him study law. He stayed there two years; but the searching of deeds and the listing of inventories had few attractions for him. All the time he could steal from his employer was used in studying Latin and Greek, which he thought he did not sufficiently know; mathematics, which he always passionately loved; Italian, English, etc. Finally he gave himself up to his taste for letters to such a point that M. Clément felt he ought to inform his friend of the poor use his son was making of his time. Thereupon my grandfather expressly charged M. Clément to propose a profession to his son, to induce him to make his choice promptly, and to engage him to be a doctor, a solicitor, or a barrister. My father asked for time to think it over, and was granted it. After some months, the propositions were renewed. Then he said that the profession of doctor did not please him, he did not want to kill any one; that the profession of solicitor was too difficult to perform scrupulously; that he would gladly choose the profession of barrister, save that he had an unconquerable aversion to busying himself all his life with other people's affairs.

' "But," said M. Clément to him, "what do you want to be, then?"

' "*Ma foi,* nothing, nothing at all. I like study; I am very well off, very happy; I don't ask anything else." ' Thereupon Diderot's father cut off his allowance and demanded that he either choose a profession or come home within the week. Diderot left the house of the solicitor, so as not to put him to any expense, and, says Mme de Vandeul, lived the next ten years on his own.[27]

At some time during this decade Diderot was a tutor in the household of a wealthy financier named Randon. But Diderot was not of the temperament to enjoy such confining work: ' "Monsieur, look at me. A lemon is less yellow than my complexion. I am making men of your children, but each day I become a child with them. I am a thousand times *too* rich and *too* well off in your house, but I must leave it. The object of my desires is not to live better, but just not to die." ' [28]

All this is completely in character and entirely credible. It shows Diderot's love of independence, his hatred of constraint. And it shows, too, a sort of lack of fondness for children which is also to be seen or sensed in his writings, even though he once asserted in middle life that he was very fond of old men and children. Diderot was constantly letting his feelings pour forth in jets of enthusiasm, but one can look long and far — that one instance excepted — for him to express any great enthusiasm for children and child-hood, except, of course, his own.[29] And not even his own daughter seems to have interested him much until she began to make precocious remarks which gave him hope that she possessed an interesting and original mind. He seems to have pitied the state of childhood — its helplessness, its limited outlook, its wrong conclusions logically derived from false premises — but he did not admire it.

Aside from two years accounted for at the solicitor's and three months being a tutor at the financier's, Diderot, according to his daughter's account, was on the town. 'He passed ten whole years . . . having no other resource than those very sciences that were earning him the disapprobation of his father. He gave lessons in mathematics; if the pupil was quick . . . he would teach him the whole day long; but if he found a stupid pupil, he would not go back. He was paid in books, in furniture, in linen, in money, or not at all; it was all the same to him. He wrote sermons. A missionary ordered six from him for the Portuguese colonies and paid fifty *écus* apiece for them. My father thought this affair one of the best he ever brought off.' [30]

This testimony bespeaks a precarious existence. Now and again he was able in other ways to supplement the income he derived from giving lessons. For example, he tells us that he prepared the general formula and mathematical tables for a treatise published in 1741 on gnomonics, the science of sundials.[31] This task presupposes considerable mathematical competence and accuracy, and it is to be presumed, although not certainly so, that he was paid for it. Moreover, the censor's approbation of Diderot's translation of Temple Stanyan's *Grecian History,* dated 25 May 1742, proves that he had prepared the manuscript before that time, and for this translation he probably received something in advance.[32] Still, his was evidently a Bohemian, hand-to-mouth existence, provided that, as will be discussed later, he did not spend some of these ten years in formal theological studies. Diderot's daughter is emphatic that her grandfather sent no money to his recalcitrant son, although 'his mother, more tender and more compliant, sent him some louis, not by the post nor by friends, but by a maid servant who did the sixty leagues on foot, delivered to him the small sum from his mother, adding to it, without mentioning it, all her own savings, and then walked back the sixty leagues in return. This woman carried out this commission on three occasions.' [33]

With an income so uncertain and evidently operating in geyserlike intervals of fast and feast, it is not surprising to learn that sometimes his cupboard was bare. One Shrove Tuesday, a day when, like Christmas in America, absent youths were particuarly likely to be homesick, Diderot arose to find that he had absolutely no money with which to buy dinner. Not wanting to disturb his friends upon such a day, he tried unsuccessfully to work, and then went out for a long walk. 'He came back to his tavern; upon entering, he sat down and felt ill. The landlady gave him a little toast soaked in wine, and he went to bed. "That day," he told me, "I swore that if ever I possessed anything, never in my life would I refuse something to an indigent person, in order not to condemn any fellow man of mine to put in a day as distressing as that." ' [34]

Diderot was not averse to receiving aid from fellow townsmen, knowing that his father would pay up. There is documentary evidence of this having occurred in 1736. On 20 August of that year, a man formerly from Langres named Foucou — fifteen years later Diderot acknowledged in his *Encyclopédie* article on 'Steel' the helpful information contributed by 'M. Foucou, previously a cutler' — signed a receipt for thirty-eight livres received from Diderot's father by the hands of Brother Angel, a Barefooted Carmelite friar. On the same receipt Didier Diderot wrote: 'This is the final receipt of the amount agreed upon with M. Foucou of Paris. I wrote him on 23 May 1736 not to advance anything to Diderot nor to take him into his house; *that he ought to remain with the solicitor. . . .* Therefore there will be no making it up to him [Foucou] if he [Diderot] stays with him at all, for it is against my wishes.'[35]

Need sometimes brought Diderot close to roguishness. Mme de Vandeul tells a long story of how Diderot convinced Brother Angel, the Carmelite friar mentioned above, a man who also came originally from Langres and was a distant relative of the Diderots, that he intended to become a friar in Brother Angel's monastery. On that understanding Diderot received payments amounting to some two thousand livres. When at last Brother Angel showed that he would advance no more, Diderot said to him, ' "Brother Angel, then you don't want to give me any more money?"

' "Assuredly not."

' "Well, then, I don't want to be a Carmelite any more. Write to my father and get yourself paid." '[36] Both Diderot and his daughter thought this sort of panhandling clever.

During the nine or ten years between the time of receiving a master of arts degree at the University of Paris and his writing the earliest of his letters now extant, Diderot existed in what to posterity has seemed a penumbra of obscurity. But the person whom Wille found so attractive has left scattered in his works various allusions to his tastes and to his doings in those early years, which help in some measure to answer the question of what manner of man he was on the eve of his public career. In the first place, it is probable that his greatest single intellectual competence lay at that time in the field of mathematics. When he published in 1748 his highly respected *Mémoires sur différens sujets de mathématiques,* he wrote in the Fifth Memoir, in which he made some corrections in Newton's calculations of the effect on pendulums of the resistance of air: 'It is true that I studied Newton with the intention of elucidating him; I shall even confess to you that this work was pushed on, if not with great success, at least with adequate vivacity; but that I no longer gave it a thought from the time that the Reverend Fathers Le Seur and Jacquier published their *Commentary* [1739], and I have not been tempted to take it up again.'[37]

In the second place, his random recollections show that during these early years he haunted the theater and was much enamored of acting — and actresses. Evidently, too, he deemed it possible that he could have made his living on the stage: 'I myself, when I was young, hesitated between the Sorbonne and the Comédie. In winter, in the worst sort of weather, I used to recite roles from Molière and Corneille out loud in the solitary walks of the Luxembourg. What did I have in mind? To be applauded? Perhaps. To live on familiar terms with women of the theater, whom I found infinitely lovable and whom I knew to be of very easy virtue? Assuredly. I don't know what I wouldn't have done to be pleasing to la Gaussin, who made her debut about that time and who was beauty personified; or to la Dangeville, who had so many attractive qualities on the stage.' [38]

The excitement that young Diderot found in going to the theater is well depicted in a passage that he wrote in 1758: 'Fifteen years ago our theaters were places of tumult. The coolest heads began to get heated upon entering them, and grave men shared there, more or less, the transports of giddy ones. . . . People moved about, fidgeted, jostled one another, one's soul was quite beside itself. . . . The piece began with difficulty and was often interrupted, but let a fine passage come along and there was an incredible tumult, encores were demanded endlessly, and people enthused over the actor and the actress. The enthusiasm passed from the pit to the dress circle, and from the dress circle to the boxes. People had come with ardor, they left in a state of intoxication: some went to visit the girls, others scattered themselves in society; it was like a thunderstorm which passes over, spending itself afar, but the mutterings of which last a long while after it has passed by. That is what pleasure is like.' [39]

Sometimes, as Diderot recalls in his *Letter on the Deaf and Dumb,* his interest in the stage was a little more philosophical and — shall we say — unconventional: 'Formerly I used to visit the theater very often, and I knew most of our good plays by heart. On the days when I proposed to study movements and gestures, I went to the third-class boxes, for the farther I was from the actors the better I was placed. As soon as the curtain went up . . . I would put my fingers into my ears, not without some astonishment on the part of those round about me . . . and stubbornly kept my ears stopped up as long as the action of the actor appeared to me to be in harmony with the lines that I was remembering. I listened only when I was thrown off the track by the gestures on stage, or thought I was.' And Diderot recalled with amusement the redoubled surprise of the people round him 'when they saw me shed tears in the pathetic parts, and that with my ears continuously stopped.' [40]

As a footnote to his love for the theater and his love of ideas, it may fairly be conjectured that Diderot often visited the Café Procope, for until 1770 the old Comédie-Française was located just across the street. The Procope, then a famous center for actors, playwrights, academicians, and other men of letters, is now reopened and operating at the old stand, 13, Rue de l'Ancienne Comédie. In its eighteenth-century heyday it was fully as famous as the Dôme and the Rotonde in the youthful days of Hemingway and Ezra Pound or the Café de Flore when Sartre was frequenting it, and it seems hardly possible that Diderot was not among the Procope's patrons.[41]

From scattered allusions in his later works, we can get some impression of Diderot's manner and appearance at this time. He was a young man of large frame — a friend later said of him that he was built like a chair-man or porter [42] — and well set up. He wore his own hair, which was blond, heavy, and thick, and he was, then as always, careless of dress, for he recalls in his *Rameau's Nephew* the days when he gave lessons in mathematics and wore 'an overcoat of gray shag, all played out on one side, with one of the sleeves torn; and black woolen stockings mended at the back with white thread.' [43] Moreover, he evidently liked to tease the girls: as he looked at Greuze's portrait of Mme Greuze, exhibited in the Salon of 1765, Diderot remembered when she was a girl in her father's bookshop on the Quai des Grands-Augustins, bordering the Seine. Diderot entered the shop one day, 'with that lively, ardent, and daft manner I used to have.

' "Mademoiselle, La Fontaine's *Fables,* and a Petronius, if you please."

' "Here they are, Monsieur. Are there any other books you'd like?"

' "I beg your pardon, Mademoiselle, but . . ."

' "Don't be hesitant."

' *"The Nun in a Shift."*

' "Fie! Monsieur; do you suppose that one keeps in stock, that one reads, nasty things like that?"

' "Why! why! is that a nasty book, Mademoiselle? I didn't realize that!" ' [44]

Finally, it may be conjectured with some assurance that Diderot took love where he could find it, a conclusion that might be drawn from his account, written in 1758, of an incident that would seem to have occurred in these early years: 'Oh! my dear friend, where is the time when I had long hair floating in the breeze? In the mornings, when my nightshirt collar was open and I took off my nightcap, my hair fell in great, disordered locks over well-knit and very white shoulders; and my neighbor would get up early in the morning from her husband's side, half-open the curtains of her window, intoxicate herself with the sight, and I would readily perceive what was going on. 'Twas thus that I seduced her from one side of the street to the other. When I was with her, for we came together at last, I acted with candor and innocence, with a manner gentle, simple, modest, and true. All has passed away, the blond hair, and the candor, and the innocence.' [45]

Diderot, it may be remarked, was always quite adequately appreciative of female charms. He was not, however, an unbridled libertine, even if the principal bridle was nothing more virtuous than a horror of venereal disease. He recalls, in a letter to Sophie Volland, how he escaped providentially from running the risk of it on two occasions that must date from these early times. 'I never think of it without having goose flesh,' he wrote.[46]

Now, what about the possibility, preposterous though it seems, that Diderot spent some time as a graduate student of theology? By his own statement, he was balancing 'between the Sorbonne and the Comédie' not long after Mlle Gaussin made her debut at the Comédie-Française, an event which took place on 28 April 1731. Diderot's reference to the Sorbonne was, of course, to the faculty of theology of the University of Paris, and it certainly is true that his degree of master of arts qualified him to take up advanced theological studies if he chose. Diderot says he wavered between a theologian's career and an actor's, and since the context of the passage shows that he did not go on the stage, it follows that it is *possible* that for a time he became instead a graduate student in theology. If only the register books of the faculty of theology were extant — but unfortunately they have disappeared.[47]

It should be recalled that Diderot was only nineteen years old when he received his master of arts degree, and it therefore seems unlikely that his father would have allowed him to go completely on his own. Of course, two of these years were spent, according to the family tradition, as apprentice to a solicitor. But were they the two years immediately following the conferral of his degree in September 1732? Probably not, for Diderot's father, writing in May 1736, says that Diderot ought to remain with the solicitor. Now, even if two of those intervening years had already been spent at the solicitor's, there is still a hiatus of some twenty months to be accounted for.

A statement in his father's will also gives color to the supposition that young Diderot spent more years living off money sent him by his parents than Mme de Vandeul's story credits, for in that document, drawn up in 1750, Didier Diderot remarks: 'You well know, you, Diderot the elder [son], the great expense I have been to for you these twenty years that you have been at Paris. If I added up nothing but what is of my certain knowledge, I have sent you more than ten thousand livres, not including what your mother and your sisters sent you and the interest on this sum. . . .'[48] Now, when it is recalled that board, room, and tuition at a place like Louis-le-Grand was only four hundred livres a year, it is easy to see that the purchasing power of ten thousand livres could account for quite a few years in a student's life.[49] Considering Diderot's relative youth, it seems not unlikely, therefore, that he continued his schooling after 1732, possibly in theology; that perhaps, if he did, he became disgusted with theological studies; and that then he and his father turned to the possibility of his becoming a solicitor.

Far more startling and sensational, however, is the probability that as late as about 1741 Diderot was seriously intending to become a doctor of theology. He himself alluded to it in a passage he wrote in the *Salon* of 1767. 'I arrive in Paris,' he wrote. 'I was going to take the fur and install myself among the doctors of the Sorbonne. I meet a woman beautiful as an angel. I want to sleep with her. I do so. I have four children by her and there I am, forced to give up Homer and Virgil, whom I always used to carry with me in my pocket; the theater, for which I had a fondness; very lucky to undertake the *Encyclopédie,* for which I shall have sacrificed twenty-five years of my life.' [50]

This passage needs explanation. In the first place, naming the Sorbonne was the usual way of referring not to the whole University of Paris, but only to its faculty of theology. In the second place, 'to take the fur' was a locution that signified taking a university degree more advanced than the master of arts.[51] In the third place, to become a doctor of theology at the Sorbonne, one had to be a priest and have completed five years of theological studies after receiving the master of arts degree.[52] In the fourth place, Diderot did not meet his future wife before 1740 at the earliest. The nub of the problem, then, is this: is it possible to lend credence to the astonishing view that Diderot was engaged in, or at least intended to embark upon, advanced theological studies at as late an age as twenty-eight or twenty-nine? If so, it is a fact his daughter either did not know or took pains to conceal.

Diderot's writings, especially his articles in the *Encyclopédie,* reflect great familiarity with theological sources and concepts, and this fact has been claimed as clear proof that he had engaged in advanced theological studies.[53] But although it is evident that Diderot could quote the Church Fathers with as much appositeness and skill as Anatole France and certainly knew his theology well enough not to blunder unwittingly into the innumerable pitfalls and booby traps of the thickly mined areas of theological contention, still the more we examine his writings, the less we feel justified in accepting this as incontrovertible proof of advanced study. A person hostile to Diderot might say of him, as Gibbon said of Saint Augustine, that his learning is too often borrowed and his arguments are too often his own. Therefore, the indirect argument, that internal evidence attests the advanced state of Diderot's theological studies, has some plausibility but is not incontestable.

More material evidence is found in letters sent from Paris by Pierre La Salette of Langres. After writing on 10 August 1741 that the shirts Diderot had received from Langres were quite unsuitable, La Salette wrote again eight days later: 'He needs linen, the dear son! As for the rest, he is well fitted out for from now to 1 January, the time that he has reiterated to me for the execution of his promises.' [54] La Salette's next letter, dated 4 September 1741, once more harps on linen, but it also reveals the nature of Diderot's promises: 'He has let me come to the conclusion that it would be better to send him the cloth for making shirts and collars instead of sending him the shirts and collars ready-made. I have examined his linen. He simply must have some: he was obliged to have the shirts that his dear mother sent him remade. . . . For the rest, he is very well and perseveres in his promises. Saint-Sulpice will be his residence on 1 January next. May God grant him the grace to carry it out for the satisfaction of his family, since it is the profession that he chooses and which no one has urged him to take in preference to all others.' [55]

These references to 'promises' suggest that Diderot really was thinking of an ecclesiastical career when he met his future wife. The celebrated Paris seminary of the order of Saint-Sulpice, founded in 1641 and situated just opposite the famous Parisian church of that name, was at that time the best known and most popular seminary in France for the training of priests. Not organized as a monastery, its object was to prepare young clerics for holy orders and concomitant ecclesiastical functions. So prominent was it that, according to the *Catholic Encyclopedia,* 'When the Revolution broke out the seminary of Paris alone had trained more than five thousand priests, and more than half the bishops who faced that dreadful tempest (about fifty) had been in Sulpician seminaries.'

In the passage from the *Salon* of 1767, Diderot spoke of being a doctor at the Sorbonne and did not mention the Seminary of Saint-Sulpice, of which Pierre La Salette wrote in 1741. Are these two bits of testimony therefore irreconcilable? Almost assuredly not; for, as we have already seen, one had to be an ordained priest to qualify for the doctorate of theology, and there was a close connection between the Sorbonne and the Seminary of Saint-Sulpice. This is demonstrated by a pertinent passage from one of the classics of French literature, published in 1731. In the *History of Manon Lescaut,* written by a man who was himself an *abbé,* the faithless Manon watches the young seminary student from Saint-Sulpice undergo his public examination in the school of theology at the Sorbonne.[56]

It may be concluded, then, that Diderot really intended about the year

1741 to take up an ecclesiastical career. There is no evidence, however, that
he ever actually did enter the Seminary of Saint-Sulpice, only evidence that
he *said* he intended to. Nor is there any evidence whatever that he was
eager to enter this profession. On the contrary, he tells us in an autobiographical passage written in 1773 or 1774 that in 'the classes of the University
my masters could never conquer my disdain for the frivolities of Scholasticism.' He devoured books of arithmetic, algebra, and geometry, he tells us,
and took pleasure in Homer, Virgil, Tasso, and Milton, 'but always coming
back to mathematics, as an unfaithful husband, tired of his mistress, returns
from time to time to his wife!' [57]

This analogy, as characteristic of eighteenth-century manners as it was
of Diderot himself, seems to show that if Diderot intended to become a
priest, it was not precisely because he had what the Methodists term a
'call.' On the other hand, there is no evidence that at this early time in his
life he was yet in flaming rebellion against the Church. It was not until
years later that the necessities of philosophical consistency turned him against
Christian belief. And it is quite possible that he contemplated the priesthood without either eagerness or reluctance. After all, the *abbé,* supported
by some benefice or commendam which provided for an untrammeled life
in secular society, was a very prominent element in the eighteenth-century
French scene. Perhaps, then, Diderot hoped to secure a benefice or sinecure
that would allow him to enjoy both security and the pleasures of scholarship; perhaps he was impressed by the fact that after all two priests were at
that very moment publishing their monumental commentary on Newton;
perhaps he was ready at last to give up his precarious and necessitous independence. At all events, meeting the girl whom he wanted to marry caused
him to lay aside any plans he may have had for a career in which celibacy
was a prerequisite, and presently Diderot was once again being urged by
his family to enter the law office of a solicitor.

CHAPTER 3

Clandestine Marriage

'IT WAS about this time, in 1741,' wrote Mme de Vandeul in her memoir of her father, 'that he made the acquaintance of my mother.'[1]

At this period Anne-Toinette Champion, who was born at La Ferté-Bernard on 22 February 1710, and was in consequence three and a half years older than her future husband, was living with her widowed mother in very modest and straitened circumstances.[2] The family was a respectable one, even though stricken by indigence. 'Mme Champion, a widow with no property,' continued Mme de Vandeul, 'came to Paris with her daughter, then three years of age. A childhood friend of my grandmother gave her a place to stay, and my mother was put into the convent of the Miramiones in order to learn to work with sufficient skill to have no need of the assistance of anyone.'[3] At sixteen, she settled with her mother 'in a small apartment, and both of them carried on the business of dealing in lace and linen. . . . My mother was tall, beautiful, pious, and modest. Various traders had wished to marry her; but she preferred her work and her liberty to marrying a husband whom she could not love.'

'My father . . . saw her and wanted to see her again. . . . As he could not pay his attentions so assiduously to my mother without some reason, he told the ladies that he was destined to become an ecclesiastic; that soon he would enter the Seminary of Saint-Nicolas; that he had need of a certain provision of linen, and he besought them to take charge of the matter.'[4]

It does not require a professional detective to deduce some close connection between the collars and shirts that Diderot persuaded Pierre La Salette had to be done over and the fact that the Champion ladies were in that sort of business. Diderot's courtship, as a matter of fact, was an anticipation of the Hollywood boy-meets-girl formula, as he himself, in his later playwright days, seemed to realize. In his *Father of a Family,* Diderot turned a

37

fond and Narcissan gaze upon recollections of his earlier self. The reckless and impetuous Saint-Albin was modeled, Diderot told his daughter,
on the young man who had courted Anne-Toinette.[5]

It is a matter of interest, almost astonishment, that Diderot was able to
convince so many people on so many occasions that he intended to become
a priest or a monk. In Langres, while still a lad, he intended to become a
Jesuit; in Paris, he convinced Brother Angel of his intention to join the Barefooted Carmelites; in 1731 or 1732, according to Diderot's recollections
recorded in a letter to Sophie Volland in 1765, he was willing to become a
Carthusian monk, although on this occasion, it is true, the prior did not take
him at his word; [6] in 1741 he persuaded La Salette that he intended to enter
Saint-Sulpice, while at nearly the same time he was leading the Champions
to believe that he was about to enter the Seminary of Saint-Nicolas-du-
Chardonnet, a nearby and highly regarded training school for priests where
Ernest Renan was to be a student a century later. From all these incidents
we must conclude that Diderot not only had a convincing way about him
but was also so familiar with seminary ways and various religious orders as
to sound completely plausible.

Their married years were to prove, abundantly and regrettably, that Denis
Diderot and Anne-Toinette Champion were far from temperamentally
congenial. What was it about her, then, that so appealed to Diderot in the
days of his courtship? The question is, it must be confessed, a silly one. What
appeals to any young man in a girl 'beautiful as an angel'? But it is also
possible that Diderot, already thirteen or fourteen years away from home
and perhaps tired of an existence more than a little Bohemian, was feeling
domestically inclined. Anne-Toinette Champion — her name sometimes appears as Anne-Antoinette — did much more for Diderot than she is usually
given credit for. Not least of these benefits was the fact that her being hard
to win drew Diderot away from that inclination toward dissoluteness and
debauchery that was quite evidently a part of his bachelor existence.[7] Those
shirts played a great role; how great may be detected in the implications of
a remark that Diderot happened to toss off in casual conversation many
years later. 'I have heard Diderot say,' wrote Nicolas de Chamfort, an
anecdotist of some repute in his century, 'that a sensible man of letters might
be the lover of a woman who writes a book, but he ought to be the husband
of her only who knows how to sew a shirt.' [8] This remark of Diderot has in
it unpremeditated sadness and poignancy because it sums up so accurately
the history of his own marriage.

'Nevertheless, they [the Champions] unceasingly referred to his entry into the Seminary,' continues Mme de Vandeul, 'but, having perceived more than once that he was pleasing to my mother, he confessed to her that he had hit upon this fib only for the purpose of being allowed in her home, and assured her with all the violence of his passion and of his character that he was determined not to take orders but, on the contrary, to marry her. My mother made only such objections as reason might suggest; in view of their mutual affection, these objections had little weight. My grandmother declared it to be most contrary to reason to marry oneself to such a hot-head, to a man who did nothing, and whose whole merit, she said, was in having a *golden tongue* with which he turned her daughter's head; but this mother, who preached so sensibly, was herself fond of my father to the point of distraction. . . . Finally they all decided that my father should visit Langres and that he should come back fortified with his family papers and the consent of his parents.' [9]

Meanwhile, even before Diderot left for Langres, the idea of his becoming a lawyer had been revived. This we learn from an undated letter he wrote to Anne-Toinette: 'I have just received a letter from the papa. After a sermon two ells longer than usual, plenary liberty to do anything I want, provided I do something. Do I persist in the resolution of going into a solicitor's office? Order given to seek out a good one and pay down the first quarter right off. . . .' [10] It is interesting that this project of becoming a solicitor crops up a second time in Diderot's life. Perhaps we may conclude that not long previously Diderot had informed his family that he had decided not to enter Saint-Sulpice on 1 January 1742. But did Diderot actually again start work in a solicitor's office? Other letters to his fiancée give absolutely no indication one way or the other. Naigeon implies that he did, by saying that Diderot fell in love 'sometime before entering the solicitor's office,' and Naigeon, though tiresome, is an authority who may not with impunity be ignored. [11]

From these letters to his fiancée it can be deduced that Diderot left Paris for Langres on 7 December 1742. [12] He found his parents much concerned about his future, but also much impressed when galley proofs arrived of the translation he was doing from the English of Temple Stanyan's *Grecian History:* 'My dear sweetheart, these proofs of my book, sent to me thrice a week, are doing wonders. My father and mother, who didn't seem too much inclined to let me go back, are going presently to be the first to hasten my return, so convinced are they that I am occupied up there with something useful. . . .' [13] Moreover, Diderot found that 'the decision that my younger brother has just taken has put the finishing touch to deciding my father to leave me my freedom.' [14] This 'freedom' may refer to Diderot's previously stated intentions of becoming an ecclesiastic. Just at this time his younger brother had entered the seminary to become a priest, and it may be that the Diderot parents did not desire both their sons to adopt a calling that precluded their having legitimate children.[15] This did not mean, however, as Diderot soon found out, that the family was willing to accept any daughter-in-law he might propose for them.

At first the Langres visit went well: no doubt Diderot's tactful gift of a book of piety for his father, an Office of the Dead, was well received.[16] It was probably during this visit, too, that Diderot went to see his sister who had become a nun, a visit mentioned by Mme de Vandeul, but in a context that is very vague.[17] It may be that during this comparatively lengthy visit Diderot let slip some views on religion that made his mother fear for his orthodoxy, for Diderot's father, writing some years later, makes an allusion to 'the remonstrances that she made to you by word of mouth.' [18] Since this visit to Langres is the only one known to have been made by Diderot between his first going to Paris and his mother's death in 1748, this testimony provides useful evidence in dating the progression of his heterodox ideas, although it should be admitted that it probably took very little to alarm the simple faith of his unsophisticated and pious mother.

Diderot's strategy was to persuade his parents to fix an annuity upon him. Following that, he intended to broach the subject of his intended marriage. But by this time Anne-Toinette's letters, addressed to him in care of one of his cousins named Humblot, were reaching him, and one of these epistles, 'full of injustices and cutting words' and evidently accusing him of being too dilatory, caused him to force the pace.[19] A later letter from Diderot mentioned that 'thy impatience, which I can only praise, since it is a proof of thy love, has just hastened my declaration.' [20] This declaration was so poorly received that Diderot appears to have demanded, in a fit of passion, that he receive his share of the family inheritance out of hand, failing which he actually threatened to have his father arrested. It must have been a tempestuous scene. The fine plans of Diderot the son were quite undone and Diderot the father took steps of his own. On 1 February 1743, he wrote to Mme Champion: 'If your daughter is as well born — and loves him as much as he believes — she will exhort him to renounce her hand. It is only at this price that he will recover his liberty, because, with the aid of friends of mine who have been made indignant by his impudence, I have had him put in a safe place, and we have, I am sure, more than enough backing to keep him there until he changes his mind.' [21]

Parental authority went rather far in the *ancien régime,* and it was not at all uncommon for heads of families to call to their assistance the supreme authority of the king in cases of particularly stubborn resistance. If passions were too hot, they were cooled off by the simple device of arrest and indefinite detention in some monastery, castle, or prison. Thus the power of the state operated to moderate the passions of junior members of a family while abetting those of the head of it. Unfaithful wives, daughters eager to elope, sons desirous of marrying beneath them could be made unwilling guests of the king for prolonged periods during which it was hoped that leisured meditation would temper the promptings of impetuous desire. The most famous example in the eighteenth century of arbitrary arrests and imprisonments used to enforce family discipline was that of the turbulent Mirabeau family. At one time the Marquis de Mirabeau had every single member of his family, save himself and one other, under lock and key.[22] This was operating on a grand scale, and the Diderots, of course, were not so magnificent. But it is quite evident that Diderot's father intended to utilize the power of the state indefinitely until his son should change his mind.

It is extremely interesting to learn that Diderot was put under coercive detention. It is no less so to know that he escaped it. 'After having experienced unheard-of torments [he wrote to Anne-Toinette], here I am at liberty. Shall I tell you? my father carried his harshness to the point of having me shut up with some monks who have employed against me all that the most determined maliciousness could imagine. I flung myself from the window the night of Sunday going on to Monday. . . . I have come thirty leagues on foot in detestable weather. . . . If you resent the lack of success of my journey and if you should show that you do, I am so overwhelmed with afflictions, I have suffered so much, so many trials still await me, that my decision is taken, I shall finish everything at one stroke; my life or death depends upon the welcome you give me. My father is in such a fury that I do not doubt at all that he will disinherit me, as he has threatened. If I lose you, too, what remains to me that can keep me in this world?

'I shall not be in safety at all in my former apartment, for I have no doubt that Brother Angel has already received orders to have me arrested, orders which he would be only too glad to carry out. Do me the favor then of finding me a furnished room near you or somewhere else. . . .

'[P. S.] I forgot to mention that to prevent my running away, they took the useless precaution of cutting off half my hair.

'In the whole family, I had on my side nobody but one aunt. I went to stay with her during our quarrels.' [23]

On his return to Paris Diderot apparently went underground for a considerable period. Perhaps the only wonder is that the police made no determined effort to catch up with him, for, after all, he had flouted the royal authority. This was an example, one is tempted to think, of how a revolution could incubate in France, for the authority of the state repeatedly showed itself arbitrary and irritating without being resolutely and effectively repressive. During this year of lying low, Diderot occupied lodgings in the Rue des Deux-Ponts on the old Île Saint-Louis, that islet in the Seine which even today preserves an air of detachment, as though living untouched by time in an age gone by.[24]

The family tradition, as reported by Mme de Vandeul, was that Anne-Toinette Champion intended to see no more of her lover: 'She assured my father very explicitly that she would never enter a family where she was not regarded favorably; she asked him to go away, and in spite of his importunities ceased to receive him.' But Diderot became ill, according to this family story: 'My mother could not remain at peace and know that he was suffering. She sent a friend to get news of him. She was told that his room was a regular kennel, that he was without hot food or any care, and was emaciated and melancholy. She thereupon made up her mind, went to see him, promised to marry him, and both mother and daughter became his nurses.' As soon as he could go out, writes Mme de Vandeul, they were married.[25]

It is noteworthy that the marriage, which occurred on 6 November 1743, was not solemnized until the groom had passed his thirtieth birthday. This was probably intentional, for by a royal ordinance of 1697 it had been established that a son who married without his father's consent before the age of thirty could be disinherited.[26] As for the customary marriage settlement, Diderot later wrote: 'My wife's relatives had our contract drawn up and I signed it without reading it. The reason was that I loved her.' [27] Concerning this marriage, the most copious source of information is provided by Jal, an indefatigable and reliable antiquarian: 'Diderot . . . had one ban published at the church of Saint-Louis [-en-l'Île, his parish church], and at the church of Saint-Séverin [Anne-Toinette's parish church], paid for dispensing with the two others, and presented himself before the parish priest of Saint-Séverin for permission to be betrothed and married on the same day in the church of Saint-Pierre-aux-Boeufs. Saint-Pierre shared with the Cardinal Le Moine and some of the small parishes of the city the privilege of solemnizing marriages that were quasi-clandestine. People went there to have marriages consecrated against which there were family repugnances or some scandal or other. Without display, without carriages, without guests, the people to be married presented themselves at an early hour at the sacristy, asked for a low mass, signed the marriage certificate witnessed by four persons, and left the church without bustle or pomp, just as they had arrived there. "Denis Diderot, a burgher of Paris, a son of full age of Didier Diderot, master cutler, and Angélique Vigneron," and "Anne-Toinette Champion, residing at Rue Poupée, in the parish of Saint-Séverin," presented themselves on 6 November, 1743 — the cold favoring the *incognito* that they wished to preserve — at Saint-Pierre-aux-Boeufs, and were united in the presence of "Marie Maleville, residing at Rue Saint-Séverin," of "Jacques Bosson, vicar of Saint-Pierre-aux-Boeufs, of Jean-Baptiste Guillot, former canon of Dôle, and of a neighbor of the bride." '[28] Saint-Pierre-aux-Boeufs was located on the Île de la Cité, just a stone's throw from Notre-Dame, on a site now occupied by the Hôtel-Dieu. Mme de Vandeul says that the marriage took place at midnight.[29]

Diderot's letters from this period of courtship and engagement trace the familiar progress of a lover from the formal *vous* to the intimate *tu,* and then — when lovers quarreled — the regress back to *vous* again. Here are the endearing nicknames, with a special tinge of Diderot's exuberance on them: 'Ninot' writing to his 'Nanette,' his 'Tonton.' And the letters reveal, too, much of the character and temperament of the bride and groom. They allow us to perceive Anne-Toinette's hardheadedness, her evident ability to be coolly skeptical and disconcertingly realistic. These were congenital qualities, no doubt, but also ones confirmed by the narrowness of a necessitous existence and reinforced by the conviction that life is hard. They were qualities that always grated on that exuberance of his, on his easy enthusiasms, on that half of him that loved to gamble, to buy expensive prints, to be late to appointments, to forget what day of the week it was, and to ignore the fact that a cab he had ordered was standing outside running up a bill. So Diderot expostulates with her, as on 2 January 1743: 'You know my sensitivity. Judge, then, of the state you have put me into. You will be my cruelest enemy if you do not hasten to redress the wrong you have done to him who in the whole world merits it the least and loves you the most.' [30] And in the last letter extant from the period before their marriage, a letter which shows that Anne-Toinette came very close to breaking off the marriage entirely, Diderot complains of the 'hardheartedness of your way of doing things.' [31]

These letters also show us in the early Diderot a Diderot already striking some of his most characteristic poses — the plausible and persuasive Diderot of the golden tongue, facilely making assurances of eternal devotion; the disarmingly candid Diderot, blandly confessing the extent of his previous vagaries in order to show how greatly he had reformed: 'The fire that consumes a young libertine (for I have truly merited the name) for his neighbor's wife is a fire of straw which soon dies down forever; but that which consumes a virtuous man (for I merit this name since you have made me well-behaved) for his own wife never goes out.' Alas! this was not only an erroneous prophecy; it was fustian. Anne-Toinette, however, married him in spite of it, perhaps because of it. And finally, there is revealed in these letters the complacent Diderot, naïvely complimenting himself, as he so frequently did, concerning his own virtue: '. . . my gratitude, my probity, for I pride myself upon having as much of it as any one alive; the tears that I shed when I was on the point of losing you, my oaths of fidelity, thy love, thy qualities of body, heart, and mind, all ought to assure you of an eternal reciprocation on my part.' [32]

For the next year and more, documentary evidence concerning the newly married couple is exceedingly meager. On 13 August 1744 — those who like to count will notice that it was a few days more than nine months after their marriage — their daughter Angélique was born, and was baptized the next day at the church of their parish, Saint-Nicolas-du-Chardonnet.[33] At this time the Diderots were living in the Rue Saint-Victor, a twelfth-century street, part of which is still in existence and in which was located the Seminary of Saint-Nicolas, that seminary which Diderot had once told the Champions that he intended to enter. But between the birth and the death of little Angélique, the Diderots evidently moved. When their six-weeks-old daughter was buried on 29 September at the parish church of Sainte-Marguerite-de-Paris, their address was given as Rue Traversière, then a street in the suburbs, almost in the open fields, out beyond the Bastille.[34] It is astonishing, too, that the parish burial register describes Diderot as a day-laborer. Perhaps to conceal himself from his relatives or the police, Diderot had moved to this out-of-the-way suburb. There must have been some powerful motive operating to induce him to move from the Left Bank, for almost all his long career in Paris was spent in that part of the city. Diderot did indeed possess the Latin Quarter sort of temperament, and the *rive gauche* should be proud of so representative a son.

Diderot's wife lived an extremely retired life, partly because they were impecunious, partly because her husband was jealous, partly because they kept their marriage a secret from the relatives at Langres. So well, indeed, was the secret kept that it was not before 1749, six years after the marriage, that old Didier Diderot heard a rumor that his son was married and the father of children.[35] Moreover, during at least the first four years of their marriage, the Diderots attempted to conceal the fact of that ceremony by having Mme Diderot live under her maiden name.[36] From her point of view, convent-nurtured as she was, it must have been a real sacrifice to have people suppose her children illegitimate. For Diderot, the inevitable result was that he spent a good deal of his time acting like a bachelor, with the unfortunate consequence that he became entirely habituated to that situation. When conditions changed later, he did not change with them, but continued to go his own way, never dreaming of allowing his wife to share any part of his social or intellectual life. Unconsciously he took advantage of her willing self-sacrifice: 'My father was of too jealous a disposition to allow my mother to continue a business that would require her to receive and deal with strangers,' wrote his daughter. 'He exhorted her to give up this business. She experienced great difficulty in consenting to do so: destitution did not frighten her as far as she herself was concerned; but her mother was aged, she was faced with the possibility of losing her, and the thought of not being in a position to provide for all her mother's needs tortured her. Nevertheless, as she persuaded herself that this sacrifice would make her husband happy, she made it. A charwoman came each day to sweep the small apartment and bring the day's provisions. My mother provided for all the rest. Often, when my father was eating out, she dined or supped on bread, and took great pleasure in thinking how on the morrow she would be able to make her customary meal for him twice as good. Coffee was too considerable a luxury for this sort of household; but she did not want him to be deprived of it, and every day she gave him six sous that he might go take his cup at the Café de la Régence and watch them play chess.' [37]

These days of courtship and early marriage saw also the cementing of one of the famous friendships of the eighteenth century, that between Diderot and Jean-Jacques Rousseau. Rousseau's early life is so well known, and is so well told in his *Confessions,* that no mention of it needs to be made here, save to say that in August 1742 he had arrived in Paris with a new scheme of musical notation that he had devised. A Swiss named Daniel Roguin introduced him to Diderot, and there immediately grew up an intimate friendship, based initially on the interest they shared in matters musical.[38]

Temperamentally these two young men were very different, congenial though they were in the first ten years of their friendship. The fact that in their frequent games of chess Rousseau invariably won is itself an indication of their differing personalities and temperaments.[39] Diderot was big-hearted, well meaning, rather grandly negligent, brash, and tactless. Although he deemed himself shy, he was in reality endowed with an over-brimming measure of self-confidence, which Rousseau, to an unusual degree, both lacked and admired. Rousseau, shy, tortured by feelings of inferiority, now and then convulsively assertive, desirous of being led while living in jealous dread that he might be, was just as brooding and paradoxical a person then as he was in the later years when he became famous.

In July 1743, Rousseau left Paris for Venice, where he had an appointment as secretary to the French embassy. Fifteen months later he was back in Paris, having quarreled with his ambassador, and it was there, in March of 1745, that he became interested in Thérèse Levasseur, a servant girl at the hotel at which he was staying, and presently began to live with her.[40] He of course knew of Diderot's attachment and speaks of Anne-Toinette in unflattering terms: 'He had a Nanette just as I had a Thérèse; that constituted between us one conformity the more. But the difference was that my Thérèse, as good-looking as his Nanette, had a gentle disposition and an amiable character, suitable for attracting a virtuous man; while his [Nanette], a shrew and a fishwife, showed nothing to other people that could make up for her bad education.'[41]

In 1812, Anne-Toinette's daughter, herself fifty-nine years old in that year, commented explosively upon these lines, in a spectacular display of filial spirit. Yet she made admissions regarding her mother's difficult temper. 'Where my father was in error was in not forming her for the world, because, born jealous, he did not wish that she should see it. . . . Solitude, domestic cares arising from a very restricted income, the chagrin caused by the love affairs of my father, her ignorance of the manners of polite society, had soured her temper; and to scold became a habit. . . .'[42]

Diderot's marital difficulties were to a large degree his own fault and arose from the fact that he got into the habit of treating his wife as though she were a concubine.

CHAPTER 4

First Fruits

DIDEROT at the age of thirty was a necessitous young man without either reputation or livelihood. His recent quarrel with his family had cut him off from any paternal support, yet he was too independent in spirit to tie himself to a profession or undergo the constraint of being a tutor or take up the daily routine of some occupation in trade or commerce. He had described himself truly to his friend Wille as a person striving to become a philosopher and a man of letters; he was as yet a complete unknown. Certainly his career was not going to be distinguished by traits of unusual precocity, that was already evident; yet he yearned to find glory as well as truth, if we may take as being partly autobiographical his picture of the ambitious child whom the sensible father tries to restrain from leaving home: 'Wretched child, what are you going to do? You are not sure to attain glory, and you rush headlong into poverty.' [1]

The tenor of his life during these difficult years suggests that his principal objectives were intellectual freedom, the 'attainment of glory,' the maintenance of personal independence, and — survival! But to achieve all these things, in proper and desired combination, was not easy. Moreover, Diderot had compounded the risks of his precarious existence by assuming the added responsibilities of a wife and, presently, a child. Had Diderot been less jealous, he might have allowed his wife to continue meeting the public in the small lace and linen trade in which she had earned her livelihood before marriage. Had he been less proud, he might have sought the patronage of the great. It was like Diderot to do neither.

The price paid for this independence was insecurity and impecuniosity. The easy and traditional way would have been to find a rich man to whom to inscribe flowery letters of dedication. But just in these very years literary men of spirit were discovering that it was possible to live a life of independence, even though its cost was high. This is the purport of D'Alembert's

'Essay on the Intercourse of Men of Letters with the Great' (1753) and Dr. Johnson's famous letter to Lord Chesterfield (1755). Yet it was hazardous and far from easy, even for men of talent and courage, to be independent and still avoid hunger. Even the proud and sensitive Jean-Jacques Rousseau was fain to be a secretary to the condescending Mme Dupin. Diderot refused to be patronized. He sought contractual relations, not feudal ones. No doubt his publishers exploited him, as he and his friends were wont to complain, but at least he avoided dependence upon the haughty and uncertain largess of a patron.

Such an attitude led him into an existence of what would now be called free-lancing — and free-lancing at its hazardous and vicissitudinous worst. Probably he received some payment for writing several reviews in a periodical entitled *Observations sur les Ecrits Modernes.* This journalistic enterprise, which was published for eight and a half years beginning 1 March 1735, was edited by the Abbé Pierre-François-Guyot Desfontaines, a man of some literary ability who is remembered for little save that he had the misfortune or bad judgment to fall foul of Voltaire. In a statement made to the Lieutenant-General of Police in 1749, Diderot declared that several of the articles in the *Observations* 'were of my making.' [2] These contributions were published anonymously, however, and it is impossible now to identify Diderot's work in these superannuated pages.

Desfontaines, a competent critic, encouraged Diderot in another branch of letters, although the advice bore no immediate fruit. It is the Abbé de La Porte, writing for his newspaper, *L'Observateur Littéraire,* in 1758, who tells us of the incident. 'I recall what was said to me one day by the celebrated Abbé Desfontaines to whom M. Diderot, then still very young, had presented a dialogue in verse. "This young man," he said to me, "is studying mathematics, and I have no doubt that he is making great progress, for he has a great deal of ability; but from the reading of a play done in verse that he brought to me some time ago, I counseled him to give up these serious studies, and devote himself to the theater, for which I believe him to have a real talent." ' [3] This advice would have had to be given before 1745, since Desfontaines died in that year.

In 1742 Diderot had for the first time the satisfaction of seeing his name in print. His satisfaction may have been alloyed with some vexation, however, for the printer had garbled his name. Over the name of P. D. Diderot there appeared an epistle in verse to a Monsieur B * * *, probably Baculard d'Arnaud (1718–1805), a very second-rate man of letters. This bit of verse appeared in *Le Perroquet,* a collection now as rare as it was then obscure, published at Frankfurt am Main.[4] A flavorsome touch of the archaic is all that distinguishes these competent but rather commonplace lines, which bespeak an author rather more practiced than inspired. Throughout his life Diderot was to turn now and then to this form of expression, being able to produce well-polished occasional verse almost on demand. Some reflections caused by a cold sore, lines written on the back of a letter to Anne-Toinette, and the epistle in *Le Perroquet* are the earliest known examples of his occasional impulses to versify.[5]

It was not as an author, however, but as a translator from the English that Diderot managed to support himself for a number of years. When and why he learned the language is a matter of conjecture; certainly he had done so by 1742, for he was then translating the work on Greece. Perhaps his reason for learning it was the curiosity excited by a book like Voltaire's *Letters concerning the English Nation,* the French edition of which (1734) had introduced into France the ideas of Locke and Newton, as well as British notions of liberty and religious toleration. How he learned the language he tells us himself, by recalling that he passed it through the Latin.[6] This suggests that he taught himself, a supposition the more likely since he appears to have been unable to write English or to speak it, the draft of a letter composed in English late in his life being the sole evidence to the contrary.[7] Still, his ability to read English was an unusual accomplishment in eighteenth-century France, enabling him to go to the fountainheads of English science, literature, and philosophy, and to read English authors who, unlike Bacon and Newton, wrote only in the vernacular.

This was an inestimable advantage for an eighteenth-century Continental thinker. English influences — the writings of a host of deistic authors like Toland and Clarke and Wollaston, arguing for natural religion; the scientific ideas of Bacon, Boyle, and, most important, Newton; the psychological ideas of Locke, emphasizing that all we can ever really know is transmitted to us by one of our five senses — had an exciting and unsettling effect upon conventional ideas, especially upon conventional ideas in France. No doubt it all started innocently enough in the hope that by using the scientific method preached by Bacon and the rational methods used by Newton, men would be vouchsafed the privilege of peering a little deeper into the nature of things. But what happened was that the scientific and rational implications of English ideas greatly affected the metaphysical and theological thinking of the time. Moreover, the doctrines of the English writers and scientists, when transplanted to France, took on an exaggerated and revolutionary character that they did not have at home. Probably the reason was that

Catholic orthodoxy was more absolutist and had less 'give' than the orthodoxy of a Protestant country. At all events, English ideas were the most exciting ones of the eighteenth century, and English thoughts in French heads produced in the long run some astonishing and explosive consequences. Diderot, with his mind and temperament, would naturally have played a leading part in this exciting and dangerous decanting of ideas. But add to this the fact that he was able, unlike many others of his coterie, to grapple with these ideas in the original, and had done so in a number of his early literary chores, and a solid basis is established for his ability to assert and make good his intellectual leadership.

The earliest of Diderot's translations from the English was Temple Stanyan's *Grecian History,* the first complete edition of which had appeared in 1739. The *Dictionary of National Biography* speaks of Stanyan as an excellent scholar and of his history as 'a compilation which held the field until the appearance of the much larger history by William Mitford' almost fifty years later. As we have already seen, the galley proofs of Diderot's translation created a sensation upon their arrival in Langres. The work, entitled *Histoire de Grèce,* appeared in three volumes in 1743.[8] The fortnightly *Journal des Sçavans,* the blue-ribbon periodical of that era, did the history the honor of quoting it copiously in three installments, but of the translator's work it finally remarked, disappointingly, that 'it was written rather negligently.'[9] A Berlin review of Diderot's translation, written in 1773 and no doubt inspired by the malevolence of Frederick the Great, spoke of it superciliously as 'a long task during which the creative spirit of M. Diderot took a rest.'[10] Maybe so; but if one be content to ask no more of a translation than that it be accurate and faithful, a comparison of the original and of the French version shows that Diderot was a quite skillful translator. For the Stanyan work Diderot received the sum of three hundred francs.[11]

Diderot's next exercise in rendering from the English was more a paraphrase than a translation. Yet it is a very important work, indeed, for understanding the growth and development of his thought. The book in question was Lord Shaftesbury's *An Inquiry concerning Virtue and Merit,* which appeared in its French dress in 1745, purportedly published in Amsterdam under the title *Principes de la philosophie morale; ou Essai de M. S * * * sur le mérite et la vertu. Avec réflexions.* It was Diderot who furnished the 'reflections' in a preliminary discourse and lengthy footnotes to which students of Diderot now turn for precious indications of the unfolding of his ideas.[12] Since this book was published in 1745 — Diderot's presentation copy to Rousseau is dated 16 March 1745 — it is to be presumed that Diderot was engaged upon the work in the months following his marriage.[13]

It will be noticed that the French version is anonymous: neither Shaftesbury's name nor that of his translator was mentioned. The reason was that there was some danger involved in presenting to the French public a work that declared so boldly for the existence of a natural morality independent of the sanctions of any particular religion or church. Shaftesbury very much believed in God, but his religion and morality were such as are revealed more by reason than by Scripture. Happily, the French press reviewed the book quite favorably and without too much emotion. The Jesuit *Journal de Trévoux,* a very influential magazine edited at Paris and (since 1734) printed there, ran its review of the book as its leading article for the issue of February 1746. 'Imagine Locke's discoursing on morality,' it said. 'Thus the author appears to us, and, if one wishes, so does the Translator or Compiler of this volume.'[14] But the *Journal des Sçavans,* while favorable, had some mental reservations: 'If he [the author] conducts the human creature, as he says, to the doors of our temples, he seems at the same time to be wishing to excuse him from entering them.'[15]

A comparison of the translation with the original shows that Diderot was quite successful in wrestling with the convolutions of Lord Shaftesbury's syntax, which still remained seventeenth-century even though he wrote in the Age of Addison.[16] Whatever Diderot gained in clarity, however, he probably lost in savor.[17] This was, of course, the fate of almost all English authors in eighteenth-century French translations, Shakespeare most of all. Nevertheless, Diderot was quite faithful to his task — more, even, than he claims to be, for he wrote in his preliminary discourse, 'I have read and reread him; I have filled myself with his thoughts; and then I closed his book, so to speak, when I took up my pen.'[18] Still, there is a great deal of the characteristic Diderot in this little treatise: the mischievous and pointed placing of footnotes where Shaftesbury's implicit heterodoxy was most apparent; the lengthy quotation from skeptical authors like Montaigne or extremely pagan ancients like Petronius; the use of concepts, that, like leitmotives, occur in Diderot's later writings, such as the notion that human beings are like musical instruments of which our passions are the strings;[19] the extremely personal approach to the reader, even in works of philosophy, as in his remark, 'I have passions, and I would be sorry not to have them: I love very passionately my God, my king, my country, my parents, my mistress, and myself.'[20] Moreover, in these notes he indulged his inveterate fondness for flushing more ideas than he could bag, a failing that was alluded to by the reviewer in Desfontaine's *Jugemens sur Quelques Ouvrages Nouveaux*, who named Diderot right out and evidently knew him. 'Let me be permitted to say to him, following Doctor Swift, in whom he frequently takes refuge, that digressions in a book are like foreign troops in a state, making one suspect that the natives lack vigor and courage. . . .'[21]

Most characteristic of all in the *Essai sur le mérite et la vertu* is Diderot's appeal for religious tolerance, which was quite in the spirit of Shaftesbury, too. In the dedicatory epistle 'To my Brother,' Diderot wrote, 'But if you will recall the history of our civil troubles, you will see half the nation bathe itself, out of piety, in the blood of the other half, and violate the fundamental feelings of humanity in order to sustain the cause of God; as though it were necessary to cease to be a man in order to prove oneself religious!'[22]

There is much in Shaftesbury's thought that made a profound and permanent impression on Diderot, who shows in his footnotes to this essay his familiarity with all of Shaftesbury's works.[23] He liked Shaftesbury's doctrine that man is endowed by nature with a moral sense; that man's emotions and passions can work for good and not exclusively for evil, as the older generation of philosophers and Christian moralists had held;[24] that it is possible to build a morality based on reason; and that there is an extremely close relationship, practically an identity, among the good, the beautiful, and the true.[25] Many, moreover, of the anticlerical or anti-Christian facets of Shaftesbury's thought are directly reflected in Diderot's later work, for example, his influential *Philosophical Thoughts*.[26]

Diderot's dedication of his work on Shaftesbury, 'To my Brother,' was perhaps only figurative. Didier Diderot, then studying theology in Paris and approaching his ordination to the priesthood, can scarcely have welcomed the dedication of such a volume even though published anonymously. There is no record of his protesting against the dedication, nor indeed of any intercourse between the two brothers during their joint residence in the capital.[27] For some reason, however, the second edition found 'aunt' substituted for 'brother' in the dedicatory passage.

Diderot's next adventure in translation was a considerable one, but accomplished without 'reflections.' Briasson, the same bookseller who had brought out the Stanyan *Histoire de Grèce*, undertook to publish Robert James's medical dictionary, a work which had appeared in three folio volumes in London between 1743 and 1745. The scope of the work, which may very well have given Diderot ideas of how to lay out an undertaking of encyclopedic character, is worth indicating by quoting its title in all its eighteenth-century lengthiness: *A Medicinal Dictionary; including Physic, Surgery, Anatomy, Chymistry, and Botany, in all their Branches relative to Medicine. Together with a History of Drugs; and an introductory Preface, tracing the Progress of Physic, and explaining the Theories which have principally prevail'd in all Ages of the World. By R. James, M. D.* These ponderous folios (Volume I weighs eleven pounds, fourteen ounces), called by Mark Twain 'A Majestic Literary Fossil,' were illustrated by sixty-three quite good copper plates of surgical instruments and operations, so that the whole work with its broad approach, its sense of the interrelationship of the sciences, its engravings, and its cross references was of a nature to kindle in a person as imaginative as Diderot a lively conception of what a similar work could do for the whole sweep of human knowledge.[28] That there is so close a connection between the *Medicinal Dictionary* and the *Encyclopédie* is conjectural but nevertheless chronologically possible. And inasmuch as Diderot, by his own account, worked almost three years on the project, he must have learned a great deal about putting a work of considerable magnitude through the press.[29] Moreover, it is highly probable that Diderot's deep and abiding interest in physiology, anatomy, and medicine was established as a result of the extensive task of translating Dr. James. Briasson brought the work out in six folio volumes between 1746 and 1748 under the title *Dictionnaire universel de médecine,* etc., 'translated from the English of Mr. James by Messrs. Diderot, Eidous and Toussaint.'[30] It is of interest to learn that Samuel Johnson, a close personal friend of Dr. James, contributed to the *Medicinal Dictionary* its dedication, its prospectus, and some of its articles, so that Diderot probably translated some of Dr. Johnson's august prose.[31]

Diderot was an extremely generous man — though distinctly more generous of his time than of his money — and the work of translating the *Medicinal Dictionary* became the occasion for a remarkable display of this quality. 'He had just undertaken this business when chance brought him two men — the one Toussaint, author of a little work called *Les Moeurs,* the other an unknown — but both of them without bread and seeking work,' wrote his daughter. 'My father, having nothing, deprived himself of two-thirds of the money that he could count upon from this translation, and engaged them to share with him this little undertaking.'[32]

Mme de Vandeul speaks here with a note of unjustified condescension about François-Vincent Toussaint and his famous book *Les Moeurs,* published in 1748 and condemned on 6 May of that year by the Parlement of Paris.[33] *Les Moeurs* was one of the first (and therefore one of the boldest) works in the eighteenth century to set forth the arguments for a natural morality unbolstered by any religious belief or public cult. No doubt Toussaint was inspired and abetted in this daring enterprise, both as to the intellectual content of the essay and the publication of it, by the example of Diderot, whose *Pensées philosophiques* had appeared two years previously. A police report on Toussaint, under date of 1 April 1749, spoke of him as being closely associated with Diderot and D'Alembert and working with them on the *Encyclopédie*.[34] It is true that he contributed some articles on jurisprudence to Volumes I and II of the *Encyclopédie,* but thereafter he had no connection with it; we do not know why.

The 'unknown' mentioned by Mme de Vandeul was the Eidous (Marc-Antoine by given name) who appears on the title page of James's *Dictionnaire*. Eidous had been an engineer in the Spanish army before coming to Paris, where he eked out a long life by doing translations from the English 'by the yard,' as Grimm contemptuously described it.[35] Thus in the fullness of time Eidous became the translator (1767) of Horace Walpole's *The Castle of Otranto*.[36] Eidous existed on the periphery of literature, never translating very well — Grimm said he rendered the English into a language all his own: the Eidoussian language — [37] never venturing to embark by himself on the deep waters of original composition. It was he who was to contribute to chapter XLVII of Diderot's novel *Les Bijoux indiscrets,* a chapter describing the adventures of what Ernest Hemingway would call 'a big, international whore.' Some of Eidous' passages in English and Italian certainly do rival Aretino, as a secret police report of the time said of them,[38] and probably come close to surpassing in pornography anything else that has appeared in print. Diderot's association with this elevating companion appears not to have extended beyond these early years. Eidous did a few unimportant articles for the *Encyclopédie* and thereafter fades out of focus in the Diderotian kaleidoscope.

During this early period — certainly before 1749 — Diderot wrote some notes and comments on a French translation of Pope's *Essay on Man*.[39] This may have been intended to be nothing more than an exercise to improve his powers of rendering from the English, but it may also have had some lasting effect upon his thought. Certainly 'Virtue alone is happiness below,' comes close to expressing Diderot's whole philosophy of living.

Sometime between September of 1744, when they had buried their first-born child in the churchyard of Sainte-Marguerite-de-Paris, and May of 1746, when their second baby was baptized, the Diderots changed their residence back to the Left Bank. The baptism of François-Jacques-Denis Diderot accordingly

took place in Saint-Médard, the parish church of the street in which they
then resided. The churchyard of Saint-Médard had been from 1728 to 1732
the scene of some healings, alleged to be miraculous, that took place over
the tomb of a Deacon Pâris. This man had been a Jansenist, and his fellow
sectaries, delighted to discover among themselves a saint (for the Jansenists
did not have many), lost no opportunity to publicize his thaumaturgical
powers. The result was that enormous crowds visited the place, creating
a frightening crescendo of religious frenzy and hysteria. This was the period
of the *convulsionnaires*. The government, as unsympathetic to Jansenist miracles as to Jansenists, closed the cemetery, causing some unknown wit to
place a placard on the gates: 'By order of the King, God is forbidden to
work miracles here.' The excitement slowly subsided, but it left the 'philosophers' of the century shuddering, for to them it seemed to prove the
ugliness of religious fanaticism, as well as to reveal that the Jansenists were
quite as far gone in obscurantism as any of their antagonists.[40]

Saint-Médard, then, of unsavory memory to a person like Diderot, who
alludes to the *convulsionnaires* in several of his *Philosophical Thoughts*,
had now become the church of his parish. In the baptismal certificate the
Diderots were mentioned as living in the Rue Mouffetard. This street, long,
populous, odorous, and poverty stricken, probably looks very much now as
it did then, and still offers to the tourist or photographer some of the oldest
roofs, the oddest angles, and the most captivating juxtaposition of planes in
all of Paris.

While the *Medicinal Dictionary* was still in the process of being translated, Diderot wrote a little book that ought to be considered, in view of
the reverberations it caused and the polemics it aroused, one of the most
important of the eighteenth century. This was the *Pensées philosophiques*,
bought by the book publisher Durand, who was to be one of the partners
in publishing the *Encyclopédie;* printed surreptitiously in 1746 by a man
named L'Epine; and then sold clandestinely by various bootlegging techniques in which the eighteenth century was becoming remarkably proficient.[41] So incisive and effective was this little book that it came under the
disapproving scrutiny of the Parlement of Paris. That court, the highest in
the land, in an 'Arrest' of 7 July 1746 condemned the book to be 'torn up
and burned . . . by the High Executioner as scandalous, and contrary to
Religion and Morals.' In amplification of this decree the Parlement declared
that the *Pensées philosophiques* 'presents to restless and reckless spirits the
venom of the most criminal and absurd opinions that the depravity of
human reason is capable of; and by an affected uncertainty places all re-

ligions on almost the same level, in order to finish up by not accepting any.' [42]

The Parlement might have been better advised to spare itself such tremendous ejaculations, for they simply served to draw attention to skeptical ideas and to the author who expressed them. People quickly learned — so many in French society were leisured and unoccupied — who the putative author was, and the ideas set forth immediately took on some of the delicious savor of forbidden fruit. Ideas, especially radical ideas, had an unusually broad and quick currency in eighteenth-century France, which is perhaps the principal explanation why a revolution occurred there rather than in some other country where misery, poverty, and inequality were even greater.

Diderot's work, bold and revolutionary though it was, was by no means the first eighteenth-century expression of skepticism about Christianity. During the first half of the century there circulated in France a very large number of manuscript works, the precursors of the flood of printed attacks that the presses presently began to pour forth. The circulation of these surreptitious manuscripts goes far to explain the rapid gain of new ideas, and the equally rapid collapse of the old, in the years after 1750.[43] And the number of these manuscripts still extant in French public libraries — Professor Wade of Princeton found some 102 separate titles, many of them in multiple copies — is testimony of their pervasion and influence. We can be pretty sure that Diderot was familiar with many of these writings, especially as manuscripts of two of them, now in the library at Fécamp, were copied out in his own hand.[44]

Diderot's book, then, has a close relationship with this underground literature; [45] but it also had characteristics of its own that made it a landmark in the chronic debate between skepticism and faith. The first of these characteristics was boldness, the very boldness of Diderot's allowing it to be printed. In eighteenth-century France it was taken for granted that a function and duty of the state was to punish the expression of opinions against 'Religion.' Therefore the police kept a close watch on authors, printers, and booksellers. Inasmuch as a larger number of persons had unavoidably to be let into the secret, the risks of printing a book were altogether different from the risks involved in the production and circulation of a manuscript. If these dangerous writings were printed in Paris, as they frequently were, they had to be clandestinely printed, often by unlicensed printers who set up their fly-by-night presses in out-of-the-way places and moved them frequently in order to escape the police. Yet some of these clandestine and peripatetic printers were themselves secret agents of the police.[46] By printing a work, one certainly ran a great risk of betrayal. But on the other hand, the very act of printing increased the circulation of one's work and extended its influence.

The *Pensées philosophiques* evidently found a considerable number of readers. In spite of the attempt of the Parlement of Paris to suppress the book, at least ten editions were published in the eighteenth century, plus five books that quoted it in entirety for the purpose of refuting it (a signally obtuse way of spreading the flames while trying to extinguish them), plus five printings in collected editions of Diderot's works, plus a translation into German.[47] Moreover, in contrast to practically all of the clandestinely circulated manuscripts, which had a decided tendency to be tedious and humorless, Diderot's was written with an epigrammatic concision and a sort of grave yet gracious persuasiveness that made his book very effective.* The tradition in his family was that he dashed off the *Pensées philosophiques* between Good Friday and Easter of 1746.[48] This is not impossible, considering that the sixty-two sections of the work comprise about ten thousand words; but it is not very likely, in view of the polish and literary elegance of the aphorisms. They have a gloss and quotability that indicate deliberation and care.

In skill of composition, as well as in boldness of publication, Diderot's *Pensées philosophiques* quickly achieved a position of pre-eminence in its genre. In the form of aphorisms it covered a good deal of ground, much of it no doubt suggested by the writings of Shaftesbury.[49] The tenor of the whole book is deistic, which is equivalent to saying that it suggests that what man can discover about God is made known by reason rather than by revelation. Some examples of the aphorisms will speak for themselves, and give some notion of the impact they must have had:

To judge from the portrait people paint me of the Supreme Being, from His inclination to anger, from the rigor of His vengeance, from certain comparisons that express the ratio between those whom He allows to perish and those to whom He condescends to stretch out a hand, the soul the most upright would be tempted to wish that He did not exist. . . . The thought that there is no God has never frightened anyone, but rather the thought that there *is* one, such as the one that has been described to me (Pensée IX).

Superstition is more injurious to God than atheism (Pensée XII).

What is God? A question which is asked of children, and which philosophers have a great deal of trouble in answering (Pensée XXV).

* An English translation is contained in Margaret Jourdain, *Diderot's Early Philosophical Works* (Chicago, 1916), 27–67.

People have a right to demand of me that I seek the truth, but not that I find it (Pensée XXIX).

Skepticism is the first step toward truth (Pensée XXXI).

In this little work Diderot defends the passions (Pensée I), a very significant position to take against the prevailing ascetic view held by orthodox Christian doctrine; he shows himself very anti-Jansenist (Pensées XIII, XIV) and therefore very opposed to the views expressed by Pascal in his famous *Pensées;* [50] he quotes Julian the Apostate with complacency, which was enough, of course, to infuriate the orthodox; if he is not an atheist — and he claims in this work that he is not, saying, 'I was born in the apostolic Roman Catholic Church; and I submit myself with all my strength to its decisions' (Pensée LVIII) — he certainly defends those who are (Pensées XV, XXI); he casts doubts on miracles (Pensées XLVI, LI, LIII, LIV), an attack regarded by some critics as the most aggressive and the most telling, as well as the hardest to answer, in the whole book; [51] by arguing from the evidence of current studies in natural history and biology, he throws new light on metaphysical and theological problems, thus making his book a remarkably original contribution to the literature of deism (Pensées XVIII, XX, XLV); and in Pensée XIX he gives a sort of preview of his philosophy of the origin of things, which he was to develop at greater length in later works.[52]

Diderot became very skillful in the art of writing dialogue, and there are some critics who feel that the *Pensées philosophiques* is a conversation among an atheist, an orthodox Christian, and a deist. Both the atheist and the Christian are confounded by the deist, and the book, in spite of its apparent looseness of construction, thus has an underlying unity.[53]

Diderot's book was important enough to draw considerable enemy fire, but this counter-bombardment gives the impression of having been more effective in betraying its own positions than in damaging its assailant.[54] The defenders of orthodoxy probably realized that their antagonist was redoubtable: some of them acknowledged his book to be 'passably well written' in 'a spirited, energetic, and sprightly style.' [55] Nor was this the last time that they would have occasion to make such a rueful admission.

CHAPTER 5

The Emerging Philosophe

As Diderot tried to discover for himself a satisfactory philosophy of life, his mind encountered trammels imposed by orthodox, revealed religion. His early works are more concerned with an examination of the truths of religion than his later ones, and there is a consistent directional trend in these first writings. From the theistic belief in a providential God, which we can see in his notes to the translation of Shaftesbury's *Inquiry concerning Virtue,* Diderot proceeds to a somewhat militant deism in the *Pensées philosophiques,* ending that little treatise with the suggestion that natural religion, revealed to us by our reason, is the best. From this point, as we shall see, he proceeds until he arrives finally at a position of outright atheism.

Anyone not well acquainted with a mind like Diderot's might suppose that he adopted skepticism and, later, atheism simply out of a desire to shock, to irritate, or to amuse. In reality, he went through this process of emancipation not to be impudent but to satisfy a sort of intellectual necessity. From first to last Diderot sought to understand the universe in which he lived, and in so doing he always seemed impelled to follow a principle that one might call the principle of greatest possible economy. Diderot was ever reluctant to make greater metaphysical assumptions than were necessary to provide a rational explanation of the world. Thus he found himself giving up Christian tenets simply because he did not find them indispensable and essential: 'If there were a reason for preferring the Christian religion to natural religion,' he wrote, 'it would be because the former offers us, on the nature of God and man, enlightenment that the latter lacks. Now, this is not at all the case; for Christianity, instead of clarifying, gives rise to an infinite multitude of obscurities and difficulties.' [1] Thus he passed from orthodox Christianity through phases of theism and deism to end in a basic physiological, psychological, and neurological materialism that left God

59

out simply because the existence of God was unnecessary, according to this view, to explain the universe.

In the *Pensées philosophiques* Diderot purported to regard himself as still a Roman Catholic (Pensée LVIII). The last 'thought' of all, however, showed him developing the deistic argument that 'natural religion' was best. This theme he amplified in a short work entitled *De la Suffisance de la religion naturelle* ('On the Sufficiency of Natural Religion'), which was not published until 1770.[2] Assézat and Tourneux, editors of Diderot's works, assert that this brief essay was written in 1747, following his *Skeptic's Walk,* although they adduce no evidence to substantiate their assertion. On the other hand, the title and argument of the 'Sufficiency of Natural Religion' are so organically connected with the *Pensées philosophiques* that it seems likely that the little treatise was written in 1746 or early 1747, thus preceding the *Skeptic's Walk,* which in several respects is the more radical of the two.[3]

It is interesting to speculate why Diderot made no attempt to publish this little series of apothegms on natural religion. Perhaps he felt that they represented only a dialectical moment in the development of his thought. In this brief work Diderot speaks frequently of natural law, 'graven in the hearts of all men,' much as Saint Paul spoke of it in the Epistle to the Romans; he declares that religion best that best accords with the goodness and the justice of God; and he ends by saying that 'the truth of natural religion is to the truth of other religions as the testimony that I discover within me is to the testimony that I receive from someone else; as what I feel to what I am told; as what I find written within me by the finger of God, to what vain, superstitious and lying men have written on paper or chiseled in marble. . . .'[4] This sort of argument was common among English deists, not at all unknown among French seventeenth-century freethinkers, and became quite commonplace in the eighteenth century. Here we see 'Reason,' unaided by any reference to the outside world of phenomena, constructing by itself a sort of intellectual fabric. This type of ratiocination, so characteristic of one aspect of the Age of Reason, was nevertheless not at all characteristic of Diderot: his efforts to understand reality were guided not by turning the reason in upon itself, but by relating his mind and understanding to the physical, biological, and psychological phenomena of the outside world. Thus the eleven pages of the 'Sufficiency of Natural Religion,' although interesting, are scarcely a characteristic work. And it may be that this was why Diderot did not seek to publish it. At all events a more dangerous work was soon to come.

In 1747 Diderot was living with Anne-Toinette and their infant son in lodgings in the Rue Mouffetard, only too glad if the police did not know who he was or his family at Langres did not know where. No doubt it was exciting to be the author of a book that had been burned by the public executioner, but it was dangerous, too. A less daring man might have deemed it prudent to wait a while before committing to paper doctrines that were even more inflammable. But Diderot had that itch for writing that is the blessing, and sometimes the curse, of a prolific man of letters, so that an incendiary successor to the *Pensées philosophiques* and the *De la Suffisance de la religion naturelle* presently began to flow from his quill. This was an allegory, almost certainly written in 1747, which he called *La Promenade du sceptique* ('The Skeptic's Walk'), with a sub-title describing it as a 'conversation concerning religion, philosophy, and the world.'[5]

In the preliminary discourse to his allegory, Diderot shows his awareness of the risks run by any author who does not limit himself to the banal. Aristes, the supposed author, examines all the disadvantages of attempting to publish so controversial an item. One of his imagined interlocutors was of the opinion that it was better to be a bad author left unmolested than a good author persecuted. But Aristes, a Diderot-like figure, was reluctant to accept that choice. There was a solution to the dilemma, though rather a drastic one, inasmuch as it involved self-exile and putting oneself into the formidable hands of Frederick the Great: 'Appeal to . . . the philosopher-prince whom you . . . recently heard scolding Machiavelli with such eloquence and good sense.* Pass into his States with your work and let the bigots rage.'[6]

This advice to an author who is a sort of mirror-image of himself may reveal uneasiness on Diderot's part as to his own tranquillity. Police records show that he would have been completely justified in being apprehensive. On 20 June 1747, a man named Perrault wrote to Berryer, the Lieutenant-General of Police, denouncing 'this miserable Didrot' as 'a very dangerous man who speaks of the holy mysteries of our religion with contempt.'[7] Two days later more ample information came in, this time from the priest of the parish in which Diderot lived, a man who stated that he had previously written to Berryer's predecessor in complaint of Diderot. 'M. Diderot is a young man who passed his early life in debauchery. At length he attached himself to a girl without money, but of social position, it seems, equal to his, and he married her without the knowledge of his father. The better to hide his so-called marriage, he has rented lodgings in my parish at the house of M. Guillotte [Guillotte and his wife were the godparents of the

* Frederick's *Anti-Machiavel* was published in 1740.

second Diderot child]; [8] his wife goes by her maiden name. . . . The re-marks that Diderot sometimes makes in this household amply prove that he is at least a deist. He utters blasphemies against Jesus Christ and the Holy Virgin that I would not venture to put in writing. . . . It is true that I have never spoken to this young man, that I do not know him personally, but I am told that he has a great deal of wit and that his conversation is most amusing. In one of his conversations he confessed to being the author of one of the two works condemned by the Parlement and burned about two years ago. I have been assured that for more than a year he has been working on another work still more dangerous to religion.' [9]

This 'still more dangerous' work, *La Promenade du sceptique,* described three separate paths and what took place on each. These were the paths of thorns, of chestnut trees, and of flowers, referring respectively to orthodox Christianity, philosophy, and life's more carnal enjoyments. The allegory about Christianity is particularly searching and savage, giving in very thin disguise a critical account of Biblical history and Christian institutions. The residents of this path of thorns are described as soldiers each equipped with a blindfold — that is to say, the symbol of faith — and a white robe, the symbol of innocence. They anxiously grope their way through life. 'The soldier's duties are limited to keeping his blindfold on right and keeping his robe from getting spots.' [10]

'The path of the chestnut trees provides a tranquil abode, and resembles very much the ancient Academy.' Here the mirror-image of Diderot heard representatives of the principal philosophical schools — the Pyrrhonians, the skeptics, the Spinozists, the Berkeleyan idealists or solipsists, the atheists, and the deists — engage in a discussion that critics regard as the solidest part of Diderot's allegory. Not infrequently the path of the chestnuts was invaded by the truculent soldiery of the path of thorns. 'Under our chestnut trees, the chiefs of the path of thorns are tranquilly listened to; their thrusts are expected and are parried, they themselves are brought to earth, they are confounded, they are enlightened, if possible; or at least their blindness is lamented. Gentleness and peacefulness regulate our proceedings; theirs are dictated by fury. We employ reason, they accumulate fagots. They preach nothing but love, and breathe nothing but blood. Their words are humane, but their hearts are cruel.' [11]

The description of the path of chestnut trees incidentally reveals that it was a place of men without women. This is quite enough to explain why Diderot's mirror-image found himself spending some time in the path of flowers. In this rather conventional and final part of the allegory, the burden of the argument is that all is not entirely well in the flower-strewn path. Proof of this contention rests in three little stories, written almost in dialogue form, about a man who swears eternal love to his mistress and then forgets her, about another who steals his friend's mistress, and about a third who by intrigue secures an appointment that he had learned about from a friend who had supposed he was going to get it himself. It is evident that Diderot recommended, if one had the resolution to do it, staying in the shade of the chestnuts.

Diderot's aptitudes were not best suited to the allegory, a literary form that he himself later described as 'the ordinary recourse of sterile minds.' [12] It may be that in experimenting with this form he was following the example of Swift in *The Tale of a Tub,* especially since we know that he was familiar with some of Swift's works.[13] It is interesting and significant that in *La Promenade du sceptique* he frequently seems on the point of breaking forth into the dialogue form, which later became his most effective and personal mode of expression. Indeed, another allegorical satire of Christianity that he is believed to have written about this time, a short tale called *Qu'en pensez-vous?* ('What Do *You* Think?'), is almost all in conversational form.[14] Although *La Promenade du sceptique* is not regarded as one of Diderot's major works, still it is by no means without interest: it shows the vigor and variety of his imagery; [15] it reveals the breadth of his reading, with references to Milton, Montaigne, Rabelais, and many others, besides, of course, a considerable familiarity with the history of philosophy; it reveals his usual dislike of the Jansenists; [16] it shows him already interested in the intellectual problems raised by a person's being deprived of one or more of his senses, problems which were presently to provide the central consideration of his *Letter on the Blind;* [17] and, finally, it again reveals his awareness of the impact of biological fact upon metaphysical speculations, a characteristic destined to make him perhaps the outstanding thinker of his century in the philosophy of science. Because of this emphasis on biological nature he eventually came to be a philosophical materialist, as we shall presently see. But for the moment it caused him to rest at a halfway station between the idea of a deistic universe with Voltaire's watchmaker God, on the one hand, and an atheistic one with no God at all, on the other.[18] This halfway station was a universe that makes God and nature the same thing, the position known as pantheism.

Presumably Diderot hoped to publish *La Promenade du sceptique.* But the police, one way or another, prevented it. According to one version, Diderot, without having to surrender the manuscript, was nevertheless forced to promise the Inspector of Publications, one Joseph d'Hémery, that it would not be published.[19] This story would seem to be confirmed by Diderot's deposition, when he got into trouble in 1749, that although he had written *La Promenade du sceptique,* he had subsequently destroyed the manuscript.[20] But another version of the story, this one told by Mme de Vandeul, is that D'Hémery searched Diderot's house, found the manuscript, and carried it away.[21] This version is confirmed by the fact that Diderot is known to have tried to get the manuscript back some thirty years later, when he was considering the publication of a collected edition of his works.[22] The result of his failure to repossess the work was that the world had to wait until 1830 before the allegory was published. And Diderot's fond recollection began to play him tricks, so that he came to believe that this was one of his best works, which is very far from being true.[23]

In writing about the path of flowers, Diderot described Aristes as meeting a beautiful woman, of whom he speaks in the somewhat rueful and wise-after-the-fact tone of a man looking back upon some untoward experience begun in a night club or bar. 'She was a blonde,' he wrote, 'but one of those blondes that a philosopher ought to avoid.'[24] We wonder if Madeleine d'Arsant de Puisieux was a blonde or if, at least, Diderot did not eventually come to think that she fitted the specification. For a time, however, Diderot was quite under the spell of this rather demanding young Parisienne, a woman seven years his junior. She was the wife of Philippe Florent de Puisieux, a non-practicing lawyer who did a great deal of translating, especially from English.[25] It is impossible to say just when the relationship between her and Diderot began. His reference to loving a number of objects 'very passionately,' including 'my mistress,' had appeared by March 1745.[26] But this may not betoken more than Diderot's Gallic feeling that if a mistress did not exist, it would be necessary to invent one. Perhaps the approximate chronology can be established indirectly: in 1751, Mme de Puisieux published a book in which she speaks quite transparently of Diderot and mentions 'five years of familiarity.'[27] If the liaison lasted five years, then it must have begun not later than 1746. This would agree with the story as told by Mme de Vandeul, who says that Diderot wrote his *Pensées philosophiques* at Eastertime in 1746 in order to procure money for his mistress.[28] Probably this is substantially correct, although it must be confessed that Mme de Vandeul's account of the Puisieux affair is demonstrably incorrect in another particular, and consequently may be so in this one. For she claims that Diderot took Mme de Puisieux for his mistress during the absence of Mme Diderot at Langres, whither her husband had sent her in the hope of being able to reconcile his family to the marriage.[29] The fact is that there is documentary evidence that as late as September 1749, Diderot's father did not know that his son was married, and therefore the visit that Mme Diderot made to Langres in 1752 seems to have been her first.[30] Evidently someone in Diderot's family, whether his daughter or himself, was ashamed of his taking a mistress and consequently fabricated this tale, thinking that the plea of connubial privation would palliate the offense.

The little that is known of Mme de Puisieux has about it a disagreeable and distasteful flavor. Of her it has been said 'with too patent humour,' wrote Lord Morely, 'that she was without either the virtue or the merit on which her admirer had just been declaiming.'[31] Mme de Puisieux became a writer of books, no doubt encouraged by Diderot. She was an ambitious authoress, full of vanity and intellectual presumption, as her various prefaces and introductions show, and it galled her very much to be thought to have relied on Diderot for any literary assistance. Thus she is at very special pains in her preliminary discourse to her first book, *Conseils à une amie,* to assert that 'M. D * * *' had nothing to do with the writing or revision of her work.[32] Nobody believed her: the entry under her name in the police records of the office of censorship declared that 'it is Diderot, her very good friend, who did all the body of this book.'[33] The Abbé Raynal, author of a fortnightly news letter, wrote to his subscribers, 'I do not know whose book this is, but I am sure that it has been corrected by M. Diderot . . . .'[34] When the world proceeded to say the same thing about her second book, *Les Caractères,* the lady became shrill: 'When [the first part of] the *Characters* appeared last year, people were disposed . . . to attribute it to a savant who, removed from the world, glories in ignoring its maxims. . . . If the Editor of the *Encyclopédie* is capable of worthily completing so great a work, it would perhaps be impossible for him to compose any as futile as mine. . . .'[35] (These words were published in 1751, and betokened quite evidently that the love affair had ended in bitterness and despite.) As for her protestations of originality, critics observed that her later works, with such unremembered titles as *Alzarac, Histoire de Mlle Terville, Mémoires de la comtesse de Zurlac,* and *Zamor et Almanzine,* did not have the sparkle, nor fulfill the promise, of the early ones. 'The works on morals, by which Mme de Puisieux signalized her first steps in the career of letters,' wrote a mild and not unsympathetic critic, 'acquired for her a glory that she has not been able to dissipate by her novels.'[36] Mme de Puisieux survived until 1795, consumed by vanity to the end. A person who met her when she was sixty years old spoke of her 'ridiculousness,' and her deficiency in judgment and intellectual power, although she was evidently convinced of possessing both to a superlative degree. By that time Mme de Puisieux was stooped and becoming toothless, but 'she kept up all the little airs and affectations that are scarcely tolerable even in a young girl.' [37]

Diderot's love for Mme de Puisieux was consuming, as he himself confessed in a letter to Voltaire in 1749, saying that he was governed 'by a violent passion that has me at its almost complete disposition.' [38] Such an attachment naturally had an upsetting effect in his own home. 'My grandmother died,' wrote Mme de Vandeul, 'my mother remained alone, without companionship. The alienation of her husband doubled the grief of her loss; her character became melancholy, her disposition less gentle. . . . Had her tenderness for my father been able to weaken, her life would have been more happy; but nothing was able to distract it for a moment. . . .' [39]

*　　*　　*　　*　　*　　*

The recollections of Rousseau in his *Confessions* allow us to see the Diderot of this period in close association with a little knot of friends: 'I spoke to Diderot about Condillac and his work; I made them acquainted with each other. They were made to get along together, and so they did. Diderot undertook to get the bookseller Durand to take the Abbé's manuscript. . . . As we lived in districts very far from one another, we used to meet, all three of us, once a week at the Palais-Royal, and then go to dine together at the Hôtel du Panier Fleuri. It must have been that these little weekly dinners were extremely pleasing to Diderot, for he, who used to miss almost all his appointments, never missed one of these. I was then forming the project of a periodical paper, to be called *Le Persifleur,* which Diderot and I were to do by turns. I sketched out the first number, and that made me become acquainted with D'Alembert, to whom Diderot had spoken about it. But unforeseen events blocked us, and the project remained where it was.' [40]

The power of Paris to draw to itself the talents of France is exemplified by the association around the table of the Panier Fleuri of these four young men — D'Alembert, the Parisian foundling; Condillac, the nobleman from Lyon; Rousseau, the plebeian from Geneva and Annecy; and Diderot, the bourgeois from Langres. Thus it had been for centuries — in university and intellectual affairs since the time of Peter Abelard, in political and social life at least since Francis I and the Age of the Renaissance and the time of Montaigne. A present-day map of the railways of France, all converging on Paris, is a chart, so to speak, of the intellectual history of France for the past few centuries. In Paris was to be found the stimulating and fructifying company of the first-rate, such as the D'Alemberts, the Condillacs, the Rousseaus, and the Diderots, teaching one another, exciting one another, profiting from the intellectual facilities and reveling in the history and monuments of so great and so venerable a city. Of all of this Diderot was now a part. He was a 'bourgeois de Paris,' as the birth certificates of his children described him. As he walked (if he took the closest route) from the Rue Mouffetard to his weekly rendezvous at the Palais-Royal, he would pass, as a tourist might do today, the great old church of Saint-Etienne-du-Mont, where Pascal and Racine are buried; the Pont-Neuf, where Henri IV was assassinated; and Saint-Germain-l'Auxerrois, where the tocsin sounded for the Massacre of Saint Bartholomew's Day. As he walked the streets of Paris, he may often have recalled Montaigne's words about the city, words he probably knew, for Montaigne was one of his favorite authors:

Paris has possessed my heart since my infancy. I am French solely because of this great city, especially great and incomparable in its variety; the glory of France and one of the noblest ornaments of earth.*

The little circle of friends mentioned by Rousseau was composed of men all destined to be eminent. Condillac, although handicapped by eyesight so poor that it is said he did not learn to read until he was twelve, became the leading psychologist of his generation. His specialty was interpreting to his countrymen the psychological doctrines of John Locke (although he was unable to read him in the original), and carrying these on to further conclusions. This sort of speculation placed him on the frontiers of knowledge, in the shadow ground between psychology and metaphysics, as may readily be seen in his works, for example *Essai sur l'origine des connaissances humaines* ('Essay on the Origin of Human Understanding,' the book Diderot helped get published in 1746). One year younger than Diderot, Condillac had taken holy orders in 1740 and, even though it is said of him that he celebrated mass only once in his life, he evidently was very careful not to write anything that could be proved hostile to the Church. Eventually Diderot and he drifted apart, perhaps on this issue. Remarkably enough, Condillac, though often quoted in the *Encyclopédie,* is not listed as having contributed any articles. It is hard to believe, considering Condillac's reputation, that Diderot did not desire him as a contributor, and accordingly it may be presumed that Condillac deemed his association with Diderot too compromising. Nevertheless, their close association, while it lasted, was of

* Paris a mon coeur dès mon enfance. Je ne suis Français que par cette grande cité, grande surtout et incomparable en variété, la gloire de la France et l'un des plus nobles ornements du monde. (These words are on the plinth of Landowski's statue of Montaigne, erected in 1937 on the Rue des Ecoles facing the Sorbonne.)

great value to both. On Diderot's side this can be seen in his *Letter on the Blind* (1749), a work much more basic in its psychological and metaphysical concepts than any previous one. As for the influence of Diderot on Condillac, the latter's *Traité des sensations* (1754) was the result of Diderot's pointing out in his *Letter on the Blind* the apparent congruence of Condillac's presuppositions with those of the British philosopher, Bishop Berkeley.[41] 'Diderot merely pointed out some troublesome affinities between two works that, in all other respects, had no relationship,' writes the leading authority on Condillac. 'With an astonishing critical sense, he had foreseen the problem which Condillac's attempt involved.'[42]

Jean Le Rond d'Alembert, of whom we shall hear much, was four years younger than Diderot. He was the illegitimate child of one of the most celebrated, not to say notorious, women of the eighteenth century, and of the Chevalier Destouches, a lieutenant general in the French army. He was left a foundling on the steps of the church of Saint-Jean-le-Rond (the baptistry of Notre-Dame de Paris), and from this circumstance took his name. The wife of a glazier, one Mme Rousseau, took care of him in infancy and mothered him into middle age. He remained with her, occupying a modest little room in her humble home, until he was forty-seven years of age and one of the most famous men in Europe, but without her ever realizing, it is said, how celebrated her adopted chick had become. Unlike Diderot, D'Alembert was unusually precocious. When only twenty-five years of age, he had become an associate member of the Academy of Sciences. At twenty-six he published his *Treatise on Dynamics,* which, according to the principal French biographical dictionary, was 'an event in the history of the sciences.'[43] D'Alembert was slight and small in stature, with a marvelously intelligent and attractive face, as we see it in La Tour's pastel of him, with a clear and piercing falsetto voice which permitted his enemies to hint that he was not quite a man, and with a skill at mimicry which was the hilarious delight of his companions.

In this small circle of friends, vis-à-vis the psychologist, the mathematician, and the musician (for Rousseau about this time undertook to write the articles on musical theory for the projected *Encyclopédie*), Diderot proved his versatility by being profoundly interested and instructed in the specialty of each. One earnest of this breadth and competence was an article he published anonymously in the October 1747 number of the *Mercure de France*. Entitled 'Project for a New Organ,'[44] it was later republished, under Diderot's own name, in his *Mémoires sur différens sujets de mathématiques* (1748), and excited a good deal of interest on the part of the editor of the *Gentle-*

man's Magazine, the leading London review of the day. What Diderot had in mind were improvements in the simple hurdy-gurdy bird organs or mechanical organs of the time. These instruments — for an excellent description of the bird organ, see Diderot's own article *'Serinette'* in the *Encyclopédie* and the corresponding engraving — had a range of only one octave and a repertory of only a few tunes.[45] Diderot's principal innovation, simple but effective, was designed to increase greatly both the acoustical range and the repertory of such an instrument. A barrel organ constructed according to his description would permit people, even those unable to play an instrument, to 'set up' quite complicated pieces of music, and thus make music more readily accessible to all. Apparently, too, Diderot had in mind the construction of instruments large enough to be played in churches. He also suggested a chronometer for accurately indicating tempi, in this respect anticipating Maelzel's metronome. Observing this early interest, it is not surprising to learn that, when the *Encyclopédie* was to be done, Diderot assigned to himself the articles on musical instruments, their construction, their acoustical characteristics, and the method of playing them.

Diderot's 'Project for a New Organ' was a very characteristic performance. In the first place, it shows him being alertly curious, original, and inventive and also reveals a constant fascination in the relation of pure theory to applied knowledge and to gadgets. Thus, as he discusses how to place the pins on the organ cylinder in order to increase its range, he shows an equal awareness of both theoretical and technological problems. Another of Diderot's hallmarks was his ability to introduce into a discussion of any subject a marked quality of subjectiveness, an intimate revelation of personality — even in an anonymous article on a technical subject. This quality delighted the editor of the London *Gentleman's Magazine* as much as the proposed invention itself. 'What suggested the notion to the author, who appears very well versed in physics and geometry,' wrote the editor in the leading article of the August 1749 issue, 'may be seen by the following extract from his work: "For my part, who am hardly more bashful, or less curious than a child, I had no rest nor ease, till I had examined the first German organ I heard; and, as I have no skill as a musician, but am a great lover of music . . . it came into my mind . . . that it would be very convenient . . . to have such an organ, or some other instrument, which might require neither more natural fitness, nor less acquired knowledge, and on which one might perform all sorts of musical compositions." '[46]

Later in the eighteenth century there was a marked improvement, both in France and England, in instruments using the barrel-and-pin mechanism,

but perhaps to attribute this to Diderot would be no more than argument
on the level of *post hoc, ergo propter hoc*.[47] In the *Gentleman's Magazine*
for September 1749, a reader from Lancashire inquired 'whether your account of M. Diderot's organ has yet set the musico-mechanical artists of
London at work, or is likely to do so. The design in all probability must
take. It has many recommendations, one especially, which will weigh both
with those that are performers in music, and those who are not; I mean
by having the barrel-pins moveable.'[48] It is therefore tempting to believe
that Diderot's influence was at work during the late eighteenth and early
nineteenth centuries, when the application of the barrel-and-pin mechanism
to the organ became very common in England. Indeed, Dr. Scholes, the well-
known British musicologist, found one of these organs still in weekly use
in a Suffolk church in 1934.[49]

Diderot always delighted in being called a philosopher, or, better yet, *the*
philosopher. In many respects he had been qualifying himself for the appel-
lation in the usual sense of the term. For in 1746-7 he was already proficient,
as his writings show, in the history of philosophy; he was already concerned with problems of ethics, of the nature of God and man's relation to
Him, and with the problem of being. Already we see him rummaging about
in the philosophy of science, trying to use mathematical, biological, and
physiological insights as aids in the investigation of ultimate things.

But more than this, Diderot wanted to be a *philosophe* in that special
sense of the French word which the English does not quite convey. What,
then, is a *philosophe?* The answer is not easy, partly because in the eighteenth
century the word was dynamic and fast-moving. At the beginning of the
century, according to Muralt, a Swiss who wrote extensively on the manners of the French, the term '*philosophe*' was one of reproach and almost
of insult, betokening a person who desired to live in moody and invidious
solitude.[50] But fifty years had been changing all that; '*philosophes*' declared
themselves to be as sociable as any other Frenchmen, and the word began
to take on pleasing connotations. Moreover, it became a party name, with
all the blood-quickening and adrenalin-stirring attributes that party names
generate. It is easy to see in part what the *philosophes* meant by 'philosophy'
if we turn to the article '*Philosophe*,' long regarded as one of Diderot's
best, in the *Encyclopédie*. In reality this article was a shortened version of
one written by some unknown person and first printed in 1743, possibly
circulated in manuscript form before that.[51] It may be fairly assumed that
Diderot was likely to have known the piece by this time (1746-7) when he
was just moving into his responsibilities with the *Encyclopédie*. His en-

thusiasm for the article may be inferred from the fact that he published the scissors-and-paste version in the *Encyclopédie,* whether he 'wrote' it himself or accepted it from another hand. And the following excerpts from the 1743 edition, copied almost verbatim in the *Encyclopédie,* will give some idea of what an eighteenth-century *philosophe* thought himself to be:

Reason is to a philosopher what grace is to a Christian in the system of Saint Augustine. . . .

. . . .

The philosophical spirit is, then, a spirit of observation and exactness, relating everything to its true principles; but it is not the mind alone that the philosopher cultivates . . . Man is not a monster who should live only in the deeps of the sea or the depths of a forest . . . his needs and well-being engage him to live in society. Thus reason demands of him that he know, study, and labor to acquire sociable qualities.

. . . .

. . . our philosopher, who knows how to divide his time between withdrawal from men and intercourse with them, is full of humanity. He is the Chremes of Terence, who feels himself a man and who interests himself in the good or bad fortune of his neighbor out of humanity alone. *Homo sum, humani a me nihil alienum puto.*
. . . Civil society is, as it were, the only divinity that he recognizes on earth; * he worships it, and honors it by probity, by an exact attention to his duties, and by a sincere desire not to be a useless or troublesome member of it. . . .

. . . .

The philosopher, then, is an honest man who acts in all things according to reason, and who combines good morals [*moeurs*] and sociable qualities with a mind disposed toward reflection and preciseness.[52]

From these quotations it is possible to see some of the reasons why the term *'philosophe'* became a pleasant word in the eighteenth century, resonant with such happy overtones. On the affirmative side, it betokened a sense of social awareness and responsibility which appealed to the sympathies and large-mindedness of many well-intentioned persons. Moreover, the *philosophe* was inherently a man of probity and virtue, par excellence the virtuous man. On the negative side, it turned out that to be a *philosophe* was easy. No one need fret over such painful prerequisites as that of knowing the difference between ontology and epistemology. The ticket of admission to the chestnut path bore no pedantic stipulations having to do with a tech-

* The *Encyclopédie,* more circumspect, reads at this point, 'For him, civil society is, as it were, a divinity on earth . . .'

nical knowledge of the subject. As Professor Dieckmann points out, the author of this treatise (and, following him, the party of the Encyclopedists in general) 'does not conceive of the philosopher as the author of a system of ideas or the creator of a comprehensive interpretation of the world. . . . The philosopher thus conceived appears as a model, an ideal norm after which one strives, as one strove during the Renaissance to be an *uomo universale,* or *cortigiano,* and in the nineteenth century a *gentleman.*' [53]

Diderot was a philosopher. He was also a *philosophe*. His early writings, skilled in the technicalities of the philosophical method, using the word in its usual sense, were also beginning quite unmistakably to show the characteristic approach described by the author of the treatise on 'The Philosopher.' The *philosophe* was beginning to emerge.

CHAPTER 6

The Early History of the *Encyclopédie*

THE French *Encyclopédie,* as it stands today on the shelves of library treasure rooms in the select company of the very old, the very rare, and the very naughty, is an enormous work consisting of seventeen folio volumes of letterpress and eleven of engravings, to say nothing of four volumes of supplement, two of index, and one of supplementary plates. Yet at its inception the *Encyclopédie* was a modest venture, planned to be no more than a translation in four volumes (plus one of engravings) of Ephraim Chambers' *Cyclopaedia, or Universal Dictionary of the Arts and Sciences,* a very successful work first published in 1728 in two folio volumes embellished by twenty-one large plates. It was Diderot who in all probability was principally responsible for the expansion from the smaller project to the larger one. At the very least, it was he who became responsible for seeing it through. And thus was produced, as a modern French critic has remarked, 'not the finest, but surely the most characteristic, work of the French eighteenth century.'[1]

Previous to that time there were in existence various technical dictionaries or dictionaries of classical literature and learning.[2] There had even been a Latin *Encyclopaedia* published in 1630 by Johann Heinrich Alsted, a work which treated of philosophy, philology, theology, jurisprudence, medicine, history, and the mechanical arts. But by the end of the seventeenth century this estimable work was outmoded, and no less a person than the great Leibniz expressed the hope that a new encyclopedia would soon be forthcoming.[3] In view of the continuing spread of knowledge and education in Western Europe, a comprehensive reference work was needed that would inform its readers of the numerous discoveries in basic science made during the seventeenth century and also attempt to guide their understanding of the whole by means of some scheme or conspectus of the interrelationships of the several branches of knowledge. As we look back on the intellectual preparation of Western

European society two hundred years ago, we are not surprised that a considerable market existed for such works as Chambers' or the more ambitious one of Diderot.

Chambers' *Cyclopaedia* was prefaced by an elaborate scheme of the divisions and subdivisions of knowledge. It was 'the first attempt that had yet been made at once to arrange Knowledge by the Alphabet, and to exhibit a view of its relations and dependencies,'[4] features which the French *Encyclopédie* also adopted. Chambers' *Cyclopaedia* was very like a present-day dictionary, especially in its emphasis on the definition of common words. There was a particular abundance of medical and pharmaceutical terms, but no attempt was made to include geographical, historical, or biographical information. Moreover, it was severely limited in the number and scope of its engravings, which were devoted to such subjects as heraldry, surveying, sun dials, algebra, geometry, trigonometry, and navigation.

The plan and intent of Chambers' work was acknowledged by everyone, including Diderot, to be excellent. The execution, he contended, left something to be desired. Though more inclusive than any other existing work, it was still not comprehensive enough, and its treatment was frequently too brief. 'The entire translation of Chambers has passed under our eyes,' wrote Diderot in the prospectus of 1750, 'and we have found a prodigious multitude of things needing improvement in the sciences; in the liberal arts, a word where there ought to be pages; and everything to be supplied in the mechanical arts.'[5] So important a subject as 'Agriculture,' for example, was allotted in Chambers thirty-two rather jejune lines. In contrast, the article that Diderot wrote on that subject for the *Encyclopédie* fills fourteen columns and, among a host of other topics, gives publicity to Jethro Tull's discoveries in new methods of husbandry. This instance shows the breadth of Diderot's interests, and reveals also how the *Encyclopédie* became a forum for new ideas.[6] Diderot had a right to say that 'the articles of Chambers are laid out regularly enough, but they are empty; ours, though irregular, are full.'[7]

In France, during the very years when Chambers was preparing his *Cyclopaedia* for the press, there was formed an ephemeral Société des Arts (1726), which cherished the hope of publishing a sort of encyclopedia in which related arts, sciences, and mechanical arts would be described.[8] Though revealing the ferment of ideas, this project had no concrete result, nor any connection with the later *Encyclopédie*. Another project that might have resulted in an *encyclopédie* was of Masonic origin. A prominent Freemason named Ramsay declared in Paris in 1737 that 'all the Grand Masters in Germany, England, in Italy and throughout Europe exhort every savant and

artist in the brotherhood to unite for furnishing materials for a universal
dictionary of liberal arts and useful sciences, theology and statecraft excepted.' [9] Moreover, the Duc d'Antin, Grand Master of the Freemasons in
France, repeated and endorsed Ramsay's ideas in a discourse pronounced in
the Masonic Grand Lodge in 1740.[10] Statements such as these naturally have
caused historians to wonder whether there was not some direct connection
between Freemasonry and the *Encyclopédie,* and this supposition has been
heightened by the discovery that André-François Le Breton, one of the publishers of the *Encyclopédie,* was made a Master Mason in a lodge at Paris
in 1729.[11] No evidence, however, has yet been turned up to suggest that
Diderot was at any time a Mason.[12] In sum it seems safe to follow the judgment of a leading modern authority on the subject that Masonry and the
Encyclopédie, however similar in attitude, were born in two different and
distinct moments as a result of two different and distinct needs in the France
of the eighteenth century.[13]

Actually, the project for translating Chambers was the result not so much
of an ideological enterprise as it was a search for profit. In June 1744 Le
Breton had signed a contract with one Godefroy Sellius, a German from
Danzig, for a translation of the works of a German metaphysician, at that
time of great repute, named Wolff.[14] This project appears not to have
achieved publication, but in January of 1745 Sellius suggested to Le Breton
the translation of Chambers' *Cyclopaedia.* Sellius claimed to have found a
'rich and opulent' partner, an Englishman named John Mills. In February
1745, Mills and Sellius entered into a contract, and just a few weeks later the
two of them contracted with Le Breton to provide a translation, corrected
and enlarged, of Chambers' *Cyclopaedia,* to consist of four volumes of letterpress and one of 120 plates.[15] During this time Le Breton was evidently in
negotiation with the authorities for a license, for there was issued in blank
on 25 February 1745 a license good for twenty years, which, in the further
processes of being sealed and spread on the records of the corporation of
booksellers, on 26 March and 13 April respectively, lost its anonymity and
appeared in Le Breton's name.[16]

On the strength of these preparations, a prospectus was printed in the
spring of 1745, antedating by five years the more famous one that Diderot
launched in 1750. This comparatively unknown prospectus of 1745, announcing an *Encyclopédie, ou Dictionnaire universel des arts & des sciences,*
is a great rarity among book collectors.[17] Besides stating the terms of subscription, the prospectus emphasized its intention of providing a polyglot
cross-reference system for the titles of articles, and included some sample

articles, translated from Chambers, such as 'Atmosphere,' 'Fable,' 'Blood,' and 'Dyeing.' Several would-be subscribers presented themselves at once,[18] and the *Journal de Trévoux,* in its number for May 1745, quite outdid itself in the warmth of its remarks. 'To judge by the Prospectus,' it wrote, '. . . there is nothing more useful, more abundant, better analyzed, better related, in a word more perfect and finer than this *Dictionary;* and such is the gift that M. Mills is making France, his adopted country, while doing honor to England, his true one.' [19]

John Mills lived to become an appreciated writer on agricultural affairs in England, and the *Dictionary of National Biography* speaks of him with approbation. His relations with Le Breton, however, were exceedingly stormy, and ended in an exchange of blows on 7 August 1745. Mills, apparently, had misrepresented both his financial situation and his command of the French language. Moreover, Le Breton had supposed that his own relation with the enterprise would be merely as printer and agent rather than entrepreneur. It was necessary, for instance, that some French citizen be the intermediary for Mills and Sellius, both of them foreigners, in negotiations with the authorities for a license. Le Breton declared, when he printed his side of the story, that the translations by Sellius were so poor that they could not be used, that Mills was remiss and tardy in the revision of these articles, and that meanwhile he, Le Breton, was so frequently asked for advances in money that he became convinced that Mills and Sellius were making him their dupe.[20] Mills's urgent demand in August for a very large sum of money, coupled with Le Breton's discovery that far from being an heir to a large estate, Mills was only a sort of clerk in the Paris branch of a British bank, led to that kind of mutual explanation that is likely to end in an explosion.

Suit and countersuit were filed after the quarrel. Mills asserted that Le Breton had not only hit him in the stomach and struck him twice over the head with a cane, but had also cheated him of subscription money and was intriguing to get sole possession of the copyright.[21] Le Breton said, among a number of things, that he 'taught this arrogant Englishman that a Frenchman, if insulted, even though his weapons be inferior, avenges himself at once, as much as in him lies.' [22] The case did not come to trial. Instead, the Chancellor of France, the highly respected D'Aguesseau, one of the most famous magistrates in the history of the *ancien régime,* took direct cognizance of it. Such action was ordinary enough, for the chancellor of France was ex officio responsible for censorship and other matters pertaining to the policing of the book trade. Le Breton asserted many years later that

D'Aguesseau, upon examining Mills and Sellius, 'quite easily detected their incompetence and their swindling.' [23] No damages were assessed against Le Breton, and soon afterward Mills left France.[24]

The Chancellor allowed Le Breton to hope that after a short time he would be allowed to take up the project again. For the moment, however, the Council of State, on D'Aguesseau's recommendation, revoked the license that had been granted the preceding February, and declared Le Breton's contract with Mills and Sellius to be void. The 'Arrest' of the Council of State alluded to various infractions of the regulations regarding subscriptions committed by Le Breton but specifically mentioned the possibility of securing a privilege anew.[25]

Although the project was now in abeyance, sufficient public interest had been aroused by the prospectus of 1745 to encourage Le Breton to resume his plans as soon as possible. An earnest of public curiosity is to be seen in the remarks of an anonymous author, writing in the *Jugemens sur Quelques Ouvrages Nouveaux:* 'What an astonishing, an admirable dictionary is that of M. Chambers, entitled the *Cyclopaedia, or the Circle of Sciences,* which ought to be translated from the English into French, and for which subscriptions were even beginning to be taken at Le Breton's, bookseller of Paris, but for which the license has been revoked because the enterprise has appeared to be poorly planned. It is very much to be hoped that this project will be undertaken again without delay, under better auspices, and that our French printing industry, which, suffering grievously from the hardness of the times, has need of being encouraged and favored, may profit from so lucrative an undertaking, for it would be regrettable to see foreign countries, protected by the formalities of our regulations, enrich themselves, to the great shame of our own industry.' [26]

Unable to count upon the 'rich and opulent' Mills but now intent on publishing a translation of Chambers himself, Le Breton evidently felt that he needed more capital. In October 1745 he took into partnership for this particular venture three of his fellow-publishers, Briasson, the elder David, and Laurent Durand.[27] This partnership agreement was supplemented by another in which it was stipulated that Le Breton was to do the printing job for the whole venture, and a total edition of 1,625 sets was planned.[28] In December 1745, the government renewed the license that had been annulled the previous 28 August and this renewal was officially sealed and promulgated on 21 January 1746.[29] The translation of Chambers' *Cyclopaedia* was once more under way.

It is hard to say when or how Diderot first became associated with the

project. It may have been as early as the summer of 1745, for Le Breton
spoke in his memoir of that year of some unnamed 'intelligent person' who
was to have corrected the whole Sellius-Mills translation, 'and without whom
the Prospectus would not have been welcomed as favorably as it has.' [30]
This 'intelligent person' may have been Diderot. Or perhaps it was through
his publishers, Briasson, David, and Durand, that he became associated with
the project. Briasson had been the publisher of Diderot's translation of the
Grecian History; all three of them had collaborated in publishing James's
Dictionnaire universel de médecine; [31] and one of them, Durand, was the
publisher of Diderot's edition of Shaftesbury, off the press that very year.[32]
The entries in the publishers' account book of the *Encyclopédie* show payments to Diderot beginning in 1746 — 60 livres in February, 30 livres on
4 March and 15 on 31 March, 90 livres on 30 April, 120 on 1 June.[33] At this
time he was certainly on the pay roll, but still a goodly distance from being
entrusted with the principal direction of the enterprise.

It has also been asserted that Diderot was introduced to the project of
the *Encyclopédie* by the Abbé Jean-Paul de Gua de Malves, a brilliant but
eccentric and unstable mathematician. According to the famous Condorcet,
who wrote a eulogy of Gua de Malves at the time of his death (1786), it was
the Abbé who recruited Diderot, among others, to assist in the work.[34] Gua
de Malves, who was described in a secret police report in 1749 as having the
manner and countenance of a crazy man, first appears in the account book
of the publishers at the same time that D'Alembert makes his appearance
there — December 1745 — and a few weeks before Diderot.[35] On 27 June
1746, the Abbé became the principal editor of the project that became the
Encyclopédie, by virtue of signing a contract of which Diderot and D'Alembert were the witnesses. In accordance with this agreement, he was to
'extend the part having to do with the arts, preferably, as much as it will
be possible for him to complete.' [36] Whether or not he had recruited them,
Gua de Malves retained both Diderot and D'Alembert to work on the
project, assigning to each of them twelve hundred livres, to be paid from
the total of eighteen thousand livres that he himself was to receive. Moreover, Diderot and D'Alembert were to enjoy a sort of veto power in judgment of the accuracy of translation of the English articles.[37]

The new chief editor was a learned man, described in the contract as
'member of the Royal Academy of Sciences, of the Royal Society of London,
Reader and Royal Professor of Philosophy at the Royal College of France.'
He was also extraordinarily headstrong and stubborn, and, as Condorcet
says, 'it would have been difficult for there not to arise frequent disputes be-

tween a savant who saw in the undertaking only an enterprise useful for the perfecting of human knowledge or public instruction, and booksellers who saw in it only a business matter. M. l'Abbé de Gua, whom misfortune had made more easily wounded and more inflexible, soon grew disgusted and abandoned this work on the *Encyclopédie*.' [38]

In the light of this documentary proof of their association with Gua de Malves, it is more than a little odd that neither Diderot nor D'Alembert ever alluded in their writings to the connection of Gua de Malves with the *Encyclopédie*, leaving us to wonder how much this taciturnity was inspired by a deliberate intent to mislead. Just what the relations between him and Diderot were can only be inferred, the sole evidence being a single remark about him made by Diderot in his later works, an allusion rather ungenerous in tone and one which made no reference to the *Encyclopédie*. Wanting an example of the tendency of some persons to run to extremes, Diderot found it in 'that old *abbé* one sees on one's walks. . . . the Abbé de Gua de Malves. He is a profound geometrician. . . . but in the street he does not have common sense. In one year he straitened his income by assignments upon it; he lost his professorship at the Royal College; he got himself excluded from the Academy, and consummated his ruin by the construction of a sand-screening machine that never separated out a single particle of gold; returning poor and dishonored, he fell on the way back while walking a narrow plank and broke a leg.' [39]

The lack of satisfactory evidence for determining to whom should belong the credit of first having proposed a much expanded project, Diderot or Gua de Malves, has occasioned something of a who-killed-Cock-Robin dispute among authorities.[40] Condorcet, who was personally acquainted with all the men involved, uncompromisingly declared that Gua de Malves had the idea first. 'He had had time to change the form of it; it was no longer a mere augmented translation — it was a new work, undertaken on a vaster plan.' [41] However, Condorcet adduces no documentation. Moreover, he was writing after the death of all the persons involved, so that any misstatements he may have made were not subject to contradiction. Condorcet says that Gua de Malves recruited Diderot and D'Alembert, but he also claims that Gua de Malves recruited other persons, such as Condillac, Mably, and Fouchy, who in fact did *not* co-operate. There does, then, exist a possibility that Condorcet was partially misinformed; and over against his testimony can be set that, equally unsupported, of Naigeon, who declared, to bolster his insinuation that Gua de Malves's association with the project did not amount to much, that 'the first project . . . was limited to the translation

of Chambers' English *Encyclopedia,* with some corrections and additions
that the Abbé de Gua, at that time the sole editor, took upon himself to do in
order to make up for the important omissions of the English author and
to finish the table of human knowledge of that epoch.' [42] In short, so conflicting and defective is the evidence that we are reduced to speculation and
the weighing of probabilities. Therefore we might say, with great diffidence,
that it seems more probable that Diderot was recruited by the publishers
rather than by Gua de Malves; that the latter might very well have recruited
D'Alembert, both of them being mathematicians, and that this may have provided the occasion for Diderot and D'Alembert to become acquainted; that
both Gua de Malves and Diderot, being persons of learning and imagination, were capable of conceiving the idea, whether independently or in
association, of expanding the project; and that Diderot, whether or not he
got the idea first, unquestionably displayed the large-mindedness necessary
for success in carrying it out.

The agreement between the publishers and Gua de Malves lasted some
thirteen months and then was canceled by mutual consent on 3 August
1747.[43] There soon followed one of the biggest moments in Diderot's life.
On 16 October the publishers entered into a contract with him and D'Alembert to replace Gua de Malves in the direction of the enterprise. Diderot
was to get 7200 livres in all: 1200 of it to be paid in a lump sum upon
publication of the first volume; and the remaining 6000 to be paid at the
rate of 144 livres per month. D'Alembert was also to be paid at the rate of
144 livres per month, but the total was to be only 2400 livres. Thus the publishers contemplated a situation in which D'Alembert would continue on
the project only another sixteen months, while Diderot, at this rate of
payment, would be on the job another three and a half years.[44]

For Diderot the contract of October 1747 represented both independence
and security. Although a sum of 144 livres per month was modest, he could
now count on a constant income for the next forty-one months, with two-
thirds of a year's salary extra and in a lump sum when the first volume was
published. To know that he could keep the wolf from the door for at least
four or five years — this was indeed something for a person who had lived
as precariously as he. Actually, in return for this advantage he undertook
responsibilities that lasted twenty-five years, for not until 1772 did he bring
out the last volume of plates. In retrospect, Diderot was inclined to think
that he had been grievously underpaid for his work on the *Encyclopédie,*
and that the time it took robbed him of the opportunity for more substantial
literary accomplishment. Maybe so, though this is far from certain. With-

out the *Encyclopédie* he might have become more undisciplined and *less* productive.[45] It must be admitted, however, that the necessity for writing a large number of articles in haste developed in Diderot, for better and for worse, a flair for a type of writing that may well be called journalistic. At its best his writing has a sublime impetuosity and, at its worst, it possesses characteristics of the impromptu and the improvised.

In the six months following the publishers' contract with Diderot, so great an expansion of plans occurred that it became necessary to ask for a new license. There had been no intimation of this during the thirteen months that Gua de Malves had been the chief editor of the project — at least so far as existing documents show — and consequently it is tempting to suppose that this expansion came as a result of Diderot's breadth of views and persuasive tongue, that 'gilded tongue' of which his mother-in-law had spoken more in admiration than anger. On some occasion during the early history of the *Encyclopédie* Diderot had a decisive interview with the learned and pious Chancellor d'Aguesseau. It is evident that the point of discussion had to do with plans for expanding the *Encyclopédie,* and that the freethinking Diderot impressed the Chancellor very favorably. This was the more extraordinary in that the Chancellor, whom Voltaire described as a tyrant desiring to prevent the nation from thinking, was customarily very stern and very conservative in his administration of the censorship.[46] But when could this interview have taken place? Probably not when the privilege of January 1746 was being mooted, for this month was the first in which Diderot's name appeared on the pay roll, and it is clear that he was not yet entrusted with any great responsibility in the enterprise. But by April 1748, when the new privilege was granted, he was one of the co-editors. Therefore it was probably at this time that he astonished D'Aguesseau by his intellectual powers and readiness of wit. At all events the new license was registered at the Royal Corporation of Booksellers on 30 April 1748, thus superseding the previous one of January 1746.[47] A comparison of the texts of the two documents shows very little difference between them, but evidently what difference there was, was considered very significant. Whereas the 1746 license set forth that Le Breton intended to publish a text 'translated from the English Dictionary of Chambers and of Harris, with some additions,' the 1748 privilege calls for a translation 'of the English Dictionary of Chambers, of Harris, of Dyche, and others, with augmentations. . . .'[48]

Lamoignon de Malesherbes, who between 1750 and 1763 was himself the magistrate in charge of regulating the book trade, is the source of two accounts of Diderot's interview with D'Aguesseau. The later account, written in 1790, is the better known, and is contained in Malesherbes' *Memoir on the Liberty of the Press*. Malesherbes recalls that 'the plan [of the *Encyclopédie*] was concerted with the most virtuous and enlightened of magistrates, the Chancellor d'Aguesseau. M. Diderot was presented to him as that one of the authors who would have the greatest share in the work.

'This author was already marked, by many of the pious, for his freedom of thought.

'However, the pious M. d'Aguesseau wished to confer with him, and I know that he was enchanted by certain marks of genius that shone forth in the conversation. . . .' [49]

The other account by Malesherbes of Diderot's interview with the Chancellor was written at a date much nearer to the event. In an unsigned and undated memorandum, written in Malesherbes' unmistakable and almost illegible hand, and which internal evidence shows to date from 1758 or early 1759, Malesherbes wrote that 'The late Chancellor had cognizance of this project [the *Encyclopédie*]. Not only did he approve it, but he corrected it, reformed it, and chose M. Diderot to be the principal editor of it.' [50]

Many years later Diderot wrote a cryptic declaration that might possibly refer to his relations with D'Aguesseau. 'I protest,' he wrote, 'that undertaking the *Encyclopédie* was not of my choosing; that a word of honor, very adroitly exacted and very unwisely granted, bound me over, hand and foot, to this enormous task and to all the afflictions that have accompanied it . . . .' [51] Whether or not this remark by Diderot refers to D'Aguesseau, one observation should be made concerning Malesherbes' statements. If Malesherbes' memory was more accurate in the account he wrote while still in office — while he still could refresh his memory from the office records about an event that had happened only ten years previously — than it was in the account written thirty years later, then it appears that the Chancellor did more than simply accept Diderot as an editor. Rather, D'Aguesseau *chose* him, thus investing him with some of the Chancellor's great prestige and authority, and making it more difficult to attack the *Encyclopédie* on ideological grounds. If so, this interpretation of events would go far to explain why Diderot, at that time a person still quite obscure, seems to have been so quickly accepted by both friend and foe as the leader of the great new enterprise.

CHAPTER 7

Two Very Different Books

As his thirty-fifth birthday approached, Diderot's time was filled by a variety of activities. Three rather cryptic entries in the publishers' account book for June, July, and August 1748 suggest that he may have been concluding his translating work on the James *Medicinal Dictionary*.[1] In addition, his new job as one of the chief editors of the *Encyclopédie* involved not only the translation and adaptation of a host of articles from Chambers' *Cyclopaedia,* combined with much planning for a greatly extended project, but carried with it concomitant necessities of looking about for collaborators and directing them in their assignments.[2] Documentary evidence of the minutiae of this important and time-consuming work has practically all disappeared. No doubt discarded in wastebaskets and trash fires as useless, the concrete evidence of the process of editing — the notes exchanged between editor and contributor, the manuscripts of proffered articles with perhaps Diderotian bluepencilings upon them, the galley proofs, the page proofs — has almost completely vanished. Nevertheless, there must have been an exhausting amount to do, especially as the *Encyclopédie* was planned to be the result of the labor of 'a company of men of letters.' And in addition to these tasks Diderot found time, or at least some time, for his domestic life with Anne-Toinette and baby François-Jacques-Denis back at the lodgings in the Rue Mouffetard; probably a good deal more time for Mme de Puisieux, and for his expanding circle of friends; and, finally, time snatched somewhere or other for the composition of one more in his series of risky and — as regards this particular work — risqué manuscripts.

This was the novel called *Les Bijoux indiscrets* ('The Indiscreet Jewels'). According to Mme de Vandeul, the book was written in a fortnight on a sort of wager with his mistress to show how easy it was to do this sort of thing.[3] The novel, having been bought by the publisher Durand for twelve hundred livres, was on sale, under the mantle or under the counter, in the early days of 1748.[4] This is about the time negotiations were under way with the Chancellor of France for a license for an expanded *Encyclopédie*. It was lucky for Diderot that D'Aguesseau, whose official duties were in some respects like those of a censor in old Roman times and whose temperament somewhat resembled that of Cato the Elder, was unaware of this excursion into the field of salacious literature.

Part of the interest — and the daring — of the book lay in its transparent allusions to living figures. The action is supposed to take place in the Congo at the capital city of Monomotapa (a name made familiar by the opening line of one of La Fontaine's fables), and the principal personages are the Sultan Mangogul and his charming favorite, Mirzoza. One did not have to be a medium to understand that the author had in mind Louis XV and Mme de Pompadour, who had become the King's acknowledged mistress three years earlier. The book is also filled with thinly disguised references to Paris, the Opéra, France and England, and to such personages as the Duc de Richelieu, Cardinal Fleury, the composers Lully and Rameau, Descartes, Newton, and Louis XIV. This in itself was sufficient to make the book audacious. Over and above this was the plot. The Sultan, to fend off boredom, to which he was unusually subject, was given a magic ring. This ring had the property, when turned toward any woman, of making that part of her anatomy talk which, if it ordinarily had the power of speech, would be most qualified to answer a Kinsey questionnaire. To a novelist perhaps unsure of his ability to write a tightly constructed novel, this plot was admirably calculated to keep up suspense. If interest flags, just bring in another trial of the magic ring. Diderot did so. There were thirty trials in two volumes, all of them attended by what might be called success.

There is a tradition that Diderot got the idea for his novel from a novelette entitled *Nocrion, conte allobroge*. This item, now exceedingly rare, was published in 1747 and written, perhaps by the Count de Caylus, perhaps by the Abbé (later Cardinal) Bernis, in the naïve manner and archaic language of a medieval fabliau.[5] Certainly Diderot could very well have taken from *Nocrion* the principal device of *Les Bijoux indiscrets*. But whether or not this was the source of *Les Bijoux,* Diderot, of course, did not invent the genre of licentious novels. Indeed, a very successful practitioner in this field, or perhaps swamp, of letters was living in Diderot's day — Crébillon the Younger, whose most famous novel, *Le Sopha,* had been published in 1740. Obviously there is a great similarity of device in the plots of Crébillon's and Diderot's novels. And there is a similarity of cynicism, too, in their common assumption that every woman, however demure and virtuous she may seem, is really morally corrupt.

Diderot would not have been Diderot if he had not strewn this work with a large number of thoughtful observations and lively criticisms of the social and intellectual life of his time. In consequence, no serious student of Diderot's ideas and their development can afford to overlook *Les Bijoux indiscrets*.[6] For example, the book contains a very good comparison and contrast of the music of Lully and Rameau (chapter xiii); there is also a critical animadversion to Louis XIV concerning his domination by Mme de Maintenon, and a disapproving reference to his Revocation of the Edict of Nantes (chapter i); there is a parody of a sermon which quite makes us believe Mme de Vandeul when she states that in the early years of vagabondage at Paris her father got fifty crowns apiece for six sermons written for the missionary who was going to the Portuguese colonies (chapter xv); there is much interesting speculation about the nature of dreams and the real character of the soul (chapters xlii and xxix);[7] the scientific and metaphysical views of the Newtonians are contrasted with those of the followers of Descartes (chapter ix); there is a good deal of criticism of the theater, views praised by Lessing, the great German playwright and critic, and which are the blood brothers of Diderot's later writings on the theater (chapters xxxvii and xxxviii);[8] and a chapter of literary criticism, rather redolent of Swift's *Battle of the Books,* in which Homer, Virgil, Horace, Pindar, Socrates, Plato, and Voltaire are admiringly mentioned and the Quarrel of the Ancients against the Moderns warmed up again (chapter xl).

Critics speak with great interest and respect of a chapter set forth as a dream, which really deals with the triumph of the scientific method over ignorance posing as knowledge.[9] It was like Diderot to include so serious a subject in a frivolous and licentious novel, telling it in the form of a dream or myth as Plato might have done. This was chapter xxxii, called by Diderot 'The best, perhaps, and the least read, of this History.' The Sultan Mangogul dreamed he had been carried into the Realm of Hypotheses. While there, he saw a child, Experiment, approaching and maturing and growing ever bigger as he advanced. At length, 'I saw Experiment draw nigh and the columns of the portico of the Temple of Hypotheses tremble, its roof cave in, and its floor yawn open beneath our feet. . . . it collapsed with a frightful roar, and I woke up.' The Sultan's sole comment about this dream, as Louis XV's might well have been, was that it had given him a headache.

People fond of Diderot are inclined to say that passages like these go far to redeem the work, and it is well to remember that André Gide noted in his *Journal* that he read *Les Bijoux indiscrets* 'with rapture.' [10] Moreover, many people argue, there is something of the scientific in Diderot's treatment of the sexual (and the sexually abnormal) in this novel. As one modern critic suggests, 'even the rather heavy-handed facetiousness of *Les Bijoux indiscrets* indicates an attention, an analyst's and psychologist's interest in the scabrous details of sexual life.' [11] Still, *Les Bijoux* has had quite enough editions, and enough illustrated editions, to prove that it is a dirty book. Within a few months of publication, six editions in French were printed in Holland alone.[12] In France, the book was highly contraband as well as popular: in 1754, for example, the police descended upon a bookseller and discovered a stock of sixty-four copies.[13] An English translation appeared in 1749, and German ones in 1776 and 1792.[14] The book is still of interest to collectors — and others: there have been ten editions in France since 1920. *Les Bijoux,* in short, is Diderot's most published work.

There is a school of critics that, when faced with the necessity of saying something about an obscene work, tends to take the it's-not-amusing-it's-just-dull line. Thus Carlyle, in his essay on 'Diderot,' spoke of Diderot's writing 'the beastliest of all past, present or future dull Novels; a difficult feat, unhappily not an impossible one'; and the late George Saintsbury agreed, in his *History of the French Novel,* that 'it really would require a most unpleasant apprenticeship to scavenging in order to discover a dirtier and duller.' [15] Actually, Diderot's work was far from dull. Quite to the contrary, it was lively — lively with ideas, lively with dialogue, lively with sallies. It was smutty — perhaps, as a French critic believes, the circumstances of Diderot's disordered youth had served to dirty his imagination — [16] but it wasn't dull. And the most honest criticism of it would be something like that which appeared in a recent history of French literature: 'Its verve and keenness do not excuse its obscenity.' [17]

Diderot was a little out of his element in writing about a king and his mistress, and this evidently was palpable to people of the time who were sensitive to social nuances. The Abbé Raynal, reviewing *Les Bijoux,* called the book 'obscure, poorly written, in a coarse and vulgar tone, and by a man ill-acquainted with the milieu he has desired to depict. The author is M. Diderot, who has very extensive knowledge and a great deal of wit, but who is not suited for the genre in which he has just written.' [18] Other contemporary criticisms were also adverse, although one of the most hostile of all admitted the verve of the work. 'One cannot deny,' wrote this critic, 'that his *Bijoux* frequently say some very sensible things; but they are wrapped up in so many dirty and cynical images and expressions, that their utility can never be comparable to the danger to which the most dispassionate mind would be exposed in reading them.' [19]

Years after the publication of *Les Bijoux indiscrets,* Diderot professed to Naigeon that he regretted having written it. 'He often assured me that if he could make good this error by the loss of a finger, he would not hesitate to sacrifice it for the sake of suppressing entirely this delirium of his imagination.' [20] Even so, some years after its publication he added two chapters to the original edition — internal evidence shows that it could not have been before 1757 — [21] and we can believe, along with Diderot's later editor, Maurice Tourneux, that if Diderot was willing to sacrifice a finger, it would have been the little one, and that on his left hand. [22]

Diderot was, as usual, running risks. It was dangerous to have written such a work, yet it was soon an open secret in Paris as to who the author was. Nor were the police the last to learn of it. An informer named Bonin, a most interesting character who operated a supposedly clandestine press, wrote to the Lieutenant-General of Police not later than 29 January 1748 that 'Dridot' had just given to the public *Les Bijoux indiscrets;* and on 14 February of that year the same informant wrote that 'it is Mr. Durand, Rue St. Jacques, who had *Les Bijoux indiscrets* printed and who sells them. He bought the copy from Dridot for 1200 livres. This publisher is very worried, as are also Messrs. David and Briasson, who fear that something might happen to Dridrot that would suspend the Dictionary of Medicine of which Dridrot is editor.' [23]

Diderot, moreover, increased the risks he was already running by having a hand in the preparation of a fairy story called *L'Oiseau blanc, conte bleu* ('The White Bird'), a *conte bleu* signifying a sort of unbelievable, fabulous tale. [24] *The White Bird* was patently inspired by the *Arabian Nights:* a sultana, finding it difficult to go to sleep, has this story told to her during a succession of seven nights, with infallible soporific effect. It is likely to have that effect on the reader too, for *The White Bird,* which recounts the adventures of Génistan, the son of the Emperor of Japan, whom a wizard had metamorphosed into a pigeon and who regained his pristine state only after being touched by the wand of the fairy Truth, is a mawkish and insipid tale even though it did receive the honor of a German translation in 1907. Presumably it was written as a sequel to *Les Bijoux indiscrets,* for it reintroduces some of the characters from that book, but it has none of the bite and none of the social comment that distinguished *Les Bijoux.* There are some commonplaces about truth and how truth does not customarily reside at courts, but these mild platitudes are far from the questing fierceness with which the mind of Diderot usually pursued truth, seeking her in the scientific and methodological developments of his time. Indeed, the contrast between this tale and anything else Diderot ever wrote is enough to raise the question of whether he really did write it. He himself emphatically disowned it. Then, under pressure, he added, 'It is by a lady whom I might name, since she herself doesn't conceal it. If I have any part in this work, it is rather in having corrected its orthography, against which ladies with the greatest intelligence are always somewhat at fault.' [25] Yet Naigeon, in spite of this testimony, published *L'Oiseau blanc* in his edition of Diderot's works appearing in 1798, the first publication of the tale. Naigeon, whom Diderot had appointed as his literary executor, was certainly in a position to know. Consequently, critics have accepted *L'Oiseau blanc* as being from the hand of Diderot, or at least greatly affected by him.[26]

The White Bird is really composed of very uninflammable stuff. But evidently rumors were rife about it at the time, for the police, under the impression that it contained derisive allusions to the King and Mme de Pompadour, tried hard to track it down. Considering its literary merits, all that can be said is that this official perturbation complimented the work a good deal more than it deserved.

Les Bijoux indiscrets was the sort of book that might seriously impair a man's scholarly reputation. What was even worse, Diderot did not yet have much of one to destroy. By his own confession, he hoped that his *Mémoires sur différens sujets de mathématiques,* on which he was working in early 1748, would 'prove to the public that I was not entirely unworthy of the choice of the associated publishers [of the *Encyclopédie*].' [27] At the same time he had undertaken a translation of Joseph Bingham's monumental *Origines ecclesiasticae, or the Antiquities of the Christian Church,* a translation which certainly was never published and possibly never completed.[28] It is probable, however, that Diderot put his knowledge of Bingham to good account in the *Encyclopédie,* especially in view of the fact that both works are well-informed about the multitudinous heresies of the Christian Church. Also in 1748 Diderot was persistently reported to be working on a 'History of the Expeditions of England,' but this rumor was evidently erroneous, for the French edition of Thomas Lediard's *Naval History of England,* published eventually at Lyon in 1751, was the translation, by all accounts, not of Diderot, but of De Puisieux, the husband of Diderot's mistress.[29]

Of greater importance in this year of varied intellectual activity was the fact, asserted by Diderot in his 1749 statement to the police, that 'I have done the *Exposition du système de musique de M. Rameau.*[30] This interesting remark — for Rameau was the most significant French composer of the eighteenth century, the 'discoverer' of thorough-bass, and a musician whose music still has both freshness and body — has set bibliographers wondering as to just which work was meant. Raynal, reviewing Diderot's *Memoirs on Mathematics,* remarked that Diderot was 'an intimate friend of M. Rameau, whose discoveries he is presently going to publish. This sublime and profound musician published formerly some works in which he did not include sufficient clarity and elegance. M. Diderot will rework these ideas, and he is most capable of setting them forth to excellent advantage.' Sometime later the same journalist remarked: 'Our very illustrious and celebrated musician, M. Rameau, claims to have discovered the principle of harmony. M. Diderot has lent him his pen in order to set forth this important discovery to its best advantage.'[31] Perhaps this work was Rameau's *Démonstration du principe de l'harmonie* (Paris, 1750), and indeed the evidence seems to suggest that it was. D'Hémery, the police inspector who confiscated *La Promenade du sceptique,* entered in his journal for 17 February 1752 that the *Elémens de musique théorique et pratique suivant les principes de M. Rameau* was done by Diderot.[32] This work, however, was always claimed by D'Alembert, and it is probable that in this instance D'Hémery was mistaken. It is certain, however, that the versatile Diderot was, in some ghost-writing way, associated with the greatest French musician of the century, an association which incidentally had a great cooling-off when Rameau began to attack Rousseau's articles on music in the *Encyclopédie.*[33]

Diderot's *Mémoires sur différens sujets de mathématiques* was published by Pissot and Durand, the latter being the Durand of the publishers of the *Encyclopédie,* and was brought out in a format de luxe, with six delightful engravings, as, for example, cupids tracing x's on a sheet of paper, or fixing pegs in the cylinder of a mechanical organ, so that, as Tourneux remarked, 'the volume is one of the most coquettish that was ever published on such arid subjects.'[34] Diderot wrote in his signed dedication to a Mme de P * * * — probably Mme de Prémontval, a mathematician and the wife of a mathematician, and not Mme de Puisieux —[35] 'I am giving up the cap and bells, never to take them up again.'

The five mathematical papers were summarized by Diderot as follows: I. The general principles of the science of sound, with a special method of fixing the pitch, in such a manner that one may play a piece of music on exactly the same pitch at whatsoever time or place; II. A new compass made of the circle and its involute, with some of its uses; III. Examination of a

principle of mechanics concerning the tension of cords . . . ; IV. Project
for a new organ . . . [this was the article that had been published anonymously in the *Mercure de France* the preceding year]; V. A letter on the
resistance of the atmosphere to the movement of pendulums, with an examination of the theory of Newton on this subject.

The *Mémoires sur différens sujets de mathématiques* received a very good
press. The censor to whom the manuscript had been submitted set the tone,
for he remarked that these papers were treated 'with great sagacity.'[36]
Diderot was beginning to make his mark. 'M. Diderot (to judge by this
essay),' wrote the *Journal des Sçavans,* 'is very much in a position to give
learned solutions to difficulties that require nice and intricate calculation.'[37]
The Jesuit *Journal de Trévoux* invited the continuation of such researches
'on the part of a man as clever and able as M. Diderot appears to us to be,
of whom we should also observe that his style is as elegant, trenchant, and
unaffected as it is lively and ingenious.'[38] And the *Mercure de France* remarked: 'Here is quite a number of new views in a volume that with its
table of contents includes not more than 250 pages. The author was already
known to be a man of a great deal of wit. Upon reading these memoirs, one
will discover that he adds to this advantage that of also being a learned
musician, an ingenious mechanician, a profound geometrician.'[39] It is no
wonder that the Abbé Raynal thought it time to modify his opinion of this
rising star. In introducing his review of the *Mémoires sur . . . mathématiques,* he began: 'I don't know whether you have heard of a M. Diderot,
who has a good deal of wit and very extensive knowledge. He has made
himself known by his writings, most of them imperfect, yet filled with
erudition and genius.'[40]

A recent and authoritative article on Diderot as a mathematician con-
cludes that by this series of papers he proved himself competent and original.
Moreover, he also demonstrated himself to be conversant with the current
developments in the field, especially the works of Euler and D'Alembert.
'He was well grounded in the earlier mathematical literature, judging from
his acquaintance with the ideas of Pythagoras, Aristoxenes, Gassendi, Halley
and Flamsteed, Newton and others referred to in his *Mémoires.'*[41] And
Julian Coolidge remarked, 'I cannot leave Diderot without expressing my
admiration for his really stimulating mathematical work, when his other
interests were so large and so varied.'[42]

We might well suppose that by this volume Diderot had proved once for
all his mathematical competence. Yet by a strange twist of fortune he has
become known to a large part of the English-reading public as a mathe-

matical dunce. Some twenty-five years after Diderot had published these mathematical papers, a story circulated around Berlin about a practical joke that may (or may not) have been played upon him during his visit to Saint Petersburg. According to this story, a Russian philosopher offered to prove to Diderot algebraically the existence of God. So, in the presence of the Court and with the secret acquiescence of the Empress, the story goes, the Russian philosopher gravely approached Diderot and said in a tone ringing with conviction, 'Sir, $\dfrac{a + b^n}{z} = x$. Therefore God exists. Reply.' The point of this story, as originally told, was that Diderot, momentarily casting about for the most effective reply to the ineptitude of this alleged proof, sensed from the attitude of the courtiers that a joke was being played upon him and that all those present were in on it. The Berlin source did not include Diderot's reply, but it did state that this misadventure caused Diderot to apprehend that others might be in store and convinced him that the intellectual climate of Russia was not congenial, so that he soon signified his desire to return to France.[43]

In the course of time the point of this story became twisted, so that it is often told by authors of books on popular mathematics as an illustration of the horrible fate that awaits a person ignorant of mathematics. The anecdote was published in 1867 and 1872 by an English author, De Morgan, with gratuitous additions; first, that the Russian philosopher involved was Euler, and second, that algebra was Hebrew to Diderot.[44] Bell, in his *Men of Mathematics,* tells the story as it was twisted by De Morgan, his only variation being in the remark that 'all mathematics was Chinese to Diderot.'[45] And Lancelot Hogben begins his *Mathematics for the Million* with this same dramatic tale, *his* variant being that 'algebra was Arabic to Diderot.'[46] How the story has been contorted and has grown to this misshapen state has been remarked on by three contemporary scholars, one of whom says, in allusion to the De Morgan-Bell-Hogben fabrication, 'That is the story, and it is a very good story, except that it isn't true.'[47]

As Diderot went through life, he lost faith in Christian immortality, and instead fixed his hopes on the sort that comes from having one's deeds live in the memory of posterity. Could he be aware that the rank and file of posterity, at least in English-speaking countries, are now likely to remember him more for being mathematically illiterate than perhaps for any other thing, he might be tempted to hedge his bet.

CHAPTER 8

Letter on the Blind

THE French Enlightenment not merely originated new ideas: it applied them to existing institutions. And eventually, of course, the process burst a good many old bottles. This attitude made the *philosophes,* with Diderot a leader among them, the radicals and the unconscious revolutionaries of their day. Indeed, their pronounced interest in practical affairs has justly earned for the *philosophes* the reputation of being reformers but at the cost of their reputation as philosophers. Diderot's own progressive outlook and concern with practical matters were evidenced at this time by a pamphlet advocating a reform that finally was brought about in 1793. This anonymous work, dated 16 December 1748, was entitled *First Letter from a Zealous Citizen Who is neither a Surgeon nor a Physician, To Monsieur D. M. . . . In which is Proposed a Means for Settling the Troubles that for a long Time have Divided Medicine and Surgery.*[1] The condition that had aroused Diderot's interest was a preposterous though long-standing division of labor in French medicine. This practice decreed that in the treatment of patients, physicians might not operate and surgeons working on the case might not express an opinion that in any way had to do with general or internal medicine. Moreover, the physicians considered themselves infinitely superior, socially and intellectually, to the surgeons. The origin of this irrational distinction, or what the sociologist is fond of calling the pecking-order, goes back to medieval times, when all physicians were clerics. This had the not unnatural tendency, incidentally, of causing them to neglect gynecology and obstetrics, a field which was left to the midwives; but what was more to the point, their status as clerics forbade their shedding blood. Since they could not perform operations, this was done by the barber-chirurgeons. Moreover, physicians, coming from the class of 'bourgeois notables,' were forbidden under pain of losing their status to exercise for gain any skill requiring the use of hands.[2] The social results of this sort of snobbery were painfully evident and, as is so often the case in jurisdictional disputes, it was the public who suffered the most. Against this Diderot inveighed. 'What are we about?' he cried. 'Where is our shame? Where is our humanity?'

Diderot's solution was for both physicians and surgeons to be united in the same body under the same name. Aesculapius, Hippocrates, and Galen practiced both medicine and surgery, he remarked. Therefore, 'what disadvantage is there today in the same person's ordering and executing a bloodletting? Let . . . doctors and surgeons form a single corps; let them be assembled in the same college, where students may learn the operations of surgery and where the speculative principles of the art of healing may be explained to them. . . .'[3]

The *Letter from a Zealous Citizen* bespeaks an interest in medicine which is not at all surprising in one who had spent so much time and energy in translating James's *Medicinal Dictionary*. This interest remained constant with Diderot throughout the years, so that one finds him a close friend of the Genevese, Théodore Tronchin, the most famous doctor of his generation in all of Europe, and of Théophile de Bordeu (1722–76), a pioneer in the study of glands and mucous membrane. Diderot also delighted in the study of anatomy, and lost no opportunity, for example, to praise the anatomical models devised by a Mlle Biheron.[4] Diderot's profoundly thoughtful and speculative *D'Alembert's Dream* is based upon a great variety of medical and physiological knowledge, and one of his last books was *Eléments de physiologie* (1774–80). 'The fact is,' he wrote late in life, 'it is very difficult to think cogently in metaphysics or ethics without being an anatomist, a naturalist, a physiologist, and a physician.'[5]

Even in the wording of its title, the *Letter from a Zealous Citizen* betokens the changing social values of an age beginning to be on the march. The eighteenth century was commencing to emphasize the concept of 'belonging,' of citizenship. Diderot was among the leaders of this movement, and the term *'citoyen'* appears very frequently in the pages of the *Encyclopédie*. Destined by the time of '93 to bear pungent and sometimes bitter fruit, 'citizen' was one of the pleasant and slightly radical words of the eighteenth century. Thus we have Diderot ending his letter with a fine humanistic flourish: 'I am a good citizen, and everything that concerns the welfare of society and the life of my fellow men is very interesting to me.'[6]

Problems of citizenship, it so happened, were being canvassed rather generally in France in 1749, for this was a year of hunger and distress, accompanied by a considerable ferment of opposition to the government.[7] In part the unrest was caused by discontent with the Treaty of Aix-la-Chapelle, which had recently brought to an end the War of the Austrian Succession and which, said the captious, was the peace that passeth all understanding. There was also disquiet owing to the opposition of the privileged classes, especially the clergy, to the imposition of a tax called the vingtième, promulgated in May of 1749, which would have had the effect of introducing into the French governmental system the principle of the obligation of everyone to pay proportionate taxes.[8] The attempt to enforce this simplest sort of elementary fairness in the incidence of taxation was bitterly resisted and obstructed by the privileged classes, whose previous connections with public finance had been more on the receiving than the paying end.

In retrospect, 1749 seems a crucial year in the history of the eighteenth century and the annals of the French monarchy, in part because of what happened to Diderot and Rousseau within that twelvemonth. No doubt to a person taking the auspices at that particular moment, only the faintest hint of thunder could be heard on the left. Yet the intellectual climate of opinion experienced a new pressure front that very year. A nineteenth-century editor of Barbier's *Journal,* a major source for the history of France in the eighteenth century, remarked that 'the year 1749 is a remarkable date in the literary history of the eighteenth century. It is at this date that writings hostile to religion appear and multiply. . . . Henceforth war breaks out between skepticism and faith. Barbier, who up to this point has spoken only of ballad writers and poets, now speaks of the *philosophes*. It is at this point that the real eighteenth century begins.' [9]

Seventeen hundred forty-nine was a year of transition in France. It marked the epoch when intellectual prestige was transferring its headquarters to a new field, while subjects hitherto regarded as almost untouchable mysteries began to be matters for critical comment. The crucial nature of this year was observed by a French historian, Rulhière, even before the Revolution. Being welcomed into the French Academy in 1787, Rulhière mentioned in his formal discourse that the year 1749 was the one in which a general revolution in manners and in letters began. 'In that very year in which were produced all these great philosophical works, we saw beginning a succession of unfortunate events that little by little and from day to day stripped from the government that public approbation and esteem that up to that time it had enjoyed; and while we passed from the love of belles-lettres to the love of philosophy, the nation, owing to a change explained by causes quite different, passed over from acclamations to complaints, from songs of triumph to the clamor of perpetual remonstrances, from prosperity to fears of a general ruin, and from a respectful silence regarding religion to importunate and deplorable quarrels. . . . The capital [Paris], which for so long a time had been the prompt and docile imitator of the sentiments, taste, and opinions of the Court, at the same time ceased to have for the latter its old-time deference. Then it was that there arose among us what we have come to call *the empire of public opinion.* Men of letters immediately had the ambition to be its organs, and almost its arbiters. A more serious purpose diffused itself in intellectual works: the desire to instruct manifested itself in them more than the desire to please. *The dignity of men of letters,* a novel but an accurate expression, quickly became an approved expression and one in common use.' [10]

Manifestations of the growing malaise in the French body politic, first identifiable in 1749, were even then interpreted by some as the beginning of a revolution. The Marquis d'Argenson recorded in his famous journal on 1 May 1751 that 'people are talking of nothing but the necessity of an early revolution because of the bad condition in which the government finds itself internally.' [11] It is very much worth remembering that the *Encyclopédie* was being prepared and its first volumes published against this background of confused and muted discontent.

In contrast, Diderot's personal affairs seemed prosperous. In 1748 and 1749 he continued to receive regularly his monthly stipend of 144 livres. To this could be added the 1200 livres he is known to have received for *Les Bijoux indiscrets,* and he may have received something for *Mémoires sur différens sujets de mathématiques,* though of this there is no record. The added security of his financial position was reflected in his moving his family from the Rue Mouffetard to a third-floor apartment in a building, built in 1681 and still standing, at 3 Rue de l'Estrapade.[12] Perhaps, one thinks as one ascends the stairs, Diderot walked up and down these steps and slid his hand along this very stair rail. Perhaps it was at this very landing that Mme Diderot assaulted the neighbor's servant girl. Or, observing the house from across the street, one gazes at the very window from which Diderot's wife, perhaps with her three-year-old son at her side, looked down to see her husband carried away by the police.[13]

Diderot, although he was not now living quite so surreptitiously, was still keeping his marriage a secret from his relatives at Langres, and that may have been the reason why he seems to have made no effort to go home at the time of his mother's death in October 1748. He inherited some property from her estate, but just how much or when it became available is not known.[14]

During these months the *Encyclopédie,* of course, continued to be in active preparation, and Diderot, besides writing manuscripts to enhance his reputation as a savant (such, for example, as the forthcoming *Letter on the Blind*), was occupied with all the organizing, directing, persuading, and exhorting that his position entailed. Probably he made it a point to pay somewhat ceremonious visits to important contributors, if we may judge from an incident in 1751 when the Chevalier de Jaucourt proposed to call upon Diderot in order to volunteer his services. 'I shall be charmed indeed to have the honor of seeing you at my house,' wrote Diderot, 'but allow me to pay *you* a visit.'[15] No doubt Diderot went the rounds on errands like this in 1748, if his being reimbursed on several occasions for cab fare is any indication.[16] In addition he made extensive use of the Royal Library, now called the Bibliothèque Nationale, and on occasion was granted the unusual privilege of borrowing books from it. In his prospectus for the *Encyclopédie,* Diderot acknowledged the invaluable assistance of the Royal Librarian, and the registers in which are recorded his numerous withdrawals still exist.[17] The work on the *Encyclopédie* was going on apace, but, as the publishers of the venture were soon to learn, all came to a stop if Diderot was not there.

Seventeen hundred forty-nine was a memorable year in the life of Diderot. And so it was to many others. To the let-'em-eat-cake segments of society it was noteworthy for the first appearance of a live rhinoceros in Paris. 'To transport him on land, a covered wagon, drawn sometimes by twenty horses, has been used. He eats up to sixty pounds of hay and twenty pounds of bread a day, and drinks fourteen pails of water. He eats everything but meat and fish,' reported Raynal in his news letter. And then he added, 'It appears that so far rhinoceroses have not been very useful.'[18] To other elements of society, especially authors, 1749 came to mean a year selected by the government to attempt by confiscations, arrests, and imprisonments to discourage the expression of radical ideas.[19] D'Argenson remarked in August that because of the great number of such arrests the Paris prisons were so full that some of the culprits had to be sent to Vincennes and other outlying prisons.[20] And it was just this year that Diderot chose for the publication of an extremely original, controversial, and dangerous book.

This work, *Lettre sur les aveugles à l'usage de ceux qui voient* ('Letter on the Blind for the Use of Those Who See'), combined a great deal of scientific observation with some very upsetting metaphysical speculation. It was printed clandestinely by a printer named Simon; was sold — under the counter, of course — by Durand, one of the four publishers of the *Encyclopédie;* and was published — or, at least, was ready for bootlegging — on 9 June 1749.[21] The book greatly enhanced Diderot's reputation as a man of letters and a learned person, as the very fact of Voltaire's letter to him in acknowledgment of a presentation copy amply signifies; but its publication was also the occasion for a frightening experience which evidently chastened him a good deal. The appearance of the *Letter on the Blind,* therefore, ushered in a period of major crisis in the life of a man who could not keep himself from continually meditating on new ideas.

The particular occasion for the book, which had to do with the psychology of blind people and with what must be the ethical ideas of a person deprived of one of his senses, was an operation performed in Paris to restore sight. News had gotten about that a Prussian oculist, sponsored by the well-known French scientist Réaumur — he of the thermometer, and the man who first worked out the technique of the artificial incubation of eggs — was going to couch the cataracts of a girl born blind. Diderot claimed that he and many others with scientific interest in the case had asked to be present when the bandage was taken off the girl's eyes so that they might observe her at the moment when she was first able to see objects. But Réaumur had refused such requests: 'In a word,' wrote Diderot, 'he has not wished to let the veil fall except in the presence of some eyes of no importance.'[22] The eyes of no importance, according to Mme de Vandeul, were those belonging to Mme Dupré de Saint-Maur, the wife of an obscure writer who owed his seat in the French Academy either to his translation of *Paradise Lost* (1729) or to certain connections formed by his wife — no one seemed to be quite sure which. This lady was on very friendly terms not only with Réaumur but also with Count d'Argenson, the Secretary of State for War who, since 1737, had been the Director of Publications. It may have been, therefore, that personal reasons, as well as reasons of state, accounted for Diderot's arrest.[23] It is certain that Diderot's relations with Réaumur from then on were unsettled and at length became antagonistic.

The *Letter on the Blind* is a disarming book, written with the seeming artlessness of someone idly improvising on a musical instrument.* One subject suggests another, so that the reader, led on and on through a sort of steeplechase over most of the various metaphysical jumps, finally gets himself soaked in the water hole called 'Does God Exist?' The work begins with a number of acute firsthand observations of the behavior of a man

---

* An English translation is in Margaret Jourdain, *Diderot's Early Philosophical Works* (Chicago, 1916), 68–142.

born blind, a man of considerable intelligence whom Diderot knew personally. In addition, Diderot used supplementary information about the behavior of the blind, and especially about the acuteness of their senses of hearing and touch, which he found in the introduction to Nicholas Saunderson's *Elements of Algebra*. Saunderson, blind from birth, had been a famous Cambridge professor of mathematics, his particular specialty being, of all things, optics. To help himself in imagining geometrical problems and in making computations, he had devised a sort of arithmetical and geometrical abacus, 'a palpable arithmetic,' as the title of his book described it. After explaining the operation of this device, Diderot began to speculate upon the kind of concepts of God and of right and wrong that a person must have who has less than the normal number of senses. This was an original way of thinking about such matters, for it clearly suggested that our ideas about God and morality are not absolute but relative to our physical make-up and endowment. No wonder that some people sniffed materialism in this point of view, especially as Diderot invented what purported to be a veridical account of Saunderson's death-bed conversation in which the professor was made to declare that 'if you want me to believe in God, you must make me touch Him.'[24]

By this method of thinking, Diderot was experimenting with a type of investigation that has since been very successfully developed in medicine, biology, and psychology. It is the method of trying to find out about the nature of the normal by studying the abnormal, of learning about the nature of the well through studying the diseased. It was always characteristic of Diderot to study the pathology and teratology of a subject in order the better to understand its normalities. And because this line of thought led him to meditate on monsters and how their malformations make them unfitted to survive, he began to speculate about the emergence and modification of biological species in a way that clearly foreshadows Darwinism.[25]

The last third of the *Letter on the Blind* speculates on the famous question propounded by William Molyneux (1656-98): suppose a blind man, in the instant of recovering his sight, to see a cube and a sphere resting on a table. Would he be able to distinguish the cube from the sphere by sight, without touching them? This brain-cracker, fundamentally similar to problems in perception that are still puzzling psychologists, deeply concerned the philosophers of the eighteenth century because the answer to it would throw light upon such fundamental topics as how human beings think and how they know what they know.[26] It was in the hope of securing some light on the Molyneux problem that Diderot had wished to be present when Réaumur had the bandage taken off the girl with the cataracts.

The *Letter on the Blind,* which was addressed to a lady, perhaps Mme de Puisieux, reveals some interesting characteristics of its author. First, of course, there was that nimbus of the personal and intimate that characterizes so much of Diderot's writing, even the most scientific, and which frequently invades the columns of the *Encyclopédie,* where one might suppose all to be impersonal and austere. In the *Letter,* too, Diderot's notorious fondness for straying from the highroad of his theme and picking sweetly scented but somewhat irrelevant nosegays is strongly marked: 'There we are, a long way from our blind people, you'll say; but you must have the goodness, Madame, to forgive me all these digressions: I have promised you a conversation, and I cannot keep my word without this indulgence.' [27]

More importantly, the *Letter on the Blind* shows Diderot to be a considerable scientist: in his knowledge of the previous 'literature' of the subject, in the accuracy of his observations, as well as in the wealth of his hypotheses concerning what these observations might mean. His work shows, for example, that he was familiar with Descartes' *Dioptrics,* the writings of Bishop Berkeley and of Condillac, Voltaire's *Elements of Newton's Philosophy,* and Saunderson's *Elements of Algebra,* a book not translated into French until 1756.

It is impressive, too, to observe how seriously Diderot's observations on the psychology of the blind have been taken by scientists and professional workers in that field. One of the curiosities in the Boston Public Library is a translation of Diderot's work, made by Samuel Gridley Howe and 'printed' in raised letters at the Perkins Institution for the Blind in 1857. The preface remarks that the work 'abounds with beauties which they [the blind] can keenly relish, & with valuable suggestions by which they may profit.' In particular, as Dr. Gabriel Farrell, the present director of the Perkins Institution, has said: 'Diderot seems to have been first to call the attention of the scientific world to the superior sensory capacities of the blind.' [28] And the late Pierre Villey, a blind professor of literature at the University of Caen, although he contested Diderot's principal thesis, namely that a blind man's intellect, personality, and ethical notions are different from those of a man with sight, nevertheless acknowledged that Diderot had foreseen the proper treatment for a Helen Keller, had evinced a remarkable taste for psychological observation, and was completely a pioneer in his speculations upon the psychology of the blind.[29]

No doubt one of Diderot's intentions in publishing the *Letter on the Blind* was to display his qualifications for being editor of the forthcoming *Encyclopédie*. By this time it was generally known that he was to have an important connection with the publication, even though the formal prospectus was not to be circulated for over a year. The *Journal de Trévoux* of April 1749, for instance, alluded to his 'preparing' the 'Universal Dictionary of the Arts and Sciences.' [30] Certainly the *Letter on the Blind* disclosed to the public what he could do and on what platform he stood. It revealed as the cornerstone of Diderot's manner of thought his assumption, based on the writings of John Locke, that the only thing the mind has to work with is the evidence conveyed to it by the senses. Put the other way around, this doctrine asserted that the mind does not have born within it any notions of morality or religion, but simply builds up these concepts upon the evidence communicated to it by the senses. This constant and exclusive reference to the teachings of experience became the foundation stone for the psychological doctrine known as sensationalism. These views of Locke had first gained circulation in France through Voltaire, who cited them approvingly in his controversial and widely read *Lettres philosophiques* (1734). By mid-century they had become the official epistemology, so to speak, of the emerging school of *philosophes*. From the very first page of the *Encyclopédie,* from the very first words of D'Alembert's 'Preliminary Discourse,' which is rightly regarded as one of the monuments of the intellectual history of man, this point of view is taken for granted. This was the basis of the scientific and critical spirit that characterized the *Encyclopédie* and made it the engine for transmuting the values of a whole society. For this doctrine, as we explore its implications in problems like the nature of being, the nature of reality, the nature of knowing, and the nature of God, is extremely corrosive and dissolvent to any religious authority based simply upon revelation and to any political authority based simply upon prescription. To those writers who wanted to rally around such a battle standard, Diderot's *Letter on the Blind* served as a recruiting placard: Sign up with me! And it is perhaps this quality that accounts for the three editions of *Letter on the Blind* appearing in 1749, and for its receiving the flattering attention of Voltaire.[31]

Besides seeking to persuade people to have faith in his intellectual competence, the *Letter on the Blind* was a personal document constituting a further step in the development of Diderot's philosophical thought. Starting from the mildly theistic footnotes to his translation of Shaftesbury, written most probably in 1744, Diderot had come, in the course of five years, through the way stations of deism (the *Philosophical Thoughts* and *On the Suf-ficiency of Natural Religion*), and then of skepticism (*La Promenade du sceptique*), until by 1749 he had reached a pretty thoroughly materialistic position: 'If you want me to believe in God, you must make me touch Him!' All this had been accomplished at a fairly mature age, between thirty-one and thirty-six, and it was done in a spirit that could be described as more proscientific than antireligious. There was nothing hysterical or frenetic in Diderot's casting off his belief in orthodox Christianity and then his belief in any God at all. On the contrary, his attitude had been rather like that of a man who, without alacrity and without regret, simply discards tools that he no longer regards as capable of doing the job.

The *Letter on the Blind* was the occasion for putting Diderot into touch for the first time with Voltaire. The latter, evidently having received an advance copy of the book, replied at length in a letter dated simply 'June.' [32] Voltaire, who by conviction was a deist and who, moreover, thought that he would have his throat cut if his servants ever came to believe that there is no God, expostulated with Diderot on the tendency of his argument toward atheism. It was a skillful letter, written by the master whose flattery was so exquisite and so appetizing that, as Lord Macaulay said, 'It was only from his hand that so much sugar could be swallowed without making the swallower sick.' And he ended by inviting Diderot to come to see him and partake of a 'philosophical repast.'

It was a heady invitation, and Diderot replied that the moment of receiving Voltaire's letter was one of the sweetest of his life. Still, he did not go. There is in his reply a certain standoffishness which his relations with Voltaire constantly exhibited until the latter's death in 1778. Through the years it was usually Voltaire who accepted the burden of initiating a correspondence, infrequent as that was, and Diderot who delayed in replying or did not reply at all. Probably a stubborn desire to remain completely independent, added to the fact that the two men did not see eye to eye on matters of philosophical belief, explains why Diderot treated somewhat distantly the century's most famous man of letters.[33]

To Voltaire's arguments about a deistic universe, Diderot replied in this letter, 'I believe in God, although I live very happily with atheists. . . . It is . . . very important not to mistake hemlock for parsley; but not at all so to believe or not in God.' [34] And having disposed of the matter so sum-marily, Diderot went on to ask Voltaire to accept copies of the *Memoirs on Different Subjects of Mathematics,* one for himself and one for Mme du Châtelet, Voltaire's mistress and an excellent mathematician and physicist.

Diderot referred to this lady with deference and was evidently overawed by her mathematical accomplishments. Thus the lives of these two persons briefly touched in a year that was to be crucial for both. In six weeks Diderot saw closing upon him the gates of a royal prison of which a kinsman of Mme du Châtelet happened to be in charge; within three months of Diderot's sending her his book, the lady herself was dead, in tragic and grotesque childbirth. 'What shall we do about the child?' Voltaire had been asked when it was first realized that Mme du Châtelet, through a liaison with the poet Saint-Lambert, was pregnant. 'Don't let that trouble you,' said Voltaire airily. 'We shall give the child a place among Madame du Châtelet's miscellaneous works.' [35]

The portion of Diderot's letter referring to Mme du Châtelet has only recently been discovered. In this same overlooked portion Diderot excuses himself from meeting with Voltaire because of exhaustion and because of tensions in his private life. 'O Philosophy, Philosophy! what good are you if you do not blunt either the pricks of grief and of vexations or the sting of the passions?' [36] No doubt he was somewhat exaggerating, in order to make his excuses more plausible; but nevertheless his allusions to overwork, family dissension, and enslavement to Mme de Puisieux throw interesting light on Diderot's condition and state of mind in early June of 1749.

CHAPTER 9

Diderot in Prison

AT SEVEN-THIRTY in the morning of Thursday, 24 July 1749, two police officers climbed the stairs of the house in the Rue de l'Estrapade. One of them was D'Hémery, the man who had previously searched for the manuscript of *La Promenade du sceptique*. He and his companion, a man named Rochebrune, were admitted by Diderot to his apartment and began to search for any manuscripts 'contrary to Religion, the State, or morals.' It is possible, some authorities think, that Diderot may have expected such a visitation, for the police found nothing but twenty-one pasteboard cases containing manuscripts that they thought pertained to Chambers' *Cyclopaedia*. On a large table serving as a desk were found more manuscripts concerning the same work, and two copies of the *Letter on the Blind*. 'In the presence of the said Diderot,' reported the police, 'we continued our search in the other rooms, and having opened the wardrobes and chests of drawers, found no papers therein.'[1] This testimony of Commissioner Rochebrune incidentally affords some insight into the conditions of Diderot's daily work, suggesting that he did much of his writing at home, 'on a large table serving as a desk.' This routine, however, was about to be suddenly and completely altered, for D'Hémery told Diderot that he was under arrest.

It was by virtue of one of the notorious writs known as *lettres de cachet* that Diderot was arrested and imprisoned. *Lettres de cachet* have become one of the most odious symbols of the *ancien régime,* as every reader of *A Tale of Two Cities* can gauge by consulting his own feelings. Though numerous — the leading modern historian of Jansenism asserts that forty thousand were issued in the seventeen years of Cardinal Fleury's administration alone[2] — perhaps the *lettres de cachet* were not in reality so abusive as they came to seem. Apologists for the good old days point out that for the most part they were used to straighten out family tangles, just as Father

Diderot had secured one in 1742 in order to cool off his hot-headed son, or to enforce with contempt-of-court penalties what might be called injunctions in cases of private morality. Such apologists also emphasize that there is no evidence that these arrest warrants were issued in blank except under very carefully controlled conditions, so that the writs never became, as is often darkly suspected, the legal instruments of unjust vengefulness. There is no record of active maltreatment of persons detained by *lettres de cachet:* no evidence, for example, of torture or starvation, though there is of forget-fulness. Indeed, orders were given that people should be granted food and treatment in approximate accordance with their social rank. Diderot, for example, was to receive the equivalent of four livres a day for *'nourriture et attentions.'* [3] Finally, a *lettre de cachet* had to bear the countersignature of one of the king's principal ministers, and in this respect unquestionably satisfied the forms as much as could be expected of a warrant for arrest in any country at any time.[4]

But *lettres de cachet* were much less satisfactory in that they did not have to state the cause for arrest. Furthermore, persons thus arrested were held incommunicado, and it was entirely legal to detain them indefinitely, which was of course a frightening and demoralizing prospect. There came to be a rather widespread feeling in France while Sartine was Lieutenant-General of Police (1759–74) that the practice of issuing *lettres de cachet* was be-coming too extensive; [5] by the time of the Revolution, they had aroused a great sense of injustice. Perhaps *lettres de cachet* would not have come to seem so great an abuse had they not been the government's favorite method of attempting to discipline men of letters.[6] At first this policy was able to enforce an apparent conformity; but eventually it boomeranged, winning for the monarchy the persistent ill-will of the most articulate element of French society.

Two days before Diderot's arrest, Count d'Argenson, acting in his capacity of director of publications, wrote to the Lieutenant-General of Police, 'to give orders for putting Mr. Didrot, author of the book on the Blind Man, in Vincennes.' Berryer made the order the occasion for instructing his men to find out from Diderot all they could about *Letter on the Blind, Pensées philosophiques, Les Bijoux indiscrets,* a work called *L'Allée des idées* (prob-ably *La Promenade du sceptique*), and *L'Oiseau blanc, conte bleu.*[7] On 23 July the *lettre de cachet,* countersigned by D'Argenson, was made out at Compiègne.[8] And on 24 July Diderot and D'Hémery made the cab journey, at the king's expense, to Vincennes, an imposing medieval fortress and former royal residence six miles east of the heart of Paris.

Having been turned over to the governor of the place, François-Bernard du Châtelet, the relative of Voltaire's mistress and a man whose correspondence gives the impression that he was well-intentioned but bumbling, Diderot was immediately placed in the central keep.[9] This lofty tower was one of the most conspicuous symbols of the grimmer side of the *ancien régime,* 'the very sight of which,' wrote the author of an eighteenth-century guide book, 'causes fear.' [10] The edifice has had its most famous and its most gracious depiction in one of Fouquet's beautiful miniatures for the Duc de Berry's Book of Hours. It remains today just as it evidently looked to Fouquet in the fifteenth century, when he made his calendar-pictures. Diderot's place of confinement, according to tradition, was in the northwest *tournelle* of the third floor, the floor directly above the room where Prince Hal is said to have died in 1422. Diderot's room was octagonal in shape, approximately thirteen feet square and twenty-eight feet high, with graceful vaultings, a brick floor, a window looking out toward the château's entrance gate, and an enormous fireplace, its mantel jutting out about six feet above the floor. The room (at least as seen in 1939; it was later closed to the public), is light and airy and would not have been too unpleasant in the summer season, the time when Diderot was there. It was, in short, a suitable place for meditation; but there was always the very great risk that he would be left to meditate infinitely longer than he desired. Every day, Mme de Vandeul states, the jailer brought Diderot two candles. But he, who got up and went to bed with the sun, had no use for them, and after a fortnight's accumulation tried to return them. 'Keep them, keep them, Monsieur!' cried the jailer; 'You have too many of them now but they'll come in very handy in the winter'! [11]

In her distress, Mme Diderot sought an interview with Berryer, who adopted the rough and tough approach. 'Well, Madam, we've got your husband and he'd better talk. You might spare him a lot of trouble and hasten his release if you would tell us where his manuscripts are. . . .' But his wife disclaimed knowing anything at all about Diderot's works, claiming never to have read any of them.[12] As for the publishers, they were much given in this emergency to bustling about in carriages, as their account books show.[13] The very day of the arrest the publishers addressed a petition to D'Argenson in which they stated that the *Encyclopédie* was on the point of being announced to the public and in which they declared that 'the detention of M. Diderot, the only man of letters we know of capable of so vast an enterprise and who alone possesses the key of this whole operation, can bring about our ruin.' [14]

The agitation of the publishers to secure Diderot's release was unremitting all through the time of his imprisonment. Four days after the arrest they had presented their case to the Chancellor and had come to the conclusion that nothing would be done until the Lieutenant-General of Police had interviewed Diderot and reported thereon. Consequently they besought Berryer to interrogate the prisoner: 'he [Diderot] is the center where all the parts of the *Encyclopédie* have to converge; his detention suspends all operations on it and will inevitably bring about our ruin if it should be at all long.' [15]

The interrogation, which took place in the tower, occurred on 31 July, exactly a week after the arrest. Apparently Diderot was still hoping that he could brazen things out. Already he had persuaded one of the prison officers — that golden tongue again — to present directly to Berryer a request to be allowed to use the large central room of the storey in which he was confined, a request evidently annoying to the Marquis du Châtelet, who did not care to have his authority thus short-circuited.[16] During the interview with Berryer, Diderot admitted nothing. Moreover, he declared under oath that he had not written the *Letter on the Blind* nor caused it to be printed nor had he sold or given the manuscript of it to anyone; that he did not know the identity of the author, that he had not had the manuscript in his possession either before it was printed or afterward, and that he had not distributed or given copies of the book to anyone. As for *Les Bijoux indiscrets* and *Pensées philosophiques,* he swore that he had not written them, and he specifically stated that he did not know who was the author of the *Pensées.* He further claimed not to have written or corrected *L'Oiseau blanc,* but admitted to having written *La Promenade du sceptique,* saying that the manuscript had been burned.[17] Inasmuch as Berryer learned the very next day from the publisher Durand that Diderot *was* the author of the *Pensées,* the *Bijoux,* and the *Lettre sur les aveugles,* the magistrate evidently adopted the policy of simply waiting until Diderot saw fit to volunteer more information.[18]

Under this sort of duress Diderot began to suffer very much. This was natural enough, for the extreme sociability of his nature and his talkativeness made him less fitted than most people for the rigors of solitary confinement. Though Diderot had been given much more freedom by the time Rousseau was allowed to see him, the visitor found Diderot 'greatly affected by his imprisonment. The keep had made a terrible impression upon him and, although he was [now] comfortable at the castle and allowed to walk where he pleased in a park that was not even surrounded by walls, he needed the society of his friends to avoid giving way to melancholy.'[19] Condorcet, a much younger contemporary of Diderot, is reported to have said that Diderot almost went crazy while he was in solitary confinement.[20] This is quite possible, especially in view of Diderot's unusually powerful and vivid imagination and sensitivity. His emotional response to situations — to music, to a generous action, to plays, to pictures, to an act of injustice, to anything either aesthetic or ethical that was beautiful or hideous — was extreme. It is therefore quite possible that there was little exaggeration in the long letter that he wrote to Berryer in which he darkly hinted that he might do violence to himself.

This letter of 10 August 1749, in which he states incidentally that 'my father is still ignorant of my marriage,' is as characteristic of Diderot as anything he ever wrote. It contains the sensibility for which he is famous — 'I feel that despair will soon finish what my bodily infirmities have greatly advanced'; the bouquets naïvely thrown at himself by his own willing hand; the torrential and expostulatory style that he made very plausible and convincing whenever he wrote in passionate defense of his own innocence and virtue; and a certain deliberate obtuseness in failing to conceive what he could possibly have done wrong. And in all this lengthy letter he does not say a word about the *Pensées,* the *Bijoux,* or the *Letter on the Blind!*[21]

Writing to D'Argenson the same day, Diderot made the same assertions, although more briefly and in a more reserved style. But in this emergency he had bait to dangle in front of the Secretary of War. 'Alas! Monseigneur, when he [Diderot is here talking of himself] was brought to this prison, he was on the point of publishing the prospectus [of the *Encyclopédie*] and of soliciting from Your Highness the permission to publish under your auspices this work that has been undertaken for the glory of France and the shame of England, and which is perhaps worthy, at least in this respect, of being offered to a minister who protects the arts and those who cultivate them.'[22] This proffer was obviously a bribe, a *quid pro quo.* It is very interesting to see that Diderot evidently regarded himself as so exclusively the director of the *Encyclopédie* that he felt free to offer the dedication without first consulting D'Alembert or the publishers. It may of course be true that he really had been intending all along to broach the subject to D'Argenson and had previously cleared the matter with his associates. But probably he had not, for if he had, the publishers would surely have alluded to it in their petition to D'Argenson. Whether D'Alembert knew of it or not there is no telling. At all events, when the first volume of the *Encyclopédie* appeared, there was the dedication to D'Argenson, the shabby reality making the high-flown phrases sound rather brassy and cracked.

Three days went by and Diderot wrote to Berryer again, on 13 August. This time he confessed. After an elaborate beginning, in which he tried to ensnare Berryer in the toils of his own generous impulses, Diderot wrote, 'I therefore avow to you, as my worthy protector, what the tediousness of a prison and all imaginable penalties would never have made me say to my judge: that the *Pensées,* the *Bijoux,* and the *Lettre sur les aveugles* are excesses that slipped out of me; but that I can on the other hand pledge my honor (and I have some) that they will be the last, and that they are the only ones.' Diderot was evidently in a state of panic, for he even offered to reveal the names of the printers and publishers of his illicit works. He made this offer, however, contingent upon Berryer's giving his word of honor not to use this information in any way whatever to their disadvantage unless they were guilty of recidivism. And Diderot, characteristically, offered to tell them himself what he had done, if Berryer demanded it.[23]

This confession got results. Sometime before 21 August, Berryer informed the Marquis du Châtelet that Diderot was to leave the keep and be allowed the freedom of the grounds: 'His Majesty also saw fit, in view of the editing work with which he is charged, to allow him freely to communicate by writing or orally in the château, with the customary precautions, with persons from the outside who come there either for that purpose or for his domestic affairs. . . . You will have the goodness to have assigned to him in the château one or two commodious rooms for sleeping and working, with a bed and such other furniture as you customarily furnish to prisoners in the keep, and nothing more, reserving for him to procure greater conveniences at his own expense if he desires them.'[24]

Berryer wrote out with his own hand the statement that Diderot had to sign in order to enjoy these new conditions: 'I promise the Lieutenant-General of Police that I will not go beyond the château nor its courts nor the enclosure of the royal garden nor the bridges [over the moat] during the time it shall please His Majesty to have me kept a prisoner, submitting myself in case of disobedience on my part regarding the foregoing to be shut up all my life in the keep whence it has pleased the clemency of the King to have me brought forth.'[25]

One of the traditions concerning Diderot's imprisonment in the tower is that he had to improvise writing materials. An account of this was first published in an obscure and rare magazine called *La Bigarure,* printed at

The Hague. In its number dated 30 October 1749, Diderot being still in prison, *La Bigarure* told how he used a toothpick for a pen, a mixture of wine and pulverized slate for ink, and for paper a copy of Plato, which the ignorant jailer had allowed him to keep on the theory that no one could get any meaning out of such stuff.[26] Differing versions of the story are told by Mme de Vandeul, Naigeon, and Eusèbe Salverte, each of whom presumably got his 'facts' from Diderot himself.[27] Their accounts are fairly well reconciled by a document found among the Diderot papers. This is entitled 'Copy of the Notes written on the Margins of a Volume of Milton's *Works* by M. Diderot during his Detention in the Château of Vincennes,' these notes being 'The Apology of Socrates, translated from memory.'[28] *Some* writing he assuredly did in the tower, whether authorized or unauthorized, for he wrote the Marquis du Châtelet in late September to ask whether the notebooks that he had filled up there, mostly with notes on Buffon's *Natural History,* might be returned to him.[29]

Because of his demonstrativeness, which always made him very conspicuous in whatever situation he found himself, Diderot's release from the tower was very likely just the sort of tableau that he admired in the pictures of Greuze, genre pictures such as 'The Village Bride' or 'The Paternal Curse,' which endeavored to 'freeze' on canvas a sentimental or violently emotional scene. For here is the situation, as recounted by Mme de Vandeul: 'At the end of twenty-eight days, my mother was told to go to Vincennes. The associated publishers accompanied her [the publishers' account book actually shows an entry for carriage expenses for this very day, 22 August 1749].[30] Upon her arrival, he was brought out of the tower. . . .' The imagination kindles at the scene: Diderot, very much the center of the picture and gesticulating, quite as in real life; his wife, with her back to the beholder and in a bad light, as always; the turnkey, with his keys in his hand; perhaps the Marquis du Châtelet himself, very elegant in courtly attire; at one side the publishers, dressed in sober, bourgeois colors; and, to give variety to the scene, no doubt a barking dog or two, come from the Lord knows where.

Mme de Vandeul went on to describe Diderot's life for the next ten weeks. 'The Marquis du Châtelet heaped kindnesses upon him, invited him to his table, and took the greatest care to make this stay as little disagreeable and as convenient as possible to my mother. They stayed there three months, then they were permitted to go home.'[31] Inasmuch as Rousseau says in the *Confessions* that he sometimes accompanied Mme Diderot from Paris to Vincennes to visit Diderot, it may be that Mme Diderot did not stay there continuously, in spite of Mme de Vandeul's statement that she did. A picture

of Diderot's routine while in the château is also reflected in the Marquis du
Châtelet's notes to Berryer. One on 30 August required correction and
amplification, for Berryer replied to it the very next day, evidently in alarm
lest Diderot was not being held strictly to his word. So Châtelet wrote
again on 3 September that Diderot had profited only once from the permission to move freely in the courts of the château. 'He has gone out three
times evenings for an hour with his wife in the park. He is well. Many
people come to work with him, but I believe he is unable to get much
done here.' [32]

Into this Eden Lilith came. Mme de Puisieux paid a visit. But Diderot
had become suspicious of her and finally 'he slipped out over the walls,
went to Champigny, saw his mistress there with her new lover, came back,
and slept in the park. The next morning he went to inform M. du Châtelet
of his escapade, and this little adventure accelerated his rupture with Mme
de Puisieux.' [33]

It is very hard to know how much of this story to believe. On the one
hand, a cooling-off in the relations between Diderot and Mme de Puisieux
did occur at approximately this time. And although it may seem odd that
Mme de Puisieux should visit Diderot at Vincennes while Mme Diderot
was there, still Diderot could conceivably have arranged interviews without his wife's knowledge. But it seems unbelievable, considering the penalty
he might incur, that Diderot would take the fearful risk of breaking his
parole. Joseph Delort, writing in 1829 with a profusion of underlinings,
claimed that Diderot 'afterward asserted (according to the note that lies
before us) that he went out several times at night to go to see in Paris
a woman he loved.' [34] M. Delort vouches for this. But who, as Gibbon might
ask, will vouch for M. Delort? And Funck-Brentano, also without documentation, declares that the Marquis du Châtelet made these escapades
possible by conniving at them.[35] Yet, considering the nervousness of Berryer's
response to what he thought was an indication of laxity in Du Châtelet's
dealing with Diderot, it does not seem likely that the governor of the prison
would have been very eager to be accessory to such goings-on. This is the
sum of the evidence, vague and uncertain as it is.

Diderot's arrest had caused some public stir and aided a great deal in
making his name well known. As early as 26 July, an Abbé Trublet wrote
to a lady of his acquaintance about Diderot's imprisonment: 'It is this last
drop of water [Letter on the Blind] that has made the vase overflow, and
this has come about, it is said, through the complaints lodged by M. de
Réaumur. You know that he is not well treated in the first few pages.' [36]

Voltaire, writing from Lunéville, almost two hundred miles from Paris, knew of Diderot's imprisonment by 29 July, only five days after it had taken place.[37] The entries, not all of them accurate, in the journal of the Marquis d'Argenson, brother of the Secretary for War, show that the case was talked about in ministerial and court circles, just as a similar entry in the equally famous journal of the bourgeois, Barbier, proves that Diderot's name was becoming known among lawyers at Paris.[38]

Diderot's misfortune had the indirect effect of allowing posterity to know who were the persons, and presumably the most influential persons, with whom he had any connection in 1749. For in his letters to Berryer and D'Argenson he mentions as people who could vouch for him, a M. de Bombarde (of whom nothing is now known), Voltaire, Mme du Châtelet (who had acknowledged his gift of a copy of his book on mathematics),[39] Fontenelle, Mme du Deffand, Buffon, Daubenton, Clairaut, Duclos, the Abbé Sallier, Helvétius, and D'Alembert. Many of these came to be great names in the eighteenth century, and some were already so. This was true of Voltaire and Mme du Châtelet, and especially of Fontenelle, then ninety-two years old, the author of the *History of Oracles* and *On the Plurality of Worlds,* a wonderfully live nonagenarian whom an American sports-writer would inevitably have called 'the grand old man of French letters.' Mme du Deffand (1697-1780) was the celebrated hostess of one of the eighteenth century's most celebrated *salons,* a lady who maintained her commanding intellectual and social position in spite of the blindness that came upon her, and who is known to English literature primarily because of her interesting and informative correspondence with Horace Walpole. Buffon was the famous naturalist, author of the interminable *Histoire naturelle,* the first volume of which appeared in that year, a person much like Samuel Johnson in respect to the massiveness and authority of his literary style. His colleague Daubenton (1716-99) was also a naturalist, who later contributed many articles to the *Encyclopédie.* Clairaut (1713-65) was an astronomer and geometrician whose particular specialty was the movements of the moon. Duclos (1704-72) had written a history of Louis XI and had recently been elected to the French Academy. The Abbé Sallier (1685-1761) was a well-known philologist and custodian of the Royal Library, and Helvétius, then the least known of the lot but eventually destined to unenviable notoriety as the author of a book entitled *De l'Esprit,* was then a farmer-general with an income of some 300,000 livres a year. But if Diderot knew these people no better than it can be demonstrated that he knew Voltaire, Mme du Châtelet, and Fontenelle, then his acquaintance with them was

slight indeed.[40] Nevertheless, it is known that Mme du Châtelet wrote to
her kinsman, the governor of Vincennes, asking him to make Diderot's
imprisonment as mild as possible, and therefore it is possible that others
of these persons did what they could in his behalf.[41]

Of one thing Diderot was confident, if we may judge from the prediction
contained in his letter to Berryer on 10 August: his father would hasten
to Paris as soon as he learned of his son's arrest. How disconcerting it must
have been to Diderot, therefore, to find that his father stayed right at Langres
and would not budge. Diderot's first letter was not even answered. His
second was replied to on 3 September in a missive of which the spelling
was frequently phonetic but the meaning unmistakable. Diderot found
that he was not the prodigal son. The elder Diderot, his letter shows, had
other sources of information about affairs at Paris than just his son's letters.
When he wrote, therefore, he wrote with a decidedly detached and astringent
air, filling his letter with more sense than comfort. He reminded the son
of his mother, 'In the remonstrances that she made to you by her own lips,
she told you several times that you were blind.' Didier Diderot's best
advice, at least in his estimation, was that Denis should straightway write a
book of Christian edification! 'This will bring down upon you the bene-
dictions of Heaven and will keep you in my good graces.' The father then
asked whether it was true that his son was married and had two children.
'I expect that you will not refuse to your sister the pleasure of rearing them,
nor to me the pleasure of seeing them under my eyes.' About money the
crusty old man became quite sardonic but sent a hundred and fifty livres
just the same.[42] And probably it was greatly needed in the household in the
Rue de l'Estrapade, for the publishers' account book shows that Diderot's
salary was discontinued by them during his imprisonment, there being no
payment entered between 14 July and late November.[43]

The letters that Diderot had written to his father are not extant. Nor is
it possible to know what effect the harshness of the letter just quoted had
upon him. Probably it convinced him that he would have to make his own
peace with the authorities, and that his liberation was not going to be
brought about by sentimental arguments or the intercession of relatives. At
all events, in this same month of September Diderot volunteered in an
undated note a far-reaching promise as to his future conduct: '[he] promises
to do nothing in the future that might be contrary in the slightest respect
to religion and good morals.' Under this promise, Berryer wrote, 'If Count
d'Argenson deems that he [Diderot] has done sufficient penance for his
intellectual excesses, he is entreated to have the King's order sent for his

release.' [44] Berryer's note suggests that Diderot's release depended upon his making a solemn promise. If so, it may explain why so many of Diderot's subsequent writings were carefully tucked away in a drawer and never published during his lifetime.

None of Diderot's friends was more alarmed or more solicitous in his behalf than Rousseau. 'Nothing can ever describe the anguish that my friend's misfortune made me feel. My somber imagination, which always expects the worst, took alarm. I thought he would be there the rest of his life. I almost lost my mind.' When he was first able to see Diderot after the release from the tower, Rousseau greeted his friend with embraces, sobs, and tears. D'Alembert and a stranger were present, and Diderot said to the latter, perhaps conceitedly but more likely appreciatively, after the strain of three weeks of solitary confinement, 'You see, Monsieur, how my friends love me.' [45]

Because of Diderot's imprisonment in Vincennes, the road thither became the scene of the most dramatic event of the Enlightenment. 'The summer of 1749 was excessively hot,' wrote Rousseau in his *Confessions*. 'It is two leagues from Paris to Vincennes. Scarcely able to afford cabs, at two o'clock in the afternoon I would set out on foot when I was alone, and I walked fast in order to get there the sooner. . . . often, quite spent by the heat and by fatigue, I would stretch out on the ground able to do no more. In order to go more slowly, I decided to take a book. One day I took the *Mercure de France* [the October issue] and as I walked and read, I lit upon the question proposed by the Academy of Dijon for its prize for the following year: *Whether the progress of the sciences and the arts has contributed to corrupting the morals or purifying them.* At the instant of reading this I saw another universe and I became another man. . . . Upon arriving at Vincennes I was in an agitation bordering upon delirium. Diderot perceived it: I told him the cause. . . . He exhorted me to give rein to my ideas and to compete for the prize.' [46]

Carlyle in his essay on 'Diderot' suggests the Biblical self-dedication of the Encyclopedists when he speaks of 'the *Acts* of the *French Philosophes*,' a phrase anticipatory of Carl Becker's *The Heavenly City of the Eighteenth-Century Philosophers*. Using such Scriptural comparisons, it may be said of Rousseau's revelation that in its suddenness and thoroughness it was similar to what happened to Saint Paul on the road to Damascus. Rousseau, in a sudden flash of mystical insight, discovered the state of nature, the pristine condition of virtue and purity. He saw with blinding certainty that the arts and sciences, contrary to usual opinion, had made us worse, not better. From then on he was to write books beginning with sentences such

as 'Everything is good as it leaves the hands of the Author of things; everything degenerates in the hands of man' (*Emile*), or 'Man is born free and
everywhere he is in chains' (*The Social Contract*). Rousseau threw himself
into this persuasion of the corruption of society with all the passion of a
pathologically sensitive person — Edmund Burke remarked that Rousseau
had no skin — a person of enormous although unsuspected talents, who
envies at the same time that he despises a highly sophisticated and polished
society in which he has not been quite successful. It is the boy from Geneva
not quite making good in Paris; the African from Tagaste, Augustine by
name, not quite successful in Rome or Milan. And because Rousseau was
one of the most eloquent writers who ever lived, his doctrines took on
enormous political importance in the eighteenth-century movement of ideas.
For he was dedicated, in brief, to the conviction that whatever is, is wrong.

As the years went by, Rousseau and Diderot quarreled in a spectacular
fashion, and Diderot subsequently fell victim to the temptation of asserting
that it was he who suggested the famous paradox to Rousseau.[47] For example, he once told Marmontel — at that time a very prominent man of
letters, though his laurel leaves are now much withered — that he had
asked Rousseau which side of the question he proposed to take.

' "The affirmative," said Rousseau.

' "That's the *pons asinorum*," I said to him. "All the mediocre talents
will take that path . . ."

' "You're right," he said to me, after having reflected upon it for a
moment, "and I'll follow your advice." '[48]

Exactly the same story is told by other contemporaries — by La Harpe,
by Collé, by Meister, and by the Abbé Morellet, who adds that this version
was accepted as established by all Baron d'Holbach's circle.[49] And Mme
de Vandeul states quite flatly that 'my father gave to Rousseau the idea of
his Discourse on the Arts.'[50] Rousseau, on the other hand, solemnly assured
a friend that he had made his choice without Diderot and solely by himself.[51]
Consequently, as might readily be expected, the question of whether Rousseau is to be denied any originality whatsoever has become a favorite battle-
ground for his partisans and his detractors, as well as a focal point for some
skillful exercises in impartial scholarship.[52]

In his *writings*, Diderot was much more cautious in his allegations about
Rousseau and the prize essay. Twice he alluded to the incident, in passages
one of which was published during his lifetime, the other posthumously. In
each instance he stops short of declaring that he gave Rousseau the idea;
he merely takes credit for knowing his Rousseau:

'When the program of the Academy of Dijon appeared, he came to consult me on the side that he should take.

' "The side you'll take," I said to him, "is the one no one else will."

' "You're right," he replied.' [53]

Although Diderot was now permitted to work on the *Encyclopédie,* his
enforced residence at Vincennes was a handicap. As Du Châtelet had remarked, he was unable to get much done. The associated publishers, in support of what they called 'the finest and most useful enterprise yet undertaken
by the book trade,' petitioned D'Argenson on this subject:

the enterprise on which Your Highness has deigned to cast some favorable regards cannot be finished so long as M. Diderot is at Vincennes. He is obliged to
consult a considerable number of craftsmen, who do not like to be shifted about;
to confer with a number of men of letters, who do not have the leisure to go to
Vincennes; and finally, to have access constantly to the Royal Library, the books
of which cannot and ought not to be carried so far away. Besides, My Lord, to
supervise the drawings and engravings, one must have the workers' tools before
one's eyes, an essential which M. Diderot can make use of only on the spot.[54]

Another and much more elaborate petition dated 7 September covered the
same ground.[55]

Perhaps the publishers would not have been so importunate had D'Alembert filled in for the absent editor. But evidently he either could not or
would not; the publishers declared that without Diderot it was impossible
to instruct the printers how to set up mathematical material correctly.[56]
From this it may be inferred that D'Alembert did not concern himself with
correcting proof, even on material he himself had written, and he seems to
have taken great care not to contract any guilt by association. At least such
would seem to be a reasonable interpretation to put upon his letter of 19
September to Formey, the secretary of the Berlin Academy: 'The detention
of M. Diderot has become much less severe; nevertheless it still lasts, and the
Encyclopédie is suspended. I never intended to have a hand in it except for
what has to do with mathematics and physical astronomy. I am in a position
to do only that, and besides I do not intend to condemn myself for ten
years to the tedium of seven or eight folios.' [57]

In a folder marked 'Diderot,' constituting part of the archives of the
Bastille that long ago were transferred to the Bibliothèque de l'Arsenal at
Paris, there is a little slip of paper addressed to the Marquis du Châtelet
and written in the hand of Berryer. Dated 29 October 1749, it stated that
the *lettre de cachet* ordering Diderot's release had been made out on 21

October, and that Du Châtelet was to release Diderot as soon as he received
Berryer's note. Another hand, not Berryer's, scratched out the date 29
October and inserted instead '3 9bre'; and indeed it was on 3 November
that Diderot was released.[58]

Now he was free to return to the Rue de l'Estrapade and to the enormous
backlog of work that had been accumulating since his arrest 102 days previously. What were the ideas, the conclusions, that this unwelcome interlude
caused to revolve in his mind? Many, no doubt, and deep-seated, for the
atrabilious moods of his solitary imprisonment seem to have darkened his
thought for several years. Rousseau speaks in his *Confessions* of the melancholy that Diderot acquired during his confinement and asserts that it is
apparent in *Le Fils naturel,* written seven years later.[59] But of one thought
in Diderot's mind we may be sure. Many years later he proposed to Catherine II of Russia that he edit, at her expense, a new and better *Encyclopédie:*
one of the advantages would be 'to substitute the name of a great and worthy
sovereign for that of a second-rate minister who deprived me of my liberty
in order to wring from me a tribute to which he could not lay claim by
merit.' [60]

The Prospectus of the *Encyclopédie,* and *Letter on the Deaf and Dumb*

IT is more than likely that Diderot spent the last weeks of 1749 and the first months of 1750 in seeking to make up for lost time. As the publishers' second petition to D'Argenson had gone to great lengths to establish, Diderot was indispensable.[1] The preparation for publishing the *Encyclopédie* could not be carried on satisfactorily without him. Their statement conveys to us a precise notion of how complex a job it was to be chief editor of the *Encyclopédie,* entailing as it did duties requiring not only the conventional blue-penciling and proofreading, but also a great deal of what is now called 'leg-work' and technological 'know-how.' For over twenty years Diderot spent the greater part of his time and energy in just this sort of daily editorial work. His was a task demanding the combined qualities of the genius and the drudge.

In the year following his detention in Vincennes there continued to be reverberations of the publication of *Letter on the Blind.* Speaking to the quinquennial Assembly of the Clergy, the Archbishop of Sens denounced the current manifestations of irreligion, as a result of which that body requested the Sorbonne to make a report on impious books, among them *Philosophical Thoughts* and *Letter on the Blind.*[2] The fictitious deathbed conversation of Saunderson, invented by Diderot, called into being an equally fictitious one in reply.[3] Though the principal French periodicals, such as the *Journal des Sçavans* and the *Journal de Trévoux,* did not deign to notice a volume that was, after all, highly contraband, the *Letter on the Blind* received a flattering amount of attention in news letters and periodicals published outside the boundaries of France. 'This book,' wrote one editor, 'has caused too much stir not to devote an article to it here.'[4] The stir was, indeed, so great that demand far outran supply. D'Alembert, writing to a friend in Switzerland who had asked for a copy, declared in February 1750 that it was very hard to procure one.[5]

The year 1750 witnessed a number of important events in the private life of Diderot. Not least remarkable among them was a complaint against his wife lodged with the police on 2 April. This document is still in existence in the National Archives of France, a single quarto sheet rather hard to find as it lies unbound and higgledy-piggledy with scores of similar depositions in a cardboard box.[6] In this complaint the servant of one of Mme Diderot's neighbors testified that on that very afternoon Mme Diderot, after picking a quarrel, had kicked the servant several times and knocked her head violently against the wall. Nevertheless, the record bears no evidence that the authorities did more than simply file the deposition. Apparently Mme Diderot was not admonished or even interrogated. Yet the existence of this document may surely be cited as proof that Mme Diderot was indeed a formidable woman, and that there may have been some basis in fact for a report of a similar and equally violent incident involving Mme Diderot a year and a half later.

This story appeared in the news magazine *La Bigarure,* which, as has been noted, was printed at The Hague and had published the account of Diderot's improvising ink when he was in solitary confinement at Vincennes. Even previous to this, the anonymous editor of *La Bigarure* had shown himself to be well informed about Diderot, accurately attributing to him the authorship of his various unacknowledged works.[7] When, therefore, under date of 3 December 1751, *La Bigarure* gleefully chronicled a fight between Mme Diderot and Mme de Puisieux, the account should not *necessarily* be regarded as a canard without any basis in fact. On balance, it seems to be testimony, however suspect and unconfirmed, that ought not to be totally disregarded. According to this account, which, incidentally, declared that Mme de Puisieux was 'frightfully ugly' and Mme Diderot, although 'a second Xantippe,' was 'as pretty as her rival is frightful,' Mme de Puisieux one day insulted Mme Diderot in the street, calling out among other things, 'Here, Mistress She-monkey, look at these two children; they are your husband's, who never did you the honor of doing as much for you.' This provocation led to a very spirited brawl, which the anonymous author describes in some lines of very indifferent verse, as though he felt, as had Homer, Virgil, Dante, and Milton, that prose could not do justice to such a sublime situation. In conclusion we learn that cold water had to be poured upon the combatants in order to separate them, and that Diderot, meanwhile, stayed inside, afraid to show his face.[8] Whether or not the anecdote was a fact, at least the publicity about it was, and Diderot probably had to face many people who had read the story.

If Mme de Puisieux actually made any such derisive remark about the lack of children in the Diderot household, she uttered a taunt the more calculatedly wounding because it was cruelly true. On 30 June 1750, little François-Jacques-Denis, only shortly past his fourth birthday, had died of a violent fever and been buried the next day at the Diderot's parish church of Saint-Etienne-du-Mont.[9] Several months later a third child was born to the grieving parents and duly carried to Saint-Etienne for baptism. Laurent Durand, the book publisher, stood godfather for the new boy, Denis-Laurent. According to Mme de Vandeul, a careless woman allowed the infant to fall on the steps of the church on the day of his baptism. Whether this be true or not, certainly the baby did not live long, Mme Diderot herself recording that he died toward the end of the year.[10] Thus the Diderots had been parents three times, and were now childless. Nor was there to be another baby until more than three years later.

It was probably also in 1750 that Diderot made the acquaintance of a man who was to be his closest and dearest friend the rest of his life. This was a young German named Friedrich Melchior Grimm, son of a Lutheran pastor at Regensburg. Grimm, following some years of study at the University of Leipzig, had come to Paris as the tutor-companion of a highly placed young German nobleman.[11] Rousseau had made Grimm's acquaintance in August of 1749,[12] and found him an extremely attractive person, then twenty-six years of age — Grimm was ten years younger than Diderot — greatly interested in music, and already endowed with that coolly ironical but accurate judgment of matters artistic that he was later to display to such advantage in his now famous news letter, the *Correspondance littéraire.*

In some ways Grimm was an adventurer, and certainly a careerist. His correspondence with the great furnishes rather elaborate proof that he knew which side his bread was buttered on. With all his elegance of manner, he could be ruthless, and through the years he could calmly exploit the time and energy of a friend like Diderot while constantly deploring that others desired to do so too. Because of this domineering manner with his friends, added to a reputed fondness for wearing face powder, Grimm's intimates called him 'The White Tyrant,' a punning reference to Tirant lo Blanch, the principal character of a Catalonian epic poem of the fifteenth century which had recently been translated into French.[13] Probably both particulars of the indictment were true. Certainly there is plenty of documentary evidence about the face powder. Grimm's papers, sequestered during the

French Revolution, are now in the National Archives, and there, among a vast collection of bills and receipts, may be found numerous ones from Dulac, Merchant Glover-Perfumer, at the Sign of the Golden Cradle, Rue Neuve-des-Petits-Champs, billing Grimm for 'fine powder purged with spirits of wine and perfumed *à la maréchalle.*' [14] In 1750 Grimm was far from being the successful and much-decorated man of affairs who impressed Ambassador Thomas Jefferson as being 'the pleasantest and most conversable member of the diplomatic corps.' [15] He had yet to establish himself: it was to be some decades before Catherine the Great would be calling him in her letters her *gobe-mouche* — it was a joke between them — her 'fag.'

Rousseau, who brought Grimm and Diderot together — their first meeting was in Rousseau's rooms — [16] was saddened to discover that each presently became fonder of the other than either was of him. Nevertheless, the year was not without its triumphs for Jean-Jacques, for on 9 July it was announced that his essay, which he had discussed with Diderot at Vincennes, had won the prize offered by the Academy of Dijon.[17] Diderot, with his usual generosity — and his usual impetuousness — arranged to see it through the press, but he gave the manuscript to the publisher instead of trying to make some money out of it for Rousseau.[18] In the last fortnight of November 1750, Rousseau's startling and paradoxical contention that the development of the arts and sciences had been noxious to mankind was ready for public perusal.[19] 'It's catching on like wildfire,' wrote Diderot to Rousseau; 'there is no example of success like it.' [20]

While Diderot was seeing Rousseau's discourse through the press, he was also busy putting the finishing touches on the prospectus of the *Encyclopédie*. Much depended, in fame and fortune, upon presenting the proposed work in an attractive way. Several times in 1749 the publishers had alleged that they were on the point of launching the prospectus, but, probably because of Diderot's imprisonment, this was much delayed. According to an unpublished document written in 1771 or 1772 by Joly de Fleury, the *procureur général* of France, Chancellor d'Aguesseau had personally approved and initialed a copy of the prospectus, satisfying by this approbation the regulations governing the previous submission of manuscript; and according to the same authority, the Lieutenant-General of Police had written on the prospectus, 'Permission for printing and posting, 11 November 1750. Signed Berryer.' [21] On 21 November 1750, the publishers drew up an agreement upon the procedure for accepting subscriptions.[22] It seems quite certain, then, as is stated in the *Encyclopédie* itself, that the prospectus was first circulated in November 1750.[23] Eight thousand copies of it were stitched (and presumably disseminated).[24] Eight thousand copies! — and they are now rarer than the whooping crane, almost as rare as the dodo. Indeed, the director of the French National Archives had considerable difficulty in 1950 in locating a copy.[25]

The salient features of the prospectus have already been described in the prologue to this book. In one of the closing paragraphs of his address to the public, Diderot spoke with humbleness of the importance and significance of this venture, and then, in abrupt transition, he saluted the future in what was a sort of dedication —

TO POSTERITY, AND TO THE BEING WHO DOES NOT DIE.

* * * * * *

Along with the editing of the *Encyclopédie* and the preparation of the prospectus, Diderot found time in 1750 to put down his speculations in a new field of thought. This *Lettre sur les sourds et muets à l'usage de ceux qui entendent et qui parlent* ('Letter on the Deaf and Dumb, for the Benefit of Those Who Hear and Speak') started out with some firsthand observations on the behavior of deaf-mutes and went on to canvass a number of interesting and original theories on linguistics and aesthetics. The work revealed an astonishing number of ingenious insights into the metaphysics of beauty and into the psychology of communication, discussing both gestures and word symbols. Just as a famous twentieth-century work entitled *The Meaning of Meaning* 'attempted to restate the problem of knowledge by means of a rigorous analysis of the functions of language,' so Diderot in his century attempted to do the same thing, breaking new ground in the study of semantics and word symbolism.[26]

This time, Vincennes having made him cautious, Diderot submitted his manuscript to the proper authorities. But although the censor passed the manuscript on 12 January 1751, there evidently was something about it that caused Malesherbes, the new director of publications, to feel that he could not authorize its publication with Diderot's name on the title page and with the accolade of *'Avec Approbation & Privilège du Roi.'*[27] Instead he gave it a 'tacit permission.' This curious and very common practice constitutes an excellent example of the sort of paradoxical and illogical procedure that the anomalies of the *ancien régime* brought into being. A tacit permission was an official connivance at an infringement of the regulations.[28] The practice was so general and so regularized that a register of most tacit permissions was kept on file by the syndics of the corporation of booksellers. Other tacit permissions, however, were accorded orally and without registration, the author and printer merely being given private and non-documentary assurances that they might publish a particular manuscript without molestation from the police. In every case, however, the censors previously read the manuscripts in the usual way and the director of publications knew perfectly what was going on. Yet all these numerous books were printed anonymously, with misleading places of publication printed on their title pages, the point being that they should bear every mark of being illicit and clandestine in order to save the government from being officially embarrassed by any statements they might contain. The advantage to the monarchy of this practice was that it increased the employment of French printers and helped keep French money inside French boundaries.[29]

Any work that received even tacit permission was not likely to contain incendiary doctrine against Church or State. In comparison with the *Letter on the Blind,* therefore, the *Letter on the Deaf and Dumb* may have seemed a little dull. Although the work had three editions in 1751 and another in 1772, and although Mme Necker, Diderot's friend and the famous wife of the famous statesman, thought it Diderot's best work — she claimed that he wrote it in a single night, which seems incredible for a book of some seventeen thousand words [30] — in general Diderot received less applause for it from his own generation than he does from the present one.

Diderot did not, however, compromise in this little book any of his convictions regarding psychology or metaphysics. He consistently assumed that knowledge is completely dependent upon the senses and that therefore a man's 'answers,' even his views on metaphysical questions, will be relative to his senses and, indeed, to the number of them. 'A society made up of five persons, each having only one of the five senses, would be, in my opinion, an amusing one': each would have a view of the world relative to his own sensory equipment, each would treat all the others as being senseless.[31] Thus Diderot was striking at and undermining various absolutist modes of thought. He did not get into trouble because this time he avoided the expression of inflammatory sentiment that in his previous treatise he had put into the mouth of the dying Saunderson. Nevertheless the *Letter on the Deaf and Dumb* incorporated and carried forward the new psychology and the new methodology which was so corrosive to older and more absolutist ways of thinking.[32]

In the course of the twentieth century the *Letter on the Deaf and Dumb* has come to be regarded more and more highly, not only as a document for establishing Diderot's extraordinary versatility and sensitivity but also as a book intrinsically valuable because of the light it throws on fundamental problems of poetics. Professors Torrey and Fellows call it 'one of the out-standing examples of literary criticism in the eighteenth century,' and con-tinue: 'In this first essentially scientific study of the deaf and dumb, Diderot was interested in the art of communication by gesture and of the relationship between gesture and language. From the great actor who projects in gestures what he expresses in words, we are led to the deaf mute who, standing before a color-organ, at last surmises what music is — like language, a means of communication. This was deduced from the fact that, often before as in conversation, he had watched people's faces and expressions while music was being played outside his world of silence. There follows a discussion of the theory that the painter is capable of portraying but a single moment within which the past and future should be suggested, whereas the poet is able to depict a succession of moments. The conclusion is drawn from this that some subjects are best described in one medium, some in the other. (The debt of Lessing's *Laokoön* to Diderot need hardly be insisted upon.) [33] But, we are told, the poet should realize that he is dealing with words, and words have both meaning and sound. The superior poet will then paint in sounds what he is expressing in meaning. Furthermore, poetry is the interweaving of hieroglyphs, that is, a series of pictures representing ideas. In this sense, Diderot adds, all poetry is "emblématique" or symbolical, but only the poet of genius succeeds in saying the inexpressible. Thus the reader, who has almost forgotten that he started out by reading a brief essay on the deaf and dumb, finds he has arrived at an esthetic theory which leads directly to Baudelaire and the Symbolists by means of certain fundamental principles which, quite possibly, have not yet been fully explored.' [34]

Diderot's doctrine that the words the poet uses are fraught with elusive and magical overtones has caught the imagination of contemporary critics, especially since he referred to such words as hieroglyphs, thus calling par-ticular attention to their symbolic nature.[35] This theory seems a little startling in contrast to the formal verse — much of it exceedingly earth-bound — that the age composed; and it is the enunciation of a doctrine such as this that makes Diderot seem so 'modern' to the aestheticians and the creative experimenters of the nineteenth and twentieth centuries.[36] It was partly because Diderot was so proficient a classicist that this theory occurred to him. For the examples he cites are taken not simply from Corneille, Racine, Voltaire, and Boileau, but from the Greek of Epictetus and the Latin of Cicero and the Italian of Tasso. Rhythms and the quantities and stresses of syllables, with their subtle and elusive intertwining of sense impression and meaning, fascinated him. Can we not, as a French critic has recently sug-

gested, can we not hear Diderot in these passages, declaiming with that
accompaniment of gesture that was habitual with him and of which he was
so fond? [37] He analyzes, much as Ruskin analyzed a passage of Milton in
Sesame and Lilies, some of the haunting passages from the *Iliad* and the
Aeneid, from Ovid and from Lucretius. 'All this inevitably disappears in
translation,' he wrote, 'even in the best.' [38]

Modern critics, speaking of the *Letter on the Deaf and Dumb,* are likely
to concur with a scholar who recently spoke of Diderot's mind as being
'like one of those complicated modern rockets which startle by the unsus-
pectedness and apparent inexhaustibility, as well as by the brilliance of their
evolutions.' [39] The same point was made by the Abbé Raynal at the time,
but in a much less complimentary vein: 'M. Diderot speaks on this occasion
of a thousand things, on metaphysics, poetry, eloquence, music, etc., which
have only a very tenuous connection with the principal subject. This letter
is not pleasing, but it is instructive. . . . Everything that comes from M.
Diderot's pen is full of new viewpoints and of well-grounded metaphysics;
but his works are never finished: they are sketches; I doubt whether his
vivacity and his precipitation will ever permit him to finish anything.' [40]
This is one of the earliest examples of what came to be in the eighteenth
and nineteenth centuries a commonplace of criticism of the works of Diderot.

The *Letter on the Deaf and Dumb* was by way of being a criticism, and
by no means a gentle one, of a work published not long before that had
sought to discover a single unifying principle of beauty applicable to all
the fine arts. This book was the Abbé Charles Batteux's *Les Beaux-Arts
réduits à un même principe* (1746), and Diderot, in his allusions to it, could
be conceived to have gone considerably beyond the call of duty.[41] All these
personalia are forgotten now, and only Diderot's interesting insights into the
problems of aesthetics remain, but it need not be overlooked that Diderot
had a taste for polemics and that his personality generated heat, causing
both him and the people with whom he was in contact to glow, whether
with a gratified sense of fellow feeling or with a consciousness of exasperated
antagonism.

A few weeks later Diderot published what amounted to the second edition
of the *Letter on the Deaf and Dumb,* with additions. His introductory remarks were dated 3 March 1751, and D'Hémery noted in his journal for
20 May that the *Additions to Serve as Clarification for some of the Passages
in the Letter on the Deaf and Dumb* was already published, with Malesherbes' tacit permission.[42] Diderot says that these additions were written in
reply to the comments and criticisms of a very intelligent young woman of

his acquaintance, Mlle de La Chaux, whose pathetic love story he tells in one of his highly regarded short stories, *Ceci n'est pas un conte* ('This Is No Yarn').[43] In the same edition was also printed Diderot's lengthy observations in rebuttal of criticisms his book had received in the April issue of the *Journal de Trévoux*.[44]

Meanwhile, the publication of the prospectus had brought about a short but sharp passage at arms between Diderot and the Jesuit editors of that same periodical, the first skirmish in what was to become a bitter and protracted war. Diderot was a formidable antagonist, but so were his opponents. They were led by the chief editor, Father Berthier, an able person who carried on the *Journal de Trévoux,* it was said, 'to the satisfaction of all, as much for his skill in digesting works as for his prudent moderation in criticisms and eulogies. . . .'[45] He was certainly moderate in his eulogy of the prospectus: in his first number for 1751 he quite patently implied that the celebrated chart or scheme of human knowledge that the prospectus contained was nothing but a barefaced plagiarism of Bacon: 'The editors, MM. Diderot and d'Alembert, make known with reference to this system that they have principally followed Chancellor Bacon, author of the book *On the Dignity and Increase of the Sciences.* And this is so true that we intend to fall in with their views, while giving pleasure to the public, by printing an extract that will compare the work of the Chancellor with the Prospectus of the *Encyclopédie,* especially in regard to the tree of human knowledge.' In this extract, which appeared in the next issue, the editors found that 'the system of this learned Englishman was followed point by point and word for word by our Authors.'[46]

At this juncture Diderot took fire, and not without cause. He had expressly stated in the prospectus his obligations to Lord Bacon, so that the imputations of the *Journal de Trévoux* seemed all the more unfair, unnecessary, and aggressive. Perhaps the antagonism of the *Journal de Trévoux* in this connection can be explained, as was propounded at the time, by the Jesuits' previous expectations of being asked to take an important share in contributing to the *Encyclopédie* — D'Alembert later stated that their fury was caused by the refusal to confide to them the theological part of the *Encyclopédie* — [47] and their subsequent vexation at finding themselves ignored.

Diderot's response to this attack was in the form of a pamphlet containing, by way of sample, his forthcoming *Encyclopédie* article on 'Art,' and also, more to the point, an open *Letter from M. Diderot to the Reverend Father Berthier, Jesuit.*[48] This was a vigorous exercise in polemics, but contained nothing of interest beyond the dispute itself, although the contemporary journalist Clément spoke of it as being 'full of fire, wit, and charm.' [49] The *Journal de Trévoux* in turn replied, 'Diderot is a man of intelligence, and there is pleasure in receiving his letters when they concern literature. Other matters are too dangerous, he knows very well.' This exordium, sounding very ominous and menacing, was followed by a sneer: 'Several of these gentlemen of the *Encyclopédie* are known to us; we hold them in high esteem; they have competence, politeness, morals, and religion. M. Diderot has given a singular proof of his modesty by not naming them after him in the frontispiece of the Prospectus. Their names would have shed a great luster upon his.' [50]

The *Second Letter of M. Diderot to the Reverend Father Berthier* was written at nine o'clock in the evening of 2 February 1751, when Diderot was still red-hot from having just read the offensive article in the *Journal de Trévoux*.[51] D'Hémery, when noting in his journal that Malesherbes had granted permission to publish this reply, described it as 'a very judicious work.' [52] This may be so; but its arguments were simply *ad hominem,* and there is nothing in the letter that has survived in interest the storm and stress of the occasion that produced it.

It is a matter of doubt whether Diderot was wise to engage in such a dispute. Evidently the publishers of the *Encyclopédie* had misgivings on this point, for Diderot mentions in an undated letter that clearly seems to refer to this time and probably to this incident that 'Messieurs the associates . . . were not in favor of printing it.' [53] But whether wise or not, the exchange of salvos served to engage the public interest, as was evidenced by the publication of a number of pamphlets, all of them now very rare, regarding the dispute. One of these, a four-page *Lettre à M. * * *, de la Société Royale de Londres,* was thought by D'Hémery to emanate from Diderot's circle or even to have been written by Diderot himself.[54] While appearing to blame Diderot, it awarded him all the honors of the combat: 'M. Diderot, who is known to be a man of genius, gifted with a very brilliant imagination, and who enjoys a merited reputation, has had the weakness to write to Father Berthier with a vivacity which even his greatest partisans have disapproved of. His letter is in truth full of ingenious sallies, its style is firm and concise, but one might almost say that each sentence is a poignard wrapped up in a bolt of lightning.' Poor Father Berthier!

A Jesuit whom Diderot greatly admired evidently wrote to him at this juncture, endeavoring to moderate the dispute. This was Father Castel, a benign and ingenious person who is remembered as the inventor of a color-organ, a harpsichord-like instrument the intent of which was to suggest sensations of melody and harmony by combining multi-colored ribbons rather than sounds. Diderot frequently mentions this machine — for example, in *Les Bijoux indiscrets,* in the *Letter on the Deaf and Dumb,* and in the *Encyclopédie* — as creating what he calls ocular music or sonatas in color.[55] Father Castel's color-organ was of scientific interest because, as Diderot himself realized, it raised a number of interesting and complicated psychological problems, in particular the phenomenon of inter-sensory association now called by the name of synesthesia.[56] Father Castel's organ was, indeed, one of the most 'philosophical' inventions of the eighteenth century.

Diderot received Father Castel's letter with great respect, although it did not modify his sense of grievance. 'But in the name of God, reverend Father,' he replied, 'what is Father Berthier thinking about to persecute an honest man who has no enemies in society other than those he has made for himself by his attachment to the Society of Jesus and who, displeased as he ought to be, has nevertheless just refused with utter contempt the weapons he has been offered against it?' This virtuous feeling arose from the fact that just after the publication of his second letter to Berthier, Diderot had received a note proffering information and money if he would use them against the Jesuits.[57] It is clear that Diderot's letters to Berthier caused something of a sensation, for although the Jesuits were used to being opposed by Jansenists, this was one of the very first occasions when their position was openly challenged by a *philosophe.*[58]

Spring of this year brought a scholarly and academic honor to Diderot, and one of which he could make very profitable display. The Prussian Royal Academy of Sciences and Belles-Lettres made him a member, just in time to allow him to mention it on the title page of Volume I of the *Encyclopédie.* Diderot's letter of thanks to Formey, the secretary, was dated 5 March 1751.[59] It was Diderot's first academy and, even in a century pullulating with academies of various kinds, almost his last. It is preposterous, but still true, that the man with one of the most seminal minds of the century should have gained admittance to no more academies than the Prussian, two Russian ones, and the Society of the Antiquaries of Scotland. It was not because he spurned invitations, for the evidence is pretty clear that he joined every academy or learned society that ever asked him. The fact was that Diderot's thought was too radical and came too close to being openly atheistic to qualify him for membership in the most respectable and sedate circles. It might be supposed that the Royal Society of London, not being so committed to an official orthodoxy as were the French academies, might have extended him a bid, especially since they invited not only D'Alembert but also the indefatigable and rather limited Encyclopedist, the Chevalier de Jaucourt. But apparently, as D'Hémery noted in his journal in 1753, the Royal Society resented Diderot's insinuation in his *Letter on the Blind* that one of their former members, the blind Saunderson, had died an atheist — resented it to the point of blackballing him permanently.[60]

Even the membership in the Prussian Academy was evidently something of a *quid pro quo*. Beginning in 1742, Formey had been collecting materials for an encyclopedic compilation, and these he offered to the editors of the *Encyclopédie* after the prospectus of 1745 had appeared.[61] The account book of the publishers shows that in 1747 they contributed three hundred livres toward the acquisition of these manuscripts and promised to send Formey a set of the *Encyclopédie* free of charge and to name him in the preface.[62] Diderot acknowledged these manuscripts very handsomely in his prospectus but without mentioning that they had been paid for, and one can only put two and two together when three months later he was made one of Formey's academy colleagues.

Public anticipation of the appearance of Volume I was increasing, whetted not only by the controversy with the *Journal de Trévoux,* but also by the sample article on 'Art' which Diderot published.[63] 'It will be the best dictionary of things that there has been up to now,' wrote the anonymous author of the *Lettre à M. * * *, de la Société royale de Londres.* 'The prodigious multiplicity of its contents, its extensiveness, and the advantage of a large number of plates showing the work of various artisans, cannot but make it useful, interesting, and curious.' [64] No less a person than Buffon, writing in December 1750, had said that the authors had shown him several articles and that the work was going to be good; and again in April, he remarked of Volume I, 'I have gone through it; it is a very good work.' [65] The official censor, writing on 24 June, gave it a very resounding compliment indeed: 'By order of My Lord the Chancellor I have read in the first volume of the Encyclopedical Dictionary the articles concerning medicine, physics, surgery, chemistry, pharmacology, anatomy, natural history, and in general everything that does not appertain to theology, jurisprudence, or history.

'The various subjects have appeared to me to be well treated therein, conformable to the arrangement, extensiveness, and clarity that they demand: and I am of the opinion that the editors of this great work are beginning to carry out in a very satisfactory manner the vast plan that they sketched in the prospectus which the public received so warmly. I found nothing in this first volume that does not merit being printed.' [66]

As the reputation of the *Encyclopédie* grew, so did the list of subscribers, which stood at 1,002 in April of 1751 and 1,431 in July.[67] Meanwhile, on 28 June 1751, the much-heralded volume was published.[68] Its title page, simple as eighteenth-century titles go, ran as follows:

ENCYCLOPEDIE

or

ANALYTICAL DICTIONARY

OF THE SCIENCES,

ARTS AND CRAFTS,

By a Society of Men of Letters.

Placed in order and published by M. Diderot, of the Prussian Royal Academy of Sciences and Belles-Lettres; and, for the mathematical portion, by M. d'Alembert, of the Royal Academy of Sciences at Paris, of that of Prussia, and of the Royal Society of London.

PARIS

Published by Briasson, the elder David, Le Breton, and Durand

MDCCLI

With Approbation and License of the King.

CHAPTER 11

What Readers Found in Volume I
of the *Encyclopédie*

THE public that greeted the first volume of the *Encyclopédie* was neither impartial nor indifferent. Readers were in a mood to be particularly responsive to — or particularly repelled by — what they found therein. And what they found was a book that purported to be a book of reference but was in fact a sort of political tract. It was a work which, in the course of imparting information, helped to transform men's values. It was a work which helped to make men favorable to change. Historians are agreed that the *Encyclopédie* played an extremely important part as one of the disposing causes of the French Revolution. It was, in short, a publication with a profound political impact.

The *Encyclopédie* was like a great modern newspaper with a strongly defined editorial policy, one which is not always acknowledged but which, far from being confined to its editorial page, creeps into its reporting and even into its special features and comic strips. There was a great deal of skillful editorializing in the columns of the *Encyclopédie*. To use a term with unpleasant connotations, we must fairly admit that the authors of the *Encyclopédie* were propagandists. Yet in their behalf it can also be said that they were propagandists not in the too frequent sense of sophists industriously and knowingly attempting to make the worse seem the better cause, but in the more gracious sense of propagandists who recognize no higher authority than truth, who are convinced that they are in search of it, and who propagandize for what they are certain will enlighten and profit mankind. And because the *Encyclopédie* was pre-eminent in its field, its effectiveness as an instrument of propaganda was all the greater. Its audience was almost a captive one: the wariest and most sophisticated of its readers, as well as the most gullible and ingenuous, found it indispensable.

Not only was the *Encyclopédie* a work that hoped to persuade its readers to a certain point of view, but also a publication that, because of the conditions of censorship, had to pick its way with extraordinary care whenever it alluded to matters involving politics or theology. Any criticism of existing conditions had to be exceedingly oblique and indirect, for this was a publishing venture completely dependent upon official authorization. How else arrange for a subscription list, without which the enormous work would be financially too precarious? How else carry through successfully all the editorial complexities of so large an undertaking? Accordingly the sophisticated soon realized that it was necessary not only to read the lines of the *Encyclopédie* but also between them. The public soon learned to identify, whether with alarm or delight, the manifold contrivances of editorial guile. The *Encyclopédie* fascinated, quite as much because of what did not meet the eye as because of the new features and devices that did.

After the flowery dedication to D'Argenson which so bruised the spirit of Diderot, Volume I was introduced by a lengthy 'Preliminary Discourse' which set the tone for the ensuing work. This essay has been much admired by contemporaries and posterity alike, one modern editor placing it on a level with Descartes' *Discourse on Method* in scientific merit, and surpassing it in literary.[1] This much-praised piece was written by D'Alembert, not Diderot. Why is not known, unless perhaps it was on the theory that so conspicuous a part should be written by an editor who had not spent time in prison.

The 'Preliminary Discourse' was moving and persuasive because it conveyed and communicated the editors' spacious faith. It is patently a document written by a man who wishes well for mankind. And the conviction it imparts is not so much — to use one of Diderot's phrases — an eloquence that one hears as a persuasion one breathes in. From its lines shines the faith that knowledge will make men better, will make them more the masters of themselves as well as of their environment, will give them light. And there is pride in these pages, too — the pride that comes from feeling that the *Encyclopédie* will help to make this knowledge secure. 'May the *Encyclopédie* become a sanctuary where men's knowledge may be protected from revolutions and from time.'[2]

The 'Preliminary Discourse' is at once an exercise in epistemology and an intellectual history, albeit a somewhat episodic one, of Europe since the beginning of the Renaissance, 'done in the light of philosophy with the technical rigor of a mind profoundly mathematical.'[3] In the epistemological part, D'Alembert inquires whence human beings derive their ideas and answers this fundamental question as Locke had: 'All our direct knowledge is reduced to that which we receive by way of our senses; from which it follows that it is to our sensations that we owe all our ideas.' [4] The original statement of the dictum that nothing exists in the mind that has not been first in the senses (*Nihil est in intellectu quod non fuerit in sensu*) appears in Aristotle and had been quite readily accepted by the medieval scholastic philosophers. In the eighteenth century, however, the expression of this psychological concept, while not precisely heterodox, almost invariably made the devout exceedingly nervous, for it came close to denying the sovereign quiddity of the soul. The Lockean view proclaimed that human beings are not born with innate ideas of religion and morality, but simply derive them from their experience. Moreover, the Lockean psychology could be interpreted as coming very close to materialism, very close to the idea that sense impressions exist, that neurological impulses exist, but that the soul as an independent entity does not. Anybody who, like Diderot in his *Letter on the Blind* and now D'Alembert in the 'Preliminary Discourse,' emphasized the role of the senses in cognition could expect to earn the praise of people seeking positive knowledge without conventional metaphysical integuments, but at the same time to win the distrust or censure of persons who felt that this view had in it something inherently irreverent and dangerous.

After his analysis of the bases of psychological knowledge, D'Alembert lengthily discussed the various branches of learning, linking them together and grouping them under the three general components of the understanding, namely, memory, reason, and imagination. This was a scheme which he, like Jefferson in classifying his library, borrowed from Bacon. This part of the discourse corresponds to a visual scheme of human knowledge that was folded into Volume I following the 'Preliminary Discourse.' In this elaborate *'Systême figuré des connoissances humaines,'* a diagrammatic depiction that aroused much admiration at the time, the editors arranged the various subjects in parallel columns. They gave the generic name of 'History' to all the branches of knowledge in the column allocated to the memory; of 'Philosophy' to all that they deemed to be principally dependent upon the reason; and of 'Poetry' to those dependent upon the imagination. Such a visual presentation of the relationships existing among the various branches of knowledge was plausible, and yet it betrays many of the prejudices and predilections of its contrivers. It is enlightening to notice how the editors have placed in visual and organic relationship two of the master words, the dynamic symbols of the age, 'Philosophy' and 'Reason,' each enhancing the prestige of the other. In contrast, 'History' is relegated to a very secondary position. It emanates from mere memory. This refusal to allow history to partake of the honors of philosophy or to consider itself as stemming from reason is one of the intellectual idiosyncrasies of the Encyclopedist school. It was typical of the whole point of view of the *Encyclopédie,* and quite representative of the intentions of Diderot, that theology and religion were slyly relegated to a small, almost infinitesimal, area in comparison with the eye-filling space taken up by the subjects of positive knowledge. 'Divine Science' bulked just about as large spatially as 'The Manufacture and Uses of Iron.' Such were the *Encyclopédie's* unacknowledged ways of waging psychological warfare: for this was not the fashion in which the relative significance of things was understood by the faculty of theology of the University of Paris.

In the second half of his 'Preliminary Discourse,' D'Alembert briefly but masterfully indicated the contributions to knowledge made by many of the great names: principally Bacon, Descartes, Newton, Locke, and Leibniz. This was brilliantly done, and D'Alembert was highly complimented on his effort by such great persons as Buffon and Montesquieu, while Raynal wrote to his subscribers that 'I believe it to be one of the most philosophical, logical, luminous, exact, compact, and best written pieces that we have in our language.' [5]

Not that the 'Preliminary Discourse' was without its blind spot. It is worthy of remark that D'Alembert dates the history that he thinks really matters as beginning practically with the Renaissance. The reason for this was plain: both he and Diderot regarded medieval times as hopelessly obscurantist and priest-ridden, and the best thing that could be said of their own century, they thought, was that it resembled the Middle Ages so little. It was exceptionally difficult for men of the French Enlightenment to feel that medieval history had had any real significance save of a negative and deplorable sort. To them the history of the Middle Ages seemed an interruption instead of a continuum, and because of this belief, they never developed a philosophy of historical continuity or an attitude of historical-mindedness, relying upon knowledge of the past to illuminate the future, as did the nineteenth century. [6] Contrast for a moment their habit of mind with that of Edmund Burke, whose feeling for history was so profound that he declared that society is indeed a contract, binding the present generation to the ones that are dead. The Encyclopedists were apt to feel, as J. B. Bury remarked, a sort of resentment against history. [7] And because eighteenth-century men wanted their own age to be an Age of Reason, they had little praise for an Age of Faith. This astigmatism was common to a large part of the Enlightenment, which felt none of the filial devotion of a Henry Adams yearning for Mont Saint-Michel and Chartres.

As to the 'Preliminary Discourse' as a whole, it is fair to say that though D'Alembert wrote it, Diderot heartily agreed with it. And if we should ask how the 'Preliminary Discourse' would have differed had Diderot written it, the correct answer would be 'very little,' save that Diderot would probably have based his argumentation more on biological modes of thought, whereas D'Alembert used the mathematical.

The *Encyclopédie* was novel in that it was a co-operative work written by several hands, and more unusual still in that it identified its contributors. According to the 'Preliminary Discourse,' articles marked with an asterisk were written or revised by Diderot in his capacity as editor; but unsigned articles without any identifying mark were also written by him; other articles were initialed according to a scheme of symbols published in the prefatory pages. The final pages of the 'Preliminary Discourse' were taken up with identifying and thanking the contributors.

As a reader turned to the body of the work, his first impression might have been of surprise that the *Encyclopédie* was organized alphabetically. It might have been supposed that, having dilated so much upon his chart of human knowledge, Diderot would have organized his presentation according to this system rather than according to the alphabet. Evidently the editors were uneasily self-conscious about this point, for they discuss at length why they did what they did, the reasons appearing to be in part solid and intrinsic, in part (like Mr. Guppy's) owing to circumstances beyond their control.[8] The *Encyclopédie* was criticized now and again for its arrangement, yet subsequent experience seems to have proved that the alphabetical presentation in reference books, although less logical, is also less confusing.[9]

The *Encyclopédie* endeavored to compensate for this lack of the systematic by freely using cross references to indicate close and organic connections.[10] Chambers had done this and it has become, of course, a commonplace in the construction of reference works; but for the *Encyclopédie* the apparatus of cross references served a further purpose. It slyly suggested points of view that, because of censorship, could not be openly canvassed.

Twentieth-century commentators naturally dwell on the most important, usually the lengthiest, articles that the *Encyclopédie* contains. To the casual contemporary reader, however, the work might have seemed most impressive because of the multiplicity of its brief entries; there were literally thousands. This is explained by the fact that the *Encyclopédie*, although it contained no maps, attempted to be a gazetteer. Moreover, it also served as a dictionary, defining numerous words, some of them very common ones, and often giving elaborate examples of synonyms. The study of synonyms had become popular in France since the publication of a book of them by an Abbé Girard in 1718. The *Encyclopédie* frequently copied Girard, usually with acknowledgments, and often printed synonyms and illustrations of its own. Diderot was proficient in this department, as when, to give a very Gallic example, he distinguished between the figurative meanings of 'to bind' and 'to attach' by adding to the Girard examples: 'One is bound to one's wife, and attached to one's mistress.' [11]

The *Encyclopédie* also contained, besides these definitions and synonyms, a large number of highly regarded articles about grammar, some of them very lengthy, and most of them done by an amiable old freethinker named Dumarsais. 'We believe ourselves able to say,' Diderot had written in the prospectus, 'that no known work will be as rich or as instructive as ours concerning the rules and usage of the French language, or, indeed, on the nature, origin, and philosophy of languages in general.' Moreover, the editors of the *Encyclopédie* were extremely aware of what is now called the problem of semantics: 'How many questions and vexations would one spare oneself if one were finally to determine the meaning of words in a clear and precise manner,' wrote D'Alembert in his 'Preliminary Discourse,' thus capping his earlier remark that 'we owe many errors, as some philosophers have noticed, to the abuse of words. . . .' [12]

A modern reader interested in biographical information finds the *Encyclopédie* lacks an alphabetical listing of personages. Volumes following the second occasionally include some biographical information, but, oddly enough, listed under the name of the city in which the person was born. As much as the *Encyclopédie* was admired, it was distinctly deficient in articles of biography and systematic history. Their inclusion would have greatly increased its size, and the editors therefore referred their readers, not very satisfactorily, to a current historical and biographical dictionary, Moreri's *Grand dictionnaire historique,* first published in 1674 and followed by a number of editions and supplements.[13]

In other respects the *Encyclopédie* had very adequate coverage, with ample articles on the inescapable subjects of theology, philosophy, and belles-lettres. It made its special reputation, however, on both scientific articles and those describing the technology of the arts and crafts. In the first volume were found lengthy articles by Diderot on 'Steel' (*Acier*), 'Agriculture,' [14] 'Silver' (*Argent*), 'Needle' (*Aiguille*), and 'Accouchement,' as well as important articles by him on more conventional subjects, such as analyses of the

philosophy of the Arabs, the Hindus, and of Aristotelianism. Other contributors wrote important articles on such topics as 'Bee' (*Abeille*), 'Anatomy'
(twenty-eight pages where Chambers had had only one column), 'Trees'
(*Arbre*), 'Attraction,' 'Alsace' (mainly about the mines in that region), 'Atmosphere,' 'Slate' (*Ardoise*), 'Magnet' (*Aimant*), 'Alkali,' etc. These subjects were described with an attention to technical and technological detail
that was always one of the most conspicuous features of the *Encyclopédie*,
a feature that made it representative of a new social class and of a new
outlook on man. This attention to up-to-date technology is admirably displayed, for example, in Diderot's own article on 'Boring Machine' (*Alésoir*).
What he was describing, with information as to how it could be constructed,
was a machine for making cannon from solid castings. An anecdote, incidentally revealing the wide distribution of the *Encyclopédie*, will show
how useful this sort of information could be. About 1773 the Ottoman
Sultan commissioned a soldier of fortune, the Baron de Tott, to build up
the Turkish artillery and arm the forts on the Dardanelles. Tott had to
manufacture the cannon he needed, without having had previous experience in the work. 'A Greek, very expert in the Art of constructing Mills,'
Tott wrote in his *Memoirs*, 'was, however, of much service to me in making
my boring Machine. The Memoirs of Saint Remi and the Encyclopédie
were my constant guides and I wanted no other till I came to make the
Moulds. . . .' [15]

In short, the *Encyclopédie* was practical. It was useful. And since it contained much information unobtainable elsewhere, it was indispensable. The
Chevalier de Jaucourt pointed out these characteristics when he wrote of the
'Art of Heraldry' in an *Encyclopédie* volume published in 1765: 'There does
not exist a single pamphlet on the art of making shirts, stockings, shoes,
bread; the *Encyclopédie* is the first and unique work describing these arts
useful to men, while the book trade is inundated with books on the vain and
ridiculous science of armorial bearings.' [16]

Diderot's interest in technology, in the crafts, and in the mechanical arts
is very typical of him. There was nothing factitious about this interest in
the practical. On the contrary, it sprang directly from his social origins, from
the microcosm of the tanners and the cutlers of Langres, from the pride in
workmanship and the canniness in money matters of the self-respecting
craftsman who begot him. Diderot always respected craftsmanship, and
although he sometimes spoke disdainfully or despairingly of 'the people'
and employed the word in much the sense that we now give to 'the masses,'
he never spoke disparagingly of the artisan or his social usefulness. It was

this attitude, faithfully reflected in a thousand places in the *Encyclopédie,* that made the work so revolutionary. New *values* were here being set forth and admired, the dignity of just plain work was being extolled. 'Upon examining the products of the arts,' wrote Diderot in his 'Art' article, 'one has observed that some were more the work of the mind than of the hand, and that others, on the contrary, were more the work of the hand than of the mind. Such is in part the origin of the pre-eminence accorded to some arts over others, and of the classification of the arts into liberal arts and mechanical arts. This distinction, though well grounded, has had the unfortunate effect of degrading people who are very estimable and very useful, and of strengthening in us a certain sort of natural laziness which already was inclining us only too much to believe that to devote a constant and continuous attention to experiments and to individual, palpable, and material objects was to detract from the dignity of the human mind, and that to practice or even to study the mechnical arts was to lower oneself to things that are laborious to study, ignoble to meditate upon, difficult to expound, dishonoring to trade in, inexhaustible in number, and in value trifling. A prejudice tending to fill the cities with prideful praters and useless contemplators, and the countryside with petty tyrants, ignorant, idle, and disdainful. 'Twas not thus that Bacon thought, one of England's foremost geniuses; nor Colbert, one of France's greatest ministers; nor, indeed, the just minds and the wise men of any era. . . . How bizarre are our judgments! We demand that people should be usefully engaged, and we disdain useful men.' [17] These views are of great interest in themselves. Moreover, Diderot attached extraordinary importance to them, a fact proved by his publication of this article in advance, as a sample of the whole encyclopedia. It is evident that he intended to fix public attention upon this aspect of the new work.

In congruence with its interest in the crafts and technology, the *Encyclopédie* manifested an equal interest in the problem of dignifying or creating an adequate and accurate vocabulary for them; '. . . a science or an art commences to be a science or an art only when acquired knowledge gives rise to making a language for it,' wrote the author of the article 'Anatomy.' [18] Diderot himself had referred in his prospectus to the importance of nomenclature and returned to the subject, discussing it at some length in his article on 'Art.' In the opinion of the principal historian of the French language, the *Encyclopédie*'s interest in accurate and sufficient nomenclature is one of its most valuable characteristics. 'The *Encyclopédie* nonetheless remains the first and chief homage of the eighteenth century to the language of artisans

. . . a powerful effort not only to disseminate the knowledge of the arts and sciences but also to rehabilitate technical terms.' [19]

[It would not have taken long for a reader of the first volume to discover that the *Encyclopédie* was interested in more than simply warming over old themes, reviving or inventing technical terms, or presenting subjects never before allotted space in a work of this kind. More than these, the *Encyclopédie* was interested in the scientific method. Indeed, it became an arsenal in which the weapons of critical thought were kept — polished, whetted, and instantly at hand. Perhaps the greatest function of the work in the estimation of its editors was that of making people more aware of the methodological problems that constantly beset the acquisition of knowledge and the pursuit of truth. *I'm finding that out with this bloody essay!*

Obviously this was a campaign that had to be conducted on many fronts. One of them was the attack on words or names that in reality were devoid of meaning. Diderot's technique was to call attention to names, especially of plants and animals, about which little more was known than simply the empty name itself. For example, he wrote about '*Aguaxima*': 'A plant of Brazil and of the islands of southern America. That is all that we are told of it; and I would willingly inquire for whom such descriptions are made. It cannot be for the natives, who very likely know more characteristics of the *aguaxima* than this description includes, and who have no need of being told that the *aguaxima* grows in their country; it is as if one said to a Frenchman that the pear tree is a tree that grows in France, in Germany, etc. Nor can it be for us; for what does it matter to us whether there be in Brazil a tree named *aguaxima,* if we know only its name? What purpose does the name serve? It leaves the ignorant in the condition they were; it teaches others nothing. If it happens, then, that I mention this plant, and several others equally poorly described, it is out of condescension for certain readers who prefer to find nothing in a dictionary article, or even to find nothing but silliness in it, than not to find the article at all.' [20] Similarly, of the word '*Aguapa*': 'A tree that grows in the West Indies, the shadow of which is said to cause the death of those who sleep in it naked, while it causes all others to swell up in a prodigious fashion. If the natives of these countries do not know it better than it is identified for us by this description, they are in great danger.' [21] And in discussing the word '*Acalipse*' he remarked, 'Here is another one of these beings . . . of which one has only the name; as if one did not already have too many names empty of sense in the sciences, arts, etc.' [22]

Comments such as these would seem absurdly out of place in a present-day work of reference. But the seekers after positive knowledge who edited the *Encyclopédie* had a useful purpose in mind. Not only did they intend to make their readers more critical and sophisticated in the nomenclature of plants and animals, they also aimed, although somewhat furtively and indirectly, at various high-sounding metaphysical and religious abstractions. No doubt the 'et cetera' that concluded the preceding quotation referred to these, thus putting a cutting edge on what is usually a dulled and lazy abbreviation. 'True philosophy,' wrote the author of the article 'To Act' (*Agir*), 'would find itself considerably briefer if all philosophers would be willing, like me, to abstain from speaking of what is manifestly incomprehensible.' [23]

Another methodological front upon which the *Encyclopédie* conducted a campaign was that of the credibility of various kinds of evidence. Obviously this tactic was primarily to unsettle convictions concerning miracles and the truthfulness of Genesis, but it had a broader purpose, one applicable to all aspects of thought and not simply the religious and the theological. The skepticism of the *Encyclopédie* exercised itself overtly and entertainingly on old wives' tales and vulgar errors, with the charm of seeming to take the reader into partnership. But the very same methods that were used to expose ignorance and superstition and sham in regard to pagan gods, ancient oracles, and nonexistent animals and plants — *Agnus Scythicus,* for example — were also the ones that, by implication, led straight to the attack upon more portentous obscurantisms.

Of course the *Encyclopédie* had had predecessors in preaching the virtues of skepticism. The most important among them was Pierre Bayle (1647–1706), one of the great names in the history of free intellectual inquiry. Bayle was a French Huguenot refugee of awesome erudition, especially in the fields of theology, mythology, ancient history, and ancient geography, as well as the history of Europe in the sixteenth and seventeenth centuries. In 1697 he published his *Dictionnaire historique et critique,* a work which demonstrated the use to which crafty cross references could be put and a work, too, which bristled with such scholarship that it contains footnotes on footnotes. Bayle was a believer, though a critical one; and his skepticism, combined with his erudition, gave him the sort of dazzling intellectual authority over young people impatient of cant that H. L. Mencken enjoyed in the 1920's in America. But it was not an influence that could be safely acknowledged, especially if one happened to live in France. Bayle, then, should be remembered as perhaps the greatest exemplar and inspiration of the critical methodology preached by the *Encyclopédie.* If his influence was more negative than positive, if he showed none of Diderot's interest in the crafts and technology and other practical matters, still his work is incontestably the real ancestor of the *Encyclopédie,* from the point of view of ideas as well as form, and it has been well said that 'he cleared the ground for the steam-roller of the Encyclopedists.' [24] It is almost literally true that his was the great unmentioned and unmentionable name of the *Encyclopédie.*[25]

Bayle's skepticism was far from nihilistic. Quite to the contrary, it was of a fruitful sort, dedicated to the search for truth. Bayle, like his successors in the eighteenth century, thought of skepticism as a kind of detergent, the use of which would reveal truth. This was precisely Diderot's point of view. As early as the *Pensées philosophiques* he had declared that 'skepticism is therefore the first step toward truth,' and his daughter says that the last words she heard him say — it was the evening before he died — were: 'The first step toward philosophy is unbelief.' [26] This was the spirit in which the *Encyclopédie* was written. Its respect for truth, combined with a far-reaching skepticism about what conventionally passed for it, was one of the most exciting features of the new work.

Equally exciting, especially in the articles written by Diderot, was a certain quality of self-revelation, an air of making the reader a confidant and sharing with him literary and scientific judgments, an air both attractive and piquant which gave a suspenseful sense of the unexpected. These unconventional qualities stirred the wrath of the bigoted, the scorn of the pedantic, and the interest of the unprejudiced. The reader of the first volume might notice in the frequent articles devoted to cooking inferential evidence that Diderot was fond of the pleasures of the table.[27] There, too, he displayed his familiarity with the cutler's craft by writing a considerable article (*Affiler*) on the art of whetting knives and bringing lancets to a fine edge.[28] It was like Diderot to describe three or four methods for catching fish-worms (*Achées*), to use his columns for paying compliments to Réaumur and Frederick the Great, or to include rhetorical bits — though quite representative of his considered views — like those in the article on 'Alecto,' 'whose name corresponds to that of Envy. . . . what envious person would not be horrified at himself when he hears it said that Envy is one of the three Furies, and that she is the daughter of Hell and of Night . . . what could be likely to make virtue more attractive and vice odious . . . ?' [29] Such editorial policies generated some of the curiosity excited by a modern syndicated column. It cannot be denied that part of the interest inspired by the work arose from a desire to see what the authors would say next. The *Encyclopédie* was edited with a flair for showmanship.

It was also inspired by an eagerness for improvement and a passion for amelioration. About the last thing that could be said about the *Encyclopédie* was that it was content with things as they were. In the largest sense, it had a revolutionary attitude. But the expression of this desire for improvement was not limited to cautious verbalizations about religion and matters of state: it shone forth in the desire for all sorts of betterments and changes; in suggestions, for example, for reforming the alphabet as well as the orthography of the French language, or — these happen to be suggestions in articles written by Diderot himself — for more effective methods of agriculture, for better techniques of making steel, for the abolition of monopolies, and for closer supervision of midwives.[30] This sense of immersion in the circumstances of real life not unnaturally constituted for readers of the *Encyclopédie* one of its principal sources of interest. A sample of what Diderot wrote about monopolies in the very interesting article on the manufacture of needles is representative:

. . . but it seems to me that there is only one contingency as a result of which exclusive privileges may be accorded without injustice. This is when they are asked for by the inventor of a useful article. . . . to accord to a company the exclusive privilege of making a product that many people are able to manufacture is tantamount to willing that this product, instead of being perfected, should continuously become worse and always be sold more dear.[31]

And under the heading of '*Accoucheuse,*' Diderot called attention to current abuses practiced by midwives who gave instruction in their profession. '. . . I saw there examples of inhumanity [which he described] that would be almost unbelievable had they occurred among barbarians. . . . Therefore I invite those who are charged with taking care of the disorders that occur in society to keep their eyes on this one.'[32]

Remarks like these, well-intentioned though they were, were apt to be regarded as coming close to trenching upon the arcana of authority in general and the prerogative of the police power in particular. Diderot was of a temperament that could scarcely refrain from telling the political and religious authorities what their policies ought to be, nor could he have avoided, even had he desired, treating in some aspect or other of the *Encyclopédie* these two subjects that were the riskiest and touchiest of all. In the France of the eighteenth century, Church and State did not regard themselves as answerable in any way to the criticism of private persons, nor were they likely to consider the public discussion of public matters as even permissible.

Since the police power was of course all on their side, persons who felt inspired to say something on religion or government had to take either devious indirections or serious risks. Diderot took both.

It might be supposed that somewhere in the *Encyclopédie* would be found a plea for freedom in the expression of thought. And so there was, in an article written by Diderot about an obscure Roman divinity, Aius Locutius, the god of speech. In this unobtrusive corner Diderot wrote eloquently in favor of freedom of thought. But the caution that he had to exercise in daring to canvass such a view is demonstrated by the curious limitation that he voluntarily proposed. Let criticisms of the Church and the government be published in a learned language only. If they should happen to be translated into the vernacular, arrest and punish the translator. Thus freedom of thought could be reconciled 'with the respect due to a people's faith and to the national cult.' [33] To a twentieth-century reader this proposal seems shockingly undemocratic and illiberal, but to the eighteenth century, as many criticisms of the *Encyclopédie* show, it seemed shockingly radical.

In his article on 'Political Authority,' Diderot stated his opinions very plainly, thereby incurring so much criticism and coming, it is said, so close to having the work's license taken away, that for some time thereafter he refrained from expressing himself quite so unambiguously. This article did indeed sound like one by John Locke or Thomas Jefferson. 'No man,' he wrote, 'has received from nature the right of commanding others. Liberty is a present from Heaven, and every individual of the same species has the right to enjoy it as soon as he enjoys reason. . . . *against privilege.*

'Power acquired by violence is only a usurpation, and lasts only as long as the force of him who commands prevails over that of those who obey, in such a fashion that if these latter become in their turn stronger and shake off their yoke, they do so with as much right and justice as did the former who had imposed it upon them. The same law that made the authority, unmakes it: it is the law of the stronger.

. . . .

'Therefore true and legitimate power necessarily has limits. . . . The prince holds from his subjects themselves the authority that he has over them; and this authority is limited by the laws of nature and of state. . . . Besides, the government, although hereditary in a family and placed in the hands of a single individual, is not a piece of private property, but is public property, which in consequence can never be wrested from the people, to whom alone it belongs essentially and in full ownership. . . . It is not the state which belongs to the prince, but rather the prince who belongs to the state; but it pertains to the prince to govern the state, because the state has chosen him for that, because he has engaged himself toward the people for the administration of affairs, and because these, for their part, have engaged themselves to obey him conformably to the laws.' [34]

This was stout doctrine, especially during a reign in which Louis XV was to tell a delegation of judges, 'I am your master, I intend to be obeyed. I am aware of all the rights that I hold from God. It belongs to none of my subjects to limit them or decide the extent of them.' [35] The *Encyclopédie* did not indulge very frequently in libertarian essays on the sources of political power, although this article on 'Authority,' another by Diderot on 'Natural Law' (*Droit naturel*), and a later one by Jean-Jacques Rousseau on '*Economie politique*' — in which there appears for the first time in his writings the famous concept of the general will — prove that it did so often enough to keep both friend and enemy on the alert.

Both friend and enemy eagerly turned to the first volume to learn what the *Encyclopédie* would say concerning the manifold matters relating to religious faith. The subject was quite inescapable. On the one hand, there existed an elaborate and established system of authoritarian faith, constantly manifesting an extreme sensitivity to anything that could be construed as inimical to it. And on the other hand there was the pressure of a growing scientific and positivistic movement, represented by the *Encyclopédie,* which sought the freedom to search for truth even at the cost of modifying or unsettling accepted articles of faith. What was occurring at that time was like the uproar and turmoil that took place in the nineteenth century over the 'higher criticism' and the concept of evolution. To translate the struggle into the idiom of a later time, the Encyclopedists were contending with fundamentalists. This aspect of the contest between them is admirably illustrated by a contemporary anecdote, even though the incident concerned Swedish Lutherans rather than Roman Catholic Frenchmen. 'One day in the eighteenth century, some Swedish scientists discovered a certain alteration in the shores of the Baltic. Immediately the theologians of Stockholm made representations to the government that "this remark of the Swedish scientists, not being consistent with Genesis, must be condemned." To whom reply was made that God had made both the Baltic and Genesis, and that, if there was any contradiction between the two works, the error must lie in the copies that we have of the book, rather than in the Baltic Sea, of which we have the original.' [36] In France there was no one with enough authority to speak to the clergy or their defenders in such terms, with the result that persons of the stripe of Diderot had to live under much the same apprehensions as that of a teacher in Tennessee attempting, about the time of the famous 'evolution trial,' to do what he could to impart scientific biological knowledge.

Since persons combating religious authoritarianism could never attack their adversary outright — and stay out of prison or continue to enjoy the right to publish — the contest became one of wits. The *Encyclopédie* is a subtle work, written, as Diderot himself declared, 'to discredit prejudices adroitly,' often concealing or almost concealing its real opinions, and prudentially conveying with a wink and a nudge what it did not dare to say aloud.[37] Diderot's attack on the illiberality of religious belief was set forth in the *Encyclopédie* under several guises, and to detect his various devices must have been as entertaining to his partisans as it was infuriating to his opponents. For example, the *Encyclopédie* contained frequent appeals to reason, though not without a certain air of smugness, implying that the writer already had all of it. Thus Diderot wrote, in an article defining 'to adore': 'The manner of adoring the true God ought never to deviate from reason, because God is the author of reason, and because He has desired it to be used even in the judgments of what is suitable to do or not to do in respect to Him.'[38]

A favorite contrivance of the Encyclopedists was to expose, in all their multitudinousness, the various heresies of the Christian Church. This was a trick they had learned from Bayle. Their descriptions, as Diderot's of the Agonyclytes — 'heretics of the seventh century, whose maxim it was never to pray on their knees, but standing up'[39] — were written impassively but not without a certain trace of unctuousness. Combined with the somewhat elaborate and ostentatious arrayal of the astonishing variety of belief that had occurred in the history of the Christian Church was a constant, undoubtedly sincere, and extremely characteristic appeal for toleration and broad-mindedness on theological subjects. This was the Enlightenment seeking to discredit scholastic discussion and religious dispute. Diderot wrote a typical example of this sort of appeal in an article on a Mohammedan sect:[40] 'Furthermore, I shall observe that the concurrence of God, His providence, His prescience, predestination, liberty, occasion disputes and heresies wherever they are discussed, and that Christians would do well in these difficult questions, says M. d'Herbelot in his *Bibliothèque orientale,* to seek to instruct one another peaceably, if that be possible, and to tolerate one another charitably on those occasions where they are of different sentiments. Indeed, what do we know of such matters? *Quis consiliarius ejus fuit?'* *

* Who was the authority for it?

Another device used by the *Encyclopédie* was the castigation of certain ancient pagan practices that, in reality, had close and obvious Christian analogues. Partly this technique bespoke an intellectual deficiency on the part of the *philosophes* in that they showed little understanding of the religious impulse in man's psychological nature, little realization that they were by way of building a kind of church of their own. Moreover, their scorn for all religious institutions, whether primitive or advanced, reveals to a twentieth-century reader that the sciences of anthropology, comparative religion, and sociology were then only embryonic. It cannot be denied, however, that the *philosophes* drew great advantage from what was essentially a propaganda device: no devout Christian could take them to task for heaping scorn on pagan customs. And so Diderot wrote, for example, of the eagle, in an article which was far from being ornithological: 'The eagle may be seen in the images of Jupiter, sometimes at his feet, sometimes at his side, and almost always carrying a thunderbolt in his talons. There is every appearance that this whole fable is founded simply upon observing the flight of the eagle, who loves to soar in the loftiest clouds and abide in the realm of the thunderbolts. That was all that was necessary to make it the bird of the god of heaven and the air, and give it a thunderbolt to carry. One had only to get the Pagans started when their gods were to be honored: rather than remain at rest, superstition conjures up the most gross and extravagant visions. Then these visions become consecrated by time and by the credulity of peoples; and woe to him who, without being bidden by God to the great and perilous calling of a missionary, loves his repose so little and knows mankind so ill as to take upon himself to instruct them. If you introduce a ray of light into a nest of owls, you will only injure their eyes and excite their cries. A hundred times happy are the people bidden by religion to believe only true, sublime, and holy things, and to imitate only virtuous actions. Such a religion is ours, wherein the Philosopher has only to follow his reason in order to arrive at the foot of our altars.' [41]

Thus Diderot ended this article with a pious flourish which the orthodox and the naïve found very edifying, but which the sophisticated presumed to be heavily ironical. This practice of saying, somewhat ostentatiously, the contrary of what he meant has raised through the years some contention as to Diderot's intellectual honesty. Even Voltaire, an expert if ever man was in covering his own tracks, was wont to complain that Diderot went to quite unnecessary lengths in his willingness to conform. The circumstances in which the two men wrote were quite different, however. Voltaire chose to live where he could nimbly skip across the border into Geneva when trouble threatened. Diderot lived in Paris, and also felt a heavy responsibility toward his Parisian publishers, whose fortunes were invested in the venture. This situation led to a number of complicated moral problems. Did not the stark necessity of bare survival justify an apparent acquiescence in orthodoxy? What were the moral rights and obligations of an editor under conditions so perilous and adverse? Could a man remain honest and still publish orthodox statements in which he had no belief? Were there any moral considerations conferring upon him the right to dissimulate his real opinions? These were problems Diderot lived with every day of the twenty-five years that the *Encyclopédie* was in preparation, and we find him now and again alluding in the *Encyclopédie* to the hazards of his exposed position. In the very first volume, he refers to criticisms of Pliny in a situation that is transparently also his own. In the article on 'Achor,' 'the fly-chasing god or god of the flies,' Diderot seems to be making a bid to his partisans for an understanding of the difficulties of his position. 'Pliny says,' he wrote, 'that the inhabitants of Cyrene sacrificed to him [Achor], in order to obtain deliverance from these insects, which sometimes occasioned contagious sicknesses in their country. This author adds that they [the flies] died as soon as the sacrifice had been made. A modern scholar remarks that Pliny could have contented himself with saying, for the honor of truthfulness, that this was the vulgar opinion. As for me, it seems to me that one ought not to demand a truth that might be dangerous to express, from an author accused of lying on so many occasions in which he would have been truthful had it not been for the consequences; and that Pliny, who, apparently, hardly believed in the divinity of the god of the flies, but who did undertake to instruct us of the prejudice of the inhabitants of Cyrene in that regard, could not express himself otherwise without jeopardizing his own tranquillity. This is, I believe, one of those occasions when one cannot draw from an author's testimony any conclusion either against himself or for the fact that he attests.'[42]

The *Encyclopédie,* far from seizing every possible opportunity to fly in the face of orthodoxy, frequently seemed to acquiesce in it. But often the reasons adduced for believing in a given matter were perfidious, arousing more doubts than they allayed. Sometimes a defense can be so extraordinarily nerveless and unconvincing that it leaves the reader, as Iago left Othello, with long and lingering doubts. Nowhere was this technique of the *Encyclopédie* more palpable than in articles in which the literal interpretation of the Old Testament was involved. It was not to be expected that the *Encyclopédie* would ever put itself into the position of flatly contradicting what was officially regarded as the revealed word of God, but by the proliferation of common-sense considerations or by the confusing juxtaposition of erudite, orthodox, and mutually contradictory authorities, it managed to stir up doubts. Nor was this sort of attack gratuitous or without justification. The battle over fundamentalism in the nineteenth century suggests that the leaders of the Enlightenment a century earlier were not mistaken in feeling that the infant biological and social sciences were fighting for breath and life against the suffocation that comes from a belief in the literal truth of the Book of Genesis. Had the Roman Catholic Church of two hundred years ago regarded scientific inquiry in the spirit of Pope Pius XII's address to the Pontifical Academy of Science in 1951, conditions would have been profoundly different. The scientists and social scientists of 1751 would not then have experienced the sense of intellectual strangulation that they did.

The *Encyclopédie,* of course, did not invent the technique of casting rationalistic doubts upon the Old Testament. That mine had been opened by Spinoza in his *Tractatus theologico-politicus* (1670) and had been industriously exploited by the English deists. Voltaire found many a nugget there, and the *Encyclopédie,* too, made many profitable trips to the pit head. One of the most interesting was the article in the first volume concerning 'Noah's Ark' (*Arche de Noé*), an article contributed by the Abbé Mallet.[43] With a very grave countenance and the mien of a person dancing a stately pavane, the Abbé set forth what the best authorities had conjectured concerning the time it had taken to build so large an edifice, especially considering that the Scriptures say that only four persons ever worked upon it; what must have been their strength, considering the size of the timbers needed; how many species of animals had to be provided for, making extrapolation for all those species not even yet known to Europeans; the dimensions and internal arrangement of the Ark, the probable number of decks, the amount of fodder needed, the disposition of weight to prevent tipping, storage space for fodder and fresh water, arrangements for cleaning and ventilating the animals' stalls, and the probable minimum number of the same; provisions for an extra number of lambs for food for the carnivorous animals; the possibility of a fish reservoir for the food supply of amphibious animals and birds, etc. By the time the Abbé laid down his pen it was evident that a considerable number of common-sense problems are presented by Noah's Ark. But, as Diderot remarked elsewhere in Volume I, 'the word of God, who explained Himself positively concerning these important matters, leaves no place for hypotheses.'[44]

* * * * * *

The several devices that Diderot and his collaborators employed to stimulate interest in the *Encyclopédie* were frequently combined in a single article. Many contributions that purport to be summaries of existing knowledge on certain subjects actually are vibrating and resonant with overtones of the Enlightenment. Let one very good sample suffice in illustration: the supplementary article, six columns in length, that Diderot wrote on '*Âme*' (Soul or Mind). The principal article on this tricky and touchy subject was treated by the Abbé Yvon in a conventional and innocuous manner. What Diderot did in addition was to speculate where in the body the *âme* resided; to show by his numerous references and citations that he was fully informed about current scientific investigations on the subject; to point out the close connection between soul and body, so that a disarrangement of a nerve fiber can bring on mental illness; to proffer some advice on child care; to give some interesting and specific case histories, one of which correlated religious hysteria with physical disease; and to end the whole by posing a problem bearing upon both aesthetics and psychopathology, namely whether painting has as much influence on the soul as music!

This was the sort of approach that opened windows and broadened horizons. Yet to the orthodox and conventional in matters of religion, any discussion of the soul that suggested any organic connection with the body was likely to seem vaguely impious and somehow impudent. Nevertheless the progress of knowledge indubitably required exploration of this very relationship. The problem was unfortunately and unnecessarily embittered by an accident of language: the French word '*âme*' means both 'soul' and 'mind.' [45] It is the portal word, the junction point, for both theology and science, for both metaphysics and psychology. Probably the intellectual crisis of the eighteenth century in France would not have engendered such bitterness had men been able to talk of the mind without theologians supposing that they were talking of the soul. Perhaps the growth of science in the eighteenth century, for which the *Encyclopédie* and Diderot fought so fiercely, would not have had to take a turn so aggressively anticlerical had the *philosophes* been able to talk of psychology, neurology, and psychopathology — in other words, of the mind — without being suspected of desiring to attack or demolish the concept of the soul. Perhaps the milder and less embittered form that the Enlightenment took in the English-speaking world was owing to nothing more than the fact that the English language has a word for each. No wonder Diderot often revealed an awareness of the problem of semantics.

The idea that the mind and the body, or the soul and the body, are bound together in close and reciprocal relationship would seem to be nothing but common sense. Yet in Diderot's day one had to be exceedingly careful what one said on this subject, lest one be traduced as a materialist and an atheist. Nevertheless this is a concept absolutely basic for the scientific understanding of mental disease, just as it is also the foundation of all neurological studies and of psychosomatic medicine. Diderot's most daring writings on this subject, such as *D'Alembert's Dream,* were much too dangerous to be published during his lifetime. But in the *Encyclopédie* he wrote what he could, never being one to fail to recognize an issue of importance or to avoid discussing it as much as was possible. 'Let us consider,' he wrote in his supplementary article on the *'Âme'* 'on what small things depend the functioning of the *âme:* a fiber out of order, a drop of extravasated blood, a slight inflammation, a fall, a contusion: and farewell to judgment, reason, and all that sagacity of which men are so vain. All this vanity depends upon a filament well or poorly placed, healthy or unhealthy.' [46]

* * * * * *

The *Encyclopédie* was a great reference book, a great repository of knowledge. But it was more than that, by far. The *Encyclopédie* conveyed to its readers a stimulus that was frequently as much emotional as it was intellectual. Consequently, the terms used to describe the *Encyclopédie*'s effect should not convey simply passive images. The words descriptive of it should be active. It was a detergent, a tool with a cutting edge, a window opener. It was something that one could learn to use for the performance of tasks one was insufficiently equipped to do before. And because this was so, it was unavoidable that the *Encyclopédie* and its principal editors were destined to figure conspicuously in the history and politics of the eighteenth century.

CHAPTER 12

'Up till Now, Hell Has Vomited Its Venom Drop by Drop'

B Y THE time that Volume I of the *Encyclopédie* was finally published on 28 June 1751, public interest had been whetted to a sharp edge of expectation. There had been the two prospectuses, the one of 1745 as well as the more elaborate one in 1750; there had been the preliminary publication of sample articles, Diderot's on 'Art' and the naturalist Daubenton's on 'Bee' (*Abeille*) and 'Agate' [1] — that on the bee to show that the *Encyclopédie* would be an indispensable repository of information already acquired, the one on agate to show how it would include information entirely new and unavailable elsewhere; and gaining the most public attention of all, there had been the hot-tempered exchange between Diderot and Father Berthier of the *Journal de Trévoux*. In addition, Diderot's previous publications, both the salacious and the radical, had indicated that his editing would be anything but colorless, so that potential friends of the new work counted upon finding their best hopes, potential enemies their worst fears, fully confirmed.

The excellence of the *Encyclopédie* was attested by attempts of foreigners to pirate it. Only a few months after the publication of the first volume the publishers became aware that they were being paid this sincerest kind of flattery. A syndicate of English publishers, hoisting the Jolly Roger, prefixed to their translation of the 'Preliminary Discourse' and its accompanying documents the announcement that 'the Proprietors have engaged in a Design of reprinting the Whole at *London,* with a View to serve their Country, by encouraging Arts, Manufactures, and Trades; and keeping large Sums at Home, that would otherwise be sent Abroad. They offer their Work at Half the Price of the *Paris* Edition; and hereby promise, in case they meet with no Discouragement, to proceed regularly in printing the subsequent Volumes.'[2] To head off this threat, the French publishers author-ized Briasson and David to go to London to treat with the English book-sellers and offer them copies of the French edition at very low cost. The Frenchmen made this journey in November and entered into an agreement, the details of which are obscure but which was ratified by their partners in February 1752.[3] This is the last heard of this particular venture in piracy. Still another English translation was proposed at about the same time, this one by a Sir Joseph Ayloffe. Apparently the French publishers did nothing about it, and Ayloffe's project, which appeared in weekly installments be-ginning on 11 January 1752 and costing six pence each, seems never to have proceeded beyond the eighth installment.[4]

The publication of the first volume of the *Encyclopédie* made it the focus of discussion in Paris. It had both censors and partisans, remarked Raynal, who added that both were in the right, for the work was blameworthy for the useless subjects included and praiseworthy because of its 'philosophic' spirit.[5] The statement of the journalist Clément of Geneva, expressed in his news letter of 15 August 1751, also reveals the volume's somewhat mixed reception: 'You have remarked, Monsieur, that with his vagrant as well as scientific imagination, M. Diderot would inundate us with words and sentences. This is the complaint of the public against his first volume, which appeared a little while ago. But an infinitely copious background of material and a fine taste for sound philosophy, which gives value to it, compensate for all these superfluities.'[6] Intellectual snobs complained that the *Encyclo-pédie* was a short-cut to culture,[7] a view rather frequently expressed as this typical epigram shows:

> Well, here we have the *Encyclopédie*,
> What luck for the ignorant!
> How this learned rhapsody
> Will hatch out false savants! *

A little later Raynal remarked that one often finds in the *Encyclopédie* what one is not looking for, and often searches fruitlessly for what one wants. 'Several of the authors write in a barbarous style, several in a precious manner, and many possess nothing but prolixity.' Still later he wrote that 'the first volume of the *Encyclopédie*, which at first succeeded very well, is quite gen-erally scoffed at. One sees such revolutions only in France.'[8]

> * Voici donc l'*Encyclopédie;*
> Quel bonheur pour les ignorants!
> Que cette docte rapsodie
> Fera naître de faux savants!

The evidence of an increasing subscription list proves that Raynal was exaggerating. Le Breton was printing an edition of 2,075 in place of the 1,625 originally planned.[9] Yet criticism did exist, symbolized by a rather ominous epigram which D'Hémery picked up and recorded in his journal:[10]

Je suis bon encyclopédiste,
Je connais le mal et le bien.
Je suis Diderot à la piste;
Je connais tout, je ne crois rien.*

The first rumblings of the attack came in the September columns of the influential *Journal des Sçavans,* and greatly upset D'Alembert. The *Journal* praised the 'Preliminary Discourse,' but — 'we are obliged to warn that this work has its defects. . . . The author supposes that sensations alone constitute the origin of ideas. . . . The system of Locke is dangerous for religion, although one has no objections to make when those who adopt it do not draw noxious conclusions from it. M. d'Alembert is of this number; he recognizes rather eloquently the spirituality of the soul and the existence of God, but he is so brief on each of these subjects, concerning which there are so many things to say, and he is so copious on others that the reader has a right to demand the reason for the distinction. . . .

'One might suspect this Preface of an affected laconism in respect to religion.' [11]

Much more trouble was made by the *Journal de Trévoux.* The animadversions of these Jesuits proceeded in a crescendo. Their first review, sour and grudging, appeared in the issue for October 1751. D'Alembert had spoken in the 'Preliminary Discourse' of 'those pedantic puerilities honored by the name of Rhetoric,' and the Jesuits evidently felt that this shaft had been aimed directly at them, rhetoric being so important a part of the education they dispensed to Europe. (They also took some of Diderot's remarks in his article on 'Aristotelianism' as intended to disparage them.) [12] This made them captious. When D'Alembert remarked that Pope Zacharias had rebuked a bishop, they pointed out peevishly that it wasn't a bishop, it was a priest. When D'Alembert praised Voltaire for writing good prose, the *Journal* pettishly remarked that other poets were known to have written good prose, too. But the *Journal* was on firmer ground when it called attention

---

* I am a good Encyclopedist,
  I know both good and evil.
  I follow hot on Diderot's trail;
  I know everything and believe in nothing.

to various editorial and typographical slips, especially to the frequent failure of the *Encyclopédie* to give adequate credit to its sources.[13]

Month after month, the *Journal de Trévoux* returned to the attack.[14] In November it complained of the *Encyclopédie*'s policy of excluding history and biography from its articles. 'The names of kings, savants, saints, etc., are excluded from the *Encyclopédie,* yet those of pagan divinities are admitted, and this occurs not only for gods of the first order, such, for example, as Amphitrite, Anubis, Apis, Apollo, Astraea, etc., but also for those of the second or third rank, such as Abellio, Achor, Acratus, Adephagie, Adramelech, Aius Locutius, and a multitude of others.' The last named article, in which Diderot had pleaded for the free expression of ideas provided they were written in 'a learned language,' presumably Latin, profoundly shocked the editors of the *Journal de Trévoux* as being contrary to the tranquillity of the state and religion. It was transparent that the editors felt that if ever there was an instance of liberty seeking to become license, this was it. The first volume of the *Encyclopédie,* they said ominously, showed no vestige of having been submitted to the customary censorship.[15] A remark such as this must have warned the editors of the *Encyclopédie* that their project was under ruthless and unscrupulous attack, for the volume *had* been submitted to the censors, as we have seen, and one of the most respected theologians of France, the Abbé Tamponnet, a former syndic of the Sorbonne, had certified on 15 March 1751 that 'by order of My Lord the Chancellor I have read the portion of the *Encyclopédie* concerning theology and ecclesiastical history, in which I have found nothing contrary to sound doctrine.' [16]

In attempting to undercut the prestige of the *Encyclopédie,* the *Journal de Trévoux* developed very effectively the technique of identifying and exposing plagiarisms. A little plagiarism goes a long way in discrediting a book's claim to originality, even though the vast mass of the work be new, and the editors of the *Journal de Trévoux,* with their talent for polemical in-fighting, naturally struck the *Encyclopédie* precisely where it hurt the most.[17] Unacknowledged borrowings were all too common in the *Encyclopédie.* It is true, although rather beside the point, that in spite of them the *Encyclopédie* was a work of great utility. This, in fact, the *Journal de Trévoux* cheerfully acknowledged, especially with regard to the arts and crafts. 'One may pillage the way the bees do,' wrote the *Journal de Trévoux,* carefully acknowledging *their* source, 'without doing anybody wrong, but the thievery of the ant, which walks off with the whole thing, ought never to be imitated.' [18] Indeed, these strictures were so devastating that Diderot and D'Alembert felt the necessity of inserting an explanation in the preface to their second volume.[19]

Besides dilating upon the matter of plagiarism, the *Journal de Trévoux* took very great exception to the article that Diderot wrote on 'Authority.'[20] It took equally great offense at a remark by the Abbé Yvon that 'most men honor letters as they do religion and virtue, that is to say, as a matter that they do not choose either to understand or practice or love.'[21] After three pages of comment set off by this fuse, the *Journal* concluded by saying, 'This is sufficient concerning this article which alarms (we happen to know) people of merit and which deserves the greatest attention on the part of the authors and editors of the *Encyclopédie* in order that henceforth nothing else of the sort creeps into it.'[22] In general, the attitude of the *Journal de Trévoux* might be described as touched with condescension: 'These reflections,' wrote the editor, 'are not intended to wound the authors of the great Dictionary. As the work advances, no doubt it will acquire a greater perfection; and we shall review it with an equal degree of care and impartiality.'[23]

Disagreeable as the *Journal de Trévoux* was making itself, its strictures were nevertheless scarcely influential enough by themselves to be catastrophic. Serious trouble did supervene, however, when, in addition to having to weather the attacks of the *Journal de Trévoux*, the *Encyclopédie* found itself involved in the celebrated scandal of the thesis of the Abbé de Prades, an episode that has been called 'the culminating point of the religious history of the eighteenth century.'[24]

On 18 November 1751 the Abbé Jean-Martin de Prades triumphantly defended during a ten-hour public examination — '*ab octavâ matutinâ ad sextem vespertinam,*' ran the posted thesis announcing the event — a theological thesis qualifying him for the licentiate in the theological faculty of the University of Paris. This was an advanced degree for which he had been several years in preparation, and for which he had satisfied all the usual requirements, such as securing the necessary approval of various Sorbonne doctors and officials before printing his thesis. Entitled *Jerusalem coelesti,* it was published in an edition of 450 copies and had been publicly posted for the statutory length of time before the public examination in the usual form of such theses, printed on extremely heavy paper, elephant folio size, on a single sheet. A considerable collection of these theses, De Prades's among them, may be seen today at the Bibliothèque Nationale in Paris.[25] Usually decorated with an engraving of a scene depicting a religious subject or suggesting religious awe, the theses, most of which were quite short, usually fitted readily into the single-page format. De Prades's thesis was considerably longer than the ordinary, approximately eight thousand words, so it was printed in extremely small type.

Indeed, the type was so small that apparently no one took the trouble to read it, including the reverend professor of theology, an Irishman named Luke Joseph Hooke, whose special and particular responsibility it was. The Abbè de Prades sailed through his examination triumphantly, and not until some days afterward did rumors begin to fly that the Sorbonne had solemnly placed its seal of approval upon a thesis that was later characterized by formal censure of the Sorbonne itself as 'blasphemous, heretical, erroneous, favorable to materialism, contrary to the authority and integrality of the laws of Moses, subversive of the foundations of the Christian religion, and impiously calling into question the veridity and divinity of the miracles of Jesus Christ.' [26]

Thereupon everyone began to read the small print. What everyone found in this dissertation, which purported to summarize all the arguments in proof of Christian revelation, was something that closely followed the psychological doctrines, and even their manner of presentation, in D'Alembert's 'Preliminary Discourse.' [27] De Prades further argued that any faith that preserves the natural law in all its purity is preferable to any revealed religion except, of course, the only true one. This was an argument practically identical with Diderot's in his manuscript work 'On the Sufficiency of Natural Religion.' [28] In other portions of his thesis De Prades expounded the fact that three different systems of chronology are to be found in the Pentateuch, from which he concluded that Moses had had nothing to do with any of them; and then the candidate proceeded to examine the nature of the proof requisite for a belief in miracles. He ended by declaring that the healings performed by Jesus Christ were similar in a number of respects to those performed by Aesculapius! [29]

The only plausible reason explaining why De Prades was able to pass an examination in defense of such propositions is that there must have been in the Sorbonne a number of ecclesiastics who were not yet opposed to the new 'philosophy' and the intellectual methods it entailed.[30] It is precisely for this reason that the incident is important in the intellectual history of the eighteenth century, for after this the lines were sharply drawn. 'Nothing is better calculated,' wrote a pamphleteer just at this time, 'for making obvious the danger of the system that places the origin of our ideas in the impression of the senses than does the use that the enemies of Religion make of it. Doubtless because it has been regarded as merely a philosophical opinion, there has been no alarm over the favor gained by this system, even in the Schools of the University, during the past few years. But the impious thesis of Monsieur de Prades has finally opened people's eyes concerning the disturbing consequences that result from it.' [31]

The Sorbonne now found itself in an extremely embarrassing position, for if ever there was an institution in the *ancien régime* expected to be vigilant in the protection of orthodoxy, it was the faculty of theology of the University of Paris. Reproached by its friends and mocked by its enemies, it was in the mortifying position of an armed service that discovers that its most famous battleship has, in a moment of negligence, gone aground.

The result, usual in such circumstances, was a search for scapegoats. A Sorbonne committee proposed on 3 January 1752 that ten propositions set forth in the thesis be censured. There then followed eleven general assemblies of the Sorbonne, during which no less than 146 doctors — were present, according to one authority; delivered speeches, according to another.[32] It developed that the unfortunate Hooke had approved De Prades's thesis without reading it, being much preoccupied at that moment with correcting the proofs of a book of his own! [33] Hooke lost his chair. De Prades's thesis was condemned by the Sorbonne, as well as by the Archbishop of Paris and the Pope.[34] The comments of the Bishop of Montauban, to whose jurisdiction De Prades was responsible, were particularly comprehensive. 'Up till now,' he wrote in a pastoral charge, 'Hell has vomited its venom, so to speak, drop by drop. Today there are torrents of errors and impieties which tend toward nothing less than the submerging of Faith, Religion, Virtues, the Church, Subordination, the Laws, and Reason. Past centuries have witnessed the birth of sects that, while attacking some Dogmas, have respected a great number of them; it was reserved to ours to see impiety forming a system that overturns all of them at one and the same time.' [35] De Prades fled to Berlin, in order to escape the warrant for his arrest, and there became reader to Frederick the Great. Some years later, he recanted and made his peace with the Church.

Meanwhile it began to be alleged that the whole imbroglio was simply the result of a conspiracy on the part of the editors of the *Encyclopédie,* a plot to overturn religion. Even the Jansenists, who regarded both the *philosophes* and the Sorbonne with equal malevolence, remarked in their underground newspaper, *Les Nouvelles Ecclésiastiques,* that the stir caused by the thesis 'has occasioned the discovery through different circumstances and by certain facts that the thesis of M. de Prades was the result of a conspiracy formed by some would-be freethinkers in order to insinuate their monstrous errors into the Faculty of Theology and moreover to make more conspicuous, if possible, the irreligion and impiety that they affect.'[36] The same allegation was made in a pamphlet entitled *Réflexions d'un Franciscain,* which, though it had a frontispiece representing Diderot being flogged by a Franciscan, probably was not written by a Franciscan at all.[37] Diderot, in his article on 'Aristotelianism,' had provocatively declared that Duns Scotus, the famous Franciscan theologian, 'made his merit consist in contradicting Saint Thomas Aquinas in every respect; one finds in him nothing but vain subtleties and a system of metaphysics rejected by everyone with common sense.'[38] It is not surprising that some sort of counterattack in answer to this should soon appear in the name of the Franciscans. The *Réflexions d'un Franciscain,* if we may believe D'Hémery, who referred to the pamphlet in his journal entry for 20 January 1752, was really written by Father Geoffroy, a Jesuit professor of rhetoric at the order's famed Collège Louis-le-Grand.[39] Here we see once again how the Jesuits took the lead in attacking the *Encyclopédie.* The pamphlet pointed out that De Prades lodged under the same roof with two priests associated with the *Encyclopédie* [the Abbés Yvon and Mallet], that he was a contributor to it himself, and that among his colleagues on the *Encyclopédie* were several quite capable of writing such a thesis.[40] Moreover, the 'Franciscan' contended that earlier theses by De Prades could not compare in Latinity or intellectual competence with the *Jerusalem coelesti.*[41] It was regarded as a particularly suspicious circumstance that the 'Preliminary Discourse' of Volume I had spoken in high praise of a forthcoming work by De Prades on religion, although in reality there is nothing to show that it was De Prades's *thesis* that D'Alembert had had in mind.[42] Moreover, the Abbé was the acknowledged author of the long and important article in Volume II of the *Encyclopédie* on 'Certitude.' This article, probably written by De Prades in good faith, explored searchingly the logical and historical grounds for believing testimony regarding miracles, especially that of the Scriptures in general and of the Resurrection in particular. It was a sober and ingenious piece of work, but it must be admitted that while it claimed to deepen faith, it could scarcely have done so save in the case of persons already determined to believe. Since Volume II saw the light in late January 1752 (even though the title page bears the date 1751), just at the time of the greatest uproar over De Prades's thesis, it was easy to portray the whole concatenation of incidents as nothing but the ramifications of an Encyclopedist plot.[43]

What is the evidence for this persistent and frequently stated suspicion? All of it is circumstantial and inconclusive. In their most extreme form, the allegations insinuate that De Prades was mentally incompetent and simply allowed himself to be a sort of ventriloquist's dummy for D'Alembert and Diderot. This can hardly be, for De Prades sustained a long and searching oral examination upon his thesis, a feat that requires both previous preparation and mental adaptability. There is no evidence that D'Alembert or Diderot wrote all or any part of De Prades's thesis for him, although there is a good deal of testimony to the effect that the Abbé Yvon did.[44] According to Naigeon, Diderot 'played no part in it except for the counsel he gave the two authors to leave the usual highway a little to one side and to make the hardened ears of the doctors listen now and again to the language of reason.'[45] Nor should it be forgotten that in their preface to Volume III of the *Encyclopédie,* Diderot and D'Alembert asserted that 'we had not even read [the thesis] at the time when people were making use of it in the effort to ruin us.'[46]

Or, if it was not insinuated that Diderot and D'Alembert wrote or practically wrote the thesis, the allegations reduced themselves to accusation of guilt by association. Association there certainly was. After all, De Prades was the contributor of a very important article, and it would be entirely natural for a contributor, living in the same city as the editor, to be in personal touch with him.[47] This association with the eloquent and crepitating Diderot must have had a powerful effect on De Prades. If not, he was the first to escape such influence. But association is not the same as conspiracy, in spite of many eighteenth- and twentieth-century attempts to equate them.

This is not to contend that Diderot had no influence on the thesis, only that there is no proof that he did. It may even be that Diderot and D'Alembert encouraged De Prades to see how far it was possible to go, as a means of feeling out public opinion to guide them in their own editing of the *Encyclopédie.*[48] This could be, although to play such a game involved considerable risks, as subsequent events were soon to prove.

In retrospect this period reveals itself as one of struggle between Diderot and the Jesuits, the stakes being, as it frequently came to be said, the editing of the *Encyclopédie* itself. The Jesuits were profoundly suspicious of the venture and, indeed, have remained so, as is evidenced by the fact that as recently as 1952 a writer in the Jesuit periodical *Etudes* referred to the *Encyclopédie* as 'the most formidable machine that ever was set up against religion.'[49] In 1752 the Jesuits appear to have been determined either to capture the *Encyclopédie* or to destroy it. Such was the interpretation several contemporary observers put on the effort to discredit Diderot and the *Encyclopédie* by representing the De Prades affair to be the result of a conspiracy. This interpretation of the incident was subscribed to not merely by such a weekly news letter as *La Bigarure,* which might have published the charge just for effect, but also by Voltaire, to whom is usually attributed the pamphlet called *Le Tombeau de la Sorbonne.* His asseverations, however, could conceivably be regarded as counterpropaganda, just as could those of Grimm, who referred in his confidential news letter to 'odious conspiracies.' [50] But the frequent declarations of the diarist Barbier, who wrote that 'this whole storm against this fine Dictionary comes by the medium of the Jesuits,' and of D'Argenson, the former secretary of state for foreign affairs, who asserted that 'this storm comes from the Jesuits,' have all the weight due to the conclusions of well-placed persons who, in their confidential diaries, may be presumed to have had no motive for altering what they conceived to be the truth.[51] As early as mid-January 1752, D'Argenson was predicting that the *Encyclopédie* would be suppressed and that the Jesuits would take it over.[52]

Powerful elements at the Court also joined in the fight against the *Encyclopédie.* Their leader was the tutor of the Dauphin, Boyer, the former bishop of Mirepoix, a man said to be devoted to the Jesuits.[53] Boyer was entrusted with the ecclesiastical patronage of the kingdom and consequently was a powerful and influential personage. He took alarm at the De Prades incident and linked it with what he regarded as the subversiveness of the *Encyclopédie.* 'The most ardent enemy of the *Encyclopédie,*' wrote Malesherbes, who ought to know, because his position as director of the book trade made him the one official to whom complaints of this sort were addressed in the first instance, 'was the former bishop of Mirepoix. He carried his complaints to the King himself, and said to him with tears in his eyes that one could no longer conceal from him that religion was about to be ruined in his kingdom.' [54] It is not very surprising, then, that an *Arrêt du Conseil du Roy* (7 February 1752) suppressed the further publication, sale, and distribution of the *Encyclopédie:* 'His Majesty has found that in these two volumes a point has been made of inserting several maxims tending to destroy the royal authority, to establish a spirit of independence and revolt, and, under cover of obscure and ambiguous terminology, to build the foundations of error, of moral corruption, of irreligion, and of unbelief.' [55]

For the second time in his life, Diderot found himself involved in the public policy of the state. Both incidents, the one leading to Vincennes in 1749 and this one, ending in the catastrophe of the suppression of the *Encyclopédie,* were crises in the history of the freedom of thought, making Diderot an important figure in the political history of the eighteenth century. But it was most uncomfortable to exist in such an exposed position. The

Encyclopédie had been solemnly and officially described in the royal decree as being close to treasonous. By inference its editor had been pilloried in a state paper and singled out as a target for public indignation, assailed (to use the parlance of American journalism) as Public Enemy No. 1. 'This morning,' wrote D'Argenson, 'appeared an *arrêt du conseil* which had not been foreseen: it suppressed the *Dictionnaire encyclopédique,* with some appalling allegations, such as revolt against God and the royal authority, corruption of morals . . . etc. It is said on this score that the authors of this dictionary, of which only two volumes have appeared, consequently must shortly be put to death, that there is no way of preventing their being hunted down and informed against.' [56]

Diderot came to think, in his later years, that his own compatriots showed him less honor than did foreigners. The obloquy of the *arrêt du conseil* of February 1752 could very well have contributed to making this sentiment burgeon within him.

CHAPTER 13

The *Encyclopédie* Recontinued

DIDEROT's very person may have been in danger during the days following the suppression of the *Encyclopédie*. D'Argenson reported on 12 February that it was rumored that a *lettre de cachet* had been issued against him, and supplemented this hearsay by the further entry, 25 February, that Diderot had taken flight in order to forestall arrest; and Barbier wrote that 'Diderot was afraid of being put a second time into the Bastille.' [1] In reality, there is no evidence from a source close to Diderot that he ever left his house in the Rue de l'Estrapade. Nevertheless this was probably a period of great anxiety and alarm, especially as he was forced to surrender what manuscripts he had in preparation for succeeding volumes. 'There have been taken away from him all the authors' manuscripts, as well as from the publishers all remaining copies of the first two volumes and twenty-five sheets already printed of the third.' [2] Apparently Diderot delivered the manuscripts personally, sometime around 21 February, either to Malesherbes, the director of publications, or to his father, Lamoignon de Blancmesnil, who since 1750 had been D'Aguesseau's successor as Chancellor of France.[3]

The impounding of the manuscripts was preliminary to the Jesuits' attempting to carry on the work. D'Argenson had recorded, a week after the suppression, that 'it is not doubted that the Jesuits will take the enterprise over and continue it. . . .' Barbier spoke of the Jesuits as having a devoted supporter in the person of Chancellor Lamoignon, and, if Grimm may be believed, it seems likely that the Jesuits were given a chance to see what they could do. 'Everything had been well concerted,' wrote Grimm a year later. 'The papers had already been taken away from M. Diderot. Thus it was that the Jesuits counted upon making away with an encyclopedia already completely finished . . . by arranging and putting in order articles that they believed to be all prepared. But they had forgotten to take away from the philosopher his head and genius as well, and to ask him for the key to a large number of articles that, far from understanding, they strove in vain to make out.'[4]

But all was not lost for Diderot, for through this lengthy crisis he had on his side a very powerful friend. This was Chrétien-Guillaume de Lamoignon de Malesherbes, a member of a very prominent family of lawyers and magistrates belonging to that class of the nobility called in the *ancien régime* the *noblesse de robe*. Since late in 1750, Malesherbes had been serving under his father, the Chancellor, as director of publications. He was only twenty-nine when he took up this office, in which he continued until 1763. During his administration the great battles over the *Encyclopédie* were fought, which almost entirely changed the intellectual complexion of France. It was scarcely possible for a man to occupy more of a key position than did he as arbiter and umpire during this momentous struggle.

At the time he took office, Malesherbes was already the presiding judge of the *cour des aides,* one of the tax courts of the *ancien régime.* This was a purchasable office, and the Lamoignon family, in accordance with the practice of the time, had simply bought it. What was out of the ordinary was that the person for whom the post was purchased should happen to be a man of intelligence, adequate legal training, and merit. Malesherbes was a man of unusual integrity, without any semblance of personal ambition, and had a fine sense of the responsibilities of his office along with a transparent desire to carry out its duties with justice to all. When unpretentiousness of character was being discussed one day at the famous Mme Geoffrin's, Malesherbes' name came up. 'So many people pretend to have it,' said Mme Geoffrin, 'but M. de Malesherbes, there's a man who is unpretentiously unpretentious.'[5]

Malesherbes' policy as director of publications was as simple and straightforward as the rest of him. This policy was molded by the fact that he held the highest view of the social usefulness of the man of letters, and once wrote that 'in a century in which every citizen can speak to the entire nation by means of print, those who have the talent for instructing men or the gift of moving them—in a word, men of letters—are, in the midst of a dispersed people, what the orators of Rome and Athens were in the midst of a people assembled.'[6] He himself alluded to his motives and policy in a letter written to one of the *philosophes* in 1758: 'As for what concerns me, you know that during many years I occupied myself exclusively with literature and lived only in the company of men of letters. When I found myself led by unforeseen circumstances—and perhaps against my will—

into a different sphere, I desired nothing else so much as to be able to render services to those with whom I had passed my life. I thought I had found the occasion of doing so when I was put in charge of the book trade, since I found myself in a position to procure for them the liberty of writing that I had always seen them sigh for, and to free them from many of the constraints under which they appeared to groan and of which they continually complained. I also considered this to be doing a service to the State, for this liberty has always seemed to me to have many more advantages than drawbacks.' [7] Thus Malesherbes brought to the performance of his duties the convictions expressed by Milton in *Areopagitica*. 'It is unjust and impossible to domineer over opinions,' wrote Malesherbes, 'and consequently [unjust and impossible] to suppress, garble, or correct the books in which they are set forth.' [8] Believing as he did that the exchange of ideas was good for a society, Malesherbes constantly favored as little repression — instead of as much — as the pressures that played upon him would permit. For this reason he granted many tacit permissions to books that could not be given the official imprimatur of the *Approbation et Privilège du Roi*. Such a policy, he believed, was necessary in order to keep up with the world: 'A man,' he wrote, 'who had read only the books that, when published, appeared with the express consent of the government the way the law prescribes, would be behind his contemporaries almost a century.' [9]

With these convictions, it is obvious that Malesherbes often found himself in the position of defending radical works. 'The Encyclopedists were mistaken in not believing in Providence,' wrote a witty historian of their doings, 'for it was manifestly for their sake that Providence gave to Malesherbes the direction of the book trade.' [10] Yet it must not be supposed that he was a prejudiced and one-sided doctrinaire. Very often he revealed himself as being more in favor of freedom of the press — freedom for both sides — than the Encyclopedists were themselves. Not infrequently it seemed that what the *philosophes* wanted was not so much freedom as immunity. What they often demanded was apparently tantamount to the right to say what they pleased when they pleased, plus protection against the counterattacks of their enemies. In fact, Malesherbes seems to have been about the only person in eighteenth-century France who desired real freedom of the press. But real freedom of the press was a reform that had to wait upon the unfolding of portentous events. Meanwhile Malesherbes did his job with dignity and skill, respecting his office and making others respect it too, resisting undue encroachments on his functions by rival agencies in the government, and revealing an almost endless willingness to endure patiently the massive and capricious manifestations of temperament displayed so frequently and copiously by the selfsame men of letters whom he was endeavoring to assist.

Much later, in 1775, Malesherbes became one of Louis XVI's ministers but, too eager for economy and reform to suit the court opinion of his day, he felt obliged to resign in the very next year. In 1792-3 he served his monarch for the last time: he was Louis XVI's principal lawyer and brilliant defender in the trial preceding the King's execution. The Terror had a rejoinder for such conspicuous devotion and in 1794 Malesherbes was tried and guillotined. One of the few monuments to be seen today in the enormous and echoing Salle des Pas-Perdus in the Palace of Justice in Paris is a statue of Malesherbes. It is a fitting recognition of a courageous and honorable man, who cast over the declining days of the *ancien régime* the refulgence of a noble soul.

This was the man of whom one of Diderot's friends wrote that 'without him the *Encyclopédie* would most likely never have dared to appear.'[11] In this particular crisis of 1752 Malesherbes had not favored the suppression or even the suspension of the *Encyclopédie,* according to D'Argenson, who got his information from one of Malesherbes' cousins. Instead he had felt that it would be sufficient simply to insert some substitute pages for the most offending passages.[12] But in this he had been overruled. It was probably owing to his influence, however, that the action taken by the King's Council only suppressed the first two volumes instead of revoking the license of the whole.[13] He may have been maneuvering, thought Barbier, to forestall action by the Parlement, which might have been more severe.[14] Considering the action the Parlement had taken six years before in having Diderot's *Pensées philosophiques* burned by the hangman, Barbier's hypothesis may have been correct.

During 1752 a number of questions regarding the final disposition of the *Encyclopédie* had to be settled. Were the Jesuits going to continue the enterprise? (If not, what were the factors preventing them?) If they did not, what terms would the government impose upon Diderot and D'Alembert as a condition of allowing the work to be recontinued? And finally, would the latter raise any difficulties in consenting to these terms?

It is impossible to say why the Jesuits did not take over the *Encyclopédie,* and Grimm's statement that they were incapable is extremely unpersuasive. Still, it is the only testimony that we have on this tantalizing subject, leaving us in the realm of vague and dubious conjecture. Probably the fate of the *Encyclopédie* was involved in the chronic struggle for power at the French court, for Mme de Pompadour, since 1745 the King's mistress, was an enemy of the Jesuits, so that by a sort of Euclidean corollary, she was well disposed toward the *Encyclopédie*.[15] This very politically minded woman, the mistress of a man who usually regarded the affairs of his kingdom as no concern of his, was sincerely interested in the arts and somewhat in the sciences. La Tour's dazzling pastel of her, first exhibited in the Salon of 1755 and now hanging in the Louvre, symbolizes these interests: a portfolio of engravings is at her feet, in the background is a guitar resting on a sofa, she holds a piece of music in her hands, and on the table by her side are a globe and a number of volumes, including a folio on the back of which can be plainly read: ENCYCLOPEDIE, TOME IV.[16] D'Argenson, evidently on the authority of D'Alembert, remarked in his entry of 7 May 1752 that 'Mme de Pompadour and some ministers [perhaps D'Argenson's brother, to whom the *Encyclopédie* had been dedicated] [17] have had D'Alembert and Diderot entreated to devote themselves again to the work of the *Encyclopédie,* while practicing the requisite resistance to any temptation to touch upon religion or authority.' [18] This suggests that the anti-Jesuit coterie at the court, having somehow or other frustrated the Jesuits, were now in a position to turn to the former editors. Apparently those in responsibility had always intended to have the project eventually carried on somehow, probably because of the fact that many citizens and foreigners already had a vested interest in the *Encyclopédie* by virtue of having subscribed to it.[19] The jurisprudence of the *ancien régime* was especially regardful of property rights, and this deference to the vested rights of subscribers goes far to explain why the *Encyclopédie* was never permanently discontinued.

As might be expected, considering the previous uproar, the agreement for recontinuing the *Encyclopédie* involved arrangements for new censors. This was the more necessary because the original censors appointed by D'Aguesseau were patently finding very little to criticize. As we have already seen, the Abbé Tamponnet had given Volume I a clean bill of health in respect to theology and ecclesiastical history. Moreover, the censor Lassone had liked the second volume even better than the first: 'As the materials are assembled, a great edifice is being formed, where one sees developing with equal methodicalness and utility the various treasures that the human race has acquired for itself by its researches.' [20] This was not the way Mirepoix and the Jesuits spoke about the work! The solution to the problem was worked out by Malesherbes, who offered Mirepoix 'to have all articles without exception censored by theologians whom he would choose himself.

'He accepted my proposition with joy, and nominated the Abbés Tamponnet, Millet, and Cotterel, who were the ones in whom he had the most confidence.

'Volumes II [Malesherbes' memory was at fault here; the new arrangement was for volumes following the second], III, IV, V, VI, and VII of the *Encyclopédie* were censored in entirety by these three doctors. There was not a single article the manuscript of which was not initialed by one of the three.' [21]

No direct evidence exists describing Diderot's attitude and policy during this crisis. One is therefore reduced to the indirect and speculative device of attempting to descry Diderot through the medium of D'Alembert. For what D'Alembert thought and said about it all was quite explicit. He took care to apprise Voltaire of his sentiments in a letter dated 24 August 1752, a letter whose main purposes were to bespeak Voltaire's protection of the Abbé de Prades and to thank him for the handsome remarks regarding the *Encyclopédie* that he had inserted in the closing lines of his great history of the age of Louis XIV (*Le Siècle de Louis XIV*). 'My colleague in the *Encyclopédie* joins me in thanking you,' wrote D'Alembert, and then, after alluding to the suspension of it, he continued, 'I suspected that after having maltreated us as they did, they would come around to begging us to continue, and this has not failed to come about. For six months I refused, I shouted like Homer's Mars, and I may say that I gave in only because of the public eagerness.' D'Alembert's giving in to the public eagerness sounds like a reluctant politician's being persuaded by his eager constituents to run. D'Alembert used this letter to suggest, perhaps not very seriously, that it might be possible to edit the *Encyclopédie* in Berlin 'under the eyes and with the protection and enlightenment of your philosopher prince.' [22] To this Voltaire, then resident at Potsdam, hastily replied that 'there is a prodigious number of bayonets here, but very few books.' [23] But the principal interest in D'Alembert's letter arises from his use of pronouns. By saying '*I* refused,' '*I* shouted,' '*I* gave in,' rather than using the collective 'we' which he employs elsewhere in these lines, he implies that Diderot's part was a subordinate one. This may be, for what evidence we have shows that D'Alembert made himself rather assertive that year. On 1 March he wrote to Formey at Berlin, 'Doubtless you have learned of the suppression of the *Encyclopédie*. I don't know whether the work will be continued, but I can assure you that it will not be by me.' [24] In May, he was grumbling, in another letter to Formey, about the rather unfavorable review that the 'Preliminary Discourse' had received at the hands of the *Journal des Sçavans* in its number of the previous September. He would not go on with the

Encyclopédie, he wrote, unless the *Journal des Sçavans* 'makes me an authenticated apology just as I shall dictate it.' Moreover, he went on, 'there shall be given to us enlightened and reasonable censors, and not brute beasts in fur, sold out to our enemies. . . . There shall be allowed to us the sustaining of all opinions not contrary to religion or government, such as the one that all ideas come from the senses, which our illustrious Sorbonne would like to make a heresy of, and an infinity of others. . . . It shall be forbidden to the Jesuits, our enemies, to write against this work, to say either good or ill of it, or else it shall be permissible for us to engage in reprisals.' [25] But D'Alembert was unable to secure any such stipulations. Perhaps because he could not obtain these guarantees, he informed some of his correspondents that he was henceforth limiting his role in the *Encyclopédie.* Thus he wrote to Formey on 10 July that in the future he would be responsible for 'the mathematical portion on condition that I shall not take part in the rest.' [26]

D'Alembert's assertions are a little self-contradictory and confusing, and they raise the problem as to the relative importance of the editorial roles of Diderot and himself. Was Diderot really the principal editor? Or was D'Alembert in fact a co-editor with, in spite of the title page — 'and for the mathematical portion, by M. d'Alembert' — equal authority and responsibilities? If not, D'Alembert certainly seemed inclined to preen himself a bit before Voltaire as if he were. Voltaire, for his part, supposed for some years that D'Alembert was in fact the work's principal editor, an impression which D'Alembert does not seem to have disturbed when he visited Voltaire in 1756. It was not until Mme d'Epinay visited Ferney in 1757 that Voltaire learned to his surprise how matters really stood.[27] At this moment in 1752 we see D'Alembert (whose name, unlike Diderot's, had not appeared on the publishers' pay roll since early 1749) writing to Voltaire in such a fashion as to imply, by the use of pronouns, that the two men were co-editors, with Diderot the rather less active. Moreover, in refusing Frederick II's proffer of the presidency of the Berlin Academy, D'Alembert wrote in explanation on 16 September 1752: 'Besides I am in charge of a great work, as you know, conjointly with M. Diderot . . . it is absolutely necessary that this work should be done and printed under our eyes, that we see each other often and work in concert upon it.' [28]

The truth, however, about the relative responsibilities of D'Alembert and Diderot in editing the *Encyclopédie* is symbolized throughout the several volumes of the work by the typographical devices used to identify the contributions of each. D'Alembert's identification was always the letter 'O,' and thus he figured symbolically with all the other contributors, to each of whom a similar identifying letter had been assigned. Diderot's articles, on the other hand, were identified either by an asterisk or by no mark whatever. In spite of this uniform and consistent symbolism, suggesting as it does that Diderot was always the principal editor, D'Alembert's description of his functions was subject to somewhat confusing changes. He evidently thought of himself, in times of prosperity, as a co-editor; in times of adversity, as a contributor.

For some time the government contemplated the issuance of a new decree reauthorizing the *Encyclopédie,* but eventually decided against it and merely allowed the work to reappear on tacit sufferance and without public and explicit approval.[29] 'The Government has appeared to desire that an enterprise of this nature should not be abandoned,' D'Alembert was permitted to write in his preface to Volume III. Grimm, writing a confidential news letter, could be more circumstantial. 'The government,' he wrote when Volume III was published, 'was obliged, not without more or less confusion, to take steps to engage M. Diderot and M. d'Alembert to undertake again a work that had been attempted in vain by some people who for a long while have occupied the least place in literature. I say with more or less confusion because the government entreated the authors to continue, but without revoking the decrees issued against the work three months before.'[30] And in fact the *Encyclopédie,* though now allowed to proceed, henceforth did so on a very tentative and provisional basis in point of law.

Painful though the episode had been, and abused as Diderot and D'Alembert considered themselves to be, their enterprise greatly profited in the long run from the temporary and evanescent triumph of the opposition. They survived, which is sometimes a very considerable feat in itself, as the Abbé Sieyès felt about his own part in the French Revolution. The enemies of Diderot and D'Alembert had been unable to eliminate or supplant them or essentially alter the character of their encyclopedia. They had not been forced to disown either their principles or their methodology. Moreover, the turmoil had given their work an invaluable amount of publicity, as Barbier, who remarked upon it in his diary, had the shrewdness to see.[31] Interest in the *Encyclopédie* kept constantly mounting. The publishers had begun with plans for an edition of 1,625, which they presently increased to 2000. When Volume III was published, in November 1753, interest had been so greatly stimulated that an edition of 3100 was necessary, with further reprintings planned to bring the first three volumes and all those thereafter to an edition of 4200.[32] The impact of the *Encyclopédie,* both

numerically and in the nature of its ideas, was such that one of the great
French critics, Ferdinand Brunetière, said — although he was consistently
hostile to Diderot — that 'it is the great affair of the time, the goal toward
which everything preceding it was tending, the origin of everything that
has followed it, and consequently the true center for any history of ideas in
the eighteenth century.' [33]

A minor circumstance during 1752 gave Diderot his opportunity for
scoring a considerable victory in polemics, and for stating with great vigor
the methodological premises upon which the *Encyclopédie* stood. A well-
known Jansenist prelate, the Bishop of Auxerre, decided to publish a
pastoral instruction condemning the thesis of the Abbé de Prades. This was
piling Ossa on Pelion, for it might be supposed that the Sorbonne, the
Bishop of Montauban, the Archbishop of Paris, and the Pope, all of whom
had pronounced on the matter, were competent to dispose of it. None of these
was a Jansenist, however, and doubtless the Bishop of Auxerre felt that it
was incumbent upon some Jansenist to prove his zeal for Catholicity at this
juncture. But this intervention was skillfully exploited by Diderot, whose
reply took the opportunity of playing off Jesuits against Jansenists, pronouncing a plague on both their houses, and drawing a sharp contrast between matters of faith and matters of scientific fact. Diderot wrote this
adroit exercise in polemics in the name of the Abbé de Prades, who was at
that time in Berlin preparing his own apology, which was to appear in two
parts. Accordingly Diderot entitled his little changeling, which was on
sale in Paris even before the Abbé de Prades had published his, the *Suite de
l'Apologie de M. l'Abbé de Prades . . . Troisième partie* ('Continuation
of the Apology of the Abbé de Prades . . . Third Part'). The little book,
which purported to be printed in Berlin, appeared about 12 October 1752,
and was followed in 1753 by another edition, a pirated one published in
Amsterdam.[34]

Problems of intellectual method were uppermost in Diderot's mind in
writing this work, as is shown by the vigorous passage in which he defends
reason against obscurantism: 'I know nothing so indecent and injurious
to religion as these vague declamations against reason on the part of some
theologians. One would say, to hear them, that men cannot enter into the
bosom of Christianity except as a flock of beasts enters into a stable, and
that one has to renounce common sense either to embrace our religion or to
persist in it. To establish such principles, I repeat, is to reduce man to the
level of the brute, and place falsehood and truth upon an equal footing.' [35]

In the preface Diderot said right out that 'this third part is as much the defense of the "Preliminary Discourse" of the *Encyclopédie,* from which I [he is writing in the name of De Prades] drew my first position, as it is the defense of my thesis.' [36] And he lengthily discussed the implications in science and theology of the old axiom, by this time very familiar to the readers of this book, *nihil est in intellectu quod non prius fuerit in sensu.*[37] Diderot once more expounded the sensistic psychology that Locke and Condillac had developed. But this antithesis of the notion that human beings are born with innate ideas of God and morality was particularly suspect among French churchmen, as we have seen, because these new ideas of psychology were likely to get confusingly mixed up with orthodox ideas about man's soul. The Bishop of Auxerre put his finger on the precise issue when he complained of De Prades's thesis that the type of man discussed therein 'is not at all the man whose creation is described for us in Genesis.' [38] This was quite true. While the Bishop wanted to talk about Genesis, Diderot wanted to talk about 'man in nature,' as he himself said, and then of the herd man (*les hommes en troupeau*) and societal man (*les hommes en société*).[39] Thus we see Diderot trying to devise and apply concepts that are recognizable to us today as those fundamental to the social sciences. As a leading French social scientist has remarked, 'the principal effort of the Encyclopedists consisted in secularizing the social sciences.' [40] That is exactly what Diderot was trying to do here. But it was a point of view most upsetting to people who, when they said 'man,' meant 'Adam.'

Diderot's life is an episode in the long history of the scientific attitude's struggle against the constrictions of authoritarianism. What he and people like him have always hoped and believed is that the methods of free inquiry can reveal more of ultimate reality than can an unbending orthodoxy. Diderot expressed this hope in the terminology of a liberal theologian when he has the pseudo-De Prades declare, 'I have believed that the wing of a butterfly, well described, would bring me closer to Divinity than a volume of metaphysics.' [41] In this sentence is the difference between fundamentalism and science, between W. J. Bryan and Clarence Darrow.

For persons of Diderot's cast of mind, the fate of Galileo was always the hobgoblin that haunted their imaginations and inhabited their fears. And consequently Diderot has De Prades distinguish between what was appropriate to theology and what to 'philosophy': 'Let us take care not to identify the truth of our religion and the divinity of our Scriptures with facts that have no relation to these subjects and which might be overturned by time and by experiments. . . . We damage both theology and philosophy if we take it into our heads to produce physicists in our [theological] schools and if philosophers begin to make theologians in their assemblies.' [42]

Thus Diderot took the opportunity inadvertently offered him by the maladroit Bishop of Auxerre to strike a blow for what the eighteenth century proudly and perhaps a little vaingloriously called enlightenment. In doing so, Diderot belabored the Bishop a little, as when he wrote that 'it seems to me that this prelate has pronounced very superficially about topics that, to tell the truth, he was not required to understand, but upon which he was much less required to speak, and infinitely less required to insult those who do understand them.' [43] This was a way of showing, as indeed was the purpose of the whole book, the pains and penalties awaiting those who attempted to overawe the partisans of the new learning. But this was, after all, a negative and defensive tactic. More important was the appeal to toleration, and the assertion that De Prades and people like him were being unjustly persecuted. Such was the burden of Diderot's peroration, which Buffon — himself a famous connoisseur of literary style — considered to be one of the most eloquent passages in the French language.[44] Similarly extravagant in its praise was the judgment of a journalist of the time who wrote that some of the passages in the *Apology,* especially the one at the end, would make one suppose that they had been written by 'a resuscitated Bossuet,' a remark which, for a generation dazzled by the literary glories of the century of Louis XIV, was the highest possible praise.[45]

Doubtless as he wrote the conclusion, Diderot was seeing himself in the figure he drew of the persecuted Abbé de Prades. There is a vein of theatricality in the *philosophes* (and in Diderot) which makes it a little difficult to take them quite so seriously as they took themselves. And a good deal of this sense of the dramatic and even of the self-righteous appears in Diderot's closing remarks. But there is persuasiveness and conviction in them, too, from an author who had had his share of perturbations and alarms:

. . . I have seen that the state of all these people [his critics] is beyond hope, and I have said, Therefore shall I forget them; such is the counsel both of my religion and of my self-interest. I shall devote myself without respite to the great work that I have undertaken; and I shall finish it, if the goodness of God allows me to do so, in a manner that some day will make all my persecutors ashamed. At the head of such a work my vindication will find its appropriate place; it is at the beginning of a treatise on the truthfulness of religion that it will be fitting to place the story of the crying injustices that I have suffered, of the atrocious calumnies with which I have been blackened, of the odious names lavished against me, of the impious conspiracies by which I have been defamed, of all the evils of which I have been accused, and of all those that have been done against me. There, then, will this story be found; and my enemies will be confounded; and the people of virtue will bless the Providence that took me by the hand, when my uncertain steps were faltering, and that brought me to this land where persecution shall not follow me.[46]

Thus he concluded, in a pleasant incandescence of self-approval.

CHAPTER 14

Italian Opera and French Taste

IDEROT was an extremely sociable man. He liked
to oblige people. And he loved to talk. He spent
so much time pouring forth his ideas to friends and acquaintances that
it is remarkable that he ever found the opportunity to accumulate new
stock. With Diderot communication was almost a compulsion. If absent
from his mistress, he wrote her long letters; if left to his own devices, his
works show that his thought patterns were set in a subtle dialectic of communication with himself; and if with friends, even casual acquaintances,
he lavished his ideas upon them in such profusion that Grimm, tidy German
and shrewd entrepreneur that he was, would frequently deplore the nonchalant outpouring of such dazzling gifts, much as a man who is part
owner of an oil well might deplore the wastefulness of a gusher that has
blown its top.

Moreover, Diderot delighted in thinking of himself as the very type and
pattern of the Good-natured Man.[1] Consequently, he did not mind ex-
pending his time and his energies in behalf of those who had no real claim
upon him. Nor did he really object to being imposed on, up to a certain
point, for it fitted into his picture of himself as an affable, approachable,
and generous person. This is illustrated by an anecdote that he told of
himself as occurring at about this time in his life. 'Once upon a time I
rescued from extreme poverty a young man of letters who was not without
talent. I fed him, lodged him, kept him warm and in clothes, for several
years. The very first flight of this talent which I had cultivated was a satire
against me and mine. The publisher . . . suggested suppressing the work. I
took care not to accept this offer. The satire appeared. The author had the
impudence to bring me the first copy of it himself. I contented myself with
saying to him: "You are an ingrate. Anyone else than I would have thrown
you out, but I am obliged to you for knowing me better than that. Take

back your work and carry it to my enemies, to that old Duc d'Orléans who lives on the other side of the street." I was living at that time in the Estrapade. The end of all this was that I wrote for him, I against my own self, a petition to the Duc d'Orléans, that the old fanatic gave him fifty louis, that the thing became known, and that the protector remained pretty ridiculous and the protected pretty vile.' * [2]

Diderot's extraversion did indeed carry with it the constant risk that he would dissipate his energies and allow himself to be distracted from more substantial accomplishment. It may be doubted, however, whether the profusion of Diderot's personality and ideas was really as wasted as Grimm feared. Among all of the *philosophes* Diderot was chief. In the vocabulary of his friends, he was more than a *philosophe*, he was THE *philosophe*. He was the leader of a party or, as his enemies would put it, of a sect. And it was by conversation as much as it was by what he published that he spread his influence and made his leadership felt. Perhaps even more; for much of what he thought was too dangerous to publish and had to remain in his desk drawer to await the random honors of posthumous publication. But his ideas, orally expressed, emanated in pulsations from the social circles that he frequented out into that highly centralized society in which everything focused upon Versailles and Paris. Add to this that Diderot was extraordinarily gifted in the arts of oral persuasion (many of his friends thought that, given different political conditions in France, he would have been an orator of the very highest rank), and it can readily be seen that not all the time he spent in company was wasted.

The ideal milieu in which to gratify his social proclivities was provided Diderot by the Baron d'Holbach, a man with whom Diderot became intimate about this time and who, like Grimm, was destined to remain a lifelong friend. D'Holbach's house, with its fine library and its quite extraordinary collections of prints and natural history, and D'Holbach's dinners attracted some of the greatest wits and intellects of his century. David Hume took Horace Walpole there in 1765, and the latter, recording the visit in his journal, spoke of D'Holbach as 'a good-natured German settled in France, who keeps a table for strangers, the *beaux esprits* of the country etc.' [3] Horace Walpole's judgment of persons was apt to be a little reductive, so that Morellet's testimony is valuable in revealing what the opportunities at D'Holbach's meant to persons of the 'philosophical' persuasion:

* The time, the street Diderot was living in, and the fact that he spoke of the publication as being 'against me and mine' suggest that this may have been *La Bigarure*'s account of the brawl between Mme Diderot and Mme de Puisieux.

Baron d'Holbach served two dinners regularly each week, Sundays and Thursdays; there assembled then . . . ten, twelve and up to fifteen or twenty men of letters and men of the world or foreigners . . . a society truly engaging, as could be realized by this symptom alone, that, being arrived at two o'clock, as was the fashion at that time, we often were almost all of us still there at seven or eight in the evening.

Now, there was the place to hear the freest, most animated and most instructive conversation that ever was. . . . There was no moot point, political or religious, that was not advanced there and discussed pro and con, almost always with great subtlety and profundity.

. . . .

It is there that I heard . . . Diderot treat questions of philosophy, art, or literature, and by his wealth of expression, fluency, and inspired appearance, hold our attention for a long stretch of time.[4]

Paul Thiry, Baron d'Holbach, later became the secret author of a long series of works which have qualified him in the eyes of posterity to be considered one of the paladins of atheism. Born in 1723, he was just ten years younger than Diderot. He was reared at Paris and educated at the University of Leyden, where he made friends with John Wilkes, the tempestuous Englishman who in the 1760's became the hero of the resistance to 'general warrants' (a sort of British counterpart of the French *lettres de cachet*) and who, in other ways as well, fell foul, like the Americans, of George III's attempts at personal rule. It was through D'Holbach that Diderot twenty years later made the acquaintance of Wilkes, who had become by then one of the best-known, not to say most notorious, men in Europe.[5]

D'Holbach settled down in Paris following the War of the Austrian Succession, became naturalized in 1749, and married, in decorous succession, two sisters, his second cousins.[6] These matches gave every indication of being for love, but they also served to keep the considerable family fortune under one roof, so that D'Holbach never had to worry, nor did any of his philosophical friends, where the next meal was coming from. That roof, still standing at Number 8, Rue des Moulins, covers a substantial five-storey building (six, counting the entresol) with its own court and porte-cochere.[7] In Diderot's day it was located in an area of tortuous and tangled streets which has since been much simplified by building the Avenue de l'Opéra. Another acquaintance of Diderot, Helvétius, lived hard by. It is difficult to say when Diderot first knew D'Holbach but it must have been at least some months before 1752, to judge from the latter's numerous contributions to Volume II of the *Encyclopédie*.[8] There is direct evidence of their connection by October of that year, for a French writer returning from Berlin mentioned meeting Diderot at the home of Mme d'Aine, D'Holbach's mother-in-law.[9]

Diderot and D'Holbach had a great deal in common, not only intellectually but also in matters of preference and taste. For instance, they both liked to overeat, they liked a walk in the country, they liked to possess fine prints and beautiful paintings, and they liked comfort. Also, without being promiscuous, they were both heartily heterosexual. In matters of philosophy and religion, they were in substantial agreement, although Diderot's doctrine is much more elusive, ambiguous, and therefore closer to life than D'Holbach's. Diderot's philosophy, hard to be sure of, has a great deal of poetic insight, and should properly be called godless rather than atheistic (to use a distinction frequently employed to discuss one aspect of the existentialism of Sartre). But there never was any question that the D'Holbach whom posterity knows was solidly and ponderously atheistic.

Oddly enough, there is testimony, although not of impeccable quality, that Diderot converted D'Holbach to atheism. The evidence comes from a book by a politician and man of letters named Garat, who in his younger days knew both men and was especially friendly with a member of their circle named Suard. Suard knew Diderot and D'Holbach at this early time and is the source of the following story: 'Having long been an adorer of God, Whom he [D'Holbach] saw in the order and laws of the universe, he had a missionary's zeal in regard to those whom he liked and who did not have the same belief. He pursued the incredulity of Diderot even into those workshops where the editor of the encyclopedia, surrounded by machines and workers, was taking sketches of all the manual arts; and drawing his text from these very machines . . . he asked him if he could doubt that they had been conceived and built by an intelligence. The application was a striking one, but it did not, however, strike either the mind or heart of Diderot. Diderot's friend, bursting into tears, fell at his feet. It has been said of Saint Paul, thrown from the horse upon which he was pursuing the Christians: *Falls a persecutor, and gets up an apostle.* It was quite the contrary that occurred in this instance: he who fell on his knees a deist, got up an atheist.'[10] There may indeed be something to this story, for as late as 1756 the curé of Saint-Germain-l'Auxerrois in Paris enthusiastically vouched for D'Holbach as 'making profession of the Catholic, apostolic and Roman faith, the duties of which he fulfills with edification.'[11]

However this may be, it is incontestable that Diderot and D'Holbach had innumerable intellectual interests in common, interests which might quite literally be called encyclopedic. Marmontel wrote of D'Holbach that he 'had read everything and never forgotten anything of interest,' and Rousseau spoke of him as maintaining his position among men of letters very adequately, owing to his knowledge and learning.[12] This passion for knowledge, especially in the fields of mineralogy and metallurgy where a mastery of German was essential, was extremely useful to the *Encyclopédie* and was acknowledged lengthily in the foreword to Volume II.

The consonant tastes of Diderot and D'Holbach were particularly revealed in this period 1752–4 by their taking the same side in an embittered debate over the comparative merits of the French and the Italian opera. On 1 August 1752, a visiting Italian company came to the French Opéra, then holding forth where the Palais Royal is today, and made their debut by singing Pergolesi's *opéra bouffe, La Serva padrona.* This company continued to give their repertory at the Opéra, singing once, twice, or sometimes three times a week until their final performance on 7 March 1754.[13] All of their thirteen pieces were short and consequently given either as curtain raisers or as concluding pieces with another work. The other attraction was always a piece from the regular French repertory, given by the regular company, so Parisian audiences had an excellent opportunity to make comparisons.

During a year that had already been enlivened by the Abbé de Prades affair and the suspension of the *Encyclopédie,* and that also saw tension heightening between the King and the Parlement of Paris caused by a very grave quarrel as to whether dying Jansenists could be denied the last rites if they refused to subscribe to the bull *Unigenitus* — a disagreement which ended with the 'exiling' of the Parlement to a provincial town in 1753 and the temporary suspension of their functions — in addition to all this, there began 'the quarrel of the buffoons,' in which the Encyclopedists found common and exciting cause. The enthusiasts for the new Italian genre tended to congregate in that part of the pit at the Opéra that was near the royal box assigned to the Queen. Consequently 'Queen's Corner' came to be the name for the *aficionados* of the Italian opera, while 'King's Corner' denominated the partisans of the French.

In D'Holbach's circle Jean-Jacques Rousseau had extolled the beauties of the Italian opera, of which he had had firsthand experience at Venice. Rousseau's friends could now judge for themselves, and what they heard charmed them utterly and seemed infinitely superior to the formalism and intellectualism of the conventional French opera which Lully (1632–87) had created. They found the Italian opera richer and more varied in musical devices, more melodious, more capable of building emotional mood, more adroit in suiting the music to the phonetics and meaning of the words. In contrast, French operatic music seemed stiff and monotonous, with long, boresome recitatives, and too much emphasis on harmony at the expense of melody. This last, they thought, was an inherent difficulty of the French language, which caused singers to bawl rather than sing. Although the French opera was excellent as a spectacle, it left much to be desired from the point of view of music. As the great Italian playwright Goldoni said of it, it was 'heaven for the eyes, hell for the ears.' [14] The French partisans of such pieces as *La Serva padrona* and Pergolesi's other comic opera heard in Paris at that time, *Il Maestro di musica,* were quite in agreement with this sentiment, and Rousseau wound up his *Lettre sur la musique française* by declaring, after a good deal of hyperbole, that 'the French have no music and cannot have any, or . . . if ever they do have any, it will be so much the worse for them.' [15]

During the quarrel of the buffoons, tempers reached an unbelievable pitch. Rousseau and Grimm, for example, were convinced that the former narrowly escaped arrest by *lettre de cachet* because of his *Lettre sur la musique française*.[16] Practically all of the Encyclopedists participated in the pamphlet war — especially Rousseau, Grimm, D'Holbach, and Diderot — and, characteristically enough, they all espoused the Italian side. They were never afraid of novelty, although their attitude was regarded by many of their enemies as practically a national betrayal. On the whole, wit was on their side, apoplexy on that of their opponents. The most effective pamphlet, and one still very amusing to read, was written by Grimm. This was *Le Petit Prophète de Boehmischbroda,* done in Scriptural language in an earnest, solemn, and deliciously naïve style. Even the outlandish place name of Boehmischbroda was funny. The Little Prophet, a famished musician in a Prague garret, was magically transported to the Paris Opéra, and what he saw and heard there, although *he* accepted it at its face value, would not, in the language of eighteenth-century English pamphleteering, bear examination.[17] This pamphlet deservedly established Grimm's reputation as a wit, and in the years to follow, Diderot's favorite and familiar epithet for him was 'prophet.' Diderot himself, whom Romain Rolland credited with a very exact knowledge of music, also entered the lists.[18] In his *Memoirs on Different Subjects of Mathematics* he had already proved his competence in musical theory from the point of view of mathematics and physics, and it will be remembered that he probably assisted Rameau in preparing some of his works for publication. Now, in early 1753, Diderot contributed three anonymous pamphlets to the controversy. They were entitled *Arrêt rendu à l'amphithéâtre de l'Opéra* ('Judgment Rendered at the Opera Amphitheatre'), *Au Petit Prophète de Boehmischbroda* ('To the Little Prophet of Boehmischbroda'), and *Les Trois Chapitres, ou La Vision de la nuit du mardi-gras au mercredi des cendres* ('The Three Chapters, or, The Vision of the Night from Shrove Tuesday to Ash Wednesday').[19] These pamphlets, though entertaining enough, are topical and ephemeral, and need not greatly detain a twentieth-century reader. What is perhaps most noteworthy about them is their air of moderation and conciliation. 'If, from the center of the pit, whence I raise my voice, I were fortunate enough to be heard by both the "Corners" . . . ,' he wrote — a statement which gives the impression that perhaps he was seeking to avoid making irreconcilable enemies of Rameau, who was after all a great contemporary composer, and his partisans.[20]

Of course Diderot in reality favored the Queen's Corner. Already in *L'Oiseau blanc* (1748) he had spoken briefly, but in praise, of Italian music.[21] At about this time — Grimm reports it in August 1753 — Diderot amused himself by composing a Latin motto to be painted (naturally it was not) on the curtain of the Opéra. The inscription clearly shows what he thought of the French opera of his day, but it is so laconic and lapidary that an explanation dilutes its humor: *Hic Marsyas Apollinem*.[22] This refers to the myth that Apollo, the god of song, flayed alive a very presumptuous and un-immortal mortal named Marsyas for presuming to challenge him to a singing contest. The piquancy of Diderot's motto is that it has no verb and therefore the nominative and accusative cases of the proper names carry all the meaning, which runs something like this: 'Here Marsyas [takes the hide off] Apollo.'

From the point of view of the *Encyclopédie,* the quarrel of the buffoons, although it served to unite the brethren in a common cause, presented an awkward contingency: it could cause trouble with Rameau. D'Alembert, as well as Diderot, had been on very friendly terms with him in earlier years. Moreover, Rameau had been asked to do the articles on music for the *Encyclopédie* but had refused, although he offered to look over and criticize the articles when prepared by someone else.[23] In consequence, the assignment was given to Rousseau, whose pieces, according to a modern critic, 'offered a faithful if somewhat jumbled and at times inept picture of Rameau's discoveries.'[24] Rousseau himself acknowledged his poor workmanship, saying that Diderot had wanted him to get them done in three months, and that he did so, but 'very hastily and very badly.'[25] Parenthetically, we may very well wonder why Editor Diderot did not see to

it that the articles were improved, either by insisting that Rousseau revise
them or by submitting them to Rameau for criticism. Perhaps he did not
because Rousseau was so touchy as to render either alternative impractical,
a hypothesis suggested by Rameau's remark that 'your Foreword makes
sufficiently evident the reason that prevented you: it is better not to give
offense to one's colleagues than to the public.'[26] Perhaps, too, Diderot and
D'Alembert, not subscribing to all of Rameau's ideas, did not want to
make the *Encyclopédie* a vehicle for them.[27]

At all events, the stand taken by the Encyclopedists in the quarrel of the
buffoons made the *Encyclopédie* vulnerable, for their decided preference
for Italian music might irritate Rameau into publicly remarking about some
of the insufficiencies of the *Encyclopédie* articles on music. Evidently it was
not the intention of the Encyclopedists to stir him up. Most of them specifically excepted him from their strictures regarding Lully and the school
of French opera in general, and Diderot praised Rameau in the *Arrêt rendu
à l'amphithéâtre de l'Opéra.*[28] He was taken as the exception proving the
rule. But how could the tradition of French operatic music be attacked without including in the censure the greatest living practitioner of it? So, at
least, Rameau appears to have thought, and in a series of little books he
presently began to show the deficiencies of Rousseau's unfortunate articles.
In 1755 he published *Erreurs sur la musique dans l'Encyclopédie,* in 1756
Suite des erreurs sur la musique dans l'Encyclopédie, and in 1757 *Réponse
de M. Rameau à MM. les éditeurs de l'Encyclopédie.* This sort of controversy
did not help the *Encyclopédie.* It was probably no exaggeration when a
journal hostile to the *Encyclopédie* remarked that Rameau's brochures 'made
a great sensation among the public.'[29] Diderot's irritation is attested by his
unflattering description of Rameau in *Rameau's Nephew,* a dialogue that
was not intended for publication in Diderot's lifetime but that still served
(perhaps all the more) as an outlet for emotional release.

Rousseau, not content to lecture the French public by precept, undertook at this time to teach it by example. The result was his extremely successful operetta, *Le Devin du Village* ('The Village Soothsayer'), for which
he wrote both words and music. In October 1752 the operetta was given
before the King at Fontainebleau, a circumstance which indirectly led to
the first open disagreement between Diderot and Rousseau. Jean-Jacques
had been invited to meet the King the day following the showing, an interview that would have been almost certainly followed by the granting of a
much needed pension. But for a number of reasons Rousseau returned to
Paris instead, a decision which Diderot disapproved of so heartily that he

sought out Rousseau to tell him so. 'Although I was moved by his zeal,' wrote Rousseau, 'I could not subscribe to his maxims, and we had a very spirited dispute, the first that I had ever had with him; and we never have had any other save of this kind, he prescribing to me what he contended I ought to do, and I resisting because I believed I ought not to do it.' [30]

It is possible that Diderot came to feel subconsciously that in the quarrel of the buffoons Rousseau had carried them too far. This is, however, completely conjectural. It is true, though, that tensions were already beginning to develop between Rousseau and the other Encyclopedists. He was inclined to think that it was because they were jealous of the success of *Le Devin du Village,* but Rousseau was a suspicious and highly imaginative man, and it is by no means certain that his fellow Encyclopedists *were* jealous of him. As Mme de Staël, writing about Rousseau ten years after his death, said of him, 'Sometimes he would leave you still loving you; but if you had said a single word that could displease him, he recalled it, examined it, exaggerated it, thought about it for a week, and ended up by quarreling with you. . . .' [31] But even if the other Encyclopedists were jealous of him, the emotional and intellectual causes of the eventual disruption were much subtler and deeper. It is quite surprising that the *philosophes* had not already realized how little of a *philosophe* Rousseau was. He did not have the faith that they did in the march of knowledge, in progress, and in reason. For years, apparently, they regarded his diatribe against the arts and sciences as more of a paradox than a conviction, failing to understand how deeply committed he was to this outlook on life. Rousseau believed in progress, too, but it was a progress that consisted in getting back to the uncomplicated and the undifferentiated, to the spirit of the simplicity and primitivism of a state of nature. This was not the point of view of men who believed in progress, as the Encyclopedists did, in terms of ever increasing knowledge, ever increasing technology, ever increasing understanding and domination of nature.

In fact, the signs of eventual disagreement could plainly be read in the disobliging way in which Rousseau spoke of 'philosophy' in the preface that he wrote to his unsuccessful comedy, *Narcisse.* This preface was written in December 1752 and published sometime in the first half of the following year, and could hardly please people who prided themselves on being called philosophers, for it discredited the very name. 'The taste for philosophy,' wrote Rousseau, 'relaxes all the bonds of esteem and benevolence that attach men to society. . . . Soon the philosopher concentrates in his person all the interest that *virtuous* men share with their fellow men: his disdain for others turns to the profit of his own pride; his self-love increases in the same ratio as his indifference for the rest of the universe. Family, fatherland, become for him words empty of meaning; he is neither a parent, nor a citizen, nor a man; he is a *philosopher.*' [32] These are strong and, indeed, quarrelsome words. Yet the *philosophes* were content to ignore them.

An incident on Shrove Sunday, 3 February 1754, in which both Diderot and Rousseau figured, gives some measure of Rousseau's growing irritation and malaise in his Encyclopedist associations. Superficially, the incident would seem to be no more than a disagreement over whether or not a certain situation was funny. But frequently like and unlike can be measured by what seems amusing to the one and deplorable to the other. What happened was this. In the summer of 1753 while walking in the Luxembourg Gardens, Diderot was introduced to a young curé from a small parish in Normandy, the Abbé Petit. He expressed delight at meeting the *philosophe,* for the Abbé wanted Diderot's comments on an original madrigal, seven hundred verses long. Diderot paled and told the Abbé that he ought to write tragedies and not waste his time on madrigals. 'Permit me, then, to say to you that I won't listen to a single verse of yours before you bring us a tragedy.' Some months later the Abbé showed up with his tragedy, and Diderot arranged for him to read it at D'Holbach's.[33] The tragedy, D'Holbach later recalled, was preceded by a discourse on theatrical composition so absurd that his listeners could not take him seriously. 'I will confess that, half-laughingly, half-soberly, I myself strung the poor curé along. Jean-Jacques hadn't said a word, hadn't smiled an instant, hadn't moved from his armchair. Suddenly he rose up like a madman and, springing towards the curé, took his manuscript, threw it on the floor, and cried to the appalled author, "Your play is worthless, your dissertation an absurdity, all these gentlemen are making fun of you. Leave here, and go back to do curate's duty in your village. . . ." Then the curé got up, no less furious, spewed forth all imaginable insults against his too sincere adviser, and from insults would have passed to blows and to tragic murder if we had not separated them. Rousseau left in a rage, which I believed to be temporary, but which has never ceased and which has done nothing but increase since that time.' [34]

This lively picture of Diderot and Rousseau in the company of their peers is complemented by another recollection of about this time, this one by the Abbé Morellet. It shows Diderot in his dressing gown in the privacy of his own home talking to men much his junior. The Abbé Morellet was twenty-five years old at the time and a theological student. His recollections of Diderot agree with those of almost everyone else who knew him well —

easy of access, generous of his time, full of ideas, and vivacious in the expression of them, sociable perhaps to a fault, and eager to persuade others to his line of thought:

The conversation of Diderot, an extraordinary man whose talent can no more be in dispute than his faults, had great ability and great charm. His discourse was animated, carried on in perfect good faith, subtle without being obscure, varied in form, brilliantly imaginative, fecund in ideas, and awakening ideas in others. One allowed oneself to be carried away by it for hours on end, as upon a gentle and limpid stream flowing through a rich countryside ornamented with fine habitations.

I have experienced few pleasures of the mind to surpass it, and I shall always remember it.

. . . .

. . . there never was a man more easy to live with, more indulgent than Diderot. He lent, and even gave, wit to others. He had in mind the desire to gain proselytes, not precisely to atheism, but to philosophy and reason. It is true that if religion and God Himself chanced to be in his path, he would not have known how to stop or turn aside; but I have never observed that he put any heat into instilling opinions of this sort. He defended them without any acrimony, and without looking unfavorably upon those who did not share them.

. . . The recollection of my Sunday meetings with Diderot leads me to speak of an *abbé* whom I sometimes met at his house, the Abbé d'Argenteuil. . . . He took it into his head to convert Diderot, and, inspired by a fine zeal, came to preach to him at the Estrapade. . . .

I shall always remember our mutual embarrassment the first time we encountered each other, and the excellent scene we provided Diderot, who saw us in his study as two shamefaced libertines meeting face to face in a house of ill repute. But after the first peals of laughter, we began to dispute. And there were the Abbé d'Argenteuil and I, carried on by the march of the conversation and entering into questions regarding toleration, while the philosopher, seeing the wrangling begun, put his hands into the sleeves of his dressing gown and made himself judge of the thrusts.[35]

Other glimpses into Diderot's private life at this time are afforded us. For one thing, we know that the family income had become greater. Beginning with 1751 the publishers paid Diderot five hundred livres quarterly. This was still far from being princely. There can be no doubt that the publishers purchased the services of a man of Diderot's ability at a very modest rate, and that they really did exploit him. Still, money was easier than it had previously been in the Diderot household, and this rate of payment continued until the beginning of 1755.[36] Of more than a little interest is the fact that in 1752 Mme Diderot visited her relatives-in-law at Langres for the first time. To judge as best we can from a letter to Mme Caroillon La Salette, now almost illegible, Diderot had hopes that she could do something to soften the intractability of Mme Diderot's character.[37] At all events, the visit terminated in mutual liking and esteem. And in the early weeks of 1753 Diderot, with his usual eagerness to do a friend a favor, moved heaven and earth in behalf of a fellow-townsman of Langres. Nicolas Caroillon, son-in-law of Pierre La Salette, wanted to be designated as the successor of his father-in-law in the lucrative post of bonded tobacco warehouseman in Langres. The episode has more than one facet of biographical interest. In the first place, some faint stirrings of an old sentimental attachment may have inspired Diderot, for Caroillon's wife, *née* La Salette, may have been one of his first calf-loves.[38] Secondly, by his assistance in this instance, Diderot put into his debt a family that eventually was to be linked to his by marriage. Thirdly, and most of all, the incident shows his eagerness to be obliging. As his daughter wrote of him, 'three-fourths of his life was spent in aiding all those who had need of his purse, his talents, or his negotiations.'[39] And with this desire to be helpful was compounded a certain gratification at being able to show off his prominent and influential connections.

Getting the position for Caroillon was an animated and complicated intrigue, involving some methods that one would like to think disappeared with the *ancien régime*. The mistress of the Controller General was promised two hundred louis, but it took another fifty before the matter was pressed to a successful conclusion; the private secretaries of the Controller General were friendly to Diderot and willing to attempt to secure for him an appointment with the minister; Buffon, 'who is very fond of me,' wrote a supporting letter; and the Controller General himself, Machault d'Arnouville, unexpectedly consented to see him. 'I believe,' wrote Diderot complacently, 'I owed this favor somewhat to his curiosity to see a man who had made such a stir.'[40]

Having thus tried to accomplish his purpose through the Controller General, Diderot also undertook to secure the support of the King's mistress. This he attempted to do through a personal friend, one of the celebrated names of the eighteenth century, a man who was Mme de Pompadour's official physician. This was François Quesnay (1694–1774), the founder of the physiocratic school of economic theory. Diderot was greatly influenced during the 1750's and the early 1760's by Quesnay's views, and opened the columns of the *Encyclopédie* to Quesnay's lengthy and substantial articles on 'Farmers' (*Fermiers*) and 'Grain.'[41] These articles afforded an excellent means for the diffusion of physiocratic ideas. Quesnay was very critical of the existing French national economy and the laws regulating it, for he felt that they put a premium on the production of luxury goods and the growth of cities at the price of impoverishing and depopulating the country-side.[42] It is easy to see how much influence Quesnay's thought exerted upon Adam Smith, for both men were seeking to understand the causes of the wealth of nations, and both — the older man more by implication — preached the virtues of increasing the net national product by allowing matters to proceed not by mercantilistic regulation but by the grace of the invisible hand. It is therefore true to say, as has often been done, that Diderot's friend Quesnay was one of the fathers of the science of political economy.

Quesnay, according to Marmontel, was 'lodged in very cramped quarters in the entresol above Mme de Pompadour, [and] occupied himself from morning to night with nothing but rural economy.' In a passage that is intensely interesting but unfortunately uncorroborated by any other memoir writer of the day, Marmontel went on: 'Below us they were deliberating concerning war and peace, the choice of generals, the dismissal of ministers, while we, in the entresol, argued about agriculture, calculated the net product, or sometimes dined gaily with Diderot, D'Alembert, Duclos, Helvétius, Turgot, Buffon; and Mme de Pompadour, not being able to induce this troop of philosophers to come down to her *salon,* came up herself to see them at table and chat with them.' [43]

For the purpose of getting the Langres appointment for his friend Caroillon, Diderot presented a memorandum to Mme de Pompadour through the good offices of Quesnay, received word from her through the same channel, and then wrote to her directly. The upshot of it all was that Caroillon got his appointment and Diderot, who evidently was not quite as convinced of Caroillon's transcendent qualifications for the post as he said he was, wrote him a page of good advice upon the scrupulous fulfillment of his official duties.[44]

It is interesting, incidentally, that Diderot kept his wife informed of the vicissitudes of this solicitation, showing that he did not always exclude her from his affairs.[45] Meanwhile, Mme Diderot had news of her own during this year, for Diderot remarked to the Caroillons in February that his wife had been very ill with morning sickness.[46] Childless Mme Diderot was forty-three years old at the time of this latest pregnancy, for which she had prayed many years. 'My mother took a vow to dress in white the next child to be born to her and consecrate it to the Holy Virgin and Saint Francis [a custom which, though it has become comparatively uncommon in France, is not unheard of to this day]. Nothing could get it out of her head that I owe my existence to this vow.' [47] Marie-Angélique Diderot, Angélique after her paternal grandmother, was born in the house on the Rue de l'Estrapade on 2 September 1753, and baptized at the parish church of Saint-Etienne-du-Mont the next day. The child's godparents, persons not otherwise known to posterity, declared themselves unable to sign their own names.[48] Now, for the fourth time, there was a baby in the house. This one was destined to a long life.

CHAPTER 15

Diderot's Thoughts on the Interpretation of Nature

ONE OF the ways in which the *philosophe* Diderot proved himself a philosopher was in his contributions to the philosophy of science. Evidence of this is especially to be found in a booklet written while he was engaged in the preparation of Volume III of the *Encyclopédie*. This essay — one of his most important and least read — was the *Pensées sur l'interprétation de la nature* ('Thoughts on the Interpretation of Nature'). An extremely rare edition of the *Pensées*, almost a pilot copy, was printed in 1753.[1] The two editions published in 1754 are more ample and better known. The work, though anonymous, was authorized. D'Hémery noted in his journal that the *Pensées*, 'attributed to Diderot,' had been published with tacit permission, another interesting and representative example of Malesherbes' policy of keeping the press as free as he could.[2]

The *Pensées sur l'interprétation de la nature* is a short book devoted to taking stock of some of the current implications of the scientific method and was intended to be a handbook for the 'philosophy,' the new learning, of the day. The somewhat solemn exordium addressed 'To Young People Preparing Themselves for the Study of Natural Philosophy,' which set Diderot's enemies laughing scornfully, reflects the seriousness of the author's purpose. 'Young man, take and read,' it began. The pages that followed opened up new points of view, sometimes by positive statements, sometimes by asking questions, sometimes by stating what Diderot labeled 'conjectures.' It was a book that suggested many of the most important problems in the philosophy of science, a tentative book sending out patrols along the frontiers of knowledge. And to at least one modern critic, comparing it with Descartes, Diderot's little book seems to be 'the *Discourse on Method* of the eighteenth century.' [3]

It might, however, be more accurate to say that the book was the *Novum*

Organum of the eighteenth century. For the *Thoughts on the Interpretation of Nature* was more Baconian than any other of Diderot's writings. Both in structure and in approach Diderot modeled his book on Bacon, whom he had been carefully studying for ten years according to the testimony of one of his friends.[4] For instance, the titles of the two books were significantly similar; the *Novum Organum* is subtitled 'True Directions concerning the Interpretation of Nature.' Moreover, the arrangement of the two books in a series of disjunctive paragraphs or 'aphorisms,' as Bacon called them, is exactly alike. And Diderot possibly was influenced by other writings of Bacon. The prayer at the end of the *Thoughts* may have been inspired by Bacon's invocation of God in his Proemium in *The Great Instauration;* Diderot's adjuration to young men, 'take and read,' is like Bacon's appeal 'Ad Filios.'[5] Critics of Diderot's book, therefore, could have spared themselves a number of irrelevant remarks had they realized that Diderot was consciously making himself a transmitter of the form and content of the Baconian philosophy of science. Diderot, in turn, could have made it easier for everyone had he explicitly acknowledged this. But perhaps he was skittish after his recent experience with the *Journal de Trévoux,* which had referred maliciously to Bacon's influence on the prospectus of the *Encyclopédie.*

In a thoughtful commentary on his friend's work, Grimm noted the parallels between Diderot and Bacon: 'There is the same depth, the same breadth, the same abundance of ideas and points of view, the same luminosity and sublimity of imagination, the same penetration, the same sagacity, and sometimes, for their contemporaries, the same obscurity, especially for those with weak sight.'[6] And he might have added that they were similar, too, in the striking aptness, variety, and vigor of their imagery. A more modern and less prejudiced critic has confirmed Grimm's high opinion: both Diderot and Bacon, writes Professor Dieckmann, 'were endowed with prodigious scientific imagination, in which the gift of exact observation and of realistic vision, the scientific spirit and the spirit of speculation, are strangely blended.'[7]

The influence of Bacon is to be seen particularly in those portions of Diderot's book that deal with methodological problems, as well as with descriptions or analyses of what should be the attitude of the scientific mind. Bacon, not as interested as Diderot in zoology, had no direct influence on the part of *Interprétation de la nature* that speculates, for example, about the origin and differentiation of species, as well as other problems posed by the rapidly emerging biological sciences.[8] But as regards general scientific method, Bacon insisted upon certain attitudes and predispositions that Diderot in his generation also stood for, and that science has learned are indispensable prerequisites for progress. The spirit of Bacon was the spirit of observation and experimentation. What, it asked, are the facts? And this solicitude for the facts was accompanied by a correlative de-emphasis on the preconceived and the a priori. Thus Bacon inveighed against the kind of scholasticism that contents itself with reading books about nature and trying to discover all about her through the use of syllogisms. This scholasticism is easy for any age to fall into, so that Diderot in his century, like Bacon in his, wrote of the necessity of having knowledge of *things*. 'The abstract sciences,' wrote Diderot, 'have occupied our best minds too long and with too little fruit. Either that which is important to know has not been studied, or no discrimination, insight, or method has been put into one's studies. Words have been multiplied endlessly, and the knowledge of *things* has remained in arrears.' [9]

By this emphasis on the knowledge of things, Diderot was implying that objects existing outside the mind do partake of objective reality. Wisdom therefore lies in the direction of attempting to link human intelligence with objective reality. This is, of course, the typical answer given by modern science to the problem of reality, the problem of being, and the problem of knowledge, namely that external objects are real and that human intelligence can know reality, at least in adumbration, by the study of them. There are many other answers that can be made to these ancient philosophical problems — that the external world has no reality but is simply illusion, or that it has reality but the human mind cannot know it, or that the human mind can find reality in terms simply and merely of itself, without relating mental processes to external objects. As Diderot remarked, 'unfortunately it is easier and shorter to consult oneself than it is to consult nature. Thus the reason is inclined to dwell within itself.' Diderot believed it essential to link the understanding with outer reality, and he remarked in his *Interprétation de la nature:* 'As long as things are only in our understanding, they are our opinions; they are notions, which may be true or false, agreed upon or contradicted. They take on consistency only by being linked to externally existing things. This linking takes place either by means of an uninterrupted chain of experiments or by an uninterrupted chain of reasoning that is fastened at one end to observation and at the other to experiment; or by a chain of experiments, dispersed at intervals between the reasoning, like weights along the length of a thread suspended by its two ends. Without these weights the thread would become the plaything of the slightest agitation occurring in the air.' [10]

According to Diderot, the interpretation of nature can be accomplished only by the reciprocal interaction in the mind of the scientist of sense impression and reflection. He expressed this idea in a much-admired image of the bee leaving the hive and returning to it, an image probably derived from Bacon: 'Men have difficulty in realizing how rigorous are the laws for the investigation of truth and how limited is the number of our instrumentalities. It all reduces itself to going from the senses to reflection and back again from reflection to the senses: ceaselessly to turn inward upon one's self and to turn outward again. This is the work of the bee: she has covered a great deal of territory in vain if she does not come back to the hive laden with wax. But she has made a lot of useless piles of wax if she does not know how to make a honeycomb out of them.' [11]

Greatly as Diderot counted upon the benefits arising from the advancement of learning, he did not suppose that advancement to be easy. On the contrary, he knew it to be very difficult. It is held back, for one reason, by human fallibility; for another, by the rarity of great scientific minds. As to the first, he wrote that 'the understanding has its prejudices, the senses their incertitude, the memory its limits, the imagination its glimmerings, instruments their imperfections. Phenomena are infinite, causes are hidden, forms are perhaps transitory. Against so many obstacles, both those inside ourselves and those outside presented by nature, we have only slow experimentation, only circumscribed reflection. Such are the levers with which philosophy proposes to move the world.' [12] Diderot realized that men capable of manipulating these levers are rare. Being a man of great imagination himself, he knew how necessary imagination and creativeness are to the discovery of nature's ways. In a passage that describes a man like Louis Pasteur or Robert Koch to a tittle, a passage which has been hailed as one of the most interesting eighteenth-century attempts to state the problem of genius and define what genius is, Diderot wrote: 'We have three principal means: observation of nature, reflection, and experiment. Observation gathers the facts, reflection combines them, experiment verifies the result of the combination. It is essential that the observation of nature be assiduous, that reflection be profound, and that experimentation be exact. Rarely does one see these abilities in combination. And so, creative geniuses are not common.' [13] Such a passage makes it clear that Diderot, in thinking about nature, did not content himself with mere empiricism, that is to say with the endless accumulation of facts, but insisted on the fecundating nature of hypotheses, even incorrect ones. 'Never is the time spent in interrogating nature entirely lost,' he wrote. An important part of his little book arises from his understanding of the reciprocal character, of the organic relationship, in the mind of a scientist between his empirical tendencies and his non-empirical intuitions.[14]

Implicit in the *Interprétation de la nature* are two attitudes very characteristic of the point of view of the whole eighteenth century. One of these attitudes is the distrust of elaborate and comprehensive philosophical systems. It is quite true that Diderot's aphorisms, like Bacon's, were disjunctive and disconnected, but this was intentional.[15] The eighteenth century distrusted the great philosophical *summae* which, like that of Saint Thomas Aquinas in the age of scholasticism or like those of Descartes and Malebranche and even Leibniz in the seventeenth century, fitted facts into a pattern only too often preconceived. D'Alembert remarked in his 'Preliminary Discourse' that 'the taste for systems, a taste more appropriate for flattering the imagination than for enlightening the reason, is today almost completely banished from sound treatises,' and he gives the credit for it to Condillac who, by publishing his *Traité des systèmes* in 1749, had, said D'Alembert, dealt the taste for systems its decisive blows.[16] The eagerness for analysis rather than systematizing and the dislike of revealed authority (with the equal dislike of a priori assumptions that had a way of hardening into something closely resembling revealed authority) caused Diderot to distrust the symmetry and consistency of an elaborate intellectual system that more often than not ignored essential facts. As he wrote in the *Encyclopédie* article *'Philosophie,'* 'the systematic spirit is no less injurious to the progress of truth. By systematic spirit I do not mean that which links truths one to the other in order to form demonstrations, for this is nothing but the true philosophical spirit, but I have in mind that spirit that builds plans, and forms systems, of the universe to which it consequently desires to adjust phenomena willy-nilly.' [17]

The other respect in which Diderot partook of the general attitude of the eighteenth century — his influence was so considerable that by accepting the attitude he reinforced it — was to regard reason more as an instrumentality than a thing in itself. Since the eighteenth century plumed itself on being the Age of Reason, we may well inquire what that century meant by the word. The seventeenth century, with its rationalistic philosophies — such as Descartes', based on the proposition *Cogito, ergo sum* — could be called an age of reason, too — but in a very different sense. An important semantic change had occurred. Whereas in the seventeenth century reason had meant the possession of a number of innate and transcendent ideas, much like the highest category of knowledge or reason described by Plato in *The Republic,* the eighteenth century regarded reason as a sort of energy, a force, a means by which to do something. It was not so much an essence as it was a process. What the eighteenth century thought reason to be was admirably and authoritatively expressed by the late Ernst Cassirer: 'To it reason was no longer an essence of innate ideas, granted anterior to experience, by which the absolute being of things is disclosed to us. Reason is much less a *possession* than it is a mode of acquisition. Reason is not the area, not the treasury of the mind, in which truth, like a minted coin, lies protected. Reason is rather the principal and original force of the mind, which impels to the discovery of truth and to the defining and assuring of it.' [18] The whole eighteenth century, he said, conceived of reason in this sense.

In the *Interprétation de la nature* Diderot proved himself familiar with the scientific discoveries and investigations going on in his day. They, in turn, suggested to him the paragraphs of 'conjectures' which are an enumeration of many promising experiments that had occurred to him as remaining to be done.[19] For example, proceeding from his knowledge of Benjamin Franklin's discoveries, which had been published in 1751 and in French translation the following year, he conjectured that there was a close relation between electricity and magnetism.[20] Diderot, however, was more of a philosopher of science than a scientist, more given to suggesting with quite extraordinary flair and insight what could be done than to doing it himself. And so he only glimpsed the promised land, staying the while in the wilderness with the *Encyclopédie.* But he had the imagination to know what should be done and yet how difficult it was: 'Open Franklin's book; leaf through the books of the chemists, and you will see what the art of experiment demands in insight, imagination, sagacity, and resourcefulness'; and he speaks of the divination that skilled experimenters acquire by which they smell out — the word he uses is *'subodorer'* — unknown procedures, new experiments, and results previously neglected.[21]

Diderot had caught the scent of a great change that was coming over the sciences in his century — the change in subject matter from pure mathematics to the natural sciences and the altered intellectual outlook that this involved. 'We are verging upon a great revolution in the sciences,' he wrote. 'To judge from the bent that it seems to me minds are showing for ethics, belles-lettres, natural history, and experimental physics, I would almost venture to say that in less than a hundred years there will not be three great geometricians [this is the eighteenth-century word for what we now call a researcher in pure mathematics] in Europe. This science will come to a full stop at the point where the Bernoullis, the Eulers, Maupertuis,

Clairaut, Fontaine, D'Alembert, and La Grange will have left it. They
will have set up the columns of Hercules: there will be no going beyond
that.' [22] There is a dash of exaggeration in Diderot — he was always just a
little larger than life — and there is exaggeration in this passage, for within
Diderot's predicted hundred years the German mathematician Gauss had
opened up new horizons in pure mathematics. Thus Diderot's remark can
be taken as just another example of the apothegm that prophecy is the most
gratuitous form of error. Nevertheless, as Cassirer remarked in discussing
this passage, Diderot was the one among the thinkers of the eighteenth
century who possessed perhaps the sharpest sense of smell (*Spürsinn*) for all
the intellectual movements and changes of the epoch.[23] His words should
be taken in the sense of a new and fuller realization of the role to be played
by the natural sciences, a new and fuller realization that mathematicians
proceed by logical concepts and axioms that, although they have a rigorous
self-consistency, possess no direct access to the empirical and concrete actuality
of things. As Diderot remarked, pure mathematics is 'a kind of general
metaphysics in which bodies are stripped of their individual qualities.' [24]
He, on the contrary, with his sense of the importance of research into organic
life, wanted to enlarge scientific method sufficiently to allow for the study
of these individual qualities. A new ideal of science was growing up calling
for purely descriptive studies and *interpretations* of nature. And this ideal,
wrote Cassirer, Diderot conceived and sketched out in its general characteristics long before it was elaborated in detail.[25] This was the revolution
that Diderot detected.

In his early writings Diderot had shown an awareness of the importance
of biological researches, especially for the new light that they threw upon
old problems of theology and metaphysics. This interest had been reflected
in 1746 in the *Pensées philosophiques* and three years later in the *Lettre sur les
aveugles*. The supposititious deathbed speech of Saunderson in the *Lettre
sur les aveugles* had posed the problem of evolution and the necessity of
studying process and change in life forms. Therefore, it is not surprising that
Diderot carries these speculations one step forward in his *Interprétation de
la nature*. The recent scientific writings of La Mettrie, of Buffon, and of
Maupertuis, the president of the Prussian Academy, had provided a spring-
board, for they trenched on the very delicate question — delicate, considering
that Genesis was thought to have decided the issue once for all — of the
origin of life and the origin of species. Diderot took these speculations, especially those of Maupertuis, and, as Grimm remarked, 'adroitly adopted the
policy of refuting the supposed Dr. Baumann [Maupertuis], under the pre-

text of the dangerous consequences inhering in this opinion, but in reality in order to push it as far as it could go.'[26] The results may be seen in some astonishing passages which read like a preview of the theory of evolution.[27]

These passages, like the one about to be quoted, reveal Diderot as a natural scientist who was a leader in introducing ideas of 'transformism' into modern scientific thought. Here we have the thinker who was aware of time and change, who had an intimation of the role of *process* in the elaboration of organic life, and who grappled with the concepts of the dynamic and the genetic. In his attempt to understand and interpret nature, Diderot surpassed the merely taxonomic, that part of science that classifies and arranges, and showed himself quite scornful of scientists like Linnaeus, whom he called a 'methodist.'[28] In contrast, Diderot sought to understand the functional and investigate the process of change itself. Diderot, wrote Cassirer, was one of the first to surmount the static eighteenth-century picture of the world and substitute for it a clear-cut dynamic one.[29] But whenever one begins to think, as Diderot did, in terms of concepts in which time and the changes brought about by time make all the difference — process, adaptation, development — one needs a new kind of logic to supplement the old logic of the Aristotelian syllogism, which takes no account of time. Diderot was a precursor of the nineteenth-century philosophers and scientists who, following Hegel, adopted the mode of logic represented by the dialectic of thesis, antithesis, and synthesis. Marxist writers in particular are appreciative of the dialectical character of Diderot's thought. Karl Marx himself once referred to Diderot as his favorite prose writer, and Henri Lefebvre, one of the most influential Marxist intellectuals in France today, declares that 'the importance of the *Pensées sur l'interprétation de la nature* in the history of the philosophy of sciences, of science itself, and of human thought, cannot be overestimated.'[30] The following passage is described by Lefebvre as one 'of real genius and truly revolutionary.' It was also one in which Diderot, somewhat masking the boldness of his thought, deemed it prudent to pretend to doff his hat to Genesis:

May it not be that, just as an individual organism in the animal or vegetable kingdom comes into being, grows, reaches maturity, perishes and disappears from view, so whole species may pass through similar stages? If the faith had not taught us that the animals came from the hands of the Creator just such as they are now, and if it were permissible to have the least uncertainty about their beginning and their end, might not the philosopher, left to his own conjectures, suspect that the animal world has from eternity had its separate elements confusedly scattered through the mass of matter; that it finally came about that these elements united — simply because it was possible for them to unite; that the embryo thus formed has passed through an infinite number of successive organizations and developments; that it has acquired in turn movement, sensation, ideas, thought, reflection, conscience, sentiments, passions — signs, gestures, sounds, articulate speech, language — laws, science and arts; that millions of years have elapsed between each of these developments; that there are perhaps still new developments to take place which are as yet unknown to us; that there has been or is to be a stationary condition of things; that the being thus developed is passing out of, or will pass out of, that condition by a continual process of decline, in which his faculties will gradually leave him just as they originally came to him; and that he will finally disappear from nature forever, or rather, will continue to exist, but in a form and with faculties wholly unlike those which characterize him in this moment of time? — But religion spares us many wanderings and much labor. If it had not enlightened us on the origin of the world and the universal system of beings, how many different hypotheses would we not have been tempted to take for nature's secret? [31]

Of this passage it has been remarked that there is contained within it 'not only the transformation of species, but also the sketch of a complete system of materialistic and ateleological evolutionary philosophy, after the Spencerian fashion.' [32]

On the face of it, Diderot's *Interprétation de la nature* does not appear very antireligious. Nor should one expect it to appear so, for, after all, it had been published by tacit permission and had been approved by a censor, even though published without the king's license. Upon examination, however, it can be seen that Diderot was, as usual, trying to open up channels for freer thought, and was consequently challenging established attitudes and modes of thinking as much as he dared. No doubt he intended that the very epigraph of the book — an apt quotation from Lucretius' poem *De rerum natura,* 'Those things that are in the light we behold from the darkness' * — should by association remind his readers that Lucretius' avowed purpose was to free mankind, crushed, as he said, beneath the weight of religion. Moreover, Diderot's popularizing of Bacon, though intelligent and necessary, was also provocative, as can be demonstrated by the fact that years later the able and distinguished Catholic conservative, Joseph de Maistre (1753–1821), in books like *Les Soirées de Saint-Pétersbourg,* devoted much attention to singling out and attacking Bacon as the prime originator of what De Maistre regarded as the going-wrong of the eighteenth century. Finally, Diderot's 'transformist' views, such as those quoted above,

* *Quae sunt in luce tuemur e tenebris.*

in combination with his theory that all atoms, even in non-organic matter, have some sort of sensitivity — a view already apparent in the *Interprétation de la nature* and destined to bulk ever greater in his thought — moved him very close to a materialistic view of the universe.[33]

Although the *Mercure de France* and the *Journal Encyclopédique* spoke favorably of the *Interprétation de la nature,* on the whole it did not meet with a very enthusiastic reception.[34] Reviewers usually complained that it was obscure. The Abbé Raynal referred in his news letter to the fact that there were only four metaphysicians left in France — Buffon, Diderot, Maupertuis, and Condillac. 'The second has strewn about in two or three brochures, some quite acute ideas, but he has only insights without having any system and without developing their relationships.'[35] The journalist Clément remarked of Diderot, 'What a pity that . . . [he] should be so marvelously, so bristlingly, so desperately, metaphysical! You are about to see his *Pensées sur l'interprétation de la nature;* at one time it is a murky verbiage as frivolous as it is learned, at another an erroneous sequence of desultory reflections, the last of which proceeds to get itself lost a hundred leagues off to the left of the first. Only when he gets trivial does he become almost intelligible. But if you have the courage to follow him gropingly into his cavern, from time to time it may light up with some illuminating gleams. . . .'[36] Frederick the Great, who disliked Diderot, remarked apropos of the adjuration 'Young man, take and read,' 'There is a book that I shall not read. It's not written for me, for I'm an old fogy.' His continuing ill will can probably be detected in the fact that a Berlin newspaper, in a 1773 review of a collected edition of Diderot's works, said of the *Interprétation de la nature* that it was 'a sublime rigmarole in which the author, always in the clouds, contemplates phantoms which he takes for nature.'[37] And La Harpe, a one-time *philosophe* who later turned against them, wrote about 1799, having had some forty-five years in which to think up the epigram, that 'never has nature been more hidden than when Diderot made himself her interpreter.'[38]

The most painful contemporary review appeared as the leading article in the first number of the new Parisian periodical *Année Littéraire.* The position given to the review symbolized the editorial policy of the *Année Littéraire* for the next thirty years: it was always ready to focus its critical attention upon the ideas of the *philosophes.* The editor, a former Jesuit named Fréron (1719–76), proved himself a doughty and formidable adversary of the *philosophes,* and they retaliated by speaking of him as if he were the vilest of men. Voltaire, particularly, made him the butt of numerous jibes, a famous one being:

> They say a snake the other day
> Bit Fréron as in sleep he lay.
> What think you did thereon betide?
> Not Fréron, but the serpent, died.[39] *

In reality Fréron conducted his magazine with both skill and urbanity, a stalwart and hard-hitting conservative but an independent one.[40] Moreover, his journal was prodigiously successful — as widely read as the *Journal des Sçavans* and more widely read than the Jesuit *Journal de Trévoux*.[41] In March 1754, Fréron presented the *Année Littéraire* to the public, and his remarks about Diderot's little book provided the basis for a long and hearty mutual disesteem. After criticizing the 'prideful presumption' of the *philosophes* in general, he turned to Diderot. 'The author is perhaps a great genius; but this astral body is always covered with the clouds of an impenetrable metaphysics. . . . Although I do not at all understand what he was trying to say, I feel that there must be a way of expressing himself more clearly, and that the confusion of his words comes merely from that of his mind.' Fréron went on with his animadversions, not forgetting to envenom the quarrel between Diderot and Réaumur by meticulously quoting some unfair and ungracious remarks that Diderot had made concerning the great entomologist.[42] Most of all, Fréron objected to the praise that Diderot lavished on his friends and the epithets he showered upon his enemies. 'They [Diderot and his friends] render one another these little services. They are associated with certain others for this traffic in incense. These Philosophical Powers have concluded among themselves an offensive and defensive alliance.'[43]

Fréron was confident that the author of the *Interprétation de la nature* would not be esteemed by posterity. In this prediction Fréron was too sure of himself, for posterity finds in Diderot's views on science a greater penetration and spaciousness than many of his contemporaries could appreciate. And with it all is a marked desire on Diderot's part to make science useful and to make it understood by the people. First and last, Diderot was a man who sought the popularization and application of knowledge, and it was

* L'autre jour, au fond d'un vallon,
Un serpent mordit Jean Fréron.
Que pensez-vous qu'il arriva?
Ce fut le serpent qui creva.

this desire within him that made him a man of potent action as well as a
man of potent thought. 'Let us hasten,' he wrote, 'to make philosophy popular.
If we want the philosophers to march on, let us bring the people up to the
point where the philosophers are now.' [44] And along with his desire to
make science useful — 'Besides, the useful circumscribes all' [45] — Diderot
breathed into his little book a Baconian humbleness toward nature, a
feeling, as Bacon had put it, that we cannot command nature except by
obeying her.

Diderot was sometimes humble but not often meek. In the face of the
criticism that he evidently anticipated, he descanted in the *Interprétation
de la nature* upon the obstacles besetting a researcher. Like many of Diderot's
most eloquent pages, it is somewhat tinged with a trace of self-pity and
self-praise. Still, it is a moving passage: [46]

. . . he who resolves to apply himself to the study of philosophy may expect not
only the physical obstacles that are in the nature of his subject, but also the multitude of moral obstacles that will present themselves, as they have done to all the
philosophers preceding him. When, then, it shall come about that he is frustrated,
misunderstood, calumniated, compromised, and torn into pieces, let him learn
to say to himself, 'Is it in my century only, am I the only one against whom there
are men filled with ignorance and rancour, souls eaten by envy, heads troubled
by superstition?' . . . I am, then, certain to obtain, some day, the only applause
by which I set any store, if I have been fortunate enough to merit it.

CHAPTER 16

'Man Is Born To Think for Himself'

THE suspension of the *Encyclopédie* in February 1752 occurred only a few days after the publication of its second volume, not unnaturally causing people to be more concerned with the decision regarding the future of the venture than with the contents of the book. A close examination of Volume II, however, evidently convinced readers, as it had convinced the censor Lassone, that the work was carrying out its initial promise, and no doubt this impression contributed affirmatively to the decision to allow continuation of the work. Representative of some of the more important articles in its 871 double-columned folio pages were those on 'Ballet' by Cahusac, soon to publish his authoritative *Danse ancienne et moderne;* 'Barometer' by D'Alembert; 'Sundials' (*Cadran*) by D'Alembert and Diderot, a throwback to the latter's mathematical days; and, by Diderot, 'Stockings' (*Bas*), 'Bronze,' 'Cacao,' 'Wood' (*Bois*, showing his interest in forestry), 'Brewing' (*Brasserie*), 'Printing Characters' (*Caractères d'imprimerie*), and 'Playing Cards' (*Cartes*), to give a sampling of his many and varied articles. Something of the self-respect of the middle class is to be seen in the editors' remark concerning the article on 'Brewing': ' "Brewing" is based upon a memorandum by M. Longchamp, whom a considerable fortune and much aptitude for letters has not detached from the occupation of his ancestors.'[1] And it is of interest to find Diderot saying in the article on 'Stockings,' 'I worked in M. Barrat's shop, the foremost craftsman of his kind and perhaps the last whom one will find of equal skill.'[2] Indeed, as Diderot had claimed in his prospectus and D'Alembert had reiterated in the 'Preliminary Discourse,' Diderot went to a great deal of trouble to familiarize himself with the construction and operation of machines.[3] Naigeon says that Diderot had scale models of the machine for knitting stockings and the machine for making cut velvet. 'Several times I have discovered him in his study intentionally dismantling the one or the other, in order to put it together again in a working condition, an operation which he executed with an ease betokening a pretty lengthy study of the art, its means of achieving its ends, and its results.' [4]

Throughout Volume II, as in Volume I, there continued to be an impatience with vulgar errors, as in the article 'Boa' for instance. Diderot recounts, 'in order to show how far exaggeration can go,' that some authors had set forth that a boa can swallow an ox: 'Historians are ordinarily the opposite of the mountain in labor. If it's a matter of a mouse, their pen gives birth to an elephant.' [5] There was the same eagerness for innovation and improvement, as when in the article 'Canvas' (*Canevas*) Diderot wrote, 'We are here going to propose a sort of canvas that will make embroidery, whether done in wool or in silk, infinitely more beautiful, less lengthy, and less costly.' [6] There was the same provocation of enemies, as when Diderot again twitted the Franciscans, in *'Capuchon,'* on the scholastic subtleties of their Duns Scotus; the same disconcerting juxtaposition of actual facts with Scriptural fantasies, as when Diderot contrasted the positive exploits of the Basque whalers with the defeatist quotation from Job, 'And are you able to pull up Leviathan with a hook?' [7] There was the same nagging at articles of Christian faith, as when, in the article 'Caucasus,' Diderot quoted the ancient geographer Strabo to the effect that the Caucasians put on mourning when children were born and rejoiced at their funerals. 'There is no Christian thoroughly penetrated with the verities of his religion who ought not to imitate the inhabitant of the Caucasus and congratulate himself upon the death of his children. Death assures the newborn child of an eternal felicity, while the fate of the man who appears to have lived the most holy life still remains uncertain. How our religion is at once both terrible and consoling!' [8] And there is Diderot's usual interest in matters having to do with anatomy, physiology, and medicine. 'The conservation of men and progress in the art of healing them,' he wrote in the article 'Cadaver,' 'are objects so important that in a well-ordered state the priests would receive cadavers only from the hands of the anatomist and there would be a law forbidding the inhumation of a body before it was opened. How many phenomena are unsuspected and will always be unknown because it is only by frequent dissection of cadavers that they can be learned.' Diderot was consistent in this view, for before his death he left instructions that an autopsy be performed upon him. And the last sentence of his article 'Cadaver' could be interpreted as making him one of the early proponents of a program of public health and preventive medicine: 'The conservation of life is an object that individuals adequately concern themselves with, but that it seems to me society neglects too much.' [9]

Though it waited until the appearance of Volume III, the *Journal des Sçavans* finally praised Volume II. This periodical, it will be remembered, had enraged D'Alembert by alleging that his 'Preliminary Discourse' had an antireligious tendentiousness. The editors had meanwhile made amends by praising his *Mélanges de littérature, d'histoire et de philosophie,* a move thought by some to be an attempt, although an unsuccessful one, to split D'Alembert and Diderot.[10] Now, belatedly, the *Journal* paid both volumes some very flattering attention.[11]

In addition to acknowledging the anonymous help of D'Holbach, the editors of the *Encyclopédie* were also able to announce in their Foreword to Volume II that Buffon had consented to contribute the article 'Nature.' This was a feather in their cap: the *Encyclopédie* was beginning to obtain the services of 'great names.' It is true that by the time the volume including 'N' was published, conditions had changed and so had Buffon, but for the nonce it was something to boast about.

The Chevalier Louis de Jaucourt was also announced as a new contributor. This man, who belonged to one of the oldest families in France, came to be of truly inestimable value to the enterprise. Unlike most members of the upper nobility, he had been carefully and broadly educated. While still a child, he was sent to Geneva and emerged from his training there a Protestant, a very latitudinarian and undogmatic one. It is, incidentally, a phenomenon of more than trivial interest that in Diderot's milieu there were so many Protestants or men of Protestant origin, like Grimm or De Jaucourt or, later, Meister — just as it is interesting to see how receptive he was to foreign influences, especially English, German, and Italian. This catholic and cosmopolitan urbanity has often been made a matter of reproach to Diderot on the part of nationalistically minded French critics, but these Protestant and foreign associations kept the windows open and prevented him from feeling stifled in the French society of his day, with all its unyielding and absolutistic tendencies.

Following his years in Geneva, De Jaucourt spent three years at Cambridge and then at Leyden, where he studied under the celebrated Boerhaave, was a fellow-student of Dr. Théodore Tronchin, and became a doctor of medicine. In 1736, at the age of thirty-two — De Jaucourt was nine years older than Diderot — he returned to Paris. The breadth of this training, combined with his unusual knowledge of languages, made him one of the most highly respected polygraphs of the century, and it was appropriate that he became a member of a number of foreign academies. Besides all these qualifications, he was a man of singular purity and uprightness, qualities of the greatest value

to the *Encyclopédie,* especially as many were only too inclined to think that
the work was edited by sinister and immoral men.[12]

As volume succeeded volume, De Jaucourt tended to take over the multitude
of short articles on every conceivable subject that Diderot himself had done
in the early days of the work; especially following the Great Desertion in
1759, De Jaucourt's symbol 'D. J.' was seen on almost every page of the last
ten volumes. De Jaucourt was a great scissors-and-paste man and, because
he frequently failed to mention his sources, can legitimately be regarded as
the *Encyclopédie*'s champion magpie. His intellect was not creative, but it
was retentive, dogged, and quite accurate. His was a truly encyclopedic mind,
in the quiz-program sense of the word, and while it is easy to scorn such
talents, as Diderot himself was inclined to do, it ought never to be forgotten
that it was the modest and unpretentious De Jaucourt who was as responsible
as anyone for making the *Encyclopédie* the great focal point and gathering
place of factual information.

It has become a truism that the *Encyclopédie* was of transcendent importance
in transmuting values and changing the outlook of the eighteenth century.
According to a present-day French critic, the *Encyclopédie* was — the meta-
phor is interesting and suggestive — the turntable of the epoch.[13] The new
conception of the world and man that it propounded came as a result not
only of following out the scientific and metaphysical implications of the
sensistic psychology, but also from making new assumptions about the
origins of man and society. There could be pieced together from the *Encyclopédie* — it was not safe to be too explicit upon subjects so delicate — an
explanation of the nature of man and the beginnings of society that did
not depend upon Genesis, an explanation of history and its meaning differing
from that described in the Old and New Testaments and Saint Augustine's
City of God. The new sociology and the new social science — if they can
be dignified at this early period with such positive names, so tentative and
groping were their beginnings — depended upon a view of man and society
that of course differed from the traditional and authoritarian one. It can
be bluntly described as the difference between conceiving of man and society
as an act of creation and conceiving of them as the consequence of growth.
The Encyclopedic view was the naturalistic view. The intimations and
affirmations of it, traceable in numerous articles in the *Encyclopédie,* would
amply repay the further researches of historians of the social sciences.[14]

This new and positivistic approach, which was to command the whole-
hearted admiration of Auguste Comte, the founder of sociology, was in
conflict, potentially or overtly, with established views, and continuously in

danger of encountering some form of attempted suppression. On the principle, then, of always keeping one's opponent a little off balance, the *Encyclopédie* seldom overlooked an opportunity to sow doubt concerning Christian evidences, and Volume II followed this rule. Diderot's article on 'The Bible' outlined a complete scheme of exegetics, according to one critic. Another has remarked of this article that, by posing a whole host of exegetical questions, Diderot undermined the principle of the verbal inspiration of the Bible once for all.[15] He continued to make a display of these exegetical principles in his article on 'Old Testament Canon' (*Canon, en théologie*), an article of such erudition that it is one of the sources for supposing his theological studies had been carried to an advanced stage. He also suggested, rather gingerly, some telling criticisms of the institution of celibacy in '*Célibat*,' and the long article on 'Certitude,' contributed by the Abbé de Prades and no doubt written in good faith, manages in its examination of the credibility of miracles to be more unsettling than reassuring. Little can be found in the *Encyclopédie* that directly challenges prevailing and official doctrine, but there is much that raises doubt while professing to allay it.

A chance remark hidden away in a very long article in Volume II stirred up a storm of antagonistic derision against the *Encyclopédie*. The offending phrase was in the article devoted to 'Deer' (*Cerf*). Diderot probably did not write it — the author was probably Charles-Georges Le Roy, Superintendent of the Chase in the Royal Park at Versailles — but he made himself doubly responsible by printing it with an asterisk, and the incident shows, if nothing else, how closely the *Encyclopédie* was scrutinized by its enemies. Although the subject would appeal primarily to sportsmen, an important part of the article — and this is characteristic of the *Encyclopédie* — was devoted to a discussion of embryology, with references to Maupertuis' book *Vénus physique* and to the observations on the embryos of deer made by William Harvey, the discoverer of the circulation of the blood. But what excited the scorn and indignation of Diderot's enemies was the statement that many marvelous things are told about deer, '*especially when they have attained the age of reason.*'[16] One might suppose that this faintly ludicrous statement, the lucubration no doubt of a deer lover, was harmless enough. But actually it touched one of the exposed nerves of the eighteenth century, for the view that animals are automata and consequently without reason had become a matter of dogmatic religious belief in France. Descartes had asserted this in his *Discourse on Method*, arguing that all that animals display in their response to situations is a mechanical reaction set up by the vibration of fibers. This makes the brute soul a materialistic one; churchmen insisted upon making an absolute distinction between man and animals, the former, of course, having a soul untouched by materialism.[17] Here was still another impediment to free inquiry, for it thus became impious to make any conclusions about human psychology based upon animal analogies. Pavlov's dogs are an example of the fact that much can be learned about human psychology from animal behavior, but in the eighteenth century this channel of inquiry was almost wholly blocked. Diderot, as usual, was willing to dare for the sake of intellectual freedom by letting the remark pass about deer's attaining the age of reason and, more importantly, by presenting the pros and cons in the article entitled '*Bête, animal, brute.*' Here he remarked that 'to assert that they have no soul and that they do not think is to reduce them to the status of machines, which one seems scarcely more authorized to do than to declare that a man whose language we do not understand is an automaton.'[18]

Included in this same volume was an article by Diderot that was an original contribution to aesthetics, and which has received a great deal of serious attention from specialists in that branch of philosophy.[19] This was the article on 'The Beautiful' (*Beau*). An unobtrusive essay, it summed up and criticized previous attempts to analyze the nature of beauty and then went on to break new ground by stating Diderot's conceptions. Here, therefore, is an excellent example of the function served by the *Encyclopédie* in the intellectual life of the eighteenth century. Not only did it assemble the accumulated facts of a couple of millennia, not only did it describe the mechanical arts and crafts as had never been done before, not only did it earnestly advocate new modes of thought in psychology and social philosophy, but it also had a contribution to make in matters involving art. Thus the universality of the *Encyclopédie* is further exemplified, as also the versatility and creative vigor of Diderot, who could strike off so substantial a piece just to satisfy the routine requirements of the *Encyclopédie*.

Diderot began by summarizing and discussing recent analyses of the nature of beauty, especially those of the Englishman Francis Hutcheson. Then, having criticized these views, he began to state his own. He disagreed with Hutcheson, who thought that we have an 'internal sense' of beauty, which, operating somewhat like an innate idea of God or morality, informs us of what is beautiful and what is not. Diderot's own theory is so simple that at first it seems slight. He declared that the perception of relationships is the basis of the beautiful.[20] In another article, on 'Beauty' (*Beauté*), he wrote, 'But I think that, philosophically speaking, everything that excites in us the perception of relationships is beautiful.'[21]

At first blush the definition of the beautiful as a perception of relationships may seem intolerably superficial. But as a matter of fact it allows
ample latitude for the development of connoisseurship and taste. The more
sensitive and perceptive the artist or the contemplator of art, the more relationships he perceives and the finer and more reliable will be his criteria
of beauty. The artist or the connoisseur becomes like the skillful experimenter
Diderot alluded to in his *Interprétation de la nature* — he develops a feel
for his subject, he 'smells it out.'

Diderot's doctrine that our sense of the beautiful depends upon our perception of relationships is characteristic of his thought, which always demonstrated flexibility, relativism, and a sense of the importance of context.
Diderot rebelled against authoritarianism as much in matters of artistic appreciation as in matters of religious belief. He was, in terms of the dispute
that convulsed French letters in the closing years of the seventeenth century,
more a Modern than an Ancient. Although he did not specifically allude to
this famous quarrel in his *Encyclopédie* article, by denying that there is such
a thing as Absolute Beauty he quite clearly attacked the traditionalist position of Boileau, the Ancients' principal defender. In accord with this line
of reasoning, Diderot pointed out that a line in a play might be tragic in
one context, deliciously comic in another.[22] Conditions, circumstances, and
contexts determine our appreciation of beauty, he wrote, thus emphasizing,
as modern aestheticians have noted, 'the infinitely conditional character of
the esthetic experience.' [23]

Any theory of the beautiful rests upon a psychological doctrine of how the
mind works in perceiving beauty. Diderot again applied the sensistic doctrine of John Locke: 'Whatever the sublime expressions used to designate
the abstract notions of order, proportion, relationships, harmony — called,
if one likes, the *eternal, original, sovereign, essential rules of beauty* — they
have passed by way of our senses in order to reach our understanding. . . .'
These remarks are a positive way of restating Diderot's denial of an internal
and absolute sense of beauty. And they show how his conception of the
understanding of beauty resembles his understanding of nature in *Interprétation de la nature*. Both the artist and the scientist must seek for reality
in the external world. The scientist cannot discover truth by simply following 'reason' within the recesses of his mind, just as the artist or connoisseur
cannot find beauty by that process. 'Therefore,' wrote Diderot, 'I call beautiful everything outside me containing in itself the material for awakening
in my understanding the idea of relationships; and [I call] beautiful in
regard to myself everything that awakens this idea. . . . Whence it follows

that, although there is no *absolute beauty,* there are two sorts of the beautiful in relation to us, a *real beauty* and a *perceived beauty.*' [24]

Diderot believed human beings so constituted that the appreciation of relationships — and therefore, by his definition, the appreciation of beauty — was natural to them. The nature of man makes him conscious of the relationships upon which beauty depends. It is as fundamental as that. Man's mind by its nature seeks symmetry, order, proportion, harmony, which is tantamount to saying that it seeks the evidence of relationships and is pleased by them. Moreover, in Diderot's view, beauty is a reality. 'Whatever may result from all these causes of diversity in our judgments, this is by no means a reason for thinking that real beauty, that which consists in the perceiving of relationships, is a chimera. The application of this principle may vary to infinity, and its accidental modifications occasion dissertations and literary wars; but the principle remains none the less constant.' [25]

Diderot's theory of the beautiful allows for an infinity of nuances and gradations, and this was like him, too. Diderot was always aware of the shadings and paradoxes and ambiguities with which all of human experience is interwoven.[26] Therefore he responded unfavorably to absolutist definitions, to descriptions of experience in terms of black and white. It is this disposition of mind that entitles his thought to be called dialectical — always qualifying itself, always in a dialogue with itself. This mental disposition makes him a thinker, an artist, a critic, very hard to pigeonhole.

By his emphasis on the relative in the appreciation of the beautiful, Diderot inevitably raised the question of taste. For taste is inherently subjective, necessarily depending upon the judgment and appreciation of the person contemplating the art object, and thus varies widely, as Diderot realized. 'Everyone agrees,' he wrote, 'that there is a beautiful, that it is the result of perceived relationships; but according as one has more or less knowledge, experience, practice in judging, meditating, *seeing,* plus natural reach of the mind, one says that a certain object is poor or rich, confused or sustained, paltry or overcharged.' [27] It is the difference between the appreciation of a painting by Rouault and of a calendar picturing a girl with her skirt caught in a wringer.

The problem of taste brings us back to the problem of standards in judgment. If there is no absolute beauty, are there then *no* criteria to go by? Must the appreciation of beauty become, after all, purely anarchical, with everybody complacently belonging to the I-don't-know-art-but-I-know-what-I-like school? Diderot was well aware of this problem, as we have seen, and in later works, when he discussed what is meant by the imitation of nature and spoke of 'the line of beauty, the ideal line,' he made trenchant attempts to deal with it.[28] Those who are critical of his article on 'The Beautiful' usually argue that his doctrine is vague and inconclusive in the matter of exploring the relationship of beauty and taste. Perhaps Diderot was attempting to deal with the problem rather too much in terms of mere logic. At all events, we later find him learning to judge art more in terms of techniques than in relationships. Still, his analysis in the article concerning the beautiful was a vigorous statement. And it is not to be forgotten that he insisted that there is such a thing as objective beauty. Not absolute beauty, or beauty to be apperceived by absolute rules. Rather, Diderot's is the attitude of a man who, by an understanding of the relative, hopes to approach the absolute, yet knowing all the while that the absolute cannot be reached and knowing, too, that we should not want to reach it if we could. Perhaps this defines a liberal, whatever the object of his meditations and wherever and whenever he may be found.

*   *   *   *   *   *

When Volume III of the *Encyclopédie* finally appeared in November 1753 after a year and a half of suspension, it contained an important preliminary notice written by D'Alembert in the name of the editors. 'The eagerness that has been shown for the continuation of this Dictionary,' he began, 'is the sole motive that could have induced us to take it up again.' In this moment of triumph, D'Alembert tended to allow his self-love to prevail, and the foreword is replete with a strange combination of apologetics, vainglory, and that irritating self-righteousness that the antagonists of the *philosophes* found so exasperating.[29]

D'Alembert not unnaturally used the occasion for a restatement of the *Encyclopédie*'s editorial doctrines. As has previously been remarked, Diderot and D'Alembert apparently were permitted to recontinue their work without having to compromise their principles. It is interesting to observe, as Grimm pointed out, that they had not even been required to tip any revised pages into the preceding volumes.[30] Their independence would seem to be confirmed by D'Alembert's statement in the foreword that 'it is principally by the philosophical spirit that we seek to distinguish this Dictionary.' Thus the *Encyclopédie* would not contain, he wrote, the lives of the saints nor the genealogical trees of ruling houses nor the detailed description of every village; 'nor the conquerors who have devastated the earth, but the immortal geniuses who have enlightened it; nor, finally, a crowd of sovereigns whom history should have proscribed. Not even the names of princes and grandees have a right to be in the *Encyclopédie*, except by the good they have done the sciences. For the *Encyclopédie* owes everything to talents, nothing to titles, and is the history of the human spirit and not of the vanity of men.' And then, with that yearning for a secular immortality so characteristic of men who deny heaven and hell, he wrote, 'May posterity love us as men of virtue, if it does not esteem us as men of letters!' [31]

Volume III, which ran to nine hundred pages and yet covered the alphabet only from CHA to CONSECRATION, began to develop some new departments or areas of interest. One was that devoted to business and business practices. Excellent articles, such as 'Exchange' (*Change*), 'Commerce,' and 'Competition' (*Concurrence*), were contributed anonymously by an economist named Forbonnais. His articles reflect the middle class, businessman's point of view characteristic of the whole *Encyclopédie*.[32] Another new development was the description of legal and administrative institutions (for example, various courts, councils, codes, and officers, such as 'Chancellor' and 'Commissioners'). These numerous articles were the work of the lawyer and legal antiquarian Boucher d'Argis (1708–91), the recipient of special editorial thanks in the forewords to Volumes III and IV. These multitudinous articles, which greatly increased the bulk of the work, were informative, authoritative, and dispassionate; and they gave the *Encyclopédie* a less contentious complexion than it had had in the first two volumes. Unquestionably they contributed greatly to the value of Volume III and its successors. 'It is already acknowledged,' wrote Clément six weeks after the publication of the third volume, 'that it is superior to the second, which in turn surpassed the first.' [33]

Diderot made fewer contributions to Volume III than to previous volumes, but the articles were substantial. There were the usual ones concerning the crafts, such as 'Post Chaise' (*Chaise de poste*), 'Hemp' (*Chanvre*), and 'Hat' (*Chapeau*). There was the usual call for reforms, as when, in the article on 'Hunting' (*Chasse*), he wrote of the damage done to crops and the savage punishments dealt out to poachers. 'If the life of a man is worth more than that of all stags, why punish a man with death for having made an attempt upon the life of a stag?' [34] Similarly, Diderot's remarks on the importance of actors (*Comédiens*) are interesting as testimony to his faith in the social value of the theater and to his desire to secure to actors their civil rights. 'If one considers,' he wrote, 'the purpose of our theater and the talents necessary to a person for successfully playing a role in it, the position of an actor will necessarily assume in every right mind the degree of consideration that is its due. It is now a matter, especially on our French stage, of inciting to virtue, inspiring horror of vice, and exposing that which is ridiculous. . . . In spite of which, they [actors] have been severely treated by some of our laws. . . .'[35] Diderot's own plays, written a few years later, exemplified this conviction that the theater could incite to virtue. Correspondingly, he always esteemed actors highly as the archpriests of what may be termed a secular church.

Particularly interesting, because it exemplified Diderot's versatility and adaptability, is the article on 'Composition in Painting.' As Diderot later told the story, 'we had hoped to have from one of our most vaunted amateurs the article "Composition in Painting." We received from him a couple of lines of definition, without exactness, without style, and without ideas, with the humiliating confession that he knew no more about it; and I was obliged to write the article, I who am neither a connoisseur nor a painter.'[36] In this article (which dealt with such subjects as the unity of time, place, and action in painting; the treatment of draperies; the subordination of figures; etc.), the reader will find many of the ideas that Diderot set forth years later in his *Salons*. His article was full of fresh and striking suggestions, and one great French critic, usually austere in his praise, wrote, 'This article is delicious. . . . Lessing's whole *Laocoön* [1766] is in it in substance.'[37]

The usual campaign of sowing doubts in regard to revealed religion was waged in Volume III. The delicate and tricky but inescapable subject of religion posed a truly Hamlet-like dilemma. Diderot solved the problem, sometimes at the price of his intellectual honesty, by never refusing lip service to the claims of revealed religion. But his treatment of such subjects as 'Christianity,' 'The Chaldeans,' 'Chaos,' and 'Sacred Chronology' (all of them lengthy and important articles appearing in Volume III), while superficially unexceptionable, was apt to raise doubts and lead to ambiguous conclusions. It became a favorite tactic of the *Encyclopédie* to indulge in chronological calculations affecting the Old Testament, for the Scriptures were demonstrably confusing and inconsistent, so that the thin wedge of higher criticism could most easily enter at this point. The article on 'The Chaldeans,' considering their proficiency in astronomy, gave Diderot an obvious opportunity; and in his article on sacred chronology, he discussed and compared various chronological systems, threw doubt on the accuracy of Old Testament manuscripts, referred learnedly to Samaritan texts and to the Septuagint, and inclined toward the conclusion reached by the Abbé de Prades — 'except that it would be impermissible to adopt it, now that the censures of several bishops of France and the Faculty of Theology have declared it prejudicial to the authority of the sacred books.' Diderot concluded this article abruptly, perhaps for the very purpose of leaving the reader uncertain and in the air. The article on 'Chaos,' too, was singularly — and probably intentionally — as chaotic as the subject it dealt with. It posed all sorts of difficult logical questions regarding the Creation, summarized with loving care the objections of Spinozists and materialists (while purporting, of course, to refute them), and concluded by leaving the question in a perplexing and confused condition.[38] The article on 'Christianity' was similarly tendentious. Instead of analyzing Christianity as a spiritual religion, it somehow managed to discuss it as if its principal importance had been as an instrument of government. Diderot plainly implied, to use Gibbon's famous phrase, that all forms of religion are regarded as equally true by the people, equally false by philosophers, and equally useful by magistrates. Accordingly he had the audacity, in eighteenth-century France, to suggest that Mohammedanism and Christianity had many points of resemblance; he quoted Montesquieu copiously; and altogether was not far short of adumbrating the sociology of religion.

What the *philosophes* meant by 'philosophy' is admirably exemplified by two quotations from articles that Diderot wrote for Volume III. The first one reveals their characteristic hatred of priestcraft and their high, humanistic views of the nature of man. Discussing the Chaldeans, Diderot wrote, in transparent allusion to authoritarian beliefs anywhere, that 'one must be oneself very little of a philosopher not to feel that the finest privilege of our reason consists in not believing anything by the impulsion of a blind and mechanical instinct, and that it is to dishonor reason to put it in bonds as the Chaldeans did. Man is born to think for himself.' [39] *

The second quotation is more Rabelaisian but equally 'philosophical.' In the article on 'Heat' (*Chaleur*) Diderot discussed the periodicity of the sex impulse in animals, and then compared it with that of a human being. 'It appears that the frequency of its accesses [in man], which begin with his adolescence and last as long and longer than his capabilities, is one of the consequences of his ability to think and of his suddenly recalling to himself certain agreeable sensations . . . . If this is so, the lady who said that if animals made love only at intervals, it was because they were beasts [this is a pun: '*bêtes*' means both 'beasts' and 'stupid'], made a more philosophical remark than she realized.' [40]

The most controversial article in Volume III turned out to be one by D'Alembert on the quality of education in the secondary schools (*collèges*) of the day. In these schools the child spent about six years in 'humanities,'

* L'homme est né pour penser de lui-même.

learning mostly Latin and some Greek; one or two years in 'rhetoric,' where he learned to write discourses called amplifications (a very suitable name, thought D'Alembert, 'since they ordinarily consist of drowning in two sheets of verbiage what one could and should say in two lines'); and two years in 'philosophy,' which smacked strongly of the content and methods of medieval scholasticism. This was the education that he himself had had, and in retrospect it seemed execrable. He wanted in the course of study more history, more modern languages, and more study of a child's native tongue. He thought that the study of English and Italian would be particularly useful, perhaps also German and Spanish. And then, knowing that his far-sweeping criticisms and suggestions for reform would engender against him a great deal of counter-criticism, he concluded by remarking that 'this is what the love for the common weal has inspired me to say on education, whether public or private. . . . I cannot think without regret of the time that I lost in my childhood: I impute this irreparable loss to the established custom and not to my masters; and I should like my experience to be useful to my country.' [41]

It was fully characteristic of the Encyclopedists in their general desire for reform not to overlook so important a matter as education. But it is also likely that in writing this article D'Alembert was satisfying his grudge against the Jesuits fully as much as gratifying his zeal for the public good. D'Alembert, a man who thought it bad policy ever to forget a slight, made a number of rather spiteful and quite unmistakable allusions, in his foreword to Volume III and in the list of errata, to certain persons who had been the sources of the *Encyclopédie*'s recent woes. In particular, he pointed out the plagiarisms in the *Dictionnaire de Trévoux,* while brazenly and impenitently defending his own.[42] And the proof that he was aiming at the Jesuits in his article on '*Collège*' lies in his severe criticism of the dramatic productions staged there, which, as everyone knew, were employed by the Jesuits as an educational device much more than by anyone else.[43]

D'Alembert's article provoked a pamphlet, probably written by a Jesuit with a keen eye for an *ad hominem* argument, for he was at great pains to show that Lord Bacon had highly praised Jesuit *collèges*.[44] Still another anonymous pamphlet, this one almost certainly written by a Jesuit, complained of Volume III generally. The pamphleteer disliked in particular the choice of subject matter. Articles such as 'Hat,' 'Collar,' 'Cat,' 'Dog,' 'Candle,' 'Post Chaise,' 'Mushroom,' 'Hemp,' and 'Coal' he thought too long. 'They have preferred to teach us how to plant cabbages, steep quinces, sow hemp, cook lemons and pumpkins, and other bagatelles of the sort;

but as for the Colosseum, they have said in a dozen lines all that one needs to know about it, or, rather, all that *they* know about it. . . . A work like the *Encyclopédie* . . . should contain only such knowledge as makes true savants.' [45]

Neither Diderot nor the *Journal de Trévoux* took any part, at least openly, in these bickerings. But the Jesuits in Lyon, the second city of France, took up the cudgels. Several times during the Lenten season of 1754 they preached against the *Encyclopédie,* and in November of that year they posted folio broadsides — there is a copy in the Bibliothèque Nationale signed by the principal orator's own hand — inviting the public to a meeting in behalf of the public schools against the Encyclopedists (*Pro Scholis publicis, adversus Encyclopaedistas*). According to a letter written to Malesherbes about this occasion, the orator inveighed for an hour and a quarter — in Latin, of course — accusing the *Encyclopédie* of disloyalty to the monarchy, pointing out its plagiarisms, and particularly attacking the article on '*Collège.*' D'Alembert was insulted by a sneering reference to his illegitimate birth allegedly made during the harangue, although this was subsequently denied and could not be substantiated. D'Alembert made as much trouble as he could for the orator, Father Tolomas, and the Royal Society of Lyon to which the priest belonged, but without obtaining much satisfaction, and thus the incident sputtered out inconclusively. [46]

His quarrel with the Jesuits at Lyon was not the only incident occurring at about this time in which D'Alembert made it a matter of policy to make people think twice before they lampooned an Encyclopedist. A budding provincial playwright named Palissot caricatured Rousseau in a play produced at Nancy in 1755. Palissot made his offense even worse in D'Alembert's eyes by having his play printed and published at Paris. D'Alembert leaped to Rousseau's defense, and caused as much difficulty for Palissot as he was able, his principal handicap being that the forgiving Rousseau wanted no trouble made at all. [47] This incident, occurring in 1755-6, made even more conspicuous the break between Rousseau and his former friends which came three years later.

* * * * * *

Volume IV of the *Encyclopédie,* published in October 1754, proceeded from CONSEIL to DIZ in eleven hundred pages, its dignity somewhat impaired by its own admissions that it was something less than perfect. [48] Thus the list of errata plaintively entreated its contributors 'to take care that their manuscripts be legible, especially in regard to proper names, and that punctuation be exact in the places where the sense is necessarily ambiguous.' This was in addition to a note that had already been published in the errata in Volume II: 'The work of the editors, as editors, consists solely in collecting and publishing the work of others together with their own; but they have never purported to undertake either recasting articles done by others or going back to the sources whence they might have been taken,' so that the editorial disclaimers, one implicit and one explicit, added up to a rather damaging admission of shortcomings.

Volume IV, of all the volumes that had yet appeared, gave the impression of being the most objective and the least controversial. Accordingly, criticisms of it were comparatively rare. The Abbé Raynal, writing in his confidential news letter, was an exception, but perhaps he was offended (being a historian who had published books on English, Dutch, and general European history) at not being asked to be a contributor.[49] That he was not is a fact that highlights the *Encyclopédie*'s lack of interest in political and military history.

A notable omission in this volume was the absence of any article on 'Constitution,' that is to say the papal bull *Unigenitus,* which had caused so much political and religious strife in France since its promulgation in 1713. This was a delicate topic indeed, especially as the Parlement of Paris had been 'exiled' to Pontoise over this very issue the preceding year, and passions were still running high. Drafts of a projected article are still in existence, but Malesherbes finally decided that the subject was too hot to handle and ordered Diderot not to publish anything concerning it.[50] Included, however, were all the usual features and some new ones: the usual abundance of articles of the type now grown familiar to us — long descriptions by Diderot, such as those on 'Ropemaking' (*Corderie*), and 'Lace' (*Dentelle*), and 'Cotton,' this last based on a memorandum furnished by Turgot, soon to become famous as a gifted public administrator. This was the type of article complained of by some as being too long, but which Diderot defended by saying that there was more to fear from their being too brief, everything in handiwork being almost equally essential and equally difficult to describe.[51] There were numerous articles once more by Boucher d'Argis on laws and legal and political institutions, as also articles by Forbonnais on business, besides contributions by interesting new authors. Dr. Théophile de Bordeu, who had recently published some important pioneering research on glands and who came to exert a considerable influence upon the thinking of Diderot, wrote an article, 'Crisis,' which was a description and discussion of the art of healing. Claude Bourgelat, who later founded the schools of veterinary medicine in France, began in Volume IV to contribute articles

on horse-training and farriery so original and extraordinary that it has been
said they were the first to give to the veterinary art a scientific direction. Another valuable acquisition was Duclos, historiographer of France and permanent secretary of the French Academy. But the shining jewel in the
Encyclopedic diadem was the name of Voltaire, announced as the author
of articles to appear in Volume V.

That Voltaire consented to contribute articles, or offered to do so — it
is uncertain which is the fact — constitutes proof by itself of the success and
prestige that the *Encyclopédie* had attained. For France's most famous man
of letters, living at Geneva since he had worn his welcome thin at Potsdam,
had a shrewd and foxy sense for keeping in the public view, and was unlikely to contribute to the prestige of an enterprise unless it offered a strong
probability of enhancing his own. For the remaining twenty-five years of his
life, until the apotheosis in Paris in 1778, Voltaire continued to live in or
near Geneva, sometimes at Les Délices in Genevan territory or at Ferney
in French, reluctant to live all the time in the one because playacting was
forbidden, and poised in the other so that he could move agilely over the
border if danger threatened. During this long period he managed to keep
himself the cynosure of Parisian eyes, the dictator in many respects of
Parisian tastes. This was, in reality, a very great accomplishment. It meant
that he must miss no opportunity of feeling the pulse of Parisian opinion.
It meant that to keep in the public eye he must have something to say on
almost every subject and a piquant rejoinder to almost every pamphleteer.
People who regret that Voltaire wasted his talents replying to every wretched
hack who took it into his head to attack him miss the point: these replies
kept him alive in the public recollection. Living practically in exile, two
hundred and fifty miles from Paris in space and a fortnight in time, his
problem was to manage by some feat of intellectual prestidigitation to seem
to be leading Parisian public opinion while in reality following it. For
twenty-five years he performed this sort of Indian rope trick. Voltaire, the
cunning Voltaire, needed all his cunning not to be forgotten, and it is a
testimony to the real success of the *Encyclopédie* that he saw self-advantage
in being associated with it.

Although Volume IV gives the impression of settling down to a somewhat less controversial tone, it must not be supposed that fire and color
were lacking. As always, the editors used the columns to flog their enemies,
as in the anti-Jansenist article by D'Alembert on '*Convulsionnaires,*' or the
article on 'Controversy' in which Diderot ironically and solemnly cites the

authority of the *Dictionnaire de Trévoux*.[52] As always, there was the desire
for economic and social improvement, as in Diderot's wondering whether
there could not be found in the French dominions a plant with an under-
bark fiber suitable for weaving, or in the long article on forced labor on the
public highways (*Corvée*), in which the author suggested ways for increasing efficiency while reducing the hardships caused the peasants.[53] As
always, there were the admonitory articles on correct scientific method,
such as Diderot's on 'Credulity' and 'Belief' (*Croire*), articles which were
likely to bemuse their readers concerning the basis for faith in the evidences
of the Christian religion. As always, there were long and solemn articles
on subjects dealing with the Old Testament, as, for example, the article
'Deluge,' which raised about as many common-sense questions about the
Flood as the article in Volume I had done about Noah's Ark. And, as
always, there were Diderot's own contributions, colorful, volatile, impudent,
sometimes profound.

Diderot's use of irony and of what Americans call the 'dead pan' is
well shown in his article on 'Damnation.' Damnation, he wrote, signifies
'eternal punishment in Hell. The dogma of damnation or of eternal punishment is clearly revealed by Scripture. Therefore it is no longer a question of
seeking to determine by reason whether or not it is possible for a finite
being to do God an infinite injury; or whether or not the eternalness of
punishment is not more contrary to His goodness than conformable to His
justice; or whether, because it has pleased Him to ordain an infinite reward
for good, He has or has not been able to ordain an infinite punishment for
evil. In place of becoming entangled in a web of captious reasonings, likely
to shake a faith not well established, one should submit to the authority of
the Holy Books and the decisions of the Church, and, trembling, effect
one's salvation, ceaselessly considering that the enormity of the offense is
in direct proportion to the dignity of the offended, and in inverse proportion
to the offender, and [ceaselessly considering] what must be the enormity of
our disobedience, if that of the first man could be effaced by nothing less
than the blood of the Son of God.'[54]

Intentionally challenging as was this kind of article, deceptively planting
doubt while saying the unexceptionable, Diderot seems to have felt that
its apparent conformity needed justification. In this volume, he himself
wrote that 'one should not suppose that sages like Socrates, Plato, and
Cicero, and others, always spoke according to the ideas of the people:
nevertheless they were sometimes obliged to conform to them in order not

to be accused of atheism.' [55] Surely for contemporary readers of the *Encyclopédie* the application of this remark to certain living 'sages' must have been unavoidable.

Among Diderot's contributions were his customary articles of preponderantly literary interest, the articles on word definition and analysis of synonyms, the import of which was primarily psychological or belletristic rather than informative. Often Diderot fitted the rhythm of his prose to the mood of what he was describing, so that he not only explained his subject but represented it, as has been strikingly brought out in regard to the article 'Enjoyment' (*Jouissance*).[56] In Volume IV Diderot wrote an article of this sort, sensitively analyzing the various meanings of the word 'delicious' and especially describing the deliciousness of sinking into repose. Grimm called it 'one of the most precious things written in French,' and a modern critic, who specializes in the study of Diderot and of Baudelaire, speaks of it as a completely modern analysis of the consciousness of the fleeting and the evanescent.[57]

Two of Diderot's articles that Grimm particularly commended were long ones devoted to the philosophical schools of the Cynics and Cyrenaics.[58] These exercises by Diderot in the history of philosophy were not without precedent, for he had written the long article on 'Aristotelianism' in Volume I. In Volumes II and III, however, he had tended to delegate these tasks to the Abbé Pestré, a shadowy figure who, after the De Prades affair, fades out of the *Encyclopédie* in the unobtrusive way that Alice observed in the Cheshire cat. From that point on, Diderot took over this assignment. His articles were so highly regarded that Naigeon, thirty-five years later, collected and republished seventy-three of them in a successor of Diderot's *Encyclopédie,* the *Encyclopédie méthodique,* which first appeared in 1781 and ran to 229 volumes before it desisted in 1832. In practically every case the information in these articles by Diderot was freely borrowed from a recent history of philosophy written in Latin by a German named Brucker, a fact which Diderot did not attempt to conceal.[59] Naigeon says that Diderot regretted that the pressure of time necessitated his following Brucker, even to the point of adopting his arrangement and organization of subject matter.[60] But it is still true that Diderot put enough of himself into these articles to make them more than a mere transcription, and a French student of the *Encyclopédie* has declared, even after making allowance for Brucker and another source named Deslandes, that Diderot is practically the creator of the history of philosophy in France.[61] Moreover, his personal additions not infrequently have a biographical interest. In the articles on 'Cynics' and

'Cyrenaics,' for example, written as they were not later than mid-1754, Diderot betrays sentiments that probably betoken a growing antagonism to the austere views of his friend Rousseau.[62]

The *Encyclopédie* was a growing success. What is more, Diderot knew it. At least it is tempting to infer so from the fact that about this time he demanded greater remuneration from his publishers, as we shall see, and also from the fact that about this period he refused in an amusingly high-and-mighty way a contribution from one of the century's greatest names. The Abbé Trublet, who was a sort of literary representative of the famous Fontenelle, tells the story: 'MM. d'Alembert and Diderot appearing to desire to have something of M. de Fontenelle's for the *Encyclopédie,* I had delivery made to the second [i.e. Diderot] of the fragments on the Greek dramatic poets, the only manuscript of M. de Fontenelle that I then had, he being still alive [he died a centenarian in 1757]. Some time afterwards I asked M. Diderot whether he would use them. He replied to me with vivacity that he would take good care *not* to insert in the *Encyclopédie* a writing in which Aeschylus was treated as being crazy; and it is true that M. de Fontenelle said that approximately, although less crudely.'[63] It was like Diderot to respond emphatically and 'with vivacity.' Thus did its editor, in his reverence for the classics, defend Aeschylus at the cost of rejecting for the *Encyclopédie* a contribution from one of the most famous men of letters in France.

CHAPTER 17

Business and Pleasure: A New Contract,
Mme Geoffrin's Salon, Sophie Volland

IN LATE 1754, with four volumes of the *Encyclopédie* off the press, Diderot could look back with gratification upon a number of arduous, eventful, and productive years. Not only had he borne the principal burden of editing a work of formidable size, but he had also found time in the years just preceding to write some influential books. Now he took time off for a visit to Langres, the first he is known to have made for twelve years and the last, it turned out, while his father was living. Having left his wife and year-old daughter in the apartment on the Rue de l'Estrapade, he spent at least ten days in Langres, where, among other things, he lent five hundred livres to a local husbandman and stood godfather to a Caroillon child, destined one day to be brother-in-law to Diderot's own daughter.[1] It is apparent that the Langres folk still thought of Diderot as being conscientiously able to accept the duties of a Christian godfather. It would be interesting, and more to the point, to know why Diderot, too, thought so.

It is quite evident that Diderot had an enjoyable time at Langres. His letter of thanks, a very long one addressed to all his relatives and friends, was that of a man writing to people he likes. It was written with a touch of robustiousness and vulgarity by no means foreign to the Diderot style, but in this instance specially tailored to please the taste of unfastidious provincial folk. It is a little as though Diderot thought of himself as writing to the people in a painting by Jan Steen. And a succeeding letter shows how thoroughly he had renewed old friendships. In it he describes to the Caroillon family how, upon his return to Paris, he shamelessly ingratiated himself, in their behalf, with a wealthy old Parisian aunt of theirs, and goes on exuberantly to speak of his hopes for the future marriage of his daughter (aged one and a half!) with a Caroillon son (aged nine), a marriage which, in fact, eventually came to pass.[2]

Diderot has left a vivid picture of the family circle at Langres in a dialogue entitled 'Conversation of a Father with his Children, or Concerning the Danger of Putting Oneself above the Law' (*Entretien d'un père avec ses enfants, ou du danger de se mettre au-dessus des lois*).[3] The discussion gave the author an opportunity to describe the compassionate but evenhanded justice of his father, the generous and tender impulses of his sister, the harsh and unbending qualities of his *abbé* brother, and his own magnanimous and somewhat quixotic impulses. Although written much later, it must surely describe the family group of this very time. Moreover, this lively and endearing dialogue probably reports a conversation much as it really occurred, for Diderot, while very imaginative and creative in matters of imagery and scientific thought, was remarkably uninventive in regard to plots and characters. He could observe meticulously, he could report with great verve, and once he had begun to take flight, he could soar. But it has been remarked that he frequently needed the memory of a real event or a real person to inspire him, so that it very often turns out that the stories he tells actually happened.[4] In this dialogue he mentions some of the persons by their real names, such as the family notary Jean-Louis Dubois, not bothering to conceal their identity even when he knew that the piece was going to be published. Therefore the presumption is all the greater that this conversation, which concerned difficult cases of conscience — Diderot loved to discuss difficult cases of conscience — really took place.

While at Langres Diderot consulted his relatives concerning his relations with the publishers of the *Encyclopédie*, even to the point of receiving elaborate legal advice from the notary Dubois. Thus he writes to his family, 'Scarcely had I returned to Paris when my publishers were informed of it and a day appointed for discussing our interests. We all put so much heat and so little reason into our first interview that I thought we would not be seeing one another again. There wasn't a single one of the articles of the contract drawn up by M. Dubois that was not attacked.' In this letter Diderot wrote as if he was determined to retire to Langres if he did not secure what he demanded.[5] But after an elaborate negotiation, involving many intermediaries and numerous compromises, a new contract was signed on 20 December 1754.

The preamble of this document recounts that Diderot had pointed out that the amount of work in the *Encyclopédie* had increased since the previous contract had been signed. Therefore the publishers agreed that beginning with the fifth volume they would pay Diderot 2500 livres a volume, 1500 livres payable when the first copy for a volume, the other 1000 when the last, was handed in. Moreover, within three months of the publication of the last volume of letterpress, Diderot was to receive a lump sum of 20,000 livres. All books hitherto supplied him as sources or for reference in editing the *Encyclopédie* were henceforth to be regarded as his property — these books were the backbone of the library he later sold to Catherine II of Russia — and the publishers put in writing that 'the said M. Diderot will be in the future, as he has been in the past, editor of all the parts of the *Encyclopédie*.'[6] It might be remarked that no previous document had so precisely defined Diderot's position.

About this time, probably because the new contract made it financially feasible, the Diderot family moved to more spacious quarters. For the remaining thirty years of Diderot's life the family lived on the fourth floor (fifth, American style) of a building in which Diderot also rented space for his study on the floor above, directly beneath the roof. The building stood on the corner of the Rue Taranne, which no longer exists, and the Rue Saint-Benoît, which still does. Were the building in which Diderot lived still standing — it was pulled down in 1866 — it would be on the Boulevard Saint-Germain directly across the street from the Café de Flore, in the heart of the domain of the existentialists. A fine statue of Diderot, done in bronze by Jean Gautherin in 1885, stands near the site.[7]

A phrase in his thank-you letter to Langres suggests that Diderot had come to distrust D'Alembert. 'I don't know how it was,' he wrote, 'that during this interval impatience did not seize me and I did not send them packing to all the devils, them, the *Encyclopédie*, their papers, and their contract; *a little more confidence in the probity of my colleague*, and that would have done it.'[8] This must mean that Diderot suspected D'Alembert of being willing to supplant him as principal editor. The lack of cordiality between the two men ultimately became marked enough to be noted by Marmontel. 'The house of Baron d'Holbach and, since some little time, that of Helvétius, were the rendezvous for this society, composed partly of the cream of Mme Geoffrin's guests and partly of some individuals whom Mme Geoffrin deemed too bold and too venturesome to be admitted to her dinners. . . .

'I have never known very well why D'Alembert held himself aloof from the society of which I speak. He and Diderot, associates in exertion and in glory in the enterprise of the *Encyclopédie*, had at first been cordially united, but they were no longer. They spoke of each other with much esteem, but they were not intimate and they scarcely saw each other any more. I never dared to ask them the reason for it.' [9]

The year 1754 was a particularly auspicious one for D'Alembert, for in the course of it he received the greatest honor his writings could earn in France, election to the French Academy. This institution, which had been founded by the great Cardinal Richelieu, existed under the direct patronage of the king of France, and inclusion among its forty members conferred such prestige that even princes of the royal blood, such as the Comte de Clermont in this very year, sought election to it. One of the Academy's most endearing and most pathetic conceits has ever been that its membership confers immortality. In the buildings of the Institut de France, on the eighteenth-century doors to the charming room in which the Academy does its work, there is wrought in intricate and garlanded design the phrase *A l'Immortalité*. It is scarcely necessary to remark, however, that laurel leaves also, like the men who wore them, can turn to dust.

D'Alembert fully deserved his election. He was more than a man of science, France's greatest living mathematician; he was also a talented and influential man of letters, as witness his 'Preliminary Discourse' to the *Encyclopédie,* as well as other writings collected and published in 1753 under the title of *Mélanges de littérature, d'histoire, et de philosophie.* Yet his election could not help but be widely interpreted as more than simply a personal recognition. It was also a victory for the *Encyclopédie* and for the new 'philosophy.' The prestige of the new outlook increased in step with his, and the fact that he had gained admittance to the citadel of French letters not unnaturally caused the *philosophes* to hope, and their enemies to dread, that this was to be only their first entry into the Academy. D'Alembert's election increased — if anything was still able to increase — the self-confidence and self-esteem of a group that was rapidly becoming a kind of party or sect.

This tendency of the *philosophes* to coalesce into a coterie became a subject of frequent and exasperated remark during the 1750's. Fréron in his *Année Littéraire* rarely let the opportunity pass to complain of it, and even the Abbé Raynal, who was more a friend than an enemy of the *philosophes,* remarked in his private news letter during 1754 upon 'the harsh tone and bad temper that some men of letters of today mistake for philosophy. . . . If the tone of criticism is abandoned [he went on], it is for the purpose of elevating to the third heaven the authors of the *Encyclopédie* and the author of the *Histoire naturelle* [Buffon]; aside from them there is nothing praiseworthy any more. They it is who have taught us to think and to write, who have re-established good taste and philosophy, and who preserve them. Nevertheless, one asks all the time, what have they done? These gentlemen, no doubt esteemworthy by virtue of their knowledge, wit, and manners, degrade their philosophy by a domineering and lawmaking tone, by an affectation of arrogating to themselves a despotism over literary matters, and by their propensity to burn incense to one another everywhere and endlessly. . . .' [10]

This flattering sense of being one of an elite was nurtured by the *salon*, a social institution of peculiar efficacy in generating a spirit of group cohesiveness. Given the centralization of French social and intellectual life, at least since the beginning of the seventeenth century, the Parisian *salon* has always been, like a gambling house, a place in which fortunes are made or lost. Often a *salon* has been of incalculable assistance in launching an author or, inversely, in wrecking another; and in no epoch was this more evidently true than in the eighteenth century. For that was a sociable age, and the ideas that were transforming society and predisposing it for change were ideas freely canvassed and exchanged in the agreeable leisure of these social hours. The connotation of the word '*salon*,' used in this special sense, was of an open house the purpose of which was intellectual discussion. Usually the word implied, too, that the hospitality was extended by a lady, acting as 'ringmistress,' or, as Henry James put it, directing 'through a smiling land, between suggestive shores, a sinuous stream of talk.' Although of course D'Holbach's was a *salon*, too, the more typical eighteenth-century *salons* were those of Mme du Deffand, Mme Geoffrin, Mlle de Lespinasse, and Mme Necker.

It took a great deal of skill and tact to run a *salon* successfully, to gain the respect of temperamental authors and intellectuals, to make them want to come again, to be able to steer a conversation without being obvious, to govern discussions so adroitly that they became neither anarchical nor contentious, to draw out the timid and circumvent the bores. No one was more proficient, more gentle but firm, in the exercise of these skills than Mme Geoffrin, so that her house came to be nicknamed, in deference both to her prestige and to her authority, 'The Kingdom of Rue Saint-Honoré.' [11] It is still standing, hard by the Place Vendôme and the Place de la Concorde, this house which became a rallying point for 'philosophy,' especially by virtue of the famous dinners she gave for men of letters every Wednesday. Artists were fed on Mondays.

This is not to say that discussions at Mme Geoffrin's were ever so bold

and fearless as they were at D'Holbach's. Mme Geoffrin was rather timorous
and very cautious, so that, as Marmontel remarked, she held Diderot, the
most original and prolific thinker of them all, at arm's length. At Mme
Geoffrin's, wrote Marmontel, the *philosophes* were 'led about and held in
leading strings.' [12] But this very prudence and timidity worked to the profit of
the Encyclopedists. 'At the moment when her *salon* was being opened,' wrote
a distinguished editor of the *Revue des Deux Mondes,* 'those who were
going to form the army of the Encyclopedists were still isolated, strangers,
or hostile to one another, and little known or little appreciated by the public.
They grouped themselves at Mme Geoffrin's: at her house they found a
center of reunion where they learned to get together, to support one another,
and to make common cause. There they submitted to discipline. A lover of
propriety and moderation, the mistress of the house prevented them from
colliding too violently with public opinion or governmental power, and she
saved them from the danger of ruining themselves by their own impatience.' [13] This is well said. It may be supplemented by a police report of
1751 about Mme Geoffrin, giving some of the down-to-earth aspects of
operating a *salon:*

> There assembles every afternoon at this lady's house a circle of wits, among
> whom are especially M. de Fontenelle and Helvétius, Farmer General, who are
> her friends.
> She often provides meals.
> Also she sells the rarest new books; that is to say, the authors send her a dozen
> copies and she takes pleasure in making her friends buy them.[14]

The functioning of a literary circle resembling that of Mme Geoffrin
is reflected in the 'Memoirs of M. de Voltaire' by Oliver Goldsmith, who
claimed to have been an eyewitness of a spirited dispute involving Fontenelle,
Diderot, and Voltaire. This must have occurred, if anything like it really
did take place, during 1755, when Goldsmith was in France. It would be
pleasant to think that Diderot and Goldsmith were acquainted, but the
latter's story is demonstrably inaccurate in part (for Voltaire was not in
Paris in 1755 and never met Diderot until 1778), leaving one to fear that
perhaps it is false *in toto*.[15]

For Diderot the importance of Mme Geoffrin's *salon* was chiefly indirect.
It existed. It was valuable. It provided a powerful support for the new
outlook represented by the *Encyclopédie*. But it functioned almost exclusively
without his presence, whether he voluntarily abstained because he disliked

the constraint that Mme Geoffrin put upon her guests, or whether he was
made to feel that she liked him better absent. Certainly there is no evidence
of antagonism between them, and she was exceedingly generous with him
in respect to money. Yet she distrusted him, for both his manners and ideas
made him difficult to manage. As Marmontel remarked, Diderot was not
admitted to her dinners. 'Diderot did not go to Mme Geoffrin's,' wrote
another of his contemporaries. 'She feared his impetuosity, the rashness of
his opinions, supported, when he was aroused, by a fiery and stirring eloquence.' [16] And she herself, writing in 1774 to her protégé, the King of
Poland, spoke of Diderot in cool and measured terms. 'He is an upright
man,' she wrote, 'but he is wrongheaded. And he is so wrongly constituted
that he neither sees nor hears anything as it really is. He is always like a
man in a dream, and who believes everything that he has dreamed.' [17]

At about this period Diderot made the acquaintance of a man whose recollection of their meeting imparts precious information as to what kind of
first impression Diderot was likely to make. The new acquaintance was
Charles de Brosses, a magistrate from Dijon, who had asked his former
schoolmate, Buffon, for an introduction to Diderot, 'that extraordinary
metaphysical head.' 'He is an agreeable fellow,' reported De Brosses, 'very
charming, very likable, a great philosopher, a great arguer, but dealing in
perpetual digressions. He made a good twenty-five of them in my room
yesterday, from nine o'clock to one.' [18]

De Brosses was a man of broad intellectual attainments, and he and
Diderot quickly became very friendly. Diderot almost importunately solicited
from him for publication in the *Encyclopédie* the manuscript of a long
article on 'Etymology.' [19] As De Brosses later described the episode, Diderot
kept the manuscript for two or three years in spite of De Brosses's reiterated
requests that it be returned for revision. The article that finally came out on
this subject in the *Encyclopédie,* however, was written not by De Brosses
but by Turgot, who evidently had used the De Brosses manuscript as a
starting point. De Brosses was rather startled at this outcome, although he
did not question that Turgot had acted in the best of faith. He was inclined,
however, to accuse Diderot of 'negligence' and thoughtlessness.[20] Here we
have a glimpse of the careless and nonchalant side of Diderot, whose possession of such disconcerting although sometimes endearing qualities made
dealing with him an experience not infrequently frustrating.

At the time that Diderot made the acquaintance of De Brosses, the
Academy of Dijon had just announced a prize contest on the subject, 'What

is the origin of inequality among men, and is it authorized by natural law?' Since De Brosses was a member of the Academy of Dijon, Diderot's conversations with him naturally came around to this topic. The subject appealed strongly to Diderot, and yet he did not compete for the prize. De Brosses reveals why: 'Diderot talks to me a great deal about the subject of this prize. He finds it very fine but impossible to deal with under a monarchy. He is a daring philosopher, with a vengeance.' [21]

Diderot's friend Jean-Jacques felt no such restrictions. He submitted an essay which, though it did not win the prize, nevertheless became one of his most famous works. In view of the foregoing evidence of Diderot's preoccupation with the subject, it is interesting to speculate upon just how much he may have influenced this essay. Rousseau declared in his *Confessions* that the *Discourse on Inequality* was the 'work that was more to Diderot's taste than any other of my writings, and for which his counsel was the most useful to me.' Somewhat later Rousseau even identified a passage in the *Discourse on Inequality* that Diderot had written, but by this time Jean-Jacques was no longer of the persuasion that Diderot had been really helpful. 'It is certain,' he wrote, 'that M. Diderot always abused my confidence and my compliance in order to impart to my writings a harsh tone and a gloomy air that they no longer had as soon as he ceased to direct me and I was left completely to myself.' [22] Recent scholarship is inclined to the view that there may indeed have been in Diderot a vein of primitivism fiercer and more stubborn than in Rousseau himself.[23] Building upon Rousseau's own admission, it is generally supposed that Diderot's share in the ideas incorporated into Rousseau's *Discourse on the Origin of Inequality* is considerable.[24]

As the *Encyclopédie* went into the letter 'E,' one of Diderot's contributions was an article intended to be published under the title of 'Encaustic.' [25] For some reason he decided to publish it separately, and accordingly there appeared anonymously in a very small edition in 1755, *L'Histoire et le secret de la peinture en cire* ('The History and Secret of Painting in Wax').[26] The article 'Encaustic' as it appeared in Volume V was done by another hand.[27]

This rather recondite subject was nevertheless topical because of the considerable discussion in Paris just at this time as to precisely what had been the method used by the ancients for painting in wax and for fixing the colors by the application of heat. The technique is very difficult, but gives special effects and is of extraordinary durability. It has been practiced today in this country with remarkable technical and aesthetic success by

Karl Zerbe of the Boston Museum School of Fine Arts. One of Diderot's acquaintances, an artist named Bachelier, thought he had rediscovered the ancient technique in 1749, but had done nothing about publicizing it. In 1753 the Comte de Caylus published the first of a series of papers in which he claimed to have deciphered the cryptic passages in Pliny the Elder regarding this ancient technique and therefore to be the first to recover the long-lost method.[28]

Caylus, however, made a mystery of the actual technique employed in duplicating the ancient method. This sort of obscurantism in matters relating to the sciences or the arts, indeed any sort of obscurantism, always infuriated Diderot, and in consequence his pamphlet was as much aimed against Caylus as the *Letter on the Blind* had been a rebuke of Réaumur. The first words of the new work were: 'Nothing is more contrary to the progress of knowledge than mystery.'[29] Then he attempted to prove that neither Bachelier, in 1749, nor Caylus had really come upon the true ancient encaustic, but that Bachelier had since discovered it in further experiments. Since Bachelier was trying to keep the discovery secret, Diderot nonchalantly put himself into the invidious position of revealing a secret that was not his property. 'I do not doubt,' he wrote, 'but what M. Bachelier bears me a grudge for publishing his secret. . . . But I have my own character and my own fashion of thinking, which I find satisfactory and from which I shall not withdraw for the sake of M. Bachelier. What I know of his methods of painting I owe solely to the pains I took to teach myself regarding it. I promised no one to keep the secret.'[30] Diderot's attitude was consistent with his freely bestowing upon the public his own ideas for the improvement of barrel organs. Nevertheless, with a characteristic impetuosity and lack of second thought and with even a certain officiousness, he deeply disobliged both Caylus and Bachelier by what he claimed to be his zeal for the public good.

The Comte was a wealthy amateur and expert who was a sort of dictator, apparently a crotchety and crabbed one, in the world of art.[31] One can well imagine what he thought of Diderot. When an Italian correspondent innocently happened to inquire in 1761 how Diderot was, Caylus replied, 'I know Diderot very little because I do not esteem him, but I believe he is well. There are certain *bougres* who don't die, while, to the misfortune of letters in Europe, honest folk like Melot [Anicet Melot (1697–1759), a French antiquarian] die in their prime.'[32] And what Diderot thought about Caylus was expressed in an epitaph Diderot wrote in 1765. Caylus had expressed the desire to be buried in an Etruscan urn that was in his garden, and Diderot wrote, in a very well-turned couplet:[33]

> Ci-gît un antiquaire acariâtre et brusque;
> Ah! qu'il est bien logé dans cette cruche étrusque! *

The pamphlet on 'Encaustic' is characteristic of Diderot's point of view and redolent of his personality. Time and again he emphasizes the importance of disseminating knowledge.[34] 'If it happens,' he writes, 'that an invention favorable to the progress of the arts and sciences comes to my knowledge, I burn to divulge it: that is my mania. Born communicative as much as it is possible to be, it is too bad that I was not born more inventive: I would have told my ideas to the first comer. Had I but one secret for all my stock in trade, it seems to me that if the general good should require the publication of it, I should prefer to die honestly on a street corner, my back against a post, than to let my fellow men suffer. . . .'[35] And he wishes that there might be established a royal academy of the mechanical arts.[36] Moreover, Diderot's interest in the applied, the factual, and the practical (as well as in the generalized and the purely theoretical) is abundantly shown in this booklet. Here is a man who knows as much as any man in his day about the chemistry of paints. Here is an author fully aware of the technical procedures of artists, as well as of their problems of composition and aesthetic intent. The *History and Secret of Painting in Wax* reveals also the classicist, able to translate and analyze Pliny's elliptic and obscure remarks. Finally, in this pamphlet — which Grimm described as 'written with much fire, a rapid pace, and much gaiety,' and which Fréron declared to be 'diffuse and overburdened with notes, some of which try to be scientific and the others amusing' — we find the subjective and the personal starting out at one, especially in the notes.[37] 'There's a sentence,' Diderot comments concerning a paragraph composed of one single sentence of eighteen lines, 'very long and tortuous, which is going to be found displeasing. Were it the only one, I would correct it.'[38] At another place he notes that 'All that follows now seems to me to be out of place; but I have not the courage to delete it.' Then in the next note, 'If I continue in this vein, I shall not finish in a hundred pages what could be said in ten, and I shall be reproached for having been obscure and diffuse, two faults that usually go together.'[39]

---

* Here lies a crabbed and brusque antiquarian.
Oh, how appropriately lodged is he in this Etruscan jug!

And what could be more personal and more revelatory of Diderot's sensitiveness than the following?

'. . . we take as great pains to destroy [our masterpieces in painting and sculpture] as they [the Ancients] did to preserve theirs. They had a varnish that they applied to their pictures, their bronzes, and their marbles . . . . Regularly every year we rub the skin off ours with sponges full of a hard and gritty fluid. . . . On the days of this cruel operation I flee from the Tuileries as one flees from a public place on a day of execution.' [40]

The controversy over encaustic painting created some stir and inspired a pamphlet ridiculing Diderot's. Its translated title is *The New Art of Painting in Cheese, Invented for Carrying Out the Laudable Project of Gradually Finding Ways of Painting Inferior to Those Now in Existence.*[41] This effusion was by an anonymous author whom Fréron found diverting and Grimm thought to be 'in the worst taste since Attila, King of the Huns.' [42] Irony upon so lordly a scale apparently discouraged other champions from entering the contest. It was all very well for Grimm to grumble, but he and his brothers of kindred spirit did not choose to reply.

It was about this time that Diderot again fell in love, suddenly and violently and enduringly. Little is known of the lady, but evidently she possessed a character very different from and much finer than that of Mme de Puisieux. None of Sophie Volland's letters to Diderot is extant, so that the impression we have of her is very like overhearing one end of a protracted telephone conversation. Incomplete and distorted as this way of knowing her personality inevitably is, it is quite apparent that she was modest where Mme de Puisieux was conceited, and self-effacing where Mme de Puisieux was self-assertive. Certainly Diderot found in Sophie Volland the qualities necessary for a lasting attachment, an attachment — attenuated perhaps, but never broken off in bitterness — enduring the rest of their lives. Sophie Volland died five months before Diderot, and in her will she left him the keepsakes of a long devotion. 'I give and bequeath to M. Diderot seven little volumes of Montaigne's *Essays* bound in red morocco, together with a ring that I call my Pauline.' [43]

'Sophie' was a special name. Not the Louise-Henriette of her baptism, but the name given to her by Diderot himself in allusion, by means of the French form of the Greek word, to the wisdom which seemed to him the quintessence of her qualities.[44] It is as Sophie Volland that she has become posthumously famous, the inspirer and recipient of letters unexcelled in their revelation both of a particularly interesting social milieu and of an infinitely rich, complex, and humane personality. 'Grudge not the elderly spinster her existence, then,' wrote Carlyle in his essay on 'Diderot.' 'Say not she lived in vain.'

Sophie Volland came from a family, perhaps a wealthy one, of the middle class. Her father, Jean-Robert Volland, who died before the lovers met, had been an important functionary in the administration of the government monopoly of salt, and was closely associated, both in business and by marriage, with the class of financiers and tax farmers whose enormous incomes tended to make them the freest spenders of the *ancien régime*. The Volland family was not dedicated to this gospel of conspicuous waste, but the father had bought an estate and built a country house at Isle-sur-Marne, near the small city of Vitry-le-François — to which Sophie's mother spirited her away for half of each year in order to separate her from Diderot — and it is also evident that the family lived comfortably in their town house on the Rue des Vieux-Augustins. This was in a quarter now much run down but at that time conservatively fashionable, close by the Place des Victoires and the grandiose and imposing church of Sainte-Eustache.[45] There is some indication in Diderot's letters that the family when he knew it was less prosperous than it had been.

Sophie had two married sisters, and it is remarkable, considering her family's affluence, that she was not married too. Perhaps, as one biographer of Diderot has surmised, some obscure but unforgotten scandal had impaired her matrimonial chances.[46] When Diderot met her, probably in 1755, perhaps in 1756, she was about forty years of age, three years younger than Diderot, having been born on 27 November 1716.[47] What little is known of her mainly concerns the state of her health, which evidently was exceedingly precarious, so much so that Diderot was constantly fussing over her. 'Very warm days are succeeded by very cool evenings,' he wrote her. 'Watch your health. Don't expose yourself to the evening damp. You know what a weak little cat's chest you have and what terrible colds you are subject to.' Two weeks later he wrote, 'Adieu, my dear. I kiss your forehead, your eyes, your mouth, and your dry little hand, which pleases me quite as much as a plump one.'[48] Biographers, having so little to go on, make much of the dry little hand (*menotte*). And they are inclined to speak of Sophie's spectacles in the spirit of Dorothy Parker's remark about girls who wear glasses. 'It is from my workshop at Le Breton's that I have been writing to you for the past two hours this long, boring letter that you will have a good deal of trouble in deciphering. Just omit, pass over, whatever makes you rub your glasses on your sleeve,' Diderot wrote upon one occasion. And upon another, imagining them gathered together at the country house:

'I hear you all chattering, I see you all in your favorite attitudes, I would paint you if I had the time. My dear one would be standing erect behind her mother's armchair, facing her sister, and with her spectacles on her nose.'[49]

Had more of Diderot's letters to Sophie Volland remained in existence, we would not now be so desperately deficient in information regarding her. They are known to have numbered more than five hundred and fifty, but Mlle Volland herself destroyed all but one hundred and eighty-seven.[50] Moreover, the first one hundred and thirty-four, which might very well have been the most interesting of all, have disappeared, and the earliest one we can consult is dated May 1759. We are thus reduced to approximations when attempting to fix the date when the acquaintance began. Mme de Vandeul asserts that her father developed this passion in 1757, when Mme Diderot and little Angélique were on a visit to Langres.[51] But Diderot's own letters suggest 1755 as the date of meeting. In 1767 he writes somewhat vaguely in terms of 'ten to twelve years,'[52] though a year later we find him still talking of a dozen years.[53] There is the same indefiniteness in this passage from a letter of 1765, regarding a carriage trip on the morrow: 'I shall have the pleasure of passing the whole day with her whom I love (which is not surprising, for who would not love her?) but whom I love, after eight or nine years, with the same passion with which she inspired me on the first day that I saw her. We were alone that day, both of us leaning on the little green table. I remember what I said to you, what you replied to me. Oh, the happy time it was, the time of that green table!'[54] Earlier references are more precise. One of September 1760 remarks that it will soon be five years since they met; and in October of 1759 he writes, 'It was four years ago that you appeared beautiful in my eyes. Today I find you more beautiful than ever. This is the magic of constancy, the most difficult and the rarest of our virtues.'[55]

A good deal of ink has been spilled, perhaps rather needlessly, in speculation as to whether Diderot and Sophie Volland were really lovers or just good friends. Were Diderot's affections 'platonic'? This is certainly a problem of appropriate biographical interest, but one concerning which a non-French biographer might well defer to French *expertise*. It may be reported, therefore, that persons deserving to be regarded as connoisseurs in such matters, as, for example, a member of the Académie Goncourt or, for another, the author of a book entitled *La Vie amoureuse de Diderot,* have weightily considered the evidence. The majority conclude — as most people would have assumed from the start — that Sophie allowed Diderot what is delicately termed 'the ultimate liberties.' [56]

Much of what is known about Diderot, the most revealing and the most precious information, comes from his correspondence with Sophie Volland. It is posterity's loss that, in contrast, so little is known of Sophie herself. Was the quality of her mind what Diderot thought it to be, or did he mistake the echoing of his own ideas as the evidence of a powerful intelligence in her? It would not have been the first or last time that Diderot admired himself by seeing in a person or a book something that was not there but was simply a projection of his own personality. Besides, Diderot was given to some exaggeration in these matters, as when he wrote in his 'Essay on Women,' 'When one writes of women, one must dip one's pen in the rainbow and dry the line with the dust of butterflies' wings.' [57] A reader of the letters may easily sentimentalize with Diderot about Sophie Volland and perhaps invest her with a character and characteristics that she is not positively known to have possessed. But at the very least it can be said with certainty that Diderot's second mistress was better than the first. And it can also be said, in view of the contents of these letters, that she can scarcely be thought a prude.

CHAPTER 18

'Changing the General Way of Thinking'

Diderot was far from well during the closing months of 1755. In late September he alluded to his illness in a letter to Caroillon at Langres: 'I have been and still am pretty badly off in my own affairs. I have had my whole chest affected. A dry cough. Terrible sweats, difficulty in speaking and breathing. But things are going much better, at the price of a drastic remedy: bread, water, and milk for my whole diet. Milk in the morning, milk at noon, milk at "tea-time," milk at supper. That's a lot of milk.'[1] In circumstances so adverse — and for most Frenchmen (save perhaps M. Mendès-France), to have to cope with that much milk is real adversity — Diderot continued his task of editing the *Encyclopédie* and writing articles for it. In particular, he composed his article 'Encyclopedia' for Volume V during this difficult time. Rousseau mentioned the article as being 'the admiration of all Paris,' and then went on to say, 'what will increase your astonishment when you read it is the fact that he wrote it while ill.'[2]

Despite this sickness, Volume V was delivered to subscribers during the first days of November.[3] Like its sisters, it was a portly folio volume, a thousand pages and more, and carried the alphabet to ESY. Its title page took cognizance of D'Alembert's new honors, mentioning that he was a member of the French Academy, the Royal Academy of Belles-Lettres of Sweden, and the Institute of Bologna. As usual, new contributors were welcomed to the fold, especially Voltaire, whose articles on 'Elegance,' 'Eloquence,' and *'Esprit'* were not only elegant but also concise, a virtue not always characterizing the *Encyclopédie*'s contents.

Once again a lengthy memoir by D'Alembert formed the introduction. This one concerned Montesquieu, who had died in February 1755 — Diderot, incidentally, happening to be the only man of letters present at the funeral.[4] Montesquieu had never engaged very deeply in the cause of the *Encyclopédie*, but with the French proclivity for making political capital out of funerals, the editors appropriated him. Their excuse was that he was a contributor, having written the article on 'Taste' (*Goût*), a rather mediocre fragment as it turned out. Posterity is accustomed to regard the author of *L'Esprit des lois* with a good deal of veneration, as did, for example, the authors of the *Federalist Papers,* but in his own lifetime and in his own country conservatives looked upon Montesquieu with great disapprobation because he seemed to be too fond of talking about the nature of liberty and too pointed in implying that France had very little of it. Moreover, his positive and factual rather than theological approach to the study of history and politics offended many. To reactionaries Montesquieu seemed radical, and it was characteristic of the editors of the *Encyclopédie* to desire to make him their own. This they did not only in their introductory memoir but also in the course of an article by Diderot on 'Eclecticism,' written like many others of his with a sudden flashing swoop from the objective to the personal which seems so out of place in a work of reference but which is probably one of the major causes of this one's success. Having commented morosely upon society's neglect and abuse of genius, he remarked, 'I wrote these reflections on 11 February 1755, upon returning from the funeral of one of our greatest men, overcome by the loss that the nation and the world of letters had sustained in his person, and profoundly shocked by the persecutions that he had undergone.' [5]

One of the principal articles in Volume V was written by Diderot on 'Natural Right' (*Droit naturel*). This was a subject in the vein of the great natural lawyers of the preceding century, men like Grotius and Pufendorf, so that a highly competent political philosopher has been able to say with some justification of Diderot's article that it was 'a rhetorical flourish with conventional ideas.' [6] Still, this was a topic difficult to discuss with frankness in the France of the eighteenth century. Diderot did discuss it. His article, being in the tradition of the natural law school, contributed to keeping concepts current that later provided the inspiration for documents like the Declaration of Independence and the Declaration of the Rights of Man and of the Citizen. Diderot wrote of man's dignity and — in 1755 — of his 'inalienable rights,' [7] and frequently referred to 'the general will.' This phrase has become so deeply associated with Jean-Jacques Rousseau and his idea of the social contract that Montesquieu's earlier use of the term in *L'Esprit des lois* seems to have become generally forgotten.[8] In Volume V of the *Encyclopédie* both Diderot, in his article on *'Droit naturel,'* and Rousseau, in his on 'Economy,' used the term with some of the identical overtones of meaning

that are found in the *Social Contract* seven years later.[9] Thus Diderot wrote
that 'Individual wills are under suspicion: they might be good or bad, but
the general will is always good. It has never deceived, it never will . . .
the general will never errs.'[10] It is therefore possible that one of the two
borrowed the term from the other, but, if so, very unclear who from whom.[11]
At all events, when one begins to use the phrase, 'the general will,' the
concept of popular sovereignty commences to stir. As De Jaucourt had the
courage to write, and Diderot to publish, in the article on 'Government,'
'all *legitimate* sovereign power must emanate from the free consent of the
people.'[12]

Articles like these were prophetic. And it is worthy of notice that Volume
V dared to begin publishing again the liberal political articles for which
Diderot had been so severely criticized when he wrote and published the
essay on 'Authority' in Volume I. His article on 'Natural Right,' Rousseau's
on 'Economy,' and De Jaucourt's on 'Natural Equality' (*Egalité naturelle*)
expound ideas that already have the smell of 1776 and 1789. Nor did the
significance of their publication in the *Encyclopédie* escape the observation
of contemporaries. If one is ever tempted to suppose that the political views
expressed in the *Encyclopédie* were so hesitant and timid as to be innocuous,
let him recall the words of a British reviewer writing in 1768, words wherein
a generous-minded liberalism may be seen contending with an English
jealousy of French progress: 'We must observe likewise, to the honour of
the authors who have had the conduct of the Encyclopedie, that the same
manly freedom of sentiment which is observable in the philosophical and
other departments of this work, is eminently conspicuous in the political.
In short, whoever takes the trouble of combining the several political articles,
will find that they form a noble system of civil liberty; and however, as
Englishmen, we may have no reason to rejoice at the prospect of a gradual
establishment of such a system among our rivals, yet as friends to the rights
of mankind, we are delighted to see such a generous system every where
expanding its influence.'[13]

As for the economic philosophy of the *Encyclopédie,* it is nowhere better
depicted than in the long article on 'Thrift' (*Epargne*) contributed by an
obscure boarding school director named Faiguet. Reminiscent of, say, Benjamin Franklin, it was an extraordinary piece to appear in 1755 in the midst
of a monarchical and aristocratic society. For its values were middle-class
values, very far indeed from those of the nobility. There is something symbolic in M. Faiguet's personal insignificance. He is faceless, which makes
him the better representative of a class, the class that made the French

Revolution. This was the class that, like M. Faiguet, regarded thrift as a cardinal virtue and, like M. Faiguet too, wanted the medieval guild restrictions on production abolished; desired the abolition of apprenticeships and journeymen's associations; wanted the abolition of Colbertism 'by removing the obstacles on every hand regarding the transport and sale of merchandise and foodstuffs'; and further desired the suppression 'of three-fourths of our religious holidays.' M. Faiguet had a keen eye for the labor supply: he wanted the state to limit the number of persons admitted to religious orders. He thought that thrift would be encouraged by placing much more severe limitations on drinking places: 'The cabarets, being always open, disorder our workers so thoroughly that one cannot ordinarily count upon them nor see the end of a job once commenced.' He favored the institution of state-owned pawn shops which could also serve as banks of deposit. 'By this means there would circulate an infinity of sums great and small that remain today in inactivity.' M. Faiguet was much opposed to luxury, the taste for which he imputed to the mistaken education of the day. 'Nothing is more to be recommended to young folk than this virtuous habit [of thrift], which would become for them a preservative against vice. . . . Prizes in eloquence and poetry have been founded in a thousand places. Who will found among us prizes for thrift and frugality?' [14] M. Faiguet deserves immortality: he is the disembodied voice of an upthrusting bourgeoisie.

Among the articles descriptive of manufacturing or artistic processes that Diderot wrote for Volume V were those on distillation of brandy (*Eau-de-vie*) and on 'Enamel' (*Email*). In the latter he introduced the personal note by mentioning a certain artist and saying, 'I do myself the honor of being a friend of the last named.' [15] D'Alembert, too, permitted himself the luxury of personal remarks now and again in this volume, as when he praised Diderot's *Thoughts on the Interpretation of Nature* or launched forth in castigation of the clandestine Jansenist newspaper, *Les Nouvelles Ecclésiastiques*. 'The anonymous author of this work,' wrote D'Alembert, '. . . could probably name himself without being better known.' [16] Also in Volume V, to take some samples, were an interesting article on 'Copyright' (*Droit de copie*), contributed by David, one of the publishers of the *Encyclopédie,* and an article on 'Duels' written by Boucher d'Argis. Of very special interest to economists is the article on how pins are made (*Epingle*), contributed by a young friend of Diderot and Rousseau named Deleyre. Following the usual *Encyclopédie* pattern of meticulously describing manufacturing processes, Deleyre mentioned eighteen separate stages in the manufacture of a pin. This article gives us some means of judging how diffused the influence of the *Encyclopédie* could be, even though not always acknowledged. Surely it is not simply a coincidence that in the first chapter of the *Wealth of Nations,* Adam Smith illustrates his doctrine regarding the division of labor by choosing the now famous example of the lowly pin. 'One man draws out the wire, another straights it, a third cuts it, a fourth points it, a fifth grinds it at the top for receiving the head; to make the head requires two or three distinct operations; to put it on is a peculiar business, to whiten the pins is another; it is even a trade by itself to put them into the paper; and the important business of making a pin is, in this manner, divided into about *eighteen* distinct operations . . .' [17]

In Volume V Diderot continued his practice of writing long and important articles on the history of philosophy, such as his account of the Eleatics. No doubt Diderot devoted this liberal amount of space to the leaders of this school because their teachings were materialistic.[18] Similarly, the article on 'Epicureanism' was long, detailed, and full of loving fondness, although it purported to do no more than allow Epicurus to speak for himself.[19] The article 'Egyptians' gave Diderot the opportunity to declare that Moses was a disciple of the Egyptian priests, thereby undercutting the orthodox Christian contention that the Mosaic books portrayed original man and the earliest societies. Also he could speak disparagingly of priests in general while ostensibly discussing the priesthood of pagan Egypt.[20]

Writers of the Enlightenment rather commonly emphasized the antiquity of the Egyptians, a point they seem to have learned from Lord Shaftesbury.[21] This appealed particularly to the *philosophes* because it permitted them to indulge their distaste for revealed religion by insinuating that the laws of Moses were simply cultural borrowings.[22] The necessities of polemics therefore gave the views of the *philosophes,* rather fortuitously, an anti-Jewish cast. This was a field in which the playful Voltaire loved to caper. The *Encyclopédie,* too, did what it could to attack the fundamentalist assertion that the Pentateuch provided the only acceptable and allowable view of historical origins. Diderot and his colleagues, because of this dialectical necessity, were unfair to the Jews, unfair in the first place because they were insufficiently informed. Diderot, who wrote his article on 'Jews' in 1754, would have been more accurate, says Herr Sänger in his monograph on this subject, had he consulted rabbis.[23] And the *philosophes* were unfair in the second place because of their inability to appreciate religious genius and religious insights in any group. This was an area of human experience in which the Enlightenment was likely to be astigmatic. Consequently Diderot could interpose in his account of the Jews the following extremely unsympathetic notice: 'It will not be useless to warn the reader that one ought not to expect to find among the Jews either accuracy in their ideas, or exactitude in their reasoning, or precision in their style — in a word, anything that ought to characterize a sound doctrine of philosophy. On the contrary, there is to be found among them only a confused mixture of the principles of reason and of revelation, an affected and often impenetrable obscurity, principles that lead to fanaticism, a blind respect for the authority of the doctors and of antiquity — in a word, all the defects indicative of an ignorant and superstitious nation.' [24]

The article 'Eclecticism' is precious to a biographer because in it Diderot allows the reader insight into what he thought of himself. A long and quite diffuse article, it is frequently illuminated by flashes of value judgment or by remarks of a very subjective character. Diderot not only defines what it is to be an eclectic, he patently thinks himself to be one. For surely he does not want to exclude himself from the company that he describes in his opening words: 'The eclectic is a philosopher who, trampling under foot prejudice, tradition, venerability, universal assent, authority — in a word, everything that overawes the crowd — dares to think for himself, to ascend to the clearest general principles, to examine them, to discuss them, to admit nothing save on the testimony of his own reason and experience; and from all the philosophies he has analyzed without favor and without partiality, to make one for himself, individual and personal, belonging to him.' Diderot next asserts what all eclectics emphasize, namely that they are not syncretists, a term of opprobrium that an eclectic uses for any eclecticism not his own. 'Nothing is so common as syncretists, nothing so rare as eclectics.' He then discusses the eclectics of the ancient world at great length, finding the greatest exemplar to be, of all people, Julian the Apostate. (It is a wonder that the censors allowed so much as the mention of the Emperor Julian in any context that might be construed as favorable.) Modern eclectics, according to Diderot (and with his emphasis), were those *cultivating experimental philosophy:* 'Eclecticism, this philosophy so reasonable, which had been practiced by geniuses of the first order long before it had a name, remained forgotten until the end of the sixteenth century. Then Nature . . . produced at last certain men covetous of humanity's finest prerogative, the liberty of thinking for oneself, and the eclectic philosophy was seen to be reborn under Giordano Bruno, Jerome Cardan, Francis Bacon, Thomas Campanella, René Descartes, Thomas Hobbes . . . William Leibniz. . . .' [25] Obviously Diderot was calling the roll of names among which he hoped posterity would place his own as of a peer.

Probably the most important single article in the whole seventeen volumes of the *Encyclopédie* was the one written by Diderot on 'Encyclopedia.' By its richly textured consideration, first of what an encyclopedia is for, and then of an encyclopedia's relationship to language, science, and knowledge in general, Diderot's article was comparable in significance and scope to D'Alembert's 'Preliminary Discourse.' And the two were alike in their faith in progress, a faith which was one of the principal tenets in the gospel of the *philosophes.* 'In fact,' wrote Diderot in the first paragraph, 'the aim of an *Encyclopedia* is to gather together the knowledge scattered over the face of the earth . . . that our descendants, being better instructed, may become at the same time more virtuous and more happy; and that we may not die without having deserved well of the human race.'

There is a printer's mystery regarding this article, for it was published with page numbers on the eye-catching right-hand page, but with no pagination on the left-hand pages. Thus there are actually thirty-one pages between those numbered 633 and 649, a circumstance which naturally makes the reader wonder. Could it be that an article half the length was submitted to the censors, then one double the length inserted instead? Or was it that Diderot's illness delayed him in writing the article? The volume may have had to be put in page proof before his article was ready; but the article may have turned out to be twice as long as planned for, thus necessitating this unusual procedure.[26]

The article 'Encyclopedia' is a little book in itself, some 34,000 words in length — 'Such are the first ideas that offered themselves to my mind,' wrote Diderot in closing — 'on the project of a universal and systematic dictionary of human knowledge: on the possibility of it, its object, the arrangement of its materials both general and detailed, its style, method, cross references, nomenclature, its manuscript, authors, censors, editors, and typography.' It can well be imagined that when Diderot spread his net so wide, he caught a lot of fish. For instance, he descanted at length in the early part of the article on problems of linguistics. Profoundly impressed with how difficult it is to achieve accurate definitions, he wrote more like the scientist than like the creative artist who knows that words are symbols or hieroglyphs and therefore cannot be completely fixed. For he knew that the increase of knowledge necessitates an accurate and expanding vocabulary to implement it and he hoped that the *Encyclopédie* or a similar venture could assist in the fixation of language. This would be extensive, including not only all aspects of definition but even an analysis of sounds and a drastic orthographic reform by which spelling would become completely phonetic. In illustration he compared the current French and English phonetic rendering of a line of Greek verse, and in so doing conceived of something closely resembling the alphabet of the International Phonetic Association. Diderot may therefore be considered one of the pioneers in the emergent science of linguistics, although a modern expert has remarked, 'as a linguistic theorist his mind was of too meteoric a nature to submit to that patient discipline, that laborious exploration of linguistic facts which alone were capable of laying the foundations of a science of language.' [27]

Diderot disarmed critics of the *Encyclopédie* by candidly acknowledging defects. First he invited his reader to visualize the problems involved in securing a proper balance and proportion among the multitudinous articles in the work. Even if one man could write every entry, the problem would still be formidable. 'And he who supposes that he has taken precautions with his colleagues so that the contributed material will square approximately with his plan is a man who has no idea of his object or of his colleagues.' Some contributions will be too laconic, some too prolix. 'The proof of it is evident in a hundred places in this work. . . . In one place we are like skeletons; in another, we have a dropsical appearance. We are alternatively dwarfs and giants, colossi and pygmies; erect, well-made, and well-proportioned, humpbacked, limping, and deformed.' As for the prolixity of some of the articles, emulation among the contributors had the effect of producing dissertations instead of articles. Time and subsequent editions would take care of this. Besides, 'new inventions and new ideas necessarily introducing a disproportion; and the first edition being, of all, the one containing the greatest number of subjects that, if not newly invented, are at least as little known as if they had this characteristic, it is evident . . . that this is the edition in which will reign the most disorder, but which, on the other hand, will exhibit, through all its irregularities, an original air that only with difficulty will pass over into subsequent editions.' [28]

Diderot was not so fatuous as to suppose that the *Encyclopédie* would not be superseded: 'If our dictionary is good, how many works will it produce that are better!' [29] Repeatedly he wrote of the necessity of succeeding editions, as when he said explicitly that 'the first edition of an encyclopedia can be only a very incomplete and formless compilation.' [30] These admissions, as also the one about being either skeletal or dropsical, were promptly seized upon by his enemies, though this self-criticism has enhanced rather than decreased the estimation of the work by impartial critics. Diderot was never in doubt about the project itself, however, and constantly spoke of it in the ringing tones of a man who believes that the spread of knowledge will make mankind happier and better.

Occasionally in this long article Diderot allowed his reader to glimpse some of the editorial problems that had to be contended with: 'I examine our work without partiality; I see that there is perhaps not a single sort of error that we have not committed; and I am forced to admit that of an *Encyclopédie* like ours, scarcely two-thirds of it would be included in a true Encyclopedia. That is a great deal, especially if one acknowledges that in laying the first foundations of such a work, one was forced to take for a basis some inferior author or other, whether Chambers, Alsted, or some other. There is almost no one of our colleagues who could have been persuaded to work, if it had been proposed to him to compose all his assignment from the beginning; each would have been intimidated, and the *Encyclopédie* would not have been done. But by presenting to each one a roll of paper that had only to be re-examined, corrected, expanded, the work of creating, which is always what one dreads, disappeared and each, from a presumption that could not have been more chimerical, allowed himself to engage to do the work; for these disconnected fragments were so incomplete, so badly written, so poorly translated, so full of omissions, errors, and inaccuracies, so contrary to the ideas of our colleagues, that most of them threw them aside. Would that they had all had the same courage! . . . How much time lost in translating inferior things! What expenditures in order to obtain a continual plagiarism!'[31] Elsewhere Diderot remarked on his colleagues' propensity to quote verse, an inclination he discouraged save in articles on literary subjects; on the prolixity of contributors, encouraged, if not justified, by the editors' own; on the difficulty, and yet the importance, of keeping a proper balance; on the impracticability of insisting that the entire manuscript be turned in before the printing was begun, with consequent blunders and omissions in regard to cross references; and on the very particular difficulty of getting accurate information about the arts and crafts.[32] Regarding this last difficulty, he wrote: 'But as the arts have been the principal object of my work, I am going to explain myself candidly, both concerning the mistakes I have made and the precautions that would need to be taken to correct them.

'He who would take upon himself the subject matter of the arts will not acquit himself of his labors in a satisfactory manner either for others or for himself, if he has not profoundly studied natural history, especially mineralogy; if he is not an excellent mechanic; if he is not well versed in theoretical and experimental physics; and if he has not taken several courses in chemistry.'[33]

These rigorous requirements of an editor were more than hypothetical to Diderot for at this very time he was attending the lectures and demonstrations given at the Jardin du Roy by Rouelle, the leading French chemist of his day. For three consecutive years Diderot attended these lectures, and copies of the notes he took are still in existence.[34] In addition, he wrote a very engaging and informative character sketch of this eccentric and single-minded scientist.[35]

Having launched on a discussion of all the qualifications necessary to one hopeful of describing the arts and crafts, Diderot particularly mentions the problem of securing information from craftsmen: 'He [who would correct the articles on the arts] will not be long in perceiving that, in spite of all the care we have taken, there have slipped into the work some gross blunders (see the article *"Brique"*), and that there are whole articles that do not have a shadow of common sense (see the article *"Blanchisserie de toiles"*); but he will learn by his own experience to thank us for the things done well and pardon us for those done ill. Especially will he learn, after having for some time gone from workshop to workshop with cash in his hand and after having paid dearly for the most preposterous misinformation, what sort of people craftsmen are, especially those at Paris, where the fear of taxes makes them perpetually suspicious, and where they look upon any person who interrogates them with any curiosity as an emissary of the tax farmers, or as a worker who wants to open shop.'[36]

It was in this article that subscribers were first told about the engravings that were to illustrate the work, none having yet been published. Diderot announced that 'we have about a thousand plates.' The account book of the publishers shows that there had indeed been much activity in this department, with disbursements beginning in 1748. In 1751, very frequent and substantial payments began, especially to a man named Goussier, who ultimately did the drawings for more than nine hundred of the finished plates.[37] Moreover, they were superior ones. 'In spite of the prodigious number of figures that fill them, we have paid attention to admitting scarcely any that do not represent a machine now in existence and working. Let our volumes be compared with the collection of Ramelli [1588] which is praised so highly, the *Theatrum machinarum* [1724-7] of Leupold, or even the volumes of machines approved by the Académie des Sciences, and then one can judge whether, of all these volumes put together, it would be possible to take twenty plates from them worthy of inclusion in such a collection as we have had the courage to conceive and the good fortune to execute. There is nothing here that is superfluous or superannuated or imaginary: everything in it is in action and alive.' [38]

This was the first occasion — but not the last — when the engravings done for the *Encyclopédie* and those for the Royal Academy of Sciences were contrasted and compared. In 1675 Colbert, the great minister of Louis XIV, had requested the Royal Academy to publish a series of illustrations and explanations concerning the machines used in the arts and crafts.[39] The preparation of these drawings and engravings continued sporadically and dilatorily for decades, with Réaumur more responsible for them than anyone else; and the result was that the *Encyclopédie* was announced and its publication far advanced before the Academy of Sciences, under the spur of competition, finally published its first fascicle, that on 'Charcoal Burning,' in 1761.

Meanwhile Diderot and the publishers of the *Encyclopédie* had procured for their examination and comparison copies of a good many of the various Academy prints that had been engraved but not yet published. Diderot says as much in the passage just quoted, and it is unlikely that he would have called attention to this proceeding, and in so public a way, if he had supposed that there was anything dishonest about it.[40] Réaumur, however, evidently regarded it so and said as much to Formey who, about this time, was toying with the idea of editing an encyclopedia himself.[41] Apparently he had written to Réaumur inquiring about engravings, for the latter replied on 23 February 1756, 'I have had more than a hundred and fifty plates engraved in folio size, they being very pleasing pictures, and I have many others that are only drawings. I could have made the whole literary world resound with my cries over the theft that has been done me of the first-named and taken steps to have justice done. The infidelity and negligence of my engravers, of whom several are dead, have made it easy for people with little delicacy regarding their methods to collect proofs of these plates, and they have been engraved anew in order to insert them in the encyclopedical Dictionary. I have learned somewhat tardily that the fruits of so many years of labor have been taken away from me. I have preferred to appear to be ignorant of it than to trouble my repose by reclaiming my property.' The only other time he had ever discussed the matter, Réaumur went on to say, was in a letter to his friend the German metaphysician Christian Wolff, now dead two years.[42]

It is hard to pronounce upon the amount of moral turpitude involved in this incident. If Réaumur was convinced that a serious theft had occurred, how does it happen that he regarded it as a matter that concerned only himself and not the Academy of Sciences? Moreover, he writes to foreign scholars about it, but evidently takes care not to say anything about it in France, alleging a desire to keep his peace of mind. But if a theft had really occurred, it would certainly seem that an investigation was in order. Indeed, this was precisely what the publishers of the *Encyclopédie* demanded at once when the allegation of theft and plagiarism was made public in 1759, two years after Réaumur's death. As a result, the official commission of the Academy of Sciences testified that 'we have recognized nothing' in the *Encyclopédie* prints 'that was copied after the plates of M. de Réaumur.' [43] There is no question that Diderot and his publishers had had in their possession some of the Academy of Science proofs, depriving Diderot of the right to claim credit for originating plans for the attractive drawings in perspective illustrating the processes in each art or craft. Both works used this device, and the Academy of Sciences can clearly claim priority. But unless there was intent to defraud, there could be no moral turpitude in possessing some of the proofs of a languishing enterprise that had been begun seventy-five years previously and had not even yet made any announcement of intending publication. [44]

Diderot's discussion of the *Encyclopédie*'s cross-reference system in his article 'Encyclopedia' is amazingly frank. He explained at great length the organic relationship of subjects that the editors hoped to accomplish by the skillful use of cross references and, surprisingly enough, he described with complete candor the ideological purpose of the *Encyclopédie*'s system. For cross references can be used, he wrote, to contrast conflicting principles and to overthrow ridiculous opinions that cannot be frontally attacked. 'The entire work would receive [from such cross references] an internal force and secret utility, the noiseless effects of which would necessarily become perceptible with time. For example, every time a national prejudice requires respect, it should respectfully be set forth, at the appropriate place, with all its accompaniments of verisimilitude and seduction; but the edifice of mud ought to be overthrown, the useless accumulation of dust be dissipated, by referring to articles where solid principles serve as a basis for opposing truths. This manner of disabusing men operates very quickly upon good understandings; and it operates infallibly on every mind and without disagreeable consequences, secretly and without creating a sensation. It is the art of tacitly deducing the most radical conclusions. If these cross references of confirmation or refutation are foreseen far ahead of time and prepared with skill, they will give to an encyclopedia the character that a good dictionary ought to have, namely the character of changing the general way of thinking.' [45]

It seems clear that Diderot had France's established religion in mind when he referred to 'a national prejudice.' His revelation of the uses to which his cross references were put not unnaturally had repercussions. It was made the subject of a considerable amount of animadversion, as was also an incidental remark of his that caused the Archbishop of Paris to write in protest to Malesherbes. 'I join to my letter,' wrote Christophe de Beaumont, 'a note of what is to be read in the fifth volume of the encyclopedic dictionary, page 635 at the word "Encyclopedia." You will see that the Sorbonne is therein spoken of in a very indecent manner by asserting that it could furnish to the *Encyclopédie* only theology, sacred history, and *superstitions*. To regard the science of religion as a source of superstition is to attack religion itself. It is very regrettable that the censors did not notice an error like this, and I hope that you will have no objection to giving the necessary orders so that it may be corrected or at least amends be made.' [46] Amends of a sort *were* made. The list of errata in Volume VI declared that the passage, which 'contrary to our intention some persons have found ambiguous,' should read 'theology, sacred history, and the history of superstitions.' Diderot's explanation, which in reality rendered his original motives more inscrutable than ever, did not reveal a high degree of penitence.

Of course when Diderot allowed himself to speak this way about the Sorbonne, he was thinking of the troubles involving the Abbé de Prades. This is but one instance of his using the article 'Encyclopedia' as a vehicle for the expression of his animosities, his likes, and his personal ambitions. He begins and ends his long article by sneering at the Jesuits and their *Dictionnaire de Trévoux;* he asserts aggressively that 'among those who have set themselves up for censors of the *Encyclopédie,* there is scarcely one with the talent necessary for enriching it with one good article'; he scolds the French Academy for not finishing its dictionary and then broadly hints that he would be capable of doing so himself if he were a member; he breaks forth in praise of a personal friend — 'O Rousseau! my dear and worthy friend'; he boasts of having taught his fellow citizens to esteem and read Francis Bacon; he apologizes for himself, managing to praise himself at the same time, and betrays his true opinion of himself, one feels quite sure, as he defines his conception of the ideal editor for a work of this sort. 'A man endowed with great good sense, celebrated by the breadth of his knowledge, the elevation of his feelings and conceptions, and his love for work; a man loved and respected both for his private and his public char-

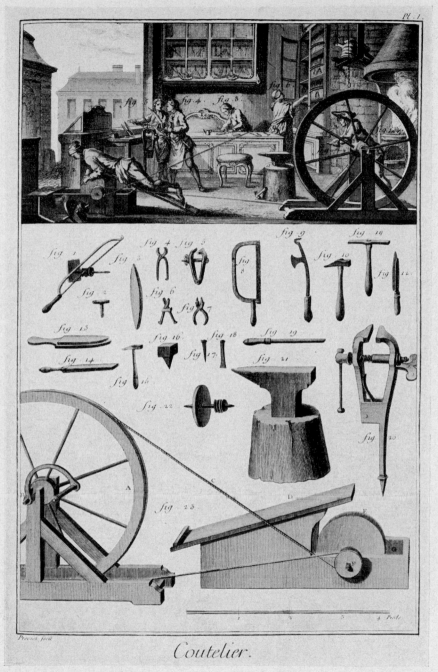

Pl. 1.

Coutelier.

This engraving (1763) from the *Encyclopédie* illustrates articles on the craft of cutlery written by Diderot himself. The shop shown is that of a Parisian cutler rather than the establishment of Diderot's father at Langres.

acter; never a frenzied enthusiast, save for truth, virtue, and humanity.' [47]

Truth, virtue, and humanity! Shining words. In their names Diderot led the assault upon minds apprehensive of change and defended himself from the allegations that he was subversive and unvirtuous. Diderot's enemies, and the enemies of the *philosophes* in general, constantly maintained that religious orthodoxy and right conduct were inseparable, and that one could not truly have the one without the other. This Diderot, believing as he did, emphatically denied, and he was always at pains to insist that to be a *philosophe* was necessarily to be virtuous. He never tired of asserting his probity and proclaiming his virtue, or of calling himself a good man, an *homme de bien*. Partly, perhaps mostly, it was because he was convinced of it; partly it was to combat the narrow-mindedness of those who would like everyone to believe that an unorthodox man must necessarily be a vicious one.

The moral note is struck more than once in Diderot's article 'Encyclopedia.' He speaks of 'inspiring the taste for knowledge, the horror of lying and of vice, and the love of virtue; for whatever has not happiness and virtue for its ultimate end is nothing,' and later on he remarks that 'it is at least as important to make men better as to make them less ignorant.' [48] There is in Diderot's manner of thinking a constant relating of truth to man and the ends of man. Truth not only exists of itself: it becomes usable only when humanly apperceived. This pronounced humanism in Diderot's thought — so pronounced that it has appropriately given the title *L'Humanisme de Diderot* to one of the best critical works concerning him — is well expressed by a passage in the article 'Encyclopedia': 'A consideration that above all must not be lost from view is that if man, or the thinking and contemplative being, is banished from the surface of the earth, this pathetic and sublime spectacle of nature becomes nothing but a mute and melancholy scene. . . . Why not [therefore] introduce man in our work as he is placed in the universe? Why not make of him a common center? . . . Man is the sole and only limit whence one must start and back to whom everything must return, if one wishes to please, interest, touch, even in the most arid considerations and the driest details. Setting aside my own existence and the happiness of my fellow beings, what does the rest of nature matter to me?' [49]

This insistence that knowledge to be meaningful must be related to man made of Diderot something more than a scientist — some people might say it made him less than one. But Diderot's humanism explains why he is so interested in ethics, why the search for the bases of moral sanction has for him so great a fascination. The ideal of the *philosophe,* as Diderot accepted it for his *Encyclopédie* article 'Philosopher,' was humanistic and social, the ideal of a thinker interested in his fellow man. Now, because this ideal was so humanistic and social — and so little religious or theological — Diderot time and again appealed for his ultimate justification to the unprejudiced judgment of his peers. And since contemporaries are likely to be prejudiced, Diderot turned to posterity for the comforting sense of ultimate justification. Thus, after describing all the difficulties attendant upon completing an encyclopedia, he writes: 'We have seen that the *Encyclopédie* could be the effort of only a philosophical century; that this century has arrived; that renown, while carrying to immortality the names of those who will finish it, will perhaps not disdain to take care of ours; and we have felt our-selves reanimated by an idea so consoling and so sweet, that we too shall be spoken of when we shall no longer exist; [reanimated] by this captivating murmur which gives us to understand, from the lips of some of our con-temporaries, what shall be said about us by men to whose instruction and happiness we have sacrificed ourselves, whom we have esteemed and loved although they are not yet born.' [50]

Posterity shall judge, wrote Diderot.[51] For posterity, in Diderot's eyes, was the supreme court.

CHAPTER 19

Growing Tension with Rousseau:
'Only the Bad Man Lives Alone'

DIDEROT was a man expansive in temperament and rich in the outpourings of his imagination, sympathy, and sensitivity. Yet he also had a vein of cool and unemotional scientific objectivity which almost always came into play when his metaphysical views were at stake. An example of this capacity to remain detached when others are suffering is shown by his neutral attitude toward the greatest public disaster of the eighteenth century. Many of his contemporaries were saddened, their fondest convictions undermined, by the earthquake at Lisbon on 1 November 1755 which wiped out the lives of many thousands within a few minutes. The earthquake not only shook Lisbon, it shook Voltaire, who had been living in a rather happy deistic faith. The impassive inscrutability and indiscriminacy of the event caused Voltaire to question shudderingly God's ways to man. To this questioning we owe *Candide*. But it is characteristic of Diderot, with his strictly naturalistic conception of a universe that he thought could be explained without having to predicate God, that the Lisbon earthquake presented him with no intellectual problem whatever.[1]

In the following year Frederick the Great precipitated the Seven Years' War by his incursion into Saxony. This was the war that saw the exploits of Montcalm and Wolfe in Canada and of Clive in India, a war which permanently affected the political destinies of a considerable fraction of mankind. This was the year of the Diplomatic Revolution, when France, since the days of Cardinal Richelieu the archenemy of the Hapsburgs, reversed her alliance system and became the ally of Maria-Theresa. It was the beginning of a war in which the luster of French arms at first was brightened by the capture of Port Mahon, only to be tarnished by the

247

humiliation of Rossbach; a war in which the monarchy of Louis XV and Madame de Pompadour frittered away the substance of colonial and maritime power in exchange for some vague dream of Continental hegemony. The prestige and the finances of France suffered grievously in the Seven Years' War, and it may be accounted one of the predisposing causes for the later alliance with the infant United States, for instance, as well as for the Revolution of 1789 itself. Militarily and intellectually, the decade of the 'fifties was the decisive one in the history of France in the eighteenth century.

It is surprising to find Diderot scarcely aware of the Seven Years' War or its implications. He, a leader in one of the two great changes occurring in the life of his time, was oddly insensitive to the other. Save for the incident in his *Fils naturel* of the capture and imprisonment of Rosalie's father by the British plus a reference in his *Père de famille* to an episode in the Port Mahon campaign, neither Diderot's writings nor his letters refer to the war. It seems to have affected him only in regard to Grimm, who was attached to the staff of a French marshal for a few months in 1757 on campaign in Westphalia.[2] During these years of 1756–63 we shall hear much of Diderot's tribulations, for this was the time of his greatest trials and, in view of his spirited conduct in the face of great adversity, his nearest approach to heroism. And as if his personal life had absorbed all his energies, he lived through these years as though buffeted by everything except the war itself.

Diderot's correspondence in 1756 shows him now and again in that mood of heated and self-righteous expostulation that he easily fell into, and there is a note of distinct acerbity and irritability in his relations with people at this time that may be a symptom of overwork or a consequence of lingering ill health. One of these occasions had to do with a lawsuit over the appointment to a priory in which his younger brother, the Abbé, had become involved. Mme de Vandeul says that her father put himself to incredible trouble in accommodating this matter, and we see Diderot working on it in a couple of letters written to his litigious and unconciliatory brother. Of the Abbé's opponent Diderot wrote, 'I believe M. le Chevalier a very honest man, even though he be a good Christian'! And a few days later, washing his hands of the affair, Diderot wrote, 'You have written me the letter of a litigant and a fanatic. If these are the two qualities that are conferred upon you by your religion, I am very content with mine, and I hope not to change it.'[3] No doubt the Abbé Diderot was a very difficult person, but letters like this were scarcely calculated to sweeten the temper.

Another of these expostulatory outbursts occurred in a long letter written by Diderot in the summer of 1756 to a contributor to the *Encyclopédie,* probably Paul Landois.[4] Landois was an obscure writer of whom very little is known save that he wrote a one-act tragedy in 1742, *Sylvie* by name, which was in prose and dealt with the affairs of run-of-the-mill humanity, not personages of exalted rank. This tragedy, with its one act, its ordinary people, its prose, and its explicit stage directions, flouted so many of the established traditions of the French theater that it deserves remembering as an early exemplar of the reforms that Diderot expounded fifteen years later. In 1756 Landois, who contributed a few unimportant articles concerning painting for the *Encyclopédie,* was evidently seven to eight days' post-time away from Paris and fuming at not being paid so promptly as he wished. It is clear from the nature of Diderot's letter that Landois was an extremely temperamental man much given to supposing that he was greatly put upon. In order to correct this impression, Diderot wrote him at great length, attacking the problem on three successive levels. The first was Diderot's personal disclaimer of guilt; the second was a discussion of Landois' way of comporting himself, viewed in the light of conventional morality; the third was a discussion of Landois' behavior from the point of view of philosophy. Inasmuch as this letter provides what appears to be a clear-cut statement of Diderot's views on ethics, it is frequently and extensively quoted.

On the first level Diderot proceeds upon the theory that the best defense is a strong offense. 'Now, let's come to the business of your manuscript. It is a work capable of ruining me. After having charged me twice with the most atrocious and most deliberate outrages, you propose to me the revision and printing of it. . . . You take me for an imbecile or you are one yourself. . . .'

Having generated a sufficient amount of heat, Diderot passes to the second level of the argument by reproaching Landois for his 'detestable morality,' and then, describing his own code of ethics: 'I find in myself an equal repugnance to wrong reasoning and wrong doing. I am between two forces, one of which shows me the good and the other inclines me toward evil. One must choose. At the beginning the moment of struggle is grievous, but the intensity of it weakens with time. There comes a time when the sacrifice of one's passion no longer costs a pang. I can even certify from experience that it is pleasant: one takes on in one's own eyes so much stature and dignity! Virtue is a mistress to whom one is attached as much by what one does for her as by the charms one believes her to possess. Woe to you if the practice of doing good is not sufficiently familiar to you, and if you have not accumulated a sufficient stock of good actions to be vain of them, to compliment yourself about them ceaselessly, to intoxicate yourself with this heady vapor and be fanatical about it.

' "We take virtue," you say, "the way a sick man takes medicine," to which, if he were well, he would prefer any other thing that would please his appetite. That is true of a sick man out of his senses: but in spite of that, if this sick man had had the merit of diagnosing his malady himself, of having discovered and prepared the medicine for it, do you think he would hesitate in taking it, however bitter it was, or that he would not compliment himself for his acumen and courage? What is a virtuous man? It is a man vain with this sort of vanity, and nothing more. . . .' This is an unusual definition of a virtuous man, and might be considered an extraordinarily 'debunking' one. But Diderot suggests that nevertheless Landois weigh the advantages such people gain for themselves, and especially what disadvantages they avoid. Thus Diderot argues that virtue is the pursuit of happiness, a kind of utilitarianism in which pleasure is strongly compounded of the esteem that others express for one as well as the esteem of oneself: 'But if ever you undertake [this calculation], do not forget to estimate for all that they are worth the esteem of others and that of oneself. Moreover, do not forget that a bad action never goes unpunished. I say never, because the first one that one commits inclines one to a second, that one to a third, and thus one advances step by step toward being held in contempt by one's fellow men, the greatest of all evils.'

Diderot now comes to the third level of his argument. His object is to cure Landois of supposing 'that the whole of nature conspires against you, that chance has heaped up all the kinds of misfortune in order to pour them on your head. Where the devil did you get such pride? My dear fellow, you prize yourself too highly, you grant yourself too much importance in the universe.' In order to disabuse Landois of so much pride, Diderot says of himself that he must 'leave off the tone of the preacher to take up, if I can, that of the philosopher.' For now comes a discussion of the relationship between morality and determinism. Diderot believed that effect follows cause so inexorably in the training and experience of the human being that 'liberty' is a meaningless word. The context would seem to indicate that he uses the word 'liberty' in the sense of 'unpredictability' or 'caprice.' At all events, this important passage is as follows: 'Look at the matter closely and you will see that the word "liberty" is a word devoid of sense; that there are not, and cannot be, free beings; that we are only what is in consonance with the general order, with our organization, education, and the chain of events. That is what disposes of us invincibly. One can no more conceive of a being acting without motive than one can of the arm of a scales acting without the action of a weight, and the motive is always external to us, foreign to us, brought on by some nature or some cause that is not we ourselves. What misleads us is the prodigious variety of our actions, joined with the habit we contracted as soon as we were born of confusing the voluntary with the free. . . .'

It will be noticed that Diderot is expressing a theory of ethics that includes both heredity and environment: in his words, organization and education. Moreover, he recognizes that human beings have wills and exercise them, but he denies that human beings can exercise their wills capriciously and without relation to the totality of cause and effect in their previous experience. This is a conception of man's moral nature as full of 'horse sense' as of philosophy. Diderot conceives of ethics as a scientific matter, effect inexorably related to cause. By such determinism he conceives of human conduct in a fashion that avoids the uncertainty and the insecurity of a theory of moral indeterminism in which anything can happen, even the most chaotic, the most unlikely, or the most unpredictable.[5] 'A wholly free will in a finite world is a fair definition of insanity,' writes a modern author.[6] The point was, according to Diderot, that Landois could not suddenly 'cease at will to be evil. After having made oneself bad, is being good merely a matter of removing oneself a hundred leagues, or of saying to oneself, I want to be? The crease is set, and the cloth has to keep it.'

Far from feeling that nothing can be done in the moral training of human beings, Diderot emphasizes that 'although the beneficent or the maleficent man is not free, man is none the less a modifiable being. It is for this reason that the maleficent man should be destroyed at a place of public execution. From this fact [of his being modifiable, derive] the good effects of example, precepts, education, pleasure, pain, grandeur, poverty, etc.; from this fact, a sort of philosophy full of commiseration, attaching one strongly to good persons, but irritating one against a bad one no more than against a hurricane that fills our eyes with dust.'

Diderot is here describing a system of morality that operates independently of the hope for reward or the fear of punishment in another world. Perhaps it is the positive and this-worldly aspect of his doctrine that causes him to avoid relying upon the ordinary criteria of 'virtue' and 'vice': 'But if there is no liberty, there is no action meriting praise or blame, no vice nor virtue, nothing that must be recompensed or chastised. What then distinguishes men? Doing good and doing evil. The evildoer is a man to be destroyed, not punished. Beneficence is a good fortune, not a virtue.'

This way of stating moral doctrine seems harsh and forbidding, and in consequence the letter to Landois is very often cited as proving that Diderot's ethics had a hard, machinelike character, divesting human life of choice. But if one judges moral conduct from the point of view of *results* instead of from the point of view of *intention,* then Diderot's doctrine does not seem nearly so strange. His emphasis is then seen as one of social utility.[7] Good conduct, according to such a view, depends upon doing, upon the concrete and positive results of moral action. But man still remains a modifiable being capable of exercising choice. Diderot proves that he believes this by saying in the next few lines of the letter, 'Adopt these principles if you find them good, or show me that they are defective. If you adopt them, they will reconcile you with others and with yourself.'

While Diderot was engaged in this troublesome quarrel with Landois, his relations with other friends were also suffering deterioration. Probably there was some sort of quarrel with Condillac, to judge by Grimm's sudden and venomous attack after having praised Diderot's former friend only a little previously. Diderot and Condillac had not been intimate for some years and were now far removed from the days of the dinners at the Panier Fleuri. Their relations were further chilled, about this time, because Diderot felt that Condillac had pilfered from the *Letter on the Deaf and Dumb* (1751) one of the main ideas for his *Treatise on Sensations,* which appeared three years later.[8]

Coincident with this turbulence in Diderot's relations with his friends was, it seems, a delay in the publication of the sixth volume of the *Encyclopédie.* For although Grimm remarked in his news letter of 1 May 1756 that the volume had just been published, a friend wrote to Rousseau from Paris on 23 September that it had not yet appeared.[9] Diderot himself speaks of being in the country seeking rest and health after having completed the sixth volume, and the same correspondent of Rousseau dates this *villeggiatura* exactly by writing on 16 September that Diderot had just returned to Paris from a three-weeks' visit at the country house of Le Breton, his publisher.[10] This delay in publication, if delay there was, may have contributed to Diderot's apparent irritability of that year, although the tardiness may have been caused by Diderot's lingering ill health. Le Breton carried him away from Paris for a vacation; yet even after that Diderot suffered a very bad attack of 'colic,' which he attributed to his injudiciously discontinuing his diet of milk.[11]

When Volume VI finally appeared it was the least controversial of all the early volumes of the *Encyclopédie* and seems to have pleased everyone but Voltaire. The volume contained important articles by Turgot on 'Etymology,' 'Expansibility,' and 'Existence,' the latter a masterly exposition of the intellectual presuppositions shared by most of the Encyclopedists. Then there were articles on 'Evidence,' 'Fêtes,' 'Fireworks,' 'Fiefs,' 'Fevers,' 'Finances,' 'Fluid,' 'Flute,' and so on, the usual sort of intake of a work that called itself a methodical dictionary of the sciences, arts, and crafts. Especially noteworthy was Quesnay's long article on 'Farmers' (*Fermiers*), an article that has recently been called by a Marxist writer 'the origin of the whole physiocratic doctrine' because it analyzes 'the role of capital in production.'[12] Diderot's share as a contributor of articles was distinctly less in this than in the other volumes, a circumstance which may have been owing to his ill health. Voltaire contributed fifteen articles and, in direct proportion to his becoming more closely identified with the work, grew correspondingly concerned about its all too patent unevenness.

Voltaire had not originally been a subscriber to the *Encyclopédie*, so that he praised it, to begin with, more on hearsay than on firsthand knowledge.[13] He liked to refer to Diderot and D'Alembert as 'Atlas and Hercules, carrying the world on your shoulders.'[14] The *Encyclopédie* was 'the greatest and finest monument of the nation and of literature'; he adjured D'Alembert to hasten to 'finish the greatest work in the world.'[15] Symbolic of their growing association was D'Alembert's visit to Voltaire during the summer of the year in which Volume VI was published. It was during this very successful stay that Voltaire suggested D'Alembert write an article on 'Geneva,' an article which was to cause much trouble when it was published in Volume VII.[16] After D'Alembert's return to Paris, Voltaire's letters became much more frank than they had previously been. 'What I am told about the articles on theology and metaphysics wrings my heart. It is grievous to print the contrary of what one thinks.

'I am also sorry that people write dissertations and give private opinions for established truths. I should like definition and the origin of the word, with examples, everywhere.'[17]

A month later Voltaire professed himself unable to believe that in so serious a work the following sentence had appeared in an article on *'Femme'*: 'Chloe presses her knee against one beau while rumpling the lace of another.' What the writer, a man named Desmahis, had really said about Chloe was not much better: 'she presses her knee against one, squeezes the hand of another while praising his lace, and at the same time tosses off some suitable words to a third.' Voltaire remarked of this article that it must have

been written by the lackey of Gil Blas.[18] To this D'Alembert replied by
a personal exculpation — 'these articles are not in my bailiwick' — and added,
'Besides, I owe my colleague the justice of saying that he is not always in a
position to reject or condense the articles presented to him.'[19] This particular aspect of the correspondence was then brought to an end by Voltaire's
very sensibly inquiring, 'Why have you not recommended a sort of instruction sheet for those who serve you, etymologies, definitions, examples, reason,
clarity, and brevity?'[20]

During 1756 the friendship of Diderot and Rousseau moved into a
penumbra that was close to eclipse. Even the play that Diderot was writing
that autumn, his *Fils naturel* ('The Natural Son'), was destined to figure
in this melancholy tale. The story of their friendship's end is tangled and
complicated, hot with the passion of their clashing certainties of being in the
right, mournful in the slow and inexorable ruin of their delight in each
other. There is something epic and something symbolic in the confused,
nightmarish deliquescence of their friendship, epic because of the intensity
and vividness of the personalities of these two men, and epic, too, because
of their articulateness. Symbolic it was in that the differences dividing them,
although they did not realize it, were ideological. Rousseau was the precursor
of Robespierre, Diderot of Danton, and a generation later one sent the other
to the guillotine. The personal and temperamental irritations occurring
during 1756–8 were exacerbated by profound and little-understood discrep-
ancies in their outlook on life. These twisted their judgments and are likely
to twist the judgments of their biographers, too, for it is almost impossible
to watch the wavering scales of justice and refrain from jumping into one
of the pans. Temperament and circumstance combine so momentously that
detached judgment becomes difficult. We tend to be Rousseau-men or
Diderot-men, just as we tend to be Hamilton-men or Jefferson-men, Erasmus-
men or Luther-men, Caesar-men or Cicero-men.

Rousseau always claimed that the revelation that came to him on the road
to Vincennes in 1749 marked the turning point of his life. This was the
revelation, glowing within him with the incandescence of a truth believed
self-evident, that man's fate had become worse as his life had grown more
sophisticated and more complex. It was a revelation such as might conceivably come to a young man reared in puritanical simplicity on the shores,
say, of Lake Tahoe, who comes to the metropolis to make his mark and
lives precariously there, never quite at home and a success, never quite
beaten and a failure, never quite sure enough of himself to be openly cen-
sorious of the life about him. The revelation of 1749 gave Rousseau the

courage of his previously unasserted convictions. He still was sensitive, over-serious, and humorless. But these temperamental qualities now focused on what seemed to him the artificiality and conventionality of Parisian life. His friends could scarcely fail to notice his discontent. Their mistake was to suppose it merely superficial or even insincere.

It was not just with Paris that Rousseau was discontented. His friends, or most of them, galled him. He resented Diderot's unsolicited advice about accepting the King's pension; he suspected D'Holbach of trying to make people believe that Rousseau had plagiarized the music for the *Village Soothsayer;* he disliked the *philosophes'* baiting of the Abbé Petit, the man who had the theory of how to write a play in five acts; and he particularly abominated, as his preface to his play *Narcisse* shows so well, the anti-religious 'philosophy' of his own circle of friends. When, therefore, the wealthy Mme d'Epinay, a lady whom he had known since 1747, offered him the occupancy of the Hermitage, a spacious and specially remodeled cottage on her estate near Montmorency, ten miles to the north of Paris, Rousseau allowed himself to be persuaded to get away from it all.[21] His friends, regarding his decision as a ludicrous whim, loudly predicted that he could not endure it a fortnight. 'Sarcasms fell on me like hail,' Rousseau later recalled in his *Confessions.* On 9 April 1756, he began living at the Hermitage, vowing never to live in cities again.

There is no doubt that Rousseau's friends were disconcerted by his leaving Paris, and even more so by his remaining away. Life away from Paris hardly seemed worth living to that intensely sociable age, especially if compounded by solitude. Paris and, for courtiers, Versailles seemed to most persons who had lived in them the only really habitable places in France. This feeling is reflected in the word the eighteenth century used when the king deprived a minister of his office and commanded him to live upon his country estate until further orders. The eighteenth century always said that a minister in such circumstances was 'exiled,' as if living in a country house or château were equivalent to being banished to the ends of the earth. Rousseau's self-exile, as the D'Holbach circle thought of it, might be construed as a standing reproach to them, and was therefore a constant and subtle irritation. If he was wise, they were foolish. Moreover, if his exile was virtue, then it cast doubt on their mode of life. This they found intolerable, so that Diderot put into the mouth of one of the characters in his *Fils naturel* this extremely barbed and personal allusion: 'I appeal to your heart: ask it, and it will tell you that the good man lives in society, and only the bad man lives alone.' [22]

Rousseau, for his part, discovered more disillusionments in his new phase of life than he had anticipated. In the first place, he expected Diderot to come to the Hermitage regularly, a necessarily one-sided arrangement since Rousseau had renounced Paris.[23] In this expectation he was frequently disappointed. In the second place, he found that whenever his benefactress was in residence at the big house, La Chevrette, his time was not his own. But worse than that was the fact that he had no domestic tranquillity. He had brought from Paris not only Thérèse Levasseur but also her aged mother. The old woman played off her daughter against Rousseau, and poor Thérèse, who had too little mind to be able to call what she had her own, was completely under her mother's domination. Rousseau discovered, with exasperation and bepuzzlement, that nothing he did won Mme Levasseur's loyalty or even her good will. She treated Rousseau with the cunning and craftiness of a peasant outwitting the lord of the manor, and Rousseau must often have felt like the well-intentioned Nekhlyudov in Tolstoy's *A Landlord's Morning*. Added to this was the fact that Mme Levasseur, during the days back in Paris, had negotiated mysteriously with Grimm and Diderot. Rousseau now discovered this from Thérèse, but he could not fathom the purpose of this secretive conduct.

After Rousseau's lively imagination had mulled over the information that Grimm and Diderot had been in secret communication with Mme Levasseur, he was quite ready to believe that a sinister conspiracy was afoot against him. This conclusion probably strengthened his determination to remain at the Hermitage through the winter. The grave illness of an old friend, Gauffecourt, called him to Paris on two separate occasions, the first in late December 1756 and the second for a two-week period the following January, during which time he dined at Mme d'Epinay's and lodged at Diderot's.[24] Indeed it was at this sickbed that Diderot first met Mme d'Epinay, a woman whose acquaintance he had always refused to make in spite of her close friendship with Rousseau and of her having become Grimm's mistress.[25] In fact, Diderot had attempted to prevent the liaison. Having received a very prejudicial view of the lady's character from a former suitor, Diderot had a protracted interview with Grimm, during the course of which he claimed to have asked his friend impatiently, 'That is to say that you sincerely believe that Mme d'Epinay is neither false nor a coquette nor a whore?' He left the interview convinced that his informant was a rascal but still unpersuaded that Mme d'Epinay was as virtuous as Grimm thought.[26] This conversation had taken place about two years before the illness that brought all Gauffecourt's friends, including the hermit from the Hermitage, to his bedside. Mme d'Epinay had meanwhile become Grimm's mistress, but

Diderot remained distant. Now, however, a train of circumstances had begun that, as Rousseau saw it, ended by arraying all his friends, Diderot and Mme d'Epinay no less than Grimm, in a sort of conspiracy against him.

Rousseau left Gauffecourt and returned to the Hermitage just before the publication of Diderot's *Fils naturel*. It was not long before he came across the line 'only the bad man lives alone,' and accordingly he wrote Diderot — this particular letter is not extant — what in his succeeding letter he described as 'the tenderest and most candid letter I ever wrote in my life, complaining, with all the gentleness of friendship, of a very ambiguous maxim from which a most injurious application could be made to me.' [27] Diderot's answer was very nonchalant. Moreover, it was bantering in tone. But Rousseau was never of the temperament to bear either banter or nonchalance gladly, and least of all was he in the mood to do so now. The emotional crisis into which he was thrown by Diderot's letters at this juncture may be seen clearly in his letters to Mme d'Epinay, as well as in her efforts to soothe him in reply.[28]

Rousseau, who had made it a matter of principle not to go to Paris and who repeatedly declared to Mme d'Epinay at this time that he would never in his life go there again,[29] suggested that Diderot come to Montmorency to see him in order to clear up the point about the solitary man's being evil. Diderot wrote: 'You can very well see, my dear fellow, that because of the weather it is not possible to go to find you, whatever the desire and even the need that I have of doing so. . . . Do you know what you ought to do? Come here and stay a couple of days incognito. I would go Saturday to pick you up at Saint-Denis and from there we would go to Paris in the same cab that brought me.' Diderot finally gets around to discussing the line in the *Fils naturel* that had wounded Rousseau, but his reference to it is very airy, and compounded with chaffing remarks, especially in regard to Mme Levasseur: 'I am glad that my work pleased you and touched you [it certainly did, and on a very sore spot]. You are not of my opinion regarding hermits. Say as much good of them as you please, you yourself will be the only one in the world of whom I shall think such good things, and even then there would be something to say on that point if one could speak to you without angering you. A woman eighty years old! . . . Adieu, citizen! And yet, a hermit is a very singular citizen.' [30] It will be noticed that Diderot by no means claims that the offending line to which Rousseau took exception had been unintentional or inadvertent.

Rousseau said of this letter that it had pierced his soul.[31] His reply is not extant, but one can be sure that it made no attempt to disguise his feelings, and it very evidently was successful in annoying its recipient. 'Whatsoever pain my letter gave you,' wrote Diderot, 'I do not repent of having written it: you were too pleased with your reply.' Rousseau having refused to come to Paris, Diderot announced, not very good-humoredly, his intention of going to Montmorency. 'Very well, then, Saturday morning I leave for the Hermitage, whatever the weather. I shall go on foot. My engagements have not permitted me to go sooner, my fortune does not permit me to go there any other way. . . .' This letter, too, made much ado about Mme Levasseur, ending, 'Live, my friend, live, and do not fear lest she die of hunger.' [32]

The letter so infuriated Rousseau — he told Diderot that it was abominable — that he wrote to Mme d'Epinay that he now devoutly hoped that Diderot would not come. 'But I ought to be reassured [that he won't]. He has promised that he will.' [33] This remark is in allusion to the many times, according to Rousseau, that Diderot made appointments and then failed to keep them. This time, however, it was Mme d'Epinay who kept the friends from meeting by sending word that Rousseau would come to Paris instead. When he did not appear, Diderot wrote a third letter which is bright with his usual conviction of having done no wrong:

Once for all, ask yourself: Who took part in looking after my health when I was sick? Who supported me when I was attacked? Who was it who took an eager interest in my glory? Who rejoiced over my successes? Reply sincerely, and recognize those who love you. . . . Oh, Rousseau! you are becoming spiteful, unjust, cruel, ferocious, and I weep with sorrow. A nasty quarrel with a man whom I never esteemed and loved as I have you, has caused me affliction and insomnia [evidently a reference to Landois]. Guess, then, what pain *you* are causing me. . . . Indicate when you wish it, and I shall hasten to you; but I shall wait until you do.[34]

Rousseau's reply, a few days later, showed how far the mutual misunderstanding had carried. 'Had you intended to irritate me in all this business,' he wrote, 'what could you have done more?' He admitted that he had got Mme d'Epinay to prevent Diderot's coming to the Hermitage: they would only have quarreled. 'Besides, you wanted to come on foot; you risked making yourself sick, and perhaps you would not have been too sorry had you done so. I did not have the courage to incur all the perils of such an interview.' Each accused the other of self-righteousness. 'You constantly appear to be so proud of your conduct in this affair,' wrote Rousseau, and then he cried out, 'Diderot! Diderot! I see it with bitter grief: living uninterruptedly in the company of spiteful men, you are learning to resemble them. Your good heart is being corrupted by their society, and you are forcing mine, by insensible degrees, to detach itself from you.' [35]

It was a pity that Montmorency was not a good deal farther from Paris. Distance made communication difficult but not impossible, just when mutual distrust was doing the same. As it was, Rousseau was near enough Paris for him to expect to see his friends constantly at the Hermitage. By his reluctance to set foot in the city he forced his friends into a one-sided intercourse whereby they paid the charges both in transportation and time.[36] And this resulted, in the case of a man like Diderot, never one to be very punctilious about his appointments, in broken promises and unfulfilled engagements. In Diderot's defense it might be said that he was an unusually busy man, occupied not only with his editorial duties but also with Rouelle's chemistry lectures and, just at this time, with his play and the complications that it brought in its train. Personal contact was difficult, correspondence generated as much misunderstanding as it did understanding — indeed, where mutual confidence was lacking, it generated more — and, to crown all, Diderot acted, although probably with the very best of intentions, with a singular lack of tact. One has the right to ask Diderot, as Rousseau did, what precisely were his motives in harping upon the fate of Mme Levasseur, and what precisely did he mean by so publicly and so gratuitously remarking that only the evil man lives alone. Candor must reply that, at least so far as documents now extant reveal, Diderot never quite justified himself satisfactorily upon either count.

CHAPTER 20

How To Write a Play: Example and Precept

THE impulse to write plays had come rather suddenly upon Diderot in his early forties. He wrote two during this period and accompanied each of them with elaborate essays upon all aspects of the theater, so that, taken together, his views could scarcely be ignored, however much they might be disparaged. The first to be published was the *Fils naturel* ('The Natural Son, or Virtue Put to the Test. A Comedy in Five Acts and in Prose. With the True History of the Piece'). The 'True History of the Piece,' to use Diderot's fiction, is better known as the *Entretiens sur le Fils naturel* ('Conversations regarding the *Fils naturel*') and consists of three dialogues with Dorval, the hero of the play, in which numerous aspects of acting and dramatic composition were discussed. Four editions of the *Fils naturel* appeared in the year of its publication (1757),[1] and in 1758 there followed the *Père de famille* ('The Father of the Family'), to which was attached the substantial *Discours sur la poésie dramatique* ('Discourse on Dramatic Poetry'). Though neither play was produced by the Comédie-Française before it was published — the *Père de famille* had its *première* there in 1761 and the *Fils naturel* its *première* (which was also its *dernière*) in 1771 — the public nevertheless became very aware of Diderot as a playwright, whether because of the intrinsic merit of his ideas or the unflagging efforts of his cabal.

Inasmuch as everyone in Paris who was interested in the theater knew that Diderot was the author of the *Fils naturel*, it might at first seem odd that his name did not appear on the title page. No doubt it was some rather dour remarks, especially those in Act III, regarding heaven and the ways of its providence, that prevented the work from being published under public license. Indeed, the fashion in which the play was received by his relatives at Langres shows that it had a tendentiousness that Malesherbes could not have dared to endorse by allowing it approbation. On 29 November 1757,

Diderot wrote to his father, 'I am very sorry to have done something that displeases you . . . I beg you to believe that it is impossible for me to be pleased with myself when you are not.' [2] On the very same day he wrote to his brother, 'I learn, my dear brother, that my most recent work has greatly afflicted you. If that is the case, I'd wish I had not written it. . . . Tell me frankly what displeased you.' [3] But the Abbé refused to be drawn into an argument. It was not suitable between brothers, he wrote. Besides, he would just bring down on himself what had happened the last time, 'because the same thing is to be found in your book, and, doubtless being unshaken and constant in your principles, you would give me the same reply, that I am a fanatic, that it is so much the worse for me if I have need of my religion in order to be an honest man, that you do not feel this need, that you are contented with your own, and that you will never change it.' [4]

The *Fils naturel* was probably offered to the Comédie-Française. [5] If so, it must have been a severe disappointment to Diderot that it was rejected. He had to content himself with printing in the list of the dramatis personae the names of the Comédie-Française actors whom he deemed suitable for the various roles. This was an unusual procedure, a little ridiculous, a little pathetic.

The publication of the *Fils naturel* occasioned an uproar. In part, this was simply the result of the collision between people who like experimentation in the arts and people who detest it. The *Fils naturel* was sufficiently novel — in techniques of staging and acting as well as new emphases in character analysis and intellectual content — to make it controversial. This was not because the *Fils naturel* was the first of its kind to exemplify these new ideas in the theater. [6] It was 'tearful comedy,' but so was the theater of Nivelle de la Chaussée, whose plays, scornfully dubbed *'comédie larmoyante,'* had preceded Diderot's by a good fifteen years. Similarly, it was not the first to be written in prose; Landois' *Sylvie* (1742) was not in verse. Moreover, *Sylvie* and Mme de Graffigny's *Cénie* (1750) had both presented seriously and respectfully the virtues and vicissitudes of persons of ordinary social rank, thus deviating from the conventions of the classic French theater. Diderot was, therefore, not so much the first practitioner of what he called the *genre sérieux* as its greatest theoretician. [7] And as such he was cried up and cried down by those who welcome, and those who abominate, the sacrosanct old's being jostled by the irreverent new.

The plays of Diderot were in sober fact revolutionary, not merely in an aesthetic sense but also in a political one. The motivations, the values, the morality, the self-evident truths set forth in the *Fils naturel* and the *Père de famille* were those of a new social class just beginning to feel its own power and to respect its own intuitions. There was nothing, to be sure, so revolutionary in Diderot's plays as there was in *The Marriage of Figaro,* where Beaumarchais has Figaro say of his master, 'What did you do to obtain all these benefits?' and then has him answer his own question by replying, 'You gave yourself the trouble to be born.' The political and social implications of the new outlook on playwriting, as revealed in Diderot's pieces, were as yet more obscure than plain, but they were there; and it is impossible to say anything more cogent about Diderot's plays than to repeat what Alexis de Tocqueville wrote in *Democracy in America.* 'If you would judge beforehand,' he remarked, 'of the literature of a people which is lapsing into democracy, study its dramatic productions. . . . The tastes and propensities natural to democratic nations, in respect to literature, will therefore first be discernible in the drama, and it may be foreseen that they will break out there with vehemence.' [8]

In France they did break out with vehemence there. Diderot's notions regarding the theater would no doubt have aroused controversy in any event because of the technical innovations they propounded, but the political implications of the plays — as yet dim and obscure — were strangely disturbing or exhilarating to readers. Moreover, Diderot's views became the official dogma of an energetic and assertive coterie, resolved to make its judgments prevail. Mme d'Epinay, probably motivated by the desire to put Diderot under obligation to her, claimed to have disposed of more than three hundred copies of the *Fils naturel* within two days of its publication, a rather large number, which a later editor prudently divided by three.[9] Grimm told the subscribers to his news letter what to think of the new work in an ecstatic fashion that suggests his judgment was somewhat biased. The *Fils naturel* was a 'work of genius. . . . [a] beautiful and sublime work': Diderot, if he kept on in this way, was destined to become the absolute master of the French theater. 'However unfamiliar may be the sort of comedy in the *Fils naturel, ou les Epreuves de la vertu;* however new may be the poetics contained in the three *Conversations* that accompany this play, the enthusiasm of the first few days has been general. All the wits admired this work, all the tenderhearted and sensitive souls honored it with their tears. Envy and stupidity have not dared to raise their voices, and the public has emerged from this bit of reading better and more enlightened than it was.' [10] Even the hostile *Année Littéraire,* still edited by the formidable Fréron, cheerfully though belatedly admitted — with the usual adversative 'but,' the usual sting in its tail — that the *Fils naturel* had caused a stir. 'I cannot express with what warmth the public received this comedy . . . Let it suffice for you to know that this drama was for some time the subject of all the reading, of all the conversations, and of almost all the praise of Paris. Nothing is said of it today.' [11]

Critics of Diderot contended that the success of the *Fils naturel* was achieved by the art of puffery. This was the claim of the Encyclopedists' most dangerous antagonist, Charles Palissot. In a pamphlet entitled *Little Letters on Great Philosophers,* he focused his attention for some forty pages on the *Fils naturel.* 'Hitch yourselves to the chariot of the new Philosophy,' he advised obscure authors, '. . . make passers-by confess that the *Fils naturel* is a masterpiece, a marvel, a discovery more precious to the world of letters than that of America to Europe; and there you are, celebrated, immortal, and perhaps some day members of the Academy.' [12] Privately many must have felt what the poet and dramatist Collé confided to his journal: that the Encyclopedists 'ought to let themselves be praised by others, and not give themselves the trouble of taking care of it themselves, as they do every minute.' [13]

Just at the time that pamphleteers and editors were preparing to attack the *Fils naturel,* Malesherbes used his authority to protect it. So titanic was the struggle against the dead weight of all the elements of society opposed to change and hostile to reform that Malesherbes often tended to throw the weight of his authority on the side of the *philosophes* in order to equalize the contest. For instance, in 1756 he had written to the man appointed to be censor of Fréron's *Année Littéraire* and, after remarking that the authors of the *Encyclopédie* were quite justified in their annoyance at one of Fréron's quotations in which the *Encyclopédie* was referred to as 'scandalous' and the author of one of its articles as 'seditious,' he inquired how it was that the censor had let it pass.[14] The censor, Trublet, replied with some animation: 'It is true that Fréron has frequently desired to attack the *Encyclopédie* and its editors in his pages, because, he says, they have often attacked him in theirs. I have never allowed these attacks to pass. One day I gave the proof of this to M. d'Alembert, by letting him read what I had blue-penciled in some of the proofs. He appeared to be grateful for this consideration. Since then Fréron has often returned to the charge, and I to my blue-pencilings. Never have I allowed any extract from any work expressly written against the *Encyclopédie.*' [15]

Malesherbes' policy regarding the *Fils naturel* is revealed in the censor's report about the manuscript of a mild little pamphlet published in 1757. Its title, translated, was *The Legitimatized Bastard, or the Triumph of Tear-*

ful Comedy, with an Examination of the Fils naturel.[16] The author was a
dull dog, and appears to have used up all his wit in the title. But perhaps
his pamphlet, which was principally interested in showing that the techniques of 'tearful comedy' had been used by the ancients, was no sharper
than it was because censorship had toned it down. 'In truth,' wrote its
censor, a man named Gaillard, in his report to Malesherbes, 'there is nothing
bitter in this criticism. It is even tempered by strong praise, and M. Diderot
cannot complain of it without being unjust; but as you have had the kindness to inform me of the reasons that make you desire that his work not be
discredited, I thought that I should inform you of this part of the manuscript
before approving it. . . .'[17]

As far as hostile reviews of the *Fils naturel* were concerned, Diderot had
most to fear from Fréron. At this juncture Malesherbes let it be known that
he hoped that Fréron and Diderot would become reconciled. Upon receiving
this intelligence, Fréron stopped the presses — sixteen pages of an article on
the *Fils naturel* had already been printed — and wrote Malesherbes a letter.[18]
He suspected a trap and was full of distrust, not least because he knew that
about 1754 Diderot and D'Alembert, learning that Frederick II had authorized
the election of Fréron to the Prussian Academy, had written to the president of the Academy that they would resign their membership if Fréron
was elected.[19] Fréron now explained to Malesherbes the reasons for his
reluctance to agree to a reconciliation: 'He is at the head of a numerous
society that spreads and multiplies day by day by reason of its intrigues.
He would ceaselessly beseech me to deal gently with his friends, his associates, his admirers. I would be able to speak neither of the *Encyclopédie*
nor of any Encyclopedist. . . .

'Permit me to observe to you further, Monsieur, that it is rather peculiar
that the moment chosen for reconciling us, M. Diderot and me, is that in
which he has just given a work to the public. One does not need to be very
farsighted to see that M. Diderot is aiming at the French Academy, and
that those who wish him well apprehend, quite rightly, that I will demon-
strate (as I believe I have done) that his *Fils naturel,* the only work he
has written in the Academy's line, is a detestable play.'[20]

It is not surprising that Diderot should, at some time, experiment with
writing plays. As mentioned earlier, he thought for some time, when he
was a youngster, of being an actor; he closely studied plays and acting; he
devoted several of the best pages of *Les Bijoux indiscrets* to a searching
criticism of the theater; [21] and he wrote some sort of play, now lost, on the
basis of which the Abbé Desfontaines is reported to have declared that Diderot

had a great talent for dramatic composition. There can therefore be no doubt that potentially Diderot was deeply interested in playwriting. If the question is posed why Diderot chose this particular and very busy moment in which to make lengthy and weighty experiments in a field of letters comparatively new to him, Fréron's theory that Diderot was aiming at the French Academy seems altogether likely. Why not? Diderot was short on memberships in academies. Moreover, D'Alembert was now a member, making the imbalance of official honors possessed by him as compared with Diderot more apparent than ever, while at the same time putting him into a favorable position to work among his new colleagues for Diderot's acceptance. Both enemy and friend hinted at the time that Diderot's object was to make himself eligible for membership in the Academy.[22] We may even conjecture that the publishers of the *Encyclopédie* hoped that their chief editor would be able to achieve such signal recognition. At all events, Diderot seems to have taken time from the *Encyclopédie* to work on the *Fils naturel* and the *Père de famille,* if the very scanty number of his contributions to Volume VII (published in October 1757) is evidence.

Diderot made his first play more difficult to criticize by pretending that the events of its plot had actually occurred.[23] Moreover, from the point of view of the theory of playwriting, this suggested that the function of the theater is to hold a mirror up to nature. But it was also a prime device for evading criticism, getting around awkward objections, and, in short, of trying to eat one's cake and have it too. These are the events that were supposed to have occurred:

It is daybreak, and the austere and virtuous Dorval is revealed ordering horses for the purpose of leaving at once, his reason being that he has fallen in love with Rosalie, the fiancée of his friend and host, Clairville. Rosalie is a motherless girl whose father has long been in the Indies and is now on his way back to France to bless Rosalie's nuptials with Clairville. Meanwhile, Rosalie is living in Clairville's house, under the care of his widowed sister, Constance. Constance is much upset by the news that Dorval is leaving, and makes to him a very thinly veiled declaration of love. 'That which follows must be hard to say for a woman like Constance,' say the stage directions parenthetically. At this point Clairville enters and begs Dorval to intercede with Rosalie in her fiancé's behalf. Something seems to have happened to her affections for him and Clairville believes that the juxtaposition of Dorval's virtue will easily put everything to rights: 'Such,' says Clairville, 'is the august prerogative of virtue: it impresses everyone who comes near it.'

In the John Alden-Priscilla Mullens interview that follows, Dorval, without acknowledging his love, learns that Rosalie loves him. This redoubles his resolve to leave the house at once, but as he is writing some farewell lines to Rosalie he is called out of the room to fly to the defense of Clairville, who is being attacked by armed assailants. Constance enters the room and reads the half-written letter, which she takes to be addressed to herself. At one point in this second act Dorval's servant ejaculates, 'No! it seems as if good sense had fled from this house. . . . God grant that we catch up with it on the road.' Several contemporary critics regarded this as the best line in the play.

From the conversation between Clairville and Dorval that begins Act III, it is clear that Dorval has just saved Clairville's life. Constance enters, shows the tormented Dorval that she has seen his letter and taken it to be meant for her, and then, not seeming able to strike much fire from so backward a lover, leaves. Clairville accepts Constance's interpretation of the letter and speculates on why Dorval had not confided in his friend. 'Did you fear that my sister, learning the circumstances of your birth . . . ?' 'Clairville,' replies Dorval, 'you offend me. I possess a soul too exalted to conceive such fears. If Constance were capable of entertaining such a prejudice, I dare to say that she would not be worthy of me.' Rosalie enters, learns from Clairville that Dorval is to marry Constance, swoons, and announces to Clairville upon reviving that she hates him. There then appears a servant of Rosalie's father, who explains that master and man had been within sight of the French coast when their vessel was captured by the British and Rosalie's father despoiled of his fortune and thrown into prison. A former business correspondent secured their release, and Rosalie's father, now penniless, is in Paris and about to rejoin his daughter. Dorval receives the news of the loss of Rosalie's fortune 'motionless, his head bowed, with a pensive attitude, and his arms crossed (such is usually his ordinary attitude).' He secretly resolves to take from his own fortune in order to restore hers, and as the curtain falls on Act III he is seen writing to his banker.

In Act IV Dorval attempts to persuade the tenacious Constance that he is not good enough for her, and that he is leaving in order to exist far from men. This is the point in the play where Constance says that 'only the bad man lives alone,' the remark that Rousseau took personally. There follows a very edifying conversation, full of eighteenth-century 'philosophy' regarding virtue. What, for example, would be the chances of their children's being virtuous? 'Dorval, your daughters will be virtuous and decent, your sons noble and proud. All your children will be charming . . . and I do not fear that a cruel soul might ever be formed in my womb and of your blood!' When the virtuous but reluctant Dorval reveals the handicap of his illegitimate albeit almost guiltless birth, Constance replies, 'Birth is bestowed upon us, but our virtues we acquire.'

In the last act Dorval demonstrates his virtue and his forcefulness by persuading Rosalie in a long harangue that they could never be happy together and that she must accept Clairville. At that moment the father of Rosalie arrives, and Dorval recognizes him as *his* father! This remarkable coincidence provides a dénouement with a vengeance: Dorval and Rosalie suddenly finding themselves half-brother and half-sister, there is scarcely any use of their engaging in speculation as to whether *their* children would be virtuous, so Rosalie resolves to live happily ever after with Clairville, and Dorval with Constance. The curtain goes down with everyone on stage bathed in happy tears, according to eighteenth-century prints of the final scene.

Most of the attention paid to the *Fils naturel* has appropriately enough been devoted to its place in the history of the French drama. But it should also be pointed out that the play has great biographical significance, not only in respect to what Diderot wrote and when and why, but also in regard to its revelation of what Diderot valued and admired. Diderot delights in Dorval. To him the hero of his play is a hero indeed. And what a hero! A man whose charms are so irresistible that he receives two declarations of love in a single day, whose courage and prowess are so great that he saves the life of his friend, whose generosity is so ample that he divides his own fortune for the sake of his friends, whose virtue and eloquence are so overpowering that he can recall one of the ladies to her duty, and whose self-abnegation and self-control are so triumphant that he can marry the other whom he does not love. Surely Dorval was the Super-Man of the *salons.* His creator wrote of him in the spirit of a boy dreaming preposterous and fantastic dreams of glory. It may even be that Diderot saw himself in this creation of his imagination. Evidence for this identification may be found in the fact that Diderot has Dorval's servant saying to him, 'Monsieur, you are good, but don't go imagining that you are as good as your father.' [24] Now, these are almost the identical words that a neighbor at Langres used in speaking to Diderot about his real-life father, so that to many readers the psychological transference will seem apparent.

Dorval is one of the first in a long line of somber heroes whose souls are touched by *Weltschmerz* and whose hearts are swollen by feelings almost too delicate and subtle for ordinary mortals to feel. The unquestionable similarity between Dorval and Goethe's Werther and the presumable influence of the former in the shaping of the latter was noticed very early.[25] Such a hero, although usually divested of his preoccupation with virtue, became standard in the course of the Romantic Movement. And from Diderot's description of Dorval in the following passage, connoisseurs will have no difficulty in recognizing the type. 'He was melancholy in his conversation and bearing, unless he spoke of virtue or experienced the transports it causes to those who are strongly enamored of it. Then you would have said that he was transfigured. His face became serene. His eyes sparkled and became gentle. His voice had an inexpressible charm. His discourse became affecting and moving, an interlinking of austere ideas and touching images that held the attention in suspense and the soul in raptures. But as in autumn evenings, during cloudy and overcast weather one sometimes sees a shaft of light escape from a cloud, shine for a moment, and then vanish away in an overcast sky, so, too, his animation died away, and he suddenly relapsed into silence and melancholy.'[26]

The impact on public opinion of the *Fils naturel* was greatly fortified by Diderot's doctrines as expounded in the three supplementary dialogues. Within the framework of these imaginary interviews, Diderot propounded many new conceptions of the drama, conceptions that he was not the first to feel but that he was the first to express, at least in so comprehensive a way.[27] And because Diderot was an author singularly endowed with the gifts of plausibility and persuasion, his precepts as stated in these conversations were fully as influential as the example of the play itself.

Many readers will be surprised to learn that Diderot did not attack the unities of time, place, and plot which had become an iron rule of the French classic stage. Quite to the contrary, he wrote that 'The laws of the three unities are difficult to observe, but they make sense,' and both *Le Fils naturel* and *Le Père de famille* conformed to them.[28] The reforms he demanded were other. One of them was greater realism. He was emphatic in the 'Conversations' that stage settings are extremely important and really part of the action. As a corollary, he wanted the stage cleared of spectators.[29] Moreover, he interspersed his dialogue with explicit stage directions — had Dorval drink a cup of tea — and peppered his pages with exclamation points and broken-off sentences, in order to give some idea of the emphatic style of speech and the semi-inarticulateness of persons who labor under strong emotions.[30] This led him, incidentally, to discuss the problem of fitting prosody to music, a technical problem of the opera that always fascinated him. Thus he called for a reform in operatic composition that anticipated the opera of Gluck.[31] And he had much to say of the importance of pantomime and gesture. 'We talk too much in our dramas; and consequently our actors do not sufficiently act.' [32] And to enhance the illusion of reality, Diderot made his play contemporaneous. The scene was laid at Saint-Germain-en-Laye, twelve miles west of Paris, and the time was 1757. All this was new.

The purpose of this greater realism was to clear the way for the second of Diderot's desired reforms, the creation of what he called domestic and bourgeois tragedy.[33] This showed the very great influence that the contemporaneous English theater had upon him, especially George Lillo's melodramatic *The London Merchant, or the History of George Barnwell* (1731), and Edward Moore's almost equally melodramatic *The Gamester* (1753). In the conversations with Dorval, Diderot twice mentioned *The London Merchant* and once *The Gamester* as models of what he had in mind, and the abiding influence of Moore's play on him is symbolized by the fact that in 1760 he translated it for the edification of some of his friends.[34] As for the matter of 'domestic and bourgeois tragedy,' Diderot did not regard himself as having written in that mode. His plays, he thought, belonged rather to what he called in 1757 the serious kind of play (*le genre sérieux*), neither the old tragedy nor the old comedy but something new and in between, something as new as the *Fils naturel* and at the same time as old as the plays of Terence.[35] By the time he had published his *Père de famille* a year later, he was calling this sort of play a drama (*drame*). The word 'drama' in French has therefore come to have a much more specific and less generic meaning than in English. It connotes the particular sort of play written along the lines recommended by Diderot.[36]

Obviously bourgeois tragedy is tragedy mirroring the vicissitudes, conflicts, and values of the middle class. The temptations to which its characters are subject are peculiarly middle-class temptations, such as the peculations of the apprentice, George Barnwell. The virtues portrayed in such plays are those of an emergent and potentially powerful social class, thus illustrating De Tocqueville's remark concerning the drama in nations tending toward democracy. To people of the seventeenth century nothing could be more deliciously funny than the bare title *Le Bourgeois Gentilhomme,* for it incongruously associated what they deemed inherently incompatible, the *bourgeois* and the *gentilhomme.* For devotees of the *drame,* however, this attitude was beginning to seem out-of-date and contrary to 'philosophy.' In the *drame* the middle class is portrayed as having dignity and being worthy of respect. Commerce, for example, is no longer considered degrading. Clairville, upon being asked what he was going to do in view of his reduced fortune, says in the *Fils naturel,* 'I shall go into commerce. . . . [It] is almost the only occupation in which great fortunes are proportionate to the effort, the industry, and the dangers that make them respectable.' [37]

Along with the creation of domestic and bourgeois tragedy, Diderot hoped to aid in creating a whole new repertoire of plays to represent the various occupations and the various family relationships: 'The occupation ought now to become the principal object, and the character should be only the accessory.' [38] Thus there should be portrayed the man of letters, the philosopher, the businessman, the judge, the lawyer, the politician, the citizen, the magistrate, the financier, the nobleman, the public administrator. 'Add to that, all the [family] relationships: the family father, the husband, the sister, the brothers.' [39] Thus Diderot raised to a new level of artistic importance both the lives of persons whose family ties were strongly knit, as in the traditional manner of middle-class families, and the lives of those who worked for their living.

The third and principal object of Diderot in writing *Le Fils naturel* and in expounding his doctrines was to make the theater an institution for teaching morality. The *philosophes,* in almost everything they thought and wrote about, were strongly utilitarian. Things should have a use, a function. Carrying this axiom over into the theater, it was not enough for Diderot and the *philosophes* that plays should entertain, they must also impel to virtuous action. The usual consensus is that this is asking the theater to carry a very heavy extra burden, but Diderot demanded it. He has Constance say, 'Doubtless there are still barbarians; and when will there not be? But the time of barbarism is past. The century has become enlightened. Reason has become refined, and the books of the nation are filled with its precepts. The books that inspire benevolence in men are almost the only ones that are read. Such are the lessons with which our theaters resound, and with which they cannot resound too often. . . .' [40] Diderot also referred jocularly to an ideal republic to be set up in the island of Lampedusa. In that ideal society, actors would fulfill the function of preachers, so useful should the theater be.[41] What, asked Dorval, is the aim of dramatic composition? And Diderot replied, 'I believe it is to inspire among men a love of virtue and a horror of vice.' [42]

Such were Diderot's ideas on how a play should be written, ideas that aroused as much scoffing and scorn as they did enthusiasm and admiration.

The short-range opposition to these notions should not, however, be allowed to obscure the long-range importance of Diderot's ideas. 'No other part of Diderot's writings has given rise to a larger mass of studies and criticisms than his plays and his essays concerning dramatic literature,' writes a recent American critic.[43] And the scholar who is generally regarded as the best authority on the history of the *drame* began his work with these words: 'French literature in the eighteenth century saw a new dramatic form being born . . . Foreshadowed and prepared by the school of tearful comedy, the *drame* acquired with Diderot a very distinct and clear-cut personality. Thus it is from the publication of the *Fils naturel* (1757) that its real existence dates.'[44]

Although the play was not produced at Paris until 1771, there were at least two performances of it 'in the provinces' in the year of its publication. These occurred, probably in a private theater, at Saint-Germain-en-Laye, the very locale in which the action of Diderot's play was supposed to have taken place. Deleyre wrote to Rousseau that he had gone 'to the first performance, where I wept copiously, although not intending to.'[45] But Fréron declared that there was nobody at the second performance![46] Whether that be true or not, the interest aroused by Diderot's drama is attested by the number of editions it had. Between 1757 and 1800 it was published in twenty-five French editions, four German and three Russian, twice in Italian and in Dutch, and in Danish and English once each.[47]

Much of what Diderot wrote in the *Fils naturel* and its subsequent dialogues lent itself to sarcastic comment. In the 'Conversations' he talked a great deal about the forthcoming *Père de famille,* praised it in advance, and, contrary to his usual custom, brazenly sought a patron for it and that in cold print. The person he had in mind was a prince of the blood royal, the Duke of Orléans, whose chief passion was his love for the theater.[48] Moreover, Diderot's enemies did not fail to notice that the fiction he used of Dorval's having written the *Fils naturel* gave him the opportunity, while seeming to compliment Dorval, really to praise his own work fulsomely.[49] And if, in his dialogue with Dorval, he made some objections to this innovation or that, it was transparently done to allow Dorval to make a triumphant and unanswerable reply. 'The author makes some objections against his play,' wrote Palissot, 'and the Lord knows how much he "pulls his punches" (*il fait patte de velours*). The so-called Dorval replies in so satisfactory a manner that M. Diderot is always obliged to agree with him.'[50] Both Palissot and Fréron thought it a weakness in Diderot's play that he had to rely upon an extraordinary coincidence, a *deus ex machina,* in order to bring his piece to an end, and Palissot spoke cuttingly of 'this old man tumbled down from the clouds.' [51] Both critics objected to the 'philosophical and glacial jargon,' and complained that there was no contrast between the personages of the play, so that all of them seemed to have been cast in the same mold. 'It is always M. Diderot, a philosopher, a metaphysician, who is speaking . . . .' [52] There was a disposition among critics, too, to claim that even if these new ideas were any good, it was not Diderot who invented them; and one pamphleteer gave himself the satisfaction of calling Diderot the Amerigo Vespucci of the new kind of play, other persons having been its Columbus.[53]

Diderot's enemies presently began to exult in a discovery they made — that the Fils naturel was very closely modeled on a comedy entitled Il Vero Amico, written by the celebrated Venetian playwright Carlo Goldoni, and first produced in 1750 at Venice. Fréron wanted to publish the news of this discovery by printing a letter purportedly written by Goldoni in complaint of the Fils naturel. This Malesherbes refused to allow. He evidently accepted the proof of plagiarism, for Fréron had sent him a copy of Goldoni's works, but his reason for refusing to allow Fréron to publish the supposititious letter was that 'it would be a falsehood worse than all the acts of plagiarism in the world, to give to the public under Goldoni's name such a letter if it were not really from him.' [54] Fréron had to content himself with a very indirect although effective approach. In one issue he published a full synopsis of the Fils naturel; then in his next issue, under pretense of reviewing Goldoni's comedies generally, he published an equally detailed synopsis of Il Vero Amico, and in doing so he used, where relevant, the identical words of his previous summary, thus creating a haunting echo effect that would naturally cause readers to look back to try to find out where they had read the same thing before.[55] By this device Fréron suggested to his readers what Malesherbes did not allow him to say outright.[56]

A collation of Goldoni's Il Vero Amico and Diderot's Fils naturel shows that the situations, the personages (save for an old miser who appears in Goldoni's play and is left out of Diderot's), and a good deal of the dialogue are extremely similar up through almost half the play.[57] This might be called cultural borrowing on the grand scale. But thereafter the plots diverge. Moreover, the spirit of the two plays is different throughout. Goldoni's is more a farce than a play 'of the serious kind': it attempts to impart no morality or 'philosophy,' and it has no special middle-class point of view. That Diderot's sins had therefore been much exaggerated by his enemies was the comforting conclusion pointed out by the contemporary Journal Encyclopédique:

Finally, from a three-act farce (half of which was itself borrowed from Molière's 'The Miser') there has emerged a symmetrical piece in five acts, written in a vigorous, grave, elevated, and energetic style, and capable of expressing feeling, without which no style can speak to the heart. Let those who desire to despoil M. Diderot of his glory, in order to give it to Goldoni, attempt a similar metamorphosis with any one of the sixty plays that the fertile Italian has written. Far from reproaching them for their theft, we will congratulate them very sincerely for having had the skill to do it.[58]

It is difficult for people in the twentieth century to be quite sure how heinously Diderot had transgressed against the ethical code of his contemporaries in regard to plagiarism. 'Even in the seventeenth and eighteenth centuries,' a scholar in the problems of literary history reminds us, 'public opinion was still indulgent in this regard; it was not until the last century that plagiarism was condemned as out-and-out dishonesty.'[59] Malesherbes seems to have partaken of this attitude when he sharply distinguished between Diderot's plagiarism and Fréron's wanting to print a letter purportedly, but not really, written by Goldoni. In Malesherbes' eyes, there was patently no comparison in the relative guilt of the two offenses. On the other hand, it is obvious that Collé took a very severe view of the matter, and it is also clear that Diderot's enemies felt that they now had him at a considerable disadvantage, from which one may conclude that plagiarism was not entirely overlooked by contemporary opinion nor completely condoned.[60] Besides, Diderot himself felt constrained to justify his procedure, and in 1758, in his *Discours sur la poésie dramatique,* he made the best of admitting what could not be denied: 'I took possession of it as if it were a piece of property belonging to me. Goldoni had not been more scrupulous. He laid hold of the *Avare* without anyone's taking it into his head to find that bad; and no one among us has imagined accusing Molière or Corneille of plagiarism for having tacitly borrowed the idea of some play either from an Italian author or from the Spanish theater.' Diderot denied that his play and Goldoni's were similar in kind, that his characters and those of Goldoni had the slightest resemblance, that there was a single important word in the *Fils naturel* that had been taken from *Il Vero Amico.* And then, becoming quite heated, he asserted that 'I really wish that there were a dozen such larcenies to reproach me with. I do not know whether the *Père de famille* has gained anything by belonging entirely to me.'[61]

Public opinion eventually began to rally somewhat to Diderot's support, as the foregoing quotation from the *Journal Encyclopédique* shows. The *Mercure de France* for February 1759, in reviewing Diderot's *Discours sur la poésie dramatique,* spoke very sympathetically regarding his explanation. 'I would never end,' wrote the reviewer, 'were I to cite all unacknowledged translations made from one language to another without anyone's believing himself obliged to announce them. This is the first time that the name of plagiarism has been given to the use of a foreign idea that has been enriched, ennobled, and, above all, applied to a genre that is not that of the original.'[62]

Nevertheless, Diderot's conduct when he later came unexpectedly face to face with Goldoni betrayed a bad conscience. Goldoni's feelings had been hurt, he tells us in his *Memoirs,* not so much by the possibility of plagiarism — after all, plagiarism is a form of very sincere compliment — but by Diderot's calling Goldoni's comedies farces! Besides, he thought that Diderot's public references to him as Charles Goldoni, instead of M. Goldoni, betrayed both irritation and contempt. 'I was sorry to see a man of the greatest merit predisposed against me. I did everything possible to draw near to him . . . to convince him that I did not deserve his indignation.' Finally, Goldoni asked a common friend, an Italian musician named Duni, to take him to call upon Diderot. Though obviously embarrassed, 'M. Diderot had the honesty to say that some of my plays had caused him much vexation. I had the courage to reply that I had noticed it.'[63] The interview seems to have ended politely but inconclusively, and although Goldoni was in Paris off and on for many years thereafter, their paths apparently did not cross again.

The *Fils naturel* greatly enhanced Diderot's reputation, but it was a source of mortification too. A few days after its publication he had written to Jean-Jacques, 'Whatsoever success my work has had*. . . I have received scarcely anything but embarrassment from it and I expect nothing but vexation.'[64] In this he was prophetic. For some years he had lived in comparative tranquillity, he and the more recent volumes of his *Encyclopédie* having given little leverage to his enemies. But the *Fils naturel* had given them a purchase. Presently other untoward events, directly or indirectly connected with Diderot, were responsible for bringing about the supreme crisis in the history of the *Encyclopédie.*

CHAPTER 21

Rising Opposition;
D'Alembert's Blunder in Volume VII

D URING all the time that Diderot and Rousseau were inexorably proceeding from misunderstanding to misunderstanding, during the time that Diderot was publishing the *Fils naturel* and was being crowned with laurel leaves by his friends and contumely by his foes, France was locked in a struggle with England and Prussia that should rightly be regarded as one of the first world wars. It was in 1757, the year of the *Fils naturel,* that the British court-martialed their admiral Byng for letting the French capture Port Mahon and had him shot on his own quarterdeck — 'to encourage the others,' wrote Voltaire grimly; it was in 1757 that Pitt formed his second ministry and out of disorganization fashioned order, and victory out of defeat; and, finally, it was in 1757 that the French won a battle at Hastenbeck and suffered a national humiliation at Rossbach.

Little as Diderot concerned himself with the vicissitudes of the war, he and his *Encyclopédie* nevertheless came under some suspicion because of it. Principally this was because Frederick the Great, now a national enemy, had singled out Diderot and D'Alembert for honors. They were members of his Academy, as the title pages of the successive volumes of the *Encyclopédie* testified, and D'Alembert in particular seldom overlooked an opportunity in articles he wrote for the *Encyclopédie* to praise the 'philosopher King.' During the Seven Years' War anyone who could be called an Encyclopedist or a *philosophe* was by that very token imputed to be a bad citizen, recalled Condorcet, 'because France at that time was the enemy of a philosopher king who, justly appreciating merit, had given public testimonials of esteem to some of the authors of the *Encyclopédie.*' [1] In addition, the Encyclopedists, especially Diderot, were hospitable to ideas from abroad, most of all to

British ones, and in a time of national emergency this could be represented, even in that milder age, as faintly smacking of the subversive.

The year 1757 began on a somber note in the political history of France, for on 5 January Louis XV was attacked in the palace at Versailles by a man who, mingling freely and unchallenged among the courtiers, got close enough to the King to wound him slightly with a double-bladed knife.[2] French opinion was appalled. So was the King, who feared that the knife, since the wound it inflicted was so trifling, must be poisoned. Damiens, the attacker, was easily disarmed, and in due time impressively and horribly executed. The King, of course, recovered, but the net result of the incident was to suggest that the current freedom of canvassing ideas, limited as it was, had somehow unsettled Damiens' mind and was in general a threat to national security. An alarmed public opinion was ready to accept strong measures. In February the syndic of the press and his deputies warned the members of their guild neither to print nor to sell anything regarding 'present affairs.'[3] On 16 April there was promulgated a Royal Declaration, a stupendous pronunciamento that stipulated that 'All those who shall be convicted of writing or of having had written or of printing any writing tending to attack religion, to rouse opinion, to impair Our authority, and to trouble the order and tranquillity of Our States shall be punished by death. With reference to all other writings of whatsoever kind, not falling under the description of Article I, it is Our pleasure that, for not having observed the formalities prescribed by Our ordinances, authors, printers, booksellers, peddlers, and all other persons disseminating such writings among the public shall be condemned to the galleys for life, or for a term suiting the gravity of the case.'[4]

This was scarcely a favorable climate for the dissemination of new ideas. Nevertheless, from D'Alembert's point of view, the seventh volume of the *Encyclopédie* might be the best yet, if we may believe his letters to Voltaire. 'Without doubt,' he added, in a letter written in July, 'we have some bad articles on theology and metaphysics, but, with censors who are theologians, and with a license, I defy you to make them better. There are other articles, less in the open daylight, where everything is made up for. Time will make the distinction between what we have thought and what we have said.'[5]

Just as the seventh volume was about to be published, there appeared in the October issue of the *Mercure de France* a formidable attack upon the *philosophes*. For some time there had been a lull in the hail of pamphlets that had pelted the Encyclopedists, but this persiflage in the *Mercure* gave the signal and set the style for a new onslaught that was destined to end in catastrophe for the *Encyclopédie*. The article was written by a certain Jacob-Nicolas Moreau, a publicist who had currently been writing (in a little magazine called the *Observateur Hollandais*) a series of comments upon foreign affairs favorable to the policy of the French government and, in fact, subsidized by it.[6] Moreau was by no means a prominent man of letters, and never became one, but his invention of the word 'Cacouac' to ridicule the *philosophes* was one of the palpable hits of the eighteenth century. He published his attack in the form of a 'Due Warning' printed in the *Mercure*. These Cacouacs, recently discovered and hitherto unsuspected enemies of the public, were strange and loathsome creatures, 'Savages fiercer and more redoubtable than the Caribs ever were. . . . Their weapons consist solely of a poison hidden under their tongues. As they are no less cowardly than malevolent, they make a frontal attack only upon those from whom they believe they have nothing to fear. Most frequently they cast their poison from behind. . . . Their whole substance is nothing but venom and corruption. The source of it is inexhaustible and is always flowing.'[7]

Just as the public was becoming Cacouac-conscious in this autumn of 1757, Volume VII was published.[8] Many of its important articles were unexceptionable. Among these were 'Geometry' by D'Alembert, and 'Geography' by the King's Geographer (Robert de Vaugondy), and those presenting the most recent developments in technology, such as the long and detailed articles on 'Iron-works' (*Forges, Grosses-*) or 'Stoves' (*Fourneau*). But, as always with the *Encyclopédie,* its articles reflected a desire for improvement and a willingness to experiment with change. Quesnay, in his article on 'Grain,' wanted free trade in that commodity. Turgot, who was already enjoying a high reputation as a magistrate, wrote the article 'Fair' (*Foire*), and concluded that the great merchant fairs 'are never as useful as the restraint of trade that they entail is harmful; and that far from their constituting the proof of the flourishing state of commerce, they can exist, on the contrary, only in those states where commerce is hindered, overburdened with taxes, and consequently indifferently great.'[9] And, as always, the *Encyclopédie* sighed for a state of affairs wherein thought would be freer, tolerance more broad. Thus the Abbé Morellet dared to praise religious freedom in the United Provinces. 'The Dutch magistrates have finally learned,' he was allowed to write, in an article that he tells us was heavily censored, 'that for the sake of peace they should abstain from participating in such disputes; allow theologians to speak and write as they please; let them confer if they want to, and come to decisions, if that pleases them; and especially persecute no one.'[10]

In a very important and influential article on 'Endowments' (*Fondation*), Turgot examined, as he said, 'the utility of [perpetual] endowments in general in regard to the public welfare, or, rather . . . the disadvantages of them.' Even endowments made for the best of motives — to say nothing of those set up out of vanity — tend to outlive their usefulness, or to encourage mendicancy instead of discouraging it, or to be abusively administered. Salutary change could be brought about, he wrote, either by improved laws applying to all of society or by temporary endowments subject to discontinuation when the need was past, such as was then being done by associations of citizens in various places in England, Scotland, and Ireland for the purpose of increasing employment. 'What has occurred in England can take place in France: for, whatsoever one may say, the English do not have the exclusive right of being citizens' — a daring thing to publish in an absolute monarchy in the midst of a war with England. In this article Turgot used time and again the stirring word 'citizen,' and said that employments and offices of all kinds should become the recompense of merit. 'What the state owes to each of its members is the destruction of obstacles that would hinder them in their industry, or that would disturb them in the enjoyment of the products that are the recompense of it.' It was not for nothing that Turgot was a close friend of Gournay, the man who invented the formula of *laissez-faire et laissez-passer*. Noteworthy in this article is the sober but earnest appeal to public opinion, and the reference to public utility as the criterion of decision. 'Public utility is the supreme law,' wrote Turgot in this article — a principal tenet of faith of the Encyclopedists in regard to all social, economic, and political policy, and one capable of cutting through all the political obscurantisms of the *ancien régime*.[11]

This article was published without attribution to Turgot, so that Diderot, as editor, accepted the further responsibility of seeming to be its author. If to praise the English was to be unpatriotic, Diderot took the burden of it. If it was subversive to assume that the state owes something to its members, if it was disloyal to speak of the state rather than the king, Diderot shouldered that onus, too.

The *Encyclopédie*'s lack of interest in political and diplomatic history of the conventional sort is exemplified by the brevity of the article devoted to 'France.' This article, written by De Jaucourt, disposes of the subject in only nine hundred words, and many of these are taken up, not by an account of French history, but by deploring France's uneven distribution of wealth (comparing it to 'Rome at the time of the fall of the Republic'), the depopulation of the provinces, the overimportance of Paris, and the poverty of the cultivators of the soil. And De Jaucourt, using the technique of cross reference, declares that causes and remedies of these evils are not hard to find: '*See the articles "Tax," "Tolerance," &c.*' [12] But if the *Encyclopédie* was not interested in political history, nevertheless it had a political point of view, and in the article on 'Government' De Jaucourt wrote, 'The people's greatest good is its liberty. Liberty is to the corporate body of the state what health is to each individual. Without health, man cannot savor pleasure. Without liberty, happiness is banished from states.' [13]

In theological and religious matters, the *Encyclopédie* continued its policy of pinpricks and knowing winks. The article on 'Grace,' for example, which may have been written by Diderot, commented somewhat obtrusively upon the futility of a subject that had not seemed so to Saint Augustine. 'Besides,' wrote this unknown author, 'so much has been written upon this subject without in any way illuminating it that we apprehend laboring quite as uselessly. The principal works of the theologians of the several parties may be read concerning these matters. The discussions, very frequently minute and futile, to which they have given rise, do not deserve a place in a philosophical work, however encyclopedic it may be.' [14] Nor did the Encyclopedists forget to twit the Jesuits, as when Voltaire began his brief but ostentatiously learned article on 'Fornication': 'The *Dictionnaire de Trévoux* says that it [fornication] is a term in theology'! [15]

Regarding the history of religions, the *Encyclopédie* sought as usual to find a rational explanation for the origin of what it regarded as irrational practices. Thus Diderot wrote of the Roman sacrifice of milch cows heavy with calf (in '*Fordicides*'), his explanation of this pagan phenomenon being that Numa had instituted the practice to alleviate some calamity, such as a lack of forage, and that the sacrifice had continued long after the condition necessitating it had passed away. 'From which I conclude,' he wrote gravely, 'that one cannot be too circumspect when commanding something in the name of the gods.' [16] This method of studying primitive religious practices, not unlike Sir James Frazer's in *The Golden Bough,* was best displayed in Volume VII in a remarkable article on the 'Parsees' (*Guèbres*). Starting with the tenets of Parsee faith, the author, Nicolas-Antoine Boulanger, broadened out to give a theory of the origin of myths and of their role in all religions.[17] It was a way of suggesting, of course, the genesis of Genesis.

Diderot's contributions to Volume VII were not numerous, but a reader finds the now familiar touches: the graceful image — 'I regard these fragments of philosophy that time has allowed to come down to us as though they were planks that the wind casts up on our shores after a shipwreck, allowing us sometimes to judge of the size of the vessel'; the subjective — 'O sweet illusion of poetry! You are no less charming to me than truth itself. May you touch me and please me until my last moments'; [18] and the personal, this time a portrait of himself in reverse in his article on 'Formalists.' In his distaste for the pettifoggers of good form, Diderot showed himself par excellence the man who always hated to wear a wig.[19]

Famous among the articles of the *Encyclopédie*, and perhaps the most fateful of them all, was D'Alembert's ill-starred contribution on 'Geneva.' Usually the *Encyclopédie* had almost nothing to say under the heading of sovereign states — three-fifths of a column allotted to England, a column to Genoa, a little over a column to Spain, seventeen lines to Denmark — but to Geneva D'Alembert devoted four double-columned pages. His knowledge was first-hand, acquired during his visit to Voltaire in the summer of 1756. Gossip had it, after the storm broke, that Voltaire had put D'Alembert up to writing the article and that Voltaire might even have written part of it himself, as Rousseau believed, the purpose being to insert in it proposals for allowing the production of plays in Geneva.[20] In that Calvinist city-state the theater was looked upon with as much favor as it was at about the same time by, say, Cotton Mather, Jonathan Edwards, or the divines of Salem, Providence, and New Haven. To this subject D'Alembert devoted a whole column: 'Plays are not allowed at Geneva, not because stage spectacles are there disapproved of in themselves, but because, it is said, of the fear of the taste for display, dissipation, and libertinage that companies of actors communicate to the youth. Nevertheless, would it not be possible to remedy this drawback by having severe and strictly executed laws governing the conduct of actors?' [21]

On the whole, D'Alembert had evidently intended to be very complimentary to Geneva, especially because, like Tacitus writing about the Germans, he wished to improve his own countrymen by calling their attention to more virtuous foreigners. Thus he pointed out that the Genevese did not allow prisoners to be put on the rack, save in very special circumstances, and he spoke with great approval — perhaps he had imbibed this doctrine, too, from Voltaire, who had long believed in it — of their practice of burying the dead in a cemetery outside the city.[22] He also approved of the rigorous examination of the theology and morals of a minister before he was ordained and evidently before he was assigned to a pastorate, remarking that 'it is to be wished that most of our Catholic churches would follow their example.' But D'Alembert was a prim and schoolmasterish man, and he could not forbear remarking on matters that the Genevese could scarcely be blamed for thinking were none of his business. Thus he reproved them for retaining a certain part of their heraldic coat of arms. He told them that they should obliterate a certain inscription upon their city hall. Speaking of their divine services, he remarked that 'the singing is in rather bad taste and the French verses that are sung are worse yet. It is to be hoped that Geneva will reform itself upon these two points.' He observed that 'Calvin was as enlightened a theologian as a heretic can be,' a remark which probably displeased the Calvinists as being too grudging and the Sorbonne as being too generous.[23] In short, it is likely that a Genevese would have read D'Alembert's article with more irritation than gratification, and it is hard not to look upon it as a monument of tactlessness. From whatever point of view this article is regarded, one is tempted to say, in the vernacular of American sports, that D'Alembert led with his chin.

Nor was this the sum total of its offenses. The article 'Geneva' almost occasioned an official protest from the Genevese government to the French government because of the remarks D'Alembert made about the condition of religious belief in that sovereign city-state: 'Several [of the clergy] no longer believe in the divinity of Jesus Christ. . . . several of the pastors of Geneva have no other religion than a perfect Socinianism, rejecting everything having to do with mysteries, and conceiving that the fundamental principle of a true religion is to propose for belief nothing shocking to reason.'[24]

Soon after the publication of Volume VII, Grimm was calling this article a blunder, and reporting that it was creating a great stir at Paris.[25] It created an even greater one at Geneva, where the corps of Calvinist ministers were highly embarrassed by this public allegation that they were deists or, at the least, a variety of eighteenth-century Unitarian. To call a person a Socinian when he was officially committed to a belief in the Trinity and in revelation was to use fighting words, and it is not surprising that the ministers sought public amends. The Council of Geneva meeting on 9 December tried to find 'whether there be not some measures to take in order to have this article changed or suppressed.'[26] It hesitated to make a formal complaint to the French government only for fear that the French would make some disagreeable demand in return. As late as 15 January 1758, the possibility that an official complaint would be lodged with the French government was not entirely past.[27] Meanwhile, the Company of Pastors appointed a Committee of Nine to draw up a reply. The 'Declaration' they formulated was sent to all the editors of Europe and Fréron printed it in his *Année Littéraire* in February of that year.[28]

The secretary of this committee was a Genevese layman, Dr. Théodore Tronchin, the famous physician who in 1756 had made himself one of the best-known men in France by his successful inoculation against smallpox of the two children of the Duke of Orléans.[29] At that time he had become acquainted with Diderot, and in due course he became a contributor to the *Encyclopédie*, his article being, appropriately enough, the one on 'Inoculation.'[30] One of his first duties as secretary of the Committee of Nine was to write to D'Alembert and Diderot to secure a retraction. D'Alembert's reply gave him no satisfaction at all.[31] From Diderot he received a letter that illumines the relations between the two editors and implies that Diderot had disapproved of his colleague's action.[32]

This letter, evidently composed with great care, if we may judge from the profusion of conditional tenses, suggests a divergence in editorial policy between the two men. Although Diderot did not explicitly claim that he tried to prevent the publication of the article, he did say he had had 'no share' in it and he certainly implied that he would not have published it had the decision depended upon him. Did he really advise against its publication, or was he trying to deceive Tronchin into believing that he had? The latter alternative seems the less likely, for Diderot was not a pusillanimous man. An attempt on his part to cultivate Tronchin's good will at D'Alembert's expense is not in character. Besides, Diderot must have realized how much it was to the interest of the *Encyclopédie* to preserve a united front in this crisis. Indeed, one may well ask why he did not assume equal responsibility as far as Tronchin was concerned, whether or not this corresponded to the reality of the case, and try to brave it out. On the contrary, he steadfastly claimed not to be responsible, although offering to take the blame publicly on himself. Finally, if it be remembered that D'Alembert never alleged, either in his letter to Tronchin or in his correspondence with Voltaire, that Diderot had approved of the article on 'Geneva' before or after its publication, the inference that Diderot disapproved of publishing the article seems strong. Had D'Alembert been able to divide responsibility with Diderot, it would have been manifestly to his advantage to do so.

It is evident that Tronchin interpreted the situation as meaning that Diderot had not favored publication. Writing to a Swiss colleague a few days after receiving Diderot's letter, Tronchin remarked that 'His co-editor, Diderot, who is, of all the men I know, the most humane,' would never have done what D'Alembert did. And Tronchin continued (but unfortunately without citing sources), 'Opinion was unanimous against the article, before it was printed. Therefore M. d'Alembert cannot say that he did not foresee its effect. He alone held out against them all. Whatsoever reasons were used to combat his obstinacy, he did not wish to give in, [and] the article was printed.'[33]

What, after all, can explain Diderot's willingness to allow Tronchin to in-fer that he had not approved of D'Alembert's article? Could Diderot have been motivated by the desire to prevent Voltaire from ever again using the *Encyclopédie* to serve his own private purposes? As Grimm remarked in the *Correspondance littéraire* — and his and Diderot's ideas did not usually diverge very far — 'I cannot express how out of place this whole article was in the *Encyclopédie,* in which the city of Geneva ought to occupy the space of three or four lines, and not entire columns for the purpose of telling us what it should or should not do — a subject absolutely foreign to the arts and sciences that constitute the subject of this dictionary.'[34] Diderot's usual policy of holding Voltaire at arm's length made itself very conspicuous at this junc-ture. Voltaire repeatedly sent regards to Diderot in letters to D'Alembert and even in a letter to the publisher Briasson.[35] Diderot did not reciprocate. Then Voltaire, in this crisis, wrote directly several times, but to his extreme annoy-ance, Diderot neglected to reply.[36] Perhaps Diderot thought it outrageous of Voltaire — and D'Alembert, too — to jeopardize the fate of the whole *En-cyclopédie* so that Voltaire might see a play in Geneva. It is therefore con-ceivable that Diderot welcomed the opportunity of a showdown with D'Alem-bert, once the latter had precipitated the issue of Voltaire's influence in so clean-cut a fashion. The distrust of D'Alembert that Diderot had already evinced in the letter written in 1755 makes this explanation even more likely.[37]

Unquestionably the *Encyclopédie* was made vulnerable by the article on 'Geneva.' It seemed presumptuous and arrogant in its cocksureness regarding matters both temporal and spiritual. It tended to reflect on the judgment of the editors. And just as it came close to involving the Ministry of Foreign Affairs, so, too, it almost precipitated an investigation by the Parlement of Paris. 'It is asserted,' wrote D'Alembert to Voltaire, reporting this new dan-ger, 'that I praise the ministers of Geneva in a fashion prejudicial to the Cath-olic Church.'[38] The enemies of the *Encyclopédie* were becoming bolder, and scarcely anyone missed the significance of the fact that a Jesuit dared to preach a sermon at Versailles, in the presence of the King, attacking the *Encyclo-pédie.*[39] The article on 'Geneva' was not the sole cause of the increasing com-plaints against the work, but it undoubtedly encouraged the accelerating tempo of the attack.

Furthermore, it is probable that D'Alembert's ill-favored article on 'Geneva' precipitated the crisis regarding censorship that overtook the *Encyclopédie* following the publication of the seventh volume. If the Parlement of Paris should investigate the *Encyclopédie,* as it threatened, then it was inevitable that a number of searching questions would be asked as to how offending passages had happened to secure approval. Evidently Malesherbes deemed it prudent, for his own protection, to ask the questions first. An undated note in his almost illegible hand stated that 'I learned with the greatest surprise' that articles had been printed that had not been reviewed by any one of the three theologian censors.[40] In another notation Malesherbes revealed how this had happened. Undated and unsigned but unquestionably in his highly individual writing, it stated that the agreement of 1752 'was observed for the third volume and, at most, for the fourth. Since that time the editors and publishers have fallen again into the habit of arbitrarily sending each article to the censor in whose province they deemed it to belong. This is what has given rise to the complaints occasioned by the seventh volume.'[41] Nor did the publishers deny that this was what had occurred. Le Breton wrote to Malesherbes on 24 December to say that 'there have not been printed any sheets, particularly of the last five volumes of the *Encyclopédie*, without their being initialed by one of the censors whom you have assigned to us,' but he could not claim that everything had been reviewed and passed by one of the theologian censors.[42] From this Malesherbes evidently concluded that these censors had been negligent, for he drafted a very stiff rebuke to the chief of them, commenting on the publication of some articles 'which it is impossible that any one of you three had approved. . . . You ought to have complained that the present rule was being evaded, and because you have not done so, you have shared in the transgression of the authors and printers.'[43] Henceforth, every single sheet was to be initialed by one of the three theologian censors. Malesherbes was fortunate that the breakdown of his previous orders did not become public knowledge, and he was quite justified in insisting that the rules agreed upon in 1752 should be carried out punctiliously. Nevertheless D'Alembert, particularly, chose to regard Malesherbes' orders as a new encroachment and another grievance.

Hostile pamphlets also plagued D'Alembert at this time. One of them was *Little Letters on Great Philosophers* by Palissot whose enmity D'Alembert had earned in 1755 when he protested in Rousseau's behalf against *Le Cercle*. Now Palissot, young in years but old in enmity, returned to the attack, an attack which D'Alembert believed to have the protection of patrons in very high places. In just a few pages Palissot managed to touch a great many sore spots. He twitted Diderot and D'Alembert for having copied Bacon 'servilely'; ridiculed Diderot's opening words in his *Pensées sur l'interprétation de la nature,* 'Young man, take and read'; laughed at the statement that deer attain the age of reason; sneered at Diderot's pamphlet on 'Encaustic'; remarked that the editors *formerly* praised Rameau; and chided them for being so morbidly sensitive to criticism. Palissot accused his enemies of monopolizing the term 'philosopher'—'All these gentlemen call themselves Philosophers. Some of them are.' He took care to remind the public that D'Alembert was the beneficiary of a Prussian pension, and he also criticized the D'Alembert eulogy of Montesquieu which had appeared as a foreword to Volume V: 'There reigns in it a tone that is revolting. It is not so much the expression of public admiration as it is an order to the Nation to believe in the merit of this illustrious writer.' Most of all, Palissot complained of the *philosophes'* forming a party, of their pronouncing upon reputations, 'of the ostentatious praise that these gentlemen mete out to one another,' of 'this tone of inspiration on the part of some, of emphasis on the part of others,' of their intolerance, of their setting up for themselves a literary throne, of their saying in effect that 'No one shall have wit save us and our friends.' And Palissot hinted that the *philosophes* were by way of becoming a church: 'At the front of certain philosophical productions one may observe a tone of authority and assurance that until now only the pulpit has exercised.' [44]

This was quite bad enough, especially after Fréron lovingly reviewed it in his *Année Littéraire*.[45] But Moreau's 'New Memoir to Serve toward the History of the Cacouacs' was even worse. In this more extensive account of the habits and manners of those formidable creatures, the author informed the public that the only weapon that the Cacouacs feared was a whistle. Whistling put them into disarray and sent them headlong into flight, a remark disclosing that in the eighteenth century as in the twentieth, whistling is to a Frenchman what booing is to an American today. The author of the 'Memoir' had forgotten his whistle and was consequently captured by the Cacouacs. He was disarmed to the strains of Italian music, and then an old man came into the room with a book, and said, 'Young man, take and read.' The Cacouacs, according to their prisoner, were anarchists; they denied the existence of the gods; the only thievery they permitted themselves was that of the thoughts of others; 'they particularly coveted the glory of destroying'; they were absolutely indifferent to patriotism, no longer recognizing any other fatherland than that of the entire universe; and by common consent they accepted lying as a general practice. The captive discovered that the Cacouacs were great talkers: 'their language has something sublime and unintelligible in it that inspires respect and arouses admiration.' He himself became proficient in their idiom: 'I continued to shine. Ideas came to me. But if sometimes they failed me, I had some big words to put in their place, and I noticed that then it was that I was applauded the most vigorously.' He was initiated into their mysteries by being permitted to peep into their seven sacred coffers (the seven volumes of the *Encyclopédie*). 'With surprise I observed a confused mass of the most heterogeneous materials — gold dust mixed with iron filings and lead slag, diamonds half-concealed in piles of ashes, and the salts of the most salubrious plants mixed up with the most noxious poisons.' The prisoner was given a valet, who robbed him while virtuously quoting to him his own philosophical principles. This valet, moreover, had written a book entitled 'New Discoveries about Tragedy, or the Art of Composing Very Fine Scenes out of Grimaces.' After a number of adventures, the captive was able to return to his own country. There he discovered that it was later than he thought: the Cacouacs were already there! 'These dangerous and ridiculous Cacouacs . . . had been given the name of *Philosophes,* and their works were being printed!' [46]

Americans have a phrase to describe this kind of persiflage — a rock in every snowball. Diderot seems to have borne it without a flutter of nerves, but D'Alembert was overawed because he believed it to be officially inspired and because he claimed to know that Malesherbes, although desirous of preventing publication, had received orders from higher up to see that it was not suppressed.[47]

At this singularly unpropitious time, D'Alembert chose to draw a large draft on Malesherbes' fund of good will. Fréron, as may readily be imagined, had unctuously and gleefully digested the 'New Memoir' for his readers, forgetting none of the most painful parts.[48] But whereas Moreau had not alluded to D'Alembert by name, Fréron inserted in a footnote a reference to one of D'Alembert's works, thus making the connection unmistakable. It was, in fact, as Malesherbes called it, nothing but a subtlety, but nevertheless D'Alembert took great umbrage.[49] Malesherbes was sufficiently moved by D'Alembert's protest to inquire of Fréron by what right he used personalities in attacking his enemies, to which Fréron made sturdy and independent reply.[50] Yet it is evident that Malesherbes, although he wrote to Fréron, was nevertheless exasperated by D'Alembert's protest. Moreover, Malesherbes was very aware of his own delicate position at this particular time, for he wrote to the Abbé Morellet, who became the intermediary in the affair, 'I am even more sorry to see how the chagrin caused by the pamphlets has blinded him to the point of not sensing how indiscreet it is and, I venture to say, unreasonable, coolly to demand redress from Fréron at the moment when the seventh volume of the *Encyclopédie* and especially the article "Geneva" have excited the most powerful outcries, and when one cannot defend the work nor take the side of the authors without exposing oneself personally to very grave reproaches.' [51] In this letter and in one to D'Alembert, Malesherbes outlined the guiding principles of his administration.[52] These were liberal and inspiring documents, even though, as Malesherbes predicted and as Morellet tells us in his *Mémoires,* D'Alembert was very discontented with them.[53] The incident shows clearly enough that of the two men, the magistrate and the writer, it was not the writer who desired freedom of the press. Malesherbes implied that what D'Alembert wanted was the right to say what he pleased and the refusal of the same right to his enemies — an analysis very close to the truth. His protest to Malesherbes against Fréron was so poorly justified and so plainly ill-timed that Malesherbes began to suspect an ulterior motive. In the draft of his letter to Morellet, Malesherbes wrote (and then scratched out) the following sentences: 'If I knew M. d'Alembert less well, I might suspect him of seeking to prepare, relative to the public, a pretext for quitting the *Encyclopédie*. But I do not believe him capable of it.' [54]

As early as 1 January 1758 D'Alembert claimed to have informed Malesherbes and the publishers of his decision to give up the *Encyclopédie;* and in his reply of 6 January 1758 to Tronchin, he added a postscript: 'I ought to add, Monsieur, that reasons of an essential character, having no relation to the article "Geneva," oblige me to give up my work on the *Encyclopédie* absolutely and once for all. Thus it seems to me that this work, brought to a stop in the middle of its course, no longer merits becoming the subject of the complaints of your clergy.' [55] It is of great interest to notice that at this writing D'Alembert evidently took it for granted that his quitting would mean the end of the *Encyclopédie*. Five days later he wrote to Voltaire that he did not know whether the *Encyclopédie* would be continued or not. 'What is certain is that it won't be by me. I have just notified M. de Malesherbes and the publishers that they may search for my successor. I am worn out by the insults and vexations of all kinds that this work brings down upon us.' [56]

Before receiving the foregoing letter Voltaire heard a rumor that D'Alembert was intending to quit and hastened to urge him to stick it out.[57] Then, in answering D'Alembert's letter, Voltaire again urged him not to resign. 'Do not abandon it. Do not do what your ridiculous enemies want. Do not give them this insolent triumph. . . . I know that it is shameful that a society of superior intelligences, working for the good of the human race, should be subject to censors not worthy of reading you; but can you not choose reasonable revisers? Cannot M. de Malesherbes aid you in this choice?' [58] But D'Alembert, replying to the first adjuration, wrote that 'In regard to the *Encyclopédie,* when you press me to take it up again, you are ignorant of the position we are in and of the fury of the authorities against us. . . .

I don't know what course Diderot will take. I doubt that he will continue without me. But I know that if he does, he is preparing for himself trials and tribulations for ten years.' [59]

Quite suddenly Voltaire had an abrupt change of heart. Instead of beseeching D'Alembert to stay on, he now began to insist that everyone connected with the *Encyclopédie* should quit with him.[60] As long as Voltaire had supposed that the author of the memoir about the Cacouacs was a Jesuit or inspired by the Jesuits, he was brave. But when he learned from D'Alembert that these attacks were protected and perhaps inspired by the Court, he began to be very cautious and, while still lustily blowing the trumpet for a charge, hastily beat a retreat.[61] Reversing his earlier and braver sentiments, he now wrote that 'it is absolutely necessary that all those who have worked with you should quit with you. Will they be so unworthy of the name of philosopher, so cowardly as to abandon you?' [62] Frightened himself, Voltaire found it a good time for calling other people cowards. 'I have already told you,' he wrote to D'Alembert on 13 February, 'that I wrote Diderot more than six weeks ago, first to beg him to give you courage regarding the article "Geneva" in case they tried to intimidate you, secondly to say to him that he must join himself to you, quit with you, and not take up the work again except with you. I repeat to you, it is infamous not to be united as brothers in such a situation. I have also written to Diderot to return my letters [and my] articles. . . . Henceforth I do not wish to furnish a line to the *Encyclopédie*. Those who will not act like me are cowards, unworthy of the name of men of letters. . . .' [63]

'D'Alembert does well to quit,' wrote Voltaire to a friend in Paris, 'and the others, by continuing, are acting like cowards.' [64]

Throughout this flurry of volubly explaining why one should give up, there was one of the protagonists who said nothing. In all this scurry of letting go, one man held fast. Diderot simply kept on. No doubt the perplexities of the situation were increased by his friends' pressure on him. Even Rousseau, 'frightened by the rumors that are going about regarding the *Encyclopédie*' and fearing for Diderot's safety, wrote a letter urging him to quit if D'Alembert did, although it is not known (the letter not being extant) whether he too called Diderot a coward! [65] In mid-February Diderot at last wrote to Voltaire, excusing himself for not having replied earlier, and describing his motives for not giving up or finishing in a foreign country, as Voltaire had suggested. They were motives which Voltaire grumbled at and which D'Alembert obviously did not regard as decisive, but nevertheless the letter shows a willingness to accept moral responsibilities and honor them in the face of adversity that ought to be acknowledged as commendable and courageous:

. . . To abandon the work is to turn one's back on the breach and do what the rascals who persecute us desire. If you but knew with what joy they learned of D'Alembert's desertion and what maneuvers they undertake to prevent him from returning!

What Diderot really thought of D'Alembert's action is revealed by that word 'desertion.' His own attitude, Diderot wrote later in his letter, was not inspired by an overwhelming fondness for the *Encyclopédie*:

My dear master, I have passed my fortieth year. I am weary of bickering. From morning to night I cry 'Rest! Rest!' and there is scarcely a day when I am not tempted to go to live obscurely and die tranquilly in the remotest part of my province.

But this was the second movement, written in a minor key, of a battle symphony. What was it, then, that Diderot thought should be done?

That which is suitable for men of courage: Despise our enemies, pursue them, and profit, as we have already done, from the imbecility of our censors. . . . Is it honest to disappoint the expectations of four thousand subscribers, and do we have no obligations in respect to the publishers? If D'Alembert starts over again and we complete the work, won't we be avenged? . . . Someone else might rejoice over his desertion, seeing gain in it of honor, money, repose. As for me, I am disconsolate over it, and I shall neglect nothing to bring him back. Now is the moment for me to show him how much I am attached to him, and I shall not fail either him or myself. But for God's sake, do not counteract me. I know how great is the influence you have over him, and it will be useless for me to prove to him that he is wrong if you tell him that he is right.

. . . .

Don't be angry any longer, and especially do not ask me any more for [the return of] your letters; for I would send them back to you and never forget such an injury. Your articles I do not have, they are in D'Alembert's hands and you well know it.[66]

Voltaire did not receive Diderot's letter with very good grace. 'The trouble all arises from M. Diderot's not making from the first the same declaration as M. d'Alembert.'[67] 'It is a pitiful thing,' he wrote a month later, 'that associates of such high merit should be masters neither of their own work nor of their thoughts. Accordingly the edifice is built half of marble and half of mud.'[68]

Diderot's decision to carry on with the *Encyclopédie* was probably as much a disappointment to D'Alembert as it was to Voltaire, if we may judge from what D'Alembert wrote five years later regarding his own decision to quit. For in justifying himself he could scarcely avoid implying his disapproval of those who did not follow his example, especially as he was, according to the journal of D'Hémery, a man 'with a great deal of vanity and presumption.' [69] When his collected works were published in 1763, D'Alembert grasped the opportunity to tell how right he had been. But perhaps all that he proved was that Malesherbes had been correct in suspecting him of seeking a pretext to quit: 'In libels publicly distributed (and openly protected) the Authors of the *Encyclopédie* were represented as men without probity or morals, although not a single line in seven volumes was cited to support such atrocious accusations. The Author of this Preface deemed it incumbent upon him to ask for justice, less for himself (for he was not personally attacked in these libels) than for the good of a work that appeared to merit some little consideration and some support. The justice he asked for being refused him, he realized, perhaps too late, that henceforth nothing could make the *Encyclopédie* secure from the gravest and most unjust imputations, and from the sort of inquisition being prepared to be used against it. Therefore he adopted the wise policy of henceforth limiting himself exclusively in this Dictionary to the mathematical part, which cannot be subjected either to the clamors of false zealots or to the chicanery of a censor, and which, besides, is the only part for which he contracted solemn engagements with the public.' [70]

The article 'Geneva' had the disconcerting effect of putting D'Alembert at odds with people whom he assuredly did not want to antagonize — with the clergy of Geneva, with the Court at Versailles, with the Parlement of Paris, with Diderot, with Malesherbes, and even, most unexpectedly, with Rousseau. For Jean-Jacques, nostalgically remembering his childhood in the puritan city of his birth, took exception to D'Alembert's arguments for allowing theatrical productions in Geneva. The result was a spirited little book attacking the theater as an immoral and enervating institution and defending republican simplicity. Rousseau's *Lettre à D'Alembert sur les spectacles* was written just at the time of greatest strain and anguish in the relations of Rousseau and Diderot, and its publication revealed with dramatic emphasis to the jubilant enemies of the *Encyclopédie* that their foes' camp was divided, their united front broken. Thus was added still another to the catalogue of woes that the article 'Geneva' brought in its train.

CHAPTER 22

'I Used To Have an Aristarchus . . .
I Wish To Have Him No Longer'

Precisely at the time that his friendship with Rousseau was slowly going to pieces, Diderot was continually beset by other distractions and anxieties. As always, there was the routine of editing the *Encyclopédie,* the chronic and Spartan necessity of earning a livelihood, of paying the rent at the Rue Taranne. Added to this was the time spent in creating — and defending — his controversial experiments in playwriting. This was the year in which he had the exhilaration of being hailed as a dramatist of genius and the bitterness of being called a plagiarist of the very first rank. This was the time when he seems to have cherished the intoxicating hope of election to the French Academy. Perhaps it was the time, too, when he came to the grim realization that his hopes would never be fulfilled. This was the year in which he was held up to scorn as a Cacouac, when the article 'Geneva' put the *Encyclopédie* in jeopardy, when his relations with D'Alembert and Voltaire were under almost as great stress as were his relations with Rousseau. The strain of such events no doubt made it more difficult to maintain his balanced judgment in regard to Rousseau, just as his worsening relations with Rousseau probably affected adversely the other crises through which he was living. Reciprocally, one magnified the other.

Rousseau was meanwhile living on at the Hermitage, to all outward appearances calm, nevertheless seething within. His agitation was partly caused by an extremely sensitive and imaginative nature, which impelled him to be suspicious of the motives of his friends and created an appalling conviction of ever-threatening menace and ever-darkling doom. Partly his excitement came from meditating upon what was to become his great love story, *La Nouvelle Héloïse.* Rousseau was in the grip of a tumultuous and irresistible passion. He was in love with love. And, as usually happens to men in that condition, it was not long before his affections lit on a person who seemed to him to be the very incarnation of his dreams.

This lady, whom he had known slightly for several years, was Sophie, Countess d'Houdetot, the sister-in-law of his benefactress, Mme d'Epinay. In her person the Countess connects the French Enlightenment with the early days of the Republic of the United States, for Ambassador Thomas Jefferson frequented her social circle and found her charming. Now twenty-seven, she had married at the age of seventeen, had separated from her husband, and, when Rousseau fell in love with her, was living at Eaubonne, not far from the Hermitage. Mme d'Houdetot was a young woman full of high spirits, far from overserious, capable of witty badinage, and endowed with a fair share of coquetry. She could, moreover, turn a pretty piece of verse, and encouraged the supposition that she was the authoress of a much esteemed 'Hymn to Breasts,' written, it was suspected, for the purpose of stimulating curiosity regarding her own.[1]

The course of true love was troubled by some rather fundamental drawbacks. In the first place, the lady was not very much in love with Rousseau, if at all, although she seems to have been flattered by his attentions. In addition, she was already the mistress of another man, a man to whom she was to remain faithful for fifty-one years. Her lover was the Marquis de Saint-Lambert, a soldier and poet who some years earlier, because of his capacity for begetting, had been the indirect cause of the death of Mme du Châtelet. His liaison with Mme d'Houdetot had begun in 1752.[2] Now, in this crucial spring and summer of 1757, he was on active duty with the French army in Westphalia, where he now and again saw Grimm, and from whom he seems to have learned that Mme d'Houdetot was seeing more of Jean-Jacques than could be regarded as discreet. This was the end of the idyllic phase of Jean-Jacques's love affair. Saint-Lambert evidently rebuked Mme d'Houdetot. She in turn told Jean-Jacques, who hotly accused Mme d'Epinay of informing Saint-Lambert. This was an accusation that Mme d'Epinay found hard to forgive, and it is difficult to say whether much friendship was left between her and Rousseau after 'the day of the five notes,' occurring in late August of 1757.[3]

Throughout this prolonged crisis the much bedeviled Rousseau tried to conceal two pieces of material information, as a result of which all the other protagonists in the imbroglio, particularly Diderot, felt as though they were groping in the dark. In the first place, Rousseau was very reluctant to admit that he was in love with Mme d'Houdetot. It was transparent enough to any-

one who lived in his society, yet he never admitted it to Mme d'Epinay nor
to Grimm nor to Saint-Lambert, and he clearly implies that he did not confess to Diderot that he was in love until the last interview that they ever
had, which took place at the Hermitage on 5 December 1757. But even then
he concealed from Diderot a second bit of material information. As he himself wrote in his *Confessions* regarding this conversation, 'I never admitted
that Mme d'Houdetot knew of it or at least that I had declared it to her.' [4]

Rousseau had of course declared his love. But his situation was perplexing
and delicate, for Mme d'Houdetot was not supposed to be fancy-free. Rousseau, moreover, was under moral obligation not to take advantage of a man's
absence to alienate the affections of his mistress. In these circumstances,
Rousseau's high reputation for virtue being what it was, he was subject to
the subtle temptation of awakening her moral scruples with regard to her
liaison with Saint-Lambert. Rousseau's passion for Mme d'Houdetot is a re-
warding subject for study in the casebook of the psychology of love. Every
man is a Saint Anthony, but the forms in which temptation appears are
various. The almost infinite capacity for subconscious self-deception, for confusing virtue and desire, is nowhere better shown than in the paradoxical,
hypocritical, and pathetic figure of the austere 'citizen,' the stern, republican
man of virtue, overwhelmingly tempted to arousing conscientious scruples
in another man's mistress in the hope of seducing her himself. Of course
Rousseau never put it this way to himself, yet he came close in his *Confessions* and in his letters to Saint-Lambert to admitting that this was what
he was about. 'I protest,' he wrote in the *Confessions,* 'I swear that if, sometimes carried away by my senses, I attempted to make her unfaithful, never
did I truly desire it.' And in a letter to Saint-Lambert, he wrote, 'I deprecate
your connection . . . but a love such as yours merits some consideration, and
the good it produces renders it less culpable.' [5] Indeed, Saint-Lambert's principal uneasiness regarding the attentions Rousseau was paying to Mme d'Houdetot seems to have arisen from just this apprehension that the citizen would
undermine her attachment for Saint-Lambert by playing upon her scruples:
'I reserve, however, your promise which you give me of never speaking to
her against our connection. . . .' [6] And Saint-Lambert might well think that
there was ground for worry when he read Rousseau's reply, in which the
citizen remarked that 'I told her that her attachment for you was *henceforth*
a virtue'! [7] When some time later the exasperated Diderot was drawing up
a list of Rousseau's malfeasances — 'Citizen Rousseau committed seven rascalities simultaneously, which have alienated all his friends' — one of the
'rascalities' was listed as follows: 'M. Rousseau then fell in love with Madame

d'Houdetot; and to prosper his affair, what did he do? He sowed scruples
in the mind of this lady regarding her passion for M. de Saint-Lambert, his
friend.'[8] Authorities are in pretty general agreement that here Diderot described the situation as it truly was.[9]

When this nightmare of tangled personalities began, Diderot's relationship
to it was extremely peripheral. At this time in his life he had not even met
Mme d'Houdetot, he had just barely made the acquaintance of Mme d'Epinay
and was reluctant to know her better, and he rarely saw Rousseau, who was
at the Hermitage, or Grimm and Saint-Lambert, who were on active duty
in the field. Although a whole book about this quarrel has been written on the
assumption that Diderot was in a plot against Rousseau and pursued him
step by step, the record seems to show more casualness than calculation. It is
nearer the truth to think of a bumbling Diderot than a conspiratorial Diderot,
of the nonchalant Diderot who antagonized his friends by not writing an
expected letter or by absent-mindedly failing an appointment, of the naïve
Diderot who was maddening in proffering unsolicited advice and ingenuous
in the admiration of his own virtue.

In the history of the friendship of Diderot and Rousseau, the year 1757
had begun with bickerings about Mme Levasseur and about the offensive
remark made by Diderot in *Le Fils naturel*. Diderot, who had been promising for a long time to go to the Hermitage, finally arrived there in early
April, and a very satisfactory reconciliation seems to have taken place.[10]
Then, in July, Rousseau stayed two nights at the Rue Taranne. The initiative for this meeting was evidently Rousseau's, his object apparently being
to make sure that Diderot would at last be brought to giving his opinion and
suggestions concerning the manuscript of *La Nouvelle Héloïse*. In his *Confessions* Rousseau says that he had sent Diderot the first two parts of the
novel about six months previously, but that Diderot had not yet read them.
Besides this, Rousseau claims to have had the generous motive of desiring to
help Diderot, the latter being involved just at this time in the crisis regarding
the plagiarism of Goldoni, and to signify to the world by this visit that the
two men had not quarreled.[11] In the anti-Rousseau camp the tradition regarding this visit was that Rousseau kept Diderot slaving at the revision until all hours, then discreditably refused to listen to something of Diderot's
when the latter wanted Rousseau's advice in return.[12]

Years afterward, in recollections clustering around these events, Diderot
and his friends asserted that he visited the Hermitage and Montmorency
very frequently during all the time that Rousseau was resident there. Thus
Mme de Vandeul wrote that 'all the time that he stayed at Montmorency,

my father had the constancy to go there on foot once or twice a week to
dine with him.'[13] Marmontel quotes a similar declaration by Diderot:
'. . . and I [he says Diderot declared] going on foot two or three times a week
from Paris to his hermitage.'[14] Moreover, Morellet claimed in his *Mémoires*
to have participated in these expeditions himself. 'Often we went, Diderot
and I, from Paris to his hermitage near Montmorency to pass whole days
with him. There, under the great chestnut trees adjacent to his little house, I
have heard long extracts from his *Héloïse,* which enraptured me as much
as they did Diderot. . . .'[15]

The testimonies of Mme de Vandeul, Marmontel, and Morellet were
written down many years after the events they purport to describe. Mme de
Vandeul's and Marmontel's remarks indicate that their sole authority was
the assertions made by Diderot. Morellet, on the other hand, claims to have
been an eyewitness. Yet his testimony is very hard to reconcile with the tone
of the letters that Rousseau was writing, not years later in his *Confessions,*
but at the very time of these alleged events. These show that all through 1757
Rousseau was greatly distressed that Diderot came so seldom to the Hermitage.
Indeed, Rousseau's letters allow us to trace only four times, and no more than
four times *for certain,* when Diderot and Rousseau saw each other face to face
in the year 1757. Perhaps the frequent visits Morellet spoke of occurred in
1756, but the difficulty regarding this possibility is that Rousseau could not
then have read to them his *Nouvelle Héloïse* because he did not begin to write
it before early 1757, when his relations with Diderot were already extremely
strained. To speak bluntly, Morellet's story does not hold water.

Regarding the four meetings between Rousseau and Diderot in 1757, we
have already spoken of three. These were: the occasion in January when
Rousseau went to Paris to be at the bedside of Gauffecourt; the one in April,
when a reconciliation occurred at the Hermitage; and that in July, when
Rousseau spent several nights at the Rue Taranne. The fourth meeting —
the last in their lives — was at the Hermitage in early December. Over and
above these, there may have been and probably was a fifth occurring early in
September at the Hermitage. If it did occur, it was because Rousseau was in
urgent need of advice, his relations with Mme d'Epinay, Mme d'Houdetot,
and Saint-Lambert having suddenly become extremely vexed and complicated as a result of the agitation caused by 'the day of the five notes' (probably
31 August). According to Diderot's Catalogue of the Seven Rascalities,
Rousseau 'accused Mme d'Epinay of either informing M. de Saint-Lambert
or having him informed of his passion for Mme d'Houdetot. Embarrassed
by his conduct with Mme d'Houdetot, he called me to the Hermitage in

order to learn what to do. I counseled him to write M. de Saint-Lambert everything, and to keep away from Mme d'Houdetot. This advice pleased him, and he promised me that he would follow it.'[16] Although many authorities make no allowance for this September interview, the fact that Rousseau did write a long letter to Saint-Lambert on 4 September makes it seem very possible that the letter was written pursuant to Diderot's advice.[17] Diderot further declared, in his enumeration of the seven rascalities, that 'Later I saw him again. He told me that he had done it and thanked me for the advice. . . .'[18] Rousseau's letter of 4 September is the only one that fills these specifications. But it is much less candid than Diderot claims to have advised.

If Jean-Jacques was driven to distraction by his love affair, it is well to remember that Diderot, too, had recently become involved in one of his own. And during September and October of 1757, when his wife and little Angélique were at Langres on a three-month visit, he had 'three or four bouts of fever,' which debilitated him precisely at the time when Rousseau's relations with Grimm were being stretched to the breaking point. Grimm returned from campaigning and was with Mme d'Epinay through those months. Being jealous of Rousseau's ascendancy over Mme d'Epinay, Grimm treated Jean-Jacques very haughtily, with that calculated hardness that was an unpleasant part of his character. The incidents in this process of disattachment may be followed at length in Book IX of Rousseau's *Confessions*.[19] At the same time the decision was shaping up that Mme d'Epinay, whose health had been poor for some time, should travel to Geneva to be under the care of Dr. Tronchin. She herself did not put much emphasis into her proposal that Rousseau, who knew Geneva well, should accompany her thither. But Diderot did, in a letter written about mid-October which threw Rousseau into a tantrum. 'I learn that Mme d'Epinay is going to Geneva, but I do not hear it said that you will accompany her. . . . Overburdened as you are with the weight of the obligations you owe her, here is an occasion for paying her back in part and for relieving yourself.' Then, after discounting in advance Rousseau's protestations of ill health, Diderot continued: 'Moreover, aren't you afraid that your conduct will be misinterpreted? You will be suspected of ingratitude or of some other secret motive. I know very well, whatever you do, that you will have in your behalf the testimony of your conscience; but does this testimony suffice by itself? And is it permissible to neglect the conscience of other men up to a certain point? . . . I salute you, love you, and embrace you.'[20]

The enraged Rousseau at once accused Diderot of a plot.[21] Once Rousseau's suspicions were aroused, his lively imagination always carried him very far. Sometimes he realized this himself. For instance, he once took it into his head that his publisher, being delayed in sending him the proofs for *Emile,* was betraying him by giving the manuscript to the Jesuits. When Malesherbes wrote to soothe him, Rousseau remorsefully replied, 'Oh! Monsieur, I have done an abominable thing. . . . Nothing has changed since the day before yesterday, yet everything now takes on in my sight a different complexion, and where I thought I saw the clearest proofs I now see only some very ambiguous indications. Oh! how cruel it is for a sick and melancholy man, living alone, to have an unregulated imagination and to be informed of nothing concerning himself.' [22]

In scarcely any circumstances could Rousseau endure being told what to do. Moreover, if two of his friends were in agreement as to any course he should pursue, he promptly concluded that a conspiracy was afoot against him. And to allege that he had obligations to some person drove him quite frantic. Much can be said in justification of this sturdy love of independence, although it can scarcely be denied that Rousseau put himself into an ambiguous light, to say the least, by accepting the occupancy of the Hermitage. Rousseau's awkward position is by no means an unusual one. Multitudinous are the men of letters and the artists of every generation whom ambitious hostesses and lionizing friends have sought to put under obligations by the very extent of their generosity. Perhaps the only defense against this constricting menace of being loved into sterility is to adopt the practice of accepting favors without incurring a sense of obligation for them. Rousseau made the mistake, however, as did James I and Charles I, at odds with their parliaments, of arguing about it. His long letter to Grimm, dated 19 October, in which he referred to his 'two years of slavery' at the Hermitage, gave Diderot ample reason for asserting that Rousseau 'wrote against Mme d'Epinay a letter that is a prodigy of ingratitude.' [23]

So Rousseau did not offer to accompany Mme d'Epinay to Geneva and Diderot wrote this down as one of the seven rascalities. Among Rousseau's secret and unacknowledged reasons for not desiring to be seen with Mme d'Epinay at Geneva was his suspicion that her motive for going was that she was with child by Grimm and that she intended to have the child in secret there. Actually this was not the case — Mme d'Epinay had some sort of bona fide abdominal ailment — but inasmuch as she had previously had an illegitimate child by M. de Francueil, a circumstance of which Rousseau might quite well have been aware, his suspicions, though he could scarcely acknowledge them in writing and though they happened to be unfounded, were nevertheless not preposterous.[24]

Mme d'Epinay left for Geneva on 30 October, and a few days later Grimm wrote Rousseau, castigating him for his 'horrible apology' and his 'monstrous system. . . . I shall never in my life see you again, and I shall deem myself fortunate if I can banish from my mind the recollection of your behavior. . . .'[25]

In view of the situation, Rousseau began to feel that he should leave the Hermitage. Mme d'Houdetot counseled against it, fearing that such a move, occurring just at the onset of the worst season of the year when most people avoided the unpleasantness of moving, would cause a great deal of gossip and perhaps make Rousseau's passion for her common knowledge. Thinking that Diderot would advise the same thing, she wrote to him, although they were not yet personally acquainted, offering to take him to the Hermitage and to be present at the interview. Diderot replied that if she was present he would find it impossible to speak frankly: 'I am of an extreme timidity,' he wrote. And in a second letter he promised to go to the Hermitage on his own initiative as soon as he could.[26] Whether because of timidity or from fear of further complications, it is quite clear that he had no desire to become acquainted with Mme d'Houdetot, and this feeling lasted at least into January, for Mme d'Houdetot wrote Rousseau that she happened to meet Diderot at Baron d'Holbach's — 'I was wearing panniers and had my diamonds on' — and 'he fled from me.'[27] Diderot wrote to Rousseau about mid-November, and did advise him not to leave. In the course of the letter he denied the existence of the plot that Rousseau was so sure his friends had organized.[28]

Early in December Diderot at last found the time to go to the Hermitage. Although Diderot says in his Catalogue of the Seven Rascalities that he went to the Hermitage to demand of Rousseau why he had not confessed to Saint-Lambert as he had told Diderot he had done, the tone and sequence of Rousseau's Confessions and of his correspondence at this period do not confirm this at all. In fact, the Saint-Lambert affair did not come to its climax until several months later. On the contrary, the conversation during the December meeting seems to have concerned itself with the Mme d'Epinay-Grimm crisis, with Rousseau's unsuccessfully trying to get old Mme Levasseur to confirm that Mme d'Epinay had attempted to suborn her and Thérèse. No doubt there was a good deal of discussion as to whether Rousseau should leave the Hermitage, now that midwinter was coming on, and Rousseau further claims that this was the occasion when he learned what was for him the very upsetting intelligence that D'Alembert, in his article on 'Geneva,' was undertaking to tell the citizens of Jean-Jacques's native city what they should do.[29]

One can well imagine that such an interview, between persons so articulate, demonstrative, and emotional, was very much like a scene from one of Diderot's dramas. Tempestuous as it must have been, it nevertheless was far from ending in a break. It was in fact the last time that the two men met, but this was not their expectation at the time. The proof lies in the fact that a few days later Mme d'Houdetot wrote to Rousseau proposing that instead of his moving to Montmorency from the Hermitage, he should go to live with Diderot for the winter. Rousseau's reply, while deeming the project unfeasible, shows that he did not suppose that he would be unwelcome. 'Do you know my situation well enough?' he asked. 'Do you know his, the temper of his wife, to be sure that that is practicable . . . ?'[30]

Rousseau moved from the Hermitage into the town of Montmorency on 15 December 1757. In February he wrote to Diderot what appears to have been a friendly letter urging him to give up the *Encyclopédie* if D'Alembert did, for this was just at the height of the turmoil caused by the article on 'Geneva.' 'He did not even deign to answer me,' wrote Rousseau to Mme d'Houdetot, 'and thus he leaves in adversity the friend who so eagerly shared his [at Vincennes]. That is all that is necessary on his part. This abandonment tells me more than all the rest. I cannot cease to love him, but I will never see him again in my life.'[31] Yet Diderot was really not unmindful of Rousseau's situation, for Deleyre, a friend they had in common, wrote on 28 February, 'He [Diderot] is as uneasy as I regarding the resources that remain to you for subsisting. He fears lest you be in need at the present moment.'[32] This month and even early in March, Deleyre as well as Mme d'Houdetot herself were writing to Rousseau of the likelihood of Diderot's paying a visit to Montmorency.[33] Then, on 2 March, Rousseau wrote a letter, apparently never answered—it was not just Voltaire who could not extract replies from Diderot—in which he stated that he had heard that Diderot was blackening his character and imputing 'horrible things' to him. 'I must, my dear Diderot, write you once more in my life. . . . I am a bad man, am I?' he asked, and then he wrote, clearly alluding to Grimm, 'I should like you to reflect a little about yourself. You trust your natural goodness. . . . What a fate for the best of men to be misled by his own candor and to become, in the hands of bad persons, the innocent instrument of their perfidy. I know that self-esteem is revolted by this idea, but it merits the examination of reason. . . . You could have been seduced and misled. . . . Diderot, think about this. I shall not speak to you about it again.' [34]

And now for the catastrophe. Saint-Lambert, having been invalided at Aix-la-Chapelle for several months, returned to Paris in March 1758.[35] He seems to have learned quite quickly that Rousseau's attentions to Mme d'Houdetot had been altogether more determined and passionate than he had ever supposed or had ever been led to believe. This being true, Rousseau's letter of 4 September took on an altogether different aspect. Although at the time he had answered it in friendly fashion, it now seemed to him to be a hypocritical document.[36] As Diderot said of Rousseau in his Catalogue of the Seven Rascalities, 'he wrote an atrocious letter, of which M. de Saint-Lambert remarked that one could reply to it only with a stick.' [37] Following upon this unpleasant discovery, Saint-Lambert used his influence with Mme d'Houdetot to cause her to break off all relations with Rousseau, which she did in a letter of 6 May, complaining that 'these rumors have come to my lover for some little time. . . . [because of] your indiscretion and that of your friends.' [38] For Rousseau this was a thunderclap. Feeling certain that it was Diderot who had informed Saint-Lambert and that he had perfidiously divulged confidential information, Rousseau not long after gave public notice that the friendship between him and Diderot was ended.

Was there, really, any perfidy involved? Ah! don't we all wish that we knew. Nor perhaps shall we ever, for the motivations are probably as deeply concealed and the points of view as various as those portrayed in *The Ring and the Book*. Diderot stoutly asserted that there was no perfidy. After Saint-Lambert's return from the army, Diderot wrote in his Catalogue of the Seven Rascalities: 'He came to see me. Persuaded that Rousseau had written to him along the lines we had agreed upon, I spoke to him [Saint-Lambert] regarding this adventure as of an episode that he must know about better than I. Not at all, for it turned out that he knew things only by halves and that, by Rousseau's falseness, I fell into an indiscretion.' [39]

Had Diderot desired to be perfidious, this was the precise point where double-dealing would be most effective and least detectable. Diderot liked to suggest, in defense of his innocence, that proof of Rousseau's badness was that he had lost all his friends. 'Our friends that we had in common have judged between him and me. I have kept them all, and none of them remains his,' Diderot wrote to a Swiss pastor early in 1759.[40] The statement is not quite true, for Deleyre, the minor Encyclopedist who had written the article 'Pin' and who for a time in 1756 and 1757 was editor of the *Journal Etranger,* remained friendly to both. But even so, one must acknowledge the possibility that the defection of Rousseau's friends is not of itself proof of his being in the wrong. It might have resulted from unscrupulous manipulation of the evidence.

An attempt to determine the merits and motives in this tortuous story of six lives is of intrinsic interest as a study in human nature. Furthermore, it throws light on the personalities and characters of persons who are important in the intellectual history of the Western world. It reveals Diderot as much as Rousseau, each claiming to be justified, each standing on the threshold of crisis. The enemies of both used the quarrel as evidence to the discredit of each. And the break between Diderot and Rousseau came just at the time of, indeed was a part of, the more important crisis in the fate of the *Encyclopédie*. Here Diderot walked in peril, walked almost alone. It was the greatest test he had been called upon to undergo — the greatest in his life. To survive it required resources of stoicism, self-confidence, endurance, and conviction that make him one of the heroes, or — if it be thought that his sense of self-righteousness is too great to allow him heroic stature — one of the near-heroes, as he was certainly one of the seminal figures, in the history of thought. The mind therefore returns again and again to the problem of the sincerity and honesty of the man who was presently to undergo such a searching test of his stamina and nerve. Was Diderot as virtuous as he thought he was?

Probably not. It is vouchsafed to few men to be *that* virtuous. But in his behalf it may safely be said that to establish that he was perfidious in his relations with Rousseau, one would need to prove a degree of forethought, of calculation, and of ruthlessness that, although they may have existed in this instance, are most contrary to the usual tenor of his ways. Through all the months of this crisis, Diderot had no consistent policy regarding Rousseau. Of course it is true that during this crucial time Diderot was in daily association with Grimm, the man who had become Rousseau's bitterest enemy, and it is altogether probable that by the attrition of constant innuendoes Grimm was able to wear away a great deal of Diderot's lingering sympathy for Rousseau. But this does not seem to have resulted in any calculated policy on Diderot's part. His attitude remained passive, not active. What he did seems to have been the result of sudden impulse. His was the attitude and conduct of a man who, as Voltaire said of him at just this moment, found it harder to write a letter than a book.[41] Moreover, the tension with Rousseau was by no means the only preoccupation of these anxious times. It is hard to believe, with so much going on, with trying to finish *Le Père de famille* and edit the eighth volume of the *Encyclopédie* and contend with

a reinvigorated censorship and parry the attacks of pamphleteers and deal
with Voltaire and persuade D'Alembert to stay with the *Encyclopédie,* that
he could think of the Rousseau problem by much more than fits or starts,
or spend his time in contriving a plot against his former friend.

Besides, Diderot probably did not lie when he stated in his Catalogue of
the Seven Rascalities, a list that was drawn up not later than 1760, and asserted at about the same time to Marmontel that Rousseau had asked for
advice about Saint-Lambert and had promised to follow it.[42] Even this cannot be established beyond a doubt, and of course it is always possible that
Diderot, without in any way being involved in calculated perfidy against
Rousseau, did thoughtlessly blurt out to Saint-Lambert confidential information that ought to have been withheld, a lapse that he thereupon undertook to justify instead of frankly acknowledging. Nevertheless the fact that
Rousseau did write to Saint-Lambert the long letter on 4 September regarding Mme d'Houdetot suggests that Rousseau had accepted Diderot's
advice and that Diderot could assume that Saint-Lambert was fully informed. If this be so, then Rousseau really misled Diderot about what he
had said in that letter, thus being the real cause of Diderot's inadvertently
committing an indiscretion. And then, to Diderot's indignation, Rousseau,
the cause of this false step, turned on Diderot and by a public break exacted
double indemnity for the offense. As Professor Torrey remarks, Diderot felt
taken in.[43] One can sense Diderot's exasperation and feeling of outrage in
the very language and style of the Catalogue of the Seven Rascalities. It
breathes the sense of injury of a man who honestly feels much put upon,
rather than the factitious indignation of a conspirator simulating wrath.[44]

Following the interview with Saint-Lambert in which, according to his
own account, Diderot was inadvertently indiscreet, he did nothing. There
was no more talk of his going to Montmorency, there were no letters exchanged, there were no upbraidings. It was Rousseau, not Diderot, who took
the initiative in notifying the public that the friendship had come to an
end. On 6 May, Mme d'Houdetot broke off relations with Rousseau, and
this was followed by Saint-Lambert's going to Montmorency a couple of
times, as a result of which Rousseau decided that it was Diderot who had
treacherously betrayed him.[45] Consequently, in the preface to his forthcoming *Letter to D'Alembert,* he gave public notice of the break: 'Taste, discrimination, correctness, will not be found in this work. Living alone, I
have been unable to show it to anyone. I used to have an Aristarchus, severe
and judicious. I have him no longer, I wish to have him no longer; but I
shall regret him ceaselessly, and he is missing a great deal more from my

heart than he is from my writings.' To this was appended a footnote, a quotation in Latin from the Book of Ecclesiasticus: 'Hast thou drawn sword
against thy friend? Be comforted; all may be as it was. Hast thou assailed
him with angry words? Thou mayst yet be reconciled. But the taunt, the
contemptuous reproach, the secret betrayed, the covert attack, all these mean
a friend lost.' [46]

When Deleyre, still friendly to both men, saw the celebrated footnote, he
wrote to Rousseau, 'What a passage from Scripture you proceed to quote!
You don't want friends any more, then, since you renounce the best one
that by your own admission you ever had.' [47] Marmontel's *Memoirs* reveal
the way in which this footnote was regarded in the circle of Diderot's friends.
'Finding myself alone with Diderot for some minutes on one occasion, I
expressed my indignation, apropos of the letter to D'Alembert on plays,
concerning the note that Rousseau had placed in the preface of this letter.
It was like a stiletto thrust. . . . Everyone knew that it was Diderot to
whom this infamous note was addressed, and many people thought that he
must have deserved it since he did not refute it.'

Diderot replied to Marmontel that he could not defend himself against
Rousseau's imputations without involving others. 'It is cruel to be calumniated,' he said, 'and that basely and in the perfidious accents of friendship
betrayed, and [it is cruel] not to be able to defend oneself. But such is my
position. You shall see that my reputation is not the only one involved. Now,
as long as one can defend one's honor only at the expense of some one
else's, one must remain silent, and I do.' [48]

Saint-Lambert, like Deleyre and Marmontel, was strongly and unfavorably impressed by the famous footnote. Rousseau had presented him with a
copy of the *Lettre à D'Alembert,* only to receive this reply: 'Truly, Monsieur, I cannot accept the present you have just made me. At the place in
your preface where, regarding Diderot, you quote a passage from Ecclesi-
astes [Ecclesiasticus], the book fell from my hands. After the conversations
of this summer, you appeared convinced that Diderot was innocent of the
alleged indiscretions that you imputed to him. He may behave badly with
you. That I would not know. But I do know that he does not give you
the right to give him a public insult. You are not ignorant of the persecutions he is undergoing, and yet you are going to add the voice of an old
friend to the cries of envy. I am unable to conceal from you, Monsieur,
how much this atrocity revolts me. I am not intimate with Diderot; but I
honor him, and I feel keenly the sorrow you cause to a man whom, at least
in my presence, you never reproached with anything but a little weakness.' [49]

Rousseau's preface was an attack masquerading as a defense, and controversy has raged over the question of who did whom wrong, much as scholars winnow the evidence regarding a question of war guilt. Diderot was not only deeply upset by the footnote in the preface, but also by the tenor of the whole book. Rousseau, in taking issue with D'Alembert as to the desirability of having a theater at Geneva, used arguments or illustrations that Diderot regarded as slurs or attacks upon himself. Accordingly he burst forth in passionate resentment of what he conceived to be Rousseau's malfeasances: 'His note is a tissue of infamy. I have lived fifteen years with that man. Of all the marks of friendship that a man can receive, there is none he has not had from me, and he never gave me any in return. . . . this man is false, vain as Satan, ungrateful, cruel, hypocritical, and bad . . . . Truly this man is a monster.'[50]

For almost all the *philosophes,* and pre-eminently for Diderot, it was a very sore point to allege, as Rousseau had done in the *Lettre à D'Alembert,* that it is impossible to be virtuous without first being religious, impossible 'to have probity without religion.' To the contrary, Diderot insisted that the two are entirely separable. He had found Lord Shaftesbury's ideas very attractive because the noble earl had made precisely this distinction, it being an important implication in the *Inquiry concerning Virtue and Merit* which Diderot had translated in 1745. A man could be virtuous, according to this view, without being inspired by the fear of hell. Indeed, he could be more virtuous, because he was animated by a love of virtue for its own sake. It was this line of thought that involved Diderot in a great deal of moralizing, an activity that he confessed he greatly enjoyed. Everyone has his idiosyncrasy, he wrote about 1773-4, and mine is to moralize.[51] Diderot wanted to prove that *philosophes* were better men than Christians were. He wanted to believe that he himself was a more virtuous man than his brother, for example, who was a priest. Consequently he scarcely ever tired of talking about virtue.

This sort of compulsion is well illustrated at this very time by Diderot's long response to a pastor in Geneva, probably Rousseau's friend, Vernes. Apparently Diderot was replying not only to words of praise but also to some tactfully phrased inquiries regarding the merits of the break with Rousseau. Probably Vernes was trying to discover whether there was any possibility of reconciliation. At all events, Diderot launched into a discussion of morality. It is not Diderot at his best. It is wordy and a little illogical. Moreover, the ideas in it give rise to the uneasy feeling that they were designed more to match the receiver's cloth than the sender's deepest beliefs. But there the letter is, in the Bibliothèque Publique et Universitaire of Geneva, with Diderot's signature upon it, testifying to what he said were the views he held regarding virtue. Diderot referred to himself as a man 'esteeming virtue to such a point that I would gladly give what I possess in exchange for having been up to the present moment as innocent as I was when I was born, or in exchange for coming to the end forgetful of the errors I have committed but conscious of not having increased the number of them!' The more one scrutinizes the latter half of this statement the more oracular and turgid it seems to become. Diderot continued by remarking that 'Virtue is, then, the greatest wealth of him who enjoys life and the most substantial consolation of him who is about to die. There is nothing in the world, accordingly, to which virtue is not preferable; and if it does not appear to us to be so, that is because we are corrupted and not enough of it is left to us to make us aware of all its value.' Then, passing to Rousseau, Diderot wrote, 'It is an atrocious action to accuse publicly an old friend, even when he is guilty. But what name can be given to the action if it happens that the friend be innocent? And what name, furthermore, should be given if the accuser avows to himself at the bottom of his heart the innocence of him whom he dares to accuse?' And then Diderot made it clear that he was seeking no reconciliation: 'For twenty years he has taught me how to pardon private slights, but this one is public, and I do not know any remedy for it.' [52]

Diderot might have been more forgiving had not the *Lettre à D'Alembert* been published at a time peculiarly unpropitious for him and for the *Encyclopédie*. Rousseau's *Lettre,* having received from Malesherbes a tacit approbation, was on sale in Paris by 28 September 1758.[53] It was not simply that this blast against the social utility of plays appeared less than a month before *Le Père de famille,* which, with its accompanying treatise on dramatic aesthetics, was intended to herald a new day in the theater. Scarcely anything could be better calculated to blunt the impact of the play or make Diderot's remarks about the drama, intended to seem self-evident, highly controvertible. This seemed grievous enough to Diderot, as his remarks in his Catalogue of the Seven Rascalities show. But more than that, the public character of the quarrel was very injurious to the *philosophes,* whether they deserved it or not. Up until this moment the public had thought of Rousseau as one of the Encyclopedists. He had been their leader in the controversy over Italian music, he had written the articles on music in the *Encyclopédie,* he had been the author of the important article on 'Political Economy,' and Diderot had apostrophized him by name in the article 'Encyclopedia.' [54] 'Oh! Rousseau, my dear and worthy friend,' Diderot had written for everyone to read in 1755; and now the dear and worthy friend was advertising to the wide world that Diderot was unworthy of further friendship because of 'the covert attack' and because of 'the secret betrayed.'

What Rousseau probably did not realize, but what Diderot and his friends, living in the hurly-burly of Paris could not forget, is that this quarrel by becoming public took on political significance. Rousseau's action, or, at least, Diderot's interpretation of it, can be thoroughly understood only in terms of its political context. Rousseau's *Letter to D'Alembert* appeared in the course of, and greatly complicated, a prolonged crisis during which Diderot's fortunes seemed to proceed with inexorable step from portent to paroxysm to catastrophe. The writings about the Cacouacs were the portent, the consequences of the publication in July 1758 of Helvétius' unlucky book *De l'Esprit* was the paroxysm, the suppression of the *Encyclopédie* in March 1759 was the catastrophe. In the whole eighteenth century this was the time of the crucial struggle to gain for one side or the other the support of public opinion. Eventually the *Encyclopédie* rose from its ashes. Eventually it became manifest that the Encyclopedists had won public opinion to their side just when the course of events would seem to indicate the contrary. But the years of 1757, 1758, and 1759 were grim and anxious for Diderot, years in which public anxieties were compounded with private distress. And it was hard for him to forget that precisely at the time when his *Encyclopédie* was most beset by his enemies, precisely at a time when he most needed to prove that a *philosophe* was an upright man and pure in heart, Rousseau gratuitously informed the public that his old friend was a scoundrel.

Inevitably, therefore, Rousseau's public denunciation, whether he realized it or not, assumed political significance. In consequence, the quarrel became a matter of consuming interest both to the friends and foes of the new philosophy. Everyone talked about it. To do so was more than a frivolity fit to fill up an idle moment. The implications of the quarrel were really of substantial interest to all. That an incident in the private lives of two middle-class writers could absorb the interest of the aristocratic society of the *ancien régime* to such a degree is a symbol of the revolution occurring in the French outlook. The Marquis de Castries, a nobleman destined to be a marshal of France, impatiently remarked one day when the quarrel of Diderot and Rousseau had become public knowledge, 'It's incredible. People don't talk of anything but of those fellows. Persons without an establishment, who don't have a house, who are lodged in a garret. One just can't get used to all that.' [55]

CHAPTER 23

Signs and Portents
of Approaching Eclipse

D'ALEMBERT's decision in January 1758 to forsake the *Encyclopédie,* which he announced as being resolute and which on the contrary was succeeded by over a year of wavering and irresolution, ushered in a period of protracted crisis and confusion. Deleyre wrote to Rousseau on 25 January, during a spell of very cold weather, that 'There is the *Encyclopédie* — spiked. It is no longer going, any more than the water mills have been running these past few days.' [1] The *Journal Encyclopédique* for 1 February mentioned that 'vexations of all kinds have finally obliged M. d'Alembert to give up the work absolutely and irrevocably.' [2] Indeed, the publishers themselves announced to the public in an eight-page pamphlet that the work had been brought to a standstill. This communication, printed in Le Breton's shop and carrying the self-explanatory title of 'Memoir of the Publishers Associated in the *Encyclopédie* regarding the Reasons for the Present Suspension of this Work,' must have been issued early in the year, for it was quoted lengthily in the *Mercure de France* in April. A goodly portion of this pamphlet was devoted to wheedling D'Alembert to return and, to judge from Diderot's informing Voltaire in June that D'Alembert had consented to continue with the mathematical part of the work, it apparently wheedled with a measure of success. [3] As late as 26 February, D'Alembert had written to Voltaire, 'I persist in the resolution not to work any more on the *Encyclopédie*'; yet presently he is to be found doing the opposite of what he had previously announced and adopting a policy diametrically the contrary of what Voltaire had been counseling. [4] The fact is that D'Alembert vacillated a good deal, much to the confusion of biographers, many of whom, putting his desertion in 1759 instead of 1758, seem to be unaware of how protracted and muddled the editorial crisis was,

with D'Alembert loudly announcing that he was quitting, then half-return-
ing, then quitting again, and — even so late as February and April of 1759 —
still considering staying on.

The publishers' appeal to D'Alembert galled Diderot very much. We have
the proof of this in a letter that he wrote about a year later to Sophie Volland.
By this time D'Alembert, who now had given up even the mathematical
part of the *Encyclopédie,* saw Diderot for the first time in several months
and rather lamely proposed being put onto the pay roll again. The fact was
that he was hard up. He lived off pensions, though very modest ones, from
the Prussian and French governments, and these were not being paid because
of the fiscal stringencies induced by the Seven Years' War. The occasion gave
Diderot an opportunity to read D'Alembert quite a lecture. When D'Alembert declared that if he came back, he would write no more prefaces, Diderot
replied, 'You might wish to write some in the course of time, and you
wouldn't be free to.'

'And why not?'

'Because your previous ones have brought down upon us all the animosities
with which we are now laden. Who is there who was not insulted in them?'

Alluding to the publishers' public declaration in the pamphlet of the year
before, Diderot said, 'Nevertheless you quit an enterprise into which they
have put all their fortunes. An affair of two millions is a bagatelle not
worthy of the attention of a philosopher like you. You entice away their
contributors, you throw them into a complication of difficulties from which
they will not soon extricate themselves.[5] All that you see is the slight satisfaction of getting yourself talked about for a moment. They are under the
necessity of addressing the public. You should see how they have regard for
you and *sacrifice me.'* [6]

In addition to causing him to tighten up the censorship of the *Encyclopédie,*
D'Alembert's article on 'Geneva' prompted Malesherbes to re-examine the
whole problem of the relation of the *Encyclopédie* to the government. The
autograph draft of his memorandum, dated about April 1758 and now in
the Bibliothèque Nationale, reveals a startling suggestion. In this letter sent
to Bernis, who was then a member of the Royal Council and soon to become
France's minister for foreign affairs, Malesherbes recommended a policy of
complete autonomy and self-responsibility for the *Encyclopédie.* His letter is
equally revelatory in the information it gives regarding Diderot's status in the
eyes of the authorities: 'As for M. Diderot, he has made some mistakes and
he has been severely punished for them, but are these transgressions irreparable? The disgraces he has already met with and the disfavor that he is

still experiencing, since entry into the academies is forbidden to him for the present moment, are they not sufficient?'[7]

Bernis' reply was affable but noncommittal, and it is not known whether Malesherbes carried his project any further, or whether Diderot realized that the academies were closed to him.[8] When this decision, so adverse to Diderot, was made is not known, but it is clear that not only the French Academy but also the Academy of Sciences were closed to him, and it may perhaps be true that the provincial academies, which at that time were flourishing everywhere in France, were aware of the official disapprobation of Diderot. This might explain why Diderot was never a member of an academy in France, no matter how provincial and obscure.

D'Alembert's decision in early 1758 to retire as an editor of the *Encyclopédie* evidently brought about a new contract between Diderot and the publishers, to judge by one of Diderot's rare letters to Voltaire. Even the latter, who had called Diderot cowardly for wanting to continue the venture, had changed his mind by June 1758, and had inquired whether Diderot would like him to contribute any more articles.

'Do I want your articles, Monsieur and dear master? [wrote Diderot on June 14]. Can there be any doubt about that? Shouldn't one make the trip to Geneva and beg them from you on one's knees, if they could be obtained at no other price? Choose, write, send, send often. I was not able to accept your offers sooner. My arrangement with the publishers is scarcely settled. We have made a fine contract together, like that of the devil and the peasant in La Fontaine. The leaves are for me, the grain is for them. But at least these leaves will be assured me.'[9]

During the early summer of 1758 the preparations for publishing the eighth volume of the *Encyclopédie* were resumed. But the work was badly crippled by D'Alembert's retirement, to judge from the statement of the publishers years later that his quitting was the reason for not publishing a volume in 1758.[10] This time Grimm helped with the reading of proof, Diderot busied himself with his ordinary editorial tasks and with the preparations for the publication of his play, *Le Père de famille,* while the storm brought on by Rousseau's reference to the Book of Ecclesiasticus had not yet broken.[11] But whatever serenity Diderot may have been enjoying in the summer of 1758 was shattered in a twinkling by the publication in late July of the book by Helvétius, *De l'Esprit* ('Concerning the Mind'). This treatise, which in spite of its name dealt more with the springs of ethical action than it did with psychology, had at first seemed so harmless that an official censor had approved it and it was published with tacit permission. All the evidence

points to the fact that Helvétius himself did not dream that his book would
be controversial, which seems to prove that he did not have a very lively
sense of the grand strategy of politics, for *De l'Esprit* put into grave jeopardy
the cause it intended to serve. The orthodox regarded the book as the most
shocking and outrageous that the century had yet seen in print, and they
contended, moreover, that it was completely representative of the point of
view of the *philosophes*. Especially was this asserted of Diderot and the
Encyclopédie. The two works were sedulously intertwined by the critics of
both, although Helvétius never contributed any articles to the *Encyclopédie*.
Nevertheless the latter was made to share by association in the general repro-
bation. In consequence, Diderot found himself living in an atmosphere of
mounting tension and suspense. And before long, crisis was succeeded by
disaster.

De l'Esprit seems rather commonplace to a twentieth-century reader and
reminiscent of that deathless line in the American theater, 'What's all the
shootin' fer?' For Helvétius was simply attempting to found a science of
morality on a basis of behaviorism without the use of transcendental sanctions. As he remarked in his preface, 'I have felt that morality should be
treated like all the other sciences, and that one should make an ethics as one
makes an experimental physics.' His doctrine now seems very much over-
simplified, but certainly familiar, indeed almost platitudinous. In fact, he
was a predecessor of Jeremy Bentham and the utilitarian ethics based upon
the pleasure-pain calculus.[12] A twentieth-century student of ethics is likely
to take the basic assumptions of Helvétius regarding the moral nature of
man as true as far as they go, but stated in a simplistic and rather perverse
fashion.

At the time of its publication, however, the orthodox, the conservative, and
the conventional were profoundly shocked by the doctrines of Helvétius
because he made his system of morality quite independent of the will of God
or the behests of religion. There were no other-worldly sanctions. Egotism,
so to speak, was to be its own reward. For Helvétius dressed up his ethics in
the paradox of an exaggerated egotism, claiming that man was virtuous,
when and if he was, only because in that fashion he best satisfied the demands of his own ego. The famous Mme du Deffand remarked of the book
that it upset everyone so much because Helvétius had revealed what was
everyone's secret.

Nor did Helvétius confine himself to views regarding psychology and
ethics. He unburdened himself of a variety of *obiter dicta,* particularly in
his footnotes, which were as inflammatory as they were extraneous. He dis-

approved of the burdensome forced labor on the highways, he declared that savages were happier than the French peasantry, he attacked the Catholic priesthood as 'not being attached to the general interest,' he wondered whether the Catholic practice of getting rid of daughters by forcing them to take the veil was not more barbarous than the infant exposure of the Chinese, he inveighed against luxury, he insisted (thinking of the belief in miracles) that evidence must be statistical and based on 'the calculation of probabilities,' he praised Julian the Apostate, he very clearly implied that there was no real metaphysical difference between men and animals, and he delivered himself of such humanitarian generalizations as 'not a hogshead of sugar arrives in Europe undyed by human blood.'[13]

Helvétius' book is by no means an unalloyed delight to read, even for those who enjoy collecting antiques. It tiresomely reflects his egotism and humorlessness. The view of human motivation is very narrow. Conduct is motivated almost exclusively by self-esteem, the thirst for fame, and the desire for women, thus mirroring its author more than man.[14] De l'Esprit is diffuse. It is repetitious. It shifts ground confusingly by taking advantage of the extraordinary semantic complexities of the word 'esprit.' Some of the time the book is talking about 'mind,' some of the time about 'wit,' and some of the time in special senses of the word peculiar to Helvétius, as when he makes 'esprit' equivalent to 'taste' and to 'expertness.' Although metaphors and similes are profuse, the effect is surprisingly uninteresting because his imagery is commonplace and unimaginative and his presentation pedestrian and dull. Diderot remarked of the book that 'A paradoxical author ought never to state his conclusion but always his proofs. He should enter into the mind of his reader slyly, and not by force. . . . If all that the author wrote had been heaped up pell-mell, so that there had been only in the mind of the author an unacknowledged principle of arrangement, his book would have been infinitely more agreeable and, without appearing so, infinitely more dangerous.'[15]

De l'Esprit was published on 27 July 1758. On 10 August the Council of State revoked the license for its publication, and this was followed in turn by fulminations from the Archbishop of Paris (22 November) and Pope Clement XIII (31 January 1759).[16] The unfortunate censor of the book, one of the chief clerks in the Ministry of Foreign Affairs, a man named Tercier, lost his job for having passed the manuscript, and Helvétius himself was deprived of the honorific position he had held of maître d'hôtel of the Queen of France.[17] He also had to make a series of solemn retractions.[18] Beyond this, upsetting enough for many men but apparently not very distressing to

Helvétius, nothing much happened to him. As the clearheaded Turgot remarked, what Helvétius had done was 'the most suitable for drawing down upon him the notoriety of being persecuted, which does not do much harm to a rich man, and to make the real weight of it fall upon a large number of honest men of letters who get the lash that Helvétius deserved. . . .' [19] Precisely the same point was made by Grimm, who was particularly alarmed because of Diderot's association with Helvétius in the public mind. 'Philosophy will feel the effects for a long time of the upheaval of opinion that this author caused almost universally by his book. . . . In order to ruin M. Diderot, it has been spread about everywhere that he was the author of all the passages in the book of M. Helvétius that revolted people, although this philosopher has no connection with the latter, and although they do not meet twice a year.' And indeed it is almost certain that Diderot, in spite of what his friend Meister later asserted, had nothing to do with the writing of Helvétius' famous book.[20]

The accusation that the Encyclopedists found most damaging was the allegation that they were closely united in a conscious conspiracy against government and religion. This was very frequently alleged, at no time more crushingly than when the Attorney General of France solemnly declared in 1759 before the highest court in the land that 'It is with grief that we are forced to say it, [but] can one conceal from oneself that there is a project formed, a Society organized, to propagate materialism, to destroy Religion, to inspire a spirit of independence, and to nourish the corruption of morals?' [21] This was but to repeat and summarize the allegations of Palissot in his Little Letters on Great Philosophers; [22] of Moreau in his description of the Cacouacs; of an Abraham de Chaumeix, whose multi-volumed Legitimate Prejudices against the Encyclopédie, together with an Essay in Refutation of this Dictionary began to appear in October 1758; of an abbé calling himself De Saint-Cyr in his 'Catechism and Determination of Cases of Conscience, for the Use of Cacouacs.' [23] This allegation of conspiracy became one of the standard myths of the party opposed to the philosophes, as may be seen in the Abbé de Barruel's Mémoires pour servir à l'histoire du Jacobinisme (1797-8).[24] And it was an allegation that the philosophes always insisted, and rightly insisted, was not so. Grimm denied it, D'Alembert denied it, although he evidently decided that it was imprudent to publish the manuscript in which the disclaimer was contained.[25] Even the publishers of the Encyclopédie denied it. In their 1758 pamphlet explaining the reasons for the suspension of work on the Encyclopédie, they wrote that 'It is the strictest truth [to say] that for the twelve years and more since the Encyclopédie was begun, those who co-operate in it have not assembled together one single time. Most of them do not know one another. Each one works individually on the topic that he has adopted, then he sends his work to one of the Editors, without being in communication with the Authors of the other parts.'[26] That it seemed necessary to make so categorical a statement gives some indication of how damaging the constant asseveration of conspiracy must have been. Yet it must be confessed that the *Encyclopédie* invited such suspicions, for it claimed on the title page of each successive volume to have been written by a *society* of men of letters.[27]

In this atmosphere of increasing tension and foreboding crisis, Diderot put the final touches on his play, *Le Père de famille*. It had been a long time in the writing. He had announced to the public in the *Entretiens sur le Fils naturel* that *Le Père de famille* was being planned. This announcement appeared early in February 1757.[28] But Deleyre's letters to Rousseau show that Diderot was hard at work on *Le Père de famille* over a year later.[29] Indeed, the play with its accompanying 'Discourse on Dramatic Poetry' was not actually published until around the beginning of November 1758.[30] One of the reasons for the long delay was the fact that for a while Diderot gave it up in disgust. This is revealed in a letter written on 29 November 1757 to a fellow playwright, Antoine Le Bret, who was worried because of rumors that the plot of his forthcoming play, *Le Faux Généreux*, was similar to Diderot's. In a hand that showed haste and was, in comparison with the firm yet delicate writing customary to him, comparatively illegible, Diderot wrote that the plot of his play, of which Le Bret had evidently been previously informed, remained unchanged. 'The first [play] involved me in so many vexations that I have been on the point twenty times of abandoning the second and throwing into the fire what I have done. My friends have prevented me. I have taken it up again. I have worked at it a little, but so little that it is scarcely worth mentioning. I do not foresee that it can be printed for two months; the printing will take up another one.'[31] Le Bret's play had its *première* on 18 January 1758, but ten months passed before Diderot's play was published.

Diderot dedicated his play to an Exalted Personage, a Sovereign. Not a very important sovereign, it is true, but still a sovereign. This was not his usual way of doing things. Perhaps he did so because he felt his position weakened and needed to boast the support of an august name. Perhaps it was no more than the influence upon him of Grimm, a man who, as someone has remarked, by dint of great efforts finally promoted himself from the rank of foremost critic in Europe to that of third-rate diplomat. Diderot's

letter was addressed to Her Serene Highness the Princess of Nassau-Saarbruck, and concerned the problem of how to educate her children.* Diderot
did not meet the Princess until 1765.[32] He submitted his dedication to her
through the good offices of Grimm sometime before mid-June 1758, and
apparently without having previously broached the subject. The lady accepted gratefully — after all, she was not a very *great* sovereign — in a somewhat tremulous shimmer of graceful eighteenth-century rhetoric.[33]

Diderot's dedicatory letter is mainly an exhortation to virtue, and has about
it the sooty smell of an academic showpiece, even though Voltaire said he
regarded it as a masterpiece of eloquence.[34] Yet Diderot could not touch a
subject without leaving the imprint of his personality. It is interesting to see
that he does not truckle or fawn. Indeed, putting into the mouth of the
Princess the sentiments that he holds and that he professes to believe that
she, too, holds, he says, 'I desire that they [the Princess' children] see poverty,
in order that they be sensitive to it and in order that they know from their
own experience that they are surrounded by men like themselves, *perhaps
more essential than they themselves,* who scarcely have straw to lie on and
who have no bread.' In view of the fact that Rousseau thought that man was
good in the state of nature, it is of importance in understanding Diderot's
outlook upon politics that in this letter he spoke critically of man in the
state of nature, calling him 'imbecile and savage.' Moreover, he declared that
men would have no need of being governed if they were not bad. Remember,
Diderot thinks the Princess should tell her children, 'power does not give
peace of mind, and labor does not take it away. . . . Virtue is the only
habit that you can contract without fear of the future. Sooner or later all the
others become importunate.'[35]

The manuscript draft of the dedicatory epistle contained a passage that
the Princess particularly and urgently desired suppressed. It is easy to see
why. For Diderot had put into her mouth the following words, addressed
to her children: 'I shall take very good care not to speak ill of sensual pleasure
and not to decry its allure. Its purpose is too august and too universal. I shall
speak to you about it as if nature herself were listening. Wouldn't she have
the right to reply to whoever should speak ill of sensual delight, "Be silent,
foolish one! Do you think that your father would have concerned himself
with your birth, that your mother would have risked her life to give you
yours, were it not for the unutterable charm that I have linked to their embraces? It was pleasure that brought you forth out of nothing." ' Even for the
eighteenth century, this was a little strong.[36]

* There is an English translation, *Concerning the Education of a Prince,* ed. John M. S. Allison
(New Haven, 1941).

In October of 1758 the *Père de famille* was in the process of being printed and Diderot was extremely impatient to get it off the press. Dr. Lavirotte, Regent of the Faculty of Medicine and a friend of Diderot as well as the author of the article *'Docteur en Médecine'* in the *Encyclopédie,* was the censor assigned by Malesherbes.[37] 'I wanted to send both one and the other [the play and the supplementary "Discourse on Dramatic Poetry"] to M. de Malesherbes,' Lavirotte reported, 'but M. Diderot hurried me so much and is so impatient to see his work printed that he carried it away right out of hand.' [38] Malesherbes evidently informed Lavirotte that some changes would have to be made in both the play and its accompanying essay before they would be allowed to appear. Somewhat plaintively he wrote to the censor that apparently Diderot could not write even an essay on dramatics without mentioning government and religion in two or three places.[39] Nor did Lavirotte think it would be easy to persuade Diderot to make changes: 'I merely wish to beg you to observe that no one will have enough authority over the mind of M. Diderot to persuade him regarding these suppressions and alterations. He will resign himself to them only as a result of the most categorical orders.' [40]

Diderot did make some changes, though very reluctantly. 'Here are the *cartons* [substitute pages, to be tipped into volumes already printed and bound] that you have required. The things that have offended you have been suppressed and those that appeared harsh to you, softened.' [41] But Diderot tried to save from the blue pencil a passage occurring in the second act, where the Father of the Family recalls the prayer he prayed when his son was born. Malesherbes objected to Diderot's reference to God, on the grounds that people would regard it as hypocritical. 'How can you make out that I shall be accused of hypocrisy? I am no more the Father of the Family than I am the Commander; and if one has me in mind when reading me, then the piece must be poor indeed.' [42] Apparently Diderot was able to persuade Malesherbes to let the passage stand. It reads as follows: 'My son, it will soon be twenty years since I bathed you with the first tears you caused me to shed. My heart leaped up as I saw in you a friend given me by nature. I received you into my arms from the bosom of your mother, and, raising you toward Heaven and mingling my voice with your cries, I said to God, "O God! who have granted me this child, if I fail in the cares You have laid upon me this day, or if he is not destined to respond to them, have no regard for the gladness of his mother, but take him back." ' [43]

The altercation regarding the prayer caused in Diderot a considerable effusion of temperament. 'I saw the man last evening at the Marquis de Croismare's,' wrote Lavirotte to Malesherbes, probably about 19 October.

'He was in such a violent fit of despair that we feared lest he throw himself out of the window.'[44] And Diderot's letter to Malesherbes, dated 20 October, bears the marks of strong emotion:

This prayer rings true. It is simple. It is moving. It is well placed. This is the opinion of M. de Saint Lambert. It is that of M. d'Argental. The latter was moved by it and the former told me that one does not conceive of such effects unless one has genius. I admit, Monsieur, that friendship for me has made them excessive in their praise. But I have tested this passage on other persons. My wife is a good woman who lacks neither common sense nor taste, and it has given her pleasure. . . .

. . . deign to consider my situation. Observe that for ten years, for thirty, I drink bitterness in a cup never empty. You do not know, Monsieur, how unfortunate my life has been. I have suffered, I think, all that it pleases destiny to make us suffer, and I was born with a sensitivity out of the ordinary. The present misfortune brings to mind misfortune in the past. One's heart swells. One's character grows embittered, and one says and does foolish things. If that has happened to me, I ask a thousand pardons.[45]

As Diderot was finishing his letter, his publisher brought news that Malesherbes was assigning a new censor to the job. This was even worse, wrote Diderot, for the new man would inevitably demand new changes, which meant new *cartons,* all at Diderot's expense. 'Monsieur, have the goodness to revoke an order injurious to a censor whom you esteem and which will be ruinous for me. . . . Monsieur, do not ruin me . . . do not destroy me.'[46] Nevertheless, Malesherbes sent the book not to one new censor but to two.[47] Censors, however, were becoming exceedingly shy, very conscious of the calamities overtaking the unfortunate censor of the book by Helvétius, on the one hand, or the sort of browbeating they were likely to get from the *philosophes,* on the other. One of the censors appointed by Malesherbes begged off for the first reason.[48] The second censor, a man named Bonamy, wrote on 29 October, 'I shall inform the publisher that I have had the honor of sending the work back to you, as being beyond my strength and my enlightenment to pass judgment on, which I confess to being true. But as I ask only for peace and comfort, and as I do not wish to have a quarrel with people who imagine themselves the sole possessors of all human reason, I dare to flatter myself that you will keep the word that you had the kindness to give me that you would not compromise me with them, for I am apprehensive of them as much as I am of the theologians.'[49] Apparently, after all this turmoil, Malesherbes was fain to let *Le Père de famille* be published without further change. In spite of the censorship Diderot had had his own way.

Not long after this display of temperament, Diderot had another adventure with the office of the director of publications. This was a real mystery story, and still remains so to a large degree — the Affair of the Dedications. Malesherbes referred to it as the most annoying and displeasing of his whole administration, and clearly the culprit would have been severely punished had Malesherbes been sure who was guilty of the hoax.[50] The facts are these: There had been timed to appear just after the publication of *Le Père de famille* two of Goldoni's plays, anonymously translated by two of Diderot's friends. *Il Vero Amico,* the play that it was alleged Diderot had plagiarized, was translated by Forbonnais, the man who had contributed to the *Encyclopédie* the admired articles on business and commercial transactions. *Il Padre di famiglia* was translated by Deleyre, the young journalist who in this same year had tried so hard to reconcile Diderot and Rousseau. These translations — usually bound together in one volume, if they can be found at all, so rare have they become — bear up creditably in a collation with the original. They are faithful and idiomatic. Nothing in the originals is suppressed, although not infrequently lines are added, especially to serve as transitions between scenes. No effort at all, however, was made to tamper with *Il Vero Amico* in any way favorable to Diderot. As for *Il Padre di famiglia,* it is so far removed in everything but name from *Le Père de famille* that there could be no question of borrowing.

These plays, when they were published, purported to be printed at Avignon and to be on sale at Liége at Etienne Bleichnarr's. There was no Etienne Bleichnarr. The name means in German 'pale fool,' of which the equivalent in French is *'pâle sot.'* Thus the word 'Bleichnarr' turned out to be simply a pun on the name of Palissot, the bitter enemy of the Encyclopedists and the author of *'Little Letters on Great Philosophers.'* In addition, each play carried as epigraph a long and puzzling Latin quotation and a dedication, one to the Comtesse de * * * and the other to the Princesse de * * * * * *, in flowery, insinuating, ambiguous, and probably insulting language.[51] Almost as soon as the plays were published, complaints were lodged with Malesherbes by two ladies of high position who happened to be well known as enemies of the *philosophes.* The Comtesse de La Marck, who by birth was a Noailles, claimed to be the person designated by the dedication in *Le Véritable Ami;* the Princesse de Robecq (who was the daughter of the Marshal of Luxembourg and had recently been the mistress of the Duke of Choiseul) by the dedication of the translation of *Il Padre di famiglia.*

In the code of eighteenth-century French manners, unfavorable personal allusions in the press or on the stage were regarded as a grave affront, no matter how veiled or slight. This was one of the indirect consequences of censorship. For everyone supposed that such attacks, if allowed publication, were tacitly approved by the government. Consequently all such situations became a matter of 'face.' Someone lost it, and a struggle would develop to see which party enjoyed the greater public credit in the effort to get it back. This was the reason why D'Alembert consistently showed himself very touchy about allusions in the press that one is tempted to think it would have been wiser to ignore. And in this instance, in conformity with this social code, Malesherbes took a grim view of the incident of the dedications and started a determined investigation to discover who had written them and was responsible for their publication.

Malesherbes quickly satisfied himself of the innocence of the translators, Forbonnais and Deleyre. The trail next led to Diderot, who had had the manuscripts of the translations for some days, but who insisted that there were no dedications either when they came into his hands or when they left them.[52] The Comtesse de La Marck had supposed Diderot to be the guilty one — D'Hémery noted in his journal that she was in 'a frightful rage' against Diderot.[53] Diderot called upon her, and managed somehow to placate her. Perhaps it was that gifted tongue of his. Probably, though, it required something more substantial, for according to Palissot's account of the matter to Voltaire, Mme de La Marck secured a signed confession from Diderot.[54] Then Mme de La Marck, in a letter to Malesherbes quite charming in its phonetic orthography, so revelatory of the well-bred illiteracy of the upper classes, informed him that she was satisfied and that Mme de Robecq and she desired him to carry the matter no further.[55]

Malesherbes' reply pointed out that a legal offense had been committed, as well as some moral ones: a premeditated attempt had been made to deceive him, the responsible magistrate, and to make innocent persons, namely Deleyre and Forbonnais, seem guilty. 'So, Madame, I beg of you to have these authors [of the dedications] informed, since they have made themselves known to you, that all they have to do is to make their confession likewise to me, and I promise you that they shall suffer from me nothing more than the disesteem that their manner of acting necessarily brings in its train.' But if they did not confess to him, he would put the affair into the hands of the Lieutenant-General of Police.[56]

At this juncture Forbonnais wrote Malesherbes insisting that someone must make public and explicit acknowledgment of personal responsibility for the translations in their entirety. Otherwise, he wrote, he and Deleyre would be unjustly suspected of being responsible for the dedications. If this was not done, he and Deleyre would resort to the law, and the affair would become a public scandal.[57] Forbonnais went on to say that witnesses had seen a lackey in Grimm's service leaving a copy of the published translations at the door of Forbonnais' lodgings.

The protest from Forbonnais caused Malesherbes to write to the Comtesse de La Marck again. 'It is you, Madame, who brought M. Diderot to his senses, first out of fear and then out of admiration and gratitude for the nobility of your way of acting.' Malesherbes explained the difficulty with Forbonnais, and strongly implied that the Comtesse was the only person in a position to assure that Forbonnais be satisfied.[58] Evidently Malesherbes was hinting that she should persuade Diderot to take the public responsibility. At all events, this is what Diderot did, whether Mme de La Marck persuaded him or Forbonnais did. It was the latter who forwarded to Malesherbes the copy of a letter that Forbonnais had drafted and Diderot had signed.[59] And in due time there appeared in the November issue of the *Observateur Littéraire* and the December issue of the *Mercure de France* the following notice:

Ill-informed persons, Monsieur, having spread about that the published translation of *Le Père de famille* of Goldoni was done by M. Deleyre and that of *Le Véritable Ami* by M. de Forbonnais, the knowledge that I have of these two plays obliges me to declare that [the translations] just published are very different, and it is established that neither the one nor the other had a part in the printing and publication of these works.

I have the honor, etc.,

Paris, 21 November 1758   Diderot [60]

It will be noticed that Diderot, although he absolves Deleyre and Forbonnais, does not hint as to who was guilty. The hostile Palissot assured Voltaire that it was Diderot himself, but Voltaire replied that he could not believe it.[61] Grimm, commenting on Voltaire's letter, told his correspondents that D'Argental, investigating the matter for Voltaire, had been informed by Mme de La Marck that she had had the signed confession in her hand, that she had immediately burned it, and that the secret of who it was would die with her.[62] Certainly the affair had an air of mystery about it to the end. Malesherbes wrote to the Lieutenant-General of Police over a year later, 'This affair remains unpunished for lack of proof,' and added that the guilty parties were under strong suspicion but yet were not known with certainty.[63]

In fact, however, Grimm was the guilty one. The German pun on the name of Palissot, the lackey delivering a copy of the translations at Forbonnais' lodgings, pointed toward him. And A. A. Barbier, an early nineteenth-century literary antiquarian, asserted that Grimm was the author, that Diderot took the guilt upon himself, that the offended ladies soon learned that this was what Diderot had done, and that the affair had had no other consequences.[64] But all this remained a little conjectural until the recent discovery and publication of a letter from Diderot to Grimm written over twenty years after the incident had occurred. Diderot's letter permits no doubt that Grimm was the real author of the dedications.[65]

Why, then, did Diderot take the guilt upon himself? It is possible that this was a really heroic decision. Yet, in what was obviously an extremely complex situation, one can only speculate as to what were his motives. Perhaps one of his reasons was that his friend Grimm was a foreigner and might have had extremely harsh treatment meted out to him, such as deportation, which in Grimm's case would have been calamitous both professionally and personally. We should like to suppose that Diderot's conduct was simply the result of courageous generosity, but in view of the innumerable and varied pressures that must have been playing upon him in this emergency, it is impossible to say with assurance just why he acted the way he did.

Still another question must be asked, a very grave one indeed. How guilty was Diderot, from the point of view of the probity he was always talking about? Unknowingly involved in this intrigue were two men whom Diderot knew to be innocent, two men who thought of themselves as Diderot's friends. Did Diderot connive at attempting to make them seem responsible for having written the dedications? Even though he was protecting his friend Grimm, Diderot incurred some moral guilt in this respect, because it is a matter of record that only under pressure did he exculpate Forbonnais and Deleyre. It may have been, therefore, to this incident that Deleyre was referring when in a letter to Rousseau he spoke of having discovered a knave among the philosophers and of having been made his dupe.[66] Diderot's conduct certainly seems to have been ambiguous — perhaps it was laudable, perhaps it was culpable. Perhaps — for he was a man given to subtle rationalizations when cases of conscience were involved — he here revealed that his early moral training had been in the hands of the Jesuits, men who had long been accused of flagrant sophistry in such matters.[67] Diderot often showed in his writings and letters his awareness of life's real and constant ambiguities, ambiguities of conduct as well as ambiguities of thought. In fact, he wrote his liveliest play upon this very theme. In this piece the hero, Hardouin, is a picture of Diderot as Diderot conceived of himself, an affable and obliging man who, from the best of motives, involves himself in the most dubious and ambiguous conduct. In the final scene the question is asked that gives the name to the play: 'Is he good? Is he bad?' And Diderot-Hardouin replies, 'Alternately.' Similarly, one can ask the same question regarding the part Diderot played in the affair of the dedications: *Est-il bon? Est-il méchant?* Perhaps the answer is the same.

CHAPTER 24

Le Père de Famille and the
'Discourse on Dramatic Poetry'

LIKE his *Fils naturel*, Diderot's *Père de famille* did not immediately receive the honors of a production at the Comédie-Française. This had to wait until 1761, but meanwhile the play quickly became a widely read and influential book. Between 1758 and 1800 there were thirty-two editions of it published in French; ten in German; three in English, plus a play by Gentleman Johnny Burgoyne more strongly influenced by Diderot than the General wished to acknowledge; three in Dutch; two each in Russian, Danish, Polish, and Italian; and one in Spanish.[1] Many of these editions, especially the ones in French, also contained the accompanying 'Discourse on Dramatic Poetry,' so that Diderot's ideas on the theater, expressed in this book as well as in the preceding *Entretiens sur le Fils naturel,* may safely be said to have reached a wide audience.

To *ancien régime* society it seemed self-evident that one of the principal preoccupations of a father was to secure suitable matrimonial arrangements for his children, and the two main 'pivots' in this new play, as Diderot himself pointed out, were to be the establishment in marriage of the Father of the Family's two children.[2] Diderot had already stated, in his *Entretiens sur le Fils naturel,* his conviction that the theater should concern itself with the points of view and behaviorisms of people's professional and family relationships — the judge, the businessman, the man of letters, the father of a family. 'The father of a family! What a subject!' he cried.[3] *Le Père de famille,* therefore, was a play in which parental prudence came into violent conflict with the impetuosity of a young lover. Its plot greatly resembled the real-life circumstances of Diderot's courtship of Anne-Toinette Champion, even to the use of a *lettre de cachet*. Interesting as such a play was to the eighteenth-century public, it is even more interesting to a person studying Diderot's life, for it is evident that the Father of the Family is Diderot's own; that Saint-Albin, the spirited young lover, is Diderot's recollection of himself; that the peevish and hateful Commander, the brother-in-law of the Father of the Family and therefore the uncle of Saint-Albin and Cécile, is Diderot's conception of the character of his younger brother, the Abbé; [4] that Cécile, the daughter of the family, 'a composite of loftiness of character, vivacity, reserve, and sensitivity,' is Diderot's idea of the character of his sister; [5] and that the heroine (whose name is Sophie and not Anne-Toinette) is probably Diderot's picture of what he supposed Sophie Volland to have been like when she was young.[6] Certainly the characterization of the part suggests that Diderot had Sophie Volland rather than his wife in mind when he wrote it. If so, Diderot consciously or unconsciously gave Mme Diderot the slight of transferring his mistress' character and his mistress' name to a role that his wife had played with him in real life. It is not very surprising that Mme Diderot did not go to see the play until its revival in 1769, nor did she go very eagerly even then, to her husband's annoyance.[7]

Still another interesting aspect of this play about family life is that no living mother nor wife figures in it. The Father of the Family is a widower. Now and again Diderot's characters refer with affection to the mother, but her absence is by no means essential to the plot. Therefore it is evident that Diderot felt unwilling or unable to deal adequately with this character in his play. Surely a psychiatrist could speculate very interestingly upon the biographical significance of Diderot's leaving the mother out of a play, the whole concern of which is with family relationships.[8]

The action takes place within the duration of twenty-four hours in the house of M. d'Orbesson, the Father of the Family. Saint-Albin, the son, has taken of late to staying out at night, and the family is revealed, as the curtain goes up, awaiting his return. After these characters have got the play started, they retire for the night, leaving the Father of the Family alone. Saint-Albin presently enters, dressed as an artisan, and explains that he has fallen in love with a virtuous young woman who supposes him to be a workingman. Sophie, temporarily stranded in Paris, is attempting to earn enough money by spinning to enable her to return home. Entreated by Saint-Albin, the Father of the Family consents to see her.

The Father finds the young lady attractive, but not of a sufficient fortune or social standing to be suitable for his son. He therefore offers to provide for her return if she will give up Saint-Albin. A very stormy scene ensues between the son and the father (who ends by pronouncing his malediction), and between the son and the uncle. The son resolves to kidnap his beloved, while the disapproving old Commander decides to secure a *lettre de cachet* that will get her out of the way. Many alarms and excursions follow, through the rest of the five acts, and the reader is likely to agree more than once with Fréron, who wrote that 'At every instant one feels the quandary he [Diderot] is in to stretch his play out. He imitates those unscrupulous manufacturers who pull their cloth violently in order to give it greater length at the expense of its quality.'[9] The play might even yet be unsatisfactorily resolved had it not turned out, by the greatest of coincidences, that the Commander is also Sophie's uncle! This revelation, a *deus ex machina* almost identical with the one in *Le Fils naturel,* establishes the fact that Sophie is of good family — obviously! for she is her lover's first cousin — so that all ends happily, save that the gruff and cantankerous Commander remains unyielding, unrepentant, and in character to the very end.

In accordance with the principles of playwriting that Diderot had already enunciated in his *Entretiens sur le Fils naturel, Le Père de famille* contained elaborate tableaux, quite in the fashion of Greuze, such as the scene at the beginning of the second act that portrays the Father of the Family's philanthropy, and the scene ending the play. Also included in the script were detailed descriptions of scene decoration and indications of stage business, and the speeches of the actors were often written in disjointed prose and unfinished sentences in order to indicate the use of gestures or the effect of strong passions. Frequently these speeches have a telling effect. Saint-Albin, especially, speaks the authentic language of an impulsive and mercurial young man overwhelmingly in love. Moreover, he speaks the language of a man who is purified by the experience. This accent upon the virtuousness of romantic love, preceding Rousseau's *Nouvelle Héloïse* by two years, represented something new and compelling in the French theater and shows that a subtle change was at work in the mores of the age.[10] 'You don't know what I owe to Sophie, you don't know. . . . She has changed me, I am no longer what I was. . . .' And when the worldly Commander asks Saint-Albin what he thinks he is going to live on, the latter replies with bright confidence, as though it were all the wealth of the Indies, 'I have fifteen hundred livres a year!'[11] The eighteenth century liked that.

Like Lucifer in *Paradise Lost,* the most absorbing character in the whole play is one who was scarcely meant to be so. This is the Commander, and it is a good touch to leave him to the very end unconciliatory and unreconciled. The Father of the Family, on the other hand, does not fill the role intended for him. He is too passive. He follows the action instead of dominating it.

Although *Le Père de famille* was a quite interesting play regarding a complicated tale of love, it was far from demonstrating what Diderot thought it demonstrated: the peculiar point of view of paternal relationship. To show that, he would have had to make his father of the family a much more positive and dynamic character, and much more in conflict with himself.[12]

Diderot was, however, proud of his plot, and declared that he had written it straight through, the first scene first and the last scene last.[13] While he was constructing it, he wrote to an acquaintance who had hinted that the plan of the work could be recontrived if necessary, 'This plot is sewn in such a manner, this framework is assembled in such a fashion, that I would not be able to rip a stitch or misplace a peg without the whole thing's collapsing.'[14] The complications in the play are symbolized by the fact that the synopsis of it in a standard contemporary dictionary of the theater ran to three tightly packed pages.[15] But in spite of its involutions, Diderot was ingenuously pleased with his plot — he admired it through several pages of his accompanying 'Discourse on Dramatic Poetry' — especially because he regarded it as psychologically sound and as having the proper sort of inevitability and inexorability about it.[16] Not every critic has agreed with him.[17]

By a passing allusion to an incident in which Saint-Albin had figured during the siege of Port Mahon, Diderot increased the feeling of contemporaneity in *Le Père de famille*. This made his references to such matters as convents and *lettres de cachet* all the more topical and daring. When Cécile declares her intention of entering a convent, the Father of the Family refuses to allow her 'to descend into a living tomb': 'Nature, by according you social qualities, did not destine you to uselessness.' Even more bold was Diderot's making the *lettre de cachet* the villain of the piece. Perhaps he remembered the villainous role a *lettre de cachet* had played in his own courtship. At all events, this instrument of the king's will was not used in Diderot's play, as it had been in Molière's *Tartuffe,* to make the play come out happily; to the contrary, it was only by *not* using the *lettre de cachet* that a happy denouement was reached. To imply that an exercise of the king's will would be equivalent to calamity was daring indeed. Moreover, Diderot insinuated that *lettres de cachet* were purchasable, and for reasons of private vengeance. For he has the Commander say of Cécile's maid, a person whom the Commander heartily dislikes, 'But I have overlooked one thing. The name of this Clairet would have done very well on my *lettre de cachet,* and it wouldn't have cost any more.'[18] Could Dickens be more pointed? When the play was finally produced, these lines were not spoken. The censor Bonamy had remarked to Malesherbes that it was none of Diderot's business either to praise or to blame *lettres de cachet*.[19] Nevertheless the book was printed as Diderot had written it.

Diderot presented Voltaire with a copy of *Le Fils naturel* and, a year later, of *Le Père de famille*. In each case Voltaire was plainly embarrassed as to how to reply. The tactics he used in acknowledging the first evidently seemed to him successful enough to bear a second trial, for the letter of thanks for the second was extremely like its elder sister. Voltaire's formula was a simple one. It consisted of praising the author rather than the author's play. 'The work you sent me, Monsieur,' he wrote in regard to *Le Fils naturel*, 'resembles its author; it appears to me to be full of virtues, sensitivity, and philosophy. Like you, I think that there is much to be reformed in the theater at Paris. . . . I exhort you to diffuse in the *Encyclopédie*, as much as you are able, the noble freedom of your soul.' [20] Acknowledging in its turn *Le Père de famille*, Voltaire wrote that it contained 'tender and virtuous things, in a new style, as with everything you write.' Then he hurriedly changed the subject to the *Encyclopédie*. 'You deserved to be better seconded,' he wrote, which was a very significant thing to say only six months after D'Alembert's desertion.[21] That Voltaire had no high opinion of *Le Père de famille*, however, is proved by his letter to Mme du Deffand regarding it. 'Have you had *Le Père de famille* read to you? Isn't it ludicrous? In faith, our century is a poor one compared to that of Louis XIV.' [22]

It might seem odd, since *Le Père de famille* was written in prose, that Diderot should entitle the little book accompanying it a 'Discourse on Dramatic Poetry.' He used the word *'poésie,'* however, in the figurative sense of signifying 'all that is lofty and touching in a work of art.' [23] In his several chapters Diderot dealt with such subjects as plot, dialogue, incident, the different kinds of plays, characterization, division of a play into acts and scenes, stage decoration, costumes, pantomime and gestures, and, most important of all, the social function of the theater. In illustrating his points he exhibited a broad command of classic and modern authors. Of course he had much to say about Corneille, Racine, Molière, and Voltaire, and he punctuated his discourse with allusions to Boileau, Fénelon, La Rochefoucauld, the Abbé Prévost, Buffon, and even, in spite of the censor's warning, to Helvétius.[24] He also referred to Aristotle, Plato, Homer, Euripides, Sophocles, Aristophanes, Plautus, Anacreon, Catullus, Lucretius, Horace, Shakespeare, George Lillo (author of *The London Merchant, or The History of George Barnwell*), and Samuel Richardson of current *Pamela-Clarissa* fame. The author whom he relied upon most, however, as providing models for his own type of play, was Terence.[25] Diderot was again at pains to show that his *drame* was really as old as Terence and yet as new as *Le Père de famille*.

Diderot's proposals for reform in the theater were inspired by his outspoken conviction that almost everything about current play production rang false. In reply to some criticisms of his 'Discourse on Dramatic Poetry' that a well-known actress and novelist of the day, Mme Riccoboni, had sent to him, Diderot remarked, 'Indeed, my friend, I have not been to the theater ten times in fifteen years. The falseness of everything done there is unendurable to me.' [26]

Diderot had a point. Much in the acting and play production of the day was needlessly conventional and artificial. There was more emphasis upon declaiming than upon acting. Diderot accused the actors of his day of acting with the face only, not with the whole body, and cited Garrick as the example they should emulate.[27] To correct the mannerisms of actors, Diderot favored rehearsals in an arena before a critical audience, a suggestion which entitles him, some people think, to be considered as the inventor of theater-in-the-round. Then, too, actors dressed magnificently and irrelevantly, with no regard to the nature of their parts.[28] Diderot believed in a greater co-ordination of the various theatrical arts than was customary. For example, he emphasized scenic effects, to be achieved in part by the skillful grouping and teamwork of the players; he called these effects tableaux, having in mind what a modern director would probably call dynamics.[29] Furthermore, he insisted that the painting of stage scenery required a greater rigor and fidelity to truth than any other kind of painting.[30] All this implied, as a great student of French literature has remarked, the complete reformation of theatrical production. 'Every improvement in the art of production for the past 150 years has sprung from Diderot, and the innovators of today still take their rise from him, even when they deny it.' [31]

When Diderot wrote, the performances of the Comédie-Française were still much impaired by the presence of spectators on the stage itself. Even the best actors were hampered by this practice, for scarcely anything could be conceived more apt to destroy the illusion of the theater. The custom was a source of income to the company of the Comédie-Française, however, although everyone suffered from having to make entrances and exits while dodging around some count or marquis engaged in his own distracting conversation. Diderot remarked in his letter to Mme Riccoboni that no one should be allowed on the stage: then improvements could be brought about at once in scene decoration.[32] As it happened, this particular reform, which marked the end of an epoch in the French theater, was about to be accomplished. Thanks to a substantial endowment given by a Comte de Lauraguais, the company of the Comédie-Française agreed thenceforth to forego the revenue accruing from selling places on the stage. Dating from the Easter vacation of 1759, spectators were banished from the stage of the Comédie-Française.[33]

The 'Discourse on Dramatic Poetry' was a flavorsome essay because Diderot injected a great deal of his own personality into it.* For example, not only was the whole work dedicated 'To my friend, Monsieur Grimm,' but Diderot also wrote in the body of the work, 'One should always have virtue and virtuous people in mind when one writes. It is you, my friend, whom I invoke when I take up my pen; it is you whom I have before my eyes when I do anything. It is Sophie whom I desire to please. If you have smiled upon me, if she has shed a tear, if both of you love me more than ever, I am recompensed.'[34] As one biographer of Diderot has remarked, it is only in the eighteenth century that a situation like this would be likely to occur: a married man's unmarried mistress and his friend, the bachelor lover of another man's wife, are invoked as the twin inspirations of a play, the purpose of which is to glorify the family.[35]

Diderot was led into making the 'Discourse on Dramatic Poetry' a very personal book by the nature of his argument. Because I am what I am, he said in effect, I write the kind of plays that I do. Naturally, this line of thought made it necessary for him to tell the reader what sort of person he was, and one finds in the essay a number of pen portraits of the author as he seemed to himself. Now, of course, Diderot not only thought that he was as he described himself, but he also thought, quite obviously, that it would be well for others if they resembled him as much as possible. Doubtless this is a method of literary criticism that egotists find congenial and yet, when used by a great temperament of Diderot's range and depth, it cannot be condemned as simply fatuous. Diderot's views, subjective as they are, were extremely influential, and he has been called, quite rightly, not merely an author but a legislator.[36] To give some idea of how seriously Diderot's ideas were taken, it is apposite to recall that Lessing, the anonymous translator into German of Diderot's plays and dramatic essays (1760), declared in his introduction that 'I might well say that no more philosophical mind than his has occupied itself with the theater since Aristotle.'[37]

Diderot conceived of himself as having an upright and straightforward character, perhaps a little simple but all the more respectable because of it. 'Born with a sensitive and upright disposition, I confess, my friend, that I have never been dismayed by any task from which I could hope to emerge

---

* The first five sections of Diderot's 'Discourse,' out of a total of twenty-two, are published in English translation by John Gaywood Linn in *Dramatic Essays of the Neo-Classic Age,* eds. Henry Hitch Adams and Baxter Hathaway (New York, 1950), 349–60.

successfully through the use of reason and integrity. These are the weapons that my parents early taught me to manage: I have so often used them against others and against myself!' [38]

Although he spoke with gratification of his use of reason, he was equally proud of his ability to respond to situations emotionally. This was the sensitivity, the *sensibilité,* that he and most of his biographers have regarded as the central and most important characteristic of his personality.[39] This extreme response to the emotional implications of a circumstance is not merely one of the most significant phenomena in the personality of Diderot. It is also one of the interesting crosscurrents in the Age of Reason, coloring much of the literature of the second half of the eighteenth century.[40] Diderot had always appreciated the role of emotions in psychological experience, and the first apothegm in his *Pensées philosophiques* had burst out: 'People are forever inveighing against the passions . . . yet it is only the passions, and grand passions, that can lift the soul to great things.' And when, in 1758, he analyzed his own personality, in reply to an assertion by Mme Riccoboni that he had a great deal of wit, he emphasized once again his *sensibilité* and surprisingly denied his wit: 'I? One cannot have less. But I have something better: simplicity; sincerity; warmth in the soul; a mind easily kindled; an inclination to be enthusiastic; a love for the good, the true, and the beautiful; a disposition ready to smile, to admire, to become indignant, to sympathize, to weep. Furthermore, I know how to be carried beyond myself, a talent without which one can do nothing worth while.' [41]

When he thought of himself as a philosopher, he liked to think he resembled the ancients. This is apparent in his description of the philosopher, Aristes, who is obviously Diderot's conception of himself: '. . . almost the only thing that he lacked of an ancient philosopher was the mantle.' [42] Particularly, he thought of himself as having a great deal of the massive simplicity, the ruggedness, and starkness of the ancients. 'Nature has given me,' he wrote, 'a taste for simplicity, and I seek to perfect it by reading the classics.' [43] Thus, by mentioning the ancients, he makes the transition from talking about simplicity in himself to talking about simplicity in plays.

This simplicity he finds in the manners and morals of the ancient peoples, against which he contrasts the conventionalities and fussiness of the manners (and the plays) of his day. Of course it is easy — and true — to say of his doctrine that his precepts were better than his example. The mountain labored and produced a melodrama. But his precepts were, nevertheless, very good. By his constant reference to the manners and to the drama of the ancients, Diderot hoped to reveal essential insights into the twin mysteries of artistic

creation and the aesthetic appreciation of it. For he accepted as self-evident
that the elemental and unsophisticated folkways of the ancients, the simple
and profound insights of the classic dramatists, could reveal the components
of genius and clarify for moderns the proper criteria of taste. Much of
Diderot's 'Discourse on Dramatic Poetry,' therefore, goes beyond mere
problems of stagecraft to the deepest and most mysterious sources of creativity and the appreciation of creativity. One complements the other. The artist
produces what the spectator appreciates. As Diderot formulated it, one facet
of the problem was genius, the other was taste; one creation, the other
appreciation.

As for genius, Diderot had a theory that it exists at all times, 'but the men
who possess it remain torpid unless extraordinary events excite the mass and
cause men of genius to appear. Then feelings accumulate in the breast,
ferment there, and those who have a voice, feeling impelled, unleash it and
feel relieved. . . . Poetry demands a certain something of the enormous, the
barbarous, and the wild. . . . When will poets be born? After a period of
disasters and great misfortunes, when the harassed peoples commence to
breathe once more.' [44] Diderot's was a theory of art not unlike that of the
Romantics; in particular, Victor Hugo.[45]

The mystery of genius fascinated Diderot, and speculation about it often
recurs in his writings.[46] But he was almost equally interested in discovering
the proper criteria of taste. Both required the faculty of imagination, of that
he was sure, for he wrote, 'Imagination! — there's the quality without which
one cannot be a poet or a philosopher or a man of reason or a man of wit
or, simply, a man.' [47] In the search for the canons of good taste, Diderot felt
and hoped that there is a discoverable standard, 'a rule anterior to everything else.' [48] 'In morals as in the arts,' he added, in his letter to Mme Riccoboni, 'there is no good or bad as far as I am concerned save that which
is good or bad at all times and everywhere. I desire that my morality and my
taste be eternal. . . . It is only the true that is of all times and places.' [49]

Diderot's mention of morals and arts in the same sentence emphasizes
once again his utilitarian approach to problems of taste and artistic creation.
In the last analysis Diderot found the supreme purpose of the playwright to
consist of combining the moral and the aesthetic. In this view the theater
becomes a kind of temple for a secular cult, wherein the good man is confirmed in his goodness and the bad man given pause. 'The pit of the theater
is the only place in which the tears of the virtuous man mingle with those
of the vicious one. There, the evil man becomes irritated against the very
injustices he has himself committed, sympathizes with the misfortunes that

he himself has caused, and grows indignant at a man of his own character. But the impression has been made; it lingers in us, in spite of ourselves; and the evil man leaves his box less disposed to do evil than if he had been scolded by a severe and harsh orator.' [50]

Such views are, of course, anathema to those aestheticians who analyze art simply in terms of itself, a process described, sometimes with unkind intent, as 'art for art's sake.' They were also anathema to the orthodox Christians of Diderot's day, who were inclined to be scandalized, as was the censor of Le Père de famille, at the proposition that the stage could be a better vehicle for preaching than the pulpit.[51] Diderot's attitude can be explained in part by his opposition to Christian morality, in part by his conviction of the positive effect the drama had had in ancient times and the effect that it still might have in his own day.

Diderot expected great things from the theater, provided that it was organized in accordance with principles he deemed correct. Should this be done, the theater could offer, in morals as in the arts, standards that are 'eternal.' Thus his 'Discourse on Dramatic Poetry,' which might at first seem only about how to contrive a plot or decorate a scene, in reality embraced some of the greatest and the most abiding themes — of the nature of genius and the criteria of taste; of the function of the artist; and, most of all, of the good, the beautiful, and the true. Nor was this all — as if in a work on aesthetics this was not enough. For Diderot had, as usual, a passion for melioration. His desire for the improvement of conditions, combined with his faith in the useful and utilitarian, caused him to hope that the playwright could indeed be a sort of 'legislator,' a Lycurgus magnificently devoting his genius to the betterment of his fellow man. 'Oh! what good would redound to men,' he wrote, 'if all the imitative arts would adopt a common purpose and one day would co-operate with the laws in making us love virtue and hate vice.' Such an attitude explains why his book was important in the general ferment of eighteenth-century ideas, even though one may contend that it was often mistaken. 'Every people has prejudices to be destroyed, vices to be attacked, ridiculous customs to be decried, and every people has need of plays, but plays appropriate to it. What a means of preparing for the changing of a law or the abrogation of a custom, if the government knows how to use it!' [52]

Thus, at the end, Diderot arrived at the threshold of politics.

CHAPTER 25

The Death of the Phoenix

W HILE Diderot the playwright was enjoying in the winter of 1785-9 a very considerable success, Diderot the Encyclopedist was faring badly. Crisis had become chronic in the affairs of the *Encyclopédie*. D'Alembert's resignation had greatly retarded the printing of Volume VIII just as the publication of *De l'Esprit* had created a feeling that the *Encyclopédie* was an incubator of subversion, spawning works like this of Helvétius which in their doctrinaire and inelastic psychology implied views about the nature of man and the universe profoundly inimical to established religion. Both externally and internally, therefore, the well-being of the *Encyclopédie* had become decidedly precarious and, as events were soon to show, the venture was in fact beginning to topple over into catastrophe.

Although the affairs of the *Encyclopédie* were consequently being carried on in an atmosphere of strain and crisis, it does not appear that Diderot labored under a sense of impending doom. 'The *Encyclopédie* advances, in the midst of all sorts and kinds of contradictions,' wrote Grimm in his news letter for 15 December 1758, and Diderot himself wrote to Turgot in January, soliciting articles and announcing, with remarkable optimism, that a new volume was about to be published and that the *Encyclopédie* was being reborn.[1]

In reality, the *Encyclopédie* was at that very moment in the gravest peril. Fate now began to rain hammer blows upon Diderot as though he were the protagonist — overwhelmed, yet tenacious and enduring — in some Greek tragedy. And perhaps it was with some consciousness of the Hellenic starkness and grimness of the struggle that he wrote some months later to Grimm, 'Fate, my friend, can change in a moment from good to ill, but not from ill to good; and mine is that of being tormented to the very end. He who devotes himself to letters sacrifices himself to the Eumenides. They will leave him only at the threshold of the tomb.'[2]

332

One of the blackest days in the history of the *Encyclopédie* was 23 January 1759, only two days after Diderot's optimistic letter to Turgot. On that day the Attorney General, a man named Omer Joly de Fleury, harangued the united assembly of magistrates who made up the Parlement of Paris. The burden of his indictment was that the kingdom was being jeopardized by the poison of impious books, foremost among them the *Encyclopédie*. With the rhetoric, earnestness, and exaggeration customary in this sort of verbal exercise, the Attorney General declared that a conspiracy was afoot:

Society, Religion, and the State present themselves today at the tribunal of justice in order to submit their complaints. Their rights have been violated, their laws disregarded. Impiety walks with head held high. . . . Humanity shudders, the citizenry is alarmed. . . .

It is with grief that we are forced to say it: can one conceal from oneself that there is a project formed, a Society organized, to propagate materialism, to destroy Religion, to inspire a spirit of independence, and to nourish the corruption of morals? . . .

In the picture that we have just drawn of the principal maxims of this work [*De l'Esprit*] you are seeing in fact, Messieurs, simply the principles and detestable consequences of many other books published earlier, epecially the Encyclopedical Dictionary. The book *De l'Esprit* is, as it were, the abridgment of this too-famous work, which according to its true purpose should have been the book of all knowledge and has become instead the book of all error. . . .[3]

Inasmuch as Helvétius had already made a solemn retraction, a fact which Joly de Fleury announced in his harangue, the weight of the Attorney General's attack obviously rested upon the *Encyclopédie*. In addition, the unrepentant Diderot was a special target of the indictment, shown by the fact that Joly de Fleury had included in his original draft of offending books, to be mentioned by name, not only the *Pensées philosophiques* but also the *Letter on the Blind*, the *Letter on the Deaf and Dumb*, and the *Thoughts on the Interpretation of Nature*.[4] The Attorney General also expressed in his indictment indignation regarding one of the *Encyclopédie*'s most emphasized and self-professed characteristics: 'all the venom rife in this Dictionary is to be found in the cross references. . . .'[5] It is not surprising that he should say so, seeing that Diderot's own article on 'Encyclopedia' had ostentatiously advertised the ideological use to which the cross references were to be put.[6] Let it be said in passing, however, that cross references were actually less used, and less skillfully used, than they should have been.[7] Even Le Breton admitted this, when replying in 1768 to an upstart proposal that the *Ency-*

clopédie should be completely redone.[8] Whether as a result of the pressure of time or of simple negligence, the system of cross references did not turn out to be so elaborate or insidious as Diderot had said it would. But Joly de Fleury is hardly to be blamed for taking Diderot at his word.

Responding to the Attorney General's indictment, the Parlement of Paris decreed that the sale and distribution of the *Encyclopédie* should be suspended, pending an examination of the volumes already published.[9] And on 6 February the membership of the examining commission was announced.[10] Three doctors of theology, three lawyers, two professors of philosophy, and one academician: nine men, and good Jansenists all.[11]

Joly de Fleury's indictment and the resultant action of the Parlement were a testimonial to the influence and effectiveness of the Jansenist De Chaumeix's *Préjugés légitimes contre l'Encyclopédie,* a work which kept dropping relentlessly from the press, volume after volume, in the years 1758 and 1759.[12] The author of this compilation was not the only tormentor of the Encyclopedists — there were also Moreau, Palissot, and others more obscure [13] — but at just this juncture he was the most excruciating, and with one voice the *philosophes* exclaimed that he misrepresented their writings or grossly quoted them out of context.[14] As the publishers presently wrote to Malesherbes, 'We take the liberty of imploring you not to sacrifice us, as a result of impressions unfavorable to the *Encyclopédie* caused by a writer who, in altering the passages he quotes or in presenting them in a false light, has passed beyond the limits of judicious criticism.' [15]

There can be no doubt that there existed among the devout in 1759 a great deal of alarm about the progress of freethinking in France. In so far as this was true, the action of the Parlement may be interpreted as sincere. Even so, it may have been too zealous for the good of its own cause, for, as Barbier remarked, 'perhaps it would have been prudent not to set forth eloquently, in the discourse of the Attorney General, the systems of deism, materialism, and irreligion, and the poison that perhaps exists in some of the articles, there being many more persons with the capacity of reading this 6 February decree of thirty pages than of thumbing through seven folio volumes.' [16]

It should also be noticed that the action of the Parlement, sincere though it no doubt was, was partly inspired by shrewd political calculation and had a certain captiousness about it. As Tom Paine observed in *The Rights of Man* regarding eighteenth-century France, 'Between the Monarchy, the Parliament, and the Church, there was a *rivalship* of despotism.' In this instance the action of the Parlement was tantamount to insinuating that the regularly constituted offices of administration — Malesherbes and his censors, operating under the authority of the chancellor, who, in turn, received his authority from the king — were remiss. Rivalry between Crown and Parlement was chronic during the eighteenth century, and this incident furnishes an excellent example of the Parlement's attempt to encroach upon the power of the throne. So, too, did Malesherbes and others interpret it at the time.[17]

From the standpoint of the *Encyclopédie,* the Parlement forced the issue at a particularly touchy moment, for the quinquennial representative assembly of the French clergy was being held in 1758-9. At each of these assemblies the clergy voted the government what they meticulously and emphatically described as a 'free gift' (*don gratuit*), thus symbolizing the clergy's fierce resistance to the idea that church property should be taxed as other property was, or, indeed, that it should be taxed at all. In such circumstances, the clergy were usually able to see to it that their free gift really bought something. Their temper being what it was in 1759 — for example, in the preceding year an *abbé* had actually published a justification of the Massacre of St. Bartholomew's Day, as well as a defense of the Revocation of the Edict of Nantes * — it is fairly safe to conclude that even had the Parlement not forced the issue, the government would still have been under pressure to do something about the *Encyclopédie*. The Assembly of the Clergy got what it wanted in 1759, and was so well satisfied that, before it dispersed, it voted the government an unprecedented sixteen million livres.[18]

The appointment by the Parlement of the nine examiners was not in itself a deathblow for the *Encyclopédie,* although it was very bad news and the harbinger of worse. It came just at the time when Volume VIII was in press.[19] In spite of this adversity, Diderot, with astonishing perseverance, pushed on with plans for continuing the work. A letter written on 12 February by Nicolas Caroillon of Langres, who was then visiting the Diderots in Paris, remarked that 'M. d'Alembert and M. Diderot are going to commence work upon the continuation of the *Encyclopédie.*' And on 24 February D'Alembert wrote, somewhat scornfully, to Voltaire, 'As for Diderot, he continues to be dead set upon wanting to do the *Encyclopédie;* but it is being asserted that the Chancellor does not agree with this way of thinking: he is going to suppress the work's license, and give Diderot peace and quiet in spite of himself.'[20]

The blow fell on 8 March. On that day a royal decree was issued condemning the *Encyclopédie* and suppressing it in its entirety. 'The advantages to be derived from a work of this sort, in respect to progress in the arts and

* Abbé Jean Novi de Caveirac, *Apologie de Louis XIV et de son Conseil, sur la révocation de l'édit de Nantes . . . avec une dissertation sur la journée de la S. Barthélemi* (n.p., 1758).

sciences,' the decree declared, 'can never compensate for the irreparable damage that results from it in regard to morality and religion.' Thus the King, sitting in his council at Versailles, and upon the advice of the Chancellor, revoked the license, claiming to do so for good and all: 'Besides, whatsoever new precautions might be taken to prevent there creeping into the last volumes features as reprehensible as those in the earlier ones, there would always be an inherent drawback in allowing the work to continue, namely that it would allow of the dissemination not only of the new volumes but also of those that have already appeared.' [21] It was scant comfort to Diderot and the publishers that the decree took the matter out of the hands of the Parlement and the Parlement's nine examiners.

Diderot's policy had been to transform the *Encyclopédie* from a mere work of reference to a conveyor of ideas — ideas that in the last analysis were profoundly political in their effect. He was now paying the price of this daring policy; his work had become inextricably entangled among political forces vying with one another for power. Nor were old religious animosities unstirred. The reference in the royal decree to the advice of the Chancellor made Barbier suspect that Lamoignon was aiding his friends the Jesuits to forestall the Jansenist Parlement.[22] In all of these rivalries and antipathies the *Encyclopédie* was in part agent, in part scapegoat. No doubt the struggle was made more bitter by the irritations and frustrations caused by the failures and the disgraces of the French arms in the great war then being waged. Diderot was caught in the buffetings of a great and bewildering political storm.

Still, Diderot and the publishers did not despair. Private property — and indeed a great deal of it — was at stake, and even if the venture could not be saved on its intellectual merits, perhaps it could be on its commercial ones. The publishers had accepted from their subscribers — and there were now some four thousand [23] — advances of money considerably greater than the value of the volumes that had so far been issued. Later in 1759 the government declared this difference to be the not inconsiderable sum of seventy-two livres on each subscription.[24] In view of all the capital outlays that the publishers had already made in anticipation of being allowed to finish the many volumed work, it followed, of course, that if they were required to make a refund they might very easily find themselves bankrupt. Just Volume VIII alone, the four thousand copies of which were ready to be distributed to subscribers but were now forbidden by the royal decree, represented a large investment. In present-day prices the total edition of this volume was worth some $400,000, if one follows the calculations of a leading French

economist and uses for the basis of price comparison the wages of the no-
toriously underpaid, unskilled labor of that day and the wages for unskilled
labor in ours.[25] In the *ancien régime* it was always an extremely grave matter
in the eyes of magistrates to touch private property, and this, of course, constitutes the reason why Diderot and his friends so often talked about the
immense sums ventured upon the *Encyclopédie*.[26] The very starkness of
their financial outlook may, paradoxically, have caused the publishers to hope
that the government would stop short of ruthlessly bankrupting them.

So the publishers and Diderot did not quite despair. Instead, they took two
important decisions. At a dinner meeting, held probably in late March
(Diderot described these events in a letter to Grimm on 1 May), 'we made
our arrangements; we encouraged one another; we swore to see the thing
through; we agreed to work up the following volumes with as much freedom of thought as the preceding ones, even at the risk of having to print
in Holland. . . . But as it was to be feared lest my enemies redouble their
fury if this arrangement should become known, and persecution, changing
the object of its attack, be transferred from the book to the authors of the
book, it was agreed that I should not show myself and that David should
see to gathering in the parts still lacking.'[27]

Thus Diderot went 'underground': 'the bolts on my door were shot each
day from six in the morning until two in the afternoon.'[28] The *Encyclopédie*
was to go on. But clearly it was to be a lonely business. D'Alembert could
at most be counted on for some articles on mathematics, and Diderot told
Grimm that there was no question of trying to persuade D'Alembert to take
on again any of the duties of an editor. D'Alembert had been at the dinner,
but, according to Diderot, had comported himself outrageously and left
early. 'It is certain that the *Encyclopédie* has no enemy more determined
than he.'[29] No person with any official connection wanted henceforth to be
associated with a condemned work, so there was no use of counting any more
on Turgot. Marmontel and Duclos were already gone. The Abbé Morellet
explained in his *Mémoires* that 'The *Encyclopédie* having been suppressed
by decree of council, I did not think that I should henceforth share the discredit that this suppression would cast upon a man of my profession who
should continue to co-operate, in spite of the government, with a work
proscribed on the grounds of attacking government and religion.'[30] Even
Voltaire, who was safe enough far off at the Genevan frontier, decided to
make no more contributions.[31] Few colleagues were left to Editor Diderot,
save the untiring compiler, De Jaucourt — and himself.

Diderot's sense of loneliness was increased during this prolonged nervous

crisis by the fact that Grimm left Paris in early March to rejoin Mme d'Epinay in Geneva, stopping off at Langres on the way in order to see Diderot's
old father, who was to live only a few weeks longer.[32] Diderot's letters to
Grimm contain an abundance of information regarding the events of this
unhappy year. They are documents, too, that vividly reveal Diderot's state
of mind, his exhaustion, his irresoluteness, his dejection, his sorrow over the
death of his father, and his loneliness, which caused him to write to his
absent friend in terms of a devotion quite feminine and seek to draw
strength from the superabundance of Grimm's bland and sometimes brutal
egotism.

Suddenly Diderot found himself in very real jeopardy of arrest and punishment. His underground routine of writing articles behind bolted doors was
cataclysmically interrupted by a scare that was anything but imaginary. 'All
of a sudden it has been necessary to carry off the manuscripts during the
night, escape from my own house, sleep elsewhere, seek out a refuge, and
think of providing myself with a post chaise and of traveling as far as the
earth would carry me.'[33] What had happened was that there was being
surreptitiously circulated in Paris a pamphlet misleadingly entitled *Memorandum for Abraham Chaumeix against the Would-be Philosophers Diderot
and D'Alembert,* and that its authorship was generally ascribed to Diderot.[34]
He described the pamphlet to Grimm as 'a long, insipid, boring, and flat
satire. No lightness, nor finesse, nor gaiety, nor taste, but, in compensation,
insults, sarcasms, and impieties. Jesus and his mother, Abraham Chaumeix,
the Court, the city, the Parlement, the Jesuits, the Jansenists, men of letters,
the nation — in a word, all the respectable authorities and all the sacred
names that there are, dragged in the mud. That's the work being attributed
to me, and that almost with unanimity.'[35] No doubt the pamphlet was
ascribed to Diderot because Abraham Chaumeix had been such a gadfly of
the *Encyclopédie;* but Diderot, in a letter the tone of which seems to reflect
his awareness of Malesherbes' exasperation about the recent Affair of the
Dedications, swore to Malesherbes 'on all that men hold most sacred, that I
had no part in it directly or indirectly.'[36] Besides this assurance, Diderot had
had to visit the Lieutenant-General of Police, the Solicitor General, and the
Attorney General, in each place protesting his innocence. 'I have been overwhelmed by so much anxiety and so much fatigue, both at once, that I
shan't get over it for a couple of months.' Diderot's acquaintances — he
mentioned specifically D'Holbach, Malesherbes, Turgot, D'Alembert, and
Morellet — all urged him to take to flight, all of them arguing that in regard
to a criminal case the safest thing to do was to enter one's plea from afar.

'Yes, the safest,' answered Diderot, 'but the most honest is not to accuse oneself when one is innocent.' [37] So he stayed.

A famous story regarding the relations of Diderot and Malesherbes is told by Mme de Vandeul, and almost certainly pertains to this period. 'Some time afterwards [Mme de Vandeul had just been describing Diderot's imprisonment at Vincennes], the *Encyclopédie* was stopped again. M. de Malesherbes warned my father the next day he would give the order to seize his manuscripts and boxes.

' "What you tell me upsets me horribly. I shall never find the time to move out all my manuscripts, and besides it is not easy to find in twenty-four hours people willing to take charge of them and with whom they will be in safety."

' "Send them all to me," replied M. de Malesherbes. "No one will come here to look for them."

'My father did indeed send half of his papers to the very man who was ordering the search for them.' [38] The usual presumption has been, following the context of Mme de Vandeul's account, that this event occurred in 1752, when the first two volumes were suspended. But the letter to Grimm, which first became known in 1931 and which mentioned Diderot's having to remove the manuscripts during the night, has given rise to the conclusion that this famous incident was a part of the crisis of 1759. [39]

During the ensuing weeks Diderot was in such a state that D'Holbach saw to it that a change of scene was provided. 'We are in the process of making journeys,' wrote Diderot to Grimm on 20 May. 'The Baron is taking me around, and he has no idea of the good he is doing. We have been to Versailles, to the Trianon, to Marly. One of these days we are going to Meudon.' [40] Diderot described the trip to Marly in a beautiful letter to Sophie Volland, a letter suffused with a muted and haunting lyricism in prose. *'Je portois tout à travers les objets des pas errans et une âme mélancolique.'* [41] There is no doubt about the wistfulness of his mood. The very sound and cadence of the syllables re-enforces the meaning of the words.

His melancholy was increased by apprehensions about his father's health, and this emotion was fortified by a sense of guilt at not being in Langres during his father's last days. 'He's very sick, isn't he? Very old, very worn out? . . . My father will die, without having me by his side. . . . Ah! my friend, what am I doing here? He wants me, he is touching upon his last moments, he calls me, and I do not go. . . . I beseech you: do not detest me.' [42] And in a letter to Dr. Théodore Tronchin, thanking him for his advice regarding the ailing parent, Diderot wrote, 'I would subtract from my own life to protract that of my father, and no one in the world has greater confidence in your knowledge than I. I have only one regret, and that is my being unable to go and settle down beside the old man, look after his health myself, and carry out everything you have prescribed for his conservation. . . .' And then, apologizing for his delay in acknowledging Tronchin's prescription, he added: 'I hope that you will find somewhat extenuating the lengthy broils into which I have been plunged, and the sort of stupid numbness that has followed upon them. Just imagine, Monsieur, that several times I have been on the point of exiling myself, that this was the advice of my friends, and that I had to muster all the courage of inno- cence to stand fast against these alarms and remain in the midst of the dangers round about me. Now tranquillity commences to be born again. I am about to regain obscurity and recover peace. Happy the man whom men have forgotten and who can escape from this world without being noticed. You think that happiness lies beyond the tomb and I think that it lies in it. That is all the difference that there is between our two systems.' [43]

Diderot's nervous exhaustion increased the tension of his relationships with others. D'Holbach displeased him. Grimm was the only friend that he had or wanted to have. Sophie Volland's mother was so inscrutable that the sphinxes he had seen at Marly reminded him of her. 'Your mother's soul is sealed with the seven seals of the Apocalypse,' he wrote her daughter. 'On her forehead is written: Mystery.' In spite of his misery he forgot himself long enough to relish this phrase, which he repeated in a letter to Grimm. But there was not just the mother to contend with: Sophie's sister was sus- picious of him, too. And even Sophie, the incomparable Sophie, had shown herself to be jealous. 'That annoys me. . . . I don't like to be under sus- picion.' And as for jealousy, Mme Diderot had her share of it, and precipi- tated a quarrel over Sophie Volland so appalling that Diderot went to com- plain of her to the monk who was her confessor. Diderot did not find people easy to live with in 1759.[44]

Accompanying his depression was poor physical health. 'Let's speak no more about milk,' he wrote to Grimm. 'Health will come back to me as soon as trouble leaves me. No more troubles, no milk will be needed.' Slowly he began to mend, from time to time he felt energy once more stirring within him, occasionally his mood of listlessness and lassitude lightened. 'Now and then I feel once more some spark of enthusiasm,' he wrote to Grimm on 20 May, and on 5 June he wrote, coining a word that seems as quaint in French as it does in English, 'I encyclopedize like a galley slave.' But the news of the death of his father, which occurred on 3 June, struck him hard. 'The final blow left for me to receive has fallen: my father is dead.' [45]

It has been shown by Freud that the death of the father is an exceptional moment in the life of any man. With Diderot it seems to have been especially so, and a Freudian would find complete substantiation of this generalization in Diderot's saying, as he did in a later letter to Grimm, 'Other sorrows do not prepare a man for this one.' [46] For the first time, Diderot began to speak of death as something that might happen to him.[47] And perhaps because he felt closer to death, he was, in a mysterious way that was of enormous importance in the evolution of his creativeness, closer to life. From the miseries of this year and from the grimness and drudgery of the bleak years that followed it, something was distilled, exquisite and precious, in the development of an artist.[48] In the bitterness of misfortunes, heaped upon him as upon some hero in Sophocles, there was forged the soul of the man who has been called by a great French scholar 'the mind and the heart of the eighteenth century.' [49]

But of all this Diderot could not be aware, nor that, after six more years of clandestine editing and toilsome writing, it would be vouchsafed to his *Encyclopédie* to be published in one release with almost no opposition. This he could not know. Instead he could only cry out, as he did to Grimm, 'How I have suffered for the past two years!' [50] 'I am so tired out that I would like to be heard without having to speak, have my letters get done without my having to write them, and arrive where I want to be without my having to move.' [51] Yet in spite of such lassitude, he turned again to his work for the *Encyclopédie,* with a stubbornness and a tenacity that is close to heroism. 'The circumstances,' wrote Lord Morley, 'under which these five-and-thirty volumes were given to the world mark Diderot for one of the true heroes of literature.' [52] Diderot was, in many respects, the 'sanguineous, vehement, volatile mortal' that Carlyle called him, but he was not volatile in this. 'We swore to see the thing through,' he had written to Grimm, and so, in blackness of mood and exhaustion of spirit, he turned once again to his great editorial task, to that *Encyclopédie* of which it has recently and well been said, in bicentennial appreciation of its worth, 'In its subject matter almost everything is superannuated, in its aspiration everything is still alive.' [53]

Years later, when all the remaining ten volumes of letterpress were ready to appear, he reiterated in his foreword his oft-repeated appeal to posterity. 'We shall have obtained the recompense we expected from our contemporaries and from posterity, if we cause them to say, some day, that we have not lived altogether in vain.'[54] No doubt this thought inspired him in 1759, too, as he turned, with unquenchable determination, to the drudgery of the seemingly endless work that lay before him. 'We swore to see the thing through.' Perhaps he might even yet see dawn.

The Nature of the Ultimate Triumph

THE distressing events of 1759 brought Diderot close to the end of his endurance. Ordinarily he was a man resilient enough not to be a prey to depression and discouragement for long. Nevertheless, that year's dispiriting and discouraging occurrences might well have unmanned him had he been unable to draw upon reserves which had been silently accumulating through the years. So much seemed against him as he drank deeply from the well of loneliness: the contumely showered upon the dishonored *Encyclopédie* by the most august authorities of the whole kingdom; the clear imputation that he himself was guilty of twenty years of treason; the defection of colleagues and collaborators; the alarms regarding his personal safety; his lassitude and lack of resolution, aggravated by the sadness and foreboding which he felt because of his father's death, all this might permanently have unnerved him had there not been going on for a long time a testing which prepared him for a crisis so momentous.

It might all have ended with a whimper. Instead, what seemed like a year of ending turned out to be a year of beginning. And the crisis, which might have ended in demoralization and despair, culminated in affirmation and success.

Eventually the complete *Encyclopédie* was written and published after all. Confronting its suppression in 1759, Diderot's spirit rose to challenge the finality of the act. 'We swore to see the thing through.' And in 1765-6 the work was published in all the plenitude of its remaining ten volumes of letterpress — a phoenix rising from the ashes. To complete the *Encyclopédie*, in view of the discouraging circumstances, required boldness, stamina, perseverance and self-confidence. And even to make the try, Diderot had to know inside himself that through the apprentice years he had been developing and tempering the qualities and characteristics requisite to cope with an emergency like this.

In the crisis of 1759, Diderot's past entitled him to believe that he had developed moral and intellectual qualities equal to doing the job. What would an inventory of these qualities include? The answer is spread on the record of the preceding chapters. He had abundantly tested the quality of his intellectual competence. He knew that he had disciplined himself to endure the drudgery of backbreaking work. And his devotion since 1746 to the idea of the *Encyclopédie*, his perseverance through the years, was another test that he had passed: he knew himself to be a man who would not quit. The years had proved his doggedness, as they were now to do again. His writings, of course, were the visible signs of his qualifications for seeing an encyclopedia through and even writing much of it, for his books had given solid evidence of encyclopedic range. He had proved his competence in areas as diverse as epistemology, psychology, aesthetics, literature, science, and technology. But most of all, he knew himself to be the master and exemplar of something that was in part an attitude toward the world and in part a method of thought. He was a *philosophe,* indeed THE *philosophe,* a standard-bearer to whom men might repair. He was a tested leader of the Enlightenment, the experienced champion of an intellectual approach toward science and knowledge that in effect was a political movement. The ten years that had passed since the days when he was writing the *Letter on the Blind* or mulling over the prospectus of the *Encyclopédie* or discussing with D'Alembert its 'Preliminary Discourse' had clarified the issues and confirmed in Diderot — if it is fair to judge by the books he wrote — the consistency and sturdiness of those attitudes of intellectual sincerity and integrity and open-minded search for truth that had characterized him from early years. All these elements of leadership had been measured in him; and now, consciously or unconsciously, he was evidently able to feel that in the present crisis he had the qualifications to carry out the task.

And indeed he had. The qualities requisite for doing so were the qualities, enlarged and intensified by the emergency, that we have seen developing in the Diderot of earlier days. The emergency brought forth the familiar Diderot — written large. To paraphrase Talleyrand, the more Diderot changed, the more he was the same. The crisis of 1759, in short, produced a Diderot who was truly the climax and end-product of his testing years.

So much for the public Diderot — the Diderot identified with the *Encyclopédie*. But there was another Diderot, one more hidden and withdrawn, whose response to the crisis of 1759 was more subtle and more difficult to define. In one sense, as we have seen, the crisis of 1759 served to intensify the qualities that had been ripening in him during the years of trial. He was still the old Diderot, only more so. But in a subtler and perhaps more significant sense, he eventually emerged from the crisis a different Diderot. Fortunately this elusive change in his personality can be closely followed, for it is just at this breaking point in his life that we begin to have the riches of his letters to Sophie Volland. Consequently, students of Diderot are now realizing that the supreme significance of the crises of 1759 lies in their having induced in him a process of maturation built solidly on the foundation of his past experience but utilizing and interpreting it in a different way. It is the difference between the young Diderot — and not so very young, at that, for he was forty-six when the crisis came upon him — and the mature Diderot. This process of maturation was essential for the production of those later works which have become the subjects of such close study and such wide admiration in the twentieth century.

Yet Diderot grew old and died without allowing more than the merest handful of people to inspect the abundant evidence of this maturation. Masterpieces flowed from his pen — and then were put away in a drawer. Whether from prudence, whether from soul-weariness at the perverseness of his own generation, Diderot laid all his bets on posterity. After 1759 he published almost nothing, save of course the *Encyclopédie,* which is scarcely to be compared with unpublished masterpieces like *The Nun, Rameau's Nephew, D'Alembert's Dream, James the Fatalist,* or *The Refutation of the Work by Helvétius Entitled 'Man.'* This very reticence denoted a Diderot greatly changed, for before 1759 there had been almost nothing that he wrote that he did *not* publish. Now he was content to publish almost nothing at all, with the result that posterity has the privilege of knowing his mind — and, by doing so, of gazing into the central vortex of eighteenth-century thought — much more intimately than his contemporaries were able to do. Indeed, to most of his contemporaries Diderot seemed in his later life to be a most unliterary literary man, satisfied to grow fat upon the largesse of Catherine the Great and exhibiting, as for example in the circumstances of his hard-headed negotiations regarding the marriage of his daughter, little but the solid and unexciting qualities of the typical bourgeois.

But the real Diderot, the Diderot that the present generation (more than any of its predecessors) has come to esteem and admire, revealed himself in just these unpublished masterpieces. They have in them, characteristic of Diderot's later period, a quality both of seeking and having found and still of seeking again. They have in them a subtle and powerful dialectic that comes from questioning life and answering life. In short, Diderot's later writings have an elusive but unmistakable quality of seeming to see far and deep into the mysteries of life, further and deeper than he had seen before, perhaps further and deeper than any other man of his century save Goethe. To use a term liked by Emerson and Carlyle, he became one who really sees, a seer. Forsaken by his friends, bereaved of his father, forced to work on the *Encyclopédie* behind locked doors and almost singlehandedly, he found resources within himself that might otherwise have lain dormant. The ultimate effect was to refine his thought, make his relations with others more subtle, and deepen his humanity.

List of Abbreviations

AIEF   *Cahiers de l'Association internationale des Études françaises.*

AJJR   *Annales de la Société Jean-Jacques Rousseau.*

Année Littéraire   *Année Littéraire,* ed. Elie-Catherine Fréron, 202 vols. (Paris, 1754–90).

D'Argenson   René-Louis de Paulmy, Marquis d'Argenson, *Journal et mémoires,* 9 vols. (Paris, 1859–67).

Asse   Eugène Asse, 'Diderot et Voltaire, d'après les papiers inédits de la censure,' *Cabinet Historique,* nouvelle série, I (1882), 3–38.

A.-T.   Denis Diderot, *Oeuvres complètes,* ed. Jules Assézat and Maurice Tourneux, 20 vols. (Paris, 1875–7).

AUP   'Conférences faites à la Sorbonne à l'occasion du 2ᵉ centenaire de l'*Encyclopédie,*' *Annales de l'Université de Paris,* XXII ([Oct.] 1952), numéro spécial.

Barbier, *Journal*   Edmond-Jean-François Barbier, *Journal historique et anecdotique du règne de Louis XV,* 4 vols. (Paris, 1847–56).

B.N., MSS, Fr.   Bibliothèque Nationale, Département des Manuscrits, Fonds Français.

B.N., MSS, Nouv. acq. fr.   Fonds Nouvelles Acquisitions Françaises.

B.N., MSS, Joly de Fleury   Fonds Joly de Fleury.

Bonnefon   Paul Bonnefon, 'Diderot prisonnier à Vincennes,' *RHLF,* VI (1899), 200–224.

BSHAL   *Bulletin de la Société Historique et Archéologique de Langres.*

CI   Denis Diderot, *Correspondance inédite,* ed. André Babelon, 2 vols. (Paris, 1931).

Corr. litt.   Friedrich Melchior Grimm, *Correspondance littéraire, philosophique et critique par Grimm, Diderot, Raynal, etc.,* ed. Maurice Tourneux, 16 vols. (Paris, 1877–82).

Courtois, 'Chronologie'   Louis-J. Courtois, 'Chronologie critique de la vie et des oeuvres de Jean-Jacques Rousseau,' *AJJR,* XV (1923), 1–366.

Cru   R. Loyalty Cru, *Diderot as a Disciple of English Thought* (New York, 1913).

DNB   *Dictionary of National Biography.*

Diderot, *Corr.*   Denis Diderot, *Correspondance,* ed. Georges Roth, I (*1713–1757*) (Paris, [1955]); II (*Décembre 1757–Novembre 1759*) (Paris, [1956]).

Diderot Studies   *Diderot Studies,* ed. Otis E. Fellows and Norman L. Torrey, I (Syracuse, 1949); II (Syracuse [1952]).

Encyc.   Denis Diderot, ed., *Encyclopédie, ou dictionnaire raisonné des sciences, des arts et des métiers, par une société de gens de lettres,* 17 vols. (Paris, 1751–65).

Encyc., Planches   Denis Diderot, ed., *Recueil de planches sur les sciences, les arts libéraux et les arts méchaniques, avec leur explication,* 11 vols. (Paris, 1762–72).

Guillemin   Henri Guillemin, 'Les Affaires de l'Ermitage (1756–1757),' *AJJR*, xxix (1941–2), 59–258.

Guyot   Charly Guyot, *Diderot par lui-même* (Paris, [1953]).

JHI   *Journal of the History of Ideas.*

Le Gras   Joseph Le Gras, *Diderot et l'Encyclopédie* (Amiens, 1928).

Luneau de Boisjermain   *Mémoire pour Pierre-Joseph-François Luneau de Boisjermain, souscripteur de l'Encyclopédie . . .* (Paris, 1771).

May   Louis-Philippe May, 'L'Histoire et les sources de l'Encyclopédie, d'après le registre de délibérations et de comptes des éditeurs, et un mémoire inédit,' *Revue de Synthèse*, xv (1938), 5–110.

MLN   *Modern Language Notes.*

MLQ   *Modern Language Quarterly.*

MLR   *Modern Language Review.*

Naigeon   Jacques-André Naigeon, *Mémoires historiques et philosophiques sur la vie et les ouvrages de D. Diderot* (Paris, 1821).

PMLA   *PMLA* (Publications of the Modern Language Association of America).

RDM   *Revue des Deux Mondes.*

RHLF   *Revue d'Histoire Littéraire de la France.*

RHPHGC   *Revue d'Histoire de la Philosophie et d'Histoire Générale de la Civilisation.*

RLC   *Revue de Littérature Comparée.*

RQH   Louis-François Marcel, 'Une Lettre du père de Diderot à son fils, détenu à Vincennes (3 septembre 1749),' *Revue des Questions Historiques*, cix (1928), 100–113.

RR   *Romanic Review.*

Rousseau, ed. Hachette   Jean-Jacques Rousseau, *Oeuvres complètes*, ed. Hachette, 13 vols. (Paris. 1885–1905).

Rousseau, *Corr. gén.*   Jean-Jacques Rousseau, *Correspondance générale*, ed. Théophile Dufour and P.-P. Plan, 20 vols. (Paris, 1924–34).

SV   Denis Diderot, *Lettres à Sophie Volland*, ed. André Babelon, 3 vols. (Paris, 1930).

Mme de Vandeul   Marie-Angélique de Vandeul, *née* Diderot, 'Mémoires pour servir à l'histoire de la vie et des ouvrages de Diderot,' A.-T., i, pp. xxix–lxii.

Venturi, *Jeunesse*   Franco Venturi, *Jeunesse de Diderot (de 1713 à 1753)* (Paris, 1939).

Venturi, *Origini*   Franco Venturi, *Le Origini dell'Enciclopedia* (Florence, 1946).

Voltaire, ed. Moland   Voltaire, *Oeuvres complètes*, ed. Moland, 52 vols. (Paris: Garnier frères, 1877–85).

Notes

CHAPTER 1

1. Diderot, *Corr.*, II, 194.
2. *Encyc.*, IX, 244–5.
3. Diderot, *Corr.*, II, 207–8. For an attempt by Diderot to represent this speech phonetically, see Diderot, *Corr.*, I, 143.
4. Louis-François Marcel, 'Le Baptême de Diderot,' *Semaine religieuse du diocèse de Langres*, 18 Oct. 1913, 675–80; George R. Havens, 'The Dates of Diderot's Birth and Death,' *MLN*, LV (1940), 31–5.
5. Louis-François Marcel, *Le Frère de Diderot* (Paris, 1913), 3 and n.
6. Ibid. 22–3; Louis-François Marcel, *Un Oncle de Diderot: Antoine-Thomas Diderot de l'Ordre des Frères Prêcheurs (1682–1756)* (Ligugé [Vienne], 1930), 3.
7. Marcel, *Le Frère de Diderot*, 14–23, 191–7.
8. 4 Sept. 1741 (Louis-François Marcel, *Le Mariage de Diderot* [Largentière (Ardèche), 1928], 17 n.; Marcel, *Un Oncle de Diderot*, 10 n.).
9. *RQH*, 110 n.; Martin Löpelmann, *Der junge Diderot* (Berlin, 1934), 9–10.
10. Löpelmann, *Der junge Diderot*, 10.
11. Diderot, *Corr.*, II, 119, 157.
12. *SV*, I, 198 (30 Sept. 1760).
13. A.-T., XVII, 333, 334, 335.
14. François Helme, 'Diderot dans notre art. A propos de son bi-centenaire,' *Presse Médicale*, vol. II for 1913, 1247.
15. A.-T., XVII, 335.
16. *SV*, II, 266 (1 Aug. 1765).
17. Memorandum *ca.* 1821 by Mme de Vandeul for her doctor (Jean Massiet du Biest, *La Fille de Diderot* [Tours, 1949], 218).
18. Massiet du Biest, 186; Louis-François Marcel, *La Soeur de Diderot: Denise Diderot (27 janvier 1715–26 mars 1797)* (Langres, 1925), 42 n.
19. Massiet du Biest, 175; A.-T., XVII, 335.
20. Facts in this paragraph are from a registry book in the Archives municipales at the Hôtel de Ville at Langres: 'Etat civil, 1699 à 1721, de la Paroisse de Saint-Martin.' Diderot's aunt, Catherine Diderot (d. 26 Dec. 1735 at the age of 46), is sometimes confused with his younger sister, the second Catherine (Diderot, *Corr.*, I, 23).
21. *RHLF*, LV (1955), 236.
22. Mme de Vandeul, lviii; Massiet du Biest, 207.
23. Marcel, *Le Frère de Diderot*, 1.
24. Mme de Vandeul, lviii–lx. The Houdon bronze is in the council room of the Hôtel de Ville at Langres.
25. Mme de Vandeul, xxix.
26. A.-T., XI, 250.
27. A.-T., XI, 253.
28. A.-T., XIV, 439.
29. Herbert Dieckmann, *Inventaire du Fonds Vandeul et Inédits de Diderot* (Geneva, 1951), 204.
30. Löpelmann, *Der junge Diderot*, 21–2; Louis-François Marcel, 'Diderot écolier,' *RHLF*, XXXIV (1927), 379.
31. Regarding the Jesuits and secondary education in France, see Pierre Clarac, 'L'*Encyclopédie* et les problèmes d'éducation,' *AUP*, XXII ([Oct.] 1952), numéro spécial, 215; also the excellent article by Marcel Bouchard, 'L'Enseignement des Jésuites sous l'Ancien Régime,' *Information Historique*, XVI (1954), 127–34.
32. Diderot was born at 9, Place Diderot (then called Place Chambeau). On 20 July 1714, his father bought the house across the square at 6, Place Diderot, occupied by the Diderot family for the rest of the eighteenth century. The marker upon it which claims that it is

Diderot's birthplace is incorrect: see Léon Guyot, 'La Maison natale de Diderot,' *BSHAL*, *Année* 1931, 34–40; Hubert Gautier, *Le Père de Diderot, 1685–1759*. . . . (Moulins, 1933), 8.
33. A.-T., XVII, 359; Marcel, 'Diderot écolier,' *RHLF*, XXXIV, 382–3.
34. Maurice Tourneux, *Diderot et Catherine II* (Paris, 1899), 349–50, 353.
35. A.-T., II, 333.
36. A.-T., II, 450–51.
37. *SV*, I, 243 (18 Oct. 1760). Mme de Vandeul, xxix–xxx, and Naigeon, 3, describe a similar incident, but with much more sensational details.
38. A.-T., III, 421, 468–88. Diderot's familiarity with the classics is emphasized by Eric M. Steel, *Diderot's Imagery: A Study of a Literary Personality* (New York, 1941), 48–51.
39. A.-T., III, 478.
40. A.-T., III, 481.
41. *Corr. litt.*, VIII, 151–3.
42. A.-T., VI, 289–302; *Corr. litt.*, VIII, 153–4. Cf. Ernst Robert Curtius, 'Diderot und Horaz,' in his *Europäische Literatur und lateinisches Mittelalter* (Berne, 1948), 556–64.
43. A.-T., XVIII, 167.
44. A.-T., V, 228–38.
45. Gustave Charlier and Léon Herrmann, 'Diderot, annotateur de Perse,' *RHLF*, XXXV (1928), 39–63.
46. A.-T., XIV, 438.
47. A.-T., VI, 298.

CHAPTER 2

1. Mme de Vandeul, xxx.
2. Marcel, *Le Frère de Diderot*, 25.
3. Ibid. 30–33. The Canon died on 28 April 1728. In the *Entretien d'un père avec ses enfants*, Diderot gives a rather different account of the succession to the prebend and the Canon's death (A.-T., V, 302). The circumstances as reconstructed by Canon Marcel seem to me to have more verisimilitude.
4. Mme de Vandeul, lx.
5. A.-T., VI, 182. Diderot may have been very gravely ill about 1729, for he is alleged to have declared in 1747 that at the age of sixteen, finding himself in danger of death, he had called a priest and received the sacraments (Bonnefon, 203).
6. A.-T., X, 391. See also Diderot's remark in a memorandum for Catherine II (Tourneux, *Diderot et Catherine II*, 159).
7. Mme de Vandeul, xxx.
8. A.-T., XVII, 231, s.v. 'Subvenir.'
9. Antoine Taillefer, *Tableau historique de l'esprit et du caractere des littérateurs françois, depuis la renaissance des lettres jusqu'en 1785*, 4 vols. (Paris, 1785), IV, 215 ff.
10. Jean Massiet du Biest, 'Lettres inédites de Naigeon à M^r et Mme de Vandeul (1786–1787), concernant un projet d'édition des oeuvres de Diderot et opinion de ceux-ci sur le même sujet, d'àpres leur correspondance inédite (1784–1812),' *BSHAL*, 1 Jan. 1948, 2. Nothing is otherwise known as to the identity of this Mme Fréjacques.
11. A convincing argument for the year 1728 is made by Marcel, 'Diderot écolier,' *RHLF*, XXXIV, 390–91; cf. Löpelmann, *Der junge Diderot*, 36 n.
12. The unidentified girl: Diderot, *Corr.*, II, 195. Diderot's early feelings for Mlle La Salette: Diderot, *Corr.*, I, 145. She married Nicolas Caroillon on 16 April 1736 (Louis-François Marcel, 'Les Premiers Aérostats à Langres,' *BSHAL*, VIII [1919], 8).
13. *SV*, I, 187 (25 Sept. 1760).
14. Canon [Louis-François] Marcel, 'La Jeunesse de Diderot, 1732–1743,' *Mercure de France*, CCXVI (1929), 68 n.
15. Mme de Vandeul, xxx–xxxi.
16. A.-T., X, 351.
17. Johann Georg Wille, *Mémoires et journal*, ed. Georges Duplessis, 2 vols. (Paris, 1857), I, 91. Wille dates this meeting in 1740, but Emilia Francis (Strong), Lady Dilke, *French En-*

gravers and Draughtsmen of the XVIIIth Century (London, 1902), 73, proves that it must have been after May 1742.

18. Taillefer, *Tableau historique*, IV, 217.
19. Mme de Vandeul, xxx; Naigeon, 5.
20. Mme de Vandeul, xxxi. Bernis, however, makes no mention of Diderot (François-Joachim de Pierre, Cardinal de Bernis, *Mémoires et lettres,* ed. Frédéric Masson, 2 vols. [Paris, 1903], I, 16-20).
21. Marcel, 'Diderot écolier,' *RHLF,* xxxiv, 396-9; R. Salesses, 'Diderot et l'Université, ou les conséquences d'une mystification,' *Revue Universitaire,* April 1935, 322-33; cf. Ralph Bowen, 'The Education of an Encyclopedist,' *Teachers of History: Essays in Honor of Laurence Bradford Packard* (Ithaca [N.Y.], 1954), 33-9. My friend, Professor François Denoeu, suggests the possibility that Diderot was a *pensionnaire* at one *collège* and went out to special lectures at the others.
22. Salesses, in *Revue Universitaire,* April 1935, 329. Cf. Aram Vartanian, *Diderot and Descartes* (Princeton, 1953), 40-43.
23. This ingenious supposition is set forth by Jean Pommier, *Diderot avant Vincennes* (Paris, 1939), 9. Yvon Belaval, *L'Esthétique sans paradoxe de Diderot* (Paris, 1950), 15, thinks that Diderot transferred from the Collège d'Harcourt to Louis-le-Grand. An anonymous polemical pamphlet of 1759 declared that Diderot did his 'philosophy' under a Dominican. If this was true, it is clear that even if Diderot was in the Jesuit Louis-le-Grand for his first year of studies in Paris, he did not remain there for his second (*Lettres sur le VIIe volume de l'Encyclopédie* [n.p., 1759], 37 n.: 'M. Diderot a fait son cours de Philosophie sous le P. Rozet, dominicain'). Evidence of Diderot's master of arts degree is on fol. 35 of a University register ('Index Magistrorum in Artibus,' B.N., MSS, Fonds latin 9158); reproduced in Guyot, 6.
24. A.-T., I, 383-4; but as M. Salesses, *Revue Universitaire,* April 1935, 325, points out, the *Lettre sur les sourds et muets* was published anonymously, and therefore Diderot's references to Louis-le-Grand and to Father Porée may have been intended merely to mystify.
25. Naigeon, 8; Salesses, 'Diderot et l'Université,' *Revue Universitaire,* April 1935, 325 n.
26. Diderot, *Corr.,* I, 23, 29.
27. Mme de Vandeul, xxxi-xxxii; she implies that Diderot read law with the *procureur* before he tried tutoring, but Naigeon, 15, says that it was the other way around. Regarding Clément, see Marcel, 'La Jeunesse de Diderot,' *Mercure de France,* CCXVI, 49-53.
28. Mme de Vandeul, xxxiii-xxxiv. There were several persons of the name of Randon contemporary with Diderot. Asséat declared (A.-T., I, xxxiv n.) that it was Randon de Boisset, and that he was the Randon to whom Diderot referred in his *Salon* of 1767 (A.-T., XI, 274). But he died a bachelor (Comte L. Clément de Ris, 'Paul Randon de Boisset, 1708-1776,' *Bulletin du Bibliophile et du Bibliothécaire,* 39e année [1872], 201). Canon Marcel, 'La Jeunesse de Diderot,' *Mercure de France,* CCXVI, 60-64, believes that Diderot's employer was an Elie Randon de Massanes d'Haneucourt; Naigeon, 13-15, stated that it was a M. Randon d'Hannecourt.
29. This characteristic of Diderot is commented upon by Steel, *Diderot's Imagery,* 175-7.
30. Mme de Vandeul, xxxiii.
31. A.-T., III, 460. This work was by Antoine Deparcieux (1703-68), *Nouveaux Traités de trigonométrie rectiligne et sphérique . . . avec un traité de gnomonique* (Paris, 1741). It contains no mention of the part played by Diderot in its preparation.
32. *Histoire de Grèce, traduite de l'Anglois de Temple Stanyan,* 3 vols. (Paris: Briasson, 1743), III, 349.
33. Mme de Vandeul, xxxii-xxxiii. Her name was Hélène Brûlé (Marcel, *La Soeur de Diderot,* 12).
34. Mme de Vandeul, xxxvii; the same story, almost verbatim, in Taillefer, *Tableau historique,* IV, 224-5. François Génin in *Nouvelle Biographie générale (Hoefer),* s.v. 'Diderot,' 82, dates this 1741, but adduces no proof.
35. Diderot, *Corr.,* I, 23; my italics. A.-T., XIII, 210, s.v. 'Acier.'
36. Mme de Vandeul, xxxiv-xxxvi.
37. A.-T., IX, 168. The work alluded to is Isaac Newton, *Philosophiae naturalis principia mathematica,* ed. Thomas Le Seur and François Jacquier, 4 vols. (Geneva, 1739-42).

38. A.-T., VIII, 398; cf. A.-T., VII, 108.
39. A.-T., VII, 400–401.
40. A.-T., I, 359.
41. For a description *ca.* 1726 of the discussions that went on at the Café Procope, see Charles Pineau Duclos, *Oeuvres complètes*, 10 vols. (Paris, 1806), x, 55–69. Cf. Jacques Hillairet, *Evocation du vieux Paris*, 2 vols. (Paris, [1952–3]), I, 619–20.
42. Jean-Nicolas Dufort de Cheverny, *Mémoires*, 2nd ed., 2 vols. (Paris, 1909), I, 459.
43. A.-T., V, 411–12.
44. A.-T., X, 349. The book in question was *Vénus dans le cloître, ou la Religieuse en chemise*, first published at Cologne in 1683.
45. A.-T., VII, 404.
46. *SV*, II, 101–2 (28 July 1762).
47. R. Salesses, 'Les Mystères de la jeunesse de Diderot, ou l'aventure théologique,' *Mercure de France*, CCLXXX (1937), 501 n.
48. Archives Départementales de la Haute-Marne, Fonds Vandeul E-4, quoted by Gautier, *Le Père de Diderot*, 17. Cf. the same document: 'Vous, mon fils l'aîné . . . vous savez ce que j'ai fait pour vous; j'ai dépensé tant pour vous que pour votre soeur la religieuse et pour Diderot le prêtre plus que le patrimoine que, moi et Angélique, nous avons eu, tant en mariage que de succession' (ibid.).
49. Marcel, 'Diderot écolier,' *RHLF*, XXXIV, 400.
50. A.-T., XI, 265–6.
51. *Encyc.*, VII, 262b, s.v. 'Fourrure.' See also ibid. IX, 893b, s.v. 'Maître ès arts.'
52. *Encyc.*, V, 5a.
53. Salesses, loc. cit., *Mercure de France*, CCLXXX, 503–11. M. Salesses thinks it probable that Diderot even knew Hebrew (ibid. 511–12); but cf. Joseph Edmund Barker, *Diderot's Treatment of the Christian Religion in* The Encyclopédie (New York, 1941), 24–6.
54. Diderot, *Corr.*, I, 25–6. In 1784 the grandson of Pierre La Salette, he being also the son-in-law of Diderot, wrote that La Salette had undertaken to try to get the elder Diderot to settle an annuity of 200 livres upon his older son but that his good offices were unsuccessful (Massiet du Biest, 'Lettres inédites . . . ,' [*supra*, ch. 2, note 10], 2–3).
55. Diderot, *Corr.*, I, 26.
56. L'Abbé Prévost, *Manon Lescaut* (Oxford: Blackwell's French Texts, 1943), I, 93–4; this edition is a facsimile of the authoritative 1753 edition.
57. A.-T., II, 399.

CHAPTER 3

1. Mme de Vandeul, xxxvii. Lester Gilbert Crocker, 'La Jeunesse de Diderot: Quelques précisions,' by L. G. Krakeur, *PMLA*, LVII (1942), 134–5, believes the couple became acquainted in 1742. For lively (though undocumented) articles regarding Mme Diderot, see Henriette Célarié, 'Le Philosophe mal marié: Diderot et son épouse,' *Monde Français*, XII (1948), 39–60, and Jules Bertaut, 'Madame Diderot,' *Revue de France*, 1 June 1924, 574–94, reprinted in his *Egéries du XVIIIe siècle* (Paris, [1928]), 183–212.
2. For Anne-Toinette's baptismal certificate, see Marcel, *Le Mariage de Diderot*, 8.
3. The principal building of this convent is now the Musée de l'Assistance Publique. Regarding Mme Diderot's family and ancestry, see Massiet du Biest, *La Fille de Diderot*, 7 n.; also Diderot, *Corr.*, I, 24. Her elder sister, Marie-Antoinette Champion, married Michel Billard (or Billaud). In her declining years she lived with the Diderots (Marcel, *Le Mariage de Diderot*, 9–10; Louis Marcel, 'Un Petit Problème d'histoire religieuse et d'histoire littéraire: La Mort de Diderot,' *Revue d'Histoire de l'Eglise de France*, XI [1925], 40 n., 46 n., 211 n.). In the marriage contract of Diderot's daughter, as printed in *Cahiers Haut-Marnais*, No. 24 (1er trimestre 1951), 19, she is referred to as the widow of Michel Belliard.
4. Mme de Vandeul, xxxvii–xxxviii.
5. Ibid. xxxviii; also Massiet du Biest, *La Fille de Diderot*, 207.
6. *SV*, II, 324 (21 Nov. 1765).
7. See Pierre Mesnard, 'Le Caractère de Diderot,' *Revue de la Méditerranée*, VII (1949), 279; see also his *Le Cas Diderot: Etude de caractérologie littéraire* (Paris, 1952), 67.

8. Comte Pierre-Louis Roederer, 'Sur Diderot,' *Journal de Paris*, 17 Fructidor An VI [3 Sept. 1798]; reprinted in Roederer, *Opuscules mêlés de littérature et de philosophie* (Paris, An VIII [1800]), 53; and in Roederer, *Oeuvres*, 8 vols. (Paris, 1853–9), IV, 215.

9. Mme de Vandeul, xxxviii–xxxix.

10. Diderot, *Corr.*, I, 29.

11. Naigeon, 26.

12. Crocker, 'La Jeunesse de Diderot,' *PMLA*, LVII, 134.

13. Christmas Eve, 1742 (Diderot, *Corr.*, I, 37).

14. Diderot, *Corr.*, I, 36. 17 Dec. 1742, according to Lester G. Crocker, *La Correspondance de Diderot*, by L. G. Krakeur (New York, 1939), 109.

15. Diderot, *Corr.*, I, 35–6. Diderot's brother entered the seminary eight days before Diderot arrived in Langres in 1742 (ibid. 35); he received the tonsure on 29 June 1743, and entered holy orders sometime in 1746, probably in May (Marcel, *Le Frère de Diderot*, 42–4).

16. Diderot's father mentioned this book in his will (Gautier, *Le Père de Diderot*, 15); cf. Marcel, 'La Jeunesse de Diderot,' *Mercure de France*, CCXVI, 78 n.

17. Mme de Vandeul, lviii. Cf. Georges May, *Diderot et 'La Religieuse'* (New Haven, 1954), 146–52.

18. 3 Sept. 1749 (*RQH*, 110).

19. Diderot, *Corr.*, I, 38, 39.

20. Diderot, *Corr.*, I, 40.

21. Arch. départ., Haute-Marne, Fonds Vandeul, II E 3; published in Diderot, *Corr.*, I, 41–2, and in Marcel, *Le Mariage de Diderot*, 21–2. This letter reproduced in facsimile in *Cahiers Haut-Marnais*, No. 24 (1er trimestre 1951), Supplément illustré.

22. Evelyn B. Hall (pseud. S. G. Tallentyre), *The Life of Mirabeau* (London, 1908), 90.

23. Diderot, *Corr.*, I, 43–4. This aunt was probably his godmother, Claire Vigneron (b. 17 Nov. 1665; date of death unknown). So far as is known, no other of Diderot's aunts was alive at this time (Marcel, *Le Frère de Diderot*, 193, 197).

24. A.-T., I, lxiii.

25. Mme de Vandeul, xxxix.

26. *CI*, II, 17 n.

27. *CI*, II, 122. The marriage contract was signed 26 Oct. 1743 (Dieckmann, *Inventaire*, 162).

28. Auguste Jal, *Dictionnaire critique de biographie et d'histoire . . . d'après des documents authentiques inédits*, 2nd ed. (Paris, 1872), 495.

29. Mme de Vandeul, xxxix. She states, however, that the marriage took place in 1744, an example of how her account of her father is not to be trusted implicitly. For Saint-Pierre-aux-Boeufs, see the Abbé Lebeuf, *Histoire de la ville et de tout le diocèse de Paris*, 5 vols. (Paris, 1883), I, 317–19; and also the same work, *Rectifications et additions*, by Fernand Bournon (Paris, 1890), 329–30. Cf. the Marquis de Rochegude and Maurice Dumolin, *Guide pratique à travers le vieux Paris*, nouv. ed. (Paris, 1923), 41.

30. Diderot, *Corr.*, I, 39.

31. Ibid. 46.

32. Ibid. 32.

33. Charles Nauroy, *Révolutionnaires* (Paris, 1891), 244; also in his *Le Curieux*, I (1883–5), 248.

34. Nauroy, *Révolutionnaires*, 246; Edmond Beaurepaire, 'Les Logis de Diderot,' *Revue des Français*, XVII (1913), 313.

35. *RQH*, 109.

36. Bonnefon, 203.

37. Mme de Vandeul, xl.

38. Courtois, 'Chronologie,' 36; Rousseau, ed. Hachette, VIII, 199.

39. A.-T., XI, 127.

40. Courtois, 'Chronologie,' 41, 48, 40, and esp. 50 n.; Louis Ducros, *Jean-Jacques Rousseau: De Genève à l'Hermitage (1712–1757)* (Paris, 1908), 131 n., argues that the summer of 1746 is the correct date.

41. Rousseau, ed. Hachette, VIII, 246.

42. *CI*, II, 14 n.

CHAPTER 4

1. A.-T., ii, 378.
2. Bonnefon, 212.
3. A.-T., vii, 17.
4. *Le Perroquet, ou mélange de diverses pièces intéressantes pour l'esprit et pour le coeur,* 2 vols. (Frankfurt am Main, 1742), i, 78–80; also A.-T., ix, 63–4. See Gustave L. Van Roosbroeck, 'Diderot's Earliest Publication,' *MLN,* xxxix (1924), 504–5. The identification of Baculard d'Arnaud is made by Venturi, *Jeunesse,* 41–2, 340, 342.
5. Diderot, *Corr.,* i, 29–30.
6. A.-T., xiv, 438.
7. Herbert Dieckmann, 'Diderot, membre honoraire de la Société d'Antiquaires d'Ecosse,' *Cahiers Haut-Marnais,* No. 24 (1er trimestre 1951), 25. For a photograph of Diderot's draft, see ibid. Supplément illustré.
8. See above, chap. 2, note 32. The *privilèges* were dated, respectively, 14 July, 14 Dec. and 19 Dec. 1742 (B.N., MSS, Fr. 21958, foll. 30–31, 81–2, 84).
9. *Journal des Sçavans,* August 1743, 451–62; Sept. 1745, 547–55; April 1746, 231–8, this quotation, 238.
10. *Les Nouvelles Littéraires de Berlin,* 21 Dec. 1773, quoted by Tourneux, *Diderot et Catherine II,* 529. The translation comprised one volume of the five-volume (unauthorized) edition of Diderot's works published at London [Amsterdam] in 1773.
11. Mme de Vandeul, xl.
12. Cf. Venturi, *Jeunesse,* 46–71, 342–58; Pierre Hermand, *Les Idées morales de Diderot* (Paris, 1923), 50–63; Cru, 119–33; Pommier, *Diderot avant Vincennes,* 20–25.
13. Hippolyte Buffenoir, *Les Portraits de Jean-Jacques Rousseau* (Paris, 1913), i, 240, plate 48. Diderot also gave a copy, with the flattering inscription 'Totum muneris hoc tui est,' to a Mme de Sainte-Croix, of whom nothing else is known; for this facsimile, see *Pierre Berès: Catalogue 48: Beaux livres anciens* (Paris, [1951?]), item 118.
14. P. 200. On the *Journal de Trévoux,* see Gustave Dumas, *Histoire du Journal de Trévoux depuis 1701 jusqu'en 1762* (Paris, 1936), *passim,* esp. 137, and Albert Cazes, 'Un Adversaire de Diderot et des philosophes: Le P. Berthier,' in *Mélanges offerts . . . à M. Gustave Lanson* (Paris, 1922), 235–49, esp. 239–40.
15. *Journal des Sçavans,* April 1746, 219.
16. Löpelmann, *Der junge Diderot,* 84, 100–101, 121–2, esp. remarks on the skill of Diderot's translation.
17. Such, too, is the judgment, in a very perspicacious essay, of a former member of the French Academy (Charles de Rémusat, 'Shaftesbury,' *RDM,* 15 Nov. 1862, 475).
18. A.-T., i, 16.
19. A.-T., i, 75. The importance of this passage has been emphasized by Venturi, *Jeunesse,* 355; by Pommier, *Diderot avant Vincennes,* 25; and by Mesnard, 'Le Caractère de Diderot,' *Revue de la Méditerranée,* vii, 283, who calls it 'le modèle unique de la sensibilité.'
20. A.-T., i, 25 n.
21. *Jugemens sur Quelques Ouvrages Nouveaux,* viii (Avignon, 1745), 86–7.
22. A.-T., i, 10.
23. Venturi, *Jeunesse,* 50; Hermand, *Les Idées morales de Diderot,* 56; John Morley, *Diderot and the Encyclopaedists,* 2 vols. (London, 1878), i, 59–61.
24. Venturi, *Jeunesse,* 59–61.
25. A.-T., i, 32–6.
26. Venturi, *Jeunesse,* 359–63; René P. Legros, 'Diderot et Shaftesbury,' *MLR,* xix (1924), 192–4.
27. Marcel, *Le Frère de Diderot,* 43–4. The brother was a student in canon law at Paris from 1744 (probably) until early 1747 (ibid. 43, 47). Succeeding editions of the translation of Shaftesbury were (1) *Philosophie morale reduite à ses principes, ou Essai de M. S. *** sur le mérite et la vertu* (Venice [Paris], 1751); (2) *Les Oeuvres de Mylord Comte de Shaftesbury,* 3 vols. (Geneva, 1769), ii, 3–166, but with no intimation that Diderot was the translator. The Shaftesbury *Essai* was included in all five of the eighteenth-century collected editions of Diderot's works.

NOTES FOR PAGES 53-7

28. Mark Twain, 'A Majestic Literary Fossil,' *Writings* (*Author's National Edition*), xxi, 524–38.

29. Bonnefon, 212. Cf. James Doolittle, 'Robert James, Diderot, and the *Encyclopédie*,' *MLN*, lxxi (1956), 431–4.

30. 'Registre des privilèges accordés aux auteurs et libraires, 1742–1748' (B.N., MSS, Fr. 21958, fol. 262). The title page is dated 1746, but the first volume was published shortly before October 1745 (*Journal des Sçavans*, Oct. 1745, 634); the second, promised for June 1746, was ready for distribution on 11 May of that year (*Journal de Trévoux*, July 1746, 1541). An Italian translation (*Dizionario universale di medicina . . . tradotto dall'originale inglese dai Signori Diderot, Eidous e Toussaint . . .*) was published at Venice in 1753.

31. *DNB*, s.v. 'James, Robert, M.D.' In 1771 Diderot reviewed admiringly (but without knowing the identity of the author) the *Histoire de Richard Savage,* just translated into French by Le Tourneur (A.-T., ix, 451–2), but aside from these slight instances, no relationship between Diderot and Johnson is known.

32. Mme de Vandeul, xl.

33. *Arrest de la cour du Parlement, qui ordonne qu'un livre intitulé, Les Moeurs . . . sera laceré & brûlé par l'Exécuteur de la Haute-Justice* (Paris: P.-G. Simon, 1748), mounted in B.N., MSS, Fr. 22176, foll. 258–9. Benedict XIV placed the book on the Index in 1757 (Franz Heinrich Reusch, *Der Index der verbotenen Bücher*, 2 vols. [Bonn, 1883–5], ii, 873).

34. B.N., MSS, Nouv. acq. fr. 10783, fol. 124. See also Maurice Pellisson, 'Toussaint et le livre des "Moeurs",' *Révolution Française*, xxxiv (1898), 385–402; and Gustave Charlier, 'Un Encyclopédiste à Bruxelles: Fr.-V. Toussaint, l'auteur des "Moeurs",' *Annales Prince de Ligne*, xviii (1937), 5–22.

35. *Encyc.*, i, xlij; *Corr. litt.*, vi, 391–2. See ibid. vi, 143–4, 285, 454 for notices of other translations by Eidous.

36. *Corr. litt.*, vii, 234.

37. Ibid. 308. For a similar judgment on Eidous, see l'Abbé Sabatier de Castres, *Les Trois Siècles de la littérature française*, 5th ed., 4 vols. (The Hague, 1778), ii, 148.

38. Bibliothèque de l'Arsenal: Archives de la Bastille 10301 (14 Feb. 1748). In 1749, Eidous was reported to be thirty-six (B.N., MSS, Nouv. acq. fr. 10782, fol. 2).

39. Dieckmann, *Inventaire*, 3–4.

40. Baptism: Nauroy, *Révolutionnaires*, 244–5; cf. Diderot, *Corr.*, i, 53. For the *convulsionnaires*, see Albert Mousset, *L'Étrange histoire des convulsionnaires de Saint-Médard* (Paris, 1953).

41. Bonnefon, 210.

42. *Arrest de la cour du Parlement . . . Du 7. Juillet 1746* (Paris: P.-G. Simon, 1746), 2, mounted in B.N., MSS, Fr. 22176, foll. 210–11.

43. Gustave Lanson, 'Questions diverses sur l'histoire de l'esprit philosophique en France avant 1750,' *RHLF*, xix (1912), 2–4.

44. Ira O. Wade, *The Clandestine Organization and Diffusion of Philosophic Ideas in France from 1700 to 1750* (Princeton, 1938), 10–18, 166, 294, *et passim*.

45. Venturi, *Jeunesse*, 73–4.

46. See the reports of Bonin and Mme de La Marche during 1748 and 1749 (Bibliothèque de l'Arsenal: Archives de la Bastille 10300–10302). Regarding the latter, see also Hugues de Montbas, 'La Littérature clandestine au XVIIIᵉ siècle,' *RDM*, 15 July 1951, 326–7. For a comprehensive account of the administration of censorship, see David T. Pottinger, 'Censorship in France during the Ancien Régime,' *Boston Public Library Quarterly*, vi (1954), 23–42, 84–101.

47. For bibliographical information regarding the *Pensées philosophiques*, see the critical edition, ed. Robert Niklaus (Geneva, 1950), 47–63; also further information in Diderot, *Lettre sur les aveugles*, ed. Robert Niklaus (Geneva, 1951), lxvi. Regarding the German translation (Halle, 1748), see Joachim Abrahams, 'Diderot, französisch und deutsch,' *Romanische Forschungen*, li (1937), 42–50, 387.

48. Mme de Vandeul, xlii. Taillefer, *Tableau historique*, iv, 263–4, says that Diderot wrote it in four days.

49. Shaftesbury's influence was alleged by [Georges-P.-G. Polier de Bottens], *Pensées chrétiennes mises en parallèle, ou en opposition, avec les Pensées philosophiques* (Rouen, 1747), 7; as

also by the reviewer of the *Pensées philosophiques* writing in the *Bibliothèque Raisonnée des Ouvrages des Savants de l'Europe*, XL (Jan.–March 1748), 112–23.

50. David Finch, *La Critique philosophique de Pascal au XVIIIᵉ siècle* (Philadelphia, 1940), 39–46; Morley, *Diderot and the Encyclopaedists*, I, 52.

51. Albert Monod, *De Pascal à Chateaubriand: Les Défenseurs français du Christianisme de 1670 à 1802* (Paris, 1916), 304, 509.

52. The importance and novelty of Diderot's biological approach is well brought out by Aram Vartanian, 'From Deist to Atheist: Diderot's Philosophical Orientation, 1746–1749,' *Diderot Studies*, I, 48–52. Cf. Lester G. Crocker, 'Pensée XIX of Diderot,' *MLN*, LXVII (1952), 433–9, and the ensuing controversy between Drs. Crocker, Vartanian, and James Doolittle, *MLN*, LXVIII (1953), 282–8.

53. Robert Niklaus, 'Les *Pensées Philosophiques* de Diderot,' *Bulletin of the John Rylands Library, Manchester*, XXVI (1941–2), 128; Guyot, 67.

54. For a bibliography of refutations of the *Pensées philosophiques*, see the Niklaus editions (*supra*, note 47), 58–63 and lxvi, resp.; also Robert Niklaus, 'Baron de Gaufridi's Refutation of Diderot's *Pensées Philosophiques*,' *RR*, XLIII (1952), 87–95. The young Turgot wrote a criticism of the *Pensées philosophiques* (Turgot, *Oeuvres*, ed. Gustave Schelle, 5 vols. [Paris, 1913–23], I, 87–97). This remained in manuscript, however, and it is not certain just when it was written. Mention might also be made of Pierre-Louis-Claude Gin, *De la Religion*, 4 vols. (Paris, 1778–9), I, 135; III, part iii, 103, 237–9, 253–4; III, part iv, 54–5, 162–4, 203–4, 215–16, 227–8, 277–8; IV, 238. For summaries of the refutations of the *Pensées*, see Venturi, *Jeunesse*, 91–104, 363–7, and Monod, *De Pascal à Chateaubriand*, 304–8.

55. David-Renaud Boullier, in Lettre XII (1 Feb. 1748), *Le Controlleur du Parnasse*, IV, 10; Polier de Bottens (*supra*, note 49), 8.

CHAPTER 5

1. A.-T., I, 269–70.
2. [Jacques-André Naigeon, ed.], *Recueil philosophique, ou Mélange de pièces sur la religion & la morale*, 2 vols. (London [Amsterdam], 1770), I, 105–29; in A.-T., I, 261–73. Naigeon attributed this falsely to Vauvenargues (*Recueil philosophique*, II, 253), because Diderot was still alive, while Vauvenargues had died in 1747. This piece 'was in part inspired by Wollaston's *The Religion of Nature Delineated*' (Lester G. Crocker, *The Embattled Philosopher: A Biography of Denis Diderot* [East Lansing (Mich.), 1954], 28).
3. So, too, thinks M. Pommier (*Diderot avant Vincennes*, 38 n.); but cf. Venturi, *Jeunesse*, 72–3, 106–7.
4. A.-T., I, 270, 264, 272.
5. Although Naigeon declared in 1786 that Diderot wrote the *Promenade du sceptique* in 1749 (Massiet du Biest, 'Lettres inédites. . . .' [*supra*, ch. 2, note 10], 4), all other authorities believe it to have been written in 1747. Wade, *Clandestine Organization*, 166, found a note in the library at Fécamp declaring that the *Promenade* was composed in 1747.
6. A.-T., I, 186–7.
7. Bonnefon, 202.
8. Nauroy, *Révolutionnaires*, 245.
9. Bonnefon, 203. Berryer was appointed Lieutenant-General of Police on 27 May 1747 (B.N., MSS, Fr. 22176, fol. 238).
10. A.-T., I, 192.
11. A.-T., I, 215, 220.
12. A.-T., VI, 30.
13. See *supra*, ch. 4, note 21; Pommier, *Diderot avant Vincennes*, 41–2. Cf. A.-T., I, 15, 185.
14. A.-T., IV, 443–8. Cf. A.-T., II, 524–6. Leif Nedergaard, 'Notes sur certains ouvrages de Diderot,' *Orbis Litterarum*, VIII (1950), 5.
15. Steel, *Diderot's Imagery*, 262–3; but cf. Venturi, *Jeunesse*, 108–10.
16. A.-T., I, 199.

17. A.-T., I, 212.
18. Vartanian, 'From Deist to Atheist,' *Diderot Studies*, I, 52–5, 60–61. See also the analysis of the *Promenade* in Venturi, *Jeunesse*, 108–19; and Paul Vernière, *Spinoza et la pensée française avant la Révolution* (Paris, 1954), 567–72; also Paul Vernière, ed., *Oeuvres philosophiques*, by Diderot (Paris, [1956]), x.
19. J. Delort, *Histoire de la détention des philosophes et des gens de lettres à la Bastille et à Vincennes*, 3 vols. (Paris, 1829), II, 213 n. Concerning D'Hémery, consult Ernest Coyecque, *Inventaire de la Collection Anisson sur l'histoire de l'imprimerie et de la librairie, principalement à Paris*, 2 vols. (Paris, 1900), x–li. See also Frederick Charles Green, *Eighteenth-Century France* (London, 1929), 205–8.
20. Bonnefon, 209.
21. Mme de Vandeul, xlvi. André Billy, ed., *Oeuvres*, by Diderot (Paris: 'Nouvelle Revue française,' 1951 [Bibliothèque de la Pléiade, No. 25]), 15, dates this in June 1747, but cites no authorities.
22. Naigeon, 142–3 nn. A manuscript copy of the *Promenade* was in Malesherbes' library in 1789 (Wade, *Clandestine Organization*, 166); perhaps this was the confiscated manuscript itself. Cf. Venturi, *Jeunesse*, 171–4.
23. Naigeon to Vandeul, August 1786 (Massiet du Biest, 'Lettres inédites . . .' [*supra*, ch. 2, note 10], 4).
24. A.-T., I, 248.
25. *Nouvelle Biographie générale (Hoefer)*, s.v. 'Puisieux, Philippe-Florent de,' and 'Puisieux, Madeleine d'Arsant de'; see also J. de Boisjoslin and G. Mossé, 'Quelques meneuses d'hommes au XVIIIᵉ siècle: Madame de Puysieux; Sophie Volland; Mesdames d'Epinay et d'Houdetot,' *Nouvelle Revue*, nouvelle série, XXXIV (1905), 519–21. De Puisieux is mentioned in the *Encyc.*, I, xlv, as having aided Diderot in the description of several of the arts.
26. A.-T., I, 25 n.
27. Madeleine d'Arsant de Puisieux, *Les Caractères*, Seconde Partie (London, 1751), ii; in print by 8 Feb. 1751 (*Corr. litt.*, II, 29).
28. Mme de Vandeul, xlii. A police report on Diderot, evidently written in 1749 because it gives his age as thirty-six, says, 'Il est marié et a eu cependant Madᵉ de Puysieux pour Maitresse pendant assez de tems' (B.N., MSS, Nouv. acq. fr. 10781, fol. 146).
29. Mme de Vandeul, xli.
30. *RQH*, 109; Diderot, *Corr.*, I, 145.
31. Morley, *Diderot and the Encyclopaedists*, I, 42.
32. Mme de Puisieux, *Conseils à une amie* (n.p., 1749), vii–x.
33. B.N., MSS, Nouv. acq. fr. 10783, fol. 51.
34. *Corr. litt.*, I, 281.
35. Mme de Puisieux, *Les Caractères*, Seconde Partie, iii, vi. Nevertheless, D'Argenson remarked that *Les Caractères* was attributed in part to Diderot (D'Argenson, VI, 182 n.). A letter from [J.-N.] Moreau, 19 April 1750, presumably to the Lieutenant-General of Police, said that the work was attributed to Diderot, although appearing under a lady's name (Bibliothèque de l'Arsenal: Archives de la Bastille, 10302). *Le Petit Reservoir* (Berlin [The Hague]), I (1750), 316–23, printed some 'Extraits du Livre intitulé; les Caracteres de Madame Puisieux, attribué à Mr. Diderot qui s'en deffend.'
36. Joseph de La Porte, *Histoire littéraire des dames françoises*, 5 vols. (Paris, 1769), V, 154. See also Sabatier de Castres, *Les Trois Siècles*, III, 385–6; and *Corr. litt.*, II, 29, III, 31, VIII, 17.
37. Marie-Jeanne Phlipon, Mme Roland, *Mémoires*, ed. Cl. Perroud, 2 vols. (Paris, 1905), II, 144.
38. Arthur M. Wilson, 'Une Partie inédite de la lettre de Diderot à Voltaire, le 11 juin 1749,' *RHLF*, LI (1951), 259.
39. Mme de Vandeul, xlii. Canon Marcel believed that Mme Diderot's mother died about 1745 (Marcel, *Le Mariage de Diderot*, 9 n.).
40. Rousseau, ed. Hachette, VIII, 246–7.
41. A.-T., I, 304–5; Georges Le Roy, *La Psychologie de Condillac* (Paris, 1937), 92–3.
42. Le Roy, 102; cf. E. Vacherot, in *Dictionnaire des sciences philosophiques*, ed. Ad. Franck, 3d printing (Paris, 1885), s.v. 'Diderot,' 388.

43. *Dictionnaire de biographie française,* ed. J. Balteau, M. Barroux, and M. Prevost (Paris, 1933–   ), I, col. 1398.
44. *Mercure de France,* Oct. 1747, 92–109; in A.-T., IX, 156–67. The standard work on this subject (M.-D.-J. Engramelle, *La Tonotechnie, ou l'art de noter les cylindres* [Paris, 1775]) bears no evidence, however, of any influence of Diderot's ideas.
45. *Encyc.,* XV, 96–7; ibid. *Planches,* V, s.v. 'Lutherie,' planche IV.
46. *Gentleman's Magazine,* XIX (1749), 339.
47. Cf. A.-T., IX, 77 n.
48. *Gentleman's Magazine,* XIX, 405.
49. Percy A. Scholes, *The Oxford Companion to Music,* 8th ed. (London, 1950), 553. Dr. Scholes does not, however, mention Diderot's project.
50. B.-L. de Muralt, *Lettres sur les Anglois et les François* (Bibliothèque de la Revue de Littérature Comparée, LXXXVI [Paris, 1933]), 168, 171. These remarks were written not long before 1700, but not published until 1725 (ibid. 45).
51. Herbert Dieckmann, ed., *Le Philosophe. Texts and Interpretation* (Washington University Studies, New Series, Language and Literature, No. 18 [St. Louis, 1948]), 2–3 *et passim.* Voltaire declared that this work was 'de l'année 1730' (Wade, *Clandestine Organization,* 15).
52. Dieckmann, *Le Philosophe,* 32, 42, 46, 58.
53. Ibid. 68.

CHAPTER 6

1. André Cresson, *Diderot: sa vie, son oeuvre* (Paris, 1949), 35.
2. For a good description of previous compendiums and works of reference, see Cru, 225–38.
3. *Supplement to the Fourth, Fifth, and Sixth Editions of the Encyclopaedia Britannica,* 6 vols. (Edinburgh, 1824), I, ii–iii. This work contains (i–ix) a good account of early encyclopedias, including the one edited by Diderot.
4. Ibid. iv.
5. A.-T., XIII, 132.
6. Diderot was commenting upon Duhamel de Monceau's *Traité de la culture des terres suivant les principes de M. Tull* (1750–61). Regarding this work, see T. H. Marshall, 'Jethro Tull and the "New Husbandry" of the Eighteenth Century,' *Economic History Review,* II (1929–30), 51–2.
7. A.-T., XIV, 456.
8. Venturi, *Origini,* 11–12.
9. Lanson, 'Questions diverses . . . ,' *RHLF,* XIX, 314. Regarding Ramsay, see Albert Chérel, *Un Aventurier religieux au XVIIIᵉ siècle: André-Michel Ramsay* (Paris, 1926), 182; and esp. concerning his Masonic activities, the note by Depping in *Biographie universelle* (*Michaud*), s.v. 'Ramsay, André-Michel de,' as also Gustave Bord, *La Franc-Maçonnerie en France des origines à 1815* (Paris, 1908), 62–8.
10. *Diderot et l'Encyclopédie: Exposition commémorative,* ed. Georges Huard (Paris: Bibliothèque nationale, 1951), 18.
11. Lanson, 'Questions diverses . . . ,' *RHLF,* XIX, 315–16; Albert Lantoine, *Histoire de la Franc-Maçonnerie française: La Franc-Maçonnerie chez elle* (Paris, 1925), 55; Albert Lantoine, *Le Rite écossais ancien et accepté* (Paris, 1930), 73; J. Emile Daruty, *Recherches sur le rite écossais ancien accepté* (Paris, 1879), 85, 84–6 nn.; Bord, *La Franc-Maçonnerie,* 121–3, 327–8. Le Gras, 31, argued that the Le Breton involved was not André-François; but Louis-Philippe May, 'Note sur les origines maçonniques de l'Encyclopédie,' *Revue de Synthèse,* XVII (1939), 182–4, was inclined to think that it was André-François Le Breton after all; and recent researches seem to have established the fact (Jean Gigot, 'Promenade encyclopédique,' *Cahiers Haut-Marnais,* No. 24 [1ᵉʳ trimestre 1951], 70 n.; and Jean Pommier, reviewing M. Gigot's article, *RHLF,* LI [1951], 378). Nevertheless, the question is not yet fully settled: see G.-H. Luquet, 'L'*Encyclopédie* fut-elle une entreprise maçonnique?' *RHLF,* LIV (1954), 29–31.
12. Bord, *La Franc-Maçonnerie,* xvii; also Le Gras, 21–2, 29–30; but cf. Pommier, *RHLF,* LI (1951), 378.

13. Venturi, *Origini*, 130. Cf. Pierre Grosclaude, *Un Audacieux Message: L'Encyclopédie* (Paris, 1951), 198–9; and Luquet, loc. cit., *RHLF*, LIV (1954), 23–31.
14. *Mémoire pour André-François Le Breton*, . . . *Contre le Sieur Jean Mills, se disant Gentilhomme Anglais* (Paris: Le Breton, 1745), 2.
15. 17 Feb. and 5 March 1745 (ibid. 2–3).
16. 25 Feb. 1745 (B.N., MSS, Fr. 21997, fol. 103: 'Registre des privilèges et permissions simples de la librairie'). Action of 26 March 1745: *Arrest du Conseil d'Etat du Roy, rendu au sujet du privilège ci-devant accordé pour l'impression de l'ouvrage intitulé, Dictionnaire universel des Arts & des Sciences. Du 28 Août 1745* (Paris: Imprimerie royale, 1745), 1, mounted in B.N., MSS, Fr. 22176, foll. 202–3. Action of 13 April 1745: 'Privilege de l'Encyclopédie de Chambers. Du 13 avril 1745,' printed in Luneau de Boisjermain, *Pièce justificative* No. III. The *privilège* of 13 April 1745 is listed in a manuscript 'Registre des privilèges accordés aux auteurs et libraires, 1742–1748' (B.N., MSS, Fr. 21958, fol. 374).
17. The title page is reproduced by Douglas H. Gordon and Norman L. Torrey, *The Censoring of Diderot's* Encyclopédie *and the Re-established Text* (New York, 1947), facing p. 10. The prospectus is printed in Luneau de Boisjermain, *Pièce justificative* No. VI.
18. *Arrest* . . . *du 28 Août 1745*, 2.
19. *Journal de Trévoux*, May 1745, 934–9; this quotation p. 937. See the equally warm remarks in *Jugemens sur Quelques Ouvrages Nouveaux*, VIII (Avignon, 1745), 70–72.
20. *Mémoire pour André-François Le Breton*, 6 ff. Even so, Le Breton signed a new contract with Mills on 7 July 1745, recognizing Mills's sole right in the enterprise; then, on 13 July, Mills retroceded to Le Breton one half of his rights (*Arrest* . . . *du 28 Août 1745*, 1–2).
21. *Sommaire pour le Sieur Jean Mills, Gentilhomme Anglois, contre le Sieur le Breton, libraire-imprimeur à Paris* (Paris: Prault, 1745), reprinted in Luneau de Boisjermain, *Pièce justificative* No. IV.
22. *Mémoire pour André-François Le Breton*, 13.
23. *Mémoire pour les libraires associés à l'Encyclopédie, contre le Sieur Luneau de Boisjermain* (Paris: Le Breton, 1771), 3–4.
24. *DNB*, s.v. 'Mills, John (*d.* 1784?),' which also says that Sellius died in 1787 in an insane asylum at Charenton, near Paris. Mills was a co-translator of the *Mémoires de Gaudence de Lucques* (Paris, 1746), a Utopian novel by Simon Berington, *The Memoirs of Signor Gaudentio di Lucca* (London, 1737). It was said of Mills in Fréron's publication, *Lettres sur quelques écrits de ce temps*, VIII (1753), 315, that 'il sçavoit médiocrement notre langue.' In the 'Avertissement' to the second French edition (Amsterdam, 1753), Dupuy-Demportes, the French translator, refers to 'Miltz' and says that he himself had to 'purger sa [Mills's] traduction des vices et des anglicismes qui lui échapperoient.'
25. *Arrest* . . . *du 28 Août 1745*, 3. A manuscript volume of 'Rapports et Decisions, Librairie,' constituting vol. 80 of the Anisson-Duperron collection, gives the minutes of discussions having to do with the revocation of the old license and the granting of a new one (B.N., MSS, Fr. 22140, foll. 102, 104, 105, 109, 112).
26. *Jugemens sur Quelques Ouvrages Nouveaux*, x, 106. This quotation was part of a lengthy article (ibid. x, 105–15) regarding the prospectus of the James *Dictionnaire universel de médecine*.
27. May, 15–16. The contract was signed 18 Oct. 1745. Le Breton kept a half-interest; each of the others had one-sixth. One of the signed copies of this contract is in B.N., MSS, Nouv. acq. fr. 3347, foll. 196–8.
28. 14 Nov. 1745 (May, 17).
29. Renewal of the *privilège*, 26 [or 28?] Dec. 1745: B.N., MSS, Fr. 21997, fol. 103. Document of 21 Jan. 1746, printed in Luneau de Boisjermain, *Pièce justificative* No. VII. The renewal was entered in the books of the corporation of book publishers on 8 Feb. 1746 (B.N., MSS, Fr. 21958, foll. 471–2).
30. *Mémoire pour André-François Le Breton*, 10.
31. B.N., MSS, Fr. 21958, fol. 262.
32. Diderot, *Pensées philosophiques*, ed. Niklaus, 48 n.
33. May, 32–3. In the second half of 1746 Diderot received a total of 1,323 livres (May, 33–5).

34. Antoine-Nicolas de Condorcet, 'Eloge de M. l'Abbé de Gua,' *Oeuvres de Condorcet*, 12 vols. (Paris, 1847–9), III, 248.
35. Venturi, *Origini*, 133. For another description, written about 1750, see *Corr. litt.*, I, 375.
36. May, 18.
37. May, 21, 19.
38. Condorcet, 'Eloge de M. l'Abbé de Gua,' *Oeuvres*, III, 247–8.
39. A.-T., XI, 125.
40. According to the 'Histoire de l'Académie Royale des Sciences et Belles-Lettres,' published (with separate pagination) in the *Nouveaux Mémoires de l'Académie Royale des Sciences et Belles-Lettres, Année MDCCLXX* (Berlin, 1772), 52, the Abbé de Gua 'forma le premier cette grande entreprise.' This 'Histoire' was probably written by Formey, the permanent secretary of the Academy. Subsequent authorities agreeing with this view are *Biographie universelle* (*Michaud*), s.v. 'Gua de Malves'; Larousse, *Grand Dictionnaire universel du XIXe siècle*, s.v. 'Gua de Malves'; Maurice Tourneux in *La Grande Encyclopédie*, XV, 1009, s.v. 'Encyclopédie'; May, 9 n. Douglas and Torrey, 11–12, believe that Diderot should be given the credit.
41. Condorcet, 'Eloge de M. l'Abbé de Gua,' *Oeuvres*, III, 248.
42. Naigeon, 45.
43. May, 21.
44. Ibid. Sometime before April 1748, Le Breton paid out 46 livres for a dinner given by the publishers for Diderot and D'Alembert (ibid. 41).
45. George R. Havens, *The Age of Ideas: From Reaction to Revolution in Eighteenth-Century France* (New York, 1955), 303.
46. Charles-Augustin Sainte-Beuve, 'Daguesseau,' *Causeries du lundi*, III, 426–7.
47. B.N., MSS, Fr. 21958, foll. 828–9. The decision to grant a new license was taken on 14 March 1748 (B.N., MSS, Fr. 21997, fol. 103).
48. For the texts of the 1746 and 1748 licenses, see Luneau de Boisjermain, *Pièces justificatives* Nos. VII and VIII.
49. Chrétien-Guillaume Lamoignon de Malesherbes, *Mémoire sur la liberté de la presse* (Paris, 1814), 89. Malesherbes is believed to have written this *Mémoire* in 1790 (J.-P. Belin, *Le Mouvement philosophique de 1748 à 1789* [Paris, 1913], 7). The principal biographer of D'Aguesseau, Aimé-Auguste Boullée, *Histoire de la vie et des ouvrages du chancelier d'Aguesseau*, 2 vols. (Paris, 1835), II, 120–21, vaguely mentions the Chancellor's interest in Diderot, without substantiation.
50. B.N., MSS, Fr. 22191, fol. 22. This autograph note is reproduced in *AUP*, XXII ([Oct.] 1952), numéro spécial, facing p. 72.
51. Maurice Tourneux, *Un Factum inconnu de Diderot* (Paris, 1901), 40; cf. D'Alembert's foreword to Vol. III of the *Encyclopédie* (*Encyc.*, III, i).

CHAPTER 7

1. May, 44–5.
2. Early recruits, though there is no evidence that it was Diderot who recruited them, were the Abbés Mallet and Yvon, who contributed articles on theology and ecclesiastical history (Venturi, *Origini*, 40, 136; cf. May, 40, 55). See D'Alembert's obituary of Mallet (*Encyc.*, VI, iii–v).
3. Mme de Vandeul, xlii.
4. As reported by the informer Bonin, 14 Feb. 1748 (Bibliothèque de l'Arsenal: Archives de la Bastille 10301); also Durand's signed statement (Bonnefon, 210).
5. The Abbé de Voisenon, hostile to Diderot, remarks inaccurately that the *Bijoux* was Diderot's first work, and then says: '. . . c'est un vol qu'il fit au Comte de Caylus, qui lui montra un manuscrit tiré de la Bibliotheque du Roi . . .' (Claude Henri de Fusée de Voisenon, *Oeuvres complèttes*, 4 vols. [Paris, 1781], IV, 175). Cf. Guillaume Apollinaire, Fernand Fleuret, and Louis Perceau, *L'Enfer de la Bibliothèque nationale*, 2nd ed. (Paris, 1913), 23; and S. Paul Jones, *A List of French Prose Fiction from 1700 to 1750* (New York, 1939), 94, s.v. 'Bernis.'

NOTES FOR PAGES 85-9

6. Cf. e.g. Pierre Trahard, *Les Maîtres de la sensibilité française au XVIIIᵉ siecle* (*1715-1789*), 4 vols. (Paris, 1931-3), II, 161-3; Marie-Louise Dufrenoy, *L'Orient romanesque en France, 1704-1789*, 2 vols. (Montreal, 1946-7), I, 112-17.

7. Sermons: Mme de Vandeul, xxxiii; nature of the soul: see comment by Vartanian, *Diderot and Descartes*, 242-3.

8. A.-T., IV, 279-80 nn. See Belaval, *L'Esthétique sans paradoxe de Diderot*, 36, 39-40; and Havelock Ellis, 'Diderot,' *The New Spirit*, 4th ed. (Boston, 1926), 52.

9. Karl Rosenkranz, *Diderot's Leben und Werke*, 2 vols. (Leipzig, 1866), I, 67, speaks of it as 'ein Meisterstück'; see also Paul Hazard, *European Thought in the Eighteenth Century: From Montesquieu to Lessing* (New Haven, 1954), 28-9.

10. André Gide, *Journals*, tr. and annotated by Justin O'Brien, 4 vols. (New York, 1947-51), II, 349.

11. Henri Lefebvre, *Diderot* (Paris, 1949), 207.

12. A.-T., IV, 135.

13. B.N., MSS, Nouv. acq. fr. 1214, fol. 111.

14. For the German translations, see Abrahams, 'Diderot, französisch und deutsch,' *Romanische Forschungen*, LI, 61-2, 387.

15. George Saintsbury, *A History of the French Novel*, 2 vols. (London, 1917-19), I, 403. Saintsbury, in his *French Literature and its Masters* (New York, 1946), 249, refers to the *Bijoux* as 'Diderot's one hardly pardonable sin.' Cf. John Garber Palache, *Four Novelists of the Old Régime* (New York, 1926), 110-12. For good critical remarks by recent authors, see Pommier, *Diderot avant Vincennes*, 59-72, and Venturi, *Jeunesse*, 123-34.

16. Mesnard, 'Le Caractère de Diderot,' *Revue de la Méditerranée*, VII, 278.

17. René Jasinski, *Histoire de la littérature française*, 2 vols. (Paris, 1947), II, 208.

18. *Corr. litt.*, I, 139-40.

19. L. Charpentier, *Lettres critiques, sur divers écrits de nos jours contraires à la Religion & aux moeurs*, 2 vols. (London, 1751), II, 22. See also Pierre Clément, *Les Cinq Années Littéraires, ou Nouvelles littéraires, etc., des années 1748, 1749, 1750, 1751, et 1752*, 4 vols. (The Hague, 1754), I, 26-30.

20. Naigeon, 37.

21. Venturi, *Jeunesse*, 134, 370.

22. A.-T., IV, 135. Cf. Roland Mortier, 'Le *Journal de Lecture* de F.-M. Leuchsenring (1775-1779) et l'esprit "philosophique",' *RLC*, XXIX (1955), 216.

23. Bibliothèque de l'Arsenal, Archives de la Bastille 10301.

24. Pommier, *Diderot avant Vincennes*, 57-9, 72-7.

25. Bonnefon, 209, 216.

26. Printed in A.-T., IV, 381-441. See Venturi, *Jeunesse*, 138, and Dufrenoy, *L'Orient romanesque en France*, 118-19.

27. Bonnefon, 212. The license to publish was granted on 10 May 1748 (B.N., MSS, Fr. 21958, fol. 837).

28. Bonnefon, 212.

29. Bonin's report, 29 Jan. 1748 (Bibliothèque de l'Arsenal: Archives de la Bastille 10301). Regarding the Lediard translation, *Corr. litt.*, II, 106-7; attribution to De Puisieux is in *Catalogue générale des livres imprimés de la Bibliothèque nationale*, XCII (1928), col. 366.

30. Bonnefon, 212.

31. *Corr. litt.*, I, 202, 313.

32. B.N., MSS, Fr. 22157, fol. 31; published by David, Le Breton, and Durand.

33. See the cryptic allusion in the 'Avertissement des éditeurs' (*Encyc.*, VI, i).

34. A.-T., IX, 75.

35. A.-T., IX, 79-80, also 81 and n., and Diderot, *Corr.*, I, 55-6, 56-7 nn.; but Venturi, *Jeunesse*, 341, is inclined to think that it was Mme de Puisieux who was meant. Diderot refers in *Jacques le fataliste* (A.-T., VI, 70-71) to the love affair of M. and Mme Prémontval. It is probable that Diderot was well acquainted with them, and that he was present at some of the mathematical lectures given by Prémontval from *ca.* 1737 to 1745. Cf. André-Pierre Le Guay de Prémontval, *Mémoires* (The Hague, 1749), esp. 1-62.

36. A.-T., IX, 77. The *Mémoires* were mentioned favorably but superficially by Clément, *Cinq Années Littéraires*, I, 199–200 (20 April 1749).
37. *Journal des Sçavans*, Année 1749, 8.
38. *Journal de Trévoux*, April 1749, 620.
39. *Mercure de France*, Sept. 1748, 135.
40. *Corr. litt.*, I, 202.
41. Lester Gilbert Crocker [formerly Krakeur] and Raymond L. Krueger, 'The Mathematical Writings of Diderot,' *Isis*, XXXIII (1941), 228; cf. Gino Loria, *Curve piane speciali*, 2 vols. (Milan, 1930), II, 125 n.
42. Julian Lowell Coolidge, *The Mathematics of Great Amateurs* (Oxford, 1949), 185.
43. Dieudonné Thiébault, *Mes Souvenirs de vingt ans de séjour à Berlin*, 3d ed., 4 vols. (Paris, 1813), II, 305–6.
44. Augustus De Morgan, *A Budget of Paradoxes* (London, 1872), 250–51. De Morgan first published his version in a letter to the *Athenaeum*, 31 Dec. 1867 (ibid. 474).
45. E. T. Bell, *Men of Mathematics* (New York, 1937), 147.
46. Lancelot Hogben, *Mathematics for the Million* (New York, 1937), 13–14.
47. Bancroft H. Brown, 'The Euler-Diderot Anecdote,' *American Mathematical Monthly*, XLIX (1942), 302–3; see also Dirk J. Struik, 'A Story concerning Euler and Diderot,' *Isis*, XXXI (1939), 431–2; and R. J. Gillings, 'The So-called Euler-Diderot Incident,' *American Mathematical Monthly*, LXI (1954), 77–80.

CHAPTER 8

1. *Premiere Lettre d'un citoyen zélé, qui n'est ni chirurgien ni medecin, A M. D. M. . . . Où l'on propose un moyen d'appaiser les troubles qui divisent depuis si long-tems, la médecine & la chirurgie*. In the Bibliothèque Nationale copy of this exceedingly rare pamphlet, which is bound into a 'Recueil de pièces et mémoires pour les maîtres en l'art et science de chirurgie,' someone has written in on the title page that Monsieur D.M. is De Morand, i.e. Sauveur-François Morand (1697–1773), a famous surgeon. Diderot's pamphlet is dated (p. 33) 'A Paris, 16 Décembre 1748.' Reprinted in A.-T., IX, 213–23; cf. Dieckmann, *Inventaire*, 60, 129–30.
2. Dr. Raoul Baudet, 'La Société sous Louis XV: Médecins et philosophes,' *Conferencia*, vol. II for 1926–7, 136–41. Cf. Dr. A. Bigot, 'Diderot et la médecine,' *Cahiers Haut-Marnais*, No. 24 (1er trimestre 1951), 42–3.
3. A.-T., IX, 217.
4. E.g., A.-T., IX, 240.
5. A.-T., II, 322.
6. A.-T., IX, 223.
7. Félix Rocquain, *L'Esprit révolutionnaire avant la Révolution, 1715–1789* (Paris, 1878), 126–33; Venturi, *Jeunesse*, 177–86.
8. Marcel Marion, *Histoire financière de la France depuis 1715*, 6 vols. (Paris, 1914–31), I, 171–5.
9. Edmond-Jean-François Barbier, *Chronique de la Régence et du règne de Louis XV (1718–1765)*, 8 vols. (Paris, 1885), IV, 378 n.
10. Claude-Carloman de Rulhière, *Oeuvres de Rulhière, de l'Académie française*, 2 vols. (Paris, 1819), II, 15, 16, 24, 26.
11. D'Argenson, VI, 403.
12. Bonnefon, 204; Beaurepaire, 'Les Logis de Diderot,' *Revue des Français*, XVII, 314.
13. Mme de Vandeul, xliii.
14. Marcel, *La Soeur de Diderot*, 19; Marcel, *Le Frère de Diderot*, 70 n.
15. A.-T., XIX, 423; the date of this note was 20 Sept. 1751 (*Diderot et l'Encyclopédie: Exposition commémorative*, 52). Similarly, see Diderot's elaborate note of thanks, 8 Jan. 1755, to Dr. d'Aumont at Valence, who contributed 34 articles to the *Encyclopédie* (A.-T., XX, 87).
16. May, 44, 45.
17. A.-T., XIII, 139. For withdrawals by Diderot between 1747 and 1751, see *Diderot et l'Encyclopédie: Exposition commémorative*, 72–3; cf. A.-T., XIII, 114 n.
18. *Corr. litt.*, I, 273.

19. D'Argenson, VI, 10–11; Edmond-Jean-François Barbier, *Journal historique et anecdotique du règne de Louis XV*, 4 vols. (Paris, 1847–56), III, 88–90 — this edition hereafter cited as 'Barbier, *Journal*.' See also Venturi, *Jeunesse*, 177–86, and Jean-Paul Belin, *Le Commerce des livres prohibés à Paris de 1750 à 1789* (Paris, 1913), 93, 100.
20. D'Argenson, VI, 15.
21. B.N., MSS, Nouv. acq. fr. 10781, fol. 146; Bonnefon, 210.
22. A.-T., I, 279. Ibid. mistakenly reads 'aveugle-né,' whereas the original edition clearly states 'Aveugle née.' The contemporary journalist, Pierre Clément, reported (*Cinq Années Littéraires*, I, 229) that Réaumur admitted only a very few persons for the lifting of the bandage. Mme de Vandeul, xlii–xliii, says that Diderot was among those present.
23. Mme de Vandeul, xliii. Regarding M. and Mme Dupré de Saint-Maur, see *Corr. litt.*, X, 518. Concerning D'Argenson, see Albert Bachman, *Censorship in France from 1715 to 1750* (New York, 1934), 72–4.
24. A.-T., I, 307.
25. A.-T., I, 309–10; Lefebvre, *Diderot*, 104, 110. Regarding Diderot's interest in the abnormal, see Hermann Karl Weinert, 'Die Bedeutung des Abnormen in Diderots Wissenschaftslehre,' *Festgabe Ernst Gamillscheg* (Tübingen, 1952), 228–44, esp. 233, 237. The publication of Benoît de Maillet's *Telliamed* (1748), with its elements of a 'transformistic' theory, evidently influenced Diderot (Vartanian, 'From Deist to Atheist,' *Diderot Studies*, I, 59), as did also Buffon's *Théorie de la Terre* (1749) (Vartanian, *Diderot and Descartes*, 116).
26. Ernst Cassirer, *Die Philosophie der Aufklärung* (Tübingen, 1932), 144–56.
27. A.-T., I, 305.
28. Gabriel Farrell, 'How the Blind See: What Is This "Sixth Sense"?' *Forum*, XCVI (1936), 85.
29. Pierre Villey [-Desmeserets], 'A propos de la *Lettre sur les Aveugles*,' *Revue du Dix-huitième Siècle*, I (1913), 410–33, especially 412, 421–2; also Pierre Villey [-Desmeserets], *The World of the Blind* (New York, 1930), 101, 180–83.
30. *Journal de Trévoux*, April 1749, 610.
31. For complete bibliographical information, consult the critical edition of the *Lettre sur les aveugles*, ed. Niklaus, 103–11.
32. Voltaire, ed. Moland, XXXVII, 22–3.
33. Norman L. Torrey, 'Voltaire's Reaction to Diderot,' *PMLA*, L (1935), 1107–43, but especially 1107, 1109, 1115.
34. Wilson, 'Une Partie inédite . . . ,' *RHLF*, LI, 259.
35. Georg Brandes, *Voltaire*, 2 vols. (New York, 1930), II, 51. Mme du Châtelet died on 4 Sept. 1749.
36. Wilson, 'Une Partie inédite . . . ,' *RHLF*, LI, 259.

CHAPTER 9

1. Bonnefon, 204–5.
2. Augustin Gazier, *Histoire générale du mouvement janséniste*, 2 vols. (Paris, 1922), II, 2.
3. Bonnefon, 205, 216.
4. Frantz Funck-Brentano, *Les Lettres de cachet* (Paris, 1926), *passim;* and the same, *The Old Regime in France* (New York, 1929), 201–32: 'Lettres de cachet.'
5. Louis Ducros, *French Society in the Eighteenth Century* (London, 1926), 142–5; Jules Flammermont, ed., *Remontrances du Parlement de Paris au XVIIIe siècle*, 3 vols. (Paris, 1888–98), III, 442–4.
6. Arthur M. Wilson, 'Men of Letters and *Lettres de cachet* in the Administration of Cardinal Fleury,' *American Historical Review*, LX (1954–5), 55.
7. Bonnefon, 207; reproduced by Guyot, 8.
8. Archives du Département de la Seine et de la Ville de Paris; printed in facsimile by Marius Barroux, *Soixante Fac-similés de documents de 1182 à 1871* (Paris, 1928), No. 17.
9. Bonnefon, 205.
10. Jacques-Antoine Dulaure, *Nouvelle Description des environs de Paris*, 2 vols. (Paris, 1786), II, 327.
11. Mme de Vandeul, xliv.
12. Ibid. xliii–xliv.

13. May, 53–4.
14. Bonnefon, 206.
15. Ibid. 206.
16. Ibid. 208.
17. Ibid. 208–9.
18. Ibid. 210.
19. Rousseau, ed. Hachette, VIII, 248–9. See also D'Argenson, VI, 34.
20. Le Gras, 54; also Alphonse Séché and Jules Bertaut, *Diderot* (Paris, n.d.), 62. The same statement was made as a matter of general knowledge by G. Peignot, *Dictionnaire critique, littéraire et bibliographique des principaux livres condamnés au feu, supprimés ou censurés,* 2 vols. (Paris, 1806), I, 103; also by Charles-Yves Cousin d'Avallon, *Diderotiana* (Paris, 1810), 29.
21. Diderot, *Corr.,* I, 83–8. The concluding page of this letter, erroneously stated to be addressed to D'Argenson, is reproduced facing p. 12 of *AUP,* XXII ([Oct.] 1952).
22. Bonnefon, 214; also in Diderot, *Corr.,* I, 82–3.
23. Bonnefon, 215; a page from this letter reproduced in Guyot, 24.
24. Bonnefon, 216. In November 1749 Le Breton was reimbursed for paying 32 livres 8 sols to the treasurer of Vincennes (May, 54), perhaps for extras supplied to Diderot. The château in question was the governor's lodgings, just to the north of the Sainte-Chapelle in the Vincennes enclosure (André Billy, *Diderot* [Paris, 1932], 137). It no longer exists.
25. 21 Aug. 1749 (Bonnefon, 217).
26. *La Bigarure ou Meslange curieux, instructif et amusant de nouvelles . . . ,* 20 vols. (The Hague, 1749–53), I, 61–2. This account is not, however, factually impeccable: it has Diderot imprisoned in the Bastille; it declares on 30 Oct. 1749, that he is already liberated; and it states that Toussaint, author of *Les Moeurs,* had for long been a prisoner in Vincennes. Delort, *Histoire de la détention des philosophes . . . ,* II, 216, would appear to have used *La Bigarure* as his source for his account of Diderot's imprisonment.
27. Mme de Vandeul, xliv; Naigeon, 131–3; Eusèbe Salverte, *Eloge philosophique de Denys Diderot* (Paris, An IX [1800–1801], 96).
28. Dieckmann, *Inventaire,* 56, 114–17, is dubious about their being translated from memory. Diderot recalled in 1762 that while he was in the tower at Vincennes 'J'avois un petit Platon dans ma poche . . .' (*SV,* II, 175 [23 Sept. 1762]).
29. 30 Sept. 1749 (A.-T., XIX, 422–3).
30. May, 53.
31. Mme de Vandeul, xliv.
32. Bonnefon, 217–18.
33. Mme de Vandeul, xlv.
34. Delort, *Histoire de la détention des philosophes . . . ,* II, 218.
35. Frantz Funck-Brentano, *Légendes et archives de la Bastille* (Paris, 1904), 153.
36. *La Correspondance de l'Abbé Trublet,* ed. J. Jacquart (Paris, 1926), 10. Canon Marcel mentioned having seen a manuscript news letter that devoted a page and a half to the event (*RQH,* 102 n.).
37. Voltaire, ed. Moland, XXXVII, 36.
38. D'Argenson, VI, 10–11, 26; Barbier, *Journal,* III, 89–90.
39. A.-T., XIX, 425.
40. For instance, Grimm wrote on 15 Feb. 1757 of Diderot seeing Fontenelle for the first time in his life *'il y a deux ou trois ans'* (*Corr. litt.,* III, 345; italics mine).
41. Voltaire, ed. Moland, XXXVII, 38.
42. *RQH,* 109, 110, 111. The money was to be paid by M. Foucou, who had befriended Diderot in 1736 (see *supra,* p. 29). For a meticulous transcription of this letter, together with a photograph of it, see J.-G. Gigot, 'Sur une lettre du père de Diderot à son fils,' *Cahiers Haut-Marnais,* No. 38 (3e trimestre 1954), 131–4, 138–40.
43. May, 52, 54.
44. Delort, *Histoire de la détention des philosophes . . . ,* II, 227; Du Châtelet's covering letter is dated simply 'Septembre' (ibid. 226); Bonnefon, 222–3.
45. Rousseau, ed. Hachette, VIII, 247, 248.

46. Ibid. 249.
47. This version of the story seems to have been circulated sedulously in the late 'seventies, when the enemies of Rousseau were apprehensively anticipating the publication of the *Confessions* (Alexis François, 'La Correspondance de J. J. Rousseau dans la querelle littéraire du XVIIIᵉ siècle: Diderot et les Lettres à Malesherbes,' *RHLF*, XXXIII [1926], 357–8).
48. Jean-François Marmontel, *Mémoires d'un père pour servir à l'instruction de ses enfants*, 4 vols. (Paris, 1804), II, 240–41.
49. J.-F. La Harpe, *Lycée, ou cours de littérature ancienne et moderne*, 15 vols. (Paris, 1816), XV, 238; Charles Collé, *Correspondance inédite* (Paris, 1864), 66–7; *Corr. litt.*, XI, 285 (June 1776); André Morellet, *Mémoires inédits*, 2 vols. (Paris, 1822), I, 119–20.
50. Mme de Vandeul, lx.
51. François-Louis, Comte d'Escherny, *Mélanges de littérature, d'histoire, de morale et de philosophie*, 3 vols. (Paris, 1811), II, 39 n.
52. This controversy is admirably analyzed and summarized by George R. Havens, ed., *Jean-Jacques Rousseau: Discours sur les sciences et les arts* (New York, 1946), 6–9, 21–3. See also his 'Diderot and the Composition of Rousseau's First Discourse,' *RR*, XXX (1939), 369–81; F. Vézinet, 'Rousseau ou Diderot?' *RHLF*, XXXI (1924), 306–14, and republished, with some additions, in his *Autour de Voltaire* (Paris, 1925), 121–41; Lester Gilbert Crocker, 'Diderot's Influence on Rousseau's First *Discours*,' by Lester Gilbert Krakeur, *PMLA*, LII (1937), 398–404; Eugène Ritter, 'Le Programme du concours ouvert en 1749 par l'Académie de Dijon,' *AJJR*, XI (1916–17), 64–71. Cf. Albert Schinz, *Etat présent des travaux sur J.-J. Rousseau* (New York, 1941), 171–2.
53. A.-T., III, 98, and in identical words in A.-T., II, 285. Diderot also gave exactly the same account in 1773 or 1774 during one of his visits at The Hague (Philippe Godet, *Madame de Charrière et ses amis . . . (1740–1805)*, 2 vols. [Geneva, 1906], I, 432).
54. Bonnefon, 219; also in A.-T., XIII, 111.
55. Bonnefon, 220–22; also A.-T., XIII, 111. Bonnefon states (p. 220) that the publishers got President Hénault, author of the famous *Abrégé chronologique de l'histoire de France*, to present their petition to D'Argenson. Perhaps this was what D'Alembert had in mind when he wrote to Hénault, *ca.* 1751: 'Diderot pense là-dessus comme moi, et nous n'oublierons jamais ni l'un ni l'autre ce que nous vous devons' (Albert Tornezy, *La Légende des 'philosophes'* [Paris, 1911], 172).
56. A.-T., XIII, 113.
57. Venturi, *Origini*, 55.
58. Bibliothèque de l'Arsenal: Archives de la Bastille 11671, fol. 20.
59. Rousseau, ed. Hachette, VIII, 277 n.
60. Tourneux, *Diderot et Catherine II*, 442.

CHAPTER 10

1. A.-T., XIII, 111–13 (7 Sept. 1749).
2. *Corr. litt.*, I, 475.
3. *Lettre de M. Gervaise Holmes à l'auteur de la* Lettre sur les aveugles, *contenant le véritable récit des dernières heures de Saounderson* (Cambridge [Berlin], 1750). This was by Formey, the secretary of the Prussian Academy (Jean-Henri-Samuel Formey, *Conseils pour former une bibliothèque peu nombreuse, mais choisie*, 3rd. ed. [Berlin, 1755], 117–18).
4. *Bibliothèque Impartiale*, Jan.–Feb. 1750, 76; this periodical was edited by Formey and printed at Leyden (Formey, *Conseils pour former une bibliothèque*, 118). See also Clément, *Cinq Années Littéraires*, I, 229–31, and Charpentier, *Lettres Critiques*, II, 101–28.
5. D'Alembert to Cramer, 12 Feb. 1750, quoted by Tamizey de Larroque in *Revue Critique d'Histoire et de Littérature*, vol. II for 1882, 478.
6. Archives Nationales, Y 12594; published by Emile Campardon, *Les Prodigalités d'un fermier général* (Paris, 1882), 119–21.
7. *La Bigarure*, I, 20–22.

8. Ibid. XIII, 58–61.
9. Mme de Vandeul, xlvi; A.-T., I, lxiv; Jal, *Dictionnaire critique*, 495; Diderot, *Corr.*, I, 99.
10. Born 29 Oct. and baptized 30 Oct. 1750 (Diderot, *Corr.*, I, 100); but according to baptismal records copied by Nauroy, *Révolutionnaires*, 245, the dates were 29 and 30 Sept. 1750. Regarding the accident, Mme de Vandeul, xlvi; A.-T., I, lxiv; but cf. Jal, *Dictionnaire critique*, 496, and Diderot, *Corr.*, I, 100.
11. André Cazes, *Grimm et les Encyclopédistes* (Paris, 1933), 9; Joseph R. Smiley, *Diderot's Relations with Grimm* ('Illinois Studies in Language and Literature, XXXIV, No. 4' [Urbana, 1950]), 9–10.
12. Louis-J. Courtois, 'Notes critiques de chronologie rousseauiste,' *Mélanges d'histoire littéraire et de philologie offerts à M. Bernard Bouvier* (Geneva, 1920), 120.
13. Joseph A. Vaeth, *Tirant lo Blanch* (New York, 1918), 5.
14. Archives Nationales, T 319⁵.
15. Jefferson to John Adams, Monticello, 8 April 1816 (*Memoir, Correspondence, and Miscellanies, from the Papers of Thomas Jefferson*, ed. T. J. Randolph, 4 vols. [Boston, 1830], IV, 272).
16. Diderot to Grimm, 25 March 1781 (Dieckmann, *Inventaire*, 252).
17. Courtois, 'Chronologie,' 59.
18. Rousseau, ed. Hachette, VIII, 258, 260.
19. Courtois, 'Chronologie,' 60; also George R. Havens, 'Rousseau's First Discourse and the *Pensées philosophiques* of Diderot,' *RR*, XXXIII (1942), 356, and George R. Havens, ed., *Jean-Jacques Rousseau: Discours sur les sciences et les arts*, 30. The censors were opposed to letting the *Discours* be published, but Malesherbes overruled them (Belin, *Le Mouvement philosophique de 1748 à 1789*, 78).
20. Rousseau, ed. Hachette, VIII, 258.
21. Douglas H. Gordon's Extra Volume, fol. 678: '. . . or en marge de la page 1ere du prospectus, il est ecrit de la main de l'illustre M. Daguesseau, *Bon D.G.*, Cette approbation est seule une preuve que les éditeurs avoient satisfait aux Reglements.
    'On trouve encore ecrit sur un autre titre du même ouvrage, de la main du Commissaire du Roy pour la librairie, *Permis d'imprimer et afficher: ce 11. 9bre 1750*. Signé *Berryer*.'
22. May, 24–5.
23. *Encyc.*, I, i n.; also *Corr. litt.*, I, 486. Buffon wrote to Formey on 6 Dec. 1750, 'Le projet du *Dictionnaire encyclopédique* paraît ici depuis quelques jours' (Georges-Louis Leclerc, Comte de Buffon, *Correspondance inédite*, ed. H. N. de Buffon, 2 vols. [Paris, 1860], I, 49–50).
24. May, 59.
25. Charles Braibant, 'Autour du Prospectus,' *Cahiers Haut-Marnais*, No. 24 (1er trimestre 1951), 5.
26. Herbert James Hunt, 'Logic and Linguistics. Diderot as "grammairien-philosophe",' *MLR*, XXXIII (1938), 217, alluding to C. K. Ogden and I. A. Richards, *The Meaning of Meaning*.
27. Approval by the censor (B.N., MSS, Fr. 22138, fol. 22). D'Hémery noted on 18 Feb. 1751 that the book was already published (B.N., MSS, Fr. 22156, fol. 33ᵛ).
28. Malesherbes, *Mémoire sur la liberté de la presse*, 49–50, 53, 56. Regarding tacit permissions, see Comte de Montbas, 'La République des Lettres au XVIIIᵉ siècle et l'avènement de la tolérance,' *Revue des Travaux de l'Académie des Sciences Morales et Politiques, Année 1950, premier semestre*, 50–51. For Diderot's opinion regarding them: A.-T., XVIII, 66 *et passim*.
29. Cf. Ferdinand Brunetière, 'La Direction de la Librairie sous M. de Malesherbes,' *RDM*, 1 Feb. 1882, 580–81; and Bachman, *Censorship in France from 1715 to 1750*, 146–53. As an example of a censor's report regarding a tacit permission, see the letter from De Cahusac to [Malesherbes], 'Paris ce 22 xbre 1751. . . . Je pense en effet qu'avec les adoucissements que j'y ai fait mettre, il peut etre susceptible, non d'un privilege; Mais d'une permission tacite' (B.N., MSS, Fr. 22137, fol. 49).
30. [Suzanne Necker, née Curchod], *Nouveaux Mélanges extraits des manuscrits de Mme Necker*, 2 vols. (Paris, An x [1801]), I, 255.

31. A.-T., I, 353. Cf. Karl von Roretz, *Diderots Weltanschauung, ihre Voraussetzungen, ihre Leitmotive* (Vienna, 1914), 14, 16.
32. See George Sidney Brett, *A History of Psychology*, 3 vols. (London, 1921), II, 289.
33. Cf. Katharine Everett Gilbert and Helmut Kuhn, *A History of Esthetics* (New York, 1939), 307. Diderot also anticipated some of the conclusions of Edmund Burke in his treatise *On the Sublime and Beautiful* (Dixon Wecter, 'Burke's Theory concerning Words, Images, and Emotion,' *PMLA*, LV [1940], 177 n.). Cf. J.-J. Mayoux, 'Diderot and the Technique of Modern Literature,' *MLR*, XXXI (1936), 528.
34. Otis E. Fellows and Norman L. Torrey, eds., *Diderot Studies*, I, ix–x. Cf. ibid. 94–121: Anne-Marie de Commaille, 'Diderot et le symbole littéraire,' esp. 110–13; and particularly James Doolittle, 'Hieroglyph and Emblem in Diderot's *Lettre sur les sourds et muets*,' *Diderot Studies*, II, 148–67.
35. A.-T., I, 374.
36. Mayoux, 'Diderot and the Technique of Modern Literature,' *MLR*, XXXI, 525–6; Hunt, 'Diderot as "grammairien-philosophe",' *MLR*, XXXIII, 215–33; Margaret Gilman, 'The Poet according to Diderot,' *RR*, XXXVII (1946), 41; Margaret Gilman, 'Imagination and Creation in Diderot,' *Diderot Studies*, II, 214–15; and Marlou Switten, 'Diderot's Theory of Language as the Medium of Literature,' *RR*, XLIV (1953), 192, 196.
37. Jean Pommier, 'Diderot et le plaisir poétique,' *Education Nationale*, 23 June 1949, 2. Concerning prosody, Dupont de Nemours declared that Diderot 'la marquait, la déclamait peut-être un peu trop. . . . Chez Diderot, la prosodie était un chant . . .' (Turgot, *Oeuvres*, ed. Schelle, II, 704).
38. A.-T., I, 376.
39. Hunt, 'Diderot as "grammairien-philosophe",' *MLR*, XXXIII, 215.
40. *Corr. litt.*, II, 32, 67. For similar contemporary judgments, see Clément, *Cinq Années Littéraires*, III, 43–4, and Lessing, writing in *Das Neueste aus dem Reiche des Witzes*, June 1751 (Gotthold Ephraim Lessing, *Werke*, ed. Julius Petersen and Waldemar von Olshausen, 25 vols. [Berlin, (1925)], VIII, 49).
41. Jean Pommier, 'Autour de la *Lettre sur les sourds et muets*,' *RHLF*, LI (1951), 262–7, 270–71; Jean Pommier, 'Etudes sur Diderot,' *RHPHGC*, X (1942), 163. Batteux is said to have been much upset by Diderot's criticism (A.-T., XIV, 529 n.). Cf. *Corr. litt.*, XII, 439.
42. B.N., MSS, Fr. 22156, fol. 70.
43. A.-T., V, 328.
44. *Journal de Trévoux*, April 1751, 841–63. Diderot's rejoinder: A.-T., I, 411–28. The *Journal de Trévoux* amplified its remarks in its volume for July 1751, 1677–97. A very colorless review of the *Lettre sur les sourds et muets* appeared in Formey's *Bibliothèque Impartiale*, III (May–June 1751), 409–17.
45. Ignacio de Luzan, *Memorias literarias de Paris* (Madrid, 1751), 282–3.
46. *Journal de Trévoux*, Jan. 1751, 188–9, 317. Still another article on the parallel is in the issue for March 1751, 708–37.
47. Venturi, *Origini*, 113.
48. *Lettre de M. Diderot au R. P. Berthier, Jésuite* (n.p., 1751) [B.N., Imprimés, Z.11855]; and in A.-T., XIII, 165–8.
49. Clément, *Cinq Années Littéraires*, III, 45.
50. *Journal de Trévoux*, 1 Feb. 1751, 571–2, 577.
51. *Seconde Lettre de M. Diderot au R. P. Berthier, Jésuite* (n.p., 1751) [B.N., Imprimés, Z.11855 (2)]; and in A.-T., XIII, 168–70.
52. B.N., MSS, Fr. 22156, fol. 25^v. According to the early nineteenth-century bibliographer, A.-A. Barbier, D'Alembert told an Abbé Goujet that it was he, using Diderot's name, who had written the two letters to Berthier (J.-M. Quérard, *Les Supercheries littéraires dévoilées*, 2nd ed., 3 vols. [Paris, 1869–70], I, 937).
53. Arthur M. Wilson, 'Un Billet inédit de Diderot, [1751],' *RHLF*, LV (1955), 56–7; but the editor, M. Pommier, cautions (p. 57 n.) that the letter Diderot refers to is quite likely the *Lettre sur les sourds et muets*.
54. N.p., n.d. [Mazarine, 24665.X, pp. 304–6]. D'Hémery's entry (B.N., MSS, Fr. 22156, fol. 42^v). Other pamphlets published at this time were *Lettre de M. * * *, l'un des*

XXIV, à M. Diderot, Directeur de la Manufacture Encyclopédique (n.p., 1751) [Mazarine, 41774, pièce 2]; and *Lettre d'un souscripteur pour le Dictionnaire Encyclopédique, à Monsieur Diderot* (n.p., 1751) [Mazarine, 34481-A, pièce 8]; cf. D'Hémery's entry, 25 Feb. 1751 quoted in Venturi, *Origini*, 152.

55. A.-T., I, 356–8; A.-T., IV, 202–3, 305; *Encyc.*, III, 511–12, s.v. 'Clavecin oculaire'; see Shelby T. McCloy, *French Inventions of the Eighteenth Century* (Lexington [Ky.], 1952), 131–2; and esp. Donald S. Schier, *Louis Bertrand Castel, Anti-Newtonian Scientist* (Cedar Rapids [Iowa], 1941), 135–96, 202. Also E. Noulet, 'Le Père Castel et le "clavecin oculaire",' *Nouvelle NRF*, I (1953), 553–9.

56. Cf. Erika von Erhardt-Siebold, 'Harmony of the Senses in English, German, and French Romanticism,' *PMLA*, XLVII (1932), 577–92, esp. 578; Erika von Erhardt-Siebold, 'Some Inventions of the Pre-Romantic Period and their Influence upon Literature,' *Englische Studien*, LXVI (1931–2), 347–63, esp. 355; Erika von Erhardt-Siebold, 'Synästhesien in der englischen Dichtung des 19. Jahrhunderts,' *Englische Studien*, LIII (1919–20), 1–157, 196–334, esp. 43–5.

57. A.-T., XIX, 425–6. Diderot wrote again to Father Castel, 2 July 1751, in reply to his letter regarding the *Lettre sur les sourds et muets* (A.-T., XIX, 426–7; original in B.N., MSS, Fr. 12763, fol. 222).

58. Venturi, *Origini*, 107.

59. A.-T., XIX, 424. The diploma of membership was dated 4 March 1751 (Dieckmann, *Inventaire*, 162). *La Bigarure*, X (3 June 1751), 45, chronicled the fact of Diderot's membership and added, 'Quelques personnes ont paru étonnées que notre Academie des *Quarante* ne leur [Diderot and Toussaint] ait pas fait cet honneur . . .'

60. D'Hémery's entry, 30 March 1753 (B.N., MSS, Fr. 22158, fol. 129). This was Naigeon's opinion also (Naigeon, 138–9). D'Alembert became a Fellow of the Royal Society in 1748 and De Jaucourt in 1756.

61. Formey, *Conseils pour former une bibliothèque*, 112; 'Histoire de l'Académie Royale des Sciences et Belles-Lettres' (sep. pagination), *Nouveaux Mémoires de l'Académie Royale des Sciences et Belles-Lettres, Année MDCCLXX*, 52.

62. May, 21–2. For a list of the articles by Formey used in the *Encyclopédie*, see E. Marcu, 'Un Encyclopédiste oublié: Formey,' *RHLF*, LIII (1953), 302–5.

63. Formey praised it highly in his *Bibliothèque Impartiale*, III (Jan.–Feb. 1751), 306–7.

64. Cf. *supra*, n. 54.

65. Buffon to Formey, 6 Dec. 1750 (J. Matter, *Lettres et pièces rares ou inédites* [Paris, 1846], 372); Venturi, *Jeunesse*, 399.

66. B.N., MSS, Nouv. acq. fr. 3345, fol. 144; the censor was Joseph-Marie-François de Lassone.

67. *Réponse signifiée de M. Luneau de Boisjermain, au Précis des libraires associés à l'impression de l'Encyclopédie* (Paris, 1772), 2; May, 25.

68. *Corr. litt.*, II, 73.

CHAPTER 11

1. F. Picavet, ed., *Discours préliminaire de l'Encyclopédie*, by Jean Le Rond d'Alembert (Paris, 1929), lviii–lix.

2. *Encyc.*, I, xxxviij.

3. Ernesto Orrei, *L'Enciclopedia e la Rivoluzione francese* (Rome, 1946), 45.

4. *Encyc.*, I, ij.

5. Marcel Hervier, *Les Ecrivains français jugés par leurs contemporains*, II: *Le dix-huitième siècle* (Paris, n.d.), 249–50; *Corr. litt.*, II, 73.

6. See René Hubert, *Les Sciences sociales dans l'Encyclopédie* (Paris, 1923), 142. This view is in disagreement with that of Nelly Noémie Schargo, *History in the* Encyclopédie (New York, 1947), *passim*; cf. also Nelly Schargo Hoyt, 'Méthode et interprétation de l'histoire dans l'*Encyclopédie*,' *RHLF*, LI (1951), 359–72. Although the *Encyclopédie* undeniably contains a host of references to past events, my own feeling is that Dr. Hoyt tries to make a rope out of a mosaic. As a recent historiographer has remarked, 'It is possible to be interested in history without having real historical-mindedness, and it is beyond dispute that such was the case with the eighteenth-century historians' (R.N. Stromberg,

'History in the Eighteenth Century,' *JHI*, XII [1951], 297). In further defense of my point of view, see Lynn Thorndike, 'L'Encyclopédie and the History of Science,' *Isis*, VI (1924), 367–71; Emile Faguet, 'L'Encyclopédie,' *RDM*, 15 Feb. 1901, 803, 814; Benedetto Croce, *History as the Story of Liberty* (New York, 1941), 70; R. G. Collingwood, *The Idea of History* (Oxford, 1946), 77, 80; Herbert J. Muller, *The Uses of the Past* (New York, 1952), 280; and David Easton, *The Political System* (New York, 1953), 13.

7. J. B. Bury, *The Idea of Progress* (London, 1920), 171.

8. *Encyc.*, I, xxxvj.

9. *Année Littéraire*, vol. VI for 1757, 302–3.

10. *Encyc.*, I, xviij.

11. A.-T., XIII, 388. For instances of Diderot's debt to Girard, see Pierre Hermand, 'Sur le texte de Diderot et sur les sources de quelques passages de ses *Oeuvres*,' *RHLF*, XXII (1915), 363.

12. A.-T., XIII, 138; *Encyc.*, I, xij, viij.

13. *Encyc.*, I, xlj.

14. See David J. Brandenburg, 'Agriculture in the *Encyclopédie*: An Essay in French Intellectual History,' *Agricultural History*, XXIV (1950), 96–108. Though ostensibly conventional (Brandenburg, 99–100), Diderot's ideas on rotation of crops were in reality very revolutionary, for they necessitated a fundamental change in property holding (Lefebvre, *Diderot*, 14–19).

15. *Memoirs of Baron de Tott. Containing the State of the Turkish Empire and the Crimea, during the Late War with Russia*, 2 vols. (London, 1785), II, 118. Pierre Surirey de Saint-Rémy, a French general, published his *Mémoires d'artillerie* in 1697. For further information regarding the influence of the *Encyclopédie* in foreign countries, see *AIEF*, No. 2 (May 1952): Gilbert Chinard, 'L'*Encyclopédie* et le rayonnement de l'esprit encyclopédique en Amérique,' 3–22; Jean Fabre, 'L'*Encyclopédie* en Pologne,' 31–45; Charly Guyot, 'Le Rayonnement de l'*Encyclopédie* en Suisse,' 47–60; D. M. Lang, 'L'*Encyclopédie* en Russie et au Caucase,' 61–5; and Jean Sarrailh, 'Note sur l'*Encyclopédie* en Espagne,' 77–83.

16. *Encyc.*, VIII, 143a.

17. A.-T., XIII, 361, 362. Cf. Georges Friedmann, 'L'*Encyclopédie* et le travail humain,' *AUP*, XXII ([Oct.] 1952), numéro spécial, 123–35.

18. *Encyc.*, I, 412a.

19. A.-T., XIII, 368–9; Alexis François, in Ferdinand Brunot, *Histoire de la langue française des origines à 1900*, VI^2 (Paris, 1932), 1181, 1174.

20. A.-T., XIII, 265–6.

21. *Encyc.*, I, 191a.

22. A.-T., XIII, 183.

23. *Encyc.*, I, 175b.

24. William A. Nitze and E. Preston Dargan, *A History of French Literature* (New York, 1922), 378; see also E. A. Beller and M. du P. Lee, Jr., eds., *Selections from Bayle's Dictionary* (Princeton, 1952), xxvii–xxviii. Cf. *Diderot et l'Encyclopédie: Exposition commémorative*, xiv; Kingsley Martin, *French Liberal Thought in the Eighteenth Century* (London, 1929), 46; Louis Ducros, *Les Encyclopédistes* (Paris, 1900), 32–7; Victor Giraud, 'Les Etapes du XVIIIe siècle, I: Du Dictionnaire de Bayle à l'Encyclopédie,' *RDM*, 15 July 1924, 356; and Havens, *The Age of Ideas*, 22–37.

25. An eloquent passage regarding Bayle, written by Diderot, was expunged by Le Breton before publication (Gordon and Torrey, 48–53, 75–8). D'Alembert praised Bayle rather gingerly in the *Encyc.*, IV, 967a, s.v. 'Dictionnaire.'

26. A.-T., I, 140; Mme de Vandeul, lvii.

27. E.g., *Encyc.*, I, 38–9, 74b, 177b, 266–9, 721–2: s.v. 'Abricots,' 'Accomoder,' 'Agneau,' 'Aliments,' and 'Artichaut.' Cf. Georges May, *Quatre visages de Denis Diderot* (Paris, 1951), 13–33: 'Diderot gastronome.' Diderot's source for these culinary matters was chiefly Noël Chomel, *Dictionnaire œconomique*, 4th ed., 2 vols. (Paris, 1740).

28. *Encyc.*, I, 159.

29. *Encyc.*, I, 95–6, s.v. 'Achées'; regarding Réaumur, ibid. 102, 108a; regarding Frederick the Great, ibid. 55b; ibid. 252–3, s.v. 'Alecto.'

30. Agriculture (A.-T., XIII, 256–65); cf. Lefebvre, *Diderot*, 14–17. Steel (A.-T., XIII, 210).

Monopolies (*Encyc.*, I, 205). Midwives (A.-T., XIII, 186). For reforms in spelling, see Marcel Cohen, 'L'*Encyclopédie* et l'orthographe académique,' *Europe*, Dec. 1951, 25–6.
31. *Encyc.*, I, 205a; for attribution to Diderot, see ibid. xliij.
32. A.-T., XIII, 186.
33. A.-T., XIII, 268.
34. A.-T., XIII, 392–5.
35. Orrei, *L'Enciclopedia e la Rivoluzione francese*, 88.
36. Ducros, *Les Encyclopédistes*, 123.
37. A.-T., XIV, 461.
38. A.-T., XIII, 223–4.
39. *Encyc.*, I, 181.
40. A.-T., XIII, 374.
41. A.-T., XIII, 266, s.v. 'Aigle.'
42. A.-T., XIII, 186–7.
43. For the Abbé Mallet, see Venturi, *Origini*, 35–7, 136.
44. A.-T., XIII, 285, s.v. 'Amenthès.'
45. Robert R. Palmer, *Catholics & Unbelievers in Eighteenth Century France* (Princeton, 1939), 147.
46. *Encyc.*, I, 242b. Cf. La Mettrie's remark: '*Un rien, une petite fibre, quelque chose que la plus subtile Anatomie ne peut découvrir*, eut fait deux Sots, d'Erasme, & de Fontenelle, qui le remarque lui même dans un de ses meilleurs *Dialogues*' (Julien Offray de La Mettrie, *Oeuvres philosophiques*, 2 vols. [Amsterdam, 1753], I, [*L'Homme Machine*, sep. pagination, 24]).

CHAPTER 12

1. 'Abeille' (*Mercure de France*, April 1751, 41–73); 'Agate' (ibid. vol. II for June 1751, 105–12).
2. *The Plan of the French Encyclopaedia, or Universal Dictionary of Arts, Sciences, Trades, and Manufactures. Being an Account of the Origin, Design, Conduct, and Execution of that Work. Translated from the Preface of the French Editors, Mess. Diderot and Alembert* (London, 1752), 'Advertisement.' Printed for W. Innys, T. Longman, C. Hitch and L. Hawes, J. and P. Knapton, S. Birt, J. Ward, J. Hodges, R. Hett, J. and J. Rivington, T. Osborne, J. Shuckburgh, M. Senex, D. Browne, and A. Millar.
3. May, 25–7; D'Hémery's journal, 25 Nov. 1751, mentions the trip David and Briasson took to London (B.N., MSS, Fr. 22156, fol. 143). See J. Lough, 'The "Encyclopédie" in Eighteenth-Century England,' *French Studies*, VI (1952), 291–3.
4. *London Daily Advertizer*, 11 and 16 Jan., 29 Feb. 1752; *DNB*, s.v. 'Ayloffe, Sir Joseph'; Lough, 'The "Encyclopédie" in Eighteenth-Century England,' *French Studies*, VI, 293–4. Cf. *Gentleman's Magazine*, XXII (1752), 46–7, and John Nichols, *Literary Anecdotes of the Eighteenth Century*, 9 vols. (London, 1812–15), III, 184 n. A Dutch publisher claimed in 1751 to have had the idea of translating and enlarging Chambers before the Paris publishers did, but there is no evidence to bolster his assertion (G. L. Van Roosbroeck, 'Who Originated the Plan of the *Encyclopédie*?' *Modern Philology*, XXVII [1929–30], 382–4).
5. *Corr. litt.*, II, 85.
6. Clément, *Cinq Années Littéraires*, III, 164–5.
7. *Corr. litt.*, II, 85.
8. Ibid. 86, 101.
9. May, 25.
10. B.N., MSS, Fr. 22156, fol. 94; also *Corr. litt.*, II, 86.
11. *Journal des Sçavans*, Sept. 1751, 625–6.
12. Venturi, *Origini*, 109.
13. *Journal de Trévoux*, Oct. 1751, 2261–4, 2279–82, 2285–6, 2288–90.
14. Ibid. Oct. 1751, 2250–95; Nov. 1751, 2419–57; Dec. 1751, 2592–2623; Jan. 1752, 146–90; Feb. 1752, 296–322; March 1752, 424–69.
15. Ibid. Nov. 1751, 2425, 2439–48, esp. 2439 and 2447.

16. B.N., MSS, Fr. 22139, fol. 146.
17. *Journal de Trévoux,* Oct. 1751, 2290; Nov. 1751, 2428–38; Dec. 1751, 2594–2608; Jan. 1752, 148–51, 172–3; Feb. 1752, 301–3, 320, 380.
18. Ibid. March 1752, 468 n.
19. *Encyc.,* I, Avertissement, ii.
20. *Journal de Trévoux,* March 1752, 456–67.
21. *Encyc.,* I, 368b.
22. *Journal de Trévoux,* Feb. 1752, 314.
23. Ibid. 382.
24. Gazier, *Histoire générale du mouvement janséniste,* II, 42.
25. B.N., MSS, Fonds Joly de Fleury 292, fol. 354; other examples in Joly de Fleury 1687, foll. 225 ff., and 1708, foll. 298, 345. Cf. Gazier, op. cit., II, 43.
26. Camille Daux, 'Une Réhabilitation: l'Abbé Jean-Martin de Prades,' *Science Catholique,* XVI (1901–2), 1025–39, 1095–1109; this quotation, 1097. Cf. Barbier, *Journal,* III, 333. The De Prades affair is well summarized by Charles Jourdain, *Histoire de l'Université de Paris au XVIIᵉ et au XVIIIᵉ siècle* (Paris, 1862), 391–2; and by Pierre Grosclaude, 'Le Bi-Centenaire de l'Encyclopédie. La pittoresque affaire de l'Abbé de Prades,' *Acropole,* III (1951), 14–16.
27. For an interesting comparison of De Prades's thesis and D'Alembert's 'Preliminary Discourse,' done in parallel columns, see B.N., MSS, Joly de Fleury 292, foll. 327–30.
28. See *supra,* p. 60.
29. The thesis summarized: A.-T., I, 435–7; also Monod, *De Pascal à Chateaubriand,* 333–4.
30. Palmer, *Catholics & Unbelievers in Eighteenth Century France,* 122–4. For an excellent estimate of the whole controversy, see ibid. 117–28.
31. *Remarques sur une thèse soutenue en Sorbonne le samedi 30 octobre 1751, par M. l'Abbé Delomenie de Brienne* (n.p., n.d.), 1 (Mazarine 41191, pièce 7; also mounted in B.N., MSS, Joly de Fleury 292, fol. 291).
32. *Mercure de France,* April 1752, 197; M.-P.-J. Picot, *Mémoires pour servir à l'histoire ecclésiastique pendant le dix-huitième siècle,* 2nd ed., 4 vols. (Paris, 1815–16), II, 246.
33. *Lettre de M. l'Abbé Hooke, Docteur de la Maison & Société de Sorbonne, Professeur de Théologie, à Monseigneur l'Archevêque de Paris* (n.p., n.d.), 27–8 (Mazarine 41191, pièce 8).
34. Latin and French texts of the Sorbonne censure mounted in B.N., MSS, Joly de Fleury 292, fol. 293, and Fr. 22092, foll. 183–91, resp.; the *mandement* of the Archbishop of Paris mounted in Fr. 22092, foll. 191–9. Consult these volumes, *passim,* for other documents concerning the De Prades case, and also B.N., MSS, Fr. 22112, foll. 139–63. Among printed sources, see Barbier, *Journal,* III, 333 *et passim;* D'Argenson, VII, 30, 68, 71, 106; Reusch, *Der Index der verbotenen Bücher,* II, 874–5.
35. *Mandement de Monseigneur l'Evêque de Montauban, portant condamnation d'une thèse . . .* (Montauban, 1752), 3, mounted in B.N., MSS, Fr. 22092, foll. 526–9.
36. *Nouvelles Ecclésiastiques,* 27 Feb. 1752, 35. Three whole issues and part of a fourth, viz. 27 Feb. and 5, 12, and 19 March (pp. 33–47) were given over to a meticulous account of the affair.
37. Frontispiece reproduced in E. Abry, C. Audic, and P. Crouzet, *Histoire illustrée de la littérature française* (Paris, numerous editions), s.v. 'L'Encyclopédie.'
38. *Encyc.,* I, 663b. Doubt has been expressed whether this article was by Diderot (A.-T., XIII, 359 n.), but it is now regarded as being his (Raymond Naves, *Voltaire et l'Encyclopédie* [Paris, 1938], 106 n.; Lois Strong Gaudin, *Les Lettres anglaises dans l'Encyclopédie* [New York, 1942], 95).
39. B.N., MSS, Fr. 22157, fol. 12; cf. *Corr. litt.,* II, 198 and n. This pamphlet is, however, variously attributed. A Father Bonhomme, presumably a Franciscan, is sometimes mentioned as its author, while the *Catalogue général des livres imprimés de la Bibliothèque Nationale,* LV (1913), cols. 1042–3, mentions another Jesuit, F.-M. Hervé, together with a Father Fruchet, as the joint authors of the work. The *Réflexions* was published without going through the ordinary channels of censorship, in consequence of which 'M. de Malesherbes is making a good deal of fuss about it' (D'Hémery's journal, ibid.; cf. Belin, *Le Mouvement*

philosophique de 1748 à 1789, 107). An expanded edition, *Réflexions d'un Franciscain sur les trois premiers volumes de l'Encyclopédie*, was published in 'Berlin' (actually Paris) in 1754. This time D'Hémery noted that its authors were Hervé and Fruchet, a Franciscan (B.N., MSS, Fr. 22159, fol. 71). Still another edition, almost identical in content, was published at The Hague in 1759, under the title of *L'Eloge de l'Encyclopédie et des Encyclopédistes*. Jesuit susceptibilities are revealed in this pamphlet by the author's remarking that he was shocked because of the ostentatious silence of the *Encyclopédie* regarding the part played by the Jesuits in the renaissance of letters (ed. 1752, 45).

40. *Réflexions d'un Franciscain* (1752), 11.

41. Ibid. 9–10. The 1754 edition printed these several theses by De Prades, the *tentative*, the *Sorbonique*, the *mineure*, and the *majeure* (179–88; cf. Palmer, *Catholics & Unbelievers in Eighteenth Century France*, 121).

42. *Encyc.*, I, xlj; cf. *Encyc.*, II, 846b; *Réflexions d'un Franciscain* (1752), 7.

43. *Encyc.*, II, 845–62, s.v. 'Certitude.' Vol. II was published on 22 or 23 Jan. 1752 (Barbier, *Journal*, III, 337); Venturi, *Jeunesse*, 211, gives 25 Jan. D'Hémery noted on 27 Jan. 1752 that Vol. II had been published 'depuis quelques jours' (B.N., MSS, Fr. 22157, fol. 18). The allegation that the De Prades thesis was the result of a plot was also made by the Bishop of Auxerre in his Pastoral Instruction in 1752 (A.-T., I, 445) and by Joseph-Robert-Alexandre Duhamel, *Lettres flamandes*, deuxième partie (Mons, 1753), 139–47, and by the Protestant writer, David Renaud Boullier, *Court examen de la thèse de Mr. l'abbé de Prades et Observations sur son Apologie* (Amsterdam, 1753), esp. 29.

44. A police report dated 1 Jan. 1753 says of Yvon: 'Il a été obligé de s'expatrier et de passer en Hollande pour l'affaire de l'Abbé de Prades, avec lequel il étoit intimmement lié, et on pretend meme qu'il a eu bonne part à la composition de sa Theze' (B.N., MSS, Nouv. acq. fr. 10783, fol. 159). Cf. ibid. fol. 43: '. . . on le [Yvon] soupçonnoit d'avoir bonne part à la Theze.' Louis Petit de Bachaumont, *Mémoires secrets pour servir à l'histoire de la république des lettres en France*, 36 vols. (London, 1777–89), I, 41, states under date of 4 Feb. 1762 that Yvon '. . . passoit pour avoir contribué en grande partie à la these de l'abbé de Prades. . . .' Yvon is said to have stated in Paris, after De Prades's reconciliation with the Church, that he, Yvon, had written the thesis (Jean-Baptiste de Boyer, Marquis d'Argens, *Histoire de l'esprit humain*, 14 vols. [Berlin, 1765–8], x, 351 n.).

45. Naigeon, 160–61 nn.

46. *Encyc.*, III, Avertissement, i.

47. Morellet recalls meeting Diderot in De Prades's rooms, but *after* the storm broke, and in no way suggests that Diderot planned to exploit the thesis in any fashion (Morellet, *Mémoires*, I, 28). According to Charles-Philippe d'Albert, duc de Luynes, *Mémoires sur la cour de Louis XV*, 17 vols. (Paris, 1860–65), xi, 369, De Prades had set forth his ideas to Diderot merely to learn what arguments Diderot would use in refutation; but Diderot had overwhelmed him with his 'sophisms.' This is very interesting, but purely hearsay.

48. Emile Regnault, *Christophe de Beaumont, Archevêque de Paris (1703–1781)*, 2 vols. (Paris, 1882), I, 346.

49. Joseph Daoust, 'Encyclopédistes et Jésuites de Trévoux (1751–1752): Deuxième centenaire de l'*Encyclopédie*,' *Etudes*, CCLXXII (1952), 179.

50. *La Bigarure*, xv, 70, 72; Voltaire, ed. Moland, xxIV, 17–28, esp. 18; *Corr. litt.*, II, 298. Regarding Voltaire and *Le Tombeau de la Sorbonne*, see Naves, *Voltaire et l'Encyclopédie*, 11–12; Grosclaude, *Un Audacieux Message*, 64–5; J. Nivat, 'Quelques Enigmes de la Correspondance de Voltaire,' *RHLF*, LIII (1953), 442–3; and Donald Schier, 'The Abbé de Prades in Exile,' *RR*, xLV (1954), 182–90. A request from Diderot to La Condamine, 16 Dec. 1752, for the loan of a copy of *Le Tombeau de la Sorbonne* (Diderot, *Corr.*, I, 147) mentions that the pamphlet was rare.

51. Barbier, *Journal*, III, 344; cf. also ibid. 336–7, 339, 346. D'Argenson, VII, 56; cf. also ibid. 57, 63. See also Luynes, *Mémoires*, xi, 385–6 (5 Feb. 1752). For an excellent discussion of the whole affair, including evidence of a 'plot,' see Venturi, *Jeunesse*, esp. 201–4.

52. D'Argenson, VII, 71–2.

53. Barbier, *Journal*, III, 344, 355.

54. Malesherbes, *Mémoire sur la liberté de la presse*, 90. For other contemporary testimony of

Mirepoix's influence, see D'Argenson, VII, 93; Voltaire, *Le Tombeau de la Sorbonne, passim; Les Nouvelles Ecclésiastiques*, 19 March 1752, 45.

55. For the printed *arrêt*, see B.N., MSS, Fr. 22177, fol. 54.

56. D'Argenson, VII, 110. Apparently the *arrêt* was not published until 13 Feb. 1752 (ibid.); but on 7 Feb. Malesherbes on his own authority had forbidden the further distribution of the *Encyclopédie* (Barbier, *Journal*, III, 344).

CHAPTER 13

1. D'Argenson, VII, 106, 122; Barbier, *Journal*, III, 355.
2. Clément, *Cinq Années Littéraires*, IV, 21 (15 March 1752); cf. *Corr. litt.*, II, 298, and D'Argenson, VII, 122.
3. Barbier, *Journal*, III, 355; Lester Gilbert Crocker, 'The Problem of Malesherbes' Intervention,' by L. G. Krakeur, *MLQ*, II (1941), 556-7.
4. D'Argenson, VII, 112; Barbier, *Journal*, III, 355; *Corr. litt.*, II, 298 (15 Nov. 1753).
5. *Corr. litt.*, XI, 407. Sainte-Beuve, 'M. de Malesherbes,' *Causeries du lundi*, II, 512-39, though old, is far from antiquated.
6. *Corr. litt.*, XI, 36, from Malesherbes' discourse upon being admitted into the French Academy (1775).
7. Malesherbes to Morellet, *ca.* 23 Jan. 1758 (Coyecque, *Inventaire de la collection Anisson*, I, xcvii-xcviii).
8. Malesherbes, *Mémoire sur la liberté de la presse*, 70.
9. Ducros, *Les Encyclopédistes*, 223.
10. Ibid. 220.
11. *Corr. litt.*, XI, 36. See Pierre Grosclaude, 'Malesherbes et l'Encyclopédie,' *AUP*, XXII ([Oct.] 1952), numéro spécial, 57-79.
12. D'Argenson, VII, 112.
13. Brunetière, 'La Direction de la librairie sous M. de Malesherbes,' *RDM*, 1 Feb. 1882, 591.
14. Barbier, *Journal*, III, 346.
15. Ducros, *Les Encyclopédistes*, 57.
16. Mme de Pompadour owned a set of the *Encyclopédie* (*Catalogue des livres de la bibliothéque de feue Madame la marquise de Pompadour* [Paris, 1765], 39; also a copy of the *Bijoux indiscrets* and the *Histoire de Grèce* [ibid. 243, 278]).
17. Cf. Ducros, *Les Encyclopédistes*, 56-7.
18. D'Argenson, VII, 223-4; for his relations with D'Alembert, see ibid. 63, 68 n.
19. For proof of this, see an unsigned and undated minute in Malesherbes' hand, probably written in 1758 (B.N., MSS, Fr. 22191, fol. 22).
20. B.N., MSS, Nouv. acq. fr. 3345, fol. 145. See also the approbation of the censor who had read the articles concerning jurisprudence in Vols. I and II (B.N., MSS, Fr. 22139, fol. 121).
21. Malesherbes, *Mémoire sur la liberté de la presse*, 90; cf. his memorandum *ca.* 1758 (B.N., MSS, Fr. 22191, fol. 23).
22. 24 Aug. 1752 (Voltaire, ed. Moland, XXXVII, 471-2).
23. 5 Sept. 1752 (ibid. 481).
24. Matter, *Lettres et pièces rares ou inédites*, 386.
25. Venturi, *Origini*, 57, 59-60.
26. Ibid. 60.
27. Clara Adèle Luce Herpin (pseud. Lucien Perey) and Gaston Maugras, 'Madame d'Epinay à Genève (1757-1759),' *Bibliothèque Universelle et Revue Suisse*, 3ᵉ période, XXI (1884), 553, quoting a letter from Mme d'Epinay to Grimm; Torrey, 'Voltaire's Reaction to Diderot,' *PMLA*, L, 1111.
28. D'Alembert to D'Argens, 16 Sept. 1752 (Jean Le Rond d'Alembert, *Oeuvres*, 5 vols. [Paris, 1821-2], V, 19); regarding the publishers' pay roll, see May, 50 *et passim*.
29. Venturi, *Origini*, 124, 126.
30. *Corr. litt.*, II, 299.
31. Barbier, *Journal*, III, 339.
32. Agreement of 6 Feb. 1754 (May, 27).

33. Ferdinand Brunetière, *L'Evolution des genres dans l'histoire de la littérature* (Paris, 1890), 210.

34. D'Hémery's journal, entry of 12 Oct. 1752: '. . . imprimé sans permission. Il ne m'a pas encore été possible de découvrir l'imprimeur' (B.N., MSS, Fr. 22157, fol. 123). For speculation as to whether or not Diderot contributed to the first two parts of De Prades's *Apologie*, see the points set forth in Dieckmann, *Inventaire*, 56-7.

35. A.-T., I, 448.

36. A.-T., I, 440.

37. A.-T., I, 449-55, 470-71.

38. A.-T., I, 449.

39. A.-T., I, 450, 454-5, 466. See Antoine Adam, 'Rousseau et Diderot,' *Revue des Sciences Humaines*, Jan.–March 1949, 26-7, for favorable comment regarding this statement of social origins.

40. René Hubert, 'L'Esprit des sciences sociales dans l'*Encyclopédie*,' *RHPHGC*, IV (1936), 113. Cf. Lefebvre, *Diderot*, 114-24.

41. A.-T., I, 477.

42. A.-T., I, 457-8.

43. A.-T., I, 456.

44. A.-T., I, 482 n.

45. Clément, *Cinq Années Littéraires*, IV, 214.

46. A.-T., I, 483-4. On Diderot's adroit use of this Jansenist attack, consult Venturi, *Jeunesse*, 214-25.

CHAPTER 14

1. A.-T., VII, 168.

2. A.-T., XVIII, 271-2. This particular Duc d'Orléans died in 1752. Mme de Vandeul's version differs (Mme de Vandeul, xlvii–xlviii).

3. *Horace Walpole's Correspondence with Madame du Deffand and Wiart*, ed. W. S. Lewis and Warren H. Smith, V (New Haven, 1939), 262.

4. Morellet, *Mémoires*, I, 133-4.

5. B.M., Add. MSS 30867, foll. 14, 18-19, 20-21. D'Holbach was 'élevé presque dès son enfance à Paris,' acc. to *Biographie universelle* (*Michaud*), s.v. 'Holbach,' 532.

6. Complete genealogical information in W. H. Wickwar, *Baron d'Holbach* (London, 1935), 19-20, 233-5. D'Holbach's naturalization in August 1749 is recorded in the Archives nationales, P. 2593, fol. 80 (*Diderot et l'Encyclopédie: Exposition commémorative*, 49).

7. Billy, *Diderot*, 314-15, quotes the undated bill of sale.

8. Rousseau stated in the *Confessions*, in a context that suggests the year 1751, that Diderot and D'Holbach had been intimate 'for a long time since' (Rousseau, ed. Hachette, VIII, 263). Acc. to Vernière, *Spinoza et la pensée française avant la Révolution*, 632 n., they became acquainted in 1749.

9. S. Lenel, 'Un Ennemi de Voltaire: La Beaumelle,' *RHLF*, XX (1913), 115 n.

10. Dominique-Joseph Garat, *Mémoires historiques sur la vie de M. Suard, sur ses écrits, et sur le XVIIIᵉ siècle*, 2 vols. (Paris, 1820), I, 208-9.

11. *Diderot et l'Encyclopédie: Exposition commémorative*, 49-50. Cf. Wickwar, *Baron d'Holbach*, 62-3.

12. Marmontel, *Mémoires*, II, 312; Rousseau, ed. Hachette, VIII, 263. Cf. Garat, *Mémoires . . . de M. Suard*, I, 207.

13. Louisette Reichenburg, *Contribution à l'histoire de la 'Querelle des Bouffons'* (Philadelphia, 1937), 30-37.

14. Carlo Goldoni, *Mémoires*, 2 vols. (Paris, 1822), II, 184. John Wilkes's views were similar (Frederick Charles Green, 'Autour de quatre lettres inédites de Diderot à John Wilkes,' *RLC*, XXV [1951], 459). For an excellent comparison and contrast of eighteenth-century French and Italian music, see Violet Paget (pseud. Vernon Lee), *Studies of the Eighteenth Century in Italy* (London, 1880), 71-9.

15. Rousseau, ed. Hachette, VI, 198.

16. Rousseau, ed. Hachette, VIII, 274; *Corr. litt.*, II, 313, 322; cf. D'Argenson, VIII, 180.
17. D'Hémery mentioned Grimm as being the author: entry of 21 Dec. 1752 (B.N., MSS, Fr. 22157, fol. 140). The *Petit Prophète* is printed in *Corr. litt.*, XVI, 313–36. Grimm was almost challenged to a duel by Chassé, one of the artists he satirized (Dieckmann, *Inventaire*, 245).
18. Romain Rolland, *Some Musicians of Former Days*, 4th ed. (London, n.d.), 257. For a much more critical view of Diderot's knowledge of music and capacity as a critic, see Adolphe Jullien, *La Ville et la cour au XVIIIᵉ siècle* (Paris, 1881), 153–66, 193–204.
19. A.-T., XII, 143–51, 152–6, 157–70, resp.; for their dates, ibid. 139–40, and Reichenburg, 50 n. Their attribution to Diderot was challenged by Ernest Thoinan in his excellent bibliography of the 'Querelle des Bouffons' in the *Supplément* (2 vols. [Paris, 1878–80], II, 450–51, s.v. 'Rousseau') to F.-J. Fétis, *Biographie universelle des musiciens*, 8 vols. (Paris, 1860–65); cf. J.-G. Prod'homme, 'Diderot et la musique,' *Zeitschrift der internationalen Musikgesellschaft*, XV (1913–14), 157, and A.-T., XII, 141, 155 n. However, Rousseau's annotations on copies of these pamphlets are the basis for attributing them to Diderot (Diderot, 'Les Trois Chapitres,' *Revue Rétrospective*, 2ᵉ série, I [1835], 94, 94–5 nn.; Paul-Emmanuel-Auguste Poulet Malassis, *La Querelle des Bouffons* [Paris, 1876], 14–17). Rousseau's note regarding *Les Trois Chapitres* was published by Guillemin, 133.
20. A.-T., XII, 155.
21. A.-T., IV, 408.
22. *Corr. litt.*, II, 272. See Diderot's article for the *Encyclopédie*, s.v. 'Intermède' (A.-T., XV, 233–4), for an enthusiastic judgment of Italian opera, especially of Pergolesi.
23. *Réponse de M. Rameau à MM. les éditeurs de l'Encyclopédie sur leur dernier Avertissement* (London and Paris, 1757), 53. Cf. René de Récy, 'La Critique musicale au siècle dernier: Rameau et les Encyclopédistes,' *RDM*, 1 July 1886, 138–64, esp. 140.
24. Alfred Richard Oliver, *The Encyclopedists as Critics of Music* (New York, 1947), 112.
25. Rousseau, ed. Hachette, VIII, 247; he evidently wrote them in early 1749 (Rousseau, *Corr. gén.*, I, 287).
26. *Réponse de M. Rameau . . .* (1757), 53.
27. This point is developed by Oliver, 101–13, who thinks that the *Encyclopédie* was more sinned against than sinning in the Rameau controversy.
28. A.-T., XII, 147; see also D'Alembert's treatment of Rameau in his *De la Liberté de la musique* (1760), reprinted in his *Mélanges de littérature, d'histoire, et de philosophie*, 5 vols. (Amsterdam [Paris], 1763–7), IV, 387–9.
29. *Année Littéraire*, vol. I for 1757, 304. Cf. Bernard Champigneulle, *L'Age classique de la musique française* (Paris, [1946]), 283–90: 'Rameau et les Encyclopédistes.'
30. Rousseau, ed. Hachette, VIII, 271.
31. Anne-Louise-Germaine Necker, Baronne de Staël-Holstein, 'Lettre sur le caractère de Rousseau,' *Oeuvres complètes*, 17 vols. (Paris, 1820–21), I, 81.
32. Rousseau, ed. Hachette, V, 105 (my emphasis).
33. *Corr. litt.*, III, 60–61; regarding this incident, see Armand Gasté, *Diderot et le curé de Montchauvet: une mystification littéraire chez le baron d'Holbach, 1754* (Paris, 1898). Cf. A.-T., V, 496.
34. D'Holbach's account was first published in the *Journal de Paris*, Supplement to No. 336, 2 Dec. 1789, 1567–8; reprinted in Morellet, *Mémoires*, II, 336–7, and *Corr. litt.*, XV, 575–6. The Abbé Petit was mentioned earlier in the *Corr. litt.*, II, 503–4.
35. Morellet, *Mémoires*, I, 29–30, 34–5.
36. May, *passim*.
37. Diderot, *Corr.*, I, 145–6. Cf. Diderot's letter to Mme Caroillon La Salette, 25 Aug. 1752 in which he apparently alluded to his wife's intractability (ibid. 142).
38. *Supra*, 23.
39. Mme de Vandeul, xlvii. For other instances of Diderot's composing memoranda, one in 1741, the other in 1755, to oblige members of the La Salette family, see Diderot, *Corr.*, I, 26, 198–9.
40. Diderot, *Corr.*, I, 151.
41. Cf. Henri Denis, 'Deux collaborateurs économiques de l'Encyclopédie: Quesnay et Rous-

seau,' *Pensée*, Sept.–Oct. 1951, 44–54; also Anita Fage, 'Les Doctrines de population des Encyclopédistes,' *Population*, VI (1951), 609–24.

42. *Encyc.*, VII, 812a, s.v. 'Grains'; cf. ibid. 816a, 820a.
43. Marmontel, *Mémoires*, II, 28, 33–4.
44. Diderot, *Corr.*, I, 151–2, 155–8. In view of this evidence of Diderot's personal relationship with Mme de Pompadour, it is possible that an undated letter alleged to have been written by him to Mme de Pompadour and apparently referring to the crisis of 1752 is not apocryphal (*Lettres de Madame la Marquise de Pompadour . . .* , 2 vols. [Paris, 1811], II, 16–18; also in A.-T., XX, 100–101). Mme de Pompadour's alleged reply was published in *Lettres de madame la marquise de Pompadour . . .* , 2 vols. (London, 1771), I, 15–16; in idem, ed. 1811, II, 19–20; and in English translation, *Letters of the Marchioness of Pompadour . . .* , 2 vols. (London, 1771), I, 15–16. Her alleged letter was also published by E. Mignoneau, 'Une Lettre inédite de Madame de Pompadour à Diderot au sujet de l'Encyclopédie,' *Revue Occidentale*, XXI (1888), 70–75, who dated it 7 April 1754. Cf. Mignoneau, ibid. XXI, 222–3. Mme de Pompadour's letter is couched in friendly and anticlerical terms. It is hard to believe that she would confide such indiscretions to paper. Professor Dieckmann, however, found a copy of what appears to be precisely this letter, in Mme de Vandeul's hand. This fact, and also the fact that 'cette copie ne fut pas faite d'après le texte imprimé dont elle diverge en plusieurs endroits, lui donne un caractère d'authenticité' (Dieckmann, *Inventaire*, 110–11).
45. Diderot, *Corr.*, I, 152.
46. Ibid. 158.
47. Mme de Vandeul, xlvi–xlvii.
48. Nauroy, *Révolutionnaires*, 245.

CHAPTER 15

1. Léon Delamarche, 'Carnet d'un bibliophile,' *Eclair*, 14 May 1923, 3; Léon Delamarche, 'Les Bibliophiles et Diderot,' *Eclair*, 26 May 1924, 4; also identified by Avenir Tchemerzine, *Bibliographie d'éditions originales et rares d'auteurs français des XVe, XVIe, XVIIe, et XVIIIe siècles*, 10 vols. (Paris, 1927–33), IV, 442–4. A copy was exhibited at the Bibliothèque Nationale in 1951 (*Diderot et l'Encyclopédie: Exposition commémorative*, 26). See Herbert Dieckmann, 'The First Edition of Diderot's *Pensées sur l'interprétation de la nature*,' *Isis*, XLVI (1955), 253–66.
2. 6 Dec. 1753 (B.N., MSS, Fr. 22158, fol. 91).
3. Jean Luc, *Diderot* (Paris, 1938), 107.
4. [Alexandre Deleyre], *La Revue des Feuilles de Mr Fréron* (London, 1756), 387; Vartanian, *Diderot and Descartes*, 136–7.
5. Cru, 202; cf. ibid. 193–206.
6. *Corr. litt.*, III, 116–17. Cf. ibid. II, 485–6.
7. Herbert Dieckmann, 'The Influence of Francis Bacon on Diderot's *Interprétation de la Nature*,' *RR*, XXXIV (1943), 329.
8. Ibid. 305.
9. A.-T., II, 18–19; my italics.
10. A.-T., II, 13–14.
11. A.-T., II, 14. On this passage, see Dieckmann, loc. cit. *RR*, XXXIV, 317; also Herbert Dieckmann, 'Goethe und Diderot,' *Deutsche Vierteljahrsschrift für Literaturwissenschaft und Geistesgeschichte*, X (1932), 497; and Fernand Papillon, 'Des Rapports philosophiques de Goethe et de Diderot,' *Séances et travaux de l'Académie des Sciences morales et politiques*, CI (1874), 259–60.
12. A.-T., II, 20.
13. A.-T., II, 18. Cf. Herbert Dieckmann, 'Diderot's Conception of Genius,' *JHI*, II (1941), 172. 'Claude Bernard, dans son *Introduction à la Médecine expérimentale*, ajoutera peu aux formules de Diderot' (Lefebvre, *Diderot*, 144).
14. A.-T., II, 40 *et passim;* Dieckmann, loc. cit. *RR*, XXXIV, 319–22, and Dieckmann, loc. cit. *JHI*, II, 174. See also Vartanian, *Diderot and Descartes*, 138, 161–71.
15. Cf. Bacon, *Novum Organum*, part I, § lxxxvi.

16. *Encyc.*, I, xxxj; see esp. Etienne Bonnot de Condillac, *Oeuvres philosophiques*, ed. Georges Le Roy, 3 vols. (Paris, 1947–51), I, 127 *et passim.*

17. A.-T., XVI, 291.

18. Cassirer, *Die Philosophie der Aufklärung*, 15–16. Cf. Walter L. Dorn, *Competition for Empire, 1740–1763* (New York, 1940), 195.

19. Cf. Herbert Dieckmann, 'Théophile Bordeu und Diderots "Rêve de d'Alembert",' *Romanische Forschungen*, LII (1938), 119.

20. A.-T., II, 27–8; see I. Bernard Cohen, 'A Note concerning Diderot and Franklin,' *Isis*, XLVI (1955), 268–72.

21. A.-T., II, 39, 34.

22. A.-T., II, 11.

23. Cassirer, *Die Philosophie der Aufklärung*, 98; see also Dieckmann, loc. cit. *Isis*, XLVI, 251–2.

24. A.-T., II, 10. Cf. Crocker and Krueger, 'The Mathematical Writings of Diderot,' *Isis*, XXXIII, 229.

25. Cassirer, *Die Philosophie der Aufklärung*, 99. Cf. A.-T., II, 10–12. See also Abraham Chaim Lerel, *Diderots Naturphilosophie* (Vienna, 1950), 49, 69. For a sharply differing view, see Vartanian, *Diderot and Descartes*, 181–9.

26. *Corr. litt.*, II, 352. So also thought Maupertuis himself (Pierre-Louis Moreau de Maupertuis, 'Reponse aux Objections de M. Diderot,' *Oeuvres*, 4 vols. [Lyon, 1768], II, 197); cf. Vartanian, *Diderot and Descartes*, 270–72, and Paul Ostoya, 'Maupertuis et la biologie,' *Revue d'Histoire des Sciences*, VII (1954), 73, 75–6. Regarding these 'terrible consequences,' see Max Wartofsky, 'Diderot and the Development of Materialist Monism,' *Diderot Studies*, II, 297–8. For the influence of Maupertuis' thought upon Diderot's, see Pierre Brunet, 'La Notion d'évolution dans la science moderne avant Lamarck,' *Archeion*, XIX (1937), 39–40. Regarding the probable relations, even though unacknowledged by Diderot, of Diderot's thought to that of La Mettrie, see Aram Vartanian, 'Trembley's Polyp, La Mettrie, and Eighteenth-Century French Materialism,' *JHI*, XI (1950), 270, 274.

27. A.-T., II, 15–16. Cf. Arthur O. Lovejoy, 'The Argument for Organic Evolution before "The Origin of Species",' *Popular Science Monthly*, LXXV (1909), 513; and Arthur O. Lovejoy, *The Great Chain of Being* (Cambridge [Mass.], 1936), 268.

28. A.-T., II, 44–5.

29. Cassirer, *Die Philosophie der Aufklärung*, 120.

30. Lefebvre, *Diderot*, 153. Marx's statement was a reply to a sort of questionnaire made up by one of his daughters (D. B. Goldenach [pseud. D. Ryazanoff], *Karl Marx, Man, Thinker, and Revolutionist* [London, 1927], 269).

31. A.-T., II, 57–8; translation by Professor Lovejoy (Arthur O. Lovejoy, 'Some Eighteenth Century Evolutionists,' *Popular Science Monthly*, LXV [1904], 326). Regarding this passage and its prophetic nature, see Oscar Schmidt, 'Die Anschauungen der Encyclopädisten über die organische Natur,' *Deutsche Rundschau*, VII (1876), 86; also the excellent article of J. Charpentier, 'Diderot et la science de son temps,' *Revue du Mois*, XVI (1913), 547.

32. Lovejoy, loc. cit. LXV, 326.

33. A.-T., II, 49–50. Cf. Dieckmann, 'The Influence of Francis Bacon on Diderot's *Interprétation de la Nature*,' *RR*, XXXIV, 329.

34. *Mercure de France*, Jan. 1754, 130–35; *Journal Encyclopédique*, vol. II for Jan. 1756, 3–18. Grimm, of course, praised it fulsomely (*Corr. litt.*, II, 308).

35. *Corr. litt.*, II, 203. Charles de Brosses declared the book 'un vray traité d'inintelligibilité' (Joseph-Théophile Foisset, *Le Président de Brosses* [Paris, 1842], 540); cf. Charles Collé, *Journal et mémoires*, 3 vols. (Paris, 1868), II, 77.

36. Clément, *Cinq Années Littéraires*, IV, 284–5.

37. A.-T., II, 4; *Nouvelles Littéraires de Berlin*, 21 Dec. 1773, quoted by Tourneux, *Diderot et Catherine II*, 527.

38. La Harpe, *Lycée*, XV, 1–2. Some modern scientists have likewise declared their inability to understand the book, e.g. the French astronomer Camille Flammarion, 'Diderot, à l'occasion de son bi-centenaire,' *Revue*, CIV (Sept.–Oct. 1913), 440.

39. Alan Conder, tr., *A Treasury of French Poetry* (New York, 1951), 138, by kind permission of Mr. Conder.

40. For a good biography of Fréron, see François Cornou, *Trente Années de luttes contre Voltaire et les philosophes du XVIIIe siècle: Elie Fréron (1718–1776)* (Paris, 1922); cf. also Paul Chauvin, 'Un Journaliste au XVIIIe siècle (L'*Année littéraire* et Fréron),' *Revue des Pyrénées*, XVII (1905), 46–74; also Jules Soury, 'Un Critique au XVIIIe siècle — Fréron,' *RDM*, I March 1877, 80–112; also Green, *Eighteenth-Century France*, 111–54: 'Voltaire's Greatest Enemy.' Cf. Francis W. Gravit, 'Notes on the Contents of Fréron's Periodicals,' *RR*, XXXIV (1943), 116–26.
41. Daniel Mornet, 'Les Enseignements des bibliothèques privées,' *RHLF*, XVII (1910), 479.
42. A.-T., II, 51; but see also Vartanian, *Diderot and Descartes*, 176–7.
43. *Année Littéraire*, vol. I for 1754, 1–14, esp. 1–2, 2, 3–4, 14.
44. A.-T., II, 38.
45. A.-T., II, 13.
46. A.-T., II, 51–2.

CHAPTER 16

1. *Encyc.*, I, xliv.
2. *Encyc.*, II, 105b. Professor Dieckmann attributes this remark to a workman (Herbert Dieckmann, 'L'*Encyclopédie* et le Fonds Vandeul,' *RHLF*, LI [1951], 325).
3. A.-T., XIII, 140–41; *Encyc.*, I, xliij; Naigeon, 49.
4. Naigeon, 50–51.
5. *Encyc.*, II, 289a.
6. *Encyc.*, II, 596b.
7. *Encyc.*, II, 35b.
8. A.-T., XIV, 39.
9. A.-T., XIV, 5.
10. *Journal des Sçavans*, March 1753, 169–75; Venturi, *Origini*, 58–9.
11. *Journal des Sçavans, combiné avec les Mémoires de Trévoux* (Amsterdam), vol. I for 1754, 305–22, esp. 307, 312–13, 321–2. The *Journal des Sçavans* was surprisingly forbearing, for meanwhile D'Alembert had grumbled for a whole folio half-page in the foreword to Vol. III about the *Journal*'s original attack upon him (*Encyc.*, III, xj–xij).
12. *La Biographie universelle (Michaud)*, s.v. 'Jaucourt,' and *La Nouvelle Biographie générale (Hoefer)*, s.v. 'Jaucourt.' Also Ducros, *Les Encyclopédistes*, 76–7.
13. Lefebvre, *Diderot*, 41.
14. See René Hubert, *Les Sciences sociales dans l'Encyclopédie* (Paris, 1923), *passim;* René Hubert, 'L'Esprit des sciences sociales dans l'*Encyclopédie*,' *RHPHGC*, IV, 107–33; René Hubert, 'Essai sur l'histoire des origines et des progrès de la sociologie en France,' ibid. VI (1938), 111–55, 281–310; René Hubert, 'Introduction bibliographique à l'étude des sources de la science ethnographique dans l'*Encyclopédie*,' ibid. I (1933), 160–72, 331–55; also, see Raymond Lenoir, 'Les Sciences sociales dans l'Encyclopédie, à propos d'un ouvrage récent,' *Revue de Synthèse Historique*, XXXIX (1925), 113–25.
15. Hubert, 'L'Esprit des sciences sociales dans l'*Encyclopédie*,' *RHPHGC*, IV, 114; Cassirer, *Die Philosophie der Aufklärung*, 251. See Barker, *Diderot's Treatment of the Christian Religion in* The Encyclopédie, 42–57, 125–9, esp. 43; also Hermann Sänger, *Juden und Altes Testament bei Diderot* (Wertheim am Main, 1933), 90–93; and Paul Vernière, 'La Critique biblique dans l'*Encyclopédie* et ses sources spinozistes,' *Revue de Synthèse*, LXIX (1951), 75–6; also Vernière, *Spinoza et la pensée française avant la Révolution*, 582–3.
16. *Encyc.*, II, 840a; my italics. 'Le mot *Cerf* est un des articles qu'on a relevés avec le plus d'aigreur' (*Mémoire des libraires associés à l'Encyclopédie, sur les motifs de la suspension actuelle de cet ouvrage* [Paris, 1758], 4).
17. For thorough discussions, see Hester Hastings, *Man and Beast in French Thought of the Eighteenth Century* (Baltimore, 1936), *passim;* and Leonora Cohen Rosenfield, *From Beast-Machine to Man-Machine: Animal Soul in French Letters from Descartes to La Mettrie* (New York, 1941), *passim* and esp. 46–50.
18. A.-T., XIII, 429. For an excellent discussion of this whole issue, see Vartanian, *Diderot and Descartes*, 207–15.

19. Gilbert and Kuhn, *A History of Esthetics*, 280–87; Władysław Folkierski, *Entre le classicisme et le romantisme: Etude sur l'esthétique et les esthéticiens du XVIIIe siècle* (Cracow and Paris, 1925), 375–91; K. Heinrich von Stein, *Die Entstehung der neueren Ästhetik* (Stuttgart, 1886), 245–50. Cf. André Fontaine, *Les Doctrines d'art en France de Poussin à Diderot* (Paris, 1909), 296–7, who finds Diderot's doctrine extremely deficient, as does also Mario Roques, 'L'Art et l'*Encyclopédie*,' AUP, XXII ([Oct.] 1952), numéro spécial, 99–100. For a comprehensive study of the importance of Diderot's article, see Lester G. Crocker, *Two Diderot Studies: Ethics and Esthetics* (Baltimore, 1952), 53–67, 96–7, *et passim*.

20. A.-T., x, 35; foreshadowed in A.-T., IX, 104; cf. ibid. 84. See Crocker, *Two Diderot Studies*, 61, 66, 113.

21. A.-T., XIII, 423.

22. A.-T., x, 30–31.

23. Gilbert and Kuhn, *A History of Esthetics*, 282.

24. A.-T., x, 25, 26, 27.

25. A.-T., x, 25, 41.

26. Jean Thomas, *L'Humanisme de Diderot*, 2nd ed. (Paris, 1938), 61–2.

27. A.-T., x, 36; my italics.

28. A.-T., XI, 10.

29. E.g. *Encyc.*, III, xiv. Professor Dieckmann inclines to the view that Diderot was co-author of this *Avertissement* (Dieckmann, *Inventaire*, 57).

30. *Corr. litt.*, II, 299. Diderot, however, felt constrained to insert this disclaimer in his list of errata (*Encyc.*, III, xvj): 'En un mot, nous n'avons prétendu dans notre article AUTORITÉ que commenter & développer ce passage, tiré d'un ouvrage imprimé par ordre de Louis XIV. & qui a pour titre, *Traité des droits de la Reine sur différens états de la monarchie d'Espagne . . .*'

31. *Encyc.*, III, iv, xiv.

32. *Encyc.*, III, 833a. François Véron de Forbonnais (1722–1800) collected his *Encyclopédie* articles in his *Elémens du commerce* (Paris, 1754; 2nd ed. [Amsterdam, 1755]; 3d ed. [Leyden, 1766]; 4th ed., 2 vols. [Paris, 1796]).

33. Clément, *Cinq Années Littéraires*, IV, 282 (31 Dec. 1753). Cf. his earlier and severer criticism of Vol. I (ibid. III, 113–15 [15 June 1751]).

34. *Encyc.*, III, 225b. Although asterisked, this article may not have been by Diderot.

35. *Encyc.*, III, 671b.

36. A.-T., XIV, 454–5.

37. Emile Faguet, 'Diderot et Naigeon,' *Revue Latine*, I (1902), 721; A.-T., XIV, 197–204, s.v. 'Composition (en peinture).'

38. 'The Chaldeans' (A.-T., XIV, 170–71); 'Chaos' (A.-T., XIV, 88–93; see Vartanian, *Diderot and Descartes*, 121–2).

39. A.-T., XIV, 79.

40. A.-T., XIV, 84.

41. *Encyc.*, III, 635–7. See also 'Etudes,' written by Faiguet (*Encyc.*, VI, 87–94).

42. *Encyc.*, III, vij, xvj.

43. *Encyc.*, III, 636a.

44. *Observation de M * * *, principal du College de * * *, sur un des articles du Dictionnaire Encyclopédique* (n.p., n.d.), 42–3 (Mazarine call number 34481-A, pièce 6).

45. *Avis au Public sur le Troisième Volume de l'Encyclopédie* (n.p., n.d.), 18–19, 21 (Mazarine call number 34481-A, pièce 7). For its Jesuit authorship, see Venturi, *Origini*, 143.

46. Relevant documents in B.N., MSS, Nouv. acq. fr. 3348, foll. 253–63. The harangue of Father Tolomas occurred on 30 Nov. 1754. See Voltaire to Dupont, Lyon, 6 Dec. 1754 (Voltaire, ed. Moland, XXXVIII, 296). For an account of the whole affair, see Joseph Bertrand, *D'Alembert* (Paris, 1889), 86–92.

47. Daniel Delafarge, *La vie et l'oeuvre de Palissot (1730–1814)* (Paris, 1912), 43–68; also Edouard Meaume, *Palissot et les philosophes* (Nancy, 1864), 13 ff.; and J.-A. Vier, 'L'Activité d'une académie provinciale au XVIIIe siècle: L'Académie de Stanislas de 1750

à 1766,' *RHLF*, xxxiii (1926), 350–52, who also points out that D'Alembert was striking at Fréron as well as at Palissot.

48. D'Hémery's journal, 17 Oct. 1754, mentioned that Vol. iv was published (B.N., MSS, Fr. 22159, fol. 71ᵛ). Rousseau wrote Vernes that it was published on 14 Oct. (Rousseau, *Corr. gén.*, ii, 103).

49. *Corr. litt.*, ii, 198–9.

50. Drafts of the proposed article (B.N., MSS, Nouv. acq. fr. 3345, foll. 157–64, 165–74). Malesherbes' letter to Diderot, 11 July 1754, was exhibited in 1932 at the Bibliothèque Nationale (*L'Encyclopédie et les Encyclopédistes* [Paris: Bibliothèque Nationale, 1932], 54); Malesherbes' draft of it (B.N., MSS, Nouv. acq. fr. 3345, fol. 150); published in Diderot, *Corr.*, i, 167–8; the same day Malesherbes stated his reasons to the Chancellor (ibid. ii, 331–3). Cf. D'Argenson, ix, 22, and Gazier, *Histoire générale du mouvement janséniste*, ii, 52 n.

51. *Encyc.*, iv, 238a–b, s.v. 'Corderie.'

52. *Encyc.*, iv, 171a; A.-T., xiv, 221.

53. A.-T., xiv, 236–7, s.v. 'Coupon'; *Encyc.*, iv, 283–8, s.v. 'Corvée.'

54. A.-T., xiv, 274; emphasis mine.

55. A.-T., xiv, 281; s.v. 'Dieux.'

56. Leo Spitzer, 'The Style of Diderot,' *Linguistics and Literary History* (Princeton, 1948), 137–46, 175.

57. A.-T., xiv, 277–78; *Corr. litt.*, vi, 115; Pommier, 'Etudes sur Diderot,' *RHPHGC*, x, 174. For the existentialist implications of this article, see Ian W. Alexander, 'Philosophy of Organism and Philosophy of Consciousness in Diderot's Speculative Thought,' *Studies in Romance Philology and French Literature Presented to John Orr* (Manchester, 1953), 18.

58. *Corr. litt.*, ii, 408.

59. Cf. *Encyc.*, iii, ix; A.-T., xiv, 267, 274. The full title of Johann Jacob Brucker's work was *Historia critica philosophiae a mundi incunabulis ad nostram usque aetatem deducta*, 5 vols. (Leipzig, 1742–4). Diderot also referred frequently to Thomas Stanley (1625–78), *The History of Philosophy*, a fourth edition of which was published at London in 1743. Occasionally Diderot referred (e.g. *Encyc.*, iii, ix) to André-François Boureau Deslandes, *Histoire critique de la philosophie*, 3 vols. (Amsterdam, 1737).

60. Jacques-André Naigeon, in the three-volume section of the *Encyclopédie méthodique* devoted to 'Philosophie ancienne et moderne' (Paris, 1791–4), i, vi–viii.

61. Hubert, *Les Sciences sociales dans l'Encyclopédie*, 327; cf. Cassirer, *Die Philosophie der Aufklärung*, 301–2.

62. Pommier, 'Etudes sur Diderot,' *RHPHGC*, x, 172. Cf. A.-T., xiv, 253, 255, 257.

63. *Mercure de France*, vol. i for Oct. 1757, 23; reprinted in Nicholas-Charles-Joseph Trublet, *Mémoires pour servir à l'histoire de la vie et des ouvrages de Mʳ. de Fontenelle*, 2nd ed. (Amsterdam, 1759), 172.

CHAPTER 17

1. Marcel, *Le Frère de Diderot*, 66 n.; *RQH*, 113 n. Rousseau mentioned to Vernes on 15 Oct. 1754 that 'Diderot est à Langres' (Rousseau, *Corr. gén.*, ii, 103).

2. Diderot, *Corr.*, i, 172–87 (6 Jan. 1755); ibid. 188–91.

3. A.-T., v, 279–308.

4. May, *Quatre visages de Diderot*, 162–8.

5. Diderot, *Corr.*, i, 178, 180. For Dubois, see Marcel, *Le Frère de Diderot*, 7 n.; for Diderot's annoyance with his publishers, see also Rousseau, *Corr. gén.*, ii, 150.

6. Diderot, *Corr.*, i, 185–6; also May, 27–8. The publishers' account book (May, *passim*) shows that these salary arrangements with Diderot were carried out for Vols. v, vi, vii, and viii; consult it also for the titles and cost of the various reference books thus provided.

7. The building on the site of Diderot's house is 149, Boulevard Saint-Germain (Beaurepaire, 'Les Logis de Diderot,' *Revue des Français*, xvii, 316 n.). Numbers 155–75, Boulevard Saint-Germain, are almost all of them survivors of the former Rue Taranne (*Guide bleu: Paris*, ed. 1937, 62). See also Auguste Vitu, *Paris* (Paris, [1889]), 271–2.

8. Diderot, *Corr.*, i, 178; my italics.

9. Marmontel, *Mémoires*, II, 306–7.
10. *Corr. litt.*, II, 144–5.
11. A commemorative plaque is affixed at No. 374; and see Hillairet, *Evocation du vieux Paris*, II, 63. But Roger Picard, *Les Salons littéraires et la société française, 1610–1789* (New York, 1943), 204, claims that No. 372 is correct.
12. Marmontel, *Mémoires*, II, 311–12.
13. René Doumic, 'La "Royauté" de Madame Geoffrin,' *RDM*, 15 June 1897, 918–19. For a recent essay on the *salon* of Mme Geoffrin, see G. P. Gooch, 'Four French Salons: I. Mme Geoffrin,' *Contemporary Review*, June 1951, 345–53.
14. B.N., MSS, Nouv. acq. fr. 10782, fol. 45.
15. Arthur L. Sells, *Les Sources françaises de Goldsmith* (Paris, 1924), 13, 14, 16; Cru, 81–4.
16. D'Escherny, *Mélanges*, III, 128.
17. Pierre de Ségur, *Le Royaume de la rue Saint-Honoré: Madame Geoffrin et sa fille* (Paris, 1897), 315.
18. Foisset, *Le Président de Brosses*, 540, 546: this letter probably written on 24 April 1754. Diderot tells an obscene story about De Brosses (A.-T., XI, 246), possibly heard from Buffon since Buffon and De Brosses had been schoolmates, and therefore it may be true. For De Brosses's proclivities in this regard, see Marcel Bouchard, *De l'Humanisme à l'Encyclopédie: L'Esprit public en Bourgogne sous l'Ancien Régime* (Paris, 1930), 654.
19. Foisset, 546; A.-T., XIX, 429–30, and XX, 106.
20. De Brosses to M. de Farges, 1761 (Foisset, 550–51).
21. Foisset, 545.
22. Rousseau, ed. Hachette, VIII, 277; Rousseau to Saint-Germain, 26 Feb. 1770 (Rousseau, *Corr. gén.*, XIX, 252 n.; cf. ibid. 245, 246). For the passage written by Diderot, as identified by Rousseau, see A.-T., IV, 101–4.
23. Gilbert Chinard, ed., *Supplément au Voyage de Bougainville*, by Diderot (Baltimore, 1935), 51–3, modifies the conclusions expressed earlier by Jean Morel, 'Recherches sur les sources du *Discours de l'Inégalité*,' *AJJR*, V (1909), 119–98, esp. 122–5. Cf. remarks by Norman L. Torrey, reviewing the Chinard edition, *MLN*, LI (1936), 470.
24. C. E. Vaughan, ed., *The Political Writings of Jean Jacques Rousseau*, 2 vols. (Cambridge [Eng.], 1915), I, 19 n., 120–21.
25. A.-T., X, 46.
26. A.-T., X, 47–83; Bibliothèque Nationale call numbers: V.24896 and V.36741. Although undated, the pamphlet mentions events in 1755 and was reviewed by Fréron, *Année Littéraire*, vol. III for 1755, 145–66, on 19 May. His hostility suggests that Fréron suspected Diderot was the author. Cf. also *Année Littéraire*, vol. VI for 1755, 87.
27. *Encyc.*, V, 607–15; by a M. Monnoye (*Encyc.*, VI, vi), otherwise unknown.
28. *Encyc.*, V, 614b; *Corr. litt.*, II, 427–8, 478.
29. A.-T., X, 47.
30. A.-T., X, 68. Regarding Bachelier, see McCloy, *French Inventions of the Eighteenth Century*, 77–8.
31. See *Corr. litt.*, VI, 364–7, for an interesting and not unsympathetic account of him; also Lady Dilke, *French Architects and Sculptors of the XVIIIth Century* (London, 1900), 66; and Eugène Muntz, 'Un Précurseur et un ennemi de Diderot: Le Comte de Caylus, d'après des documents nouveaux,' *Revue Bleue*, 29 May 1897, 674–8.
32. Caylus, Anne-Claude-Philippe, comte de, *Correspondance inédite du comte de Caylus avec le P. Paciaudi, théatin (1757–1765)*, 2 vols. (Paris, 1877), I, 237–8.
33. *Corr. litt.*, VI, 366 n.; A.-T., X, 45 n.; A.-T., XVIII, 251.
34. A.-T., X, 47, 69, 81–2.
35. A.-T., X, 69.
36. A.-T., X, 71.
37. *Corr. litt.*, III, 15; *Année Littéraire*, vol. III for 1755, 147.
38. A.-T., X, 57 n.
39. A.-T., X, 69 nn.
40. A.-T., X, 80.
41. *L'Art nouveau de la peinture en fromage, ou en ramequin, inventée pour suivre le louable*

projet de trouver graduellement des façons de peindre inférieures à celles qui existent (Marolles, 1755): B.N. call number 8ºVp 7724.

42. *Année Littéraire,* vol. III for 1755, 167-71; *Corr. litt.,* III, 25, 94-5.

43. Archives nationales, Y77, foll. 167-8; dated at Paris, 20 June 1772.

44. Michel Corday, *La Vie amoureuse de Diderot* (Paris, 1928), 49.

45. *SV,* 2 vols. (1938), I, 7-8 nn.; more informative than the 1930 edition. The *Annuaire de la Noblesse, 1884,* 138, referred to Sophie Volland's father as a Palatine count; see also Diderot, *Corr.,* II, 133-4.

46. Billy, *Diderot,* 272.

47. *SV* (1938), I, 7 n.

48. *SV,* II, 97 (25 July 1762); *SV,* II, 127 (15 Aug. 1762).

49. *SV,* II, 75-76 (14 July 1762); *SV,* I, 293 (3 Nov. 1760).

50. *SV* (1938), I, 12-13, according to a holograph note of Diderot's son-in-law.

51. Mme de Vandeul, xlvii. Rousseau, *Corr. gén.,* III, 114, and Diderot, *Corr.,* I, 255.

52. *SV,* III, 70 (8 Sept. 1767); *SV,* III, 105 (28 Sept. 1767).

53. *SV,* III, 126-7 (24 Aug. 1768).

54. *SV,* II, 240 (31 May 1765).

55. Diderot, *Corr.,* II, 277 (14? Oct. 1759); *SV,* I, 162 (2 Sept. 1760). The collection of letters to Sophie Volland in the Fonds Vandeul is headed by the notation, written at the time the letters were collected, 'Lettres . . . écrites par Mr Diderot à Made^{lle} Voland depuis le 1er juillet 1755 . . . .' (Diderot, *Corr.,* II, 8).

56. Billy, *Diderot,* 265-70; André Billy, 'Diderot de pied en cap,' *Conferencia,* vol. I for 1939, 657; Corday, *La Vie amoureuse de Diderot,* 121-46. Cf. Pierre Mesnard, 'Sophie Volland et la maturité de Diderot,' *Revue des Sciences Humaines,* Jan.-March 1949, 12-13; Pierre Mesnard, *Le Cas Diderot,* 164-5; E. Caro, *La Fin du dix-huitième siècle: Etudes et portraits,* 2nd ed., 2 vols. (Paris, 1881), I, 307; Alyse Gregory, 'Denis Diderot,' *Horizon,* IX (1944), 37-38; Guyot, 38-39; and Crocker, *The Embattled Philosopher,* 149-50.

57. A.-T., II, 260.

CHAPTER 18

1. Diderot, *Corr.,* I, 197-8 (22 Sept. 1755). He was still on his milk diet in late December (ibid. 200); and on 24 Jan. 1756 (ibid. 204).

2. Rousseau to Vernes, 23 Nov. 1755 (Rousseau, *Corr. gén.,* II, 239).

3. D'Hémery's journal, 6 Nov. 1755 (B.N., MSS, Fr. 22159, fol. 145); *Corr. litt.,* III, 129; Rousseau, *Corr. gén.,* II, 239).

4. *Corr. litt.,* II, 491; Rousseau, *Corr. gén.,* II, 160.

5. A.-T., XIV, 349. Montesquieu, replying to D'Alembert on 16 Nov. 1753, had declined to write the articles 'Démocratie' and 'Despotisme,' but had volunteered to do 'Goût' (Charles de Sécondat, Baron de Montesquieu, *Correspondance,* ed. François Gebelin and André Morize, 2 vols. [Paris, 1914], II, 492).

6. George H. Sabine, *A History of Political Theory,* revised ed. (New York, 1950), 582. For Diderot's borrowing from Pufendorf, see René Hubert, *Rousseau et l'Encyclopédie* (Paris, 1928), 32-5. See also Robert Derathé, *Jean-Jacques Rousseau et la science politique de son temps* (Paris, 1950), 58, 81.

7. A.-T., XIV, 299, 300.

8. Montesquieu, *L'Esprit des Lois,* book XI, ch. vi.

9. Cf. *Encyc.,* V, 338b, 339b, 340a, 340b, 341b, 346b, s.v. 'Economie.' But regarding incipient divergencies of point of view, see Antoine Adam, 'Rousseau et Diderot,' *Revue des Sciences Humaines,* Jan.-March 1949, 30-32. Cf. Vaughan, *The Political Writings of Jean Jacques Rousseau,* I, 322-3, 426, 445 n., 447, 450-54; and Georges Beaulavon, 'La Question du *Contrat social:* une fausse solution,' *RHLF,* XX (1913), 594-5.

10. *Encyc.,* V, 116a, 116b; also in A.-T., XIV, 299, 301. As Hubert, *Rousseau et l'Encyclopédie,* 46-9, points out, however, Diderot appears to mean by *volonté générale* a general consensus, while Rousseau means a specific contract.

11. Vaughan, *The Political Writings of Jean Jacques Rousseau,* I, 424-6; Sabine, *A History of Political Theory,* 585.

12. *Encyc.*, VII, 789a; my italics.
13. Owen Ruffhead, writing in the *Monthly Review*, XXXIX (1768), 545 (Lough, 'The "Encyclopédie" in Eighteenth-Century England,' *French Studies*, VI, 296).
14. *Encyc.*, V, 745–50, esp. 747b, 748b, 749a, 750b. Other writings by Faiguet are analyzed by André Lichtenberger, *Le Socialisme au XVIIIᵉ siècle* (Paris, 1895), 334–8.
15. *Encyc.*, V, 536b.
16. *Encyc.*, V, 445a, s.v. 'Elasticité'; ibid. 223a, s.v. 'Nouvelles ecclésiastiques.'
17. My italics. Cf. Franco Venturi, 'Deleyre e la società degli Enciclopedisti,' *Aretusa*, Jan.–Feb. 1946, 81–93; also John Lough, 'Le Rayonnement de l'*Encyclopédie* en Grande-Bretagne,' *AIEF*, No. 2 (May 1952), 71. The principle of division of labor had already been isolated and described by Diderot in 'Art' in Volume I (A.-T., XIII, 372), a passage of great interest to Marxist writers, who see in the *Encyclopédie* a powerful instrument in bringing about French industrialization: e.g. Marcel Prenant, 'L'Encyclopédie et les origines de la science moderne,' *Pensée*, Nov.–Dec. 1951, 32; also René Metz, 'Les Racines sociales et politiques d'une idéologie nationale: L'Encyclopédie,' *Pensée*, Jan.–Feb. 1952, 68–81.
18. A.-T., XIV, 400.
19. A.-T., XIV, 508.
20. A.-T., XIV, 386–7.
21. Sänger, *Juden und Altes Testament bei Diderot*, 67 n. For Shaftesbury's unacknowledged influence in Diderot's article on the 'Egyptians,' see Pierre Hermand, 'Sur le texte de Diderot et sur les sources de quelques passages de ses "Oeuvres",' *RHLF*, XXII (1915), 367; and the same, *Les Idées morales de Diderot*, 265 n.
22. Hubert, *Les Sciences sociales dans l'Encyclopédie*, 42, 48, 51, 79.
23. Sänger, 86; for date of 1754, ibid. 32 n.
24. A.-T., XV, 378.
25. A.-T., XIV, 304, 306, 334–7, 346, 345.
26. Similar vagaries of pagination occur in *Encyc.*, VII, 233 ff., 451 ff., 458–63, 575 ff.
27. Hunt, 'Diderot as "grammairien-philosophe",' *MLR*, XXXIII, 233; A.-T., XIV, 416–50.
28. A.-T., XIV, 454–6. Diderot also alluded to the problem of colleagues' contributions in his article 'Editeur' (A.-T., XIV, 379).
29. A.-T., XIV, 468.
30. A.-T., XIV, 479.
31. A.-T., XIV, 477.
32. A.-T., XIV, 462, 456, 473, 471, 490–91 resp.
33. A.-T., XIV, 489.
34. A.-T., VI, 407; cf. A.-T., XIX, 442, and *Encyc.*, VI, vj. A manuscript 'Cours de Chymie de M. Rouelle rédigé par M. Diderot et éclairci par plusieurs notes,' consisting of nine volumes with a total of 1,258 folios, is MS 564 in the Bibliothèque publique de la Ville de Bordeaux; the headings of this 'Cours de Chymie' are listed by Charles Henry, *Introduction à la chymie. Manuscrit inédit de Diderot, publié avec notice sur les cours de Rouelle* (Paris, 1887), 81–101. The introduction to this Bordeaux manuscript appears to be by Diderot, and was first published by Charles Henry, 'Introduction à la chymie. Manuscrit inédit de Diderot,' *Revue scientifique*, 3ᵐᵉ série, XXXIV (1884), 97–108; later reprinted by M. Henry in 1887 (op. cit. *supra*, 17–78). M. Henry believes that this introduction was written after 1758 (ibid. 14). From the point of view of Diderot studies, the principal problem is to determine whether this introduction should be regarded as an original Diderot work. In response to M. Henry's article, Edouard Grimaux, 'Le Cours de chymie de Rouelle,' *Revue Scientifique*, 3ᵐᵉ série, XXXIV (1884), 184–5, declared that he, too, possessed a manuscript notebook of Rouelle's lectures. Collation showed, he said (p. 185), that 'à mon avis, les pages que vous avez publiées renferment toutes les idées, et rien que les idées de Rouelle, avec le style de Diderot en plus.' The Bibliothèque Nationale also possesses a copy of these manuscript notes (Maurice Tourneux, 'Les Manuscrits de Diderot conservés en Russie,' *Archives des Missions Scientifiques et Littéraires*, 3ᵐᵉ série, XII [1885], 463 and n.). In 1885 M. Henry published another portion of the Bordeaux manuscript which he thought was written by Diderot, but the evidence, both external and internal, is far from conclusive (Charles Henry, 'L'Utilité de la Chymie, par Denis Diderot,' *Revue Scientifique*, 3ᵐᵉ série, XXXV [1885], 802–4).

35. A.-T., VI, 405–10. Cf. Charles Bedel, 'L'Avènement de la chimie moderne,' *L' 'Encyclopédie' et le progrès des sciences et des techniques* (Paris, 1952), 123–4.

36. *Encyc.*, v, 647aʳ; this passage not faithfully transcribed in A.-T., XIV, 491.

37. Louis-Jacques Goussier (1722–99). See *Encyc.*, I, xliv; also May, 42, 48, 58, 61, *et passim*.

38. A.-T., XIV, 479.

39. Arthur H. Cole and George B. Watts, *The Handicrafts of France as Recorded in the Descriptions des Arts et Métiers, 1761–1788* (Boston, 1952), 5–6.

40. Such, too, is the opinion of Pommier, *Diderot avant Vincennes*, 92 n.

41. Georges Roth, 'Samuel Formey et son projet d' "Encyclopédie reduite",' *RHLF*, LIV (1954), 371–4.

42. Jean-Henri-Samuel Formey, *Souvenirs d'un citoyen*, 2 vols. (Berlin, 1789), II, 169. Part of this letter is reproduced by Jean Torlais, *Réaumur, un esprit encyclopédique en dehors de l'Encyclopédie'* (Paris, 1936), facing 252, but with the erroneous information (pp. 254–5) that Albrecht von Haller, the Swiss physiologist, was the recipient: see Georges Huard, 'Les Planches de l'Encyclopédie et celles de la *Description des Arts et Métiers* de l'Académie des Sciences,' *L' 'Encyclopédie' et le progrès des sciences et des techniques*, 37.

43. *Encyc., Planches*, I, 6.

44. See Bertrand Gille, 'L'Encyclopédie, dictionnaire technique,' *L' 'Encyclopédie' et le progrès des sciences et des techniques*, 188–9, 199. Intent to defraud is vigorously argued by Huard, 'Les Planches de l'Encyclopédie et celles de la *Description des Arts et Métiers* de l'Académie des Sciences,' ibid. 42–3. Cf. George B. Watts, 'The *Encyclopédie* and the *Descriptions des arts et métiers*,' *French Review*, XXV (1951–2), 447.

45. A.-T., XIV, 462–3.

46. 2 March 1756 (B.N., MSS, Nouv. acq. fr. 3345, fol. 175). For the offending passage, see *Encyc.*, v, 635ᵛ, or A.-T., XIV, 418.

47. The Jesuits (A.-T., XIV, 415, 502); 'one good article' (ibid. 494); the Académie Française (ibid. 415, 418–21, 481; cf. Pommier, 'Etudes sur Diderot,' *RHPHGC*, x, 163 n.); Rousseau (A.-T., XIV, 485); Bacon (ibid. 494); apology plus self-gratulation (ibid. 471); the ideal editor (ibid. 502).

48. A.-T., XIV, 461, 483.

49. A.-T., XIV, 453. This passage quoted in evidence of the humanism of the *Encyclopédie* by Bury, *The Idea of Progress*, 159; and by A. Wolf, *A History of Science, Technology, and Philosophy in the Eighteenth Century* (New York, 1939), 39. It is also emphasized by René de Messières, 'L'Encyclopédie et la crise de la société au milieu du XVIIIᵉ siècle,' *French Review*, XXIV (1950–51), 395. Cf. Jean Thomas, *L'Humanisme de Diderot*, 2nd. ed. (Paris, 1938), *passim*. Diderot's humanism, esp. as revealed in his article 'Encyclopédie,' is emphasized by Paul Vernière, 'L'Encyclopédie de Diderot et d'Alembert,' *Revue de Synthèse*, XXVI (1950), 142. See also Diderot's remark regarding *humanité* (A.-T., XIV, 493).

50. A.-T., XIV, 473.

51. A.-T., XIV, 474.

CHAPTER 19

1. His sole reference to the Lisbon earthquake seems to be the slight one in *Jacques le fataliste* (A.-T., VI, 51).

2. A.-T., VII, 53–6, 232.

3. Mme de Vandeul, lix; Diderot, *Corr.*, I, 220, 221. Cf. Marcel, *Le Frère de Diderot*, 53–63.

4. A.-T., XIX, 432–8; also printed in *Corr. litt.*, III, 249–55 (1 July 1756), and Diderot, *Corr.*, I, 209–17. Although Grimm specifically refers to Landois as the recipient of this letter (ibid. 255), it is argued by Frederika Macdonald, *Jean Jacques Rousseau*, 2 vols. (New York, 1906), II, 7–13, 249–51, that Grimm hoped his readers would conclude that it was really Rousseau to whom the letter was addressed. Mrs. Macdonald's is a rather speculative conclusion, especially as it does not take cognizance of a passage (A.-T., XIX, 442) of a letter written to Rousseau by Diderot in Jan. 1757. Nevertheless, her conclusion is also subscribed to by Hélène Pittard (pseud. Noëlle Roger), 'Jean-Jacques Rousseau et les drames de l'Ermitage,' *RDM*, 1 June 1925, 660–61; by Cazes, *Grimm et les Encyclopédistes*, 288–9; and by Georges Roth, ed., *Les Pseudo-Mémoires de Madame d'Epinay: Histoire de*

Madame de Montbrillant, by Louise de La Live d'Epinay, 3 vols. (Paris, [1951]), III, 576. The letter to Landois was printed by Babelon as having been addressed to Naigeon (*CI,* I, 308–12). But Naigeon was then only eighteen; moreover, he did not claim to have known Diderot before this year, and Diderot refers in this letter to having known his correspondent for four years at least (A.-T., XIX, 433, 437; Rudolf Brummer, *Studien zur französischen Aufklärungsliteratur im Anschluss an J.-A. Naigeon* [Breslau, 1932], 3–4). See also Dieckmann, *Inventaire,* pp. 148–9.

5. Otis E. Fellows and Alice G. Green, 'Diderot and the Abbé Dulaurens,' *Diderot Studies,* I, 78; Avédik Mesrobian, *Les Conceptions pédagogiques de Diderot* (Paris, [1913]), 45.

6. Edmond N. Cahn, *The Sense of Injustice* (New York, 1949), 10.

7. Hermand, *Les Idées morales de Diderot,* 85–7, 200; cf. Crocker, *Two Diderot Studies: Ethics and Esthetics,* 18–19; also Alice Green Fredman, *Diderot and Sterne* (New York, 1955), 29, 220.

8. *Corr. litt.,* III, 111–12 and 111 n.; cf. A.-T., I, 345–6, 352–3. It is significant that Naigeon (in the three-volume section of the *Encyclopédie méthodique* devoted to 'Philosophie ancienne et moderne,' II, 5–7) stressed Condillac's dependence upon Diderot regarding this very point. Condillac, on the other hand, declared that 'il y avoit déjà long-temps que mademoiselle Ferrand m'avoit communiqué cette idée. Plusieurs personnes savoient même que c'étoit là l'objet d'un Traité auquel je travaillois, et l'auteur de la Lettre sur les Sourds et Muets ne l'ignoroit pas' ('Réponse à un reproche qui m'a été fait sur le projet exécuté dans le Traité des Sensations,' *Oeuvres philosophiques,* I, 318).

9. *Corr. litt.,* III, 222; cf. Courtois, 'Chronologie,' 86. Rousseau, *Corr. gén.,* II, 338.

10. A.-T., VII, 19; Rousseau, *Corr. gén.,* II, 336. Cf. *Corr. litt.,* IV, 56–7. Le Breton's country house was at Massy, near Sceaux (Billy, *Diderot,* 209).

11. Rousseau, *Corr. gén.,* II, 349, 350.

12. Ronald Grimsley, 'Turgot's Article "Existence" in the *Encyclopédie,*' *The French Mind: Studies in Honour of Gustave Rudler* (Oxford, 1952), 126–51; also Georg Misch, 'Zur Entstehung des französischen Positivismus,' *Archiv für Geschichte der Philosophie,* XIV (1901), 24–6, 30, 36; Denis, 'Deux collaborateurs économiques de l'Encyclopédie: Quesnay et Rousseau,' *Pensée,* Sept.–Oct., 1951, 45.

13. Voltaire, ed. Moland, XXXIX, 117.

14. Ibid. XXXVIII, 125.

15. 9 Dec. 1755 (ibid. 519); 13 Nov. 1756 (ibid. XXXIX, 131).

16. Naves, *Voltaire et l'Encyclopédie,* 19–20.

17. 9 Oct. 1756 (Voltaire, ed. Moland, XXXIX, 117); cf. Voltaire to D'Alembert, 24 May 1757 (ibid. 211).

18. 13 Nov. 1756 (ibid. 130); *Encyc.,* VI, 474b. See also Voltaire to D'Alembert, 29 Nov. 1756 (Voltaire, ed. Moland, XXXIX, 135–6).

19. 13 Dec. 1756 (ibid. 139).

20. 22 Dec. 1756 (ibid. 144).

21. Date of Rousseau's first acquaintance with Mme d'Epinay (Eugène Ritter, 'J. J. Rousseau et Madame d'Houdetot,' *AJJR,* II [1906], 18).

22. Act IV, scene iii. For an excellent analysis of the difference of point of view of Diderot and Rousseau, see Ernst Cassirer, *Rousseau, Kant, Goethe* (Princeton, 1945), 7–9.

23. Rousseau, *Corr. gén.,* II, 279, 282, 338, 342, 349.

24. Courtois, 'Chronologie,' 89–90.

25. Mme d'Epinay to Rousseau [Dec. 1756] (Rousseau, *Corr. gén.,* II, 359).

26. Louise de La Live d'Epinay, *Mémoires,* ed. Paul Boiteau, 2 vols. (Paris, 1865), II, 101–11, esp. 106; also Mme d'Epinay, *Pseudo-Mémoires,* II, 601–8, esp. 604. Regarding this passage, see D. C. Cabeen, gen. ed., *A Critical Bibliography of French Literature,* IV: *The Eighteenth Century,* ed. George R. Havens and Donald F. Bond (Syracuse, 1951), 255, item 2237.

27. [26 March 1757] (Rousseau, *Corr. gén.,* III, 49). Cf. Rousseau to Saint-Germain, 26 Feb. 1770 (ibid. XIX, 244).

28. Rousseau, *Corr. gén.,* III, 20–49.

29. Ibid. 21, 36.

30. A.-T., xix, 438–9. Regarding Diderot's attitude, see the comments by F. C. Green, *Jean-Jacques Rousseau: A Critical Study of his Life and Writings* (Cambridge, 1955), 150–51.
31. Rousseau, *Corr. gén.*, iii, 21.
32. A.-T., xix, 440–41. I accept the date of 14 March 1757 for this letter, according to Rousseau, *Corr. gén.*, iii, 23–5.
33. Rousseau, *Corr. gén.*, iii, 32, 50.
34. A.-T., xix, 442; also Rousseau, *Corr. gén.*, iii, 40–41, which dates it either 22 or 23 March 1757.
35. [26 March 1757] (Rousseau, *Corr. gén.*, iii, 49–52).
36. Cf. Deleyre's difficulties in getting away from Paris in order to visit Rousseau (Rousseau, *Corr. gén.*, ii, 336, 338; ibid. iii, 38).

CHAPTER 20

1. Besides the three editions listed by Tchemerzine, *Bibliographie d'éditions originales et rares d'auteurs français*, iv, 447, there was also one in 1757 published in Amsterdam by Marc Michel Rey; a copy of this edition is in the Boston Public Library.
2. Diderot, *Corr.*, ii, 20.
3. Ibid. 21.
4. 10 Dec. 1757 (ibid. 23).
5. So asserted by Collé, *Journal et mémoires*, ii, 74; by the *Année Littéraire*, vol. ii for 1758, 29; and by Charles Palissot de Montenoy, *Oeuvres complettes*, 7 vols. (London, 1779), ii, 125 n.; cf. Thieriot to Voltaire, 10 April 1757 (*RHLF*, xv [1908], 150). On 23 April 1757, Diderot, writing to Marmontel, refused the pass to the Comédie-Française performances that the famous actress, Mlle Clairon, had offered him (Herbert Dieckmann, 'Three Diderot Letters, and *Les Eleuthéromanes*,' *Harvard Library Bulletin*, vi [1952], 71). Authors whose plays were produced were given permanent passes; therefore, it is possible that Mlle Clairon's offer just at this time was something in the nature of a consolation prize having some connection with a refusal by the Comédie-Française to produce the *Fils naturel*.
6. Corneille had set forth ideas in his *épître dédicatoire* to *Don Sanche* (1650) tantamount to the theory of a *tragédie bourgeoise* (Lester Gilbert Crocker, 'Aspects of Diderot's Esthetic Theory,' by L. G. Krakeur, *RR*, xxx [1939], 251; Cru, 301 n.). There is no evidence, however, that Corneille's notions, which seemed paradoxical even to himself, had any effect upon the French theater or influenced Diderot.
7. Edith Melcher, 'Trends in Recent Criticism of the Eighteenth-Century French Theatre,' *RR*, xxix (1938), 160–66. See Gustave Lanson, *Nivelle de la Chaussée et la comédie larmoyante*, 2nd ed. (Paris, 1903), i, 277. Diderot specifically mentions *Sylvie* as a concrete example of his ideas (A.-T., vii, 119), but it is noticeable that he hardly ever mentions Nivelle de la Chaussée (Lanson, 276, 277). Regarding *Sylvie*, see esp. Henry Carrington Lancaster, *French Tragedy in the Time of Louis XV and Voltaire, 1715–1774*, 2 vols. (Baltimore, 1950), i, 262–5; and also his critical edition of *Sylvie* (*Johns Hopkins Studies in Romance Literatures and Languages*, xlviii [1954]).
8. De Tocqueville, *Democracy in America*, ii, book i, ch. xix: 'Some Observations on the Drama amongst Democratic Nations.' For a discussion of the significance of Diderot's plays from the point of view of historical materialism, see P.-B. Marquet, 'Diderot et le théâtre au XVIIIe siècle,' *Europe*, Sept. 1951, 115–28.
9. Mme d'Epinay, *Pseudo-Mémoires*, iii, 61; Mme d'Epinay, *Mémoires* (1865), ii, 187. Publication occurred about mid-Feb. 1757 (Courtois, 'Chronologie,' 90).
10. *Corr. litt.*, iii, 354, 357 (1 March 1757).
11. *Année Littéraire*, vol. iv for 1757, 146.
12. Palissot, *Oeuvres complettes*, ii, 123–4.
13. Collé, *Journal et mémoires*, ii, 75.
14. B.N., MSS, Nouv. acq. fr. 3531, fol. 62; quoted by Le Gras, 101–2, but with faulty volume reference. Cf. *Année Littéraire*, vol. iii for 1756, 193. D'Alembert's letter of complaint to Malesherbes, 25 June [1756] (B.N., MSS, Fr. 22191, fol. 134; also in Le Gras, 101).
15. Paris, 28 June 1756 (B.N., MSS, Nouv. acq. fr. 3531, foll. 63–4).

16. [Jean-Jacques Garnier], *Le Bâtard légitimé, ou le triomphe du comique larmoyant, avec un examen du Fils naturel* (Amsterdam [Paris], 1757) [B.N., Imprimés, Yᶠ 9433].

17. B.N., MSS, Nouv. acq. fr. 3346, fol. 12.

18. Fréron to Malesherbes, 21 March 1757 (Etienne Charavay, 'Diderot & Fréron,' *Revue des Documents Historiques,* III [1875–6], 157).

19. Fréron to Malesherbes, 27 Jan. 1758 (Charavay, 166).

20. 21 March 1757 (Charavay, 160–61).

21. A.-T., IV, 283–9.

22. Palissot, *Oeuvres complettes,* II, 124; A.-T., VII, 17.

23. Cf. A.-T., VII, 19–21, 92, 93, 97.

24. A.-T., VII, 111; cf. *supra,* p. 13.

25. Garat, *Mémoires . . . de M. Suard,* II, 18–19. See also Hans Sckommodau, ' "Il n'y à que le méchant qui soit seul." (Zu den Anschauungen der französischen Aufklärung über Menschenhass und Weltflucht),' *Romanistisches Jahrbuch,* I (1947–8), 213–4.

26. A.-T., VII, 19.

27. E. B. O. Borgerhoff, *The Evolution of Liberal Theory and Practice in the French Theater, 1680–1757* (Princeton, 1936), 113 *et passim.*

28. A.-T., VII, 87.

29. A.-T., VII, 94–8, 114. Cf. Edith Melcher, *Stage Realism in France between Diderot and Antoine* (Bryn Mawr, 1928), pp. 31–2.

30. A.-T., VII, 105–6.

31. A.-T., VII, 162–5; cf. Romain Rolland, *Some Musicians of Former Days,* 255, 277; also Julien Tiersot, 'Gluck and the Encyclopædists,' *Musical Quarterly,* XVI (1930), 349. Diderot once wrote a sketch of the libretto of a comic opera (J. Robert Loy, 'Diderot's Unedited *Plan d'un opéra comique,' RR,* XLVI [1955], 3–24). This may have been written in the 1750's, but I am inclined to date it in the late 1760's.

32. A.-T., VII, 104; see also ibid. 100. According to A. Lombard, *L'Abbé du Bos, un initiateur de la pensée moderne (1670–1742)* (Paris, 1913), 335–6, this and a good many other of Diderot's ideas can be found in Du Bos's *Réflexions critiques sur la poésie et sur la peinture* (1719).

33. A.-T., VII, 120, 161.

34. A.-T., VII, 95, 120, 411–525. Cf. Cru, 304–16.

35. A.-T., VII, 135.

36. Just before this new development, 'drame' had been defined very broadly and loosely by Mallet in the *Encyclopédie (Encyc.,* V, 105b).

37. A.-T., VII, 71–2.

38. A.-T., VII, 150.

39. A.-T., VII, 150–51.

40. A.-T., VII, 68; also ibid. 128.

41. A.-T., VII, 108–9.

42. A.-T., VII, 149.

43. Cru, 288.

44. Félix Alexandre Gaiffe, *Le Drame en France au XVIIIᵉ siècle* (Paris, 1910), I.

45. 1 Oct. 1757 (Rousseau, *Corr. gén.,* III, 128). Cf. A.-T., VII, 17–18.

46. *Année Littéraire,* vol. II for 1758, 29–30.

47. Not infrequently these editions included the *Entretiens sur le Fils naturel,* thus increasing the dissemination of Diderot's ideas. According to A.-T., VII, 10, a Spanish edition, evidently of the *Entretiens,* was published in 1788. Interest in the concept of the *Fils naturel* is attested by the existence of a novel falsely attributed to Diderot: *The Natural Son . . . Translated from the French of M. Diderot,* 2 vols. (London: T. N. Longman, 1799).

48. A.-T., VII, 166–7; cf. Collé, *Journal et mémoires,* II, 74.

49. Cf. A.-T., VII, 110, 129, 151, *et passim.*

50. Palissot, *Oeuvres complettes,* II, 161.

51. Ibid. 131; *Année Littéraire,* vol. IV for 1757, 159.

52. Palissot, *Oeuvres complettes,* II, 139, 140; *Année Littéraire,* vol. IV for 1757, 170. Even the friendly Lessing made some very unfavorable judgments of the *Fils naturel:* see no. 85 (23 Feb. 1768) of Lessing's *Hamburgische Dramaturgie.*

53. *Supplément d'un important ouvrage. Scène dernière du Fils naturel, avec une lettre à Dorval* (Venise [Paris], 1758), 59.
54. These documents in Manlio D. Busnelli, *Diderot et l'Italie* (Paris, 1925), 273-4.
55. *Année Littéraire*, vol. IV for 1757, 145-73, 289-316.
56. Yet Palissot had been allowed to remark in his *Petites lettres sur de grands philosophes* 'que le *Fils Naturel* lui-même n'est qu'une copie défigurée du *Vero Amico*, de M. Goldoni' (Palissot, *Oeuvres complettes*, II, 162). The anonymous *Supplément d'un important ouvrage* (n. 53, *supra*) mischievously claimed to be printed at Venice, 'chez François Goldino, à l'Enseigne del Fido Amico.'
57. Through Act II, scene vi, of Goldoni; and Act III, scene iii, of Diderot. Cf. Pietro Toldo, 'Se il Diderot abbia imitato il Goldoni,' *Giornale Storico della Letteratura Italiana*, XXVI (1895), 350-76; and Susanna Gugenheim, 'Drammi e teorie drammatiche del Diderot e loro fortuna in Italia,' *Etudes Italiennes*, III (1921), 167-9.
58. *Journal Encyclopédique*, vol. VIII for 1758, 3me partie, 122-4 (15 Dec. 1758).
59. André Morize, *Problems and Methods of Literary History* (Boston, 1922), 83.
60. Collé, *Journal et mémoires*, II, 108-9.
61. A.-T., VII, 337, 339; cf. ibid. 317. Diderot was likewise defended by the Abbé de la Porte in *L'Observateur Littéraire* for 5 Nov. 1758 (Busnelli, *Diderot et l'Italie*, 108-10). A later version of the Abbé's remarks was published in the *Oeuvres de théâtre de M. Diderot, avec un Discours sur la poésie dramatique*, 2 vols. (Paris, 1771), I, 319-36; reprinted in A.-T., VII, 11-18.
62. *Mercure de France*, Feb. 1759, 91.
63. Goldoni, *Mémoires*, II, 177-8.
64. A.-T., XIX, 441.

CHAPTER 21

1. 'Eloge de M. d'Alembert,' *Histoire de l'Académie Royale des Sciences, Année MDCCLXXXIII* (Paris, 1786), 103. D'Alembert's allusions to Frederick the Great (*Encyc.*, I, 55b, **s.v.** 'Académie,' and *Encyc.*, IV, 969b, s.v. 'Dictionnaire'; cf. Venturi, *Origini*, 78).
2. Cheverny, *Mémoires*, I, 179-86. Cheverny was then official Introducer of Ambassadors.
3. B.N., MSS, Fr. 22177, fol. 197.
4. B.N., MSS, Fr. 22177, foll. 200-201. Cf. Belin, *Le Commerce des livres prohibés*, 114; Belin, *Le Mouvement philosophique de 1748 à 1789*, 110; and an undated letter from D'Alembert to Voltaire, probably in late March 1757 (Voltaire, ed. Moland, XXXIX, 199).
5. Voltaire, ed. Moland, XXXIX, 235; cf. D'Alembert to Voltaire, 11 Jan. 1758 (ibid. 363).
6. For Moreau's authorship of *L'Observateur Hollandais*, see D'Hémery's journal (B.N., MSS, Fr. 22159, fol. 87).
7. *Mercure de France*, vol. I for Oct. 1757, 15-19.
8. D'Hémery mentioned the publication of Vol. VII in his entry of 24 Nov. 1757 (B.N., MSS, Fr. 22160, fol. 63ᵛ); cf. *Corr. litt.*, III, 457. But some authorities declare that Vol. VII was published 10 Oct. 1757 (Courtois, 'Chronologie,' 95; Cazes, *Grimm et les Encyclopédistes*, 71 n.; and Clara Adèle Luce Herpin [pseud. Lucien Perey] and Gaston Maugras, *La Vie intime de Voltaire aux Délices et à Ferney, 1754-1778* [Paris, 1885], 168).
9. *Encyc.*, VII, 41b. The articles 'Foire' and 'Fondation' were published anonymously (ibid. XIV); A.-T., XV, 12-21, erroneously attributes the latter to Diderot. For attribution to Turgot, see Turgot, *Oeuvres*, ed. Schelle, I, 59, 577-93.
10. *Encyc.*, VII, 735b, s.v. 'Gomaristes'; Morellet, *Mémoires*, I, 42-3.
11. *Encyc.*, VII, 72b-75b. Regarding Turgot and Gournay, see W. Walker Stephens, *The Life and Writings of Turgot* (London, 1895), 20.
12. *Encyc.*, VII, 282a-b.
13. *Encyc.*, VII, 790b.
14. *Encyc.*, VII, 802b.
15. *Encyc.*, VII, 188b.
16. *Encyc.*, VII, 128b.
17. *Encyc.*, VII, 979a-81a. The best analysis of Boulanger's thought is by Franco Venturi,

L'Antichità svelata e l'idea del progresso in N. A. Boulanger (1722–1759) (Bari, 1947).

18. *Encyc.*, VII, 907a, 907b, s.v. 'Grecs (philosophie des)'; A.-T., xv, 53. An important article, 'Génie,' is attributed to Diderot by ibid. 35–41. Grimm, however, attributed it to Saint-Lambert (*Corr. litt.*, III, 458), and Saint-Lambert himself, writing to his publisher in 1798, claimed it as his (Pierre Marot, 'A propos du deuxième centenaire de l'*Encyclopédie*. Saint-Lambert au Musée lorrain,' *Pays lorrain*, XXXII [1951], 196); cf. Venturi, *Jeunesse*, 344–5. It is likely, however, that Diderot edited or re-worked the article (Barker, *Diderot's Treatment of the Christian Religion in* The Encyclopédie, 116 n.; and Dieckmann, 'Diderot's Conception of Genius,' *JHI*, II, 163 n.: 'I am still convinced that great parts of the article "Génie" must have been either inspired or revised by Diderot himself').
19. A.-T., xv, 23.
20. Naves, *Voltaire et l'Encyclopédie*, 38–49; René Pintard, 'Voltaire et l'*Encyclopédie*,' *AUP*, XXII ([*Oct.*] 1952), numéro spécial, 39–57, esp. 51; John Stephenson Spink, *Jean-Jacques Rousseau et Genève* (Paris, 1934), 153; Rousseau, *Corr. gén.*, IV, 91.
21. *Encyc.*, VII, 576b, s.v. 'Genève.'
22. *Encyc.*, VII, 576b, 577b, s.v. 'Genève'; Naves, *Voltaire et l'Encyclopédie*, 44.
23. *Encyc.*, VII, 577b, 575a–b, 578b, s.v. 'Genève.'
24. *Encyc.*, VII, 578a, s.v. 'Genève.'
25. *Corr. litt.*, III, 458.
26. Naves, *Voltaire et l'Encyclopédie*, 35.
27. Voltaire to Théodore Tronchin, 15 Jan. 1758 (Voltaire, *Correspondance avec les Tronchin*, ed. André Delattre [Paris, 1950], 309); cf. D'Alembert to Voltaire, 11 Jan. 1758 (Voltaire, ed. Moland, XXXIX, 362).
28. *Année Littéraire*, vol. II for 1758, 59–69. D'Alembert republished this protest, with comments, in his *Mélanges de littérature, d'histoire, et de philosophie*, v (1767), 571–600.
29. *Corr. litt.*, III, 205–7; Naves, *Voltaire et l'Encyclopédie*, 37.
30. *Encyc.*, VIII, 769–71. See Pierre Astruc, 'Les Sciences médicales et leurs représentants dans l'*Encyclopédie*,' *L' 'Encyclopédie' et le progrès des sciences et des techniques*, 177.
31. Tronchin to D'Alembert (Gustave Desnoiresterres, *Voltaire et la société au XVIIIᵉ siècle*, 2nd ed., 8 vols. [Paris, 1871–6], v, 175–6); D'Alembert to Tronchin, 6 Jan. 1758 (Voltaire, *Correspondance avec les Tronchin*, ed. Delattre, 299–300).
32. 30 Dec. 1757 (Diderot, *Corr.*, II, 26–8).
33. Tronchin to Pictet, 24 Jan. 1758 (Herpin [pseud. Perey] and Maugras, *La Vie intime de Voltaire aux Délices et à Ferney*, 179).
34. *Corr. litt.*, IV, 53.
35. See Voltaire to Briasson, 13 Feb. 1756 (Voltaire, ed. Moland, XXXVIII, 551); and to D'Alembert: [19?] Feb., 23 July, 29 Aug., 29 Dec. 1757; and 3 Jan. 1758 (ibid. XXXIX, 181, 236, 255, 341, and 343 resp.).
36. Ibid. 363–4, 375–6; Naves, *Voltaire et l'Encyclopédie*, 53–62. See Voltaire's indignant letters to D'Alembert: 5, 13, 19, and 25 Feb. 1758; and to D'Argental, 9 and 26 Feb. 1758 (ibid. 387–8, 396–7, 400, 406–7, 392, and 408–9 resp.).
37. *Supra*, p. 220.
38. 11 Jan. 1758 (Voltaire, ed. Moland, XXXIX, 362).
39. In Jan. 1758 (Le Gras, 112); cf. D'Alembert to Voltaire, 11 Jan. 1758, and Voltaire to D'Alembert, 13 Feb. 1758 (ibid. 362, 396).
40. B.N., MSS, Fr. 22191, fol. 24.
41. Ibid. fol. 23.
42. Ibid. foll. 25–6. Precisely the same claim was made publicly by the publishers (*Mémoire des libraires associés à l'Encyclopédie, sur les motifs de la suspension actuelle de cet ouvrage* [Paris, 1758], 4–5).
43. B.N., MSS, Fr. 22191, fol. 20ʳ–20ᵛ. Fol. 20ʳ is reproduced in *AUP*, XXII ([Oct.] 1952), numéro spécial, facing 62.
44. Palissot, *Oeuvres complettes*, II, 106, 107, 110, 111, 112, 114, 117–18, and 120, resp.
45. *Année Littéraire*, vol. VIII for 1757, 238–52.
46. [Jacob-Nicolas Moreau], *Nouveau Mémoire pour servir à l'histoire des Cacouacs* (Amsterdam [Paris], 1757), 4, 5, 16–17, 20–21, 23, 26, 38, 58–9, 71, 73, 82, 97–9, 102.

47. D'Alembert to Voltaire, 28 Jan. 1758 (Voltaire, ed. Moland, XXXIX, 383–4); also the same to the same, 11 Jan., 20 Jan., and 8 Feb. 1758 (ibid. 362–3, 374–5, and 390–91, resp.).
48. *Année Littéraire,* vol. I for 1758, 3–22, esp. 8.
49. D'Alembert to Malesherbes, 23 Jan. 1758 (B.N., MSS, Fr. 22191, fol. 140; published by Sainte-Beuve, 'M. de Malesherbes,' *Causeries du lundi,* II, 530–31).
50. Fréron to Malesherbes, 27 Jan. 1758 (B.N., MSS, Fr. 22191, fol. 141; published by Charavay, 'Diderot & Fréron,' *Revue des Documents Historiques,* III, 165–7, and [in part] by Sainte-Beuve, 'M. de Malesherbes,' *Causeries du lundi,* II, 531).
51. B.N., MSS, Fr. 22191, fol. 138. For the letter in entirety (Morellet, *Mémoires,* I, 46–50; also Coyecque, *Inventaire de la collection Anisson,* I, xcvii–xcix).
52. B.N., MSS, Fr. 22191, foll. 136–7. Published, under date of 16 Feb. 1758 in Morellet, *Mémoires,* I, 50–54, and in Coyecque, op. cit. I, xcv–xcvii.
53. Morellet, *Mémoires,* I, 46, 53. Cf. D'Alembert to Voltaire, Paris, 23 Jan. 1757 (Voltaire, ed. Moland, XXXIX, 163).
54. Draft of the letter to Morellet (B.N., MSS, Fr. 22191, foll. 148–51; the quotation is from fol. 148^v).
55. Yves Laissus, 'Une Lettre inédite de d'Alembert,' *Revue d'Histoire des Sciences,* VII (1954), 1–5; Voltaire, *Correspondance avec les Tronchin,* ed. Delattre, 300.
56. Voltaire, ed. Moland, XXXIX, 362. Cf. D'Alembert's letter to the Genevese, J. Vernes, 15 Jan. 1758 (Eugène Ritter, *Revue Critique d'Histoire et de Littérature,* nouvelle série, XLVI [1898], 291–2). The *Journal Encyclopédique,* vol. I for 1758, 3e Partie (1 Feb. 1758), 116, referred to D'Alembert's retiring from the *Encyclopédie,* and added: 'Ainsi cette grande entreprise . . . va donc de nouveau être interrompue!'
57. 8 Jan. 1758 (Voltaire, ed. Moland, XXXIX, 356).
58. 19 Jan. 1758 (ibid. 369, 370).
59. 20 Jan. 1758 (ibid. 374–5).
60. Voltaire to D'Alembert, 29 Jan. 1758 (ibid. 385).
61. Ibid. 352; cf. Naves, *Voltaire et l'Encyclopédie,* 55. At first Grimm also thought the author a Jesuit (*Corr. litt.,* III, 458).
62. 5 Feb. 1758 (Voltaire, ed. Moland, XXXIX, 387).
63. Ibid. 396.
64. Voltaire to Tressan, 13 Feb. 1758 (ibid. 397–8).
65. Rousseau to Mme d'Houdetot, 13 Feb. 1758 (Rousseau, *Corr. gén.,* III, 279).
66. Diderot, *Corr.,* II, 37–40. A rather clumsy reply to Palissot, Moreau, and Fréron, coupled with a defense of Diderot, was contained in a pamphlet entitled *L'Aléthophile, ou l'Ami de la Vérité* (Amsterdam, 1758), esp. 13, 30–31; cf. *Corr. litt.,* III, 486. Fréron replied to it effectively (*Année Littéraire,* vol. II for 1758, 24–38).
67. Voltaire to D'Argental, 26 Feb. 1758 (Voltaire, ed. Moland, XXXIX, 410).
68. Voltaire to D'Argental, 12 March 1758 (ibid. 422).
69. Venturi, *Origini,* 144.
70. D'Alembert, *Mélanges de littérature, d'histoire, et de philosophie,* I (1763), 320.

CHAPTER 22

1. *SV,* I, 202 (30 Sept. 1760); the author was really Charles Bordes (Hippolyte Buffenoir, *La Comtesse d'Houdetot, une amie de Jean-Jacques Rousseau* [Paris, 1901], 331–8).
2. Ritter, 'J. J. Rousseau et Madame d'Houdetot,' *AJJR,* II, 18.
3. According to Guillemin, 70, 154–7, the 'day of the five notes' was probably 31 Aug. 1757; his reasoning appears to me to be conclusive. But other authorities argue for earlier dates: cf. Mme d'Epinay, *Pseudo-Mémoires,* III, 178 n.; and Ritter, loc. cit. *AJJR,* II, 42.
4. Rousseau, ed. Hachette, VIII, 349. According to Diderot, however, Rousseau confided in him at an earlier date: he told Marmontel that Rousseau came to Paris to ask his advice (Marmontel, *Mémoires,* III, 2–3). The only visit that Rousseau is known to have made to Paris during the time of his love affair with Mme d'Houdetot was in July 1757. In his catalogue of the 'sept scélératesses,' Diderot says that, having given Rousseau this advice,

'Je le revis dans la suite' (*Corr. litt.,* xvi, 220). Since they did not meet after 5 Dec. 1757, the original confession must then have occurred on an earlier occasion. Both these assertions by Diderot date from 1758 or thereabouts (Guillemin, 73).

5. Rousseau, ed. Hachette, viii, 318; Rousseau, *Corr. gén.,* iii, 120.

6. 11 Oct. 1757 (Rousseau, *Corr. gén.,* iii, 145; also ibid. 144).

7. 28 Oct. 1757 (ibid. 153; my italics).

8. *Corr. litt.,* xvi, 219, 220.

9. Ritter, 'J. J. Rousseau et Madame d'Houdetot,' *AJJR,* ii, 99. Cf. Schinz, *Etat présent des travaux sur J.-J. Rousseau,* 337.

10. Deleyre to Rousseau, 31 March 1757, announcing the forthcoming visit (Rousseau, *Corr. gén.,* iii, 52-3); Rousseau to Mme d'Epinay, 10 April 1757 (ibid. 67): 'Au reste, vous savez que le Philosophe m'est venu voir.'

11. Rousseau, ed. Hachette, viii, 330-31; Courtois, 'Chronologie,' 92-3. On Rousseau's motives for visiting Paris, see Guillemin, 69, 187.

12. Mme de Vandeul, lxi.

13. Ibid. lx-lxi.

14. Marmontel, *Mémoires,* iii, 8.

15. Morellet, *Mémoires,* i, 106.

16. *Corr. litt.,* xvi, 220.

17. Rousseau, *Corr. gén.,* iii, 118-21, under date of 5 Sept. 1757. The date should be 4 Sept., according to Guillemin, 221.

18. *Corr. litt.,* xvi, 220.

19. Mme Diderot at Langres: Rousseau, *Corr. gén.,* iii, 114; Diderot, *Corr.,* i, 255. Diderot's illness: Rousseau, *Corr. gén.,* iii, 146. For evidence independent of Rousseau's *Confessions* regarding Grimm's frosty treatment of Rousseau, see Henri Piguet, *Mélanges de littérature* (Lausanne, 1816), 255-8.

20. A.-T., xix, 443.

21. Rousseau to Diderot, *ca.* 19 Oct. 1757 (Rousseau, *Corr. gén.,* iii, 135).

22. Rousseau, *Corr. gén.,* vi, 325.

23. Ibid. iii, 136-43; *Corr. litt.,* xvi, 219.

24. Ritter, 'J. J. Rousseau et Madame d'Houdetot,' *AJJR,* ii, 60-61. The child by Francueil was born on 29 May 1753 (Guillemin, 67 n.).

25. P.-P. Plan inserts this letter in his edition of Rousseau, *Corr. gén.,* iii, 170-71, though he calls it 'fausse.' A convincing case, however, for its genuineness is made by Norman L. Torrey, 'Rousseau's Quarrel with Grimm and Diderot,' *Essays in Honor of Albert Feuillerat* (*Yale Romanic Studies,* xxii [New Haven, 1943]), 165-72; see also Guillemin, 215-16. Among articles discussing the Grimm-D'Epinay aspect of the quarrel with Rousseau should be mentioned Rodolphe-Louis Hébert, 'Grimm and Rousseau,' *French Review,* xxv (1951-2), 262-9; Gustave Charlier, 'Mme d'Epinay et J.-J. Rousseau,' in his *De Ronsard à Victor Hugo* (Brussels, 1931), 193-220; and Eugène Ritter, 'Nouvelles recherches sur les *Confessions* et la correspondance de Jean-Jacques Rousseau,' *Zeitschrift für neufranzösische Sprache und Literatur,* ii (1880), 326.

26. Undated (Hippolyte Buffenoir, *La Comtesse d'Houdetot, sa famille, ses amis* [Paris, 1905], 46-7; and in Rousseau, *Corr. gén.,* iii, 243-4). Guillemin, p. 205, dates Diderot's first letter about 10 Nov. 1757.

27. 28 Jan. 1758 (Rousseau, *Corr. gén.,* iii, 270).

28. A.-T., xix, 444-5. Cf. Rousseau's letters to Mme d'Epinay and to Mme d'Houdetot (Rousseau, *Corr. gén.,* iii, 157, 159-60, 161).

29. Rousseau, ed. Hachette, viii, 349-50, 355.

30. 17 Dec. 1757 (Rousseau, *Corr. gén.,* iii, 230), in reply to a letter of 14 Dec. (ibid. 225). See also Rousseau to Mme d'Houdetot, 28 Jan. 1758 (ibid. 268): 'A la bonne heure, pour moi, je ne changerai point pour lui, et j'attendrai paisiblement qu'il revienne.'

31. 13 Feb. 1758 (ibid. 279).

32. Ibid. 295.

33. Ibid. 289, 295, 299. Cf. Ritter, 'J. J. Rousseau et Madame d'Houdetot,' *AJJR,* ii, 83 n.

34. Rousseau, *Corr. gén.*, III, 296–8.
35. Ibid. 299, 308. See also Torrey, 'Rousseau's Quarrel with Grimm and Diderot,' *Essays in Honor of Albert Feuillerat*, 177.
36. This is the hypothesis of Torrey, 'Rousseau's Quarrel with Grimm and Diderot,' 180; also of Lucien Brunel, '*La Nouvelle Héloïse* et Mme d'Houdetot,' *Annales de l'Est*, II (1888), 508. For other theories as to which was the 'lettre atroce,' see Ritter, 'J. J. Rousseau et Madame d'Houdetot,' *AJJR*, II, 100–101, 103.
37. *Corr. litt.*, XVI, 220.
38. Rousseau, *Corr. gén.*, III, 320.
39. *Corr. litt.*, XVI, 220.
40. 9 Jan. 1759 (Diderot, *Corr.*, II, 108).
41. Voltaire to D'Argental, 15 June 1758 (Voltaire, ed. Moland, XXXIX, 454).
42. *Corr. litt.*, XVI, 220. Cf. Guillemin, 70–71; Torrey, 'Rousseau's Quarrel with Grimm and Diderot,' *Essays in Honor of Albert Feuillerat*, 173. For dating the Catalogue, see Anatole Feugère, 'Pourquoi Rousseau a remanié la Préface de la *Lettre à D'Alembert*,' *AJJR*, XX (1931), 147–48.
43. Torrey, loc. cit. 181. See also Professor Torrey's remarks in the *Romanic Review*, XXIX (1938), 189 n. And Professor F. C. Green remarks (*Jean-Jacques Rousseau*, 169): 'I see no reason to doubt Diderot's story of what happened.'
44. Nevertheless, there are chronological difficulties about accepting Diderot's story (*Corr. litt.*, XVI, 220) that he made a trip to the Hermitage to upbraid Rousseau for not making the confession that he said he had and to find out whether he was 'fou ou méchant.' Diderot used the very same words, 'fou ou méchant,' in telling this story to Marmontel (Marmontel, *Mémoires*, III, 5), in a conversation that probably took place in 1758 (Guillemin, 73). Inasmuch as the Saint-Lambert crisis did not occur until March or April of 1758, when Diderot and Rousseau were no longer seeing each other, it seems unlikely that this alleged interview really occurred. Was it simply braggadocio that made Diderot boast to Marmontel — and set down in his private notes — that he had told Rousseau off? Or was he uneasy about having committed a real indiscretion, and wanted to imply, by claiming that he taxed Rousseau with it, that Rousseau was just as much to blame, or more, than he? Cf. Mme d'Epinay, *Pseudo-Mémoires*, III, 255 n., 258 n., 280 n.
45. Rousseau, ed. Hachette, VIII, 356–7.
46. The preface is dated 20 March 1758, but Rousseau added in June the paragraph alluding to Diderot (Feugère, 'Pourquoi Rousseau a remanié la Préface de la *Lettre à D'Alembert*,' *AJJR*, XX, 128). The quotation is Ecclesiasticus xxii: 26–7 (Vulgate, tr. Father Ronald Knox).
47. Liége, 28 Oct. 1758 (Rousseau, *Corr. gén.*, IV, 65).
48. Marmontel, *Mémoires*, II, 316–17; III, 1–2. Cf. the 'Sept Scéleratesses': 'Sa note est d'autant plus vile qu'il savait que je n'y pouvais répondre sans compromettre cinq ou six personnes' (*Corr. litt.*, XVI, 221–2).
49. 10 Oct. 1758 (Rousseau, *Corr. gén.*, IV, 74–5).
50. *Corr. litt.*, XVI, 221.
51. A.-T., VI, 315.
52. 9 Jan. 1759 (Ville de Genève: Bibliothèque Publique et Universitaire: Collection Rilliet); for the attribution to Vernes as the recipient, see Guillemin, 112; published in Diderot, *Corr.*, II, 106–9.
53. According to D'Hémery's entry of that date (B.N., MSS, Fr. 22160, fol. 108). Malesherbes had appointed D'Alembert to be the censor (Rousseau, *Corr. gén.*, IV, 23, 35, 49), a clever move which tied D'Alembert's hands. Rousseau predicted to Rey, his Amsterdam publisher, that Durand, the Paris bookseller, would refuse to serve as the Paris agent for Rousseau's book, 'attendu qu'il est le libraire de M. Diderot . . .' (13 Sept. 1758: Rousseau, *Corr. gén.*, IV, 53). Durand did, however, handle the commission (*Année Littéraire*, vol. VI for 1758, 327).
54. A.-T., XIV, 485.
55. Sébastien-Roch-Nicolas Chamfort, *Maximes et pensées, caractères et anecdotes* (Porrentruy, [1946]), 194.

CHAPTER 23

1. Rousseau, *Corr. gén.*, III, 274.
2. Gustave Charlier and Roland Mortier, *Le Journal Encyclopédique (1756–1793)* (Paris, 1952), 85.
3. *Mémoire des libraires associés à l'Encyclopédie, sur les motifs de la suspension actuelle de cet ouvrage* (Paris, 1758), 5. *Mercure de France*, vol. II for April 1758, 97–104. Diderot to Voltaire, 14 June 1758 (A.-T., XIX, 454).
4. Voltaire, ed. Moland, XXXIX, 411.
5. According to André Billy, ed., *Oeuvres*, by Diderot (Paris: 'Nouvelle Revue française,' 1951 [Bibliothèque de la Pléiade, No. 25]), 17, Marmontel and Duclos quit the *Encyclopédie* in March 1758.
6. Diderot, *Corr.*, II, 272–5 (14? Oct. 1759; my italics).
7. B.N., MSS, Fr. 22191, fol. 9; quoted and paraphrased by Sainte-Beuve, 'M. de Malesherbes,' *Causeries du lundi*, II, 527–9. Thieriot wrote to Voltaire on 27 Dec. 1757 that the Jesuits were back of the agitation over the Cacouacs, their motive being to prevent Diderot from being elected to the Academy of Sciences (Fernand Caussy, 'Lettres inédites de Thieriot à Voltaire,' *RHLF*, XV [1908], 154).
8. Versailles, 8 April 1758 (B.N., MSS, Fr. 22191, fol. 10).
9. Diderot, *Corr.*, II, 61. Cf. Voltaire to Diderot, 26 June 1758 (Voltaire, ed. Moland, XXXIX, 462). The allusion is to La Fontaine's *conte*, 'Le Diable de Papefiguière.'
10. *Mémoire à consulter pour les libraires associés à l'Encyclopédie* (Paris: Le Breton, 1770), 4.
11. Cazes, *Grimm et les encyclopédistes*, 73; Smiley, *Diderot's Relations with Grimm*, 83, 84.
12. Claude-Adrien Helvétius, *De l'Esprit*, 2 vols. (Amsterdam and Leipzig, 1759), I, xx, 50–51 nn., 88, 89, 151, 198, 253, and esp. 262.
13. Helvétius, *De l'Esprit*, I, 22 n., 23 n., 171, 154 n., 26–8 and nn., 6–9 nn., 238, 3, 29 n., resp.
14. See the remarkable criticism of the book by Turgot, *Oeuvres*, ed. Schelle, III, 636–41.
15. A.-T., II, 272, 273.
16. *Arrest du Conseil d'Etat du Roi, rendu au sujet du privilége ci-devant accordé pour l'impression de l'Ouvrage intitulé, de l'Esprit* (Paris: Imprimerie royale, 1758); a copy is mounted in B.N., MSS, Fr. 22177, fol. 247. For the *mandement* of the Archbishop of Paris, see Hervier, *Les Ecrivains français jugés par leurs contemporains*, II, 259–60. For the condemnation issued by Pope Clement XIII: *Damnatio et prohibitio Operis, cui Titulus: De l'Esprit . . .* (Rome, 1759); a copy is mounted in B.N., MSS, Fr. 22094, pièce 6. For a very good account of Helvétius' difficulties and woes, see Belin, *Le Mouvement philosophique de 1748 à 1789*, 114–27.
17. Barbier, *Journal*, IV, 307–8.
18. E.g. *Lettre au révérend pere * * *, Jésuite* (n.p., n.d.), 6–7; mounted in B.N., MSS, Fr. 22191, foll. 73–6.
19. Turgot, *Oeuvres*, ed. Schelle, III, 639.
20. *Corr. litt.*, IV, 80. A.-T., I, xvii n.; Virgil W. Topazio, 'Diderot's Supposed Contribution to Helvétius' Works,' *Philological Quarterly*, XXXIII (1954), 319–22.
21. *Arrests de la Cour de Parlement, portant condamnation de plusieurs Livres & autres Ouvrages imprimés. Extrait des registres de Parlement. Du 23 Janvier 1759* (Paris: P. G. Simon, 1759), 2; mounted in B.N., MSS, Fr. 22177, foll. 257–72, and Fr. 22094, pièce 1.
22. See also Palissot's open letter to Fréron (*Année Littéraire*, vol. VIII for 1757, 121–31).
23. Abraham-Joseph de Chaumeix, *Préjugés légitimes contre l'Encyclopédie et essai de réfutation de ce dictionnaire*, 8 vols. (Paris and Brussels, 1758–9); vols. I and II were published in Oct. 1758 (Naves, *Voltaire et l'Encyclopédie*, 64). [Odet-Joseph de Vaux de Giry, Abbé de Saint-Cyr], *Catéchisme et décisions de cas de conscience, à l'usage des Cacouacs, avec un discours du patriarche des Cacouacs, pour la réception d'un nouveau disciple* (Cacopolis, 1758).
24. Augustin de Barruel, *Mémoires pour servir à l'histoire du Jacobinisme*, 4 vols. (London, 1797–8), I, 2, 61, 189–94, *et passim*.
25. *Corr. litt.*, III, 458 (15 Dec. 1757). D'Alembert's manuscript, written in 1760, was pub-

lished by Lucien Brunel, *Les Philosophes et l'Académie française au dix-huitième siècle* (Paris, 1884), 361–6; see esp. 364–5.

26. *Mémoire des libraires associés à l'Encyclopédie*, 4. Cf. Ducros, *Les Encyclopédistes*, 213 n.
27. Cf. H. de Montbas, 'A propos d'un bicentenaire. Les Encyclopédistes n'ont pas voulu la Révolution,' *Revue de Paris*, Nov. 1951, 122–3.
28. A.-T., VII, 167; cf. *Corr. litt.*, III, 357 (1 March 1757).
29. 3, 25 Jan., 28 Feb. 1758 (Rousseau, *Corr. gén.*, III, 252, 274, 294).
30. D'Hémery's entry for 2 Nov. 1758 noted that the *Père de famille* had been published by Lambert, with tacit permission (B.N., MSS, Fr. 22160, fol. 113). Grimm discussed the play in his number for 15 Nov. 1758 (*Corr. litt.*, IV, 47–9).
31. First published by Cru, 472–4, as also by him in 'Lettres inédites de Diderot,' *Revue du XVIIIᵉ Siècle*, III–IV (1915–17), 111–12. Cru read '1753' for '1757,' however. The original is in the B.M., Egerton MSS 19, fol. 46; now available in Diderot, *Corr.*, II, 18–19.
32. *SV*, II, 255–6 (25 July 1765).
33. To Grimm, 13 June 1758 (Sophia Christina Charlotte, Princess of Nassau-Saarbruck, *Concerning the Education of a Prince*, ed. John M. S. Allison [New Haven, 1941], 37–42). Also to Diderot, 15 Nov. 1758 (ibid. 42–3), and to her son, 15 Nov. 1758 (ibid. 44–8). See also Asse, 4–6, 9–10, 13–14, 15–17.
34. Voltaire, ed. Moland, XL, 410–11.
35. A.-T., VII, 182, 180, 182, 181, 184, resp. (my italics).
36. B.N., MSS, Nouv. acq. fr. 1182, fol. 7ᵛ; Diderot, *Concerning the Education of a Prince*, ed. Allison, 34–5.
37. Louis-Anne Lavirotte (1725–59) was also one of the editors of the *Journal des Sçavans* (*Biographie universelle* [*Michaud*], s.v. 'Lavirotte').
38. Asse, 18.
39. Brunetière, 'La Direction de la librairie sous M. de Malesherbes,' *RDM*, 1 Feb. 1882, 595.
40. Asse, 20–21.
41. Diderot to Malesherbes, 20 Oct. 1758 (B.N., MSS, Nouv. acq. fr. 1182, fol. 25ʳ); also Asse, 25.
42. B.N., MSS, Nouv. acq. fr. 1182, fol. 25ᵛ; also Asse, 26.
43. A.-T., VII, 221. One censor objected to the line (A.-T., VII, 244): 'Anges du ciel, prenez cette enfant sous vôtre garde, et conduisez-la' (Asse, 23–4).
44. Asse, 24.
45. B.N., MSS, Nouv. acq. fr. 1182, fol. 25ʳ and 25ᵛ; Asse, 25–6.
46. The ellipses are Diderot's (B.N., MSS, Nouv. acq. fr. 1182, fol. 26ᵛ); also Asse, 27; now available in Diderot, *Corr.*, II, 68–71.
47. Lambert to Malesherbes, 24 Oct. 1758 (Asse, 27–8).
48. Moncrif to Malesherbes, 25 Oct. 1758 (Asse, 28); republished by E. P. Shaw, 'An Unpublished Letter of Moncrif concerning Diderot's "Père de Famille",' *MLN*, LXVII (1952), 424–5.
49. Pierre-Nicolas Bonamy (1694–1770) to Malesherbes (Asse, 29).
50. Malesherbes to Mme de La Marck, 21 Nov. 1758 (B.N., MSS, Nouv. acq. fr. 3344, fol. 281); also in Busnelli, *Diderot et l'Italie*, 277–8.
51. Title pages and epigraphs printed in *Corr. litt.*, XVI, 258; also Delafarge, *La Vie et l'oeuvre de Palissot*, 104–6. The insulting nature of the epigraphs explained by Meaume, *Palissot et les philosophes*, 45–6 nn.
52. Diderot to Malesherbes, 16 Nov. 1758 (*Corr. litt.*, XVI, 258–9).
53. 23 Nov. 1758 (B.N., MSS, Fr. 22160, fol. 118ᵛ).
54. Delafarge, *La Vie et l'oeuvre de Palissot*, 107.
55. B.N., MSS, Nouv. acq. fr. 3344, fol. 274; in Busnelli, *Diderot et l'Italie*, 275.
56. 20 Nov. 1758 (B.N., MSS, Nouv. acq. fr. 3344, foll. 282–3); in Busnelli, 275–6.
57. 20 Nov. 1758 (B.N., MSS, Nouv. acq. fr. 3344, foll. 279–80); in Busnelli, 276–7.
58. 21 Nov. 1758 (B.N., MSS, Nouv. acq. fr. 3344, fol. 281); in Busnelli, 277–8.
59. 21 Nov. 1758 (A.-T., XIX, 454 n.). For an undated letter from Diderot to Suard, written about this period regarding presentation copies of the translated plays as well as a copy of the *Père de famille*, see *Corr. litt.*, XVI, 259–60.

60. Also in A.-T., XIX, 454, and Busnelli, 106–7.
61. Busnelli, 104 n. Cf. *Corr. litt.*, IV, 257–8, and Morellet, *Mémoires*, I, 92.
62. *Corr. litt.*, IV, 259.
63. Delafarge, *La Vie et l'oeuvre de Palissot*, 109.
64. Quérard, *Les Supercheries littéraires dévoilées*, III, col. 1129.
65. 25 March 1781 (Dieckmann, *Inventaire*, 245).
66. 24 May 1759 (Rousseau, *Corr. gén.*, IV, 255). Cf. Deleyre to Malesherbes, 23 Nov., and Malesherbes to Deleyre, 28 Nov. 1758 (Busnelli, 278–9).
67. See Morley, *Diderot and the Encyclopaedists*, I, 17.

CHAPTER 24

1. In English there appeared (1) *The Father, A Comedy. Translated from the French of Monsieur Diderot* (Lynn, 1770); (2) *The Family Picture. A Play Taken from the French of Mons. Diderot's Pere de famille* (London, 1781); (3) John Burgoyne, *The Heiress* (London, 1786); and (4) Charles Stearns, *Dramatic Dialogues for the Use of Schools* (Leominster [Mass.], 1798), 281–98: 'The Father of a Family' (follows Diderot's plot very closely but without any allusion to his having been the author). Regarding Burgoyne's play, the *Monthly Review*, LXXIV (Jan.–June 1786), 207–13, reviewed *The Heiress* and gave Diderot all the credit for the plot (209). The *Père de famille* also influenced Charles Jenner's *The Man of Family* (1771) and Sophia Lee's *The Chapter of Accidents* (1780). Cf. David Erskine Baker, *Biographia Dramatica*, 3 vols. in four parts (London, 1812), II, 289; John Genest, *Some Account of the English Stage, from the Restoration in 1660 to 1830*, 10 vols. (Bath, 1832), VI, 381; and Allardyce Nicoll, *A History of Late Eighteenth Century Drama, 1750–1800* (Cambridge [Eng.], 1927), 120.
2. A.-T., VII, 309.
3. A.-T., VII, 150–51.
4. Mme de Vandeul, xxxviii.
5. A.-T., VII, 325.
6. Cf. Louis Ducros, *Diderot: l'homme et l'écrivain* (Paris, 1894), 264.
7. *SV*, III, 202 (2 Sept. 1769).
8. Cf. Arthur Eloesser, *Das bürgerliche Drama: Seine Geschichte im 18. und 19. Jahrhundert* (Berlin, 1898), 73.
9. *Année Littéraire*, vol. III for 1761, 303.
10. Trahard, *Les Maîtres de la sensibilité française au XVIIIᵉ siècle*, II, 205; Gaiffe, *Le Drame en France au XVIIIᵉ siècle*, 260.
11. A.-T., VII, 199, 230. Diderot said he had once overheard this ejaculation in a similar situation in real life (Salverte, *Eloge philosophique de Denys Diderot*, 102–3).
12. Eloesser, *Das bürgerliche Drama*, 71.
13. A.-T., VII, 336.
14. Diderot to Le Bret, 29 Nov. 1757 (Diderot, *Corr.*, II, 19).
15. Joseph de La Porte and S.-R. Chamfort, *Dictionnaire dramatique . . .* , 3 vols. (Paris, 1776), II, 398–401.
16. A.-T., VII, 322–6. Cf. Edna C. Fredrick, *The Plot and Its Construction in Eighteenth Century Criticism of French Comedy* (Bryn Mawr, 1934), 69, 74.
17. Cf. La Harpe, *Lycée*, X, 401–4.
18. A.-T., VII, 232, 210, 284.
19. Asse, 35.
20. 28 Feb. 1757 (Voltaire, ed. Moland, XXXIX, 181–2).
21. 16 Nov. 1758 (ibid. 532–3).
22. 27 Dec. 1758 (ibid. 563).
23. Littré, *Dictionnaire de la langue française*, s.v. 'Poésie.'
24. See Bonamy to Malesherbes (Asse, 32). The passage Bonamy objected to, and which may indeed have been modified (Asse, 36), appears to be one regarding the imagination (A.-T., VII, 333). Diderot also quotes Helvétius by name (ibid. 353).

25. A.-T., VII, 311, 367; cf. *Journal Encyclopédique*, vol. VIII for 1758, 3ᵉ partie, 139 (15 Dec. 1758). Felix Vexler, *Studies in Diderot's Esthetic Naturalism* (New York, 1922), 71.
26. A.-T., VII, 400. Mme Riccoboni's letter was dated 18 Oct. 1758, and his reply 27 Nov. (Dieckmann, *Inventaire*, 107); they were first published in the Brière edition (1821).
27. A.-T., VII, 399, 402.
28. A.-T., VII, 400, 376. Cf. Max Aghion, *Le Théâtre à Paris au XVIIIᵉ siècle* (Paris, [1926]), 418–23.
29. A.-T., VII, 361–2.
30. A.-T., VII, 374.
31. Gustave Lanson, *Esquisse d'une histoire de la tragédie française* (New York, 1920), 125–6.
32. A.-T., VII, 398. Cf. ibid. 374. Melcher, *Stage Realism in France between Diderot and Antoine*, 31–2, points out that in Diderot's view the setting is an integral part of the action.
33. Green, *Eighteenth-Century France*, 164–7; H. Carrington Lancaster, *The Comédie Française, 1701–1774: Plays, Actors, Spectators, Finances* (*Transactions of the American Philosophical Society*, New Series, XLI, Part 4 [1951]), 594, 797; *Corr. litt.*, IV, 111, 118. These last items were very likely written by Diderot himself, for Grimm was in Geneva at the time.
34. A.-T., VII, 310.
35. Ducros, *Diderot*, 265.
36. Aghion, *Le Théâtre à Paris au XVIIIᵉ siècle*, 39. Cf. Gustave Larroumet, 'Diderot. — Sa théorie dramatique. — "Le Père de famille",' *Revue des Cours et Conférences*, VIII (1899–1900), 2ᵉ série, 837.
37. *Das Theater des Herrn Diderot*, 2 vols. (Berlin, 1760), II: *'Vorrede des Uebersetzers'* (separate pagination), 3ᵛ.
38. A.-T., VII, 320.
39. E.g. Trahard, *Les Maîtres de la sensibilité française au XVIIIᵉ siècle*, II, 49–286, esp. ch. iii: 'La Sensibilité de Diderot' (49–70). But see the criticism of Trahard by Herbert Dieckmann, 'Zur Interpretation Diderots,' *Romanische Forschungen*, LIII (1939), 52–3 nn.
40. Cf. Arthur M. Wilson, 'Sensibility in France in the Eighteenth Century: A Study in Word History,' *French Quarterly*, XIII (1931), 35–46.
41. A.-T., VII, 404; cf. Venturi, *Jeunesse*, 80–82.
42. A.-T., VII, 390. An Aristes had also figured as the hero of *La Promenade du sceptique*.
43. A.-T., VII, 339.
44. A.-T., VII, 371, 372.
45. Cf. Hubert Gillot, *Denis Diderot* (Paris, 1937), 308–10.
46. See Dieckmann, 'Diderot's Conception of Genius,' *JHI*, 151–82, esp. 166.
47. A.-T., VII, 333.
48. A.-T., VII, 310.
49. A.-T., VII, 403.
50. A.-T., VII, 312.
51. Bonamy to Malesherbes (Asse, 31–2).
52. A.-T., VII, 313, 369.

CHAPTER 25

1. *Corr. litt.*, IV, 59. Turgot, *Oeuvres*, ed. Schelle, I, 594; also in Diderot, *Corr.*, II, 110.
2. Diderot, *Corr.*, II, 119.
3. *Arrests de la Cour de Parlement . . .* (1759), 1, 2, 13. Joly de Fleury's *réquisitoire* is quoted in part in Hervier, *Les Ecrivains français jugés par leurs contemporains*, II, 261–2. The allegation of conspiracy was repeated (but without naming the *Encyclopédie*) in the *Censure de la faculté de théologie de Paris, contre le livre qui a pour titre, De l'Esprit* [11 May 1759] (Paris: J. B. Garnier, 1759), 8, mounted in B.N., MSS, Fr. 22094, pièce 10.
4. Belin, *Le Mouvement philosophique de 1748 à 1789*, 129. The edition of the *Pensées philosophiques* attacked was the *Etrennes des esprits forts* (London [Amsterdam], 1757): cf. Diderot, *Pensées philosophiques*, ed. Niklaus (1950), 50.
5. *Arrests de la Cour de Parlement . . .* (1759), 18.
6. A.-T., XIV, 462–3; cf. *Encyc.*, I, xviij.
7. Herbert Dieckmann, writing in *RR*, XXXIV (1943), 176; Gaudin, *Les Lettres anglaises dans*

l'Encyclopédie, 207. A contrary and more conventional view in Grosclaude, *Un Audacieux Message*, 152-6.

8. 'Réponse au Prospectus de M. Fromageot,' 2 March 1768 (Douglas H. Gordon's Extra Volume, foll. 64-5).

9. Barbier, *Journal*, IV, 302. A facsimile of the warrant served upon Le Breton on 25 Jan. 1759, in Gordon and Torrey, *The Censoring of Diderot's* Encyclopédie, facing 20.

10. *Arrests de la Cour de Parlement* . . . (1759), 30; Barbier, *Journal*, IV, 304-5. The text of the *arrêt* of 6 Feb. 1759 also in [Louis Chaudon], *Dictionnaire anti-philosophique* (Avignon, 1767), 415-18.

11. Malesherbes, *Mémoire sur la liberté de la presse*, 93.

12. The first two volumes were published in Oct. 1758; the other six in Nov. 1758 and Jan. 1759 (Naves, *Voltaire et l'Encyclopédie*, 64).

13. Also published in 1759 were [Père Bonhomme], *L'Eloge de l'Encyclopédie et des Encyclopédistes* (The Hague, 1759), a new edition, brought up to date by references to *De l'Esprit*, of the *Réflexions d'un Franciscain* (see *supra*, ch. 12, n. 39); David Renaud Boullier, *Pièces philosophiques et littéraires* (n.p., 1759), a collection of earlier papers critical of the Encyclopedists' tendency towards materialism, by a courteous but rather dull Protestant writer; and *Lettres sur le VIIᵉ volume de l'Encyclopédie* (n.p., 1759) (Mazarine 41774, pièce 6). This last took umbrage (p. 16) that the *Encyclopédie* (VII, 285b) had praised Julian the Apostate; was much upset (pp. 31-6) by D'Alembert's article on 'Frères de la Charité' (*Encyc.*, VII, 301) and De Jaucourt's on 'Franciscains' (ibid. 284); and asserted (pp. 17-18) that the article 'Franconie' praised the Free-Masons. This article, signed by De Jaucourt (ibid. 287) does not even mention the Masons, but a brief article of fourteen lines on 'Francs-Maçons' (ibid. 281b), in itself an avowed and indeed tolerably close translation (cf. Chambers, *Cyclopaedia*, s.v. 'Masons, *Free* or *Accepted*'), states that 'Tout ce qu'on peut pénétrer de leurs mysteres ne paroît que louable . . .'

14. *Corr. litt.*, IV, 59; Le Gras, 126.

15. 18 Feb. 1759 (B.N., MSS, Nouv. acq. fr. 3348, fol. 170).

16. Barbier, *Chronique* . . . (1885), VII, 129-30.

17. Barbier, *Journal*, IV, 303; Belin, *Le Mouvement philosophique de 1748 à 1789*, 130 n. See Malesherbes' five memoranda for the Dauphin (Chrétien-Guillaume Lamoignon de Malesherbes, *Mémoires sur la librairie et sur la liberté de la presse* [Paris, 1809], IV). Frequent allusions (ibid. 5, 7-9, 15-17, *et passim*) reveal how much Malesherbes disliked the Parlement's action.

18. Monod, *De Pascal à Chateaubriand*, 365; Belin, *Le Commerce des livres prohibés*, 113; Belin, *Le Mouvement philosophique de 1748 à 1789*, 128, 130.

19. *Corr. litt.*, IV, 81 (15 Feb. 1759).

20. Archives . . . Haute-Marne, Fonds II E 16; a photograph published in *Cahiers Haut-Marnais*, No. 24 (Iᵉʳ trimestre 1951), Supplément illustré. Voltaire, ed. Moland, XL, 45.

21. *Arrest du Conseil d'Etat du Roi* . . . *Du 8 Mars 1759* (Paris: Imprimerie royale, 1759), 2; mounted in B.N., MSS, Fr. 22177, foll. 273-4; complete text in A.-T., XIII, 118-19.

22. Barbier, *Journal*, IV, 310; A.-T., XIII, 118.

23. *Corr. litt.*, III, 457.

24. *Arrest du Conseil d'Etat du Roi* . . . *Du 21 Juillet 1759* (Paris: Imprimerie royale, 1759); mounted in B.N., MSS, Fr. 22177, fol. 324; text in A.-T., XIII, 119-20.

25. Jean Fourastié, 'L'*Encyclopédie* et la notion de progrès économique,' *AUP*, XXII ([Oct.] 1952), numéro spécial, 144.

26. Gustave Lanson, *RHLF*, IX (1902), 152.

27. Diderot, *Corr.*, II, 120, 121-2. For the new financial terms, see ibid. 121.

28. Ibid. 122.

29. Ibid. 120.

30. Morellet, *Mémoires*, I, 88. Diderot wrote Grimm that he suspected Turgot, D'Alembert, Bourgelat, and Morellet of being in a plot against the *Encyclopédie* (Diderot, *Corr.*, II, 130).

31. Voltaire to Bertrand, 22 March 1759 (Voltaire, ed. Moland, XL, 65).

32. *Corr. litt.*, IX, 253.

33. Diderot, *Corr.*, II, 122.
34. *Mémoire pour Abraham Chaumeix, contre les prétendus philosophes Diderot et d'Alembert* (Amsterdam, 1759).
35. Diderot, *Corr.*, II, 122–3. It was probably Diderot who, in Grimm's absence, described this pamphlet for the *Corr. litt.*, IV, 108–111; see Dieckmann, *Inventaire*, 16.
36. 7 April 1759 (Diderot, *Corr.*, II, 117). Antoine-Alexandre Barbier, the eminent bibliographer, declared in his 'Remarques sur la Correspondance de MM. Grimm et Diderot,' in Friedrich Melchior Grimm, *Supplément à la Correspondance littéraire de MM. Grimm et Diderot* (Paris, 1814), 323, that Diderot was the author.
37. Diderot, *Corr.*, II, 123.
38. Mme de Vandeul, xlv.
39. Lester Gilbert Crocker, 'The Problem of Malesherbes' Intervention,' by L. G. Krakeur, *MLQ*, II (1941), 551–8. Malesherbes remarked in his *Mémoire sur la liberté de la presse*, 53, that it was common to allow a publisher to publish a book 'secretly,' with the understanding that if a search and seizure had to be made, warning would be given in advance. The Diderot incident does not seem to be different in essence from such cases.
40. Diderot, *Corr.*, II, 140.
41. Ibid. 135 (10 May 1759). A critic writing in a review edited by T. S. Eliot called a paragraph of this letter 'almost a piece of music' (Francis Birrell, 'Things Diderot Could Do,' *Criterion*, XII [1932–3], 633).
42. Diderot, *Corr.*, II, 119.
43. Henry Tronchin, *Un Médecin du XVIIIᵉ siècle: Théodore Tronchin (1709–1781)* (Paris, 1906), 375–6; also Diderot, *Corr.*, II, 139.
44. Diderot, *Corr.*, II, 124–6, 138, 140, 146, 151. Diderot was so fond of the Apocalypse-mystery phrase that he used it again several years later in his essay *Sur les femmes* (1772): see A.-T., II, 260.
45. Diderot, *Corr.*, II, 150–51, 140, 150, 156 resp. Contrary to Babelon (*CI*, I, 42 n.), the correct date is 3 June (George R. Havens, 'The Chronology of Diderot's Journey to Langres in 1759,' *MLN*, LIX [1944], 33).
46. Diderot, *Corr.*, II, 157.
47. Ibid. 165.
48. Pierre Mesnard, 'Sophie Volland et la maturité de Diderot,' *Revue des Sciences Humaines*, Jan.–March 1949, 12, 20. Regarding the Freudian significance of the death of Diderot's father, see ibid. 13; also Pierre Mesnard, *Le Cas Diderot: Etude de caractérologie littéraire* (Paris, 1952), 163–76.
49. Paul Hazard, 'Les Origines philosophiques de l'homme de sentiment,' *RR*, XXVIII (1937), 336.
50. Diderot, *Corr.*, II, 167.
51. Ibid. 164.
52. Morley, *Diderot and the Encyclopaedists*, I, 112; similarly, Jean Thomas, 'Le Rôle de Diderot dans l'*Encyclopédie*,' *AUP*, XXII ([Oct.] 1952), numéro spécial, 14–15, 25; also Crocker, *La Correspondance de Diderot*, by L. G. Krakeur, 37.
53. Paul Vernière, 'L'Encyclopédie de Diderot et d'Alembert,' *Revue de Synthèse*, XXVI (1950), 148–9.
54. A.-T., XIII, 175.

Bibliography

I. UNPUBLISHED SOURCES

BALTIMORE - Mr. Douglas H. Gordon's Extra Volume. For a description of the contents of this volume, see Douglas H. Gordon and Norman L. Torrey, *The Censoring of Diderot's* Encyclopédie *and the Re-established Text* (New York, 1947), 109–12. The Extra Volume is usually housed in the Walters Art Gallery; Mr. Gordon keeps a set of microfilm of it at his office.

CHAUMONT - Archives Départementales de la Haute-Marne, Série E (Fonds Vandeul). A manuscript catalogue of these family papers has been compiled by M. Jean Massiet du Biest and is available at the Archives in Chaumont (Jean Massiet du Biest, *La Fille de Diderot* [Tours, 1949], vii).

GENEVA - Bibliothèque Publique et Universitaire:
Collection Rilliet: Letter from Diderot to Vernes (?), 9 Jan. 1759.
Tronchin Archives, vol. 167.

LANGRES - Archives Municipales, Hôtel de Ville.

LONDON - British Museum:
Additional Manuscripts 30867, foll. 14, 18–19, 20–21: Early letters from D'Holbach to Wilkes.
Egerton Manuscripts, vol. 19, fol. 46: Diderot to Le Bret, 29 Nov. 1757.

NEW YORK - The Pierpont Morgan Library:
Diderot to Le Breton, undated (1751?).

PARIS - Archives de la Comédie-Française.
Archives Départementales de la Seine, 417868x: copy of the birth certificate of Sophie Volland.
Archives Nationales: T 319^5, Y 77, Y 12594, Y 13777, U 1051, AD VIII (Année 1745).
Bibliothèque de l'Arsenal: Cartons 10300–303, 10305, 11671.
Bibliothèque Nationale:
Archives Administratives, vol. 56.
Département des Imprimés: Prêt 5 (notation of books borrowed by Diderot).
Département des Manuscrits: Fonds Français: vols. 12763, 14307, 15230, 21813, 21928, 21958–60, 21997, 22068–9, 22086, 22092, 22112, 22137–40, 22155–65, 22176–7, 22191. Volumes 22061–193 of this *fonds* are inventoried in Ernest Coyecque, *Inventaire de la Collection Anisson sur l'histoire de l'imprimerie et de la librairie, principalement à Paris*, 2 vols. (Paris, 1900).

Fonds Joly de Fleury: vols. 292, 1687, 1708. This collection has been inventoried by A. Molinier, *Inventaire sommaire de la Collection Joly de Fleury* (Paris, 1881).

Fonds Latin, vol. 9158.

Fonds Nouvelles Acquisitions Françaises, vols. 31, 558, 717, 1182–3, 1185–6, 1214, 1311, 2777, 3344–8, 3531, 4200, 4411, 5184, 6203, 9197, 9216, 10165, 10781–3, 12961, 13004, 21196.

By decree of the President's Council of Ministers, 30 April 1952, there was deposited in the Bibliothèque Nationale the Fonds Vandeul. For a detailed description of this collection of manuscripts, see Herbert Dieckmann, *Inventaire du Fonds Vandeul et Inédits de Diderot* (Geneva, 1951).

PHILADELPHIA - The Historical Society of Pennsylvania:
Dreer Collection of Autographs: Diderot to Voltaire, 11 June 1749 (published by Arthur M. Wilson, 'Une Partie inédite de la lettre de Diderot à Voltaire, le 11 juin 1749,' *RHLF*, LI [1951], 257–60).

Regarding the manuscripts of Diderot sent to Russia after his death, see Maurice Tourneux, 'Les Manuscrits de Diderot conservés en Russie,' *Archives des Missions Scientifiques et Littéraires*,

3me série, XII (1885), 439–74. Vol. XVII of this collection has been intensively studied by Johan Viktor Johansson, *Etudes sur Denis Diderot: Recherches sur un volume-manuscrit conservé à la bibliothèque publique de l'Etat à Leningrad* (Göteborg and Paris, [1927]). Fifteen rolls of microfilm from this collection are now available at the Bibliothèque Nationale.

II. SOME EDITIONS OF DIDEROT'S WORKS

The most nearly complete edition is the *Oeuvres complètes,* ed. Jules Assézat and Maurice Tourneux, 20 vols. (Paris, 1875–7). Since its publication a very large number of Diderot's letters and writings have been discovered, so that a new collection of his works is very much to be desired. Moreover, the new edition, in view of the rapidly accelerating appreciation of Diderot's place in French letters, ought to be a meticulously edited one. Year by year the need for such an edition makes itself increasingly felt.

Special mention should be made of a well-edited edition, now in progress, of Diderot's correspondence: Diderot, *Correspondance,* ed. Georges Roth, I (*1713–1757*) (Paris, [1955]); II (*Décembre 1757–Novembre 1759*) (Paris, [1956]).

A useful and comparatively complete selection of Diderot's works is that edited by André Billy: Diderot, *Oeuvres* (Paris: 'Nouvelle Revue française,' 1935 [Bibliothèque de la Pléiade, No. 25]); an enlarged edition was published in 1946 and 1951. Also of interest and usefulness is the well-edited edition by Paul Vernière: Diderot, *Oeuvres philosophiques* (Paris: Classiques Garnier, [1956]). In English there is the attractively translated *Rameau's Nephew and Other Works, in New Translations by Jacques Barzun and Ralph H. Bowen* (Garden City, N.Y.: Doubleday Anchor Books, 1956).

The following list is comprised of recent editions of single works by Diderot written in the early part of his life, together with what available English translations there are of writings from this early period:

Denis Diderot, *Pensées philosophiques,* ed. Robert Niklaus (Geneva, 1950).

Denis Diderot, *Lettre sur les aveugles,* ed. Robert Niklaus (Geneva, 1951).

Diderot's Early Philosophical Works, tr. and ed. Margaret Jourdain (Chicago, 1916).

Diderot, Interpreter of Nature: Selected Writings, tr. Jean Stewart and Jonathan Kemp (New York, 1938).

Dramatic Essays of the Neo-Classic Age, ed. Henry Hitch Adams and Baxter Hathaway (New York, 1950), 349–60: Diderot's 'Essay on Dramatic Poetry,' tr. John Gaywood Linn. An abridgement.

III. SOME GENERAL BIOGRAPHICAL BOOKS AND ARTICLES

a. IN ENGLISH:

Morley, John: *Diderot and the Encyclopaedists,* 2 vols. (London, 1878).

Becker, Carl: 'The Dilemma of Diderot,' in *Everyman His Own Historian* (New York, 1935), 262–83.

Carlyle, Thomas: 'Diderot,' in *Critical and Miscellaneous Essays.*

Crocker, Lester Gilbert: *The Embattled Philosopher: A Biography of Denis Diderot* (East Lansing [Mich.], 1954).

Ellis, Havelock: 'Diderot,' in *The New Spirit,* 4th ed. (New York, [1926]), 34–68.

Laski, Harold: 'Diderot,' in *Studies in Law and Politics* (New Haven, 1932), 48–65.

b. IN GERMAN:

Kassner, Rudolf: *Denis Diderot* (Berlin, [1906]).

Rosenkranz, Karl: *Diderot's Leben und Werke,* 2 vols. (Leipzig, 1866).

c. IN FRENCH:

Billy, André: *Diderot* (Paris, 1932); revised and enlarged edition (Paris, 1943). An excellent and comprehensive biography, but unfortunately not provided with documentation.

Other highly regarded works, but much briefer in their treatment:

Ducros, Louis: *Diderot: l'homme et l'écrivain* (Paris, 1894).

Gillot, Hubert: *Denis Diderot: l'homme, ses idées philosophiques, esthétiques, littéraires* (Paris, 1937).

Lefebvre, Henri: *Diderot* (Paris, 1949).

Luppol, I. K.: *Diderot* (Paris, 1936). Translated from the Russian.
Mornet, Daniel: *Diderot: l'homme et l'oeuvre* (Paris, [1941]). An important and influential estimate of Diderot's place in French letters.
Sainte-Beuve, Charles-Augustin: 'Diderot,' *Premiers lundis,* I, 372–93.
Sainte-Beuve, Charles-Augustin: 'Diderot,' *Portraits littéraires,* I, 239–64.
Other general works:
Collignon, A.: *Diderot: sa vie, ses oeuvres, sa correspondance* (Paris, 1895).
Cresson, André: *Diderot: sa vie, son oeuvre* (Paris, 1949).
Meyer, E.: *Diderot* (Paris, [1923]).
Reinach, Joseph: *Diderot* (Paris, 1884).
Scherer, Edmond: *Diderot* (Paris, 1880).
Seillière, Ernest: *Diderot* (Paris, 1944).

IV. PUBLISHED SOURCES, AND SECONDARY WORKS

The following four works include such comprehensive bibliographies regarding Diderot that the publication here of a long bibliography is unnecessary.

1. David C. Cabeen, gen. ed., *A Critical Bibliography of French Literature,* IV: *The Eighteenth Century,* ed. George R. Havens and Donald F. Bond (Syracuse, 1951). All entries in this volume are fully and critically described. The excellent sections on 'Diderot' (items 2203–343) and 'Encyclopédie' (items 1288–1322) were done by Herbert Dieckmann and Norman L. Torrey, and by Lester G. Crocker, resp.
2. Herbert Dieckmann, 'Bibliographical Data on Diderot,' *Studies in Honor of Frederick W. Shipley* ('Washington University Studies – New Series: Language and Literature–No. 14' [St. Louis, 1942]), 181–220.
3. Herbert Dieckmann, *Stand und Probleme der Diderot-Forschung* (Bonn, 1931).
4. Jean Thomas, *L'Humanisme de Diderot,* 2nd ed. (Paris, 1938), 161–82: 'Etat présent des travaux sur Diderot.'

By far the greater share of books and articles used in the preparation of this book is listed in the four bibliographical works just mentioned. The following list of titles is therefore simply complementary in nature. It is confined to older works overlooked in the four bibliographies mentioned above, or to works published since the appearance of the eighteenth-century volume in the *Critical Bibliography of French Literature* (1951). And in the interest of brevity, even such titles have been mentioned in the following list only if they have been used more than once and in more than one chapter.

Adam, Antoine: 'Rousseau et Diderot,' *Revue des Sciences Humaines,* January–March 1949, 21–34.
Arrests de la Cour de Parlement, portant condamnation de plusieurs Livres & autres Ouvrages imprimés. Extrait des registres de Parlement. Du 23 Janvier 1759 (Paris: P. G. Simon, 1759).
Bibliothèque Impartiale, 18 vols. (Leyden, 1750–58). This periodical was edited by Jean-Henri-Samuel Formey.
La Bigarure ou Meslange curieux, instructif et amusant de nouvelles, de critique, de morale, de poesies, Et autres matieres de Littérature, d'Evénements singuliers & extraordinaires, d'Avantures galantes, d'Histoires Secrettes, & de plusieurs autres Nouveautés amusantes, avec des Réflexions Critiques sur chaque Sujet, 20 vols. (The Hague, 1749–53). Passages in *La Bigarure* alluding to Diderot have recently been published by Roland Mortier, 'Un Témoignage curieux sur Diderot, vers 1750,' *Marche Romane,* III (1953), 1–10.
Les Cahiers Haut-Marnais, No. 24 (1er trimestre 1951), plus 'Supplément illustré.' This special number of this periodical, edited by M. Jean Gigot and published at Châlons-sur-Marne, contains valuable documents regarding Diderot.
Charpentier, L.: *Lettres critiques, sur divers écrits de nos jours contraires à la Religion et aux moeurs,* 2 vols. (London, 1751).
Cheverny, Jean-Nicolas Dufort, comte de: *Mémoires,* 2nd ed., 2 vols. (Paris, 1909).

'Conférences faites à la Sorbonne à l'occasion du 2ᵉ centenaire de l'*Encyclopédie,' Annales de l'Université de Paris,* XXII ([Oct.] 1952), numéro spécial.

Crocker, Lester Gilbert: *Two Diderot Studies: Ethics and Esthetics* ('The Johns Hopkins Studies in Romance Literatures and Languages, Extra Volume XXVII' [Baltimore, 1952]).

Delort, Joseph: *Histoire de la détention des philosophes et des gens de lettres à la Bastille et à Vincennes,* 3 vols. (Paris, 1829).

Denis, Henri: 'Deux collaborateurs économiques de l'Encyclopédie: Quesnay et Rousseau,' *Pensée,* Sept.–Oct. 1951, 44–54.

Diderot et l'Encyclopédie: Exposition commémorative, ed. Georges Huard (Paris: Bibliothèque Nationale, 1951).

Diderot Studies, ed. Otis E. Fellows and Norman L. Torrey, II (Syracuse, [1952]).

Dieckmann, Herbert: *Inventaire du Fonds Vandeul et Inédits de Diderot* (Geneva, 1951).

L' 'Encyclopédie' et le progrès des sciences et des techniques, ed. Suzanne Delorme and René Taton (Paris: Presses Universitaires de France, 1952). A collection of twenty articles first published in the *Revue d'Histoire des Sciences.*

Epinay, Louise de La Live d': *Les Pseudo-Mémoires de Madame d'Epinay: Histoire de Madame de Montbrillant,* ed. Georges Roth, 3 vols. (Paris, [1951]).

Escherny, François-Louis, comte d': *Mélanges de littérature, d'histoire, de morale et de philosophie,* 3 vols. (Paris, 1811).

Foisset, Joseph-Théophile: *Le Président de Brosses* (Paris, 1842).

Fredman, Alice Green: *Diderot and Sterne* (New York, 1955).

Gazier, Augustin: *Histoire générale du mouvement janséniste,* 2 vols. (Paris, 1922).

Green, Frederick Charles: *Jean-Jacques Rousseau: A Critical Study of His Life and Writings* (Cambridge, 1955).

Grosclaude, Pierre: *Un Audacieux Message: L'Encyclopédie* (Paris, 1951).

Guyot, Charly: *Diderot par lui-même* (Paris, [1953]). An anthology, competently edited and profusely illustrated.

Havens, George R.: *The Age of Ideas: From Reaction to Revolution in Eighteenth-Century France* (New York, 1955).

Hillairet, Jacques: *Evocation du vieux Paris,* 2 vols. (Paris, [1952–3]).

Hubert, René: 'L'Esprit des sciences sociales dans l'*Encyclopédie,' RHPHGC,* IV (1936), 107–33.

Jal, Auguste: *Dictionnaire critique de biographie et d'histoire . . . d'après des documents authentiques inédits,* 2nd ed. (Paris, 1872).

Lefebvre, Henri: *Diderot* (Paris, 1949).

Lettres sur le VIIᵉ volume de l'Encyclopédie (n.p., 1759).

Lough, John: 'The "Encyclopédie" in Eighteenth-Century England,' *French Studies,* VI (1952), 289–308.

Lough, John, ed.: *The* Encyclopédie *of Diderot and d'Alembert: Selected Articles* (Cambridge, 1954).

Matter, J.: *Lettres et pièces rares ou inédites* (Paris, 1846).

May, Georges: *Diderot et 'La Religieuse'* (Paris and New Haven, 1954).

May, Georges: *Quatre visages de Denis Diderot* (Paris, 1951).

Meaume, Edouard: *Palissot et les philosophes* (Nancy, 1864).

Mémoire des libraires associés à l'Encyclopédie, sur les motifs de la suspension actuelle de cet ouvrage (Paris: Le Breton, 1758).

Mesnard, Pierre: 'Le Caractère de Diderot,' *Revue de la Méditerranée,* VII (1949), 268–98, 664–95.

Mesnard, Pierre: *Le Cas Diderot: Etude de caractérologie littéraire* (Paris, 1952).

Mesnard, Pierre: 'Sophie Volland et la maturité de Diderot,' *Revue des Sciences Humaines,* Jan.–March 1949, 12–20.

Mortier, Roland: *Diderot en Allemagne (1750–1850)* (Paris, 1954).

Nedergaard, Leif: *Diderot: Filosoffens Liv og Virke* (Copenhagen, 1953).

Palissot de Montenoy, Charles: *Oeuvres complettes,* 7 vols. (London, 1779).

Reusch, Franz Heinrich: *Der Index der verbotenen Bücher,* 2 vols. (Bonn, 1883–5).

Sainte-Beuve, Charles-Augustin: 'M. de Malesherbes,' *Causeries du lundi,* II, 512–39.

Sauro, Antonio: *Diderot* (Bari, 1953). In French; a work disfigured by numerous errors.

Smiley, Joseph Royall: *Diderot's Relations with Grimm* ('Illinois Studies in Language and Literature, xxxiv, No. 4' [Urbana, 1950]).

Taillefer, Antoine: *Tableau historique de l'esprit et du caractère des littérateurs français depuis la Renaissance des Lettres jusqu'en 1785,* 4 vols. (Paris, 1785).

Vernière, Paul: 'L'Encyclopédie de Diderot et d'Alembert,' *Revue de Synthèse,* xxvi (1950), 134-54.

Vernière, Paul: *Spinoza et la pensée française avant la Révolution* (Paris, 1954).

Vartanian, Aram: *Diderot and Descartes: A Study of Scientific Naturalism in the Enlightenment* (Princeton, 1953).

Wade, Ira O.: 'The Rediscovery of Diderot,' *Symposium,* vi (1952), 197-208.

Index

Abélard, Peter, 66
Académie Française, 94, 97, 214, 221, 232, 244, 264, 265, 291, 309
Académie Goncourt, 230
Academy of Sciences (Paris), 68, 78, 241–3, 309
Adams, Henry, 134
Aeneid, 124
Aeschylus, 217
Aesculapius, 93, 155
Aguesseau, Henri-François d', chancellor of France, 76–7, 84, 120, 161, 165; authorizes expansion of the *Encyclopédie*, 81; designates Diderot as chief editor, 82
Aine, Mme d', mother-in-law of D'Holbach, 176
Aix-la-Chapelle, 300; treaty of, 94
Alembert, Jean Le Rond d', 47–8, 68, 89, 90, 117–18, 158, 164, 179–80, 185, 193, 201, 217, 220–21, 263, 304, 312, 318, 367 n.52, 392 n.53, 397 n.30; connection with the *Encyclopédie*, 54, 78–80, 107, 115, 154, 158, 165–8; and the 'Preliminary Discourse,' 100, 131–4, 135, 150, 152, 157, 166, 170, 191, 199, 201, 221, 238, 344; and Voltaire, 253–4, 276, 280, 287–90; and the Jesuits, 125, 152, 157, 211–12; membership in academies, 68, 127, 129, 221, 232, 264, 265, 275; and the article 'Geneva,' 280–90, 299, 308; other *Encyclopédie* articles by, 199, 207–8; 214, 235, 277; ideas concerning education, 210–11; relations with Diderot, 66, 111, 113, 166–8, 220–21, 289, 291, 302, 335, 337, 338; retirement from the *Encyclopédie*, 287–90, 307–9, 326, 332
Alsted, Johann Heinrich, 73, 240
Alzarac (Mme de Puisieux), 65
Amsterdam, 169
Anacreon, 18, 326

Angel, Brother, 29–30, 38, 41
Année Littéraire (Fréron), 196–7, 221, 262–3, 281, 285
Antin, Louis de Pardaillan de Gondrin, duc d', 75
Apologie de Louis XIV . . . sur la Révocation de l'Edit de Nantes (Caveirac), 335 and n.
Aquinas, St. Thomas, 157, 191
Areopagitica (Milton), 163
Aretino, Pietro, 54
Argenson, Marc-Pierre de Paulmy, comte d', 97, 104, 105, 111, 112, 117; and the *Encyclopédie*, 107–8, 115–16, 131, 165
Argenson, René-Louis de Voyer, marquis d', 111; comments of, 95, 96, 159, 160, 161, 164, 165
Argental, Charles-Auguste, comte d', 316, 319
Argenteuil, —, abbé d', 183
Aristophanes, 326
Aristotle, 8, 132, 326, 328
Aristoxenes, 90
Arrêt rendu à l'amphithéâtre de l'Opéra (Diderot), 179, 180
Assembly of the Clergy, 117, 335
Assézat, Jules, 60
Athens, 162
Au Petit Prophète de Boehmischbroda (Diderot), 179
Augustine, St., 34, 71, 114, 202, 279
Austrian Succession, War of the, 94, 175
Auxerre, Charles de Caylus, bishop of, 169–71
Avare (Molière), 273
Avignon, 317
Ayloffe, Sir Joseph, 151

B

Bachelier, Jean-Jacques, 226
Bacon, Francis, 4, 49, 133, 137, 211, 237,

405

Bacon, Francis (*continued*)
    284; and Diderot, 187–9, 191, 195, 198,
    244; and the *Encyclopédie*, 125, 132
Baculard d'Arnaud, François-Thomas-Marie
    de, 48
Baltic Sea, 143
Barbier, Antoine-Alexandre, 320
Barbier, Edmond-Jean-François, diarist, 94,
    111; comments of, 159, 161, 164, 168,
    334, 336
Barrat, —, 199
Barruel, Augustin, abbé de, 312
Bartholdi, Frédéric-Auguste, 11
Batteux, Charles, abbé, 124
Battle of the Books (Swift), 85
Baudelaire, Charles, 123, 216
Bayle, Pierre, 5, 139–40, 144
Beaumarchais, Pierre-Augustin Caron de, 262
Beaumont, Christophe de, archbishop of Paris,
    156, 169, 244, 311
Beaux-Arts réduits à un même principe (Bat-
    teux), 124
Becker, Carl, 113
Bell, E. T., 91
Bentham, Jeremy, 310
Berkeley, George, 68, 99
Berlin, 91, 156, 166, 169; Academy of, 115,
    127, 167, 193, 264, 275
Bernis, François-Joachim de Pierre, cardinal
    de, 25, 26, 28, 84, 308–9
Bernoulli, family of mathematicians, 5, 192
Berryer, Nicolas-René, lieutenant-general of
    police, 61, 120; and Diderot's imprison-
    ment, 104–8, 110, 112–13, 115–16,
    356 n.9
Berthier, Guillaume-François, père, 125–7, 150
Bigarure, 108–9, 118, 159, 174 n.
Biheron, Marie-Catherine, 93
Bijoux indiscrets (Diderot), 54, 83–7, 95, 104,
    106, 107, 108, 127, 264
Billard (née Champion), Marie-Antoinette,
    sister of Mme Denis Diderot, 352 n.3
Bingham, Joseph, 88
Boerhaave, Hermann, 201
Boileau, Nicolas, 123, 205, 326
Bombarde, — de, 111
Bonamy, Pierre-Nicolas, 316, 325
Bonin, —, 87
Bordeu, Théophile de, 93, 213
Bosson, Jacques, 43
Bossuet, Jacques-Bénigne, bishop of Meaux, 5,
    171
Boston, Public Library, 99; Museum School
    of Fine Arts, 226
Boucher, François, 3

Boucher d'Argis, Antoine-Gaspard, 208, 213,
    235
Boulanger, Nicolas-Antoine, 279
Bourbonne-les-Bains, 12, 13
Bourdaloue, Louis, 5
Bourgelat, Claude, 213–14, 397 n.30
Bourgeois Gentilhomme (Molière), 269
Boyer, Jean-François, sometime bishop of
    Mirepoix, 159, 165
Boyle, Robert, 5, 49
Briasson, publisher, 52–3, 77, 78, 87, 129,
    151, 283
Brosses, Charles de, 224–5, 381 n.18
Brucker, Johann Jacob, 216
Brûlé, Hélène, 351 n.33
Brunetière, Ferdinand, 169
Bruno, Giordano, 237
Bryan, William Jennings, 170
Buffon, Georges-Louis Leclerc, comte de, 109,
    111, 128, 133, 171, 184, 185, 193, 196,
    201, 221, 224, 326
Burgoyne, John, general, 322
Burke, Edmund, 114, 133, 367 n.33
Bury, J. B., 133
Byng, John, admiral, 275

C
Cahusac, Louis de, 199
Calvin, John, 281
Cambridge, 98, 201
Campanella, Thomas, 237
Candide (Voltaire), 247
Caractères (Mme de Puisieux), 65
Cardan, Girolamo, 237
Carlyle, Thomas, 6, 86, 113, 229, 341, 346
Caroillon, Nicolas, 184–5, 218–19, 232, 335,
    350 n.12
Caroillon de la Charmotte, Nicolas, godson of
    Diderot, 218
Cassirer, Ernst, 192, 193, 194
Castel, Louis-Bertrand, père, 126–7
Castle of Otranto (Walpole), 54
Castries, Charles-Eugène-Gabriel de La Croix,
    marquis de, 306
Catherine II, 18, 91, 116, 120, 220, 345
Cato the Elder, 84
Catullus, 326
Caveirac, Jean Novi de, abbé, 335 and n.
Caylus, Anne-Claude-Philippe, comte de, 84,
    226–7
Ceci n'est pas un conte (Diderot), 125
Chambers, Ephraim, 5, 73, 74, 75, 76, 77,
    80, 81, 83, 103, 134, 136, 240
Chamfort, Nicolas de, 38

Champigny, 110

Champion, Anne-Toinette, *see* Diderot (née Champion), Anne-Toinette

Champion, Marie, mother-in-law of Denis Diderot, 37, 40, 43, 45

Chartres, 134

Chassigny (Haute-Marne), 11

Châtelet, Emilie du, 101–2, 111–12, 292

Châtelet, François-Bernard du, 105, 106, 108, 109, 110, 112, 115, 116

Chaumeix, Abraham-Joseph de, 312, 334, 338

Choiseul, Etienne-François, duc de, 317

Cicero, 19, 123, 215

City of God (St. Augustine), 202

Clairaut, Alexis-Claude, 111, 193

Clairon, Claire-Joseph, 386 n.5

Clarke, Samuel, 49

Clement XIII, 311

Clément, Pierre, 126, 151, 196, 208

Clément de Ris, —, 23, 27

Clermont, Louis de Bourbon-Condé, comte de, 221

Colbert, Jean-Baptiste, 137, 242

Colby, Frank Moore, 5

Collé, Charles, 114, 263, 273

Comédie-Française, 30, 31, 33, 260, 261, 322, 327–8

Compiègne, 104

Comte, Auguste, 202

Concerning the Education of a Prince (Diderot), 313–14

Condillac, Etienne Bonnot de, abbé, 79, 99, 170, 191, 196; and Diderot, 66–8, 252, 385 n.8

Condorcet, Antoine-Nicolas de, 78, 79, 107, 275

Confessions (Rousseau), 45, 66, 109, 113, 116, 225, 255, 293, 294, 295, 296, 298

Conseils à une amie (Mme de Puisieux), 65

Conversation of a Father with His Children (Diderot), 219

Conversations regarding Le Fils naturel (Diderot), 260, 268–71, 313, 322, 324

Convulsionnaires, 55

Coolidge, Julian, 90

Corneille, Pierre, 5, 30, 123, 273, 326, 386 n.6

Correspondance littéraire (Grimm), 119, 283

Cotterel, Alexandre-François, abbé, 166

Crébillon the Younger, 84

Croismare, Marc-Antoine-Nicolas, marquis de, 315

Cyclopaedia, or Universal Dictionary of the Arts and Sciences (Chambers), 5, 73, 74, 75, 76, 77, 80, 83, 103, 134, 136, 240

D

D'Alembert's Dream (Diderot), 93, 149, 345

Damiens, Robert-François, 276

Dangeville, Marie-Anne Botot, 31

Danse ancienne et moderne (Cahusac), 199

Dardanelles, 136

Darrow, Clarence, 170

Daubenton, Louis-Jean-Marie, 111, 150

David, publisher, 77, 78, 87, 129, 151, 235, 337

De la Suffisance de la religion naturelle (Diderot), 60, 61, 101, 155

De l'Esprit (Helvétius), 111, 306, 309–12, 332, 333

De Morgan, Augustus, 91

De rerum natura (Lucretius), 195

Declaration of Independence, 233

Declaration of the Rights of Man and of the Citizen, 233

Deffand, Marie de Vichy, marquise du, 111, 222, 310, 326

Deleyre, Alexandre, 271, 317–20; and the *Encyclopédie*, 235–6; and Diderot, 299, 300, 303, 320–21; and Rousseau, 299, 300, 303, 307, 313

Delort, Joseph, 110

Democracy in America (De Tocqueville), 262

Démonstration du principe de l'harmonie (Rameau), 89

Denmark, 280

Descartes, René, 5, 84, 85, 99, 131, 133, 187, 191, 203, 237

Desfontaines, Pierre-François-Guyot, abbé, 48, 52, 264

Deslandes, André-François Boureau, 216

Desmahis, Joseph-François-Edouard de Corsembleu, 253

Destouches, Louis Camus, chevalier, 68

Devin du village (Rousseau), 180–81, 255

Dickens, Charles, 103, 325

Dictionary of National Biography, 50, 76

Dictionnaire de Trévoux, 211, 215, 244, 279

Dictionnaire historique et critique (Bayle), 139–40

Dictionnaire universel de médecine (James), 52–3, 54, 55, 78, 83, 87, 93

Diderot (née Vigneron) (1677–1748), Angélique, mother of Denis Diderot, 12, 29, 40, 43, 95–6, 112

Diderot, Angélique (1720–48), sister of Denis Diderot, 14, 40

Diderot, Angélique (1744), daughter of Denis Diderot, 12, 44

Diderot, Angélique (1753–1824), *see* Vandeul (née Diderot), Angélique

Diderot (née Champion), Anne-Toinette, wife
of Denis Diderot, 49, 64–5, 83, 95, 105,
109–10, 118–19, 174 n., 184, 185–6, 230,
296, 299, 316, 322–3, 340; birth and
ancestry, 37; courtship, 37–44; early
married life, 44–6, 54–5, 60–61

Diderot, Antoine-Thomas, uncle of Denis Diderot, 11, 12

Diderot, Catherine (1716–18), sister of Denis
Diderot, 14

Diderot, Catherine (1719– ?), sister of Denis
Diderot, 14

Diderot, Denis (1654–1726), grandfather of
Denis Diderot, 11–12

Diderot, Denis (1713–84): see also Encyclopédie; birth, 11–12; ancestry, 11–13;
childhood, 14–19; becomes an abbé, 20–
21, 27; early life in Paris, 23–36; relations with his father, 12–13, 107, 112,
218–19, 261, 267, 323, 339–41; and his
mother, 12, 95–6; and his sister Denise,
13; and his brother, 14, 52, 219, 248,
261, 323; courtship and marriage, 37–46;
domestic life, 44–6, 47, 54–5, 60–61, 83,
95, 118–19, 182–6, 218–19, 220; and
Mme de Puisieux, 64–6, 110, 118–19;
and Sophie Volland, 228–31; early literary efforts, 47–58, 60–64, 83–8, 92–3,
96–102, 120–25; and the 1750 prospectus
of the Encyclopédie, 4–8, 120–21; and the
Encyclopédie, 77–82, 83, 96, 107–8, 115–
16, 117, 128–9, 130–49, 161–2, 164–9,
220–21, 282–3, 332–9; personal characteristics, 10, 16–17, 43–4, 47–8, 59–60,
69, 106–7, 109, 173–5, 176, 184–5, 223–
4, 301–2, 343–6; conception of himself,
70, 108, 173–4, 198, 244–5, 304–5, 320–
21, 323, 328–9; and mathematics, 30,
89–91; and knowledge of medicine, 52–
3, 92–3; business relations with publishers, 219–20, 309, 380 n.6; income, 80–
81, 95, 112, 183, 220; interest in music,
68–70, 88–9, 177–81; and the Abbé de
Prades affair, 156–9, 169–72; relations
with the censorship, 55–7, 63–4, 81–2,
96–7, 106–8, 121–2, 124, 126, 131, 159–
60, 162–4, 165–6, 187, 260–61, 263–4,
283–4, 315–16; and the police, 61–2, 63–
4, 87, 103, 161; imprisonment, 103–16;
scientific ideas, 85, 146–7, 169–70, 187–
96, 202–3; attitude toward religious orthodoxy, 50–52, 55–8, 59–60, 62–3, 100–
101, 143–7; esthetic concepts, 123–4,
204–7, 209, 225–8; ethical concepts, 245–
6, 249–52, 270, 304–5, 330–31; ideas regarding 'philosophy,' 70–72, 97–100, 122,

146–7, 210, 237; ideas about the theater,
30–32, 208–9, 260–72, 322–31; relationship to politics, 93, 142–3, 159–60, 275–
6, 306, 310, 330–31, 336; interest in
crafts and technology, 68–70, 136–8, 199–
200, 213, 240–42; Encyclopédie articles
by, 134–48, 199–200, 203, 208–10, 213,
214–17, 233–4, 235–46, 253, 278–80; appeals to posterity, 121, 239–40, 246, 341–
2; humanism of, 245–6; and membership in academies, 127–8, 264–5, 291,
308–9; accused of plagiarism, 272–4; accused of leading a sect, 197, 285–6, 312–
13, 333; and the 'Cacouacs,' 276–7, 285–
6; and the Jansenists, 25–7, 55, 63, 169–
71; and the Jesuits, 15, 17–19, 21–3, 25–
7, 125–7, 153–4, 157–9, 161, 164–5, 244;
and the 'Affair of the Dedications,' 317–
21, 338; relationship to D'Alembert as
editor, 282–3, 287–90, 307–8; quarrels
with Rousseau, 225, 254–9, 291–306; ill-
nesses, 232, 252, 296, 339–41, 350 n.5;
works of, see individual titles, also Encyclopédie

Diderot, Denise, sister of Denis Diderot, 13–
14, 112, 219, 323

Diderot, Denis-Laurent (1750), son of Denis
Diderot, 119, 366 n.10

Diderot, Didier, father of Denis Diderot, 12–
13, 17, 20, 22–4, 29–30, 33, 43, 45, 65,
103–4, 107, 112, 218–19, 261, 267, 323,
338, 339–41; attitude regarding his son's
marriage, 39–41

Diderot, Didier-Pierre, abbé, brother of Denis
Diderot, 14, 40, 52, 219, 248, 261, 323,
353 n.15, 354 n.27

Diderot, François-Jacques-Denis (1746–50),
son of Denis Diderot, 54–5, 83, 119

Dieckmann, Herbert, 72, 188

Dijon, 10, 224; Academy of, 113, 115, 120,
224–5

Dioptrics (Descartes), 99

Discours sur la poésie dramatique (Diderot),
260, 273, 313, 315, 322, 325, 326–31

Discours sur l'origine de l'inégalité (Rousseau), 225

Discourse on Dramatic Poetry (Diderot), 260,
273, 313, 315, 322, 325, 326–31

Discourse on Method (Descartes), 131, 187,
203

Dubois, Jean-Louis, 219

Duclos, Charles Pineau, 111, 185, 214, 337

Dulac, merchant glover-perfumer, 120

Dumarsais, César Chesneau, 135

Duni, Egidio Romualdo, 274

Duns Scotus, 157, 200

Dupin, Louise-Marie-Madeleine, 48
Dupré de Saint-Maur, Mme Nicolas-François, 97
Dupré de Saint-Maur, Nicolas-François, 97
Durand, Laurent, 55, 66, 77, 78, 83, 87, 89, 97, 106, 119, 129
Dyche, Thomas, 81

E

Eaubonne, 292
Ecclesiasticus, Book of, 303, 309
Edinburgh Review, 7
Eidous, Marc-Antoine, 53, 54, 355 n.38
Elémens de musique . . . suivant les principes de M. Rameau (Diderot?), 89
Elémens de physiologie (Diderot), 93
Elements of Algebra (Saunderson), 98, 99
Elements of Newton's Philosophy (Voltaire), 99
Emerson, Ralph Waldo, 346
Emile (Rousseau), 114, 297
Encyclopaedia Britannica, 5
Encyclopédie, prospectus (1745), 75–6, 128, 150; prospectus (1750), 3–8, 107, 120–21, 125, 126, 128, 150, 188, 344; 'Preliminary Discourse,' 100, 131–4, 135, 150, 152, 155, 157, 166, 170, 191, 199, 201, 221, 238, 344; *Systéme figuré des connoissances humaines*, 132–3, 134; censorship of, 128, 165–6, 283–4; suppression of (1752), 159–60, 161–9, 177, 199; suppression of (1759), 306, 332–6, 337–9; system of cross references in, 134, 243–4, 279, 333–4; plates of, 241–3; early history, 73–82; general mention of, 15, 22, 27, 34, 53, 55, 65, 67, 68, 83, 84, 88, 89, 93, 95, 96, 97, 99, 100, 105, 106, 111, 115, 116, 117, 156, 158, 179, 180, 192, 202, 212, 217, 218, 220, 223, 249, 263, 264, 265, 274, 275–6, 287, 289, 290, 291, 305–6, 307–9, 310, 312–13, 317, 326, 338, 339, 341, 343, 344, 345, 346; Volume I, 54, 108, 127, 128–9, 130–49, 150–54, 165; Volume II, 54, 154, 157, 166, 176, 177, 199–207, 213, 216; Volume III, 158, 166, 168, 187, 201, 207–12, 216, 284; Volume IV, 165, 166, 208, 212–17, 284; Volume V, 166, 220, 225, 232–46, 285; Volume VI, 166, 244, 252–3; Volume VII, 166, 253, 265, 276–84, 286; Volume VIII, 301, 309, 332, 335, 336; articles on: Abeille, 136, 150; Acalipse, 138; Accouchement, 135; Accoucheuse, 141; Achées, 140; Achor, 146, 153; Acier, 29, 135; Adorer, 144; Affiler, 140; Agate, 150; Agir, 139; Agnus Scy-

thicus, 139; Agonyclytes, 144; Agriculture, 74, 135; Aguapa, 138; Aguaxima, 138; Aigle, 145; Aiguille, 135, 141; Aimant, 136; Aius Locutius, 142, 153; Alecto, 140; Alésoir, 136; Alkali, 136; Alsace, 136; Âme, 148–9; Anatomie, 136, 137; Arbre, 136; Arche de Noé, 147, 215; Ardoise, 136; Argent, 135; Aristotélisme, 136, 152, 157, 216; Art, 125, 128, 137–8, 150, 383 n.17; Atmosphère, 136; Attraction, 136; Autorité politique, 142–3, 154, 234, 379 n.30; Ballet, 199; Baromètre, 199; Bas, 199; Beau, 204–7; Beauté, 204; Bête, animal, brute, 204; Bible, 203; Blanchisserie de toiles, 241; Boa, 200; Bois, 199; Brasserie, 199; Brique, 241; Bronze, 199; Cacao, 199; Cadavre, 200; Cadran, 199; Canevas, 200; Canon, en théologie, 203; Capuchon, 200; Caractères d'imprimerie, 199; Cartes, 199; Caucase, 200; Célibat, 203; Cerf, 203–4, 378 n.16; Certitude, 157, 203; Chaise de poste, 208, 211; Chaldéens, Philosophie de, 209–10; Chaleur, 210; Change, 208; Chanvre, 208, 211; Chaos, 209–10; Chapeau, 208, 211; Chasse, 208; Christianisme, 209–10; Chronologie sacrée, 209; Collège, 210–11, 212; Comédiens, 208–9; Commerce, 208; Composition (en peinture), 209; Concurrence, 208; Constitution, 213; Controverse, 214–15; Convulsionnaires, 214; Corderie, 213; Corvée, 215; Coton, 213; Crédulité, 215; Crise, 213; Croire, 215; Cyniques, 216–17; Cyrénaique (Secte), 216–17; Damnation, 215; Délicieux, 216; Déluge, 215; Dentelle, 213; Docteur en médecine, 315; Droit de copie, 235; Droit naturel, 143, 233–4; Duel, 235; Eau-de-vie, 235; Eclectisme, 233, 237; Economie politique, 143, 233–4, 305; Editeur, 383 n.28; Egalité naturelle, 234; Egyptiens (Philosophie des), 236; Eléatique (Secte), 236; Elégance, 232; Eloquence, 232; Email, 235; Encaustique, 225; Encyclopédie, 18, 232, 238–46, 305, 333; Epargne, 234–5; Epicuréisme, 236; Epingle, 235–6, 300; Esprit, 232; Etymologie, 224, 253; Evidence, 253; Existence, 253; Expansibilité, 253; Femme, 253–4; Fermiers, 184, 253; Fêtes, 253; Feux d'artifice, 253; Fief, 253; Fièvre, 253; Finances, 253; Fluide, 253; Flûte, 253; Foire, 277; Fondation, 278; Fordicides, 279; Forges, Grosses-, 277; Formalistes, 280; Fornication, 279; Fourneau, 277; France, 278–9; Genève, 253,

Encyclopédie (continued)
  280–81, 283, 286, 287, 288, 290, 291,
  299, 308; Génie, 389 n.18; Géographie,
  277; Géométrie, 277; Goût, 233; Gouvernement, 234, 279; Grâce, 279; Grains,
  184, 277; Guèbres, 279; Héraldique, Art,
  136; Inoculation, 282; Jouissance, 216;
  Juifs (Philosophie des), 236–7; Langres,
  10; Nature, 201; Philosophe, 70–71, 246;
  Philosophie, 191; Serinette, 69
Encyclopédie méthodique, 216
England, 275, 278, 280
Entretien d'un père avec ses enfants (Diderot),
  219
Entretiens sur le Fils naturel (Diderot), 260,
  268–71, 313, 322, 324
Epictetus, 123
Epicurus, 236
Epinay, Louise de La Live d', 167, 292; and
  Rousseau, 255–8, 292, 293, 295, 296–8;
  and Grimm, 256–7, 296–8, 338; and
  Diderot, 256–7, 262, 294
Erreurs sur la musique dans l'Encyclopédie
  (Rameau), 180
Esprit des lois (Montesquieu), 233
Essai sur le mérite et la vertu (Diderot), 50–
  52, 59, 78, 100, 304
Essai sur l'origine des connaissances humaines
  (Condillac), 67
Essay on Man (Pope), 54
Essay on Women (Diderot), 231
Est-il bon? Est-il méchant? (Diderot), 320–21
Etudes, 158
Euler, Leonhard, 90, 91, 192
Euripides, 18, 326

F

Faiguet, —, 234–5
Farrell, Gabriel, 99
Father of the Family (Diderot), 37–8, 248,
  260, 261–2, 265, 268, 269, 271, 273, 301,
  305, 309, 313–16, 322–6, 331, 394 n.30
Faux généreux (Le Bret), 313
Fécamp, 56
Federalist Papers (Hamilton, Madison, and
  Jay), 233
Fellows, Otis E., 123
Fénelon, François de Salignac de la Mothe-,
  326
Ferney, 167, 214
Fils naturel (Diderot), 116, 248, 254, 255,
  257, 260–74, 275, 294, 322, 324, 326
First Letter from a Zealous Citizen . . . (Di-
  derot), 92–3
Flamsteed, John, 90
Fleury, André–Hercule, cardinal de, 84, 103

Fontaine (des Bertins), Alexis, 193
Fontainebleau, 180
Fontenelle, Bernard le Bovier de, 111, 217,
  223
Forbonnais, François Véron-Duverger de, 208,
  213, 317–20
Formey, Jean-Henri-Samuel, 115, 127, 128,
  166, 167, 242
Fouchy, Jean-Paul Grand-Jean de, 79
Foucou, —, 29–30, 364 n.42
Fouquet, Jean, 105
France, conditions in, 4, 25–6, 41, 49–50, 55,
  56–7, 66–7, 92–5, 103–4, 131, 143–4,
  148–9, 162–4, 177, 202, 221–3, 233–4,
  247–8, 261–2, 269–70, 275–6, 306, 310,
  317–18, 333–7
France, Anatole, 34
Francis I, 66
Francueil, Claude-Louis Dupin de, 297
Frankfurt am Main, 49
Franklin, Benjamin, 192, 234
Frazer, Sir James, 279
Frederick II, king of Prussia, 3, 50, 61, 140,
  156, 167, 196, 247, 264, 275
Freemasons, 74–5
Fréjacques, Mme, 23
Fréron, Elie-Catherine, 196–7, 221, 227, 228,
  271, 281, 285, 286, 287, 324; and Di-
  derot, 196–7, 262–5, 272, 273; and
  D'Alembert, 286–7
Freud, Sigmund, 341
Funck-Brentano, Frantz, 110

G

Gaillard, Gabriel-Henri, 264
Galen, 93
Galileo, 170
Gamester (Moore), 269
Garat, Dominique-Joseph, 176
Garrick, David, 327
Gassendi, Pierre, 90
Gauffecourt, Jean-Vincent Capperonnier de,
  256, 257, 295
Gauss, Karl Friedrich, 193
Gaussin, Jeanne-Catherine Gaussem, 31, 33
Gautherin, Jean, 220
Genesis, Book of, 139, 143, 147, 170, 193,
  194, 202, 279
Geneva, 114, 201, 281–2, 296, 297, 298, 304,
  305, 309; and Voltaire, 145, 214, 280;
  and the article 'Geneva,' 280–83, 290
Genoa, 280
Gentleman's Magazine (London), 68–9, 70
Geoffrin, Marie-Thérèse, 162, 222–4
Geoffroy, —, abbé, 157
George III, 175

Gibbon, Edward, 34, 110, 210
Gide, André, 86
Girard, Gabriel, abbé, 135
Gluck, Christoph Willibald, 269
Goethe, Wolfgang, 268, 346
Golden Bough (Frazer), 279
Goldoni, Carlo, 178, 317; and Diderot, 272–4, 294
Goldsmith, Oliver, 223
Gournay, Jean-Claude-Marie-Vincent de, 278
Goussier, Louis-Jacques, 241
Graffigny, Françoise d'Issambourg d'Happon-court de, 261
Grecian History (Stanyan), 29, 39, 50, 78
Greuze, Jean-Baptiste, 24, 32, 109, 324
Greuze, Mme Jean-Baptiste, 32
Grimm, Friedrich Melchior, 12, 54, 119–20, 164, 173, 174, 178, 248, 252, 292, 309, 332, 337, 339; and Diderot, 201, 256, 294, 301, 313–14, 319–21, 328, 338, 340–41; and Mme d'Epinay, 256–7, 292, 338; and Rousseau, 296–8, 299; quoted, 159, 161–2, 168, 188, 193–4, 207, 216, 227, 228, 262, 281, 283, 312, 332
Grotius, Hugo, 233
Gua de Malves, Jean-Paul, abbé, 78–80, 81
Guillot, Jean-Baptiste, 43
Guillotte, François-Jacques, 61–2

H

Hague, The, 109, 118
Halley, Edmond, 90
Harris, John, 81
Harvey, William, 203
Hegel, Georg Wilhelm Friedrich, 194
Helvétius, Claude-Adrien, 111, 175, 185, 220, 223, 316, 326; and *De l'Esprit*, 306, 309–12, 332, 333
Hémery, Joseph d', 64, 89, 124, 126, 128, 152, 157, 187, 290, 318; and Diderot, 103, 104
Hemingway, Ernest, 31, 54
Hénault, Charles-Jean-François, 365 n.55
Henri IV, 67
Henry V (of England), 105
Herbelot, Barthélemy d', 144
Hermitage, The, 255, 256, 257, 258, 259, 291, 292, 293, 294, 295, 297, 298, 299
Hippocrates, 93
Histoire de Grèce (trans. of Stanyan by Diderot), 29, 39, 50, 52, 78
Histoire de Mlle Terville (Mme de Puisieux), 65
Histoire et le secret de la peinture en cire (Diderot), 225–8, 284
Histoire naturelle (Buffon), 109, 111, 221

History and Secret of Painting in Wax (Diderot), 225–8, 284
History of Manon Lescaut (Prévost), 35
Hobbes, Thomas, 237
Hogben, Lancelot, 91
Holbach, Paul Thiry, baron d', 114, 174–7, 178, 182, 255, 298; salon of, 175, 220, 222, 223; and the *Encyclopédie*, 177, 201; and Diderot, 174–7, 338–40
Holland, 86, 337
Homer, 18, 34, 36, 85, 118, 326
Hooke, Luke Joseph, 155, 156
Horace, 5, 17, 18, 19, 85, 326
Houdetot, Sophie d', 292; and Rousseau, 292–302; meets Diderot, 294, 298
Houdon, Jean-Antoine, 14
Howe, Samuel Gridley, 99
Hugo, Victor, 330
Humanisme de Diderot (Thomas), 245
Hume, David, 174
Hutcheson, Francis, 204
Huyghens, Christian, 5

I

Iliad, 124
Inquiry concerning Virtue and Merit (Shaftesbury), 50–52, 59, 78, 100, 304
Isle-sur-Marne, 229

J

Jacques le fataliste (Diderot), 21, 345
Jacquier, François, 30
Jal, Auguste, 42–3
James, Henry, 222
James, Robert, 52–3, 54, 55, 78, 83, 87, 93
James the Fatalist (Diderot), 21, 345
Jansen, Cornelis, bishop of Ypres, 26
Jansenists, 25–7, 55, 63, 127, 156, 169–71, 177, 334, 336, 338
Jaucourt, Louis, chevalier de, 96, 128, 201–2, 368 n.60; and the *Encyclopédie*, 136, 201–2, 234, 278–9, 337
Jefferson, Thomas, 120, 132, 142, 292
Jesuits, 279, 297, 336, 338; at Langres, 15–16; and D'Alembert, 211–12; and Diderot, 17–18, 21–3, 25–7, 38, 125–7, 169, 244, 320; and the *Encyclopédie*, 152–4, 156–9, 161–2, 164–5, 167, 283, 288
Jews, 236–7
Job, Book of, 200
Johnson, Samuel, 4, 48, 53, 111, 355 n.31
Joly de Fleury, Omer, 120, 312, 333–4
Journal de Trévoux, 51, 76, 90, 100, 117, 128, 197, 212; attacks the *Encyclopédie*, 125–6, 150, 152–4, 188
Journal des Sçavans, 50, 51, 90, 117, 166–7, 197; and the *Encyclopédie*, 7, 152, 201

Journal Encyclopédique, 196, 272–3, 307
Journal Etranger, 300
Jugemens sur Quelques Ouvrages Nouveaux, 52, 77
Julian the Apostate, 58, 237, 311

K

Keller, Helen, 99

L

La Chaux, Mlle de, 125
La Ferté-Bernard (Sarthe), 37
La Fontaine, Jean de, 32, 84, 309
La Grange, Joseph-Louis, 193
La Harpe, Jean-François de, 114, 196
La Marck, comtesse de, 317–19
La Mettrie, Julien Offroy de, 193
La Porte, Joseph de, abbé, 48
La Rochefoucauld, François, duc de, 326
La Salette, Pierre, 35, 37, 38, 184, 352 n.54
La Salette, Simone, wife of Nicolas Caroillon, 23, 184, 350 n.12
La Tour, Maurice Quentin de, 68, 165
Lamoignon de Blancmesnil, Guillaume de, chancellor of France, 161, 162, 335, 336
Lampedusa, 270
Lancret, Nicolas, 3
Landois, Paul, 249–52, 258, 261
Landowski, Paul Maximilien, 67 n.
Langres, 9–11, 14, 50, 64, 65, 112, 184, 230, 232, 260, 267, 296, 338, 339; and Diderot, 15–16, 20–23, 38, 39–40, 136; Jesuit college of, 15–16; Hôtel du Breuil Museum at, 13, 17; Place Chambeau (now Place Diderot), 11, 15; Diderot's visits to, (1742) 39–41; (1754) 218–19; (1759) 9–10
Laocoön (Lessing), 123, 209
Lassone, Joseph-Marie-François de, 165, 199
Lauraguais, Louis-Léon-Félicité de Brancas, comte de, 327
Lavirotte, Louis-Anna, 315–16
Le Bret, Antoine, 313
Le Breton, André-François, 75, 229; and the *Encyclopédie,* 75–81, 129, 152, 284, 307, 333–4, 359 n.27, 369 n.25, 385 n.10; and Diderot, 252
Le Roy, Charles-Georges, 203
Le Seur, Thomas, 30
Lediard, Thomas, 88
Lefebvre, Henri, 194
Legitimate Prejudices . . . (Chaumeix), 312, 334
Legitimatized Bastard (anonymous), 263–4
Leibniz, Gottfried Wilhelm, 5, 73, 133, 191, 237

Leipzig, University of, 119
L'Epine, printer, 55
Lespinasse, Julie-Jeanne-Eléonore de, 222
Lessing, Gotthold Ephraim, 85, 123, 209, 328
Letter from M. Diderot to the Reverend Father Berthier, Jesuit (Diderot), 125–6
Letter on the Blind (Diderot), 63, 68, 96–101, 103, 104, 106, 107, 108, 110, 117–18, 122, 128, 132, 193, 226, 333, 344
Letter on the Deaf and Dumb (Diderot), 26, 31, 121–5, 127, 252, 333
Letters concerning the English Nation (Voltaire), 49, 100
Lettre à d'Alembert sur les spectacles (Rousseau), 290, 302–3, 304, 305, 306
Lettre à M. ***, de la Société Royale de Londres (anonymous), 126, 128
lettre de cachet, 103–4, 115, 161, 175, 178, 322, 324, 325–6
Lettre sur la musique française (Rousseau), 178
Lettre sur les aveugles (Diderot), 63, 68, 96–101, 103, 104, 106, 107, 108, 110, 117–18, 122, 128, 132, 193, 226, 333, 344
Lettre sur les sourds et muets (Diderot), 26, 31, 121–5, 127, 252, 333
Lettres philosophiques (Voltaire), 49, 100
Leupold, Jakob, 241
Levasseur, Mme, mother of Thérèse, 256, 257, 258, 259, 294, 298
Levasseur, Thérèse, 46, 256, 298
Leyden, University of, 175, 201
Liége, 317
Lillo, George, 269, 326
Linnaeus, Carl, 194
Lisbon, earthquake of (1755), 247
Little Letters on Great Philosophers (Palissot), 263, 284–5, 312, 317
Locke, John, 5, 49, 51, 67, 100, 132, 133, 142, 152, 170, 205
London, 52, 150–51
London Merchant (Lillo), 269, 326
Longchamp, —, 199
Louis XIV, 11, 26, 84, 85, 166, 171, 242
Louis XV, 84, 85, 143, 180, 248, 276
Louis XVI, 164
Lucretius, 18, 21, 124, 195, 326
Lully, Jean-Baptiste, 84, 85, 177–8, 180
Lunéville, 111
Luxembourg, Charles-François-Frédéric de Montmorency, maréchal-duc de, 317
Lyon, 88, 212

M

Mably, Gabriel Bonnot de, 79
Macaulay, Thomas Babington, 101

Machault d'Arnouville, Jean-Baptiste, 184
Machiavelli, Niccolo, 61
Maelzel, Johann Nepomuk, 69
Maestro di musica (Pergolesi), 178
Maintenon, Françoise d'Aubigné, marquise de, 85
Maistre, Joseph de, 195
Malebranche, Nicolas de, 191
Malesherbes, Chrétien-Guillaume de Lamoignon de, 81–2, 126, 159, 161, 165–6, 212, 244, 260, 286, 297, 305, 325, 334; description of, 162–4; policy of, 187, 263–4, 286–7, 334–5; and tacit permissions, 121–2, 124, 187; and Diderot, 213, 308–9, 315–19, 338–9; and the *Encyclopédie*, 283–4; and D'Alembert, 286–7, 290; and Fréron, 264, 272, 273
Mallet, —, abbé, 147, 157, 360 n.2
Marly, 339, 340
Marmontel, Jean-François, 177, 185, 220–21, 223, 224, 337; and Diderot, 114, 295, 302, 303
Marne (river), 9, 23
Marriage of Figaro (Beaumarchais), 262
Marx, Karl, 194
Maupertuis, Pierre-Louis Moreau de, 192, 193, 196, 203
Meaning of Meaning (Ogburn and Richards), 121
Medicinal Dictionary (James), 52–3, 55, 83, 87, 93
Meister, Jakob Heinrich, 114, 201, 312
Mélanges de littérature, d'histoire et de philosophie (D'Alembert), 201, 221
Melot, Anicet, 226
Mémoire pour Abraham Chaumeix contre . . . Diderot et d'Alembert (anonymous), 338
Mémoires de la comtesse de Zurlac (Mme de Puisieux), 65
Mémoires pour servir à l'histoire du Jacobinisme (Barruel), 312
Mémoires sur différens sujets de mathématiques (Diderot), 30, 68, 88–91, 95, 101, 178
Memoirs on Different Subjects of Mathematics (Diderot), 30, 68, 88–91, 95, 101, 178
Memorandum for Abraham Chaumeix against . . . Diderot and D'Alembert (anonymous), 338
Mencken, Henry Louis, 139
Mercure de France, 68, 90, 113, 196, 273, 276–7, 319; and the *Encyclopédie,* 7, 307
Meudon, 339
Millet, —, abbé, 166
Mills, John, 75–7, 359 nn.20 and 24

Milton, John, 36, 63, 109, 118, 124, 163
Mirabeau, family of, 41
Mirepoix, Jean-François Boyer, bishop of, 159, 165
Mitford, William, 50
Moeurs (Toussaint), 53–4
Molière, Jean-Baptiste Poquelin, 30, 269, 273, 325, 326
Molyneux, William, 98–9
Mont Saint-Michel, 134
Montaigne, Michel de, 51, 63, 66, 67 and n., 228
Montauban, Michel Verthamon de Chavagnac, bishop of, 156, 169
Montesquieu, Charles de Sécondat, baron de, 133, 210, 232–3, 285, 382 n.5
Montmorency, 255, 257, 258, 259, 294, 295, 299, 302
Moore, Edward, 269
Moreau, Jacob-Nicolas, 276; attacks the 'Cacouacs,' 276–7, 285–6, 312, 334
Morellet, André, abbé, 114, 277, 286–7, 295, 337, 338, 397 n.30; his description of Diderot, 175, 182–3
Moreri, Louis, 135
Morley, John, viscount, 65, 341
Moses, 18, 155, 236
Muralt, B.-L. de, 70

N

Naigeon, Jacques-André, 22–3, 25, 26, 27, 39, 79, 87, 88, 109, 158, 199, 216
Nancy, 212
Narcisse (Rousseau), 181, 255
Nassau-Saarbruck, Sophia Christina Charlotte, princess of, 313–14
Nattier, Jean-Marc, 3
Naval History of England (Lediard), 88
Necker (née Curchod), Suzanne, 122, 222
Neveu de Rameau (Diderot), 32, 180, 345
New Art of Painting in Cheese . . . (anonymous), 228
Newton, Isaac, 5, 30, 36, 49, 84, 85, 90, 133
Nivelle de la Chaussée, Pierre-Claude, 261
Nocrion, conte allobroge, 84
Nouvelle Héloïse (Rousseau), 291, 294, 295, 324
Nouvelles Ecclésiastiques, 26, 156–7, 235
Novum Organum (Bacon), 187–8
Numa, 279
Nun (Diderot), 14, 345
Nun in a Shift (anonymous), 32

O

Observateur Hollandais (Moreau), 277
Observateur Littéraire, 48, 319

Observations sur les Ecrits Modernes, 48

Oiseau blanc, conte bleu (Diderot), 87–8, 104, 106, 179

On the Dignity and Increase of the Sciences (Bacon), 125

On the Sufficiency of Natural Religion (Diderot), 60, 61, 101, 155

Opéra (Paris), 84, 177, 178, 179

Origines ecclesiasticae (Bingham), 88

Orléans, Louis (1703–52), duc d', 174

Orléans, Louis-Philippe (1725–85), duc d', 271, 282

Ovid, 124

P

Padre di famiglia (Goldoni), 317, 319

Paine, Thomas, 334

Palissot, Charles, 317, 318, 319; and the *philosophes*, 212, 263, 271–2, 284–5, 312, 334

Paradise Lost, 97, 324

Paris, 3, 9, 10, 16, 23, 34, 66–7, 84, 95, 97, 151, 174, 214, 241, 255, 256, 257, 258, 259, 271, 278, 295, 306; Archives de France, 118, 120, 121; Avenue de l'Opéra, 175; Bastille, 44, 115; Bibliothèque de l'Arsenal, 115; Bibliothèque du Roi, 96, 111, 115; Bibliothèque Nationale, 96, 154, 212, 308; Boulevard Saint-Germain, 220; Boulevard Saint-Michel, 25; Café de Flore, 32, 220; Café de la Régence, 45; Café de la Rotonde, 31; Café du Dôme, 31; Café Procope, 31–2; churches: Saint-Etienne-du-Mont, 67, 119, 186; Saint-Eustache, 229; Saint-Germain-l'Auxerrois, 67, 176; Saint-Jean-le-Rond, 68; Saint-Louis-en-l'Île, 42; Saint-Médard, 55; Saint-Nicolas-du-Chardonnet, 44; Saint-Pierre-aux-Boeufs, 42, 43; Saint-Séverin, 42, 43; Sainte-Marguerite-de-Paris, 44, 54; Collège de Beauvais, 25; Collège de Bourgogne, 23, 24, 25; Collège d'Harcourt, 23, 25–7; Collège Louis-le-Grand, 25–7, 33, 157; Convent of the Miramiones, 37; Ecole de Médecine, 24; Hôtel-Dieu, 43; Hôtel du Panier Fleuri, 66; Île de la Cité, 43; Île Saint-Louis, 24; Institut de France, 221; Jardin des Plantes, 241; Louvre, 165; Luxembourg Gardens, 30, 182; Lycée Saint-Louis, 25; Musée de l'Assistance Publique, 352 n.3; Notre-Dame, 43, 68; Opéra, 84, 177, 178, 179; Palais de Justice, 164; Palais Royal, 66, 67, 177; Place de la Concorde, 222; Place de la Sorbonne, 25; Place des Vic-

toires, 229; Place Vendôme, 222; Pont-Neuf, 67; Quai des Grands Augustins, 32; Rues: de la Harpe, 17; de l'Ancienne Comédie, 31; de l'Estrapade, 95, 103, 112, 116, 161, 174, 186, 218; de l'Observance (now Antoine-Dubois), 24; des Deux-Ponts, 42; des Moulins, 175; des Vieux-Augustins, 229; Monsieur-le-Prince, 24; Montmartre, 17; Mouffetard, 55, 61, 67, 83, 95; Neuve des Petits Champs, 120; Poupée, 43; Saint-Benoît, 220; Saint-Honoré, 222; Saint-Jacques, 25, 87; Saint-Séverin, 43; Saint-Victor, 44; Taranne, 220, 291, 294, 295, 380 n.7; Traversière, 44; seminaries: Saint-Nicolas-du-Chardonnet, 37–8, 44; Saint-Sulpice, 35–6, 38, 39; Tuileries, 228; University of Paris, 26

Pâris, François de, abbé, 55

Parker, Dorothy, 229

Parlement of Paris, 53, 177, 213, 283, 290, 338; condemns the *Pensées philosophiques*, 55–7, 164; suspends the *Encyclopédie*, 333–6

Pascal, Blaise, 5, 58, 67

Paul, St., 60, 113, 176

Pavlov, Ivan Petrovitch, 204

Pensées philosophiques (Diderot), 52, 54, 55–8, 59, 60, 61, 64, 101, 104, 106, 107, 108, 117, 140, 193, 329, 333

Pensées sur l'interprétation de la nature (Diderot), 187–98, 205, 235, 284, 333

Père de famille (Diderot), 37–8, 248, 260, 261–2, 265, 268, 269, 271, 273, 301, 305, 309, 313–16, 322–6, 331, 394 n.30

Pergolesi, Giovanni Battista, 177, 178

Perkins Institution for the Blind, 99

Perrault, —, 61

Perroquet, 48–9

Persius, 18

Pestré, —, abbé, 216

Petit, —, abbé, 182, 255

Petit Prophète de Boehmischbroda (Grimm), 178

Petronius, 32, 51

philosophe, definition of, 70–72, 174, 181–2, 210, 221–2, 236–7, 238, 269–70

Philosophical Thoughts (Diderot), 52, 54, 55–8, 59, 60, 61, 64, 101, 104, 106, 107, 108, 117, 140, 193, 329, 333

Pindar, 85

Pissot, publisher, 89

Pius XII, 147

Plan d'une université pour le gouvernement de Russie (Diderot), 18

Plato, 8, 18, 85, 109, 191, 215, 326
Plautus, 326
Pliny the Elder, 18, 146, 226, 227
Pompadour, Jeanne-Antoinette, marquise de, 84, 88, 164–5, 184–5, 248, 373 n.16, 376 n.44
Pontoise, 213
Pope, Alexander, 54
Porée, Charles, 26
Port Mahon, 247, 248, 275, 325
Potsdam, 166, 214
Pound, Ezra, 32
Prades, Jean-Martin de, abbé, 166, 177, 203, 209, 244; Sorbonne thesis of, 154–6; and Diderot, 157–8, 169–71
Préjugés légitimes contre l'Encyclopédie (Chaumeix), 312, 334
Première lettre d'un citoyen zélé . . . (Diderot), 92–3
Prémontval (née Pigeon), Marie-Anne-Victoire de, 89
Prévost, Antoine-François, abbé, 35, 326
Project for a New Organ (Diderot), 68–70
Promenade du sceptique (Diderot), 60, 61–4, 89, 101, 103, 104, 106, 357 n.22
Prussian Royal Academy of Sciences and Belles-Lettres, 115, 127, 167, 193, 264, 275
Pufendorf, Samuel, 233
Puisieux, Madeleine d'Arsant de, 64–6, 83, 89, 99, 102, 110, 118–19, 174 n., 228, 357 n.28
Puisieux, Philippe Florent de, 64, 88, 357 n.25
Pythagoras, 90

Q
Qu'en pensez-vous? (Diderot), 63
Quesnay, François, 184–5, 253, 277
Quintus Curtius, 17

R
Rabelais, François, 63
Racine, Jean-Baptiste, 5, 67, 123, 326
Rameau, Jean-Philippe, 84, 85, 89, 178, 284; and the Encyclopédie, 89, 179–80
Rameau's Nephew (Diderot), 32, 180, 345
Ramelli, Agostino, 241
Ramsay, Andrew Michael, 74–5
Randon de Boisset, Paul, 28, 351 n.28
Raynal, Guillaume-Thomas-François, abbé, 221; quoted, 65, 86, 89, 90, 96, 124, 133, 151, 152, 196, 213, 221–2
Réaumur, René-Antoine de Ferchault de, 97, 99, 110, 140, 363 n.22; and Diderot, 197, 226, 242–3

Réflexions d'un Franciscain (Geoffroy), 157
Réfutation de l'ouvrage d'Helvétius intitulé L'Homme (Diderot), 345
Regensburg, 119
Religieuse (Diderot), 14, 345
Renan, Ernest, 38
Réponse de M. Rameau à MM. les éditeurs de l'Encyclopédie (Rameau), 180
Republic (Plato), 192
Rêve de d'Alembert (Diderot), 93, 149, 345
Revocation of the Edict of Nantes, 335
Revue des Deux Mondes, 223
Riccoboni, Marie-Jeanne Laboras de Mézières, 327, 329, 330
Richardson, Samuel, 326
Richelieu, Armand, duc de, 84
Richelieu, Armand-Jean du Plessis, cardinal, duc de, 221, 247
Ring and the Book (Browning), 300
Robecq, Anne-Marie, princesse de, 317–18
Robert, Hubert, 15
Rochebrune, Miché de, 103
Roguin, Daniel, 45
Rolland, Romain, 178
Rome, 114, 162, 278
Rossbach, battle of, 248, 275
Rouault, Georges, 206
Rouelle, Guillaume-François, 241, 259
Rousseau, Jean-Jacques, 8, 48, 51, 89, 94, 106–7, 109, 116, 119–20, 143, 177, 212, 225, 232, 233–4, 235, 252, 271, 274, 275, 280, 284, 290, 307, 309, 313, 314, 317, 320, 324; and Italian music, 177–81; and the Encyclopédie, 68, 179–80; friendship with Diderot, 45–6, 66–8, 113–15, 244, 288; and Mme d'Houdetot, 292–302; tension with Diderot, 180–82, 217, 225, 254–9, 291–306
Rousseau, Mme, foster-mother of D'Alembert, 68
Royal Society (London), 78, 127–8
Rulhière, Claude-Carloman de, 94–5
Ruskin, John, 124

S
Sänger, Hermann, 236
Saint-Cyr, Odet-Joseph de Vaux de Giry, abbé de, 312
Saint-Denis, 257
Saint-Germain-en-Laye, 269, 271
Saint-Lambert, Jean-François, marquis de, 102, 389 n.18; and Mme d'Houdetot, 292–4; and Rousseau, 292–4, 295, 296, 298, 300, 302–3; and Diderot, 294, 300–302, 316
Saint Petersburg, 91

Saint-Rémy, Pierre Surirey de, 136, 369 n.15
Sainte-Croix, Mme de, 354 n.13
Saintsbury, George, 86
Sallier, Claude, abbé, 111
Salons (Diderot), 34, 35, 209
Salverte, Eusèbe, 109
Sartine, Antoine-Raymond-Jean-Gualbert-Gabriel de, 104
Sartre, Jean-Paul, 32, 176
Saunderson, Nicholas, 98, 99, 117, 122, 128, 193
Scholes, Percy A., 70
Seconde Lettre de M. Diderot au R. P. Berthier, Jésuite (Diderot), 126
Sellius, Godefroy, 75, 76, 77, 359 n.24
Seneca, 18
Sens, archbishop of, 117
Serva padrona (Pergolesi), 177, 178
Sesame and Lilies (Ruskin), 124
Seven Years' War, 247–8, 275, 308
Shaftesbury, Anthony Ashley Cooper, third earl of, 57, 236, 304; Diderot's translation of, 50–52, 59, 100, 304
Shakespeare, William, 51, 326
Siècle de Louis XIV (Voltaire), 166
Sieyès, Emmanuel-Joseph, abbé, 168
Simon, printer, 96
Skeptic's Walk (Diderot), 60, 61–4, 89, 101, 103, 104, 106, 357 n.22
Smith, Adam, 7, 185, 236
Social Contract (Rousseau), 114, 234
Société des Arts, 74
Society of the Antiquaries of Scotland, 127
Socrates, 85, 109, 215
Soirées de Saint-Pétersbourg (De Maistre), 195
Sopha (Crébillon), 84
Sophocles, 326, 341
Sorbonne (faculty of theology of the University of Paris); 117, 133, 153, 167, 209, 244, 281; and the Abbé de Prades, 154–6, 169; and Diderot, 30, 33–6
Spain, 280
Spinoza, Baruch, 147
Staël-Holstein, Anne-Louise-Germaine, baronne de, 181
Stanyan, Temple, 29, 39, 50, 52, 78
Steen, Jan, 218
Strabo, 200
Suard, Jean-Baptiste-Antoine, 176
Suite de l'Apologie de M. l'Abbé de Prades (Diderot), 169–72
Suite des erreurs sur la musique dans l'Encyclopédie (Rameau), 180
Sur les femmes (Diderot), 231
Swift, Jonathan, 52, 63, 85
Switzerland, 7

Sylvie (Landois), 249, 261

T

tacit permissions, 121–2, 163, 366 n.29
Tacitus, 19, 280
Taillefer, Antoine, 22
Tale of Two Cities (Dickens), 103, 325
Tamponnet, —, abbé, 153, 165, 166
Tartuffe (Molière), 325
Tasso, Torquato, 36, 123
Tennessee, 144
Tercier, Jean-Pierre, 311
Terence, 18, 269, 326
Theatrum machinarum (Leupold), 241
Thoughts on the Interpretation of Nature (Diderot), 187–98, 205, 235, 284, 333
Tirant lo Blanch, 119
Tocqueville, Alexis de, 262, 269
Toland, John, 49
Tolomas, —, père, 212
Tolstoy, Leo, 256
Tombeau de la Sorbonne (Voltaire), 159
Torrey, Norman L., 123, 302
Tott, François, baron de, 136
Tourneux, Maurice, 60, 87, 89
Toussaint, François-Vincent, 53–4
Tractatus Theologico-politicus (Spinoza), 147
Traité des sensations (Condillac), 68, 252
Traité des systèmes (Condillac), 191
Treatise on Dynamics (D'Alembert), 68
Trois Chapitres . . . (Diderot), 179
Tronchin, Théodore, 93, 201, 287, 296, 339–40; and inoculation, 281–2; protests against the article 'Geneva,' 281–3
Trublet, Nicolas-Charles-Joseph, abbé, 110, 217, 263
Tull, Jethro, 74
Turgot, Anne-Robert-Jacques, 185, 312, 333, 338, 356 n.54, 397 n.30; and the *Encyclopédie*, 213, 224, 253, 277, 278, 332, 337
Twain, Mark, 53

U

Unigenitus, papal bull, 26, 177, 213

V

Vandeul, Abel-François-Nicolas Caroillon de, son-in-law of Denis Diderot, 23, 25
Vandeul (née Diderot), Angélique, 12, 28, 185–6, 218, 296; quoted, 13, 14, 20, 21, 22, 23, 24, 25, 26, 27, 29, 30, 33, 37, 38, 39, 40, 42, 43, 45, 46, 53, 64, 66, 83, 85, 97, 105, 109, 114, 119, 140, 184, 230, 248, 294–5, 339
Vaugondy, Robert de, 277

Venice, 46, 177, 272
Vénus physique (Maupertuis), 203
Vernes, Jacob, 304-5
Vero Amico (Goldoni), 272-3, 317, 319
Versailles, 174, 203, 255, 276, 283, 290, 336, 339
Vigneron, Claire, 12, 353 n.23
Vigneron, Didier, 11, 21, 350 n.3
Vigneron, Jean, 11
Villey (-Desmeserets), Pierre, 99
Vincennes, 96, 254, 299; Diderot imprisoned at, 104-16, 117, 118, 339, 364 n.24
Virgil, 18, 19, 34, 36, 85, 118
Vitry-le-François, 229
Volland, Jean-Robert, 229
Volland, Mme Jean-Robert, 229, 340
Volland, Sophie (Louise-Henriette), 10, 12, 17, 23, 33, 38, 308, 323, 328, 339, 340, 345; description of, 228-31; will of, 228
Voltaire, François-Marie Arouet de, 25, 48, 49, 63, 66, 81, 85, 97, 99, 100, 101, 102, 111, 123, 145, 147, 152, 159, 166, 167, 197, 214, 223, 232, 236, 247, 275, 282, 299, 307, 318, 319; and D'Alembert, 276, 287-90, 307, 335; and the *Encyclopédie*, 253-4, 279, 288-90, 337; and Diderot, 283, 288-90, 291, 301, 309, 314, 326

W

Wade, Ira O., 56
Walpole, Horace, 54, 111, 174
Wealth of Nations (Smith), 236
White Bird (Diderot), 87-8
Wilkes, John, 175
Wille, Johann Georg, 24-5, 30, 47
Wolff, Christian, 75, 242
Wollaston, William, 49

Y

Yvon, Claude, abbé, 148, 154, 360 n.2, 372 n.44; and the De Prades affair, 157, 158

Z

Zacharias, Pope, 152
Zamor et Almanzine (Mme de Puisieux), 65
Zerbe, Karl, 226